# Controlling
# Technology

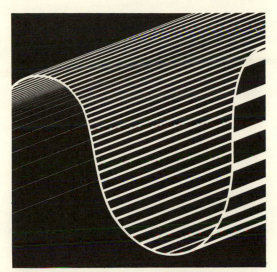

# Controlling Technology

## Contemporary Issues

Edited by

## William B. Thompson

## Prometheus Books
Buffalo, New York

Published 1991 by Prometheus Books

Editorial offices located at 700 East Amherst Street, Buffalo, New York, 14215, and distribution facilities located at 59 John Glenn Drive, Amherst, New York 14228.

Library of Congress Cataloging-in-Publication Data

Controlling Technology / edited by William B. Thompson.
      p.        cm.
Includes bibliographical references.
ISBN 0-87975-616-0
    1. Technology. I. Thompson, William B., 1929–
T185.C68    1991
600—dc20                              90-19871
                                              CIP

Printed on acid-free paper in the United States of America

# Contents

*Preface*                                                                9

*Introduction*                                                          11

PART 1. THE MODERN PREDICAMENT

Introduction                                                            17

    1. The Fate of the Earth
       *Jonathan Schell*                                           19

PART 2. DEFINING TECHNOLOGY

Introduction                                                            37

    2. Can Technology Replace Social Engineering?
       *Alvin M. Weinberg*                                         41

    3. A Technology of Behavior
       *B. F. Skinner*                                             49

    4. Defining Technique
       *Jacques Ellul*                                             56

    5. Technology: Practice and Culture
       *Arnold Pacey*                                              65

6.  Trapped in the 'NASA-Speak' Machine
*Jack Beatty*                                          76

PART 3.  THE AUTONOMY OF MODERN TECHNOLOGY

Introduction                                          81

7.  The Autonomy of Technique
*Jacques Ellul*                                       85

8.  Toward a Philosophy of Technology
*Hans Jonas*                                          98

9.  Reverse Adaptation and Control
*Langdon Winner*                                     120

10.  The Ruination of the Tomato
*Mark Kramer*                                        131

PART 4.  THE BLESSINGS OF TECHNOLOGY

Introduction                                         145

11.  In Praise of Technology
*Samuel C. Florman*                                  148

12.  Technology and Human Values
*Melvin Kranzberg*                                   157

13.  The Role of Technology in Society
*Emmanuel G. Mesthene*                               166

PART 5.  DEMYSTIFYING AUTONOMOUS TECHNOLOGY

Introduction                                         191

14.  Is Technology Autonomous?
*Michael Goldhaber*                                  195

15.  The Secret Behind Star Wars
*William J. Broad*                                   204

16.  Do Machines Make History?
*Robert Heilbroner*                                  213

17.  Social Choice in Machine Design: The Case of
Automatically Controlled Machine Tools, and a
Challenge for Labor
*David F. Noble*                                     223

## PART 6. TECHNOLOGY AND POLITICS

Introduction     245

18. Presumed Neutrality of Technology
 *Norman Balabanian*     249

19. The Great Transportation Conspiracy
 *Jonathan Kwitny*     265

20. The Political Impact of Technical Expertise
 *Dorothy Nelkin*     275

21. Technē and Politeia: The Technical Constitution
 of Society
 *Langdon Winner*     291

## PART 7. ALIENATED LABOR

Introduction     307

22. Estranged Labor
 *Karl Marx*     311

23. Working
 *Studs Terkel*     323

24. Alienation and Freedom
 *Robert Blauner*     331

25. Scientific Management
 *Harry Braverman*     350

## PART 8. APPROPRIATE TECHNOLOGY

Introduction     367

26. Authoritarian and Democratic Technics
 *Lewis Mumford*     371

27. The American Ideal of a Democratic Technology
 *Carroll Pursell*     379

28. Buddhist Economics
 *E. F. Schumacher*     392

29. Small Is Dubious
 *Samuel C. Florman*     399

30. Appropriate Technology and Inappropriate Politics
 *Thomas Simon*     404

## PART 9. THE HUMAN PROSPECT

Introduction                                                    425

31. The Final Constraints
    *Barbara Ward*                                             428

32. The Problems of Mankind's Survival
    *Mikhail S. Gorbachev*                                     439

33. Cultural Revolution
    *Arnold Pacey*                                             448

# Preface

The title of this book is quite deliberately ambiguous. This is to reflect a central issue in the philosophy of technology. Does technology control us, or do we control technology? What is, and what ought to be, the role of technology in human affairs?

The study of technology has not traditionally been thought of as a part of a liberal arts curriculum and certainly not a legitimate topic for philosophical reflection. However, it is clear that modern technology, with its grounding in scientific knowledge, is a major force shaping the society in which we live and the way we experience the world. If we understand philosophy as the attempt to analyze and make sense of our experience, we can no longer neglect a critical examination of technology. In the Atomic Age this is quite literally a matter of life and death.

One of the reasons for this neglect can be attributed to philosophers' traditional disdain for *praxis*, for practical applications and actions, which has its roots in the ancient Greek evaluation of the manual arts and fabrication as fitting only for slaves. Philosophers, as free men, should deal with purely abstract and theoretical matters.

Another factor lies in the modern fragmentation of human knowledge, which is itself an expression of a technological mode of thinking. All problems, we have believed, ought to be divided, and subdivided, into ever smaller parts to be investigated only by experts with the relevant specializing training. By this mode of thinking, such practical considerations as the safety of nuclear power are purely technical and therefore ought to be left to nuclear engineers. The philosopher should limit himself to his own area of expertise—conceptual analysis—and not attempt to assess highly technical issues where he lacks the requisite specialized knowledge—as though there were no important conceptual issues about the nature and direction of technology.

This prejudice is reinforced by the prevalent view that technology is value-neutral, that whether it is good or bad simply depends upon how it is used.

If this view were correct, there would, indeed, be no philosophical or ethical issues about technology per se. However, this commonsense notion will not stand critical analysis. All technologies, from hammers and MX missiles to organizational techniques such as the division of labor, are designed for a purpose. Thus, engineering and management design cannot be divorced from the larger ethical issues confronting our society. While we may argue about how technology ought to be defined, on no account is it to be regarded as neutral.

This book is addressed to both those in the arts and sciences and those in technical fields. Its aim, to paraphrase Plato, is to see technology writ large. In the sense that all the readings concern fundamental issues, they are all of philosophical interest. However, the readings are not all written by professional philosophers. Some of the more seminal, if less careful, thinking has been done by those outside the discipline of philosophy. I have excluded treatments that are overly technical, so this material should be accessible to undergraduates. The selections are intended to be read in order, for the later readings typically discuss authors and arguments presented earlier in the text.

The issues discussed in this volume are organized in such a way as to bring into sharp focus the basic and opposing positions concerning the relationships between technology and fundamental human values—especially those ideals that center around the concept of democracy: human autonomy and freedom, human equality and the right of all persons to exercise some control over the factors that determine their destiny, and respect for the universal aspiration for a rich and meaningful existence.

I would like to thank the National Endowment for the Humanities for a grant awarded to me over ten years ago to develop a course dealing with technology and human values. It was this grant that stimulated my interest in the issues discussed in this volume. Additional thanks are due to Potsdam College of the State University of New York for a sabbatical leave to work on this book.

# Introduction

This is a book about faith. Although people have always displayed a certain ambivalence toward technology, the most prevalent attitude in recent history, especially in the United States, has been a quasi-religious faith in the capacity of technology to provide the good life for all. Surely, the rising standard of living in the industrialized countries gives some grounds for this confidence. As we have all "learned," it is technology, in conjunction with the free-enterprise system, that has made America great. The dominant view in our society equates technological innovation and growth in the GNP with human progress. This belief is so common that the *Webster's New Collegiate Dictionary* defines "technology" as "the totality of the means employed to provide objects necessary for human sustenance and comfort." The value of technology is thus built into the very meaning of the term.

This faith, however, has suffered a number of traumatic shocks. The Atomic Age burst upon the world on August 6, 1945, with a sudden explosion and a mushroom cloud over Hiroshima. Although aerial bombardment during World War II had accustomed us to the indiscriminate annihilation of civilian populations, we were wholly unprepared for such wholesale destruction by one bomb packing the power of some twenty thousand tons of TNT. But this was good, we believed, for the atomic bomb shortened the war and saved American lives.

Following the war, the Atoms for Peace program, funded by the U.S. government to exploit and publicize the positive uses of atomic fission, reassured us that scientific knowledge could be used for constructive as well as destructive purposes. Cheap, unlimited atomic energy promised such material abundance for all that there would no longer be cause for war.

This optimism faded, however, when the Soviet Union developed its own atom bomb and nuclear proliferation became a common cause of anxiety. Nuclear strategists preached theories of massive retaliation and mutual assured destruction (MAD) to rationalize the accelerating arms race between the United

States and Soviet Russia. Today these two superpowers have at their disposal such destructive power that the very continuance of the human race has been put in jeopardy. And we must consider all the other nations that now possess the bomb and could themselves precipitate a nuclear holocuast. While some people might survive the initial blast and radiation of an all-out exchange of nuclear weapons, recent studies make clear that they would inevitably face starvation during an ensuing nuclear winter. Limited concerns about the effects of technology on the quality of life pale before the awful prospect of no life at all, and it is all life on Earth that is threatened by the absolute, awesome power of our nuclear weapons. Can we who live under the constant threat of nuclear annihilation continue to believe in the essential goodness of technology? Has not technology escaped rational human control?

While nuclear arms pose the most immediate threat to life on this planet, they are only a part of a wider ecological crisis, a crisis which some claim may be just as fatal in the long run. Broad public awareness of this crisis began in the 1960s with a series of best-sellers focusing on some of the hidden costs of technological progress. While Dupont continued to advertise "better living through chemistry," it seemed that chemicals were poisoning the environment. DDT, intended to eliminate malaria, was contaminating the food chain, killing songbirds, and thus threatening to create what Rachel Carson called a "silent spring." The effects of Mirex, PCBs (polychlorinated biphenyls), lead and mercury poisoning, black and brown lung, acid rain, asbestosis, and carcinogens of all kinds have become part of the daily evening news. Empedocles' four elements (earth, air, fire, and water) now all appear unsafe for living things. Even America's most beloved technological icon, the automobile, has come under attack. Ralph Nader declared it an unmitigated hazard in his book *Unsafe at Any Speed*. Not only do car crashes take 50,000 lives each year, but the automobile itself has proven to be a major source of air pollution. The promise of cheap, safe nuclear power has been dimmed by escalating costs and events like the near disaster at Three Mile Island in 1979 and the actual nuclear catastrophe at Chernobyl in the Soviet Union in 1986. Perhaps the most dramatic failure of modern technology, watched by millions on television, was the explosion of the space shuttle *Challenger*.

In 1972 Studs Terkel published *Working,* a book that documents the brutalizing nature of work for many in our society. Is this another price we must pay for technological progress? While automation promises to liberate the worker from monotonous, meaningless work, the fear is that it will simply eliminate jobs or further reduce the worker's skill. While the threat of unemployment has reduced agitation about the quality of work, this is not an issue that is likely to disappear. Recently, workers at the Nova automobile assembly plant in California have complained, in defiance of management and union leaders, that the success of this operation is due to inhumane working conditions.

These contemporary crises have led many to conclude that our technology is out of control. Rather than being essentially good, technological advancement appears to be more akin to a cancerous growth endemic to all technological societies. This conclusion gives credence to the view that technology has become autonomous, and that it evolves according to its own internal logic which operates independently of human purposes. Those who hold that technology has become autonomous argue that, barring a nuclear holocaust, we are being ineluctably propelled toward a "brave new world," an all-pervasive totalitarian state in which persons and their values are subservient to the requirements of technological development. On this view, the "controling" in this volume's title should be understood as an adjective: it is technology that is controlling us.

Our traditional faith in technology is, however, very much alive. The orthodox response to these crises is to keep faith with the notion of technological progress, but in addition to admit that along with the intended (good) consequences there may develop some unintended (bad) ones, and that further technological growth is necessary to eliminate these undesirable "side effects." Such thinking underlies the nuclear strategy that proposes a Strategic Defense Initiative: while offensive missiles now threaten the human race, our country's salvation must lie in the deployment of a "Star Wars" defense. If we do not lose the old American "can-do spirit," the promise of technology will continue to be fulfilled. No radical rethinking of the very nature of technology, therefore, is necessary. For every technological problem—indeed for every human problem—there is an appropriate technological solution. Accordingly, it does not make sense to blame technology for the problems we face; technology provides the very means of solving those problems.

Of course, if technology is autonomous and *necessarily* brings about the good life for us all, we need not worry—or think. But if technology is autonomous and *necessarily* leads to a degradation of the quality of our lives, stoic resignation seems the only appropriate attitude. However, there is reason to believe that there are points in the system where values can, and do, exert leverage. The esoteric complexity of large-scale technical systems discourages many ordinary citizens from attempting to evaluate them, leaving these most important issues in the hands of experts. But, while expert knowledge about probable consequences of our technology is important, when available, the fundamental questions still involve basic human values. Indeed, as we shall see, normative choices based on personal values frequently masquerade as purely technical decisions.

Although it may be proved that some technological developments are, in an important sense, out of human control, it does not follow that this is an inevitable or universal condition. Once we untangle the multiple elements that propel technical change, we shall see that human purposes are at work here and that technology typically does serve human interests. However, "human" interests are not necessarily "humane," nor can we move automatically from the interests of some to those of all mankind. Thus, a crucial moral issue is concerned with distributive justice: Who profits and who loses as a consequence of new technologies? Are the burdens and benefits of technological change distributed fairly? Who in fact controls, and ought to control, technology?

Arguments about how burdens and benefits should be distributed presuppose some view about what constitutes a burden and a benefit—ultimately, some view of intrinsic value. Given the high esteem we grant our liberty, we are rightly suspicious of anyone who attempts to dictate what constitutes the good life, but this means that we are all obliged to give serious thought to the kind of life that is most worth living. As we shall see in our examination of appropriate technology, this movement most importantly involves a critique of the materialistic values of a consumer society and offers an alternative vision of the good life.

Following the first nuclear explosion, Albert Einstein commented that, "the unleashed power of the atom has changed everything save our modes of thinking; thus we drift toward catastrophe." This volume challenges us to reevaluate our habitual modes of thinking in order to gain some insight into how this drift might be prevented. Although many of the essays in this volume are concerned with theory, the book's purpose overall is crucially practical.

To deal effectively with what appear to be overwhelming problems confronting our civilization does require faith, but a faith informed by our most careful thinking. The readings in this volume contain no definitive answers to the problems facing us, but it is our hope that the reader will come away with a clearer understanding of the issues and of the questions that we all ought to be asking. If the ideal of a democratic society is to be viable, the management of technology must be everybody's business.

# Part One
# The Modern Predicament

# Introduction

Power makes the modern predicament unique. Throughout recorded history there have been wars and rumors of war, but the effects of Homo sapiens' aggressive instincts have been circumscribed by his limited means. While environmental pollution is not a new phenomenon, until the development of modern industry this remained a localized problem and did not seriously affect the biosphere. Nature once ruled supreme. Modern technology has radically changed this situation. As Jonathan Schell points out in the following selection, the balance of power has decisively shifted from nature to man. Therefore it is no longer nature that threatens man, but man who threatens nature.

Schell wrote *The Fate of the Earth* at the height of the arms race between the United States and the Soviet Union. The collapse of communism and the end of the Cold War have now reduced, if not eliminated, our anxiety about an all-out exchange of nuclear weapons. However, we need to realize that most of these weapons are still in place and that the United States and the Soviets do not have a monopoly on their manufacture or use. Indeed, one can plausibly argue that the likelihood of using nuclear weapons by a Third World country or terrorist organization has increased. Even if the dream of eliminating all nuclear weapons is realized, the threat of nuclear annihilation cannot be eliminated. As Schell makes clear, the only *final* solution to the nuclear peril is the destruction of the civilization that has the knowledge to produce such weapons of mass destruction. Scientific and technological "progress" is, in this sense, irreversible.

Although nuclear weapons pose the most obvious and dramatic threat to life on earth, Schell argues that they are to be seen as only part of a more general ecological crisis that may be even more intractable. Men do not actively conspire to destroy the planet that sustains them; toxic wastes, acid rain, ozone

17

depletion, and changes wrought by the greenhouse effect are unintended "side-effects" of our intended goals. Nonetheless, we may by incremental steps so alter the ecology that life on Earth is no longer viable. Our world may end in a whimper, not a bang.

Most important for our purposes is Schell's understanding of the causes of the modern predicament. On his account, the origins of our peril lie in basic scientific understanding, not in social circumstances. Scientific revolutions are to be sharply distinguished from social revolutions, the former being sprung on the world by relatively few individuals working in the privacy of their laboratories. Science is also a collective enterprise, in which each generation of scientists builds on the work of previous generations in progessively increasing our understanding of nature. This linear view of scientific development contrasts sharply with the circular nature of social revolutions that require the tactic consent of large numbers of ordinary citizens. These revolutions are reversible and occur only in societies where there has been a long period of preparation.

The critical problem, which many writers have described as cultural lag, is the failure of our understanding of social and political relations—our wisdom—to keep pace with the explosive increase in our scientific knowledge of physical reality. Philosophers, lacking a rigorous scientific discipline, attack their predecessors while scientists are busily building on the shoulders of those who have gone before.

Although scientists are the principal cause of our predicament, they are not primarily responsible in a moral sense, and therefore we should not look to them for a solution. According to Schell, pure scientists aim solely at understanding, at discovering the laws of nature. The direction scientific discovery takes is determined not by human volition but by the structure of physical reality. In this sense science is autonomous. Ethical questions arise only when it comes to the applications of scientific knowledge. Thus, the moral responsibility for the uses we make of science rests with political leaders, *applied* scientists, and, at least in a democracy, with us all.

We shall see this view of scientific and technological development elaborated and criticized from various perspectives in subsequent sections of this book. But a basic question being asked is: Are scientists "pure," are they never "political actors"?

# 1

# The Fate of the Earth

## Jonathan Schell

If a council were to be empowered by the people of the earth to do whatever was necessary to save humanity from extinction by nuclear arms, it might well decide that a good first step would be to order the destruction of all the nuclear weapons in the world. When the order had been carried out, however, warlike or warring nations might still rebuild their nuclear arsenals—perhaps in a matter of months. A logical second step, accordingly, would be to order the destruction of the factories that make the weapons. But, just as the weapons might be rebuilt, so might the factories, and the world's margin of safety would not have been increased by very much. A third step, then, would be to order the destruction of the factories that make the weapons—a measure that might require the destruction of a considerable part of the world's economy. But even then lasting safety would not have been reached because in some number of years—at most, a few decades —everything could be rebuilt, including the nuclear arsenals, and mankind would again be ready to extinguish itself. A determined council might next decide to try to arrest the world economy in a pre-nuclear state by throwing the blueprints and technical manuals for reconstruction on the bonfires that had by then consumed everything else, but that recourse, too, would ultimately fail, because the blueprints and manuals could easily be redrawn and rewritten. As long as the world remained acquainted with the basic physical laws that underlie the construction of nuclear weapons—and these laws include the better part of physics as physics is understood in our century—mankind would have failed to put many years between itself and its doom. For the fundamental origin of the peril of human extinction by nuclear arms lies not in any particular social or political circumstances of our time but in the attainment by mankind as a whole, after millennia of scientific progress, of a certain level of knowledge of the physical universe. As long as that knowledge is in our possession, the atoms themselves, each one stocked with its prodigious supply of energy, are, in a manner of speaking, in a perilously advanced state of mobilization for nuclear hostilities, and any conflict anywhere in the world can become a nuclear one. To return to safety through technical measures alone, we would have to disarm matter itself, converting it back into its relatively safe, inert, nonexplosive nineteenth-century Newtonian state—something that not even the physics of our time can teach us how to do. (I mention these farfetched, wholly imaginary programs of demolition and suppression in part because the final destruction of all mankind is so much more farfetched, and therefore seems to give us license to at least consider extreme alternatives, but mainly because their obvious inadequacy serves to demonstrate how deeply the nuclear peril is ingrained in our world.)

It is fundamental to the shape and character of the nuclear predicament that its origins lie in scientific knowledge rather than in social circumstances. Revolutions born in the laboratory are to be sharply distinguished from revolutions born in society. Social revolutions are usually born in the minds of millions, and are led up to by what the Declaration of Independence calls "a long train of abuses," visible to all; indeed, they usually cannot occur unless they are widely understood by and supported by the public. By contrast, scientific revolutions usually take shape quietly in the minds of a few men, under cover of the impenetrability to most laymen of scientific theory, and thus catch the world by surprise. In the case of nuclear weapons, of course, the surprise was greatly increased by the governmental secrecy that surrounded the construction of the first bombs. When the world learned of their existence, Mr. Fukai had already run back into the flames of Hiroshima, and tens of thousands of people in that city had already been killed. Even long after scientific discoveries have been made and their applications have transformed our world, most people are likely to remain ignorant of the underlying principles at work, and this has been particularly true of nuclear weapons, which, decades after their invention, are still surrounded by an aura of mystery, as though they had descended from another planet. (To most people, Einstein's famous formula $E=mc^2$, which defines the energy released in nuclear explosions, stands as a kind of symbol of everything that is esoteric and incomprehensible.)

But more important by far than the world's unpreparedness for scientific revolutions are their universality and their permanence once they have occurred. Social revolutions are restricted to a particular time and place; they arise out of particular circumstances, last for a while, and then pass into history. Scientific revolutions, on the other hand, belong to all places and all times. In the words of Alfred North Whitehead, "Modern science was born in Europe, but its home is the whole world." In fact, of all the products of human hands and minds, scientific knowledge has proved to be the most durable. The physical structures of human life—furniture, buildings, paintings, cities, and so on—are subject to inevitable natural decay, and human institutions have likewise proved to be transient. Hegel, whose philosophy of history was framed in large measure in an attempt to redeem the apparent futility of the efforts of men to found something enduring in their midst, once wrote, "When we see the evil, the vice, the ruin that has befallen the most flourishing kingdoms which the mind of man ever created, we can scarce avoid being filled with sorrow at this universal taint of corruption; and, since this decay is not the work of mere Nature, but of Human Will—a moral embitterment—a revolt of the Good Spirit (if it have a place within us) may well be the result of our reflections." Works of thought and many works of art have a better chance of surviving, since new copies of a book or a symphony can be transcribed from old ones, and so can be preserved indefinitely; yet these works, too, can and do go out of existence, for if every copy is lost, then the work is also lost. The subject matter of these works is man, and they seem to be touched with his mortality. The results of scientific work, on the other hand, are largely immune to decay and disappearance. Even when they are lost, they are likely to be rediscovered, as is shown by the fact that several scientists often make the same discovery independently. (There is no record of several poets' having independently written the same poem, or of several composers' having independently written the same symphony.) For both the subject matter and the method of science are available to all capable minds in a way that the subject matter and the method of the arts are not. The human experiences that art deals with are, once over, lost forever, like the people who undergo them, whereas matter, energy, space, and time, alike everywhere and in all ages, are always available for fresh inspection. The subject matter of science is the physical world, and its findings seem to share in the immortality of the physical world. And artistic vision grows out of the unrepeatable individuality of each artist, whereas the reasoning power of the mind—its ability to add two and two and get four—is the same in all competent persons. The rigorous exactitude of scientific methods does not mean that creativity is any less individual, intuitive, or mysterious in great scientists than in great artists, but it does mean that scientific findings, once arrived at, can be tested and confirmed by shared canons of logic and experimentation. The agreement among scientists thus achieved permits science to be a collective enterprise, in which each generation, building on the accepted findings of the generations before, makes amendments and additions, which in their turn become the starting point for the next generation. (Philosophers, by contrast, are constantly tearing down the work of their predecessors, and circling back to re-ask questions that have been asked and answered countless times before. Kant once wrote in despair, "It seems ridiculous that while every science moves forward ceaselessly, this [metaphysics], claiming to be wisdom itself, whose oracular pronouncements everyone consults, is continually revolving in one spot, without advancing one step.") Scientists, as they erect the steadily growing structure of scientific knowledge, resemble nothing so much as a swarm of bees working harmoniously together to construct a single, many-chambered hive, which grows more elaborate and splendid with every year that passes. Looking at what they have made over the centuries, scientists need feel no "sorrow" or "moral embitterment" at any "taint of corruption" that supposedly undoes all human achievements. When God, alarmed that the builders of the Tower of Babel would reach heaven with their construction, and so become as God, put an end to their undertaking by making them all speak different languages, He apparently overlooked the scientists, for they, speaking what is often called the "universal language" of their disciplines from country to country and generation to generation, went on to build a new tower   the edifice of scientific knowledge. The phenomenal success, beginning not with Einstein but with Euclid and Archimedes, has provided the unshakable structure that supports the world's nuclear peril. So durable is the scientific edifice that if we did not know that human beings had constructed it we might suppose that the findings on which our whole technological civilization rests were the pillars and crossbeams of an invulnerable, inhuman order obtruding into our changeable and perishable human realm. It is the crowning irony of this lopsided development of human abilities that the only means in sight for getting rid of the knowledge of how to destroy ourselves would be to do just that—in effect, to remove the knowledge by removing the knower.

Although it is unquestionably the scientists who have led us to the edge of the nuclear abyss, we would be mistaken if we either held them chiefly responsible for our plight or looked to them, particularly, for a solution. Here, again, the difference between scientific evolutions and social revolutions shows itself, for the notion that scientists bear primary responsibility springs from a tendency to confuse scientists with political actors. Political actors, who, of course, include ordinary citizens as well as government officials, act with definite social ends in view, such as the preservation of peace, the establishment of a just society, or, if they are corrupt, their own aggrandizement; and they are accordingly held responsible for the consequences of their actions, even when these are unintended ones, as they so often are. Scientists, on the other hand (and here I refer to the so-called pure scientists, who search for the laws of nature for the sake of knowledge itself, and not to the applied scientists, who make use of already discovered natural laws to solve practical problems), do not aim at social ends, and, in fact, usually do not know what the social results of their findings will be; for that matter, they cannot know what the findings themselves will be, because science is a process of discovery, and it is in the nature of discovery that one cannot know beforehand what one will find. This element of the unexpected is present when a researcher sets out to unravel some small, carefully defined mystery—say, the chemistry of a certain enzyme—but it is most conspicuous in the synthesis of the great laws of science and in the development of science as a whole, which, over decades and centuries, moves toward destinations that no one can predict. Thus, only a few decades ago it might have seemed that physics, which had just placed nuclear energy at man's disposal, was the dangerous branch of science while biology, which underlay improvements in medicine and also helped us to understand our dependence on the natural environment, was the beneficial branch; but now that biologists have begun to fathom the secrets of genetics, and to tamper with the genetic substance of life directly, we cannot be so sure. The most striking illustration of the utter disparity that may occur between the wishes of the scientist as a social being and the social results of his scientific findings is certainly the career of Einstein. By nature, he was, according to all accounts, the gentlest of men, and by conviction he was a pacifist, yet he made intellectual discoveries that led the way to the invention of weapons with which the species could exterminate itself. Inspired wholly by a love of knowledge for its own sake, and by an awe at the creation which bordered on the religious, he made possible an instrument of destruction with which the terrestrial creation could be disfigured.

A disturbing corollary of the scientists' inability even to foresee the path of science, to say nothing of determining it, is that while science is without doubt the most powerful revolutionary force in our world, no one directs that force. For science is a process of submission, in which the mind does not dictate to nature but seeks out and then bows to nature's laws, letting its conclusions be guided by that which *is,* independent of our will. From the political point of view, therefore, scientific findings, some lending themselves to evil, some to good, and some to both, simply pour forth from the laboratory in senseless profusion, offering the world now a neutron bomb, now bacteria that devour oil, now a vaccine to prevent polio, now a cloned frog. It is not until the pure scientists, seekers of knowledge for its own sake, turn their findings over to the applied scientists that social intentions begin to guide the results. The applied scientists do indeed set out to make a better vaccine or a bigger bomb, but even they, perhaps, deserve less credit or blame than we are sometimes inclined to give them. For as soon as our intentions enter the picture we are in the realm of politics in the broadest sense, and in politics it is ultimately not technicians but governments and citizens who are in charge. The scientists in the Manhattan Project could not decide to make the first atomic bomb; only President Roosevelt, elected to office by the American people, could do that.

If scientists are unable to predict their discoveries, neither can they cancel them once they have been made. In this respect, they are like the rest of us, who are asked not whether we would like to live in a world in which we can convert matter into energy but only what we want to do about it once we have been told that we do live in such a world. Science is a tide that can only rise. The individual human mind is capable of forgetting things, and mankind has collectively forgotten many things, but we do not know how, as a species, to *deliberately* set out to forget something. A basic scientific finding, therefore, has the character of destiny for the world. Scientific discovery is in this regard like any other form of discovery; once Columbus had discovered America, and had told the world about it, America could not be hidden again.

Scientific progress (which can and certainly will occur) offers little more hope than scientific regression (which probably cannot occur) of giving us relief from the nuclear peril. It does not seem likely that science will bring forth some new invention—some antiballistic missile or laser beam—that will render nuclear weapons harmless (although the unpredictability of science prevents any categorical judgment on this point). In the centuries of the modern scientific revolution, scientific knowledge has steadily increased the destructiveness of warfare, for it is in the very nature of knowledge, apparently, to increase our might rather than to diminish it. One of the most common forms of the hope for deliverance from the nuclear peril by technical advances is the notion that the species will be spared extinction by fleeing in spaceships. The thought seems to be that while the people on earth are destroying themselves communities in space will be able to survive and carry on. This thought does an injustice to our birthplace and habitat, the earth. It assumes that if only we could escape the earth we would find safety—as though it were the earth and its plants and animals that threatened us, rather than the other way around. But the fact is that wherever human beings went there also would go the knowledge of how to build nuclear weapons, and, with it, the peril of extinction. Scientific progress may yet deliver us from many evils, but there are at least two evils that it cannot deliver us from: its own findings and our own destructive and self-destructive bent. This is a combination that we will have to learn to deal with by some other means.

We live, then, in a universe whose fundamental substance contains a supply of energy with which we can extinguish ourselves. We shall never live in any other. We now know that we live in such a universe, and we shall never stop knowing it. Over the millennia, this truth lay in waiting for us, and now we have found it out, irrevocably. If we suppose that it is an integral part of human existence to be curious about the physical world we are born into, then, to speak in the broadest terms, the origin of the nuclear peril lies, on the one hand, in our nature as rational and inquisitive beings and, on the other, in the nature of matter. Because the energy that nuclear weapons release is so great, the whole species is threatened by them, and because the spread of scientific knowledge is unstoppable, the whole species poses the threat: in the last analysis, it is all of mankind that threatens all of mankind. (I do not mean to overlook the fact that at present it is only two nations—the United States and the Soviet Union—that possess nuclear weapons in numbers great enough to possibly destroy the species, and that they thus now bear the chief responsibility for the peril. I only wish to point out that, regarded in its full dimensions, the nuclear peril transcends the rivalry between the present superpowers.)

The fact that the roots of the nuclear peril lie in basic scientific knowledge has broad political implications that cannot be ignored if the world's solution to the predicament is to be built on a solid foundation, and if futile efforts are to be avoided. One such effort would be to rely on secrecy to contain the peril—that is, to "classify" the "secret" of the bomb. The first person to try to suppress knowledge of how nuclear weapons can be made was the physicist Leo Szilard, who in 1939, when he first heard that a nuclear chain reaction was possible, and realized that a nuclear bomb might be possible, called on a number of his colleagues to keep the discovery secret from the Germans. Many of the key scientists refused. His failure foreshadowed a succession of failures, by whole governments, to restrict the knowledge of how the weapons are made. The first, and most notable, such failure was the United States' inability to monopolize nuclear weapons, and prevent the Soviet Union from building them. And we have subsequently witnessed the failure of the entire world to prevent nuclear weapons from spreading. Given the nature of scientific thought and the very poor record of past attempts to suppress it, these failures should not have surprised anyone. (The Catholic Church succeeded in making Galileo recant his view that the earth revolves around the sun, but we do not now believe that the sun revolves around the earth.) Another, closely related futile effort—the one made by our hypothetical council—would be to try to resolve the nuclear predicament through disarmament alone, without accompanying political measures. Like the hope that the knowledge can be classified, this hope loses sight of the fact that the nuclear predicament consists not in the possession of nuclear weapons at a particular moment by certain nations but in the circumstance that mankind as a whole has now gained possession once and for all of the knowledge of how to make them, and that all nations—and even some groups of people which are not nations, including terrorist groups—can potentially build them. Because the nuclear peril, like the scientific knowledge that gave rise to it, is probably global and everlasting, our solution must at least aim at being global and everlasting. And the only kind of solution that holds out this promise is a global political one. In defining the task so broadly, however, I do not mean to argue against short-term palliatives, such as the Strategic Arms Limitation Talks between the United States and the Soviet Union, or nuclear-nonproliferation agreements, on the ground that they are short-term. If a patient's life is in danger, as mankind's now is, no good cause is served by an argument between the nurse who wants to give him an aspirin to bring down his fever and the doctor who wants to perform the surgery that can save his life; there is need for an argument only if the nurse is claiming that the aspirin is all that is necessary. If, given the world's discouraging record of political achievement, a lasting political solution seems almost beyond human powers, it may give us confidence to remember that what challenges us is simply our extraordinary success in another field of activity—the scientific. We have only to learn to live politically in the world in which we already live scientifically.

Since 1947, the *Bulletin of the Atomic Scientists* has included a "doomsday clock" in each issue. The editors place the hands farther away from or closer to midnight as they judge the world to be farther from or closer to a nuclear holocaust. A companion clock can be imagined whose hands, instead of metaphorically representing a judgment about the likelihood of a holocaust, could represent an estimate of the amount of time that, given the world's technical and political arrangements, the people of the earth can be sure they have left before they are destroyed in a holocaust. At present, the hands would stand at, or a fraction of a second before, midnight, because none of us can be sure that at any second we will not be killed in a nuclear attack. If, by treaty, all nuclear warheads were removed from their launchers and stored somewhere else, and therefore could no longer descend on us at any moment without warning, the clock would show the amount of time that it would take to put them back on. If all the nuclear weapons in the world were destroyed, the clock would show the time that it would take to manufacture them again. If in addition confidence-inspiring political arrangements to prevent rearmament were put in place, the clock would show some estimate of the time that it might take for the arrangements to break down. And if these arrangements were to last for hundreds or thousands of years (as they must if mankind is to survive this long), then some generation far in the future might feel justified in setting the clock at decades, or even centuries, before midnight. But no generation would ever be justified in retiring the clock from use altogether, because, as far as we can tell, there will never again be a time when self-extinction is beyond the reach of our species. An observation that Plutarch made about politics holds true also for the task of survival, which has now become the principal obligation of politics: "They are wrong who think that politics is like an ocean voyage or a military campaign, something to be done with some end in view, something which levels off as soon as that end is reached. It is not a public chore, to be got over with; it is a way of life."

The scientific principles and techniques that make possible the construction of nuclear weapons are, of course, only one small portion of mankind's huge reservoir of scientific knowledge, and, as I have mentioned, it has always been known that scientific findings can be made use of for evil as well as for good, according to the intentions of the user. What is new to our time is the realization that, acting quite independently of any good or evil intentions of ours, the human enterprise as a whole has begun to strain and erode the natural terrestrial world on which human and other life depends. Taken in its entirety, the increase in mankind's strength has brought about a decisive, many-sided shift in the balance of strength between man and the earth. Nature, once a harsh and feared master, now lies in subjection, and needs protection against man's powers. Yet because man, no matter what intellectual and technical heights he may scale, remains embedded in nature, the balance has shifted against him, too, and the threat that he poses to the earth is a threat to him as well. The peril to nature was difficult to see at first, in part because its symptoms made their appearance as unintended "side effects" of our intended goals, on which we had fixed most of our attention. In economic production, the side effects are the peril of gradual pollution of the natural environment—by, for example, global heating through an increased "greenhouse effect." In the military field, the side effects, or prospective side effects—sometimes referred to by the strategists as the "collateral effects"—include the possible extinction of the species through sudden severe harm to the ecosphere, caused by global radioactive contamination, ozone depletion, climatic change, and the other known and unknown possible consequences of a nuclear holocaust. Though from the point of view of the human actor there might be a clear difference between the "constructive" economic applications of technology and the "destructive" military ones, nature makes no such distinction: both are beachheads of human mastery in a defenseless natural world. (For example, the ozone doesn't care whether oxides of nitrogen are injected into it by the use of supersonic transports or by nuclear weapons; it simply reacts according to the appropriate chemical laws.) It was not until recently that it became clear that often the side effects of both the destructive and the constructive applications were really the main effects. And now the task ahead of us can be defined as one of giving the "side effects," including, above all, the peril of self-extinction, the weight they deserve in our judgments and decisions. To use a homely metaphor, if a man discovers that improvements he is making to his house threaten to destroy its foundation he is well advised to rethink them.

A nuclear holocaust, because of its unique combination of immensity and suddenness, is a threat without parallel; yet at the same time it is only one of countless threats that the human enterprise, grown mighty through knowledge, poses to the natural world. Our species is caught in the same tightening net of technical success that has already strangled so many other species. (At present, it has been estimated, the earth loses species at the rate of about three per day.) The peril of human extinction, which exists not because every single person in the world would be killed by the immediate explosive and radioactive effects of a holocaust—something that is exceedingly unlikely, even at present levels of armament—but because a holocaust might render the biosphere unfit for human survival, is, in a word, an *ecological* peril. The nuclear peril is usually seen in isolation from the threats to other forms of life and their ecosystems, but in fact it should be seen as the very center of the ecological crisis—as the cloud-covered Everest of which the more immediate, visible kinds of harm to the environment are the mere foothills. Both the effort to preserve the environment and the effort to save the species from extinction by nuclear arms would be enriched and strengthened by this recognition. The nuclear question, which now stands in eerie seclusion from the rest of life, would gain a context, and the ecological movement, which, in its concern for plants and animals, at times assumes an almost misanthropic posture, as though man were an unwanted intruder in an otherwise unblemished natural world, would gain the humanistic intent that should stand at the heart of its concern.

Seen as a planetary event, the rising tide of human mastery over nature has brought about a categorical increase in the power of death on earth. An organism's ability to renew itself during its lifetime and to reproduce itself depends on the integrity of what biologists call "information" stored in its genes. What endures—what lives—in an organism is not any particular group of cells but a configuration of cells which is dictated by the genetic information. What survives in a species, correspondingly, is a larger configuration, which takes in all the individuals in the species. An ecosystem is a still larger configuration, in which a whole constellation of species forms a balanced, self-reproducing, slowly changing whole. The ecosphere of the earth—Dr. Lewis Thomas's "cell"— is finally, the largest of the living configurations, and is a carefully regulated and balanced, self-perpetuating system in its own right. At each of these levels, life is coherence, and the loss of coherence—the sudden slide toward disorder —is death. Seen in this light, life is information, and death is the loss of information, returning the substance of the creature to randomness. However, the death of a species or an ecosystem has a role in the natural order that is very different from that of the death of an organism. Whereas an individual organism, once born, begins to proceed inevitably toward death, a species is a source of new life that has no fixed term. An organism is a configuration whose demise is built into its plan, and within the life of a species the death of individual members normally has a fixed, limited, and necessary place, so that as death moves through the ranks of the living its pace is roughly matched by the pace of birth, and populations are kept in a rough balance that enables them to coexist and endure in their particular ecosystem. A species, on the other hand, can survive as long as environmental circumstances happen to permit. An ecosystem, likewise, is indefinitely self-renewing. But when the pace of death is too much increased, either by human intervention in the environment or by some other event, death becomes an extinguishing power, and species and ecosystems are lost. Then not only are individual creatures destroyed but the sources of all future creatures of those kinds are closed down, and a portion of the diversity and strength of terrestrial life in its entirety vanishes forever. And when man gained the ability to intervene directly in the workings of the global "cell" as a whole, and thus to extinguish species wholesale, his power to encroach on life increased by still another order of magnitude, and came to threaten the balance of the entire planetary system of life.

Hence, there are two competing forces at work in the terrestrial environment—one natural, which acts over periods of millions of years to strengthen and multiply the forms of life, and the other man-made and man-operated, which, if it is left unregulated and unguided, tends in general to deplete life's array of forms. Indeed, it is a striking fact that both of these great engines of change on earth depend on stores of information that are passed down from generation to generation. There is, in truth, no closer analogy to scientific progress, in which a steadily growing pool of information makes possible the creation of an ever more impressive array of artifacts, than evolution, in which another steadily growing pool of information makes possible the development of ever more complex and astonishing creatures—culminating in human beings, who now threaten to raze both the human and natural structures to their inanimate foundations. One is tempted to say that only the organic site of the evolutionary information has changed—from genes to brains. However, because of the extreme rapidity of technological change relative to natural evolution, evolution is unable to refill the vacated niches of the environment with new species, and, as a result, the genetic pool of life as a whole is imperilled. Death, having been augmented by human strength, has lost its appointed place in the natural order and become a counter-evolutionary force, capable of destroying in a few years, or even in a few hours, what evolution has built up over billions of years. In doing so, death threatens even itself, since death, after all, is a part of life: stones may be lifeless but they do not die. The question now before the human species, therefore, is whether life or death will prevail on the earth. This is not metaphorical language but a literal description of the present state of affairs.

One might say that after billions of years nature, by creating a species equipped with reason and will, turned its fate, which had previously been decided by the slow, unconscious movements of natural evolution, over to the conscious decisions of just one of its species. When this occurred, human activity, which until then had been confined to the historical realm—which, in turn, had been supported by the broader biological current—spilled out of its old boundaries and came to menace both history and biology. Thought and will became mightier than the earth that had given birth to them. Now human beings became actors in the geological time span, and the laws that had governed the development and the survival of life began to be superseded by processes in the mind of man. Here, however, there were no laws; there was only choice, and the thinking and feeling that guide choice. The reassuring, stable, self-sustaining prehistoric world of nature dropped away, and in its place mankind's own judgments, moods, and decisions loomed up with an unlooked-for, terrifying importance.

Regarded objectively, as an episode in the development of life on earth, a nuclear holocaust that brought about the extinction of mankind and other species by mutilating the ecosphere would constitute an evolutionary setback of possibly limited extent—the first to result from a deliberate action taken by the creature extinguished but perhaps no greater than any of several evolutionary setbacks, such as the extinction of the dinosaurs, of which the geological record offers evidence. (It is, of course, impossible to judge what course evolution would take after human extinction, but the past record strongly suggests that the reappearance of man is not one of the possibilities. Evolution has brought forth an amazing variety of creatures, but there is no evidence that any species, once extinguished, has ever evolved again. Whether or not nature, obeying some law of evolutionary progress, would bring forth another creature equipped with reason and will, and capable of building, and perhaps then destroying, a world, is one more unanswerable question, but it is barely conceivable that some gifted new animal will pore over the traces of our self-destruction, trying to figure out what went wrong and to learn from our mistakes. If this should be possible, then it might justify the remark once made by Kafka: "There is infinite hope, but not for us." If, on the other hand, as the record of life so far suggests, terrestrial evolution is able to produce only once the miracle of the qualities that we now associate with human beings, then all hope rides with human beings.) However, regarded subjectively, from within human life, where we are all actually situated, and as something that would happen to us, human extinction assumes awesome, inapprehensible proportions. It is of the essence of the human condition that we are born, live for a while, and then die. Through mishaps of all kinds, we may also suffer untimely death, and in extinction by nuclear arms the number of untimely deaths would reach the limit for any one catastrophe: everyone in the world would die. But although the untimely death of everyone in the world would in itself constitute an unimaginably huge loss, it would bring with it a separate, distinct loss that would be in a sense even huger—the cancellation of all future generations of human beings. According to the Bible, when Adam and Eve ate the fruit of the tree of knowledge God punished them by withdrawing from them the privilege of immortality and dooming them and their kind to die. Now our species has eaten more deeply of the fruit of the tree of knowledge, and has brought itself face to face with a second death—the death of mankind. In doing so, we have caused a basic change in the circumstances in which life was given to us, which is to say that we have altered the human condition. The distinctness of this second death from the deaths of all the people on earth can be illustrated by picturing two different global catastrophes. In the first, let us suppose that most of the people on earth were killed in a nuclear holocaust but that a few million survived and the earth happened to remain habitable by human beings. In this catastrophe, billions of people would perish, but the species would survive, and perhaps one day would even repopulate the earth in its former numbers. But now let us suppose that a substance was released into the environment which had the effect of sterilizing all the people in the world but otherwise leaving them unharmed. Then, as the existing population died off, the world would empty of people, until no one was left. Not one life would have been shortened by a single day, but the species would die. In extinction by nuclear arms, the death of the species and the death of all the people in the world would happen together, but it is important to make a clear distinction between the two losses; otherwise, the mind, overwhelmed by the thought of the deaths of the billions of living people, might stagger back without realizing that behind this already ungraspable loss there lies the separate loss of the future generations.

The possibility that the living can stop the future generations from entering into life compels us to ask basic new questions about our existence, the
most sweeping of which is what these unborn ones, most of whom we will
never meet even if they are born, mean to us. No one has ever thought to
ask this question before our time, because no generation before ours has ever
held the life and death of the species in its hands. But if we hardly know
how to comprehend the possible deaths in a holocaust of the billions of people who are already in life how are we to comprehend the life or death of
the infinite number of possible people who do not yet exist at all? How are
we, who are a part of human life, to step back from life and see it whole,
in order to assess the meaning of its disappearance? To kill a human being
is murder, and there are those who believe that to abort a fetus is also murder, but what crime is it to cancel the numberless multitude of unconceived
people? In what court is such a crime to be judged? Against whom is it committed? And what law does it violate? If we find the nuclear peril to be somehow abstract, and tend to consign this whole elemental issue to "defense experts"
and other dubiously qualifed people, part of the reason, certainly, is that the
future generations really are abstract—that is to say, without the tangible
existence and the unique particularities that help to make the living real to
us. And if we find the subject strangely "impersonal" it may be in part because
the unborn, who are the ones directly imperilled by extinction, are not yet
persons. What are they, then? They lack the individuality that we often associate with the sacredness of life, and may at first thought seem to have only
a shadowy, mass existence. *Where* are they? Are they to be pictured lined
up in a sort of fore-life, waiting to get into life? Or should we regard them
as nothing more than a pinch of chemicals in our reproductive organs, toward which we need feel no special obligations? What standing should they
have among us? How much should their needs count in competition with ours?
How far should the living go in trying to secure their advantage, their happiness, their existence?

The individual person, faced with the metaphysical-seeming perplexities
involved in pondering the possible cancellation of people who do not yet exist—
an apparently extreme effort of the imagination, which seems to require one
first to summon before the mind's eye the countless possible people of the
future generations and then to consign these incorporeal multitudes to a more
profound nothingness—might well wonder why, when he already has his own
death to worry about, he should occupy himself with this other death. Since
our own individual death promises to inflict a loss that is total and final, we
may find the idea of a second death merely redundant. After all, can everything
be taken away from us twice? Moreover, a person might reason that even
if mankind did perish he wouldn't have to know anything about it, since in
that event he himself would perish. There might actually be something consoling
in the idea of having so much company in death. In the midst of universal
death, it somehow seems out of order to want to go on living oneself. As

Randall Jarrell wrote in his poem "Losses," thinking back to his experience in the Second World War, "it was not dying: everybody died."

However, the individual would misconceive the nuclear peril if he tried to understand it primarily in terms of personal danger, or even in terms of danger to the people immediately known to him, for the nuclear peril threatens life, above all, not at the level of individuals, who already live under the sway of death, but at the level of everything that individuals hold in common. Death cuts off life; extinction cuts off birth. Death dispatches into the nothingness after life each person who has been born; extinction in one stroke locks up in the nothingness before life all the people who have not yet been born. For we are finite beings at both ends of our existence—natal as well as mortal—and it is the natality of our kind that extinction threatens. We have always been able to send people to their death, but only now has it become possible to prevent all birth and so doom all future human beings to uncreation. The threat of the loss of birth—a beginning that is over and done with for every living person—cannot be a source of immediate, selfish concern; rather, this threat assails everything that people hold in common, for it is the ability of our species to produce new generations which assures the continuation of the world in which all our common enterprises occur and have their meaning. Each death belongs unalienably to the individual who must suffer it, but birth is our common possession. And the meaning of extinction is therefore to be sought first not in what each person's own life means to him but in what the world and the people in it mean to him.

In its nature, the human world is, in Hannah Arendt's words, a "common world," which she distinguishes from the "private realm" that belongs to each person individually. (Somewhat surprisingly, Arendt, who devoted so much of her attention to the unprecedeted evils that have appeared in our century, never addressed the issue of nuclear arms; yet I have discovered her thinking to be an indispensable foundation for reflection on this question.) The private realm, she writes in *The Human Condition*, a book published in 1958, is made up of "the passions of the heart, the thoughts of the mind, the delights of the senses," and terminates with each person's death, which is the most solitary of all human experiences. The common world, on the other hand, is made up of all institutions, all cities, nations, and other communities, and all works of fabrication, art, thought, and science, and it survives the death of every individual. It is basic to the common world that it encompasses not only the present but all past and future generations. "The common world is what we enter when we are born and what we leave behind when we die," Arendt writes. "It transcends our life-span into past and future alike; it was there before we came and will outlast our brief sojourn in it. It is what we have in common not only with those who live with us, but also with those who were here before and with those who will come after us." And she adds, "Without this trancendence into a potential earthly immortality, no politics, strictly speaking, no common world, and no public realm is possible." The creation of a common world is the use that we human beings, and we alone among the earth's creatures, have made of the biological circumstance that while each of us is mortal, our species is biologically immortal. If mankind had not established a common world, the species would still outlast its individual members and be immortal, but this immortality would be unknown to us and would go for nothing, as it does in the animal kingdom, and the generations, unaware of one another's existence, would come and go like waves on the beach, leaving everything just as it was before. In fact, it is only because humanity has built up a common world that we can fear our destruction as a species. It may even be that man, who has been described as the sole creature that knows that it must die, can know this only because he lives in a common world, which permits him to imagine a future beyond his own life. This common world, which is unharmed by individual death but depends on the survival of the species, has now been placed in jeopardy by nuclear arms. Death and extinction are thus complementary, dividing between them the work of undoing, or threatening to undo, everything that human beings are or can ever become, with death terminating the life of each individual and extinction imperilling the common world shared by all. In one sense, extinction is less terrible than death, since extinction can be avoided, while death is inevitable; but in another sense extinction is more terrible—is the more radical nothingness—because extinction ends death just as surely as it ends birth and life. Death is only death; extinction is the death of death.

# Part Two
# Defining Technology

# Introduction

There are considerable confusions about the meaning of the word "technology." It might seem that these could be cleared up by simply referring to a good dictionary. However, since dictionaries report on the ways we do in fact use language, one finds the same multiple, vague, and ambiguous meanings that we find in ordinary discourse. Thus, these definitions do little to clarify our thinking.

It is also the case that there is no consensus among the authors in this section, indeed throughout this volume, as to how "technology" ought to be defined. This is not, however, because these writers do not know what they are talking about. The concepts of technology they propose are used to introduce theories of technology. Disputes that may appear to be a matter of semantics are, at a deeper level, disputes about the meaning of technology in our lives. In this sense we are looking for concepts that will illuminate the significance of a most important aspect of the human condition. Although most of the concepts we will encounter fall within the range of common usage, some will strain against these bounds. Some definitions may hide, while others may uncover, important points of view regarding technology. It will thus be important to not ask for *the* meaning, but as the philosopher Ludwig Wittgenstein might say, to look for the way this thinker is using the term.

If we focus our attention on "technology" in a narrow sense as tools or material artifacts it seems obvious that technology is neutral in two senses: (1) since technology simply provides us with means, it does not affect our lives in any significant way. New technologies simply provide more efficient means for accomplishing pre-existing ends. A calculator is just a faster way to balance the check book. (2) Technology is ethically neutral, for its value depends on how it is used. A hammer can be used to build a house or to bash your neighbor's head in.

If, on the other hand, we focus on the design of even simple tools, a very different picture emerges. It is clear that specific tools are created for specific purposes. A carpenter's hammer is designed to drive nails, not to kill your neighbor—that is what hand guns are for. On this view the ends are built into the very construction of the implement. Thus, a technology *is* a use, and in this sense is thoroughly intentional.

A further difficulty is that some authors talk of technology in the abstract, arguing that there is an essential nature to all technology, while others will focus on the operation of this or that particular technology—and may deny that there is any such thing as technology in general.

One last cautionary note. Beware of *persuasive* definitions! Some ways of defining "technology" attempt to smuggle into the very meaning of the word important theoretical and evaluative conclusions. The definition cited in the general introduction, "the totality of means employed to provide objects necessary for human sustenance and comfort," is a prime example. The MX missile may be necessary for human sustenance and comfort, but surely this needs to be argued. We should not be seduced into accepting this conclusion without reasons.

According to Alvin Weinberg, technology does give us the means to provide objects "necessary for human sustenance and comfort," but this is not true by definition. He gives us some reasons to support faith in technological solutions to social problems. In contrast to social engineering, which aims at the tremendously complex problem of changing human behavior, "technical fixes eliminate the original social problem" or "so alter the problem as to make its resolution more feasible." Technology, by increasing our productive capacity, can obviate questions of social justice by providing more than enough goods to go around. The H-bomb has brought us peace without making people good, or even more rational. If we don't lose faith in the idea of progress and put our minds and money into technological development, we can develop efficient nuclear desalinization plants to produce all the water people want. We would thus not need to urge conservation or deal with questions of distributive justice.

Weinberg admits that "technological solutions to social problems tend to be incomplete and 'metastable,' to replace one social problem with another." The precarious peace brought about by nuclear weapons is clearly "metastable." However, even here technical fixes are relevant. Weinberg would, I think, agree that President Reagan's Strategic Defense Initiative is a force for peace. Further, cheap nuclear energy would go a long way in reducing tensions between nations of haves and have-nots. "Technology will never *replace* social engineering," but through a cooperative effort between technologists and social engineers we can hope to bring about a better society and a better life for us all.

B. F. Skinner would agree with Weinberg that "technology" can solve our social problems, but not the kind of technology that is based on the physical sciences. Indeed, many of our problems have been generated by such technologies. Mass production techniques may have raised the standard of living in the West, but are also the source of environmental pollution. Better birth control techniques are worthwhile only if people use them. The root of our problems lies with human behavior. New technologies represent remarkable achievements, but our social problems "grow steadily worse."

One of Weinberg's reasons for pessimism about human engineering is that he seems to assume that there is a fixed human nature: "Men have not been good, and . . . they are not paragons of virtue, or even of reasonableness." Moral preaching is ineffective, for human nature is immutable.

Skinner argues neither for the mutability nor immutability of human behavior. For him the major stumbling blocks in developing a technology of behavior are the unscientific beliefs that there is an autonomous human nature to begin with and that what people do is determined by the free choices of an "inner man." Once we recognize that the notion of human autonomy is a myth, that human behavior is determined by contingencies of reinforcement in the environment, we can manipulate those contingencies to modify behavior in socially constructive ways. There is no reason why we should not be able to predict and control human behavior in as precise a manner as the physicist in his work with nuclear reactions. The point is not to make people good, but to control their behavior; moral notions of virtue are irrelevant.

No one is morally responsible for what he or she does, for it is the environment that is responsible for behavior—and this can be changed once we go "beyond freedom and dignity." As Skinner recognizes, this "raises questions concerning 'values.' Who will use a technology and to what ends?" However, it is difficult to see, if Skinner is correct in saying that we are simply links in a deterministic causal chain, how we could rationally evaluate the ends of our technology. Indeed, is not Skinner's verbal behavior merely the product of the contingencies of reinforcement?

Jacques Ellul argues that *no* distinctions can be made in the contemporary world between science and technology. On his view "this traditional distinction is radically false. . . . It is true only for the physical sciences and for the nineteenth century." While a few intellectuals may continue to value knowledge as an end, their views are irrelevant; for our technological society values science only as a means. To raise questions about ends is considered irrational in a society dominated by what Ellul calls "technique," which "is nothing more than means and the ensemble of means."

If we are to understand the current situation, Ellul thinks we need a very broad notion of technology. Although the machine remains the model for technique, the machine is not the problem. The basic problem is the all-embracing "ensemble of means" that integrates and coordinates all *human* activities, eliminating all that is spontaneous, free, and distinctively human. This "technical phenomenon" is the quest for the one best means in every field: economics, social and political organization, and man himself. We cannot, Ellul claims, bring ourselves to question the universal applicability of the machine model that divides, quantifies, and rationalizes all activities in seeking the most efficient means. As an analogy Ellul might point to the popularity of sex manuals that prescribe the steps to follow in our most intimate, human relationships. Man himself "becomes the object of technique," as exemplified in the article by B. F. Skinner in this section. The machine is the model for dealing with both mice and men.

Undoubtedly, Ellul reveals some of the most significant ways in which technology shapes our lives and thought. But there is the danger that he may have a too abstract, too inclusive concept for thinking clearly about our situation.

Arnold Pacey's thinking about technology is rooted in case studies of how specific technologies have functioned in various cultural contexts. Modeled on the idea of medical practice, his admirably lucid concept of technology-practice allows us a most comprehensive view of technology without obscuring important distinctions. Technology in the narrow sense, e.g., as defined by Weinberg, is to be understood as it interacts with cultural and organizational factors. Thinking of technology only in the traditional, restricted sense, which Pacey refers to as the technical aspect, leads not only to intellectual confusions but to misapplications of technology—especially in the transfer of technology to "underdeveloped" societies. The wider perspective reveals that technology is neither culturally nor ethically neutral, but constitutes a way of life.

As one opposed to the linear view taken by Ellul, which sees technology as *the* cause of all social change, or Skinner's environinmental determinism, Pacey gives us a dynamic model which he thinks more accurately reflects the multiplicity of causes. The technology-practice perspective shows that there is no "technological imperative," no inevitable "one best way." There is a place, on his view, for human choices; important ethical and political decisions have to be made. The question is, Who will make them, and for whom will they be made?

Jack Beatty's reflections on the hearings following the *Challenger* disaster show that the causes were not, following Pacey's usage, merely technical. As we all know, the proximate cause of the explosion was the failure of an O-ring; still, it was the bureaucratic organization and language of NASA that prevented the warnings of lower echelon engineers from finding their way up the chain of command. To understand this situation, we need a concept of technology that is broader than the "technical." As we shall see in Part 3, an argument can be made that we are all trapped in a machine-like system.

# 2

# Can Technology Replace Social Engineering?

## Alvin M. Weinberg

During World War II, and immediately afterward, our federal government mobilized its scientific and technical resources, such as the Oak Ridge National Laboratory [ORNL], around great technological problems. Nuclear reactors, nuclear weapons, radar, and space are some of the miraculous new technologies that have been created by this mobilization of federal effort. In the past few years there has been a major change in focus of much of our federal research. Instead of being preoccupied with technology, our government is now mobilizng around problems that are largely social. We are beginning to ask what we can do about world population, about the deterioration of our environment, about our educational system, our decaying cities, race relations, poverty. Recent administrations have dedicated the power of a scientifically oriented federal apparatus to finding solutions for these complex social problems.

Social problems are much more complex than are technological problems. It is much harder to identify a social problem than a technological problem: how do we know when our cities need renewing, or when our population is too big, or when our modes of transportation have broken down? The problems are, in a way, harder to identify just because their solutions are never clear-cut: how do we know when our cities are renewed, or our air clean enough, or our transportation convenient enough? By contrast, the availability of a crisp and beautiful technological *solution* often helps focus on the problem to which the new technology is the solution. I doubt that we would have been nearly as concerned with an eventual shortage of energy as we now are if we had not had a neat solution—nuclear energy—available to eliminate the shortage.

There is a more basic sense in which social problems are much more difficult than are technological problems. A social problem exists because many people behave, individually, in a socially unacceptable way. To solve a social problem one must induce social change—one must persuade many people to behave differently than they have behaved in the past. One must persuade many people to have fewer babies, or to drive more carefully, or to refrain from disliking blacks. By contrast, resolution of a technological problem involves many fewer individual decisions. Once President Roosevelt decided to go after atomic energy, it was by comparison a relatively simple task to mobilize the Manhattan Project.

The resolution of social problems by the traditional methods—by motivating or forcing people to behave more rationally—is a frustrating business. People don't behave rationally; it is a long, hard business to persuade individuals to forgo immediate personal gain or pleasure (as seen by the individual) in favor of longer term social gain. And indeed, the aim of social engineering is to invent the social devices—usually legal, but also moral and educational and organizational—that will change each person's motivation and redirect his activities along ways that are more acceptable to the society.

The technologist is appalled by the difficulties faced by the social engineer; to engineer even a small social change by inducing individuals to behave differently is always hard even when the change is rather neutral or even beneficial. For example, some rice eaters in India are reported to prefer starvation to eating wheat which we send to them. How much harder it is to change motivations where the individual is insecure and feels threatened if he acts differently, as illustrated by the poor white's reluctance to accept the black as an equal. By contrast, technological engineering is simple: the rocket, the reactor, and the desalination plants are devices that are expensive to develop, to be sure, but their feasibility is relatively easy to assess, and their success relatively easy to achieve once one understands the scientific principles that underlie them. It is, therefore, tempting to raise the following question: In view of the simplicity of technological engineering, and the complexity of social engineering, to what extent can social problems be circumvented by reducing them to technological problems? Can we identify Quick Technological Fixes for profound and almost infinitely complicated social problems, "fixes" that are within the grasp of modern technology, and which would either eliminate the original social problem without requiring a change in the individual's social attitudes, or would so alter the problem as to make its resolution more feasible? To paraphrase Ralph Nader, to what extent can technological *remedies* be found for social problems without first having to remove the *causes* of the problem? It is in this sense that I ask, "Can technology replace social engineering?"

## THE MAJOR TECHNOLOGICAL FIXES OF THE PAST

To better explain what I have in mind, I shall describe how two of our profoundest social problems—poverty and war—have in some limited degree been solved by the Technological Fix, rather than by the methods of social engineering. Let me begin with poverty.

The traditional Marxian view of poverty regarded our economic ills as being primarily a question of maldistribution of goods. The Marxist recipe for elimination of poverty, therefore, was to eliminate profit, in the erroneous belief that it was the loss of this relatively small increment from the worker's paycheck that kept him poverty-stricken. The Marxist dogma is typical of the approach of the social engineer: one tries to convince or coerce many people to forgo their short-term profits in what is presumed to be the long-term interest of the society as a whole.

The Marxian view seems archaic in this age of mass production and automation, not only to us but apparently to many Eastern bloc economists. For the brilliant advances in the technology of energy, of mass production, and of automation have created the affluent society. Technology has expanded our productive capacity so greatly that even though our distribution is still inefficient, and unfair by Marxian precept, there is more than enough to go around. Technology has provided a "fix"—greatly expanded production of goods—which enables our capitalistic society to achieve many of the aims of the Marxist social engineer without going through the social revolution Marx viewed as inevitable. Technology has converted the seemingly intractable social problem of *widespread* poverty into a relatively tractable one.

My second example is war. The traditional Chinese position views war as primarily a moral issue: if men become good, and model themselves after the Prince of Peace, they will live in peace. This doctrine is so deeply ingrained in the spirit of all civilized men that I suppose it is a blasphemy to point out that it has never worked very well—that men have not been good, and that they are not paragons of virtue or even of reasonableness.

Though I realize it is terribly presumptuous to claim, I believe that Edward Teller may have supplied the nearest thing to a quick Technological Fix to the problem of war. The hydrogen bomb greatly increases the provocation that would precipitate large-scale war—and not because men's motivations have been changed, not because men have become more tolerant and understanding, but rather because the appeal to the primitive instinct of self-preservation has been intensified far beyond anything we could have imaginged before the H-bomb was invented. To point out these things today [1966], with the United States involved in a shooting war [in Vietnam], may sound hollow and unconvincing; yet the desperate and partial peace we have now is much better than a full-fledged exchange of thermonuclear weapons. One cannot deny that the Soviet leaders now recognize the force of H-bombs, and that this has surely contributed to the less militant attitude of the USSR. One can only hope that the Chinese leadership, as it acquires familiarity with H-bombs, will also become less militant. If I were to be asked who has given the world a more effective means of achieving peace, our great religious leaders who urge men to love their neighbors and, thus, avoid fights, or our weapons technologists who simply present men with no rational alternative to peace, I would vote for the weapons technologists. That the peace we get is at best terribly fragile, I cannot deny; yet, as I shall explain, I think technology can help stabilize our imperfect and precarious peace.

## THE TECHNOLOGICAL FIXES OF THE FUTURE

Are there other Technological Fixes on the horizon, other technologies that can reduce immensely complicated social questions to a matter of "engineering"? Are there new technologies that offer society ways of circumventing social problems and at the same time do *not* require individuals to renounce short-term advantage for long-term gain?

Probably the most important new Technological Fix is the Intra-Uterine Device for birth control. Before the IUD was invented, birth control demanded very strong motivation of countless individuals. Even with the pill, the individual's motivation had to be sustained day in and day out; should it flag even temporarily, the strong motivation of the previous month might go for naught. But the IUD, being a one-shot method, greatly reduces the individual motivation required to induce a social change. To be sure, the mother must be sufficiently motivated to accept the IUD in the first place, but, as experience in India already seems to show, it is much easier to persuade the Indian mother to accept the IUD once, than it is to persuade her to take a pill every day. The IUD does not completely replace social engineering by technology; and indeed, in some Spanish American cultures where the husband's manliness is measured by the number of children he has, the IUD attacks only part of the problem. Yet, in many other situations, as in India, the IUD so reduces the social component of the problem as to make an impossibly difficult social problem much less hopeless.

Let me turn now to problems which from the beginning have had both technical and social components—broadly, those concerned with conservation of our resources: our environment, our water, and our raw materials for production of the means of subsistence. The social issue here arises because many people by their individual acts cause shortages and, thus, create economic, and ultimately social, imbalance. For example, people use water wastefully, or they insist on moving to California because of its climate, and so we have water shortages; or too many people drive cars in Los Angeles with its curious meteorology, and so Los Angeles suffocates from smog.

The water resources problem is a particularly good example of a complicated problem with strong social and technological connotations. Our management of water resources in the past has been based largely on the ancient Roman device, the aqueduct: every water shortage was to be relieved by stealing water from someone else who at the moment didn't need the water or was too poor or too weak to prevent the steal. Southern California would steal from Northern California, New York City from upstate New York, the farmer who could afford a cloud-seeder from the farmer who could not afford a cloud-seeder. The social engineer insists that such shortsighted expedients have got us into serious trouble; we have no water resources policy, we waste water disgracefully, and, perhaps, in denying the ethic of thriftiness in using water, we have generally undermined our moral fiber. The social engineer, therefore, views such technological shenanigans as being shortsighted, if not downright immoral. Instead, he says, we should persuade or force people to use less water, or to stay in the cold Middle West where water is plentiful instead of migrating to California where water is scarce.

The water technologist, on the other hand, views the social engineer's approach as rather impractical. To persuade people to use less water, to get along with expensive water, is difficult, time-consuming, and uncertain in the extreme. Moreover, say the technologists, what right does the water resources expert have to insist that people use water less wastefully? Green lawns and clean cars and swimming pools are part of the good life, American style, . . . and what right do we have to deny this luxury if there is some alternative to cutting down the water we use?

Here we have a sharp confrontation of the two ways of dealing with a complex social issue: the social engineering way which asks people to behave more "reasonably," the technologists' way which tries to avoid changing people's habits or motivation. Even though I am a technologist, I have sympathy for the social engineer. I think we must use our water as efficiently as possible, that we ought to improve people's attitudes toward the use of water, and that everything that can be done to rationalize our water policy will be welcome. Yet as a technologist, I believe I see ways of providing more water more cheaply than the social engineeers may concede is possible.

I refer to the possibility of nuclear desalination. The social engineer dismisses the technologist's simpleminded idea of solving a water shortage by transporting more water primarily because, in so doing, the water user steals water from someone else—possibly foreclosing the possibility of ultimately uitilizing land now only sparsely settled. But surely water drawn from the sea deprives no one of his share of water. The whole issue is then a technological one; can fresh water be drawn from the sea cheaply enough to have a major impact on our chronically water-short areas like Southern California, Arizona, and the Eastern seaboard?

I believe the answer is yes, though much hard technical work remains to be done. A large program to develop cheap methods of nuclear desalting has been undertaken by the United States, and I have little doubt that within the next ten to twenty years we shall see huge dual-purpose desalting plants springing up on many parched seacoasts of the world. At first these plants will produce water at municipal prices. But I believe, on the basis of research now in progress at ORNL and elsewhere, water from the sea at a cost acceptable for agriculture—less than ten cents per 1,000 gallons—is eventually in the cards. In short, for areas close to the seacoasts, technology can provide water without requiring a great and difficult-to-accomplish change in people's attitudes toward the utilization of water.*

The Technological Fix for water is based on the availability of extremely cheap energy from very large nuclear reactors. What other social consequences can one foresee flowing from really cheap energy eventually available to every country regardless of its endowment of conventional resources? Though we now see only vaguely the outlines of the possibilities, it does seem likely that from very cheap nuclear energy we shall get hydrogen by electrolysis of water, and, thence, the all important ammonia fertilizer necessary to help feed the hungry of the world; we shall reduce metals without requiring coking coal; we shall even power automobiles with electricity, via fuel cells or storage batteries, thus reducing our world's dependence on crude oil, as well as eliminating our air pollution insofar as it is caused by automobile exhaust or by the burning of fossil fuels. In short, the widespread availability of very cheap energy everywhere in the world ought to lead to an energy autarky in every country of the world; and eventually to an autarky in the many staples of life that should flow from really cheap energy.

## WILL TECHNOLOGY REPLACE SOCIAL ENGINEERING?

I hope these examples suggest how social problems can be circumvented or at least reduced to less formidable proportions by the application of the Technological Fix. The examples I have given do not strike me as being fanciful, nor are they at all exhaustive. I have not touched, for example, upon the extent to which really cheap computers and improved technology of communication can help improve elementary teaching without having first to improve our elementary teachers. Nor have I mentioned Ralph Nader's brilliant observation that a safer car, and even its development and adoption by the auto company, is a quicker and probably surer way to reduce traffic deaths than is a campaign to teach people to drive more carefully. Nor have I invoked some really fanciful Technological Fixes: like providing air conditioners and free electricity to operate them for every black family in Watts on the assumption (suggested by Huntington) that race rioting is correlated with hot, humid weather; or the ultimate Technological Fix, Aldous Huxley's soma pills that eliminate human unhappiness without improving human relations in the usual sense.

---

*That this has not been realized should, perhaps, temper our enthusiasm for technological fixes. (Ed.).

My examples illustrate both the strength and the weakness of the Technological Fix for social problems. The Technological Fix accepts man's intrinsic shortcomings and circumvents them or capitalizes on them for socially useful ends. The Fix is, therefore, eminently practical and, in the short term, relatively effective. One does not wait around trying to change people's minds: if people want more water, one gets them more water rather than requiring them to reduce their use of water; if people insist on driving autos while they are drunk, one provides safer autos that prevent injuries even after a severe accident.

But the technological solutions to social problems tend to be incomplete and metastable, to replace one social problem with another. Perhaps the best example of this instability is the peace imposed upon us by the H-bomb. Evidently the *pax hydrogenica* is metastable in two senses: in the short term, because the aggressor still enjoys such an advantage; in the long term, because the discrepancy between have and have-not nations must eventually be resolved if we are to have permanent peace. Yet, for these particular shortcomings, technology has something to offer. To the imbalance between offense and defense, technology says let us devise passive defense which redresses the balance. A world with H-bombs and adequate civil defense is less likely to lapse into thermonucelar war than a world with H-bombs alone, at least if one concedes that the danger of the thermonuclear war mainly lies in the acts of irresponsible leaders. Anything that deters the irresponsible leader is a force for peace: a technologically sound civil defense therefore would help stabilize the balance of terror.

To the discrepancy between haves and have-nots, technology offers the nuclear energy revolution, with its possibility of autarky for haves and have-nots alike. How this might work to stabilize our metastable thermonuclear peace is suggested by the possible political effect of the recently proposed Israeli desalting plant. The Arab states I should think would be much less set upon destroying the Jordan River Project if the Israelis had a desalination plant in reserve that would nullify the effect of such action. In this connection, I think countries like ours can contribute very much. Our country will soon have to decide whether to continue to spend $5.5 \times 10^9$* per year for space exploration after our lunar landing. Is it too outrageous to suggest that some of this money be devoted to building huge nuclear desalting complexes in the arid ocean rims of the troubled world? If the plants are empowered with breeder reactors, the out-of-pocket costs, once the plants are built, should be low enough to make large-scale agriculture feasible in these areas. I estimate that for $4 \times 10^9$† we could build enough desalting capacity to feed more than ten million new mouths per year (provided we use agricultural methods that husband water), and we would, thereby, help stabilize the metastable, bomb-imposed balance of terror.

---

*5.5 billion, equivalent to approximatly $13.5 billion in today's dollars.

†$4 billion, equivalent to approximately $10 billion in today's dollars.

Yet, I am afraid we technologists shall not satisfy our social engineers, who tell us that our Technological Fixes do not get to the heart of the problem; they are at best temporary expedients; they create new problems as they solve old ones; to put a Technological Fix into effect requires a positive social action. Eventually, social engineering, like the Supreme Court decision on desegregation, must be invoked to solve social problems. And, of course, our social engineers are right. Technology will never *replace* social engineeering. But technology has provided and will continue to provide to the social engineer broader options, to make intractable social problems less intractable; perhaps, most of all, technology will buy time—that precious commodity that converts violent social revolution into acceptable social evolution.

Our country now recognizes and is mobilizing around the great social problems that corrupt and disfigure our human existence. It is natural that in this mobilization we should look first to the social engineer. But, unfortunately, the apparatus most readily available to the government, like the great federal laboratories, is technologically oriented, not socially oriented. I believe we have a great opportunity here; for, as I hope I have persuaded [my readers], many of our seemingly social problems do admit of partial technological solutions. Our already deployed technological apparatus can contribute to the resolution of social questions. I plead, therefore, first for our government to deploy its laboratores, its hardware contractors, and its engineering universities around social problems. And I plead, secondly, for understanding and cooperation between technologist and social engineer. Even with all the help he can get from the technologist, the social engineer's problems are never really solved. It is only by cooperation between technologist and social engineer that we can hope to achieve what is the aim of all technologists and social engineeers—a better society, and thereby, a better life, for all of us who are part of society.

# 3

# A Technology of Behavior

## B. F. Skinner

In trying to solve the terrifying problems that face us in the world today, we naturally turn to the things we do best. We play from strength, and our strength is science and technology. To contain a population explosion we look for better methods of birth control. Threatened by a nuclear holocaust, we build bigger deterrent forces and anti-ballistic-missile systems. We try to stave off world famine with new foods and better ways of growing them. Improved sanitation and medicine will, we hope, control disease, better housing and transportation will solve the problems of the ghettos, and new ways of reducing or disposing of waste will stop the pollution of the environment. We can point to remarkable achievements in all these fields, and it is not surprising that we should try to extend them. But things grow steadily worse, and it is disheartening to find that technology itself is increasingly at fault. Sanitation and medicine have made the problems of population more acute, war has acquired a new horror with the invention of nuclear weapons, and the affluent pursuit of happiness is largely responsible for pollution. As [C. D.] Darlington has said, "Every new source from which man has increased his power on the earth has been used to diminish the prospects of his successors. All his progress has been made at the expense of damage to his environment which he cannot repair and could not foresee."[1]

Whether or not he could have foreseen the damage, man must repair it or all is lost. And he can do so if he will recognize the nature of the difficulty.

The application of the physical and biological sciences alone will not solve our problems because the solutions lie in another field. Better contraceptives will control population only if people use them. New weapons may offset new defenses and vice versa, but a nuclear holocaust can be prevented only if the conditions under which nations make war can be changed. New methods of agriculture and medicine will not help if they are not practiced, and housing is a matter not only of buildings and cities but of how people live. Overcrowding can be corrected only by inducing people not to crowd, and the environment will continue to deteriorate until polluting practices are abandoned.

In short, we need to make vast changes in human behavior, and we cannot make them with the help of nothing more than physics or biology, no matter how hard we try. (And there are other problems, such as the breakdown of our educational system and the disaffection and revolt of the young, to which physical and biological technologies are so obviously irrelevant that they have never been applied.) It is not enough to "use technology with a deeper understanding of human issues," or to "dedicate technology to man's spiritual needs," or to "encourage technologists to look at human problems." Such expressions imply that where human behavior begins, technology stops, and that we must carry on, as we have in the past, with what we have learned from personal experience or from those collections of personal experiences called history, or with the distillations of experience to be found in folk wisdom and practical rules of thumb. These have been available for centuries, and all we have to show for them is the state of the world today.

What we need is a technology of behavior. We could solve our problems quickly enough if we could adjust the growth of the world's population as precisely as we adjust the course of a spaceship, or improve agriculture and industry with some of the confidence with which we accelerate high-energy particles, or move toward a peaceful world with something like the steady progress with which physics has approached absolute zero (even though both remain presumably out of reach). But a behavioral technology comparable in power and precision to physical and biological technology is lacking, and those who do not find the very possibility ridiculous are more likely to be frightened by it than reassured. That is how far we are from "understanding human issues" in the sense in which physics and biology understand their fields, and how far we are from preventing the catastrophe toward which the world seems to be inexorably moving.

Unable to understand how or why the person we see behaves as he does, we attribute his behavior to a person we cannot see, whose behavior we cannot explain either but about whom we are not inclined to ask questions. We probably adopt this strategy not so much because of any lack of interest or power but because of a longstanding conviction that for much of human behavior there *are* no relevant antecedents. The function of the inner man is to provide an explanation which will not be explained in turn. Explanation stops with him. He is not a mediator between past history and current behavior, he is a *center* from which behavior emanates. He initiates, originates, and creates, and in doing so he remains, as he was for the Greeks, divine. We say that he is autonomous—and, so far as a science of behavior is concerned, that means miraculous.

The position is, of course, vulnerable. Autonomous man serves to explain only the things we are not yet able to explain in other ways. His existence depends upon our ignorance, and he naturally loses status as we come to know more about behavior. The task of a scientific analysis is to explain how the behavior of a person as a physical system is related to the conditions under which the human species evolved and the conditions under which the individual lives. Unless there is indeed some capricious or creative intervention, these events must be related, and no intervention is in fact needed. The contingencies of survival responsible for man's genetic endowment would produce tendencies to *act* aggressively, not feelings of aggression. The punishment of sexual behavior changes sexual *behavior*, and any feelings which may arise are at best by-products. Our age is not suffering from anxiety but from the accidents, crimes, wars, and other dangerous and painful things to which people are so often exposed. Young people drop out of school, refuse to get jobs, and associate only with others of their own age not because they feel alienated but because of defective social environments in homes, schools, factories, and elsewhere.

We can follow the path taken by physics and biology by turning directly to the relation between behavior and the environment and neglecting supposed mediating states of mind. Physics did not advance by looking more closely at the jubilance of a falling body, or biology by looking at the nature of vital spirits, and we do not need to try to discover what personalities, states of mind, feelings, traits of character, plans, purposes, intentions, or the other perquisites of autonomous man really are in order to get on with a scientific analysis of behavior.

The effect of the environment on behavior remained obscure for a long time. We can see what organisms do to the world around them, as they take from it what they need and ward off its dangers, but it is much harder to see what the world does to them. It was Descartes who first suggested that the environment might play an active role in the determination of behavior, and he was apparently able to do so only because he was given a strong hint. He knew about certain automata in the Royal Gardens of France which were operated hydraulically by concealed valves. As Descartes described it, people entering the gardens "necessarily tread on certain tiles or plates, which are so disposed that if they approach a bathing Diana, they cause her to hide in the rosebushes, and if they try to follow her, they cause a Neptune to come forward to meet them, threatening them with his trident." The figures were entertaining just because they behaved like people, and it appeared, therefore, that something very much like human behavior could be explained mechanically. Descartes took the hint: living organisms might move for similar reasons.

(He excluded the human organism, presumably to avoid religious controversy.)

The triggering action of the environment came to be called a "stimulus"—the Latin for goad—and the effect on an organism a "response," and together they were said to compose a "reflex." Reflexes were first demonstrated in small decapitated animals, such as salamanders, and it is significant that the principle was challenged throughout the nineteenth century because it seemed to deny the existence of an autonomous agent—the "soul of the spinal cord"—to which movement of a decapitated body had been attributed. When Pavlov showed how new reflexes could be built up through conditioning, a full-fledged stimulus-response psychology was born, in which all behavior was regarded as reactions to stimuli. One writer put it this way: "We are prodded or lashed through life." The stimulus-response model was never very convincing, however, and it did not solve the basic problem, because something like an inner man had to be invented to convert a stimulus into a response. Information theory ran into the same problem when an inner "processer" had to be invented to convert input into output.

The effect of an eliciting stimulus is relatively easy to see, and it is not surprising that Descartes' hypothesis held a dominant position in behavior theory for a long time, but it was a false scent from which a scientific analysis is only now recovering. The environment not only prods or lashes, it *selects*. Its role is similar to that in natural selection, though to a very different time scale, and was overlooked for the same reason. It is now clear that we must take into account what the environment does to an organism not only before but after it responds. Behavior is shaped and maintained by its consequences. Once this fact is recognized, we can formulate the interaction between organism and environment in a much more comprehensive way.

There are two important results. One concerns the basic analysis. Behavior which operates upon the environment to produce consequences ("operant" behavior) can be studied by arranging environments in which specific consequences are contingent upon it. The contingencies under investigation have become steadily more complex, and one by one they are taking over the explanatory functions previously assigned to personalities, states of mind, feelings, traits of character, purposes, and intentions. The second result is practical: the environment can be manipulated. It is true that man's genetic endowment can be changed only very slowly, but changes in the environment of the individual have quick and dramatic effects. A technology of operant behavior is, as we shall see, already well advanced, and it may prove to be commensurate with our problems.

That possibility raises another problem, however, which must be solved if we are to take advantage of our gains. We have moved forward by dispossessing autonomous man, but he has not departed gracefully. He is conducting a sort of rear-guard action in which, unfortunately, he can marshal formidable support. He is still an important figure in political science, law, religion, economics, anthropology, sociology, psychotherapy, philosophy, ethics, history, education, child care, linguistics, architecture, city planning, and family life. These fields have their specialists, and every specialist has a theory, and in almost every theory the autonomy of the individual is unquestioned. The inner man is not seriously threatened by data obtained through casual observation or from studies of the structure of behavior, and many of these fields deal only with groups of people, where statistical or actuarial data impose few restraints upon the individual. The result is a tremendous weight of traditional "knowledge," which must be corrected or displaced by a scientific analysis.

Two features of autonomous man are particularly troublesome. In the traditional view, a person is free. He is autonomous in the sense that his behavior is uncaused. He can therefore be held responsible for what he does and justly punished if he offends. That view, together with its associated practices, must be re-examined when a scientific analysis reveals unsuspected controlling relations between behavior and environment. A certain amount of external control can be tolerated. Theologians have accepted the fact that man must be predestined to do what an omniscient God knows he will do, and the Greek dramatist took inexorable fate as his favorite theme. Soothsayers and astrologers often claim to predict what men will do, and they have always been in demand. Biographers and historians have searched for "influences" in the lives of individuals and peoples. Folk wisdom and the insights of essayists like Montaigne and Bacon imply some kind of predictability in human conduct, and the statistical and actuarial evidences of the social sciences point in the same direction.

Autonomous man survives in the face of all this because he is the happy exception. Theologians have reconciled predestination with free will, and the Greek audience, moved by the portrayal of an inescapable destiny, walked out of the theater free men. The course of history has been turned by the death of a leader or a storm at sea, as a life has been changed by a teacher or a love affair, but these things do not happen to everyone, and they do not affect everyone in the same way. Some historians have made a virtue of the unpredictability of history. Actuarial evidence is easily ignored; we read that hundreds of people will be killed in traffic accidents on a holiday weekend and take to the road as if personally exempt. Very little behavioral science raises "the specter of predictable man." On the contrary, many anthropologists, sociologists, and psychologists have used their expert knowledge to prove that man is free, purposeful, and responsible. Freud was a determinist— on faith, if not on the evidence—but many Freudians have no hesitation in assuring their patients that they are free to choose among different courses of action and are in the long run the architects of their own destinies.

This escape route is slowly closed as new evidences of the predictability of human behavior are discovered. Personal exemption from a complete determinism is revoked as a scientific analysis progresses, particularly in accounting for the behavior of the individual. Joseph Wood Krutch has acknowledged the actuarial facts while insisting on personal freedom: "We can predict with a considerable degree of accuracy how many people will go to the seashore on a day when the temperature reaches a certain point, even how many will jump off a bridge . . . although I am not, nor are you, compelled to do either."[2] But he can scarcely mean that those who go to the seashore do not go for good reason, or that circumstances in the life of a suicide do not have some bearing on the fact that he jumps off a bridge. The distinction is tenable only so long as a word like "compel" suggests a particularly conspicuous and forcible mode of control. A scientific analysis naturally moves in the direction of clarifying all kinds of controlling relations.

By questioning the control exercised by autonomous man and demonstrating the control exercised by the environment, a science of behavior also seems to question dignity or worth. A person is responsible for his behavior, not only in the sense that he may be justly blamed or punished when he behaves badly, but also in the sense that he is to be given credit and admired for his achievements. A scientific analysis shifts the credit as well as the blame to the environment, and traditional practices can then no longer be justified. These are sweeping changes, and those who are committed to traditional theories and practices naturally resist them.

There is a third source of trouble. As the emphasis shifts to the environment, the individual seems to be exposed to a new kind of danger. Who is to construct the controlling environment and to what end? Autonomous man presumably controls himself in accordance with a built-in set of values; he works for what he finds good. But what will the putative controller find good, and will it be good for those he controls? Answers to questions of this sort are said, of course, to call for value judgments.

Freedom, dignity, and value are major issues, and unfortunately they become more crucial as the power of a technology of behavior becomes more nearly commensurate with the problems to be solved. The very change which has brought some hope of a solution is responsible for a growing opposition to the kind of solution proposed. This conflict is itself a problem in human behavior and may be approached as such. A science of behavior is by no means as far advanced as physics or biology, but it has an advantage in that it may throw some light on its own difficulties. Science *is* human behavior, and so is the opposition to science. What has happened in man's struggle for freedom and dignity, and what problems arise when scientific knowledge begins to be relevant in that struggle? Answers to these questions may help to clear the way for the technology we so badly need.

Almost all our major problems involve human behavior, and they cannot be solved by physical and biological technology alone. What is needed is a technology of behavior, but we have been slow to develop the science from which such a technology might be drawn. One difficulty is that almost all of what is called behavioral science continues to trace behavior to states of mind, feelings, traits of character, human nature, and so on. Physics and biology once followed similar practices and advanced only when they discarded them. The behavioral sciences have been slow to change partly because the explanatory entities often seem to be directly observed and partly because other kinds of explanations have been hard to find. The environment is obviously important, but its role has remained obscure. It does not push or pull, it *selects,* and this function is difficult to discover and analyze. The role of natural selection in evolution was formulated only a little more than a hundred years ago, and the selective role of the environment in shaping and maintaining the behavior of the individual is only beginning to be recognized and studied. As the interaction between organism and environment has come to be understood, however, effects once assigned to states of mind, feelings, and traits are beginning to be traced to accessible conditions, and a technology of behavior may therefore become available. It will not solve our problems, however, until it replaces traditonal prescientific views, and these are strongly entrenched. Freedom and dignity illustrate the difficulty. They are the possessions of the autonomous man of traditional theory, and they are essential to practices in which a person is held responsible for his conduct and given credit for his achievements. A scientific analysis shifts both the responsibility and the achievement of the environment. It also raises questions concerning "values." Who will use a technology and to what ends? Until these issues are resolved, a technology of behavior will continue to be rejected, and with it possibly the only way to solve our problems.

## NOTES

1. C. D. Darlington, *The Evolution of Man and Society,* noted in *Science* 168 (1970): 1332.
2. Joseph Wood Krutch, *New York Times Magazine,* July 30, 1967.

# 4

# Defining Technique

## Jacques Ellul

## DEFINITIONS

Once we stop identifying technique and machine, the definitions of technique we find are inadequate to the established facts. Marcel Mauss, the sociologist, understands the problem admirably, and has given various definitions of technique, some of which are excellent. Let us take one that is open to criticism and, by criticizing it, state our ideas more precisely: "Technique is a group of movements, of actions generally and mostly manual, organized, and traditional, all of which unite to reach a known end, for example, physical, chemical, or organic."

This definition is perfectly valid for the sociologist who deals with the primitive. It offers, as Mauss shows, numerous advantages. For example, it eliminates from the realm of techniques questions of religion or art. But these advantages apply only in a historical perspective. In the modern perspective, this definition is insufficient.

Can it be said that the technique of elaboration of an economic plan (purely a technical operation) is the result of such movements as Mauss describes? No particular motion or physical act is involved. An economic plan is purely an intellectual operation, which nevertheless is a technique.

When we consider Mauss's statement that technique is restricted to manual activity, the inadequacy of his definition is even more apparent. Today most technical operations are not manual. Whether machines are substituted for men, or technique becomes intellectual, the most important sphere in the world today (because in it lie the seeds of future development) is scarcely that of manual labor. True, manual labor is still the basis of mechanical operation, and we would do well to recall Jünger's principal argument against the illusion of technical progress. He holds that the more technique is perfected, the more it requires secondary manual labor; and, furthermore, that the volume of manual operations increases faster than the volume of mechanical operations. This may be so, but the most important feature of techniques today is that they do not depend on manual labor but on organization and on the arrangement of machines.

I am willing to accept the term *organized,* as Mauss uses it in his definition, but I must part company with him in respect to his use of the term *traditional.* And this differentiates the technique of today from that of previous civilizations. It is true that in all civilizations technique has existed as tradition, that is, by the transmission of inherited processes that slowly ripen and are even more slowly modified; that evolve under the pressure of circumstances along with the body social; that create automatisms which become hereditary and are integrated into each new form of technique.

But how can anyone fail to see that none of this holds true today? Technique has become autonomous; it has fashioned an omnivorous world which obeys its own laws and which has renounced all tradition. Technique no longer rests on tradition, but rather on previous technical procedures; and its evolution is too rapid, too upsetting, to integrate the older traditions. This fact, which we shall study at some length later on,* also explains why it is not quite true that a technique assures a result known in advance. It is true if one considers only the user: the driver of an automobile knows that he can expect to go faster when he steps on the accelerator. But even in the field of the mechanical, with the advent of the technique of servo-mechanisms,† this axiom does not hold true. In these cases the machine itself adapts as it operates; this very fact makes it difficult to predict the final result of its activity. This becomes clear when one considers not use but technical progress— although, at the present time, the two are closely associated. It is less and less exact to maintain that the user remains for very long in possession of a technique the results of which he can predict; constant invention ceaselessly upsets his habits.

Finally, Mauss appears to think that the goal attained is of a physical order. But today we recognize that techniques go further. Psychoanalysis and sociology have passed into the sphere of technical application; one example

---

*See part 3, chapter 7.

†Mechanisms which involve so-called "feedback," in which information measuring the degree to which an effector (e.g., an oil furnace) is in error with respect to producing a desired value (e.g., a fixed room temperature) is "fed back" to the effector by a monitor (e.g., a thermostat). (Trans.)

of this is propaganda. Here the operation is of a moral, psychic, and spiritual character. However, that does not prevent it from being a technique. But what we are talking about is a world once given over to the pragmatic approach and now being taken over by method. We can say, therefore, that Mauss's definition, which was valid for technique until the eighteenth century, is not applicable to our times. In this respect Mauss has been the victim of his own sociological studies of primitive people, as his classification of techniques (food gathering, the making of garments, transport, etc.) clearly shows.

Further examples of inadequate definition are those supplied by Jean Fourastié and others who pursue the same line of research as he. For Fourastié, technical progress is "the growth of the volume of production obtained through a fixed quantity of raw material or human labor"—that is, technique is uniquely that which promotes this increase in yield. He then goes on to say that it is possible to analyze this theorem under three aspects. In *yield in kind,* technique is that which enables raw materials to be managed in order to obtain some predetermined product; in *financial yield,* technique is that which enables the increase in production to take place through the increase of capital investment; in *yield of human labor,* technique is that which increases the quantity of work produced by a fixed unit of human labor. In this connection we must thank Fourastié for correcting Jünger's error—Jünger opposes technical progress to economic progress because they would be, in his opinion, contradictory; Fourastié shows that, on the contrary, the two coincide. However, we must nevertheless challenge his definition of technique on the ground that it is completely arbitrary.

It is arbitrary, first of all, because it is purely economic and contemplates only economic yield. There are innumerable traditional techniques which are not based on a quest for economic yield and which have no economic character. It is precisely these which Mauss alludes to in his definition; and they still exist. Among the myriad modern techniques, there are many that have nothing to do with economic life. Take, for example, a technique of mastication based on the science of nutrition, or techniques of sport, as in the Boy Scout movement—in these cases we can see a kind of yield, but this yield has little to do with economics.

In other cases, there are economic results, but these results are secondary and cannot be said to be characteristic. Take, for example, the modern calculating machine. The solving of equations in seventy variables, required in certain econometric research, is impossible except with an electronic calculating machine. However, it is not the economic productivity that results from the utilization of this machine by which its importance is measured.

A second criticism of Fourastié's definition is that he assigns an exclusively productive character to technique. The growth of the volume of production is an even narrower concept than yield. The techniques which have shown the greatest development are not techniques of production at all. For example, techniques in the care of human beings (surgery, psychology, and so on) have nothing to do with productivity. The most modern techniques of destruction have even less to do with productivity; the atomic and hydrogen bombs and the Germans' V1 and V2 weapons are all examples of the most powerful technical creations of man's mind. Human ingenuity and mechanical skill are today being exploited along lines which have little reference to productivity.

Nothing equals the perfection of our war machines. Warships and warplanes are vastly more perfect than their counterparts in civilian life. The organization of the army—its transport, supplies, administration—is much more precise than any civilian organization. The smallest error in the realm of war would cost countless lives and would be measured in terms of victory or defeat. What is the yield there? Very poor, on the whole. Where is the productivity? There is none.

Vincent, in his definition, likewise refers to productivity: Technical progress is the relative variation in world production in a given sphere between two given periods." This definition, useful of course from the economic point of view, leads him at once into a dilemma. He is obliged to distinguish technical progress from progress of technique (which corresponds to the progression of techniques in all fields) and to distinguish these two from "technical progress, properly speaking," which concerns variations in productivity. This is an inference made from natural phenomena for, in his definition, Vincent is obliged to recognize that technical progress includes *natural* phenomena (the greater or lesser richness of an ore, of the soil, etc.) by definition the very contrary of *technique!*

These linguistic acrobatics and hairsplittings suffice to prove the inanity of such a definition, which aims at a single aspect of technical progress and includes elements which do not belong to technique. From this definition, Vincent infers that technical progress is slow. But what is true of economic productivity is not true of technical progress in general. If one considers technique shorn of one whole part, and that it's most progressive, one can indeed assert that it is slow in its progress. This abstraction is even more illusory when one claims to measure technical progress. The definition proposed by Fourastié is inexact because it excludes everything that does not refer to production, and all effects that are not economic.

This tendency to reduce the technical problem to the dimensions of the technique of production is also present in the works of so enlightened a scholar as Georges Friedmann. In his introduction to the UNESCO* Colloquium on technique, he appears to start out with a very broad definition. But in the second paragraph, without warning, he begins to reduce everything to the level of economic production.

What gives rise to this limitation of the problem? One factor might be a tacit optimism, a need to hold that technical progress is unconditionally

---

*United Nations Educational, Scientific, and Cultural Organization (Ed.)

valid—which leads to the selection of the most positive aspect of technical progress, as though it were its only one.

This may have guided Fourastié, but it does not seem to hold true in Friedmann's case. I believe that the reasoning behind Friedmann's way of thinking is to be found in the turn of the scientific mind. All aspects—mechanical, economic, psychological, sociological—of the techniques of production have been subjected to innumerable specialized studies; as a result, we are beginning to learn in a more precise and scientific way about the relationships between man and the industrial machine. Since the scientist must use the materials he has at hand; and since almost nothing is known about the relationship of man to the automobile, the telephone, or the radio, and absolutely nothing about the relationship of man to the *Apparat* or about the sociological effects of other aspects of technique, the scientist moves unconsciously toward the sphere of what is known scientifically, and tries to limit the whole question to that.

There is another element in this scientific attitude: only that is knowable which is expressed (or, at least, can be expressed) in numbers. To get away from the so-called "arbitrary and subjective," to escape ethical or literary judgments (which, as everyone knows, are trivial and unfounded), the scientist must get back to numbers. What, after all, can one hope to deduce from the purely qualitative statement that the worker is fatigued? But when biochemistry makes it possible to measure fatigability numerically, it is at last possible to take account of the worker's fatigue. Then there is hope of finding a solution. However, an entire realm of effects of technique—indeed, the largest—is not reducible to numbers; and it is precisely that realm which we are investigating in this [chapter]. Yet, since what can be said about it is apparently not to be taken seriously, it is better for the scientist to shut his eyes and regard it as a realm of pseudo-problems, or simply as nonexistent. The "scientific" position frequently consists of denying the existence of whatever does not belong to current scientific method. The problem of the industrial machine, however, is a numerical one in nearly all its aspects. Hence, all of technique is unintentionally reduced to a numerical question. In the case of Vincent, this is intentional, as his definition shows: "We embrace in technical progress all kinds of progress . . . *provided* that they are treatable numerically in a reliable way."

H. D. Lasswell's definition of technique as "the ensemble of practices by which one uses available resources in order to achieve certain valued ends" also seems to follow the conventions cited above, and to embrace only industrial technique. Here it might be contested whether technique does indeed permit the realization of values. However, to judge from Lasswell's examples, he conceives the terms of his definition in an extremely broad manner. He gives a list of values and the corresponding techniques. As values, for example, he lists riches, power, well-being, affection; and as techniques, the techniques of government, production, medicine, the family, and so on. Lasswell's conception of *value* may seem somewhat strange; the term is obviously not apt. But what he has to say indicates that he gives techniques their full scope. Moreover, he makes it quite clear that it is necessary to show the effects of technique not only on inanimate objects but also on people. I am, therefore, in substantial agreement with this conception.

## TECHNICAL OPERATION AND TECHNICAL PHENOMENON

With the use of these few guideposts, we can now try to formulate, if not a full definition, at least an approximate definition of technique. But we must keep this in mind: we are not concerned with the different individual techniques. Everyone practices a particular technique, and it is difficult to come to know them all. Yet in this great diversity we can find certain points in common, certain tendencies and principles shared by them all. It is clumsy to call these common features Technique with a capital T; no one would recognize his particular technique behind this terminology. Nevertheless, it takes account of a reality—the technical phenomenon—which is worldwide today.

If we recognize that the method each person employs to attain a result is, in fact, his particular technique, the problem of means is raised. In fact, technique is nothing more than *means* and the *ensemble of means*. This, of course, does not lessen the importance of the problem. Our civilization is first and foremost a civilization of means; in the reality of modern life, the means, it would seem, are more important than the ends. Any other assessment of the situation is mere idealism.

Techniques considered as methods of operation present certain common characteristics and certain general tendencies, but we cannot devote ourselves exclusively to them. To do this would lead to a more specialized study than I have in mind. The technical phenomenon is much more complex than any synthesis of characteristics common to individual techniques. If we desire to come closer to a definition of technique, we must in fact differentiate between the technical operation and the technical phenomenon.

The technical operation includes every operation carried out in accordance with a certain method in order to attain a particular end. It can be as rudimentary as splintering a flint or as complicated as programming an electronic brain. In every case, it is the method which characterizes the operation. It may be more or less effective or more or less complex, but its nature is always the same. It is this which leads us to think that there is a continuity in technical operations and that only the great refinement resulting from scientific progress differentiates the modern technical operation from the primitive one.

Every operation obviously entails a certain technique, even the gathering of fruit among primitive peoples—climbing the tree, picking the fruit as quickly and with as little effort as possible, distinguishing between the ripe and the unripe fruit, and so on. However, what characterizes technical action within a particular activity is the search for greater efficiency. Completely natural and spontaneous effort is replaced by a complex of acts designed to improve, say, the yield. It is this which prompts the creation of technical forms, starting from simple forms of activity. These technical forms are not necessarily more complicated than the spontaneous ones, but they are more efficient and better adapted.

Thus, technique creates means, but the technical operation still occurs on the same level as that of the worker who does the work. The skilled worker, like the primitive huntsman, remains a technical operator; their attitudes differ only to a small degree.

But two factors enter into the extensive field of technical operation: consciousness and judgment. This double intervention produces what I call the technical phenomenon. What characterizes this double intervention? Essentially, it takes what was previously tentative, unconscious, and spontaneous and brings it into the realm of clear, voluntary, and reasoned concepts.

When André Leroi-Gourhan tabulates the efficiency of Zulu swords and arrows in terms of the most up-to-date knowledge of weaponry, he is doing work that is obviously different from that of the swordsmith of Bechuanaland who created the form of the sword. The swordsmith's choice of form was unconscious and spontaneous; although it can now be justified by numerical calculations, such calculations had no place whatever in the technical operation he performed. But reason did, inevitably, enter into the process because man spontaneously imitates nature in his activities. Accomplishments that merely copy nature, however, have no future (for instance, the imitation of birds' wings from Icarus to Ader). Reason makes it possible to produce objects in terms of certain features, certain abstract requirements; and this in turn leads, not to the imitation of nature, but to the ways of technique.

The intervention of rational judgment in the technical operation has important consequences. Man becomes aware that it is possible to find new and different means. Reason upsets pragmatic traditions and creates new operational methods and new tools; it [generates] experimentation. Reason in these ways multiplies technical operations to a high degree of diversity. But it also operates in the opposite direction: it considers results and takes account of the fixed end of technique—efficiency. It notes what every means devised is capable of accomplishing and selects from the various means at its disposal with a view to securing the ones that are the most efficient, the best adapted to the desired end. Thus the multiplicity of means is reduced to one: the most efficient. And here reason appears clearly in the guise of technique.

In addition, there is the intervention of consciousness. Consciousness shows clearly, and to everybody, the advantages of technique and what it can accomplish. The technician takes stock of alternative possibilities. The immediate result is that he seeks to apply the new methods in fields which traditionally had been left to chance, pragmatism, and instinct. The intervention of consciousness causes a rapid and far-flung extension of technique.

The twofold intervention of reason and consciousness in the technical world, which produces the technical phenomenon, can be described as the quest of the one best means in every field. And this "one best means" is, in fact, the technical means. It is the aggregate of these means that produces technical civilization.

The technical phenomenon is the main preoccupation of our time; in every field men seek to find the most efficient method. But our investigations have reached a limit. It is no longer the best relative means that counts, as compared to other means also in use. The choice is less and less a subjective one among several means that are potentially applicable. It is really a question of finding the best means in the absolute sense, on the basis of numerical calculation.

It is, then, the specialist who chooses the means; he is able to carry out the calculations that demonstrate the superiority of the means chosen over all others. Thus a science of means comes into being—a science of techniques, progressively elaborated.

This science extends to greatly diverse areas; it ranges from the act of shaving to the act of organizing the landing in Normandy, or to cremating thousands of deportees. Today no human activity escapes this technical imperative. There is a technique of organization (the great fact of organization described by Toynbee fits very well into this conception of the technical phenomenon); just as there is a technique of friendship and a technique of swimming. Under the circumstances, it is easy to see how far we are from confusing technique and machine. And, if we examine the broader areas where this search for means is taking place, we find three principal subdivisions of modern technique, in addition to the mechanical (which is the most conspicuous but which I shall not discuss because it is so well known) and to the forms of intellectual technique (card indices, libraries, and so on).

(1) *Economic technique* is almost entirely subordinated to production, and ranges from the organization of labor to economic planning. This technique differs from the others in its object and goal. But its problems are the same as those of all other technical activities.

(2) *The technique of organization* concerns the great masses and applies not only to commercial or industrial affairs of magnitude (coming, consequently, under the juristiction of the economic) but also to states and to administration and police power. This organizational technique is also applied to warfare and insures the power of an army at least as much as its weapons. Everything in the legal field also depends on organizational technique.

(3) *Human technique* takes various forms, ranging all the way from medicine and genetics to propaganda (pedagogical techniques,

vocational guidance, publicity, etc.) Here man himself becomes the object of technique.

We observe, in the case of each of these subdivisions, that the subordinate techniques may be very different in kind and not necessarily similar one to another as techniques. They have the same goal and preoccupation, however, and are thus related. The three subdivisions show the wide extent of the technical phenomenon. In fact, nothing at all escapes technique today. There is no field where technique is not dominant—this is easy to say and is scarcely surprising. We are so habituated to machines that there seems to be nothing left to discover.

## REFERENCES

Fourastié, Jean. *Révolution à l'Ouest* [*Revolution in the West*]. Paris: Presses Universitaires de France, 1957.

Friedmann, Georges. *La crise du progrès* [*The Crisis of Progress*]. Paris: Gallimard, 1936.

Jünger, F. *Die Perfection der Technik*. Frankfurt: Klostermann, 1949.

Lasswell, Harold Dwight. *Power and Personality*. New York: Academy of Medicine, Compass Books edition, 1962.

Leroi-Gourhan, André. *Milieu et techniques. Évolution et techniques*. A. Michel, 1945.

Mauss, Marcel. *Sociologie et anthropologie*. Paris: Presses Universitaires de France, 1949–1950.

Vincent, André L. A., and René Froment. *Le progrès technique en France dupuis cent aus* [*A Century of Technical Progress in France*]. Imprimerie Nationale, 1944.

# 5

# Technology: Practice and Culture

## Arnold Pacey

### QUESTIONS OF NEUTRALITY

Winter sports in North America gained a new dimension during the 1960s with the introduction of the snowmobile. Ridden like a motorcycle, and having handlebars for steering, this little machine on skis gave people in Canada and the northern United States extra mobility during their long winters. Snowmobile sales doubled annually for a while, and in the boom year of 1970–1 almost half a million were sold. Subsequently the market dropped back, but snowmobiling had established itself, and organized trails branched out from many newly prosperous winter holiday resorts. By 1978, there were several thousand miles of public trails, marked and maintained for snowmobiling, about half in the province of Quebec.

Although other firms had produced small motorized toboggans, the type of snowmobile which achieved this enormous popularity was only really born in 1959, chiefly on the initiative of Joseph-Armand Bombardier of Valcourt, Quebec.[1] He had experimented with vehicles for travel over snow since the 1920s, and had patented a rubber-and-steel crawler track to drive them. His first commercial success, which enabled his motor repair business to grow into a substantial manufacturing firm, was a machine capable of carrying seven passengers which was on the market from 1936. He had other successes later, but nothing that caught the popular imagination like the little snowmobile of 1959, which other manufacturers were quick to follow up.

However, the use of snowmobiles was not confined to the North American tourist centers. In Sweden, Greenland, and the Canadian Arctic, snowmobiles have now become part of the equipment on which many communities depend for their livelihood. In Swedish Lapland they are used for reindeer herding. On Canada's Banks Island they have enabled Eskimo trappers to continue providing their families' cash income from the traditional winter harvest of fox furs.

Such use of the snowmobile by people with markedly different cultures may seem to illustrate an argument very widely advanced in discussions of problems associated with technology. This is the argument which states that technology is culturally, morally, and politically neutral—that it provides tools independent of local value-systems which can be used impartially to support quite different kinds of lifestyle.

Thus in the world at large, it is argued that technology is "essentially amoral, a thing apart from values, an instrument which can be used for good or ill."[2] So if people in distant countries starve; if infant mortality within the inner cities is persistently high; if we feel threatened by nuclear destruction or more insidiously by the effects of chemical pollution, then all that, it is said, should not be blamed on technology, but on its misuse by politicians, the military, big business, and others.

The snowmobile seems the perfect illustration of this argument. Whether used for reindeer herding or for recreation, for ecologically destructive sport, or to earn a basic living, it is the same machine. The engineering principles involved in its operation are universally valid, whether its users are Lapps or Eskimos, Dene (Indian) hunters, Wisconsin sportsmen, Quebecois vacationists, or prospectors from multinational oil companies. And whereas the snowmobile has certainly had a social impact, altering the organization of work in Lapp communities, for example, it has not necessarily influenced basic cultural values. The technology of the snowmobile may thus appear to be something quite independent of the lifestyles of Lapps or Eskimos or Americans.

One look at a modern snowmobile with its fake streamlining and flashy colors suggests another point of view. So does the advertising which portrays virile young men riding the machines with sexy companions, usually blonde and usually riding pillion. The Eskimo who takes a snowmobile on a long expedition in the Arctic quickly discovers more significant discrepancies. With his traditional means of transport, the dog-team and sledge, he could refuel as he went along by hunting for his dogs' food. With the snowmobile he must take an ample supply of fuel and spare parts; he must be skilled at doing his own reapirs and even then he may take a few dogs with him for emergency use if the machine breaks down. A vehicle designed for leisure trips between well-equipped tourist centers presents a completely different set of servicing problems when used for heavier work in more remote areas. One Eskimo "kept his machine in his tent so it could be warmed up before starting in the morning, and even then was plagued by mechanical failures."[3] There are stories of other Eskimos, whose mechanical aptitude is well known, modifying their machines to adapt them better to local use.

So is technology culturally neutral? If we look at the construction of a basic machine and its working principles, the answer seems to be yes. But if we look at the web of human activities surrounding the machine, which include its practical uses, its role as a status symbol, the supply of fuel and spare parts, the organized tourist trails, and the skills of its owners, the answer is clearly no. Looked at in this second way, technology is seen as a part of life, not something that can be kept in a separate compartment. If it is to be of any use, the snowmobile must fit into a pattern of activity which belongs to a particular lifestyle and set of values.

The problem here, as in much public discussion, is that "technology" has become a catchword with a confusion of different meanings. Correct usage of the word in its original sense seems almost beyond recovery, but consistent distinction between different levels of meaning is both possible and necessary. In medicine, a distinction of the kind required is often made by talking about "medical practice" when a general term is required, and employing the phrase "medical science" for the more strictly technical aspects of the subject. Sometimes, references to "medical practice" only denote the organization necessary to use medical knowledge and skill for treating patients. Sometimes, however, and more usefully, the term refers to the whole activity of medicine, including its basis in technical knowledge, its organization, and its cultural aspects. The latter comprise the doctor's sense of vocation, his personal values and satisfactions, and the ethical code of his profession. Thus "practice" may be a broad and inclusive concept.

Once this distinction is established, it is clear that although medical practice differs quite markedly from one country to anther, medical science consists of knowledge and techniques which are likely to be useful in many countries. It is true that medical science in many Western countries is biased by the way that most research is centered on large hospitals. Even so, most of the basic knowledge is widely applicable and relatively independent of local cultures. Similarly, the design of snowmobiles reflects the way technology is practiced in an industrialized country—standardized machines are produced which neglect some of the special needs of Eskimos and Lapps. But one can still point to a substratum of knowledge, technique, and underlying principle in engineering which has universal validity, and which may be applied anywhere in the world.

We would understand much of this more clearly, I suggest, if the concept of practice were to be used in all branches of technology as it has traditionally been used in medicine. We might then be better able to see which aspects of technology are tied up with cultural values, and which aspects are, in some respects, value-free. We would be better able to appreciate technology as a human activity and as part of life. We might then see it not only as comprising machines, techniques, and crisply precise knowledge, but also as involving characteristic patterns or organization and imprecise values.

Medical practice may seem a strange exemplar for the other technologies, distorted as it so often seems to be by the lofty status of the doctor as an expert. But what is striking to anybody more used to engineering is that medicine has at least got concepts and vocabulary which allows vigorous discussion to take place about different ways of serving the community. For example, there are phrases such as "primary health care" and "community medicine" which are sometimes emphasized as the kind of medical practice to be encouraged wherever the emphasis on hospital medicine has been pushed too far. There are also some interesting adaptations of the language of medical practice. In parts of Asia, paramedical workers, or paramedics, are now paralleled by "para-agros" in agriculture, and the Chinese barefoot doctors have inspired the suggestion that barefoot technicians could be recruited to deal with urgent problems in village water supply. But despite these occasional borrowings, discussion about practice in most branches of technology has not progressed very far.

## PROBLEMS OF DEFINITION

In defining the concept of technology-practice more precisely, it is necessary to think with some care about its human and social aspect. Those who write about the social relations and social control of technology tend to focus particularly on organization. In particular, their emphasis is on planning and administration, the management of research, systems for regulation of pollution and other abuses, and professional organization among scientists and technologists. These are important topics, but there is a wide range of other human content in technology-practice which such studies often neglect, including personal values and individual experience of technical work.

To bring all these things into a study of technology-practice may seem likely to make it bewilderingly comprehensive. However, by remembering the way in which medical practice has a technical and ethical as well as an organizational element, we can obtain a more orderly view of what technology-practice entails. To many politically-minded people, the *organizational aspect* may seem most crucial. It represents many facets of administration, and public policy; it relates to the activities of designers, engineers, technicians, and production workers, and also concerns the users and consumers of whatever is produced. Many other people, however, identify technology with its *technical aspect,* because that has to do with machines, techniques, knowledge, and the essential activity of making things work.

Beyond that, though, there are values which influence the creativity of designers and inventors. These, together with the various beliefs and habits of thinking which are characteristic of technical and scientific activity, can be indicated by talking about an ideological or *cultural aspect* of technology-practice. There is some risk of ambiguity here, because strictly speaking, ideology, organization, technique, and tools are all aspects of the culture of a society. But in common speech, culture refers to values, ideas, and creative activity, and it is convenient to use the term with this meaning. It is in this sense that the title of this [chapter] refers to the cultural aspect of technology-practice.

All these ideas are summarized by figure 1, in which the whole triangle stands for the concept of technology-practice and the corners represent its organizational, technical, and cultural aspects. This diagram is intended to illustrate how the word technology is sometimes used by people in a restricted sense, and sometimes with a more general meaning. When technology is discussed in the more restricted way, cultural values and organizational factors are regarded as external to it. Technology is then identified entirely with its technical aspects, and the words "technics" or simply "technique" might often be more appropriately used. The more general meaning of the word, however, can be equated with technology-practice, which clearly is not value-free and politically neutral, as some people say it should be.

Some formal definitions of technology hover uncertainly between the very general and the more restricted usage. Thus J. K. Galbraith defines technology as "the systematic application of scientific or other organized knowledge to practical tasks."[4] This sounds a fairly narrow definition, but on reading further one finds that Galbraith thinks of technology as an activity involving complex organizations and value-systems. In view of this, other authors have extended Galbraith's wording.

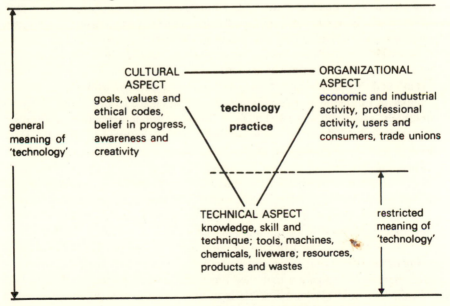

FIGURE 1. *Diagrammatic definitions of "technology" and "technology practice"*

For them a definition which makes explicit the role of people and organizations as well as hardware is one which describes the technology as "the application of scientific and other organized knowledge to practical tasks by . . . ordered systems that involve people and machines."[5] In most respects, this sums up technology-practice very well. But some branches of technology deal with processes dependent on living organisms. Brewing, sewage treatment, and the new biotechnologies are examples. Many people also include aspects of agriculture, nutrition, and medicine in their concept of technology. Thus our definition needs to be enlarged further to include "liveware" as well as hardware; technology-practice is thus *the application of scientific and other knowledge to practical tasks by ordered systems that involve people and organizations, living things and machines.*

This is a definition which to some extent includes science within technology. That is not, of course, the same as saying that science is merely one facet of technology with no purpose if its own. The physicist working on magnetic materials or semiconductors may have an entirely abstract interest in the structure of matter, or in the behavior of electrons in solids. In that sense, he may think of himself as a pure scientist, with no concern at all for industry and technology. But it is no coincidence that the magnetic materials he works on are precisely those that are used in transformer cores and computer memory devices, and that the semiconductors investigated may be used in microprocessors. The scientist's choice of research subjects is inevitably influenced by technological requirements, both through material pressures and also via a climate of opinion about what subjects are worth pursuing. And a great deal of science is like this, with goals that are definitely outside the technology-practice, but with a practical function within it.

Given the confusion that surrounds usage of the word "technology," it is not surprising that there is also confusion about the two adjectives "technical" and "technological." Economists make their own distinction, defining change of technique as a development based on choice from a range of known methods, and technological change as involving fundamentally new discovery or invention. This can lead to a distinctive use of the word "technical." However, I shall emlploy this adjective when I am referring solely to the technical aspects of practice as defined by figure 1. For example, the application of a chemical water treatment to counteract river pollution is described here as a "technical fix" (not a "technological fix"). It represents an attempt to solve a problem by means of technique alone, and ignores possible changes in practice that might prevent the dumping of pollutants in the river in the first place.

By contrast, when I discuss developments in the practice of technology which include its organizational aspects, I shall describe these as "technological developments," indicating that they are not restricted to technical form. The terminology that results from this is usually consistent with everyday usage, though not always with the language of economics.

## EXPOSING BACKGROUND VALUES

One problem arising from habitual use of the word technology in its more restricted sense is that some of the wider aspects of technology-practice have come to be entirely forgotten. Thus behind the public debates about resources and the environment, or about world food supplies, there is a tangle of unexamined beliefs and values, and a basic confusion about what technology is for. Even on a practical level, some projects fail to get more than half way to solving the problems they address, and end up as unsatisfactory technical fixes, because important organizational factors have been ignored. Very often the users of equipment (figure 2) and their patterns of organization are largely forgotten.

Part of [our] aim is to strip away some of the attitudes that restrict our view of technology in order to expose these neglected cultural aspects. With the snowmobile, a first step was to look at different ways in which the use and maintenance of the machine is organized in different communities. This made it clear that a machine designed in response to the values of one culture needed a good deal of effort to make it suit the purposes of another.

A further example concerns the apparently simple handpumps used at village wells in India. During a period of drought in the 1960s, large power-driven drilling rigs were brought in to reach water at considerable depths in the ground by means of bore-holes. It was at these new wells that most of the handpumps were installed. By 1975 there were some 150,000 of them, but surveys showed that at any one time as many as two-thirds had broken down. New pumps sometimes failed within three or four weeks of installation. Engineers identified several faults, both in the design of the pumps and in standards of manufacture. But although these defects were corrected, pumps continued to go wrong. Eventually it was realized that the breakdowns were not solely an engineering problem. They were also partly an administrative or management issue, in that arrangements for servicing the pumps were not very effective. There was another difficulty, too, because in many villages, nobody felt any personal responsibility for looking after the pumps. It was only when these things were tackled together that pump performance began to improve.

This episode and the way it was handled illustrates very well the importance of an integrated appreciation of technology-practice. A breakthrough only came when all aspects of the administration, maintenance, and technical design of the pump were thought out in relation to one another. What at first held up solution of the problem was a view of technology which began and ended with the machine—a view which, in another similar context, had been referred to as tunnel vision in engineering.

Any professional in such a situation is likely to experience his own form of tunnel vision. If a management consultant had been asked about the handpumps, he would have seen the administrative failings of the maintenance system very quickly, but might not have recognized that mechanical improve-

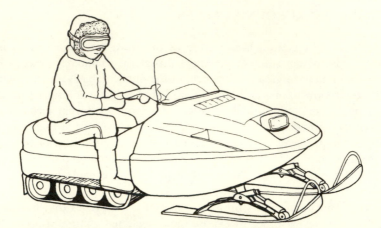

FIGURE 2. *Technology is about "systems that involve people and machines," and many of the people concerned are users of machines, such as handpumps or snowmobiles.*

ments to the pumps were required. Specialist training inevitably restricts people's approach to problems. But tunnel vision in attitudes to technology extends far beyond those who have had specialized training; it also affects policy-making, and influences popular expectations. People in many walks of life tend to focus on the tangible, technical aspect of any practical problem, and then to think that the extraordinary capabilities of modern technology ought to lead to an appropriate "fix." This attitude seems to apply to almost everything from inner city decay to military security, and from pollution to a cure for cancer. But all these issues have a social component. To hope for a technical fix for any of them that does not also involve social and cultural measures is to pursue an illusion.

So it was with the handpumps. The technical aspect of the problem was exemplified by poor design and manufacture. There was the organizational difficulty about maintenance. Also important, though, was the cultural aspect of technology as it was practiced by the engineers involved. This refers, firstly, to the engineers' way of thinking, and the tunnel vision it led to; secondly, it indicates conflicts of values between highly trained engineers and the relatively uneducated people of the Indian countryside whom the pumps were meant to benefit. The local people probably had exaggerated expectations of the pumps as the products of an all-powerful, alien technology, and did not see them as vulnerable bits of equipment needing care in use and protection from damage; in addition, the local people would have their own views about hygiene and water use.

Many professionals in technology are well aware that the problems they deal with have social implications, but feel uncertainty about how these should be handled. To deal only with the technical detail and leave other aspects on one side is the easier option, and after all, is what they are trained for. With the handpump problem, an important step forward came when one of the staff of a local water development unit started looking at the case-histories of individual pump breakdowns. It was then relatively easy for him to pass from a technical review of components which were worn or broken to looking at the social context of each pump. He was struck by the way some pumps had deteriorated but others had not. One well-cared-for pump was locked up during certain hours; another was used by the family of a local official; others in good condition were in places where villagers had mechanical skills and were persistent with improvised repairs. It was these specific details that enabled suggestions to be made about the reorganization of pump maintenance.[6]

A first thought prompted by this is that a training in science and technology tends to focus on general principles, and does not prepare one to look for specifics in quite this way. But the human aspect of technology—its organization and culture—is not easily reduced to general principles, and the investigator with an eye for significant detail may sometimes learn more than the professional with a highly systematic approach.

A second point concerns the way in which the cultural aspect of technology-practice tends to be hidden beneath more obvious and more practical issues. Behind the tangible aspect of the broken handpumps lies an administrative problem concerned with maintenance. Behind that lies a problem of political will—the official whose family depended on one of the pumps was somehow well served. Behind that again were a variety of questions concerning cultural values regarding hygiene, attitudes to technology, and the outlook of the professionals involved.

This need to strip away the more obvious features of technology-practice to expose the background values is just as evident with new technology in Western countries. Very often concern will be expressed about the health risk of a new device when people are worried about more intangible issues, because health risk is partly a technical question that is easy to discuss openly. A relatively minor technical problem affecting health may thus become a proxy for deeper worries about the way technology is practiced which are more difficult to discuss.

An instance of this is the alleged health risks associated with visual display units (VDUs) in computer installations. Careful research has failed to find any real hazard except that operators may suffer eyestrain and fatigue. Yet complaints about more serious problems continue, apparently because they can be discussed seriously with employers while misgivings about the overall systems are more difficult to raise. Thus a negative reaction to new equipment may be expressed in terms of a fear of "blindness, sterility, etc.," because in our society, this is regarded as a legitimate reason for rejecting it. But to take such fears at face value will often be to ignore deeper, unspoken anxieties about "deskilling, inability to handle new procedures, loss of control over work."[7]

Here, then, is another instance where, beneath the overt technical difficulty there are questions about the organizational aspect of technology—especially the organization of specific tasks. These have political connotations, in that an issue about control over work raises questions about where power lies in the workplace, and perhaps ultimately, where it lies within industrial society. But beyond arguments of that sort, there are even more basic values about creativity in work and the relationship of technology and human need.

In much the same way as concern about health sometimes disguises workplace issues, so the more widely publicized environmental problems may also hide underlying organizational and political questions. C. S. Lewis once remarked that "Man's power over Nature often turns out to be a power exerted by some men over other men with Nature as its instrument," and a commentator notes that this, "and not the environmental dilemma as it is usually conceived," is the central issue for technology.[8] As such, it is an issue whose political and social ramifications have been ably analyzed by a wide range of authors.[9]

Even this essentially political level of argument can be stripped away to reveal another cultural aspect of technology. If we look at the case made out in favor of almost any major project—a nuclear energy plant, for example—

there are nearly always issues concerning political power behind the explicit arguments about tangible benefits and costs. In a nuclear project, these may relate to the power of management over trade unions in electricity utilities; or to prestige of governments and the power of their technical advisers. Yet those who operate these levers of power are able to do so partly because they can exploit deeper values relating to the so-called technological imperative, and to the basic creativity that makes innovation possible. This, I argue, is a central part of the culture of technology. If these values underlying the technological imperative are understood, we may be able to see that here is a stream of feeling which politicians can certainly manipulate at times, but which is stronger than their short-term purposes, and often runs away beyond their control.

## NOTES

1. M. B. Doyle, *An Assessment of the Snowmobile Industry and Sport* (Washington, D.C.: International Snowmobile Industry Association, 1978), pp. 14, 47; on Joseph-Armand Bombardier, see Alexander Ross, *The Risk Takers* (Toronto: Macmillan and the Financial Post, 1978), p. 155.

2. R. A. Buchanan, *Technology and Social Progress* (Oxford: Permagon Press, 1965), p. 163.

3. P. J. Usher, "The Use of Snowmobiles for Trapping on Banks Island," *Arctic* (Arctic Institute of North America) 25 (1972): 173.

4. J. K. Galbraith, *The New Industrial State*, 2d British edition (London: André Deutsch 1972), chapter 2.

5. John Naughton, "Introduction: Technology and Human Values," in *Living with Technology: a Foundation Course* (Milton Keynes: The Open University Press, 1979).

6. Charles Heineman, "Survey of Handpumps in Vellakovil," unpublished report, January 1975, quoted by Arnold Pacey, *Handpump Maintenance* (London: Intermediate Technology Publications, 1977).

7. Leela Damodaran, "Health Hazards of VDUs?—Chairman's Introduction," conference at Loughborough University of Technology, December 11, 1980.

8. Quoted by Peter Hartley, "Educating Engineers," *The Ecologist* 10 (December 1980): 353.

9. E.g., David Elliott and Ruth Elliott, *The Control of Technology* (London and Winchester: Wykeham, 1976).

# 6

# Trapped in the 'NASA-Speak' Machine

## Jack Beatty

One of the great brooding themes of American literature is the dread of mechanism—the fear that the free individual will be caught up and crushed in some sort of system. This is usually rendered as a quasi-military social organization.

One thinks of the cowed crew of the Pequod in *Moby Dick,* so much social grist for Ahab's satanic obsession; of the lunatic contrivances to which autonomy is reduced in the rational hell of Joseph Heller's *Catch-22;* above all, of the vision of history as a realm of total control that Tyrone Slothrop in Thomas Pynchon's *Gravity's Rainbow* is vouchsafed before his rendezvous with oblivion.

As the names Poe, Thoreau, Emerson, and Twain attest, this fear of mechanism has been preying on the American mind since the Industrial Revolution reached these shores in the nineteenth century. It is the shadow-side of our relish of freedom.

I was put in mind of this premonitory theme while watching an extended television report on the hearings into the causes of the [*Challenger*] space-shuttle disaster. There it was: the free individual literally caught by the machine and not just crushed but scattered to the indifferent winds. There, too, was the machine—as system—the vast bureaucracy of the National Aeronautics and Space Administration, which masked its carelessness with a bristling rhetoric of efficiency. That rhetoric itself offered a third sense of mechanism—the machine-as-language.

---

"We want to be given a chance to communicate what the process was," Lawrence B. Mulloy, a key NASA official, told an interviewer. "I don't have any problems with the process," said Pat Smith, the brother of the shuttle pilot, when he was asked if the findings of haste and flawed decision-making made by the blue-ribbon committee investigating the incident had caused him to lose confidence in NASA. "The process they use," he said, "is a good process." The word came up again and again, and so did a medley of its fellow abstractions: "factor," "parameter," "criticality." One official alluded to his "elements manager"; another spoke of "my action relative to 51 C."

Listening to this impenetrable argot, I wondered if it had somehow contributed to the disaster, muffling the anxiety and anger of the engineers both inside and outside NASA who gave urgent warnings that it was too cold to launch the shuttle. A high NASA official spoke of a problem of communication he had had with worried engineers from Rockwell International, which built the shuttle. Did they advise against launching under those weather conditions? They may have "intended to offer me that concern," he said, but that is not how they were understood. Perhaps their meaning could not break through a language as dead to directness as NASA-speak.

There was yet a fourth sense in which the shuttle disaster fit this quintessentially American pattern: It showed an extraordinary face of a routine horror—the machine-as-division-of-labor. One of the unintended consequences of the highly ramified modern division of labor is to make men dumb—to stupefy them by repetition and routine. The division of labor also has an unintended moral liability: It makes men fearfully jealous of the little autonomy the system permits them.

The division of labor certainly had this effect on the NASA official who chose not to tell his superiors, who had the authority to cancel the liftoff, of the doubts expressed to him by the Morton-Thiokol engineers. "It was my decision to make," he was quoted as saying. Partly he was just telling the truth in that answer; partly, though, he was still defending his ever-threatened authority.

It's hard to judge that man harshly. The division of labor works relentlessly against most employees having power and the dignity that comes of its exercise. For every decision in the modern office, there is a counter-decision. For every boss, another boss somewhere else. For every job, hundreds of applicants—fresher, smarter, and more tractable than oneself. We may rush out to buy the latest musings of Lee A. Iacocca and grovel before the icon of the entrepreneur, but who are we kidding? For most of us, the system rules; the division of labor holds sway.

In their revelations of bureaucratic inertia and the suppression of good judgment by quantitative data, the shuttle hearing made us angry. The moral revelations were harder to take: They struck too close to home for simple anger. In their picture of fear of the boss, of employees' hoarding petty authority, of lack of straightforward communication up the bureaucratic chain of command, of somnambulistic devotion to "the process," the hearings gave us glimpses of everyman at work.

Mediocrity is a heavy personal cross to bear, as some of us know all too intimately, but the hearings showed us how much worse socially patterned mediocrity can be. It can get people killed. Is the shuttle disaster a portent of what America has become under the division of labor—a nation of specialists bereft of common sense and courage alike?

# Part Three

# The Autonomy
# of Modern Technology

# Introduction

It is a common practice to label the people in this part as anti-technology, but this requires some qualification. Even Jacques Ellul, who is regarded as a paradigm of the anti-technologist, is not opposed to technology per se, but sees tragic consequences in the modern technological system. Traditional techniques were limited to the satisfaction of specific human needs, but it is a profound mistake to think of modern technology in this way. It is not technology in the narrow sense that these authors see as dangerous, but more broadly the modern "system." They do, however, call into question the orthodox faith in inevitable progress, and in this sense can be thought of as opposed to technology.

All the authors in this part support the idea of autonomous technology, although they disagree about how inevitable such autonomy is or how universally applicable. To speak of autonomous technology conjures up the image of a Frankenstein monster with a will of its own, and certainly Ellul's way of speaking sometimes suggests this; however, no one in this Part intends to attribute will or volition to technology. More precisely, these authors argue that there is no will, no human purpose driving (at least some) technological development. As we saw in part 1, Schell argued that pure science was autonomous in this sense. If technology is indeed autonomous, there are no effective "political actors" in control of technological change either.

Jacques Ellul takes a very hard line in regard to the autonomy of technique. As we saw in part 2, the problem is not the machine, but the extension of machine-like thinking and procedures. Perhaps this can best be understood if we recall Pacey's concept of technology-practice. According to Ellul, Pacey's "technical aspect" is no mere aspect but a determinant of the whole of technology-practice. Although in principle the cultural and organizational aspects

81

could interact and modify the technical, in practice they have become ineffective in contemporary society. While Ellul claims that technique evolves independently of economics, politics, and the social situation, his point can be better put by saying that these cultural and organizational factors can no longer be distinguished from technique. Traditional cultural values and ways of organizing our lives have all been swept away and transformed by the imperatives of technological "progress." Technique has created a new civilization.

Although persons participate in technological development, they turn out to be co-conspirators on Ellul's view, since their traditional values have been replaced by the worship of "progress." Man himself becomes a means to the increasingly efficient perfection of means. Thus it happens that technique evolves according to its own internal laws, free from any decisive interference from external factors. Every next step in technological development is inevitably determined by every preceding step, beyond the intervention or desire of any single human agency. In this sense, it is not that technique is literally autonomous but that it builds its own momentum. Hiroshima was destroyed by The Bomb, not because it was necessary to win the war, but because it was the necessary next step in the development of atomic energy.

Of course new technologies create new problems, but this only fuels the demand for further development to find "technical fixes" for these problems in a never-ending circle. This is an all-or-nothing situation. Once a society opts for technological development, that is its last option. Traditional ideologies (democracy, capitalism, or communism) become irrelevant in the technological society and political distinctions between societies become blurred. Mikhail Gorbachev's choice of technological development sounds the death knell of traditional communism in his country. Although Ellul denies being a determinist, he sees no way to prevent "a world-wide totalitarian dictatorship which will allow technique its full scope . . . . "

Hans Jonas is primarily concerned to reveal some important, and much neglected, philosophical issues embedded in technology. The task is immense, but we can begin by selecting the most obvious aspects of this "focal fact of modern life" under the categories of: (1) formal dynamics, (2) material works, and (3) ethics.

Although Jonas is more circumspect than Ellul, he clearly agrees with the central tenets of the autonomous technology thesis. Viewed from an abstract, formal perspective, modern technology is clearly not a possession or state—a mere tool—but a restless, dynamic process. This force does not aim at an equilibrium, but is constantly disequilibrating. Following its own "laws of motion," each new stage in the evolution of technology gives us the next developments. There is a technological imperative at work here; "can" becomes "must" in our technological society. Thus, it seems that "technology is destiny."

Having described the traits of modern technology, Jonas analyzes what he considers to be the major forces driving technological development: pressures of competition, population growth and scarcity of natural resources, the idea of progress, and the need for coordination and control. Although the competitive pressures for profit inhere in capitalism, the rest operate independently of the economic system. The technological system is out of control.

Jonas's discussion of the material works of technology makes the point that technological objects are not mere means but radical transformations of our way of life, creating a life that is qualitatively different. The revolution in biology may even, for example, make it possible to engineer a "human" being. Surely, then, we need to redirect our most serious philosophical thinking in grappling with these unprecedented possibilities.

The point in describing our situation with regard to technology is to do something about it. In contrast to the impression Ellul gives, Jonas sees no "hard" determinism in the process of technology. His description is to extract the important philosophical and ethical choices that confront us. The first step in gaining control, in opposing the enormous inertial forces at work, is to become aware of how the "system" works. But to do something requires social and political action, and to be effective we may have to employ those "techniques" we despise: propaganda, persuasion, indoctrination, and manipulation, i.e., Skinner's technology of behavior. However, "the best hope of man rests in his most troublesome gift: the spontaneity of human acting which confounds all prediction."

Langdon Winner does not argue that technology in general is autonomous, but that autonomy is characteristic of some technological complexes. While the conventional wisdom continues to think of technology as a means to preestablished human ends, modern, large-scale systems frequently reverse the means-ends distinction. Rather than a linear view of technological development in which desired ends drive the quest for means, we find a circularity here in which the means provided by technology drive the quest for ends— as means to further means. On this model, ends are invented *ex post facto* for public relations as a means to keep the system going. While all specific technologies are purposive in their original design, the complexity of the system sometimes produces means for which some special purpose has to be designed if there is to be "progress."

In supporting this view, Winner describes in some detail five ways in which, to quote Herbert Marcuse, the technological society's "sweeping rationality, which propels efficiency and growth, is itself irrational." Curiously enough, Winner claims that he "is not arguing that there is anything inherently wrong with this." However, it is clear that if our social and political ideals are to guide technological development, this increasingly prevalent tendency of large-scale systems needs to be understood.

Mark Kramer, in his piece of investigative journalism, gives us a case study of one of the ways reverse-adaptation works. He asks, "Why did modern agriculture have to take the taste (of the tomato) away"? The answer is not to be understood in terms of a conspiracy. No single person, or group, wanted to deprive us of tasty tomatoes, but this was the unintended consequence of a highly integrated technological system. Although individual actors in the business have purposes—efficiency, control, profits, wages, etc.—no one willed a tasteless tomato. There are causes for the tomatoes we find in the supermarket, but, in an important sense, no reasons.

Although this may seem a trivial matter, may the pattern not be generalized? Consider the arms race, or the environment, or politics. Why, for instance, do our political candidates sound so vapid and noncommittal, even though the electronic media that present their messages have grown so sophisticated in such a short space of time? Is it inevitable that technological "progress" will continue to reduce the quality of the air we breathe and the water we drink? Unintended "side effects" may become the most important effects.

Ellul, writing from the vantage point of the early 1960s, lists some of contemporary science's sanguine predictions for the year 2000: the elimination of disease and universal hunger, an end to fuel shortages, and routine trips to the moon. Needless to say, science seems to have reneged on many of its promises. Worsening global pollution, the *Challenger* disaster, and the proliferation of AIDS indicate that the "perfect world" the savants envisioned is much further off. Indeed, when contemplating the problems still before us, we might consider, at least in passing, the power of the emerging social and environmental activism of the last two decades which has consistently challenged the hegemony of science and the role this same activism has played in thwarting the "inevitability" of technological progress.

# 7

# The Autonomy of Technique

## Jacques Ellul

The primary aspect of autonomy is perfectly expressed by Frederick Winslow Taylor, a leading technician. He takes, as his point of departure, the view that the industrial plant is a whole in itself, a "closed organism," an end in itself. Giedion adds: "What is fabricated in this plant and what is the goal of its labor—these are questions outside its design." The complete separation of the goal from the mechanism, the limitation of the problem to the means, and the refusal to interfere in any way with efficiency; all this is clearly expressed by Taylor and lies at the basis of technical autonomy.

Autonomy is the essential condition for the development of technique, as Ernst Kohn-Bramstedt's study of the police clearly indicates. The police must be independent if they are to become efficient. They must form a closed, autonomous organization in order to operate by the most direct and efficient means and not be shackled by subsidiary considerations. And in this autonomy, they must be self-confident in respect to the law. It matters little whether police action is legal, if it is efficient. The rules obeyed by a technical organization are no longer rules of justice or injustice. They are "laws" in a purely technical sense. As far as the police are concerned, the highest stage is reached when the legislature legalizes their independence of the legislature itself and recognizes the primacy of technical laws. This is the opinion of Best, a leading German specialist in police matters.

The autonomy of technique must be examined in different perspectives on the basis of the different spheres in relation to which it has this charac-

From *The Technological Society* by Jacques Ellul, translated by John Wilkinson. Copyright © 1964 by Alfred A. Knopf, Inc. Reprinted by permission of the publisher.

teristic. First, technique is autonomous with respect to economics and politics. We have already seen that, at the present, neither economic nor political evolution conditions technical progress.* Its progress is likewise independent of the social situation. The converse is actually the case, a point I shall develop at length. Technique elicits and conditions social, political, and economic change. It is the prime mover of all the rest, in spite of any appearance to the contrary and in spite of human pride, which pretends that man's philosophical theories are still determining influences and man's political regimes decisive factors in technical evolution. External necessities no longer determine technique. Technique's own internal necessities are determinative. Technique has become a reality in itself, self-sufficient, with its special laws and its own determinations.

Let us not deceive ourselves on this point. Suppose that the state, for example, intervenes in a technical domain. Either it intervenes for sentimental, theoretical, or intellectual reasons, and the effect of its intervention will be negative or nil; or it intervenes for reasons of political technique, and we have the combined effect of two techniques. There is no other possibility. The historical experience of the last years shows this fully.

To go one step further, technical autonomy is apparent in respect to morality and spiritual values. Technique tolerates no judgment from without and accepts no limitation. It is by virtue of technique rather than science that the great principle has become established: *chacun chez soi*.† Morality judges moral problems; as far as technical problems are concerned, it has nothing to say. Only technical criteria are relevant. Technique, in sitting in judgment on itself, is clearly freed from this principal obstacle to human action. (Whether the obstacle is valid is not the question here. For the moment we merely record that it is an obstacle.) Thus, technique theoretically and systematically assures to itself that liberty which it has been able to win practically. Since it has put itself beyond good and evil, it need fear no limitation whatever. It was long claimed that technique was neutral. Today this is no longer a useful distinction. The power and autonomy of technique are so well secured that it, in its turn, has become the judge of what is moral, the creator of a new morality. Thus, it plays the role of creator of a new civilization as well. This morality—internal to technique—is assured of not having to suffer from technique. In any case, in respect to traditional morality, technique affirms itself as an independent power. Man alone is subject, it would seem, to moral judgment. We no longer live in that primitive epoch in which things were good or bad in themselves. Technique in itself is neither, and can therefore do what it will. It is truly autonomous.

However, technique cannot assert its autonomy in respect to physical or biological laws. Instead, it puts them to work; it seeks to dominate them.

---

*See Part 2, chapter 4.

†"Each [is master] in his own house." (Ed.)

Giedion, in his probing study of mechanization and the manufacture of bread, shows that "wherever mechanization encounters a living substance, bacterial or animal, the organic substance determines the laws." For this reason, the mechanization of bakeries was a failure. More subdivisions, intervals, and precautions of various kinds were required in the mechanized bakery than in the non-mechanized bakery. The size of the machines did not save time; it merely gave work to larger numbers of people. Giedion shows how the attempt was made to change the nature of the bread in order to adapt it to mechanical manipulations. In the last resort, the ultimate success of mechanization turned on the transformation of human taste. Whenever technique collides with a natural obstacle, it tends to get around it either by replacing the living organism by a machine, or by modifying the organism so that it no longer presents any specifically organic reaction.

The same phenomenon is evident in yet another area in which technical autonomy asserts itself: the relations between techniques and man. We have already seen, in connection with technical self-augmentation, that technique pursues its own course more and more independently of man. This means that man participates less and less actively in technical creation, which, by the automatic combination of prior elements, becomes a kind of fate. Man is reduced to the level of a catalyst. Better still, he resembles a slug inserted into a slot machine: he starts the operation without participating in it.

But this autonomy with respect to man goes much further. To the degree that technique must attain its result with mathematical precision, it has for its object the elimination of all human variability and elasticity. It is a commonplace to say that the machine replaces the human being. But it replaces him to a greater degree than has been believed.

Industrial technique will soon succeed in completely replacing the effort of the worker, and it would do so even sooner if capitalism were not an obstacle. The worker, no longer needed to guide or move the machine to action, will be required merely to watch it and to repair it when it breaks down. He will not participate in the work any more than a boxer's manager participates in a prize fight. This is no dream. The automated factory has already been realized for a great number of operations, and it is realizable for a far greater number. Examples multiply from day to day in all areas. Man indicates how this automation and its attendant exclusion of men operates in business offices; for example, in the case of the so-called tabulating machine.* The machine itself interprets the data, the elementary bits of information fed into it. It arranges them in texts and distinct numbers. It adds them together and classifies the results in groups and subgroups, and so on. We have here an administrative circuit accomplished by a single, self-controlled machine. It is scarcely necessary to dwell on the astounding growth of automation in the last ten years. The multiple applications of the automatic assembly line, of

---

*We might substitute for Ellul's tabulating machine the personal computer. (Ed.)

automatic control of production operations (so-called cybernetics) are well known. Another case in point is the automatic pilot. Until recently the automatic pilot was used only in rectilinear flight; the finer operations were carried out by the living pilot. As early as 1952 the automatic pilot effected the operations of take-off and landing for certain supersonic aircraft. The same kind of feat is performed by automatic direction finders in anti-aircraft defense. Man's role is limited to inspection. This automation results from the development servomechanisms which act as substitutes for human beings in more and more subtle operations by virtue of their "feedback" capacity.

This progressive elimination of man from the circuit must inexorably continue. Is the elimination of man so unavoidably necessary? Certainly! Freeing man from toil is in itself an ideal. Beyond this, every intervention of man, however educated or used to machinery he may be, is a source of error and unpredictability. The combination of man and technique is a happy one only if man has no responsibility. Otherwise, he is ceaselessly tempted to make unpredictable choices and is susceptible to emotional motivations which invalidate the mathematical precision of the machinery. He is also susceptible to fatigue and discouragement. All this disturbs the forward thrust of technique.

Man must have nothing decisive to perform in the course of technical operations; after all, he is the source of error. Political technique is still troubled by certain unpredictable phenomena, in spite of all the precision of the apparatus and the skill of those involved. (But this technique is still in its childhood.) In human reactions, howsoever well calculated they may be, a "coefficient of elasticity" causes imprecision, and imprecision is intolerable to technique. As far as possible, this source of error must be eliminated. Eliminate the individual, and excellent results ensue. Any technical man who is aware of this fact is forced to support the opinions voiced by Robert Jungk, which can be summed up thus: "The individual is a brake on progress." Or: "Considered from the modern technical point of view, man is a useless appendage." For instance, ten per cent of all telephone calls are wrong numbers, due to human error. An excellent use by man of so perfect an apparatus!

Now that statistical operations are carried out by perforated-card machines instead of human beings, they have become exact. Machines no longer perform merely gross operations. They perform a whole complex of subtle ones as well. And before long—what with the electronic brain—they will attain an intellectual power of which man is incapable.

Thus, the "great changing of the guard" is occurring much more extensively than Jacques Duboin envisaged some decades ago. Gaston Bouthoul, a leading sociologist of the phenomena of war, concludes that war breaks out in a social group when there is a "plethora of young men surpassing the indispensable tasks of the economy." When for one reason or another these men are not employed, they become ready for war. It is the multiplication of men who are excluded from working which provokes war. We ought at least to bear this in mind when we boast of the continual decrease in human participation in technical operations.

However, there are spheres in which it is impossible to eliminate human influence. The autonomy of technique then develops in another direction. Technique is not, for example, autonomous in respect to clock time. Machines, like abstract technical laws, are subject to the law of speed, and coordination presupposes time adjustment. In his description of the assembly line, Giedion writes: "Extremely precise time tables guide the automatic cooperation of the instruments, which, like the atoms in a planetary system, consist of separate units but gravitate with respect to each other in obedience to their inherent laws." This image shows in a remarkable way how technique became simultaneously independent of man and obedient to the chronometer. Technique obeys its own specific laws, as every machine obeys laws. Each element of the technical complex follows certain laws determined by its relations with the other elements, and these laws are internal to the system and in no way influenced by external factors. It is not a question of causing the human being to disappear, but of making him capitulate, of inducing him to accommodate himself to techniques and not to experience personal feelings and reactions.

No technique is possible when men are free. When technique enters into the realm of social life, it collides ceaselessly with the human being to the degree that the combination of man and technique is unavoidable, and that technical action necessarily results in a determined result. Technique requires predictability and, no less, exactness of prediction. It is necessary, then, that technique prevail over the human being. For technique, this is a matter of life or death. Technique must reduce man to a technical animal, the king of the slaves of technique. Human caprice crumbles before this necessity; there can be no human autonomy in the face of technical autonomy. The individual must be fashioned by techniques, either negatively (by the techniques of understanding man) or positively (by the adaptation of man to the technical framework), in order to wipe out the blots his personal determination introduces into the perfect design of the organization.

But it is requisite that man have certain precise inner characteristics. An extreme example is the atomic worker or the jet pilot. He must be of calm temperament, and even temper, he must be phlegmatic, he must not have too much initiative, and he must be devoid of egotism. The ideal jet pilot is already along in years (perhaps thirty-five) and has a settled direction in life. He flies his jet in the way a good civil servant goes to his office. Human joys and sorrows are fetters on technical aptitude. Jungk cites the case of a test pilot who had to abandon his profession because "his wife behaved in such a way as to lessen his capacity to fly. Every day, when he returned home, he found her shedding tears of joy. Having become in this way accident conscious, he dreaded catastrophe when he had to face a delicate situation." The individual who is a servant of technique must be completely unconscious of himself. Without this quality, his reflexes and his inclinations are not properly adapted to technique.

Moreover, the physiological condition of the individual must answer to technical demands. Jungk gives an impressive picture of the experiments in training and control that jet pilots have to undergo. The pilot is whirled on centrifuges until he "blacks out" (in order to measure his toleration of acceleration). There are catapults, ultrasonic chambers, etc., in which the candidate is forced to undergo unheard-of tortures in order to determine whether he has adequate resistance and whether he is capable of piloting the new machines. That the human organism is, technically speaking, an imperfect one is demonstrated by the experiments. The sufferings the individual endures in these "laboratories" are considered to be due to "biological weaknesses," which must be eliminated. New experiments have pushed even further to determine the reactions of "space pilots" and to prepare these heroes for their roles of tomorrow. This has given birth to new sciences, biometry for example; their one aim is to create the new man, the man adapted to technical functions.

It will be objected that these examples are extreme. This is certainly the case, but to a greater or lesser degree the same problem exists everywhere. And the more technique evolves, the more extreme its character becomes. The object of all the modern "human sciences" is to find answers to these problems.

The enormous effort required to put this technical civilization into motion supposes that all individual effort is directed toward this goal alone and that all social forces are mobilized to attain the mathematically perfect structure of the edifice. ("Mathematically" does not mean "rigidly." The perfect technique is the most adaptable and, consequently, the most plastic one. True technique will know how to maintain the illusion of liberty, choice, and individuality; but these will have been carefully calculated so that they will be integrated into the mathematical reality merely as appearances!) Henceforth it will be wrong for a man to escape this universal effort. It will be inadmissible for any part of the individual not to be integrated in the drive toward technicization; it will be inadmissible that any man even aspire to escape this necessity of the whole society. The individual will no longer be able, materially or spiritually, to disengage himself from society. Materially, he will not be able to release himself because the technical means are so numerous that they invade his whole life and make it impossible for him to escape the collective phenomena. There is no longer an uninhabited place, or any other geographical locale, for the would-be solitary. It is no longer possible to refuse entrance into a community to a highway, a high-tension line, or a dam. It is vain to aspire to live alone when one is obliged to participate in all collective phenomena and to use all the collective's tools, without which it is impossible to earn a bare subsistence. Nothing is gratis any longer in our society; and to live on charity is less and less possible. "Social advantages" are for the workers alone, not for "useless mouths." The solitary is a useless mouth and will have no ration card—up to the day he is transported to a penal colony. (An attempt was made to institute this procedure during the French Revolution, with deportations to Cayenne.)

Spiritually, it will be impossible for the individual to disassociate himself from society. This is due not to the existence of spiritual techniques which have increasing force in our society, but rather to our situation. We are constrained to be "engaged," as the existentialists say, with technique. Positively or negatively, our spiritual attitude is constantly urged, if not determined, by this situation. Only bestiality, because it is unconscious, would seem to escape this situation, and it is itself only a product of the machine.

Every conscious being today is walking the narrow ridge of a decision with regard to technique. He who maintains that he can escape it is either a hypocrite or unconscious. The autonomy of technique forbids the man of today to choose his destiny. Doubtless, someone will ask if it has not always been the case that social conditions, environment, manorial oppression, and the family conditioned man's fate. The answer is, of course, yes. But there is no common denominator between the suppression of ration cards in an authoritarian state and the family pressure of two centuries ago. In the past, when an individual entered into conflict with society, he led a harsh and miserable life that required a vigor which either hardened or broke him. Today the concentration camp and death await him; technique cannot tolerate aberrant activities.

Because of the autonomy of technique, modern man cannot choose his means any more than his ends. In spite of variability and flexibility according to place and circumstance (which are characteristic of technique) there is still only a single employable technique in the given place and time in which an individual is situated.

At this point, we must consider the major consequences of the autonomy of technique. This will bring us to the climax of this analysis.

Technical autonomy explains the "specific weight" with which technique is endowed. It is not a kind of neutral matter, with no direction, quality, or structure. It is a power endowed with its own peculiar force. It refracts in its own specific sense the wills which make use of it and the ends proposed for it. Indeed, independently of the objectives that man pretends to assign to any given technical means, that means always conceals in itself a finality which cannot be evaded. And if there is a competition between this intrinsic finality and an extrinsic end proposed by man, it is always the intrinsic finality which carries the day. If the technique in question is not exactly adapted to a proposed human end, and if an individual pretends that he is adapting the technique to this end, it is generally quickly evident that it is the end which is being modified, not the technique. Of course, this statement must be qualified by what has already been said concerning the endless refinement of techniques and their adaptation. But this adaptation is effected with reference to the techniques concerned and to the conditions of their applicability. It does not depend on external ends. Perrot has demonstrated this in the case of judicial techniques, and Giedion in the case of mechanical techniques. Concerning the overall problem of the relation between the ends and the means, I take the liberty of referring to my own work, *Présence au monde moderne*.

Once again we are faced with a choice of "all or nothing." If we make use of technique, we must accept the specificity and autonomy of its ends, and the totality of its rules. Our own desires and aspirations can change nothing.

The second consequence of technical autonomy is that it renders technique at once sacrilegious and sacred. (*Sacrilegious* is not used here in the theological but in the sociological sense.) Sociologists have recognized that the world in which man lives is for him not only a material but also a spiritual world; that forces act in it which are unknown and perhaps unknowable; that there are phenomena in it which man interprets as magical; that there are relations and correspondences between things and beings in which material connections are of little consequence. This whole area is mysterious. Mystery (but not in the Catholic sense) is an element of man's life. Jung has shown that it is catastrophic to make superficially clear what is hidden in man's innermost depths. Man must make allowance for a background, a great deep above which lie his reason and his clear consciousness.

The characteristics we have examined permit me to assert with confidence that there is no common denominator between the technique of today and that of yesterday. Today we are dealing with an utterly different phenomenon. Those who claim to deduce from man's technical situation in past centuries his situation in this one show that they have grasped nothing of the technical phenomenon. These deductions prove that all their reasonings are without foundation and all their analogies are astigmatic.

The celebrated formula of Alain has been invalidated: "Tools, instruments of necessity, instruments that neither lie nor cheat, tools with which necessity can be subjugated by obeying her, without the help of false laws; tools that make it possible to conquer by obeying." This formula is true of the tool which puts man squarely in contact with a reality that will bear no excuses, in contact with matter to be mastered, and the only way to use it is to obey it. Obedience to the plow and the plane was indeed the only means of dominating earth and wood. But the formula is not true for our techniques. He who serves these techniques enters another realm of necessity. This new necessity is not natural necessity; natural necessity, in fact, no longer exists. It is technique's necessity, which becomes the more constraining the more nature's necessity fades and disappears. It cannot be escaped or mastered. The tool was not false. But technique causes us to penetrate into the innermost realm of falsehood, showing us all the while the noble face of objectivity of result. In this innermost recess, man is no longer able to recognize himself because of the instruments he employs.

The tool enables man to conquer. But, man, dost thou not know there is no more victory which is thy victory? The victory of our days belongs to the tool. The tool alone has the power and carries off the victory. Man bestows on himself the laurel crown, after the example of Napoleon III, who stayed in Paris to plan the strategy of the Crimean War and claimed the bay leaves of the victor.

But this delusion cannot last much longer. The individual obeys and no longer has victory which is his own. He cannot have access even to his apparent triumphs except by becoming himself the object of technique and the offspring of the mating of man and machine. All his accounts are falsified. Alain's definition no longer corresponds to anything in the modern world. In writing this, I have, of course, omitted innumerable facets of our world. There are still artisans, petty tradesmen, butchers, domestics, and small agricultural landowners. But theirs are the faces of yesterday, the more or less hardy survivals of our past. Our world is not made of these static residues of history, and I have attempted to consider only moving forces. In the complexity of the present world, residues do exist, but they have no future and are consequently disappearing. . . .

## A LOOK AT THE YEAR 2000

In 1960 the weekly *Express* of Paris published a series of extracts from texts by American and Russian scientists concerning society in the year 2000. As long as such visions were purely a literary concern of science-fiction writers and sensational journalists, it was possible to smile at them.* Now we have like works from Nobel Prize winners, members of the Academy of Sciences of Moscow, and other scientific notables whose qualifications are beyond dispute. The visions of these gentlemen put science fiction in the shade. By the year 2000, voyages to the moon will be commonplace; so will inhabited artificial satellites. All food will be completely synthetic. The world's population will have increased fourfold but will have been stabilized. Sea water and ordinary rocks will yield all the necessary metals. Disease, as well as famine, will have been eliminated; and there will be universal hygienic inspection and control. The problems of energy production will have been completely resolved. Serious scientists, it must be repeated, are the source of these predictions, which hitherto were found only in philosophic utopias.

The most remarkable predictions concern the transformation of educational methods and the problem of human reproduction. Knowledge will be accumulated in "electronic banks" and transmitted directly to the human nervous system by means of coded electronic messages. There will no longer be any need of reading or learning mountains of useless information; everything will be received and registered according to the needs of the moment. There will be no need of attention or effort. What is needed will pass directly from the machine to the brain without going through consciousness.

In the domain of genetics, natural reproduction will be forbidden. A stable population will be necessary, and it will consist of the highest human

---

*Some excellent works, such as Robert Jungk's *Le futur a déjà commencé*, were included in this classification.

types. Artificial insemination will be employed. This, according to Muller, will "permit the introduction into a carrier uterus of an ovum fertilized *in vitro,* ovum and sperm . . . having been taken from persons representing the masculine ideal and the feminine ideal, respectively. The reproductive cells in question will preferably be those of persons dead long enough that a true perspective of their lives and works, free of all personal prejudice, can be seen. Such cells will be taken from cell banks and will represent the most precious genetic heritage of humanity . . . . The method will have to be applied universally. If the people of a single country were to apply it intelligently and intensively . . . they would quickly attain a practically invincible level of superiority . . . . " Here is a future Huxley never dreamed of.

Perhaps, instead of marveling or being shocked, we ought to reflect a little. A question no one ever asks when confronted with the scientific wonders of the future concerns the interim period. Consider, for example, the problems of automation, which will become acute in a very short time. How, socially, politically, morally, and humanly, shall we contrive to get there? How are the prodigious economic problems, for example, of unemployment, to be solved? And, in Muller's more distant utopia, how shall we force humanity to refrain from begetting children naturally? How shall we force them to submit to constant and rigorous hygienic controls? How shall man be persuaded to accept a radical transformation of his traditional modes of nutrition? How and where shall we relocate a billion and a half persons who today make their livings from agriculture and who, in the promised ultrarapid conversion of the next forty years, will become completely useless as cultivators of the soil? How shall we distribute such numbers of people equably over the surface of the earth, particularly if the promised fourfold increase in population materializes? How will we handle the control and occupation of outer space in order to provide a stable *modus vivendi?* How shall national boundaries be made to disappear? (One of the last two would be a necessity.) There are many other "hows," but they are conveniently left unformulated. When we reflect on the serious although relatively minor problems that were provoked by the industrial exploitation of coal and electricity, when we reflect that after a hundred and fifty years these problems are still not satisfactorily resolved, we are entitled to ask whether there are any solutions to the infinitely more complex "hows" of the next forty years. In fact, there is one and only one means to their solution, a world-wide totalitarian dictatorship which will allow technique its full scope and at the same time resolve the concomitant difficulties. It is not difficult to understand why the scientists and worshippers of technology prefer not to dwell on this solution, but rather to leap nimbly across the dull and uninteresting intermediary period and land squarely in the golden age. We might indeed ask ourselves if we will succeed in getting through the transition period at all, of if the blood and the suffering required are not perhaps too high a price to pay for this golden age.

If we take a hard, unromantic look at the golden age itself, we are struck with the incredible naïveté of these scientists. They say, for example, that they will be able to shape and reshape at will human emotions, desires, and thoughts and arrive scientifically at certain efficient, pre-established collective decisions. They claim they will be in a position to develop certain collective desires, to constitute certain homogeneous social units out of aggregates of individuals, to forbid men to raise their children, and even to persuade them to renounce having any. At the same time, they speak of assuring the triumph of freedom and of the necessity of avoiding dictatorship at any price.* They seem incapable of grasping the contradiction involved, or of understanding that what they are proposing, even after the intermediary period, is in 'fact the harshest of dictatorships. In comparison, Hitler's was a trifling affair. That it is to be a dictatorship of test tubes rather than of hobnailed boots will not make it any less a dictatorship.

When our savants characterize their golden age in any but scientific terms, they emit a quantity of down-at-the-heel platitudes that would gladden the heart of the pettiest politician. Let's take a few samples. "To render human nature nobler, more beautiful, and more harmonious." What on earth can this mean? What criteria, what content, do they propose? Not many, I fear, would be able to reply. "To assure the triumph of peace, liberty, and reason." Fine words with no substance behind them. "To eliminate cultural lag." What culture? And would the culture they have in mind be able to subsist in this harsh social organization? "To conquer outer space." For what purpose? The conquest of space seems to be an end in itself, which dispenses with any need for reflection.

We are forced to conclude that our scientists are incapable of any but the emptiest platitudes when they stray from their specialties. It makes one think back on the collection of mediocrities accumulated by Einstein when he spoke of God, the state, peace, and the meaning of life. It is clear that Einstein, extraordinary mathematical genius that he was, was no Pascal; he knew nothing of political or human reality, or, in fact, anything at all outside his mathematical reach. The banality of Einstein's remarks in matters outside his specialty is as astonishing as his genius within it. It seems as though the specialized application of all one's faculties in a particular area inhibits the consideration of things in general. Even J. Robert Oppenheimer,† who seems receptive to a general culture, is not outside this judgment. His political and social declarations, for example, scarcely go beyond the level of those of the man in the street. And the opinions of the scientists quoted by *l'Express* are not even on the level of Einstein or Oppenheimer. Their pomposities, in fact, do not rise to the level of the average. They are vague generalities inherited from the nineteenth century, and the fact that they represent the furthest lim-

---

*The material here and below is cited from actual texts.

†J. Robert Oppenheimer (1904–1967). Physicist and director of the Manhattan Project that developed the atomic bomb. (Ed)

its of thought of our scientific worthies must be symptomatic of arrested development or of a mental block. Particularly disquieting is the gap between the enormous power they wield and their critical ability, which must be estimated as null. To wield power well entails a certain faculty of criticism, discrimination, judgment, and option. It is impossible to have confidence in men who apparently lack these faculties. Yet it is apparently our fate to be facing a "golden age" in the power of the sorcerers who are totally blind to the meaning of the human adventure. When they speak of preserving the seed of outstanding men, whom, pray, do they mean to be the judges? It is clear, alas, that they propose to sit in judgment themselves. It is hardly likely that they will deem a Rimbaud or a Nietszche worthy of posterity. When they announce that they will conserve the genetic mutations which appear to them most favorable, and that they propose to modify the very germ cells in order to produce such and such traits; and when we consider the mediocrity of the scientists themselves outside the confines of their specialties, we can only shudder at the thought of what they will esteem most "favorable."

None of our wise men ever pose the question of the end of all their marvels. The "wherefore" is resolutely passed by. The response that would occur to our contemporaries is: for the sake of happiness. Unfortunately, there is no longer any question of that. One of our best-known specialists in diseases of the nervous system writes: "We will be able to modify man's emotions, desires, and thoughts, as we have already done in a rudimentary way with tranquillizers." It will be possible, says our specialist, to produce a conviction or an impression of happiness without any real basis for it. Our man of the golden age, therefore, will be capable of happiness amid the worst privations. Why, then, promise us extraordinary comforts, hygiene, knowledge, and nourishment if, by simply manipulating our nervous systems, we can be happy without them? The last meager motive we could possibly ascribe to the technical adventure thus vanishes into thin air through the very existence of technique itself.

But what good is it to pose questions of motives? of Why? All that must be the work of some miserable intellectual who balks at technical progress. The attitude of the scientists, at any rate, is clear. Technique exists because it is technique. The golden age will be because it will be. Any other answer is superfluous.

## REFERENCES

Bouthol, Gaston. *La Guerre* [*War*]. Paris: Presses Universitaires de France, 1953.

Duboin, Jacques. *La grande relève des hommes par la machine* [*The Great Replacement of Man by the Machine*]. Paris: Les Editions Nouvelles, 1932.

Ellul, Jacques. *Présence au monde moderne* [*Presence in the Modern Word*]. Geneva: Roulet, 1948.

Giedion, Siegfried. *Mechanization Takes Command*. New York: Oxford University Press, 1948.

Jung, Carl Gustav. *Modern Man in Search of a Soul.* New York: Harcourt Brace, 1956.

Jungk, Robert. *Die Zukunft hat schon begonnen: Amerikas Allmacht und Ohnmacht.* Stuttgart: Scherz and Goverts, 1952. [Translated as *Tomorrow Is Already Here: Scenes from a Man-Made World.* London: R. Hart-Davis, 1954.]

Kohn-Bramstedt, Ernst. *Dictatorship and Political Police: The Technique of Control by Fear.* London: K. Paul, Trench, Trubner, 1945.

Taylor, Frederick Winslow. *The Principles of Scientific Management, 1911.* Reprint New York: Norton, 1947, 1967.

# 8

# Toward a Philosophy of Technology

## Hans Jonas

Are there philosophical aspects to technology? Of course there are, as there are to all things of importance in human endeavor and destiny. Modern technology touches on almost everything vital to man's existence—material, mental, and spiritual. Indeed, what of man is *not* involved? The way he lives his life and looks at objects, his intercourse with the world and with his peers, his powers and modes of action, kinds of goals, states and changes of society, objectives and forms of politics (including warfare no less than welfare), the sense and quality of life, even man's fate and that of his environment: all these are involved in the technological enterprise as it extends in magnitude and depth. The mere enumeration suggests a staggering host of potentially philosophic themes.

To put it bluntly: if there is a philosophy of science, language, history and art; if there is social, political, and moral philosophy; philosophy of thought and of action, of reason and passion, of decision and value—all facets of the inclusive philosophy of man—how then could there not be a philosophy of technology, the focal fact of modern life? And at that a philosophy so spacious that it can house portions from all the other branches of philosophy? It is almost a truism, but at the same time so immense a proposition that its challenge staggers the mind. Economy and modesty require that we select, for a beginning, the most obvious from the multitude of aspects that invite philosophical attention.

---

From *The Hastings Center Report* 9, no. 1 (1979): 34–93. Reproduced by permission. © The Hastings Center.

The old but useful distinction of "form" and "matter" allows us to distinguish between these two major themes: (1) the *formal dynamics* of technology as a continuing collective enterprise, which advances by its own "laws of motion"; and (2) the *substantive content* of technology in terms of the things it puts into human use, the powers it confers, the novel objectives it opens up or dictates, and the altered manner of human action by which these objectives are realized.

The first theme considers technology as an abstract whole of movement; the second considers its concrete uses and their impact on our world and our lives. The formal approach will try to grasp the pervasive "process properties" by which modern technology propels itself—through our agency, to be sure—into ever-succeeding and superceding novelty. The material approach will look at the species of novelties themselves, their taxonomy, as it were, and try to make out how the world furnished with them looks. A third, overarching theme is the *moral* side of technology as a burden on human responsibility, especially its long-term effects on the global condition of man and environment. This—my own main preoccupation over the past years—will only be touched upon.

## THE FORMAL DYNAMICS OF TECHNOLOGY

First some observations about technology's form as an abstract whole of movement. We are concerned with characteristics of *modern* technology and therefore ask first what distinguishes it *formally* from all previous technology. One major distinction is that modern technology is an enterprise and process, whereas earlier technology was a possession and a state. If we roughly describe technology as comprising the use of artificial implements for the business of life, together with their original invention, improvement, and occasional additions, such a tranquil description will do for most of technology through mankind's career (with which it is coeval), but not for modern technology. In the past, generally speaking, a given inventory of tools and procedures used to be fairly constant, tending towards a mutually adjusting, stable equilibrium of ends and means, which—once established—represented for lengthy periods an unchallenged optimum of technical competence.

To be sure, revolutions occurred, but more by accident than by design. The agricultural revolution, the metallurgical revolution that led from the neolithic to the iron age, the rise of cities, and such developments, *happened* rather than were consciously created. Their pace was so slow that only in the time-contraction of historical retrospect do they appear to be "revolutions" (with the misleading connotation that their contemporaries experienced them as such). Even where the change was sudden, as with the introduction first of the chariot, then of armed horsemen into wartime—a violent, if short-lived, revolution indeed—the innovation did not originate from within the military art of the advanced societies that it affected, but was thrust on it from outside by the (much less civilized) peoples of Central Asia. Instead of spreading through the technological universe of their time, other technical breakthroughs, like Phoenician purple-dying, Byzantine "greek fire," Chinese porcelain and silk, and Dumascene steel-tempering, remained jealously guarded monopolies of the inventor communities. Still others, like the hydraulic and steam playthings of Alexandrian mechanics, or compass and gunpowder of the Chinese, passed unnoticed in their serious technological potentials.[1]

On the whole (not counting rare upheavals), the great classical civilizations had comparatively early reached a point of technological saturation—the afore-mentioned "optimum" in equilibrium of means with acknowledged needs and goals—and had little cause later to go beyond it. From there on, convention reigned supreme. From pottery to monumental architecture, from food growing to shipbuilding, from textiles to engines of war, from time measuring to stargazing: tools, techniques, and objectives remained essentially the same over long times; improvements were sporadic and unplanned. Progress therefore—if it occurred at all*—was by inconspicuous increments to a universally high level that still excites our admiration and, in historical fact, was more liable to regression than to surpassing. The former at least was the more noted phenomenon, deplored by the epigones with a nostalgic remembrance of a better past (as in the declining Roman world). More important, there was, even in the best and most vigorous times, no proclaimed *idea* of a future of *constant progress* in the arts. Most important, there was never a deliberate method of going about it like "research," the willingness to undergo the risks of trying unorthodox paths, exchanging information widely about the experience, and so on. Least of all was there a "natural science" as a growing body of theory to guide such semitheoretical, prepractical activities, plus their social institutionalization. In routines as well as panoply of instruments, accomplished as they were for the purposes they served, the "arts" seemed as settled as those purposes themselves.†

## Traits of Modern Technology

The exact opposite of this picture holds for modern technology, and this is its first philosophical aspect. Let us begin with some manifest traits.

---

*Progress did, in fact, occur even at the heights of classical civilizations. The Roman arch and vault, for example, were distinct engineering advances over the horizontal establature and flat ceiling of Greek (and Egyptian) architecture, permitting spanning feats and thereby construction objectives not contemplated before (stone bridges, aqueducts, the vast baths, and other public halls of Imperial Rome). But materials, tools, and techniques were still the same, the role of human labor and crafts remained unaltered, stonecutting and brickbaking went on as before. An existing technology was enlarged in its scope of performance, but none of its means or even goals made obsolete.

†One meaning of "classical" is that those civilizations had somehow implicitly "defined" themselves and neither encouraged nor even allowed to pass beyond their innate terms. The—more or less—achieved "equilibrium" was their very pride.

1. Every new step in whatever direction of whatever technological field tends *not* to approach an equilibrium or saturation point in the process of fitting means to ends (nor is it meant to), but, on the contrary, to give rise, if success-ful, to further steps in all kinds of direction and with a fluidity of the ends themselves. "Tends to" becomes a compelling "is bound to" with any major or important step (this almost being its criterion); and the innovators them-selves expect, beyond the accomplishment, each time, of their immediate task, the constant future repetition of their inventive activity.

2. Every technical innovation is sure to spread quickly through the techno-logical world community, as also do theoretical discoveries in the sciences. The spreading is in terms of knowledge and of practical adoption, the first (and its speed) guaranteed by the universal intercommunication that is itself part of the technological complex, the second enforced by the pressure of competition.

3. The relation of means to ends is not unilinear but circular. Familiar ends of longstanding may find better satisfaction by new technologies whose gene-sis they had inspired. But equally—and increasingly typical—new technologies may suggest, create, even impose new ends, never before conceived, simply by offering their feasibility. (Who had ever wished to have in his living room the Philharmonic orchestra, or open heart surgery, or a helicopter defoliating a Vietnam forest? or to drink his coffee from a disposable plastic cup? or to have artificial insemination, test-tube babies, and host pregnancies? or to see clones of himself and others walking about?) Technology thus adds to the very objectives of human desires, including objectives for technology it-self. The last point indicates the dialectics or circularity of the case: once in-corporated into the socio-economic demand diet, ends first gratuitously (per-haps accidentally) generated by technological invention become necessities of life and set technology the task of further perfecting the means of realizing them.

4. Progress, therefore, is not just an ideological gloss on modern technology, and not at all a mere option offered by it, but an inherent drive which acts willy-nilly in the formal automatics of its *modus operandi* as it interacts with society. "Progress" is here not a value term but purely descriptive. We may resent the fact and despise its fruits and yet must go along with it, for—short of a stop by the fiat of total political power, or by a sustained general strike of its clients or some internal collapse of their societies, or by self-destruction through its works (the last, alas, the least likely of these)—the juggernaut moves on relentlessly, spawning its always mutated progeny by coping with the challenges and lures of the now. But while not a value term, "progress" here is not a neutral term either, for which we could simply substitute "change." For it is in the nature of the case, or a law of the series, that a later

stage is always, in terms of technology itself, *superior* to the preceding stage.*
Thus we have here a case of the entropy-defying sort (organic evolution is
another), where the internal motion of a system, left to itself and not interfered with, leads to ever "higher," not "lower" states of itself. Such at least
is the present evidence.† If Napoleon once said, "Politics is destiny," we may
well say today, "Technology is destiny."

These points go some way to explicate the initial statement that modern
technology, unlike traditional, is an enterprise and not a possession, a process
and not a state, a dynamic thrust and not a set of implements and skills.
And they already adumbrate certain "laws of motion" for this restless
phenomenon. What we have described, let us remember, were formal traits
which as yet say little about the contents of the enterprise. We ask two questions
of this descriptive picture: *why* is this so, that is, what *causes* the restlessness
of modern technology: what is the nature of the thrust? And, what is the
philosophical import of the facts so explained?

### The Nature of Restless Technology

As we would expect in such a complex phenomenon, the motive forces are
many, and some causal hints appeared already in the descriptive account.
We have mentioned *pressure of competition*—for profit, but also for power,
security, and so forth—as one perpetual mover in the universal appropriation
of technical improvements. It is equally operative in their origination, that
is, in the process of invention itself, nowadays dependent on constant outside subsidy and even goal-setting: potent interests see to both. War, or the
threat of it, has proved an especially powerful agent. The less dramatic, but
no less compelling, everyday agents are legion. To keep one's head above
the water is their common principle (somewhat paradoxical, in view of an
abundance already far surpassing what former ages would have lived with
happily ever after). Of pressures other than the competitive ones, we must
mention those of population growth and of impending exhaustion of natural
resources. Since both phenomena are themselves already by-products of
technology (the first by way of medical improvements, the second by the
voracity of industry), they offer a good example of the more general truth
that to a considerable extent technology itself begets the problems which it
is then called upon to overcome by a new forward jump. (The Green Revolution
and the development of synthetic substitute materials or of alternate sources
of energy comes under this heading.) These compulsive pressures for prog-

---

*This only seems to be but is not a value statement, as the reflection on, for example,
an ever more destructive atom bomb shows.

†There may conceivably be internal degenerative factors—such as the overloading of finite
information-processing capacity—that may bring the (exponential) movement to a halt or even
make the system fall apart. We don't know yet.

ress, then, would operate even for a technology in a noncompetitive, for example, a socialist setting.

A motive force more autonomous and spontaneous than these almost mechanical pushes with their "sink or swim" imperative would be the pull of the quasi-utopian *vision* of an ever better life, whether vulgarly conceived or nobly, once technology has proved the open-ended capacity for procuring the conditions for it: perceived possibility whetting the appetite ("the American dream," "the revolution of rising expectations"). This less palpable factor is more difficult to appraise, but its playing a role is undeniable. Its deliberate fostering and manipulation by the dream merchants of the industrial-mercantile complex is yet another matter and somewhat taints the spontaneity of the motive, as it also degrades the quality of the dream. It is also moot to what extent the vision itself is *post hoc* rather than *ante hoc*, that is, instilled by the dazzling feats of a technological processs already underway and thus more a response to than a motor of it.

Groping in these obscure regions of motivation, one may as well descend, for an explanation of the dynamism as such, into the Spenglerian* mystery of a "Faustian soul" innate in Western culture, that drives it, nonrationally, to infinite novelty and unplumbed possibilities for their own sake; or into the Heideggerian† depths of a fateful, metaphysical decision of the will for boundless power over the world of things—a decision equally peculiar to the Western mind: speculative intuitions which do strike a resonance in us, but are beyond proof and disproof.

Surfacing once more, we may also look at the very sober, functional facts of industrialism as such, of production and distribution, output maximization, managerial and labor aspects, which even apart from competitive pressure provide their own incentives for technical progress. Similar observations apply to the requirements of *rule* or control in the vast and populous states of our time, those giant territorial superorganisms which for their very cohesion depend on advanced technology (for example, on information, communication, and transportation, not to speak of weaponry) and thus have a stake in its promotion: the more so, the more centralized they are. This holds for socialist systems no less than for free-market societies. May we conclude from this that even a communist world state, freed from external rivals as well as from internal free-market competition, might still have to push technology ahead for purposes of control on this colossal scale? Marxism, in any case, has its own inbuilt commitment to technological progress beyond necessity. But even disregarding all dynamics of these conjectural kinds, the most monolithic case imaginable would, at any rate, still be exposed to those noncompetitive, natural pressures like population growth and dwindling resources that beset industrial-

---

*Oswald Spengler (1880–1936). German writer, whose best known work is *The Decline of the West*, in which he predicted the breakdown of Western civilization. (Ed.)

†Martin Heidegger (1889–1976). German existentialist philosopher. (Ed.)

ism as such. Thus, it seems, the compulsive element of technological progress may not be bound to its original breeding ground, the capitalist system. Perhaps the odds for an eventual stabilization look somewhat better in a socialist system, provided it is worldwide—and possibly totalitarian in the bargain. As it is, the pluralism we are thankful for ensures the constancy of compulsive advance.

We could go on unravelling the causal skein and would be sure to find many more strands. But none nor all of them, much as they explain, would go to the heart of the matter. For all of them have one premise in common without which they could not operate for long: the premise that there *can* be indefinite progress because there *is* always something new and better to find. The, by no means obvious, givenness of this objective condition is also the pragmatic conviction of the performers in the technological drama; but without its being true, the conviction would help as little as the dream of the alchemists. Unlike theirs, it is backed up by an impressive record of past successes, and for many this is sufficient ground for their belief. (Perhaps holding or not holding it does not even greatly matter.) What makes it more than a sanguine belief, however, is an underlying and well-grounded, theoretical view of the nature of things and of human cognition, according to which they do not set a limit to novelty of discovery and invention, indeed, that they of themselves will at each point offer another opening for the as yet unknown and undone. The corollary conviction, then, is that a technology tailored to a nature and to a knowledge of this indefinite potential ensures its indefinitely continued conversion into the practical powers, each step of it begetting the next, with never a cutoff from internal exhaustion of possibilities.

Only habituation dulls our wonder at this wholly unprecedented belief in virtual "infinity." And by all our present comprehension of reality, the belief is most likely true—at least enough of it to keep the road for innovative technology in the wake of advancing science open for a long time ahead. Unless we understand this ontologic-epistemological premise, we have not understood the inmost agent of technological dynamics, on whch the working of all the adventitious causal factors is contingent in the long run.

Let us remember that the virtual infinitude of advance we here seek to explain is in essence different from the always avowed perfectibility of every human accomplishment. Even the undisputed master of his craft always had to admit as possible that he might be surpassed in skill or tools or materials; and no excellence of product ever foreclosed that it might still be better, just as today's champion runner must know that his time may one day be beaten. But these are improvements within a given genus, not different in kind from what went before, and they must accrue in diminishing fractions. Clearly, the phenomenon of an expotentally growing *general* innovation is qualitatively different.

## Science as a Source of Restlessness

The answer lies in the interaction of *science* and *technology* that is the hallmark of modern progress, and thus ultimately in the kind of nature which modern science progressively discloses. For it is here, in the movement of *knowledge*, where relevant novelty first and constantly occurs. This is itself a novelty. To Newtonian physics, nature appeared simple, almost crude, running its show with a few kinds of basic entities and forces by a few universal laws, and the application of those well-known laws to an ever greater variety of composite phenomena promised ever widening knowledge indeed, but no real surprises. Since the mid-nineteenth century, this minimalistic and somehow finished picture of nature has changed with breathtaking acceleration. In a reciprocal interplay with the growing subtlety of exploration (instrumental and conceptual), nature itself stands forth as ever more subtle. The progress of probing makes the object grow richer in modes of operation, not sparer as classical mechanics had expected. And instead of narrowing the margin of the still-undiscovered, science now surprises itself with unlocking dimension after dimension of new depths. The very essence of matter has turned from a blunt, irreducible ultimate to an always reopened challenge for further penetration. No one can say whether this will go on forever, but a suspicion of intrinsic infinity in the very being of things obtrudes itself and therewith an anticipation of unending inquiry of the sort where succeeding steps will not find the same old story again (Descartes's "matter in motion"), but always add new twists to it. If then the art of technology is correlative to the knowledge of nature, technology too acquires from this source that potential of infinity for its innonvative advance.

But it is not just that indefinite scientific progress offers the *option* of indefinite technological progress, to be exercised or not as other interests see fit. Rather the cognitive process itself moves by interaction with the technological, and in the most internally vital sense: for its own *theoretical* purpose, science must generate an increasingly sophisticated and physically formidable technology as its tool. What it finds with this help initiates new departures in the practical sphere, and the latter as a whole, that is, technology at work, provides with its experiences a large-scale laboratory for science again, a breeding ground for new questions, and so on in an unending cycle. In brief, a mutual feedback operates between science and technology; each requires and propels the other; and as matters now stand, they can only live together or must die together. For the dynamics of technology, with which we are here concerned, this means that (all external promptings apart) an agent of restlessness is implanted in it by its functionally integral bond with science. As long, therefore, as the cognitive impulse lasts, technology is sure to move ahead with it. The cognitive impulse, in its turn, culturally vulnerable in itself, liable to lag or to grow conservative with a treasured canon—that theoretical eros itself no longer lives on the delicate appetite for truth alone, but is spurred on by its hardier offspring, technology, which communicates to it impulsions from the broadest arena of struggling, insistent life. Intellectual curiosity is seconded by interminably self-renewing practical aim.

I am conscious of the conjectural character of some of these thoughts. The revolutions in science over the last fifty years or so are a fact, and so are the revolutionary style they imparted to technology and the reciprocity between the two concurrent streams (nuclear physics is a good example). But whether these scientific revolutions, which hold primacy in the whole syndrome, will be typical for science henceforth—something like a law of motion for its future—or represent only a singular phase in its longer run, is unsure. To the extent, then, that our forecast of incessant novelty for technology was predicated on a guess concerning the future of science, even concerning the nature of things, it is hypothetical, as such extrapolations are bound to be. But even if the recent past did not usher in a state of permanent revolution for science, and the life of theory settles down again to a more sedate pace, the scope for technological innovation will not easily shrink; and what may no longer be a revolution in science, may still revolutionize our lives in its practical impact through technology. "Infinity" being too large a word anyway, let us say that present signs of potential and of incentives point to an indefinite perpetuation and fertility of the technological momentum.

**The Philosophical Implications**

It remains to draw philosophical conclusions from our findings, at least to pinpoint aspects of philosophical interest. Some preceding remarks have already been straying into philosophy of science in the technical sense. Of broader issues, two will be ample to provide food for further thought beyond the limitations of this [chapter]. One concerns the status of knowledge in the human scheme, the other the status of technology itself as a human goal, or its tendency to become that from being a means, in a dialectical inversion of the means-end order itself.

Concerning knowledge, it is obvious that the time-honored division of theory and practice has vanished for both sides. The thirst for pure knowledge may persist undiminished, but the involvement of knowing at the heights with doing in the lowlands of life, mediated by technology, has become inextricable; and the aristocratic self-sufficiency of knowing for its own (and the knower's) sake has gone. Nobility has been exchanged for utility. With the possible exception of philosophy, which still can do with paper and pen and tossing thoughts around among peers, all knowledge has become thus tainted, or elevated if you will, whether utility is intended or not. The technological syndrome, in other words, has brought about a thorough *socializing* of the theoretical realm, enlisting it in the service of common need. What used to be the freest of human choices, an extravagance snatched from the pressure of the world—the esoteric life of thought—has become part of the

great public play of necessities and a prime necessity in the action of the play.*
Remotest abstraction has become enmeshed with nearest concreteness. What
this pragmatic functionalization of the once highest indulgence in impractical pursuits portends for the image of man, for the restructuring of a hallowed
hierarchy of values, for the idea of "wisdom," and so on, is surely a subject
for philosophical pondering.

Concerning technology itself, its actual role in modern life (as distinct from
the purely instrumental definition of technology as such) has made the relation
of means and ends equivocal all the way up from the daily living to the very
vocation of man. There could be no question in former technology that its role
was that of humble servant—pride of workmanship and esthetic embellishment
of the useful notwithstanding. The Promethean enterprise of modern technology
speaks a different language. The word "enterprise" gives the clue, and its un-
endingness another. We have mentioned that the effect of its innovations is
disequilibrating rather than equilibrating with respect to the balance of wants
and supply, always breeding its own new wants. This in itself compels the constant attention of the best minds, engaging the full capital of human ingenuity
for meeting challenge after challenge and seizing the new chances. It is psychologically natural for that degree of engagement to be invested with the dignity of dominant purpose. Not only does technology dominate our lives in fact,
it nourishes also a belief in its being of predominant worth. The sheer gran-
deur of the enterprise and its seeming infinity inspire enthusiasm and fire ambition. Thus, in addition to spawning new ends (worthy or frivolous) from the
mere invention of means, technology as a grand venture tends to establish *itself*
as the transcendent end. At least the suggestion is there and casts its spell on
the modern mind. At its most modest, it means elevating *homo faber* to the
essential aspect of man; at its most extravagant, it means elevating *power* to
the position of his dominant and interminable goal. To become ever more masters of the world, to advance from power to power, even if only collectively
and perhaps no longer by choice, *can* now be seen to be the chief vocation
of mankind. Surely, this again poses philosophical questions that may well lead
unto the uncertain grounds of metaphysics or of faith.

I here break off, arbitrarily, the formal account of the technological movement in general, which as yet has told us little of what the enterprise is about.
To this subject I now turn, that is, to the new kinds of powers and objectives
that technology opens to modern man and the consequently altered quality of
human action itself.

---

*There is a paradoxical side effect to this change of roles. That very science which forfeited
its place in the domain of leisure to become a busy toiler in the field of common needs, creates
by its tools a growing domain of leisure for the masses, who reap this with the other fruits of
technology as an additional (and no less novel) article of forced consumption. Hence leisure, from
a privilege of the few, has become a problem for the many to cope with. Science, not idle, provides
for the needs of this idleness too: no small part of technology is spent on filling the leisure-time
gap which technology itself has made a fact of life.

## THE MATERIAL WORKS OF TECHNOLOGY

Technology is a species of power, and we can ask questions about how and on what object any power is exercised. Adopting Aristotle's rule in *De anima* that for understanding a faculty one should begin with its objects, we start from them too—"objects" meaning both the visible *things* technology generates and puts into human use, and the *objectives* they serve. The objects of modern technology are first everything that had always been an object of human artifice and labor: food, clothing, shelter, implements, transportation—all the material necessities and comforts of life. The technological intervention changed at first not the product but its production, in speed, ease, and quantity. However, this is true only of the very first stage of the industrial revolution with which large-scale scientific technology began. For example, the cloth for the steam-driven looms of Lancashire remained the same. Even then, one significant new product was added to the traditional list—the machines themselves, which required an entire new industry with further subsidiary industries to build them. These novel entities, machines—at first capital goods only, not consumer goods—had from the beginning their own impact on man's symbiosis with nature by being consumers themselves. For example: steam-powered water pumps facilitated coal mining, required in turn extra coal for firing their boilers, more coal for the foundries and forges that made those boilers, more for the mining of the requisite iron ore, more for its transportation to the foundries, more—both coal and iron—for the rails and locomotives made in these same foundries, more for the conveyance of the foundries' product to the pitheads and return, and finally more for the distribution of the more abundant coal to the users outside this cycle, among which were increasingly still more machines spawned by the increased availability of coal. Lest it be forgotten over this long chain, we have been speaking of James Watt's modest steam engine for pumping water out of mine shafts. This syndrome of self-proliferation—by no means a linear chain but an intricate web of reciprocity—has been part of modern technology ever since. To generalize, technology exponentially increases man's drain on nature's resources (of substances and of energy), not only through the multiplication of the final goods for consumption, but also, and perhaps more so, through the production and operation of its own mechancial means. And with these means—machines—it introduced a new category of goods, not for consumption, added to the furniture of our world. That is, among the objects of technology a prominent class is that of technological apparatus itself.

Soon other features also changed the initial picture of a merely mechanized production of familiar commodities. The final products reaching the consumer ceased to be the same, even if still serving the same age-old needs; new needs, or desires, were added by commodities of entirely new kinds which changed the habits of life. Of such commodities, machines themselves became increasingly part of the consumer's daily life to be used directly by himself, as an article not of production but of consumption. My survey can be brief as the facts are familiar.

## New Kinds of Commodities

When I said that the cloth of the mechanized looms of Lancashire remained the same, everyone will have thought of today's synthetic fiber textiles for which the statement surely no longer holds. This is fairly recent, but the general phenomenon starts much earlier in the synthetic dyes and fertilizers with which the chemical industry—the first to be wholly a fruit of science—began. The original rationale of these technological feats was substitution of artificial for natural materials (for reasons of scarcity or cost), with as nearly as possible the same properties for effective use. But we need only think of plastics to realize that art progressed from substitutes to the creation of really new substances with properties not found in any natural one, raw or processed, thereby also initiating uses not thought of before and giving rise to new classes of objects to serve them. In chemical (molecular) engineering, man does more than in mechanical (molar) engineering which constructs machinery from natural materials; his intervention is deeper, redesigning the infra-patterns of nature, making substances to specification by arbitrary disposition of molecules. And this, be it noted, is done deductively from the bottom, from the thoroughly analyzed last elements, that is, in a real *via compositiva* after the completed *via resolutiva*, very different from the long-known empirical practice of coaxing substances into new properties, as in metal alloys from the bronze age on. Artificiality or creative engineering with abstract construction invades the heart of matter. This, in molecular biology, points to further, awesome potentialities.

With the sophistication of molecular alchemy we are ahead of our story. Even in straightforward hardware engineering, right in the first blush of the mechanical revolution, the objects of use that came out of the factories did not really remain the same, even where the objectives did. Take the old objective of travel. Railroads and ocean liners are relevantly different from the stage coach and from the sailing ship, not merely in construction and efficiency but in the very feel of the user, making travel a different experience altogether, something one may do for its own sake. Airplanes, finally, leave behind any similarity with former conveyances, except the purpose of getting from here to there, with no experience of what lies in between. And these instrumental objects occupy a prominent, even obtrusive place in our world, far beyond anything wagons and boats ever did. Also they are constantly subject to improvement of design, with obsolescence rather than wear determining their life span.

Or take the oldest, most static of artifacts: human habitation. The multi-storied office building of steel, concrete, and glass is a qualitatively different entity from the wood, brick, and stone structures of old. With all that goes into it besides the structures as such—the plumbing and wiring, the elevators, the lighting, heating, and cooling systems—it embodies the end products of a whole spectrum of technologies and far-flung industries, where only at the remote sources human hands still meet with primary materials, no longer recognizable in the final result. The ultimate customer inhabiting the product is ensconced in a shell of thoroughly derivative artifacts (perhaps relieved by a nice piece of driftwood). This transformation into utter artificiality is generally, and increasingly, the effect of technology on the human environment, down to the items of daily use. Only in agriculture has the product so far escaped this transformation by the changed modes of its production. We still eat the meat and rice of our ancestors.*

Then, speaking of the commodities that technology injects into private use, there are machines themselves, those very devices of its own running, originally confined to the economic sphere. This unprecedented novum in the records of individual living started late in the nineteenth century and has since grown to a pervading mass phenomenon in the Western world. The prime example, of course, is the automobile, but we must add to it the whole gamut of household appliances—refrigerators, washers, dryers, vacuum cleaners—by now more common in the lifestyle of the general population than running water or central heating were one hundred years ago. Add lawn mowers and other power tools for home and garden; we are mechanized in our daily chores and recreations (including the toys of our children) with every expectation that new gadgets will continue to arrive.

These paraphernalia are machines in the precise sense that they perform work and consume energy, and their moving parts are of the familiar magnitudes of our perpetual world. But an additional and profoundly different category of technical apparatus was dropped into the lap of the private citizen, not labor-saving and work-performing, partly not even utilitarian, but—with minimal energy input—catering to the senses and the mind: telephone, radio, television, tape recorders, calculators, record players—all the domestic terminals of the electronics industry, the latest arrival on the technological scene. Not only by their insubstantial, mind-addressed output, also by the subvisible, not literally "mechanical" physics of their functioning do these devices differ in kind from all the macroscopic, bodily moving machinery of the classical type. Before inspecting this momentous turn from power engineering, the hallmark of the first industrial revolution, to communication engineering, which

---

*Not so, objects my colleague Robert Heilbroner in a letter to me: "I'm sorry to tell you that meat and rice are both *profoundly* influenced by technology. Not even they are left untouched." Correct, but they are at least generically the same (their really profound changes lie far back in the original breeding of domesticated strains from wild ones—as in the case of all cereal plants under cultivation). I am speaking here of an order of transformation in which the results bear no resemblance to the natural materials at their source, nor to any naturally occurring state of them.

almost amounts to a second industrial-technological revolution, we must take a look at its natural base: electricity.

In the march of technology to ever greater artificiality, abstraction, and subtlety, the unlocking of electricity marks a decisive step. Here is a universal force of nature which yet does not naturally appear to man (except in lightning). It is not a datum of uncontrived experience. Its very "appearance" had to wait for science, which contrived the experience for it. Here, then, a technology depended on science for the mere providing of its "object," the entity itself it would deal with—the first case where theory alone, not ordinary experience, wholly preceded practice (repeated later in the case of nuclear energy). And what sort of entity! Heat and steam are familiar objects of sensuous experience, their force bodily displayed in nature; the matter of chemistry is still the concrete, corporeal stuff mankind had always known. But electricity is an abstract object, disembodied, immaterial, unseen; in its usable form, it is entirely an artifact, generated in a subtle transformation from grosser forms of energy (ultimately from heat via motion). Its theory indeed had to be essentially complete before utilization could begin.

Revolutionary as electrical technology was in itself, its purpose was at first the by now conventional one of the industrial revolution in general: to supply motive power for the propulsion of machines. Its advantages lay in the unique versatility of the new force, the ease of its transmission, transformation, and distribution—an unsubstantial commodity, no bulk, no weight, instantaneously delivered at the point of consumption. Nothing like it had ever existed before in man's traffic with matter, space, and time. It made possible the spread of mechanization to every home; this alone was a tremendous boost to the technological tide, at the same time hooking private lines into centralized public networks and thus making them dependent on the functioning of a total system as never before, in fact, for every moment. Remember, you cannot hoard electricity as you can coal and oil, or flour and sugar for that matter.

But something much more unorthodox was to follow. As we all know, the discovery of the universe of electromagnetics caused a revolution in theoretical physics that is still underway. Without it, there would be no relativity theory, no quantum mechanics, no nuclear and subnuclear physics. It also caused a revolution in technology beyond what it contributed, as we noted, to its classical program. The revolution consisted in the passage from electrical to electronic technology which signifies a new level of abstraction in means and ends. It is the difference between power and communication engineering. Its object, the most impalpable of all, is information. Cognitive instruments had been known before—sextant, compass, clock, telescope, microscope, thermometer, all of them for information and not for work. At one time, they were called "philosophical" or "metaphysical" instruments. By the same general criterion, amusing as it may seem, the new electronic information devices, too, could be classed as "philosophical instruments." But those earlier cognitive devices, except the clock, were inert and passive, not generating information actively, as the new instrumentalities do.

Theoretically as well as practically, electronics signifies a genuinely new phase of the scientific-technological revolution. Compared with the sophistication of its theory as well as the delicacy of its apparatus, everything which came before seems crude, almost natural. To appreciate the point, take the man-made satellites now in orbit. In one sense, they are indeed an imitation of celestial mechanics—Newton's laws finally verified by cosmic experiment: astronomy, for millennia the most purely contemplative of the physical sciences, turned into a practical art! Yet, amazing as it is, the astronomic imitation, with all the unleashing of forces and the finesse of techniques that went into it, is the least interesting aspect of those entities. In that respect, they still fall within the terms and feats of classical mechanics (except for the remote-control course corrections).

Their true interest lies in the instruments they carry through the void of space and in what these do, their measuring, recording, analyzing, computing, their receiving, processing, and transmitting abstract information and even images over cosmic distances. There is nothing in all nature which even remotely foreshadows the kind of things that now ride the heavenly spheres. Man's imitative practical astronomy merely provides the vehicle for something else with which he sovereignly passes beyond all the models and usages of known nature.* That the advent of man portended, in its inner secret of mind and will, a cosmic event was known to religion and philosophy: now it manifests itself as such by fact of things and acts in the visible universe. Electronics indeed creates a range of objects imitating nothing and progressively added to by pure invention.

And no less invented are the ends they serve. Power engineering and chemistry for the most part still answered to the natural needs of man: for food, clothing, shelter, locomotion, and so forth. Communication engineering answers to needs of information and control solely created by the civilization that made this technology possible and, once started, imperative. The novelty of the means continues to engender no less novel ends—both becoming as necessary to the functioning of the civilization that spawned them as they would have been pointless for any former one. The world they help to constitute and which needs computers for its very running is no longer nature supplemented, imitated, improved, transformed, the original habitat made more habitable. In the pervasive mentalization of physical relationships, it is a *trans-nature* of human making, but with this inherent paradox: that it threatens the obsolescence of man himself, as increasing automation ousts him from the places of work where he formerly proved his humanhood. And there is a further threat: its strain on nature herself may reach a breaking point.

---

*Note also that in radio technology, the medium of action is nothing material, like wires conducting currents, but the entirely immaterial electromagnetic "field," i.e., space itself. The symbolic picture of "waves" is the last remaining link to the forms of our perceptual world.

**The Last Stage of the Revolution**

That sentence would make a good dramatic ending. But it is not the end of the story. There may be in the offing another, conceivably the last, stage of the technological revolution, after the mechanical, chemical, electrical, electronic stages we have surveyed, and the nuclear we omitted. All these were based on physics and had to do with what man can put to his use. What about biology? And what about the user himself? Are we, perhaps, on the verge of a technology, based on biological knowledge and wielding an engineering art which, this time, has man himself for its object? This has become a theoretical possibility with the advent of molecular biology and its understanding of genetic programming; and it has been rendered morally possible by the metaphysical neutralizing of man. But the latter, while giving us the license to do as we wish, at the same time denies us the guidance for knowing what to wish. Since the same evolutionary doctrine of which genetics is a cornerstone has deprived us of a valid image of man, the actual techniques, when they are ready, may find us strangely unready for their responsible use. The anti-essentialism of prevailing theory, which knows only of *de facto* outcomes of evolutionary accident and of no valid essences that would give sanction to them, surrenders our being to a freedom without norms. Thus the technological call of the new microbiology is the twofold one of physical feasibility and metaphysical admissibility. Assuming the genetic mechanism to be completely analyzed and its script finally decoded, we can set about rewriting the text. Biologists vary in their estimates of how close we are to the capability; few seem to doubt the right to use it. Judging by the rhetoric of its prophets, the idea of taking our evolution into our own hands is intoxicating even to many scientists.

In any case, the idea of making over man is no longer fantastic, nor interdicted by an inviolable taboo. If and when *that* revolution occurs, if technological power is really going to tinker with the elemental keys on which life will have to play its melody in generations of men to come (perhaps the only such melody in the unvierse), then a reflection on what is humanly desirable and what should determine the choice—a reflection, in short, on the image of man, becomes an imperative more urgent than any ever inflicted on the understanding of mortal man. Philosophy, it must be confessed, is sadly unprepared for this, its first cosmic task.


TOWARD AN ETHICS OF TECHNOLOGY

The last topic has moved naturally from the descriptive and analytic plane, on which the objects of technology are displayed for inspection, onto the evaluative plane where their ethical challenge poses itself for decision. The particular case forced the transition so directly because there the (as yet hypothetical) technological object was man directly. But once removed, man is involved in all the other objects of technology, as these singly and jointly remake the worldly frame of his life, in both the narrower and the wider of its senses: that of the artificial frame of civilization in which social man leads his life proximately, and that of the natural terrestrial environment in which this artifact is embedded and on which it ultimately depends.

Again, because of the magnitude of technological effects on both these vital environments in their totality, both the quality of human life and its very preservation in the future are at stake in the rampage of technology. In short, certainly the "image" of man, and possibly the survival of the species (or of much of it), are in jeopardy. This would summon man's duty to his cause even if the jeopardy were not of his own making. But it is, and, in addition to his ageless obligation to meet the threat of things, he bears for the first time the responsibility of prime agent in the threatening disposition of things. Hence nothing is more natural than the passage from the objects to the ethics of technology, from the things made to the duties of their makers and users.

A similar experience of inevitable passage from analysis of fact to ethical significance, let us remember, befell us toward the end of the first section. As in the case of the matter, so also in the case of the form of the technological dynamics, the image of man appeared at stake. In view of the quasi-automatic compulsion of those dynamics, with their perspective of indefinite progression, every existential and moral question that the objects of technology raise assumes the curiously eschatological quality with which we are becoming familiar from the extrapolating guesses of futurology. But apart from thus raising all challenges of present particular matter to the higher powers of future exponential magnification, the despotic dynamics of the technological movement as such, sweeping its captive movers along in its breathless momentum, poses its own questions to man's axiological conception of himself. Thus, form and matter of technology alike enter into the dimension of ethics.

The questions raised for ethics by the objects of technology are defined by the major areas of their impact and thus fall into such fields of knowledge as ecology (with all its biospheric subdivisions of land, sea, and air), demography, economics, biomedical and behavioral sciences (even the psychology of mind pollution by television), and so forth. Not even a sketch of the substantive problems, let alone of ethical policies for dealing with them, can here be attempted. Clearly, for a normative rationale of the latter, ethical theory must plumb the very foundations of value, obligation, and the human good.

The same holds of the different kind of questions raised for ethics by the sheer fact of the formal dynamics of technology. But here, a question of another order is added to the straightforward ethical questions of both kinds, subjecting any resolution of them to a pragmatic proviso of harrowing uncertainty. Given the mastery of the creation over its creators, which yet does not abrogate their responsibility nor silence their vital interest, what are the chances and what are the means of gaining *control* of the process, so that the results of any ethical (or even purely prudential) insights can be translated into effective action? How in short can man's freedom prevail against the determinism he has created for himself? On this most clouded question, whereby hangs not only the effectuality or futility of the ethical search which the facts invite (assuming it to be blessed with *theoretical* success!), but perhaps the future of mankind itself, I will make a few concluding, but—alas—inconclusive, remarks. They are intended to touch on the whole ethical enterprise.

## Problematic Preconditions of an Effective Ethics

First, a look at the novel state of determinism. Prima facie, it would seem that the greater and more varied powers bequeathed by technology have expanded the range of choices and hence increased human freedom. For economics, for example, the argument has been made[2] that the uniform compulsion which scarcity and subsistence previously imposed on economic behavior with a virtual denial of alternatives (and hence—conjoined with the universal "maximization" motive of capitalist market competition—gave classical economics at least the appearance of a deterministic "science") has given way to a latitude of indeterminacy. The plenty and powers provided by industrial technology allow a pluralism of choosable alternatives (hence disallow scientific protection). We are not here concerned with the status of economics as a science. But as to the altered state of things alleged in the argument, I submit that the change means rather that one, relatively homogeneous determinsm (thus relatively easy to formalize into a law) has been supplanted by another, more complex, multifarious determinism, namely, that exercised by the human artifact itself upon its creator and user. We, abstractly speaking the possessors of those powers, are concretely subject to their emancipated dynamics and the sheer momentum of our own multitude, the vehicle of those dynamics.

    I have spoken elsewhere[3] of the "new realm of necessity" set up, like a second nature, by the feedbacks of our achievements. The almighty we, or Man personified is, alas, an abstraction. *Man* may have become more powerful; *men* very probably the opposite, enmeshed as they are in more dependencies than ever before. What ideal Man can do is not the same as what real men permit or dictate to be done. And here I am thinking not only of the immanent dynamism, almost automatism, of the impersonal technological complex I have invoked so far, but also of the pathology of its client society. Its compulsions, I fear, are at least as great as were those of unconquered nature. Talk of the blind forces of nature! Are those of the sorcerer's creation less blind? They differ indeed in the serial shape of their causality: the action of nature's forces is cyclical, with periodical recurrence of the same, while that of the technological forces is linear, progressive, cumulative, thus replacing the curse of constant toil with the threat of maturing crisis and possible catastrophe.

Apart from this significant vector difference, I seriously wonder whether the tyranny of fate has not become greater, the latitude of spontaneity smaller; and whether man has not actually been weakened in his decision-making capacity by his accretion of collective strength.

However, in speaking, as I have just done, of "his" decision-making capacity, I have been guilty of the same abstraction I had earlier criticized in the use of the term "man." Actually, the subject of the statement was no real or representative individual but Hobbes' "Artificial Man," "that great Leviathan, called a Common-Wealth," or the "large horse" to which Socrates likened the city, "which because of its great size tends to be sluggish and needs stirring by a gadfly." Now, the chances of there being such gadflies among the numbers of the commonwealth are today no worse nor better than they have ever been, and in fact they are around and stinging in our field of concern. In that respect, the free spontaneity of personal insight, judgment, and responsible action by speech can be trusted as an ineradicable (if also incalculable) endowment of humanity, and smallness of number is in itself no impediment to shaking public complacency. The problem, however, is not so much complacency or apathy as the counterforces of active, and anything but complacent, interests and the complicity with them of all of us in our daily consumer existence. These interests themselves are factors in the determinism which technology has set upon the space of its sway. The question, then, is that of the possible chances of unselfish insight in the arena of (by nature) selfish *power*, and more particularly: of one long-range, interloping insight against the short-range goals of many incumbent powers. Is there hope that wisdom itself can become power? This renews the thorny old subject of Plato's philosopher-king and—with that inclusion of realism which the utopian Plato did not lack—or the role of myth, not knowledge, in the education of the guardians. Applied to our topic: the *knowledge* of objective dangers and of values endangered, as well as of the technical remedies, is beginning to be there and to be disseminated; but to make it prevail in the marketplace is a matter less of the rational dissemination of truth than of public relations techniques, persuasion, indoctrination, and manipulation, also of unholy alliances, perhaps even conspiracy. The philosopher's descent into the cave may well have to go all the way to "if you can't lick them, join them."

That is so not merely because of the active resistance of special interests but because of the optical illusion of the near and the far which condemns the long-range views to impotence against the enticement and threats of the nearby: it is this incurable shortsightedness of animal-human nature more than ill will that makes it difficult to move even those who have no special axe to grind, but still are in countless ways, as we all are, beneficiaries of the untamed system and so have something dear in the present to lose with the inevitable cost of its taming. The taskmaster, I fear, will have to be actual pain beginning to strike, when the far has moved close to the skin and has vulgar optics on its side. Even then, one may resort to palliatives of the hour.

In any event, one should try as much as one can to forestall the advent of emergency with its high tax of suffering or, at the least, prepare for it. This is where the scientist can redeem his role in the technological estate.

The incipient knowledge about technological danger trends must be developed, coordinated, systematized, and the full force of computer-aided projection techniques deployed to determine priorities of action, so as to inform preventive efforts wherever they can be elicited, to minimize the necessary sacrifices, and at the worst to preplan the saving measures which the terror of beginning calamity will eventually make people willing to accept. Even now, hardly a decade after the first stirrings of "envrontmental" consciousness, much of the requisite knowledge, plus the rational persuasion, is available inside and outside academia for any well-meaning powerholder to draw upon. To this, we—the growing band of concerned intellectuals—ought persistently to contribute our bit of competence and passion.

But the real problem is to get the well-meaning into power and have that power as little as possible beholden to the interests which the technological colossus generates on its path. It is the problem of the philosopher-king compounded by the greater magnitude and complexity (also sophistication) of the forces to contend with. Ethically, it becomes a problem of playing the game by its impure rules. For the servant of truth to join in it means to sacrifice some of his time-honored role: he may have to turn apostle or agitator or political operator. This raises moral questions beyond those which technology itself poses, that of sanctioning immoral means for a surpassing end, of giving unto Caesar so as to promote what is not Caesar's. It is the grave question of moral casuistry, or of Dostovesky's Grand Inquisitor, or of regarding cherished liberties as no longer affordable luxuries (which may well bring the anxious friend of mankind into odious political company)—questions one excusably hesitates to touch but in the further rule of things may not be permitted to evade.

What is, prior to joining the fray, the role of philosophy, that is, of a philosophically grounded ethical knowledge, in all this? The somber note of the last remarks responded to the quasi-apocalyptic prospects of the technological tide, where stark issues of planetary survival loom ahead. There, no philosophical ethics is needed to tell us that disaster must be averted. Mainly, this is the case of the ecological dangers. But there are other, noncatastrophic things afoot in technology, where not the existence but the image of man is at stake. They are with us now and will accompany us and be joined by others at every new turn technology may take. Mainly, they are in the biomedical, behavioral, and social fields. They lack the stark simplicity of the survival issue, and there is none of the (at least declaratory) unanimity on them which the specter of extreme crisis commands. It is here where a philosophical ethics or theory of values has its task. Whether its voice will be listened to in the dispute on policies is not for it to ask; perhaps it cannot even muster an authoritative voice with which to speak—a house divided, as philosophy is. But the philospher must try for normative knowledge, and if his labors fall predictably short of producing a compelling axiomatics, at least his clarifications can counteract rashness and make people pause for a thoughtful view.

Where not existence but "quality" of life is in question, there is room for honest dissent on goals, time for theory to ponder them, and freedom from the tyranny of the lifeboat situation. Here, philosophy can have its try and its say. Not so on the extremity of the survival issue. The philosopher, to be sure, will also strive for a theoretical grounding of the very proposition that there ought to be men on earth, and that present generations are obligated to the existence of future ones. But such esoteric, ultimate validation of the perpetuity imperative for the species—whether obtainable or not to the satisfaction of reason—is happily not needed for consensus in the face of ultimate threat. Agreement in favor of life is pretheoretical, instinctive, and universal. Averting disaster takes precedence over everything else, including pursuit of the good, and suspends otherwise inviolable prohibitions and rules. All moral standards for individual or group behavior, even demands for individual sacrifice of life, are premised on the continued existence of human life. As I have said elsewhere,[4] "No rules can be devised for the waiving of rules in extremities. As with the famous shipwreck examples of ethical theory, the less said about it, the better."

Never before was there cause for considering the contingency that all mankind may find itself in a lifeboat, but this is exactly what we face when the viability of the planet is at stake. Once the situation becomes desperate, then what there is to do for salvaging it must be done, so that there be life—which "then," after the storm has been weathered, can again be adorned by ethical conduct. The moral inference to be drawn from this lurid eventuality of a moral pause is that we must never allow a lifeboat situation for humanity to arise.[5] One part of the ethics of technology is precisely to guard the space in which any ethics can operate. For the rest, it must grapple with the cross-currents of value in the complexity of life.

A final word on the question of determinism versus freedom which our presentation of the technological syndrome has raised. The best hope of man rests in his most troubleome gift: the spontaneity of human acting which confounds all prediction. As the late Hannah Arendt never tired of stressing: the continuing arrival of newborn individuals in the world assures ever-new beginnings. We should expect to be surprised and to see our predictions come to naught. But those predictions themselves, with their warning voice, can have a vital share in provoking and informing the spontaneity that is going to confound them.

## NOTES

1. But as serious an actuality as the Chinese plough "wandered" slowly westward with little traces of its route and finally caused a major, highly beneficial revolution in medieval European agriculture, which almost no one deemed worth recording when it happened (cf. Paul Leser, *Entstehung und Verbreitung des Pfluges* [Münster, 1931; reprint The International Secretariate for Research on the History of Agricultural Implements, Brede-Lingby, Denmark, 1971).

2. I here loosely refer to Adolph Lowe, "The Normative Roots of Economic Values," in Sidney Hook, ed., *Human Values and Economic Policy* (New York: New York University Press, 1967), and more, perhaps, to the many discussions I had with Lowe over the years. For my side of the argument, see "Economic Knowledge and the Critique of Goals," in R. I. Heilbroner, ed., *Economic Means and Social Ends* (Englewood Cliffs, N.J.: Prentice-Hall, 1969), reprinted in Hans Jonas, *Philosophical Essays* (Englewood Cliffs, N.J.: Prentice-Hall, 1969, and 1974).

3. "The Practical Uses of Theory," *Social Research* 26 (1959), reprinted in Hans Jonas, *The Phenomenon of Life: Toward a Philosophical Biology* (New York: Harper and Row, 1966). The reference is to pp. 209-10 in the latter edition.

4. "Philosophical Reflections on Experimenting with Human Subjects," in Paul A. Freund, ed., *Experimentation with Human Subjects* (New York: George Braziller, 1970), reprinted in Hans Jonas, *Philosophical Essays*. The reference is to pp. 124-25 in the latter edition.

5. For a comprehensive view of the demands which such a situation or even its approach would make on our social and political values, see Geoffrey Vickers, *Freedom in a Rocking Boat* (London: Allen Lane, 1970).

9

# Reverse Adaptation and Control
## Langdon Winner

The process which I call *reverse adaptation* is the key to the critical interpretation of how ends are developed for large-scale systems and for the activities of the technological society as a whole. Here the conception of autonomous technology as the rule of a self-generating, self-perpetuating, self-programming mechanism achieves its sharpest definition. The basic hypothesis is this: *that beyond a certain level of technological development, the rule of freely articulated, strongly asserted purposes is a luxury that can no longer be permitted.* I want now to state the logic of this position.

Of interest to the theory are technological systems or networks of a highly advanced development—systems characterized by large size, concentration, extension, and the complex interconnection of a great number of artificial and human parts. Such conditions of size and interconnectivity mark a new "state" in the history of technical means. Components that were developed and operated separately are now linked together to form organized wholes. The resulting networks represent a quantum jump over the power and performance capabilities of smaller, more segmental systems. In this regard, the genius of the twentieth century consists in the final connecting of technological elements taken from centuries of discovery and invention.

Characteristic also of this new stage of development is the interdependence of the major functioning components. Services supplied by one part are crucial to the successful working of other parts and to the system as a

From *Autonomous Technology: Technics Out-of-Control as a Theme in Political Thought.* Copyright © 1977 by MIT Press. Reprinted by permission of the publisher.

whole. This situation has both an internal and external dimension. Within the boundaries of any specific system, the mutual dependencies are tightly arranged and controlled. But internally well-integrated systems are also in many cases dependent upon each other. Through relationships of varying degrees of certainty and solidity, the systems establish meta-networks, which supply "inputs" or receive "outputs" according to the purposes at hand. One need only consider the relationships among the major functional components— systems of manufacturing, energy, communications, food supply, transportation—to see the pulse beat of the technological society.

Large-scale systems can succeed in their ambitious range of activities only through an extension of *control*. Interdependence is a productive relationship only when accompanied by the ability to guarantee its outcome. But if a system must depend on elements it does not control, it faces a continuing uncertainty and the prospect of disruption. For this reason, highly organized technologies of the modern age have a tendency to enlarge their boundaries so that variables which were previously external become working parts of the system's internal structure.

The name usually given to the process of thought and action that leads to the extension of control is *planning*, which means much more than the sort of planning done by individuals in everyday life. Planning in this context is a formalized technique designed to make new connections with a high degree of certainty and manipulability. Clear intention, foresight, and calculation combine with the best available means of action. In some typical passages from Ellul we read:

> The more complex manufacturing operations become, the more necessary it is to take adequate precautions and to use foresight. It is not possible to launch modern industrial processes lightly. They involve too much capital, labor, and social and political modifications. Detailed forecasting is necessary.[1]

> Planning permits us to do more quickly and more completely whatever appears desirable. Planning in modern society is *the* technical method.[2] In the complexity of economic phenomena arising from techniques, how could one justify refusal to employ a trenchant weapon that simplifies and resolves all contradictions, orders incoherences, and rationalizes the excesses of production and consumption.?[3]

Size, complexity, and costliness in technological systems combine to make planning—intelligent anticipation plus control—a virtual necessity. This is more than just convenience. Planning is crucial to the coherence of the technological order at a particular stage in its development.

One can ask, What would be the consequences of an inability to plan or to control the span of interdependencies? A reasonable answer would be that many specific kinds of enterprise known to us would fail. The system could not complete its tasks or achieve its purposes. Another consequence, more drastic, might be that the disturbance and disorientation would eventually ruin the internal structure of the system. The whole organized web of connections would collapse.

More important than either of these are the implications for the technological ensemble of the civilization as a whole. Ultimately, if large-scale, complex, interconnected, interdependent systems could not successfully plan, technological apraxia would become endemic. Society would certainly move to a different sort of technological development. This is clear enough to those who read Jacques Ellul, Lewis Mumford, Herbert Marcuse, Paul Goodman, or Ivan Illich and experience horror at the critique of social existence founded on large-scale systems. What if the critics were taken seriously? What if the necessary operating conditions of such systems were tampered with? Surely society would move "backward."[4]

This idea of moving "backward" is a fascinating one. At work here is a quaint, two-dimensional, roadlike image that almost everyone (including this writer) falls into as easily as sneezing. One moves, it seems forward (positive) or backward (negative). Never does one move upward and to the right or off into the distance at, say, a thirty-four degree angle. No; it is forward or backward in a straight line. What is understood, furthermore, is that forward means larger, more complex, based on the latest scientific knowledge and the centralized control of an increasingly greater range of variables. Hence it is clear that not to plan, not to control the circumstances of large-scale systems, is to risk a kind of ghastly cultural regression. This lends extra urgency to these measures and extra vehemence toward any criticism of the world that they produce. Surely, it is believed (and this is no exaggeration), the critics would have us *back* in the stone age.[5]

Now, everything I have said so far presupposes that large-scale technological systems are at the outset based on independent ends or purposes. It makes sense to say that technologies "serve" this or that end or need or to say that they are "used" to achieve a preconceived purpose or set of purposes. Nothing argued here seeks to deny this. In the original design, all technologies are *purposive*.

But within the portrait of advanced technics just sketched, this situation is cast in a considerably different light. Under the logic that takes one from size, interconnection, and interdependence to control and planning, it can happen that such things as ends, needs, and purposes come to be dysfunctional to a system. In some cases, the originally established end of a system may turn out to be a restraint upon the system's ability to grow or to operate properly. Strongly enforced, the original purpose may serve as a troublesome obstacle to the elaboration of the network toward a higher level of development. In other instances, the whole process that leads to the establishment of ends for the system may become an unacceptable source of uncertainty, interference, and instability. Formerly a guide to action, the end-setting process is now a threat. If the system must depend on a source that is truly independent in its ability to enforce new ends, then it faces the perils of dependency.

In instances of this kind, a system may well find it necessary to junk the whole end-means logic and take a different course. It may decide to take direct action to extend its control over the ends themselves. After all, when strongly asserted needs, purposes, or goals begin to pose a risk to the system's effective operation, why not choose transcendence? Why not treat the ends as an "input" like any other, include them in the plan, and tailor them to the system's *own needs?* Obviously *this* is the "one best way."

At this point the idea of rationality in technological thinking once again begins to wobble, for if one takes rationality to mean the accommodation of means to ends, then surely reverse-adapted systems represent the most flagrant violation of rationality. If, on the other hand, one understands rationality to be the effective, logical ordering of technological parts, then systems which seek to control their own ends are the very epitome of the rational process. It is this contrast that enables Herbert Marcuse to conclude that the technological society's "sweeping rationality, which propels efficiency and growth, is itself irrational."[6] How one feels about this depends on which model of rationality one wishes to follow. The elephant can do his dance if you ask him to, but he sometimes crushes a beautiful maiden during the performance.

Let us briefly examine some of the patterns reverse adaptation can take. Remember that as I use the term *system* here I am referring to large socio-technical aggregates with human beings fully present, acting, and thinking. The behavior suggested, however, is meant as an attribute of the aggregate. Later I shall ask whether a change in the identities or ideologies of those "in control" is likely to make any difference.

1. *The system controls markets relevant to its operations.* One institution through which technologies are sometimes thought to be regulated is the market. If all went according to the ideal of classical economics, the market ought to provide the individual and social collectivity a powerful influence over the products and services that technological systems offer. Independent agents acting through the market should have a great deal to say about what is produced, how much, and at what price.

In point of fact, however, there are many ways in which large-scale systems circumvent the market, ways that have become the rule rather than the exception in much of industrial production. In J. K. Galbraith's version of what has become a mundane story: "If, with advancing technological and associated specialization, the market becomes increasingly unreliable, industrial planning will become increasingly impossible unless the market also gives way to planning. Much of what the firm regards as planning consists in minimizing or getting rid of market influences."[7]

Galbraith mentions three common procedures through which this is accomplished. The first is vertical integration, in which the market is superseded. "The planning unit takes over the source of supply or the outlet; a transaction that is subject to bargaining over prices and amounts is thus replaced with a transfer within the planning unit."[8]

A second means is market control, which "consists in reducing or eliminating the independence of action of those to whom the planning unit sells or from whom it buys."[9] Such control, Galbraith asserts, is a function of size. Large systems are able to determine the price they ask or pay in transactions with smaller organizations. To some extent, they are also able to control the amount sold.[10]

A third means suspends the market through contract. Here the systems agree in advance on amounts and prices to prevail in exchanges over a long period of time. The most stable and desirable of these involve contracts with the state.

Galbraith illustrates each of these with examples from General Motors, U.S. Steel, General Electric, and others, examples I shall not repeat. The matter is now part of modern folklore. That the market is an effective means for controlling large-scale systems is known to be a nostalgic, offbeat, or fantastic utopian proposal with little to do with reality.

2. *The system controls or strongly influences the political processes that ostensibly regulate its output and operating conditions.* Other possible sources of independent control are the institutions of politics proper. According to the model, clear-minded voters, legislators, executives, judges, and administrators make choices, which they impose upon the activities of technological systems. By establishing wise goals, rules, and limits for all such systems, the public benefit is ensured.

But the technological system, the servant of politics, may itself decide to find political cures for its own problems. Why be a passive tool? Why remain strictly dependent on political institutions? Such systems may act directly to influence legislation, elections, and the content of law. They may employ their enormous size and power to tailor political environments to suit their own efficient workings.

One need only review the historical success of the railroads, oil companies, food and drug producers, and public utilities in controlling the political agencies that supposedly determine what they do and how. A major accomplishment of political science is to document exactly how this occurs. The inevitable findings are now repeated as Ralph Nader retraces the footsteps of Grant McConnell. It is apparently still a shock to discover that "regulatory" commissions are dominated by the entities they regulate.[11]

The consequences of this condition are well known. In matters of safety, price, and quality of goods and services, the rules laid down reflect the needs of the system rather than some vital, independent, and forceful expression of public interest. It is not so much that the political process is always subverted in this way: the point is that occurrences of this sort happen often enough to be considered normal. No one is surprised to find Standard Oil spending millions to fight antipollution legislation. There is little more than weariness in our discovery that the Food and Drug Administration regularly allows corporations of the food industry to introduce untested and possibly unsafe additives into mass-processed foods.[12] I am not speaking here of the influence of private organizations only. Indeed, the best examples in this genre come from public agencies able to write their own tickets, for example, the Army Corps of Engineers.

3. *The system seeks a "mission" to match its technological capabilities.* It sometimes happens that the original purpose of a megatechnical organization is accomplished or in some other way exhausted. The original, finite goals may have been reached or its products become outmoded by the passage of time. In the reasonable, traditional model of technological employment one might expect that in such cases the "tool" would be retired or altered to suit some new function determined by society at large.

But this is an unacceptable predicament. The system with its massive commitments of manpower and physical resources may not wish to steal gracefully into oblivion. Unlike the fabled Alexander, therefore, it does not weep for new worlds to conquer. It sets about creating them. Fearing imminent extinction, the system returns to the political arena in an attempt to set new goals for itself, new reasons for social support. Here a different kind of technological invention occurs. The system suggests a new project, a new mission, or a new variety of apparatus, which, according to its own way of seeing, is absolutely vital to the body politic. It places all of its influence into an effort to convince persons in the political sphere of this new need. A hypothesis suggests itself: if the system is deemed important to society as a whole, and if the new purpose is crucial to the survival of the sytem, then that purpose will be supported regardless of its objective value to the society.

Examples of this phenomenon are familiar in contemporary political experience and are frequently the subject of heated debate. The National Aeronautics and Space Administration faces the problem of finding new justifications for its existence as a network of "big technology." NASA has successfully flown men to the moon. Now what? Many interesting new projects have been proposed by the agency: the space shuttle, the VSTOL [vertical short takeoff and landing] aircraft system, explorations to Mars, Venus, and Jupiter, asteroid space colonies. But whatever the end put forward, the fundamental argument is always the same: the aerospace "team" should not be dismantled, the great organization of men, technique, and equipment should not be permitted to fall to pieces. Give the system something to do. Anything. In the early 1960s resources were sought to fly the astronauts to unknown reaches of space; now funds are solicited to fly businessmen from Daly City to Lake Tahoe or the president to a space station for lunch.

Similar instances can be found in the recent histories of the ABM [antiballistic missile] project, the SST [supersonic transport], Boeing, General Dynamics, and Lockheed.[13] The nation may not need a particular new fighter plane, transport, bomber, or missile system. But the aerospace firms certainly need the contracts. And Los Angeles, Seattle, Houston, and other cities certainly need the aircraft companies. Therefore the nation needs the aircraft.

The connections of the system to society as a whole give added punch to the effort to have reverse-adapted technological ends embraced as the most revered of national goals.

4. *The system propagates or manipulates the needs it also serves.* But even if one grants a certain degree of interference in the market and political processes, is it not true that the basic human *needs* are still autonomous? The institutionalized means to their satisfaction may have been sidetracked or corrupted, but the original needs and desires still exist as vital and independent phenomena. After all, persons in society do need food, shelter, clothing, health, and access to the amenities of modern life. Given the integrity of these needs, it is still possible to establish legitimate ends for all technical means.

The theory of technological politics finds such views totally misleading, for reverse adaptation does not stop with deliberate interference in political and economic institutions. It also includes control of the needs in society at large. Megatechnical systems do not sit idly by while the whims of public taste move toward some specifically desired product or service. Instead they have numerous means available to bring about that most fortunate of circumstances in which the social need and what the system is best able to produce coincide in a perfect one-to-one match. All the knowledge of the behavioral sciences and all of the tools of refined psychological technique are put to work on this effort. Through the right kinds of advertising, product design, and promotion, through the creation of a highly energized, carefully manipulated universe of symbols, man as consumer is mobilized to want and seek actively the goods and services that the instruments of technology are able to provide at that moment. "Roughly speaking," Ellul observes, "the problem here is to modify human needs in accordance with the requirements of planning."[14]

If the system were truly dependent upon a society with autonomous needs, if it were somehow forced to take a purely responsive attitude, then the whole arrangement of modern technology would be considerably different. In all likelihood there would be fewer such systems and with less highly developed structures. Autonomous needs are in this sense an invitation to apraxia. Adequate steps must be taken to insure that wants and needs of the right sort arrive at the correct time in predetermined quantity. In Ellul's words: "If man does not have certain needs, they must be created. The important concern is not the psychic and mental structure of the human being but the uninterrupted flow of any and all goods which invention allows the economy to produce. Whence the measureless trituration of the human soul, the true issue of which is propaganda. And propaganda, reduced to advertising, relates happiness and a meaningful life to consumption."[15]

The point here raises an important issue, which neither the apologists nor the critics of the technological society have addressed very well. Assumed in most of the writing is the continued growth of human wants and needs in response to the appearance of new technological achievements. With each new invention or innovation it becomes possible to awaken and satisfy an appetite latent in the human constitution. Potentially there is no limit to this. A want or need will arise to meet any breakthrough. But precisely how this occurs is never fully elucidated. Apparently the human being is by nature a creature of infinite appetite.

But even thinkers who believe this to be true are sometimes sobered by its implications. What if all the wrong needs are awakened? Marxists grapple with this dilemma in their analyses of "false consciousness" and "commodity fetishism," trying to explain how the proletariat should have taken such a serious interest in the debased consumer goods and status symbols of bourgeois society. Much of the neo-Marxian criticism of the Frankfurt school—the writings of Theodor Adorno, Max Horkheimer, Marcuse, Jürgen Habermas, and others—focuses on the corruption of Marx's vision of human fulfillment in technological societies.[16] Persons in such societies certainly do lead lives of great material abundance, as predicted by Marx's theory. But the quality of their desire and of their relationships to material things is certainly not what the philosopher had in mind.

Many of Ellul's lamentations, similarly, come from his conclusion that man, or at least modern man, is indeed infinitely malleable and appetitive and, therefore, an easy mark. There is nothing that a well-managed sales campaign cannot convince him to crave with all his heart. Manipulated by "propaganda," the sum total of all psychological and mass media techniques, man wildly pursues a burgeoning glut of consumer products of highly questionable worth.[17]

It is incorrect, however, to say that needs of this sort are false. Persons who express the needs undoubtedly have them. To those persons, they are as real as any other needs ever experienced. "False" is not a response to someone who says he absolutely must have an automatic garage door opener, extra-dry deodorant for more protection, or air-flow torsion-bar suspension. No; the position of the theory is not that such needs are false but rather that they are not autonomous. A need becomes a need in substantial part because a megatechnical system external to the person needed that need to be needed.

A possible objection here is that human needs are always some variant of what is available at the time and generally desired by the society. Personal needs do not exist independent of the social environment and specific state of technics in which they occur. That is undoubtedly correct. Nevertheless, it is clear that the degree of conscious, rational, well-planned stimulation and manipulation of need is now much greater than in any previous historical period. Systems in the technological order are able to engender and give direction to highly specific needs, which in the aggregate constitute much of the "demand" for products and services. The combined impact of such manipulation produces a climate of generalized, intense needfulnees bordering on mass hysteria, which keeps the populace permanently mobilized for its necessary tasks of consumption.

True, other cultures at other times have been as effective in suppressing need for religious or purely practical reasons. But this fact merely gives additional focus to the peculiar turn that a culture based on high-tech systems has taken.

5. *The system discovers or creates a crisis to justify its own further expansion.* One way in which large systems measure their own vitality is on the scale of growth. If a system is growing, it is maintaining its full structure, replacing worn-out parts, and expanding into new areas of activity. Thinking on this subject has become highly specialized, but the basic maxim is still simple: healthy things grow.

There are times, however, when a system may find that its growth has slowed or even stopped. Even worse, it may discover that its rationale for growth has eroded. Public need for the goods or services the system provides may have leveled off; social and political support for expansion may have withered. In such cases the system has, from its own point of view, failed in its very success.

But the system is not helpless in this predicament. It does control its own internal structure, and it has command of a great deal of information about its role in society. With a little care it can manipulate either its own structure or the relevant information to create the appearance of a public "crisis" surrounding its activities. This is not to say that the system lies or deceives. It may, however, read and publicize its own condition and the condition of its environment very selectively. From the carefully selected portrait may come an image of a new and urgent social need.

Two scenarios of this sort have become familiar in recent years: the threat and the shortage. Under the psychology of the threat, the system finds an external and usually very nebulous enemy whose existence demands the utmost in technological preparation. Foreign military powers and crime in the streets have been traditional favorites. Statistics are cited to demonstrate that the enemy is well armed and busy. Society, on the other hand, is asleep at the switch, woefully bereft of tools and staff. The only logical conclusion is that the relevant system must, therefore, be given the means necessary to meet the threat as soon as possible.

The Department of Defense, to cite one noteworthy example, keeps several such plot lines in various stages of preparation at all times. If public or congressional interest in new projects or impressive hardware fails, the latest "intelligence" is readily available to show that a "gap" has appeared in precisely the area in question. This practice works best when defense systems on two continents are able to justify their growth in terms of each other's activities. Here one can see firsthand one of nature's rarities: the perfect circle.

If well orchestrated, the shortage can be equally impressive. Here the system surveys the data on its own operations and environment and announces that a crucial resource, product, or service is in dangerously short supply. Adequate steps must be taken to forestall a crisis for the whole society. The system must be encouraged to expand and to extend its sphere of control.

It may well be that there is a demonstrable shortage. What is important, however, is that the system may command a virtual monopoly of information concerning the situation and can use this monopoly for self-justification. Persons and groups outside usually do not have access to or interest in the information necessary to scrutinize the "need" in a critical way. This allows the system to define the terms of the "shortage" in its own best way. Outsiders are able to say, "Yes, I see; there is a shortage." But they are usually not prepared to ask: What is its nature? What are the full circumstances? What alternatives are available? Thus the only response is, "Do what is necessary." A number of "shortages" of this kind have been well publicized of late. There are now "crises" in natural gas, petroleum, and electricity, which a guileless public is discovering from predictable sources of information. In this instance, as in others, the almost inevitable outcome may well be "crisis - system growth supported by a huge public investment," all with a dubious relation to any clearly demonstrated need.

Some of the more interesting cases of reverse adaptation combine the above strategies in various ways. Numbers 1 and 2 as well as 2 and 3 could be anticipated as successful pairings. A particularly ironic case is that which brings together numbers 4 and 5, the propagation of need and the discovery of shortage. This is presently a popular strategy with power companies who spend millions advertising power-consuming luxury appliances while at the same time trumpeting the dire perils of the "energy crisis." Such cases might be called double reverse adaptations.

I am not saying that the patterns noted are universal in the behavior of megatechnical systems. It may also happen that the traditionally expected sequence of relating ends to means does occur, or some mix may take place. The hypothesis of the theory of technological politics is that as large-scale systems come to dominate various areas of modern social life, reverse adaptation will become an increasingly important way of determining what is done and how.

I am not arguing that there is anything inherently wrong with this. My point is that such behavior violates the models of technical practice we normally employ. To the extent to which we employ tool-use and ends-means conceptions, our experience will be out of sync with our expectations.

## NOTES

1. Jacques Ellul, *The Technological Society*, trans. John Wilkinson (New York: Alfred A. Knopf, 1964), p. 166.

2. Ibid., p. 184.

3. Ibid., p. 177.

4. A sample of this response is found in Melvin Kranzberg, "Historical Aspects of Technology Assessment," *Technology Assessment Hearings Before the Subcommittee on Science, Research and Development of the U.S. House of Representatives* (Washington, D.C.: U.S. Government Printing Office, 1970). After a brief survey of the ideas of Ellul, Mumford, and Marcuse, Kranzberg

concludes: "While such wholesale indictments may stimulate nihilistic revolutionary movements, they really tell us very little about what can be done to guide and direct technological innovation along socially beneficial lines" (ibid., p. 385).

5. Another interesting side to the "forward"-"backward" view counsels that the forward direction is ineluctable. In his statement to a U.S. Senate hearing in 1970, Harvey Brooks took care to deny the proposition that "technological progress" is a "largely autonomous development." But he went on to say, "While this pessimistic view of technology is not without evidence to support it, I believe it represents only a partial truth. Furthermore, it is an essentially sentimental and irrational view, because man in fact has *no choice* but to push forward with his technology. The world is already *irrevocably committed to a technological culture* [emphasis added]." Reprinted ibid., p. 331.

6. Herbert Marcuse, *Negations: Essays in Critical Theory*, trans. Jeremy J. Shapiro (Boston: Beacon Press, 1969), p. xiii.

7. John Kenneth Galbraith, *The New Industrial State* (New York: The New American Library, 1968), p. 37.

8. Ibid., p.39.

9. Ibid.

10. Ibid., p. 41.

11. Compare Grant McConnell, *Private Power and American Democracy* (New York: Alfred A. Knopf, 1966), and the reports of the Ralph Nader Study groups: James S. Turner, *The Chemical Feast: The Ralph Nader Study Group Report on the Food and Drug Administration* (New York: Grossman Publishers, 1970); Robert Fellmeth, *The Interstate Commerce Commission: The Ralph Nader Study Group Report on the Interstate Commerce Commission and Transportation* (New York: Grossman Publishers, 1970).

12. Gene Marine and Judy Van Allen, *Food Pollution* (New York: Holt, Rinehart & Winston, 1972).

13. See Clark R. Mollenhoff, *The Pentagon: Politics, Profits and Plunder* (New York: Pinnacle Books, 1972); Murray Weidenbaum, "Arms and the American Economy: A Domestic Convergence Hypothesis," *Quarterly Review of Economics and Business* 8 (Spring 1968); Ralph Lapp, *The Weapons Culture* (Baltimore, Md.: Penguin Books, 1968); Seymour Melman, *Pentagon Capitalism: The Political Economy of War* (New York: McGraw-Hill, 1970).

14. Ellul, *Technological Society*, p. 225.

15. Ibid., p. 221.

16. See Theodor Adorno, *Minima Moralia*, trans. E. F. N. Jephcott (London: NLB, 1974); Max Horkheimer, *Critical Theory*, trans. Matthew J. O'Connell et al.(New York: Herder and Herder, 1972); Jürgen Habermas, *Legitimation Crisis*, trans. Thomas McCarthy (Boston: Beacon Press, 1975). An interesting, polemical review of the progress of the Frankfurt school is given in Göran Therborn's article, "A Critique of the Frankfurt School," *New Left Review*, No. 63 (September–October 1970): 65–96.

17. "Propaganda is a set of methods employed by an organized group that wants to bring about the active or passive participation in its actions of a mass of individuals, psychologically unified through psychological manipulations and incorporated in an organization." Jacques Ellul, *Propaganda*, trans. Konrad Kellen (New York: Alfred A. Knopf, 1967), p. 61.

10

# The Ruination of the Tomato

## Mark Kramer

It wasn't a conspiracy, it was just good business sense—but why did modern agriculture have to take the taste away?

Sagebrush and lizards rattle and whisper behind me. I stand in the moonlight, the hot desert at my back. It's tomato harvest time, 3 A.M. The moon is almost full and near to setting. Before me stretches the first lush tomato field to be taken this morning. The field is farmed by a company called Tejon Agricultural Partners, and lies three hours northeast of Los Angeles in the middle of the bleak, silvery drylands of California's San Joaquin Valley. Seven hundred sixty-six acres, more than a mile square of tomatoes—a shaggy, vegetable-green rug dappled with murky red dots, 105,708,000 ripe tomatoes lurking in the night. The field is large and absolutely level. It would take an hour and a half to walk around it. Yet, when I raise my eyes past the field to the much vaster valley floor, and to the mountains that loom farther out, the enormous crop is lost in a big flat world.

This harvest happens nearly without people. A hundred million tomatoes grown, irrigated, fed, sprayed, now taken, soon to be cooled, squashed, boiled, barreled, and held at the ready, then canned, shipped, sold, bought, and after being sold and bought a few more times, uncanned and dumped on pizza. And such is the magnitude of the vista, and the dearth of human presence, that it is easy to look elsewhere and put this routine thing out of mind. But

131

that quality—of blandness overlaying a wonderous integration of technology, finances, personnel, and business systems—seems to be what the "future" has in store.

Three large tractors steam up the road toward me, headlights glaring, towing three thin-latticed towers that support floodlights. The tractors drag the towers into place around an assembly field, then hydraulic arms raise them to vertical. They illuminate a large, sandy work yard where equipment is gathering—fuel trucks, repair trucks, concession trucks, harvesters, tractor-trailers towing big open hoppers. Now small crews of Mexicans, their sunburns tinted light blue in the glare of the three searchlights, climb aboard the harvesters; shadowy drivers mount tractors and trucks. The night fills with the scent of diesel fumes and with the sound of large engines running evenly.

The six harvesting machines drift across the gray-green tomato-leaf sea. After a time, the distant ones come to look like steamboats afloat across a wide bay. The engine sounds are dispersed. A company foreman dashes past, tally sheets in hand. He stops nearby only long enough to deliver a one-liner. "We're knocking them out like Johnny-be-good," he says, punching the air slowly with his right fist. Then he runs off, laughing.

The nearest harvester draws steadily closer, moving in at about the speed of a slow amble, roaring as it comes. Up close, it looks like the aftermath of a collision between a grandstand and a San Francisco tram car. It's two stories high, rolls on wheels that don't seem large enough, astraddle a wide row of jumbled and unstaked tomato vines. It is not streamlined. Gangways, catwalks, gates, conveyors, roofs, and ladders are fastened all over the lumbering rig. As it closes in, its front end snuffles up whole tomato plants as surely as a hungry pig loose in a farmer's garden. Its hind end excretes a steady stream of stems and rejects. Between the ingestion and the elimination, fourteen laborers face each other on long benches. They sit on either side of a conveyor that moves the new harvest rapidly past them. Their hands dart out and back as they sort through the red stream in front of them.

Watching them is like peering into the dining car of a passing train. The folks aboard, though, are not dining but working hard for low wages, culling what is not quite fit for pizza sauce—the "greens," "molds," "mechanicals," and the odd tomato-sized clod of dirt which has gotten past the shakers and screens that tug tomato from vine and dump the harvest onto the conveyor.

The absorbing nature of the work is according to plan. The workers aboard this tiny outpost of a tomato sauce factory are attempting to accomplish a chore at which they cannot possibly succeed, one designed in the near past by some anonymous practitioner of the new craft of *management*. As per cannery contract, each truckload of tomatoes must contain no more than 4 percent green tomatoes, 3 percent tomatoes suffering mechanical damage from the harvester, one percent tomatoes that have begun to mold, and .5 percent clods of dirt.

"The whole idea of this thing," a farm executive had explained earlier in the day, "is to get as many tons as you can per hour. Now, the people culling on the machines strive to sort everything that's defective. But to us, that's as bad as them picking out too little. We're getting $40 to $47 a ton for tomatoes—a bad price this year—and each truckload is 50,000 pounds, 25 tons, 1100 bucks a load. If we're allowed 7 or 8 percent defective tomatoes in the load and we don't have 7 or 8 percent defective tomatoes in the load, we're giving away money. And what's worse, we're paying these guys to make the load too good. It's a double loss. Still, you can't say to your guys, 'Hey, leave 4 percent greens and one percent molds when you sort the tomatoes on that belt.' It's impossible. On most jobs you strive for perfection. They do. But you want to stop them just the right amount short of perfection—because the cannery will penalize you if your load goes over spec. So what you do is run the belt too fast, and sample the percentages in the output from each machine. If the load is too poor, we add another worker. If it's too good, we send someone home."

The workers converse as they ride the machine toward the edge of the desert. Their lips move in an exaggerated manner, but they don't shout. The few workers still needed at harvest time have learned not to fight the machine. They speak under, rather than over, the din of the harvest. They chat, and their hands stay constantly in fast motion.

Until a few years ago, it took a crowd of perhaps 600 laborers to harvest a crop this size. The six machines want about a hundred workers tonight—a hundred workers for 100 million tomatoes, a million tomatoes per worker in the course of the month it will take to clear the field. The trucks come and go. The harvesters sweep back and forth across the field slowly. Now one stands still in midfield. A big service truck of the sort that tends jet planes drives across the field toward it, dome light flashing. It seems that whatever breaks can be fixed here.

After the first survey, there is nothing new to see. It will be this way for the entire month. Like so many scenes in the new agriculture, the essence of this technological miracle is its productivity, and that is reflected in the very uneventfulness of the event. The miracle is permeated with the air of everyday-ness. Each detail must have persons behind it—the inventions and techniques signal insights into systems, corporate decisions, labor meetings, contracts, phone calls, handshakes, hidden skills, management guidelines. Yet the operation is smooth-skinned. Almost nothing anyone does here requires manual skills or craft beyond the ability to drive and follow orders. And everyone—top to bottom—has his orders.

The workday mood leaves the gentleman standing next to me in good humor. We'll call him Johnny Riley, and at this harvest time he is still a well placed official at this farm. He is fiftyish and has a neatly trimmed black beard. His eyebrows and eyelashes match the beard, and his whole face, round, ruddy, and boyish, beams behind heavy, black-framed glasses. He's a glad-hander, a toucher, with double-knit everything, a winning smile that demands acknowledgement, and praise to give out. It is enjoyable to talk with him.

"There are too many people out here on the job with their meters running. We can't afford trouble with tomato prices so low. If something hasn't been planned right, and it costs us extra money to get it straightened out, it's my ass," he says.

The tomato harvester that has been closing for some time, bearing down on our outpost by the edge of the field, is now dangerously near. Behind the monster stretches a mile-and-a-quarter-long row of uprooted stubble, shredded leaves, piles of dirt, and smashed tomatoes. Still Johnny Riley holds his ground. He has to raise his voice to make himself heard.

"I don't like to blow my own horn," he shouts, "but there are secrets to agriculture you just have to find out for yourselves. Here's one case in point. It may seem small to you at first, but profits come from doing the small things right. And one of the things I've found over the years is that a long row is better. Here's why. When you get to the end of a row, the machine here. . . ." Riley gestures up at the harvester, notices our plight, and obligingly leads me to one side. He continues, ". . . the machine here has to turn around before it can go back the other way. And that's when people get off and smoke. Long rows keep them on the job more minutes per hour. You've got less turns with long rows, and the people don't notice this. Especially at night, with lights on, row length is an important tool for people management. Three-fourths of the growers don't realize that. I shouldn't tell you so—it sounds like I'm patting myself on the back—but they don't."

And sure enough, as the harvester climbs off the edge of the tomato field and commences its turn on the sandy work road, the crew members descend from the catwalk, scramble to the ground, and light up cigarettes. Johnny Riley nods knowingly to me, then nods again as a young fellow in a John Deere cap drives out of the darkness in a yellow pickup to join us in the circle of light the harvester has brought with it. It's as if he arrived to meet the harvester—which, it turns out, is what he did do. He is introduced as Buck Klein. Riley seems avuncular and proud as he talks about him.

"He's the field supervisor. Just a few years ago he was delivering material for a fertilizer company. Soon he was their dispatcher, then took orders. He organized the job. He came here to do pesticides, and we've been moving him up." Buck Klein keeps a neutral face for the length of this history, for which I admire him. He is of average height, sturdily built, sports a brush moustache that matches his short, dark blond hair. He wears a western shirt, a belt with a huge buckle that says "Cotton" on it, and cowboy boots. He has come on business.

"We just got a truck back," he says, "all the way from the cannery at Fullerton—three hundred miles of travel and it's back with an unacceptable load. It's got 12 percent mechanical damages, so something's beating on the tomatoes. And this is the machine that's been doing it."

Johnny Riley appears to think for a moment. "We had three loads like that today. Seven percent, 11 percent, and 17 percent mechanicals. You got to take the truck back, get some workers to take out the center of the load and put in some real good tomatoes before you send it back. It ties up workers, and it ties up a truck."

Buck and I join the crew for one lap of harvesting. Then, while the crew members smoke, Buck and a staff mechanic go at the machine with wrenches and screwdrivers. Finally, it is fixed. As we drive off in his truck, Buck talks about the nature of corporate farming. "We have budget sheets for every crop. It's what the management spends their time worrying about, instead of how to make the crops better. It's all high finance. It makes sense, if you think about what they have in it. But I'll tell you something. It's expensive to farm here."

Buck points across the darkness, to the lights of the assembly yard. "Just beyond those lights there's a guy owns a piece—a section of land, and he grows tomatoes there, too. A guy who works with the harvester here, he knows tomatoes pretty well. And he says that guy has a break-even of about 18 tons—18 tons of $40 tomatoes pay his costs, and he's watching every row, growing better than 30 tons to the acre. Our break-even is 24 tons. Why? Because we're so much bigger. They give me more acres than I feel I can watch that closely. The partnership charges 35 bucks an acre management fee, good prices for this and that in the budget. And there is a stack of management people here, where that guy drives his own tractor while he thinks about what to do next. You can't beat him. This is not simple enough here.

"Here, they're so big, and yet they are always looking for a way to cut a dollar out of your budget. Trying to get more and more efficient. It's the workers who they see as the big expense here. They say, okay, management is us, but maybe we can cut out some of those people on the harvesting machines. We can rent these machines from the custom harvester company for $6 a ton bare. We got to pay the workers by the hour even when we're holding up the picking. Twenty workers to a machine some nights and $2.90 a worker is 58 bucks for an hour of down time. You keep moving or send people home.

"Of course this will all be a thing of the past soon. There's a new machine out—Blackwelder makes it—and it's not an experimental model. I mean, it's on the job, at $104,000 and up a shot, and it still pays. It does the same work, only better, with only two workers on it. It's faster, and there's no labor bill. It's an electronic sort. It has a blue belt and little fingers and electric eyes, and when it spots a tomato that isn't right, the little fingers push it out of the way. You just set the amount of greens you want left alone, and it does that, too. We're going to have two of them running later in the harvest, soon as they finish another job."

"What about the workers who have always followed the tomato harvest?" I ask.

"They're in trouble," says Buck, shaking his head. "They'll still be needed, but only toward the end of the harvest. At the beginning, most of what these cullers take away is greens. The electric eye can do that. But at the end of the harvest, most of what they take away is spoiled reds, stuff that gets over-ripe before we pick it, and they say the machines don't do that as well. That leaves a lot of workers on welfare, or whatever they can get, hanging around waiting for the little bit we need them. They get upset about being sent away. This one guy trying to get his sister on a machine, he's been coming up to me all evening saying things about the other workers. I just ignore it, though. It's all part of the job, I guess."

The trouble in which California farm labor finds itself is old trouble. And yet, just a few years ago, when harvesting of cannery tomatoes was still done by hand, ten times the labor was required on the same acreage to handle a harvest that yielded only a third of what Tejon Agricultural Partners and other growers expect these days. The transformation of the tomato industry has happened in the course of about twenty years.

Much has been written recently about this phenomenon, and with good reason. The change has been dramatic, and is extreme. Tomatoes we remember from the past tasted rich, delicate, and juicy. Tomatoes hauled home in today's grocery bag taste bland, though, and dry. The new taste is the taste of modern agriculture.

The ruination of the tomato was a complex procedure. It required co-operation from financial, engineering, marketing, scientific, and agricultural parties that used to go their separate ways more and cross paths with less intention. Now larger institutions control the money that consumers spend on tomatoes. It is no more possible to isolate a "cause" for this shift than it is possible to claim that it's the spark plugs that cause a car to run. However, we can at least peer at the intricate machinery that has taken away our tasty tomatoes and given us pale, scientific fruit.

Let us start then, somewhat arbitrarily, with processors of tomatoes, especially with the four canners—Del Monte, Heinz, Campbell, and Libby, McNeill & Libby—that sell 72 percent of the nation's tomato sauce. What has happened to the quality of tomatoes in general follows from developments in the cannery tomato trade.

The increasingly integrated processors have consolidated, shifted, and "reconceptualized" their plants. In the fast world of marketing processed tomatoes, the last thing executives want is to be caught with too many cans of pizza sauce, fancy grade, when the marketplace is starved for commercial catsup. What processors do nowadays is capture the tomatoes and process them until they are clean and dead, but still near enough to the head of the assembly line so they have not yet gone past the squeezer that issues tomato juice on the sluice gate leading to the spaghetti sauce vat, the paste vat, the aspic tank, or the cauldrons of anything in particular. The mashed stuff of tomato products is stored until demand is clear. Then it's processed the rest of the way. The new manufacturing concept is known in the trade as aseptic barreling, and it leads to success by means of procrastination.

The growers supplying the raw materials for these tightly controlled processors have contracted in advance of planting season for the sale of their crops. It's the only way to get in. At the same time, perhaps stimulated by this new guaranteed marketplace—or perhaps stimulating it—these surviving growers of tomatoes have greatly expanded the size of their plantings. The interaction of large growers and large processors has thus crowded many smaller growers out of the marketplace, not because they can't grow tomatoes as cheaply as the big growers (they can) but because they can't provide large enough units of production to attract favorable contracts with any of the few canners in their area.

In turn, the increasing size of tomato growing operations has encouraged and been encouraged by a number of developments in technology. Harvesters (which may have been the "cause" precipitating the other changes in the system) have in large part replaced persons in the fields. But the new machines became practical only after the development of other technological components—especially new varieties of tomato bred for machine harvesting, and new chemicals that make machine harvesting economical.

What is remarkable about the tomato from the grower's point of view is its rapid increase in popularity. In 1920, each American ate 18.1 pounds of tomato. These days we eat each 50.5 pounds of tomato. Half a million acres of cropland grow tomatoes, yielding nearly 9 milllion tons, worth over $900 million on the market. Today's California tomato acre yields 24 tons, while the same acre in 1960 yielded 17 tons and in 1940, 8 tons.

The increased consumption of tomatoes reflects changing eating habits in general. Most food we eat nowadays is prepared, at least in part, somewhere other than in the home kitchen, and most of the increased demand for tomatoes is for processed products—catsup, sauce, juice, canned tomatoes, and paste for "homemade" sauce. In the 1920s, tomatoes were grown and canned commercially from coast to coast. Small canneries persisted into the 1950s.

Tomatoes were then a labor-intensive crop, requiring planting, transplanting, staking, pruning. And, important in the tale of changing tomato technology, because tomatoes used to ripen a few at a time, each field required three or four forays by harvesting crews to recover successively ripening fruits. The forces that have changed the very nature of tomato-related genetics, farming practices, labor requirements, business configurations, and buying patterns started with the necessity, built so deeply into the structure of our economic system, for the constant perfection of capital utilization.

Some critics sometimes seem to imply that the new mechanization is a conspiracy fostered by fat cats up top to make their own lives softer. But though there are, surely, greedy conspirators mixed in with the regular folks running tomato farms and tomato factories and tomato research facilities, the impulse for change at each stage of the tomato transformation—from the points of view of those effecting the change—is "the system." The system always pressures participants to *meet the competition.*

Even in the 1920s, more tomatoes were grown commercially for processing than for fresh consumption, by a ratio of about two to one. Today the ratio has increased to about seven to one. Fifty years ago, California accounted for about an eighth of all tomatoes grown in America. Today, California grows about 85 percent of tomatoes. Yet as recently as fifteen years ago, California grew only about half the tomato crop. And fifteen years ago, the mechanical harvester first began to show up in the fields of the larger farms.

Before the harvester came, the average California planting was about 45 acres. Today, plantings exceed 350 acres. Tomato production in California used to be centered in family farms around Merced. It has now shifted to the corporate farms of Kern County, where Tejon Agricultural Partners operates. Of the state's 4,000 or so growers harvesting canning tomatoes in the late sixties, 85 percent have left the business since the mechanical harvester came around. Estimates of the number of part-time picking jobs lost go as high as 35,000.

The introduction of the harvester brought about other changes too. Processors thought that tomatoes ought to have more solid material, ought to be less acid, ought to be smaller. Engineers called for tomatoes that had tougher skins and were oblong so they wouldn't roll back down tilted conveyor belts. Larger growers, more able to substitute capital for labor, wanted more tonnage per acre, resistance to cracking from sudden growth spurts that follow irrigation, leaf shade for the fruit to prevent scalding by the hot sun, determinate plant varieties that grow only so high to keep those vines in rows, out of the flood irrigation ditches.

As geneticists selectively bred for these characteristics, they lost control of others. They bred for thick-walledness, less acidity, more uniform ripening, oblongness, leafiness, and high yield—and they could not also select for flavor. And while the geneticists worked on tomato characteristists, chemists were perfecting an aid of their own. Called ethylene, it is in fact also manufactured by tomato plants themselves. All in good time, it promotes reddening. Sprayed on a field of tomatoes that has reached a certain stage of maturity (about 15 percent of the field's tomatoes must have started to "jell"), the substance causes the plants to start the enzyme activity that induces redness. About half of the time a tomato spends between blossom and ripeness is spent at full size, merely growing red. (Tomatoes in the various stages of this ripening are called, in the trade, immature greens, mature greens, breakers, turnings, pinks, light reds, and reds.) Ethylene cuts this reddening time by a week or more and clears the field for its next use. It recovers investment sooner. Still more important, it complements the genetic work, producing plants with a determined and common ripening time so machines can harvest in a single pass. It guarantees precision for the growers. The large-scale manufacturing system that buys the partnership's tomatoes requires predictable results. On schedule, eight or ten or fourteen days after planes spray, the crop will be red and ready. The gas complements the work of the engineers, too, loosening the heretofore stubborn attachment of fruit and stem. It makes it easier for the new machines to shake the tomatoes free of the vines.

The result of this integrated system of tomato seed and tomato chemicals and tomato hardware and tomato know-how has been, of course, the reformation of tomato business.

According to a publication of the California Agrarian Action Project, a reform-oriented research group located at Davis (some of whose findings are reflected in this [chapter]), the effects of an emerging "low-grade oligopoly" in tomato processing are discoverable. Because of labor savings and increased efficiency of machine harvesting, the retail price of canned tomatoes should have dropped in the five years after the machines came into the field. Instead, it climbed 111 percent, and it did so in a period that saw the overall price of processed fruits and vegetables climb only 76 percent.

There are "social costs" to the reorganization of the tomato processing industry as well. The concentration of plants concentrates work opportunities formerly not only more plentiful but more dispersed in rural areas. It concentrates problems of herbicide, pesticide, and salinity pollution.

As the new age of cannery tomato production has overpowered earlier systems of production, a kind of flexibility in tomato growing, which once worked strongly to the consumer's advantage, has been lost. The new high-technology tomato system involves substantial investment "up front" for seed, herbicides and pesticides, machinery, water, labor, and for the "management" of growing, marketing, and financing the crop.

In order to reduce the enormous risks that might, in the old system, have fallen to single parties, today's tomato business calls for "jointing" of the tomatoes. Growers nowadays share the burden of planting, raising, harvesting, and marketing—"farming" together with a "joint contractor." The tomatoes grown by Johnny Riley and Buck Klein on land held by Tejon Agricultural Partners were grown under a joint contract with Basic Vegetable Products, Inc., of Vacaville, California. TAP's president at the time, Jack Morgan, was previously executive vice president of Basic Vegetable.

"Jointing" deals are expensive both to set up and to administer. The tomato-growing business situation is becoming so Byzantine that the "per unit cost of production," the cost to a grower of producing a pound of tomatoes, is no longer the sole determinant of who gets to grow America's tomatoes. Once, whoever could sell the most cheaply won the competitive race to market. Today, the cost of doing all business supersedes, for large-scale operations, simple notions such as growing tomatoes inexpensively. Market muscle, tax advantages, clout with financiers, control of supply, all affect the competitive position of TAP as much as does the expense of growing tomatoes.

The consequence of joint contracting for the consumer is a higher-priced tomato. Risks that until recently were undertaken by growers and processors and distributors separately, because they were adversaries, are passed on to consumers now by participants that have allied. Growers are more certain they will recover the cost of production.

Howard Leach, who was president of TAP's parent company, Tejon Ranch, at the time of the tomato harvest, understood very well the economic implications for consumers of joint contracting.

"Productivity lessens," Leach explained to me. "Risk to the producer lessens, which is why we do it. The consumer gets more cost because the processor who puts money in will try to lower supply until it matches the anticipated demand. If you're Hunt-Wesson, you gear up to supply what you forecast that sales will be. You want an assured crop, so you contract for an agreed price. You're locked in, and so is the farming organization. But they are locked into a price they are assured of, and they are big enough to affect the supply."

Under this sort of business condition, the marketplace is fully occupied by giants. It is no place for the little guy with a truckload or two of tomatoes —even if his price is right. Farmers who once planted twenty or thirty acres of cannery tomatoes as a speculative complement to other farming endeavors are for the most part out of the picture, with no place to market their crops and no place to finance their operating expenses. As John Wood, a family farmer turned corporate manager, who currently runs TAP, puts it, "The key thing today is the ability to muscle into the marketplace. These days, it's a vicious fight to do so." And Ray Peterson, the economist and former vice president of Tejon Ranch, sums up the importance of the business side of farming now that the new technology has increased the risk and scale of each venture. "Today," he says, "vegetable farming is more marketing than farming."

The "jointing" of vegetable crops integrates the farming operation with the marketing, processing, and vending operations so closely that it takes teams of lawyers to describe just where one leaves off and another begins. And joint contracting is only one of several sorts of financial and managerial integration with suppliers and marketers that occur in the new tomato scene. Today chemical companies consult as technical experts with farming organizations. Equipment companies consult with farming organizations about what machines will do the jobs that need doing. Operations lease equipment from leasing companies run by banks that also lend them funds to operate. Financial organizations that lend growers vast sums of capital for both development and operations receive in return not merely interest but negotiated rights to oversee some decision-making processes. Agricultural academics sit on agribusiness corporate boards.

Today the cannery tomato farmer has all but ceased to exist as a discrete and identifiable being. The organizations and structures that do what farmers once did operate as part and parcel of an economy functioning at a nearly incomprehensible level of integration. So much for the tasty tomato.

# Part Four

# The Blessings of Technology

# Introduction

The critics in the previous section have not gone unheard, as is evidenced by the (sometimes angry) response of the partisans of modern technology. The authors in this section can be regarded as being pro-technology, but, as with "anti-technology," this needs some qualification. If we think of technology as ethically neutral, it does not make sense to favor technology as such; it is possible, however, to believe that the application of technology has been most beneficial. Furthermore, advocates such as Samuel Florman (see chapter 1 of this section) decry attempts to alter the current direction of technology. The authors in this section are in favor of the modern *uses* of technology. We cannot turn the clock back, we must go forward. To borrow General Electric's phrase, "Progress is our most important product." While modern technology does produce some undesirable "side-effects," these can be rectified only through continual technological development.

As we have seen, Jacques Ellul and Hans Jonas take a broad, abstract view of technology that includes Arnold Pacey's cultural and organizational aspects. Without denying the social impact of technical inventions—the "material works" of technology—the authors we shall read in this section insist that the cultural and organizational factors be kept separate. Against Ellul and Jonas, they argue that if problems exist, they cannot be blamed on some mysterious, all-encompassing force called technology. Technology is a means to satisfy what people want, what they freely choose as an end.

Samuel Florman recognizes that we face serious social problems. The orthodox belief that technology is *necessarily* good is a myth. However, Florman argues that anti-technologists like Ellul have simply substituted a new myth, namely that technology has escaped human control and become autonomous. This belief of Ellul, Florman argues, is so absurd that it hardly deserves serious refutation. The fundamental mistake, he thinks, is the reification of technology, that is, treating the abstract notion of technology as if it were a thing existing independently of its human context. There is no such thing as technology in the abstract; there exist only specific technologies. Some observers have become so obsessed with the unanticipated and undesirable consequences of modern technology that they have forgotten the intended, and central, results that do satisfy people's desires.

Florman argues that although the anti-technologists assume a high moral purpose, there is a strong totalitarian bias in their thinking. The anti-technologists denigrate the intelligence of ordinary citizens when they claim that technology forces men to work, to consume, and to live in cities. The fact is that persons freely choose their style of life. They want to raise their material standard of living and are quite willing to work hard in order to achieve this. Modern technology has provided the opportunity for people to live better while at the same time expanding their political freedoms. To think that life was more humane, more satisfying, or more free in preindustrial society is pure, unfounded romanticism.

The problems we confront, Florman claims, are not caused by technology (or, by his own profession, engineering) but by indomitable human nature. ". . . The vast majority of people in the world want to move forward, whatever the consequences." The basic problem, Florman thinks, is obvious: there are simply too many people wanting too many things. To address the real dangers we must reject the negative, vacuous, and mystifying doctrines of the anti-technologists. Progress is not automatic, but with a good dose of common sense, courage, and citizen activism, the promise of technology may still be realized.

Melvin Kranzberg is in substantial agreement with Florman. He finds it most puzzling that just when technology is about to eliminate human want, the "bleeding heart humanists" attack the technological basis of this prosperity. He agrees with William Fielding Ogburn's notion of "cultural lag," but the problem is due to our failure to adjust our social arrangements to keep pace with technological change. The problem is not with technology, but with the "humanists" who fail to understand modern technology.

New technologies, on Kranzberg's view, have already created tensions in society and ushered in new ways of life; however, anti-technologists like Jonas and Ellul discern a qualitative difference in modern technology. They fear that man himself is becoming obsolete, and that traditional human values are being destroyed by the imperatives of the new technologies. But, according to Kranzberg, this is irrational, for there is no technological imperative. He agrees with Lynn White's historical analysis that claims that "technology opens doors, it does not compel man to enter." Technology, then, is simply a means to an end, which people may use as they see fit.

Although Kranzberg admits that there are difficulties inherent in regarding technology as only a means, he does believe that people have choices about how to apply a technology that involves "factors which are social, political, and ethical, as well as technological, in character." While technology is always "Janus-faced," on balance technology, contrary to the claims of the "humanists," has tended to enlarge human freedom, to increase democracy and equality, and to provide the leisure which is the foundation of culture.

Emmanuel Mesthene gives us what he regards as a balanced view of the role of technology: it is neither an unalloyed blessing nor an unmitigated evil. To comprehend the importance of technology in society, we need a concept that goes beyond the idea of simple hardware, e.g., Weinberg's notion of a "technical fix." Mesthene defines "technology" as the organization of knowledge for practical purposes." "Practical," however, does not *mean* beneficial, for "It has both positive and negative effects, and it usually has the two *at the same time and in virtue of each other.*"

In essential agreement with Florman and Kranzberg, Mesthene sees technology as not only "capable" of, but actually giving us, choices. The problem is to reorganize society to take maximum advantage of technological opportunities. Traditional structures and values tend, however, to impede technological and human progress. Thus, "technical fixes" alone are insufficient. We also require "human engineering."

The trick, Mesthene argues, is to do cost-benefit analyses in order to maximize the social benefits of new technologies while at the same time minimizing the costs. For example, the perceived benefits of the chemical Alar in producing beautiful apples must be weighed against the possibility that it causes cancer. Control of technology may clash with the ideals of individual freedom and the free market. But despite the tension between these forces, Mesthene clearly remains, despite his reservations, an advocate of laissez-faire capitalism and what may be called laissez-faire technology. Advancing technology makes possible great advances in the direction of equality among men and more democratic societies.

The authors in this section are in substantial agreement with those in Part 9 who deny that technology is autonomous. They are content, however, to leave things pretty much alone. While our social and political system may require some fine tuning to take advantage of the fruits of technological innovations, no radical changes are necessary.

# 11

# In Praise of Technology

## Samuel C. Florman

A generation ago most people believed, without doubt or qualification, in the beneficial effects of technological progress. Books were written hailing the coming of an age in which machines would do all the onerous work, and life would become increasingly utopian.

Today there is a growing belief that technology has escaped from human control and is making our lives intolerable. Thus do we dart from one false myth to another, ever impressed by glib and simple-minded prophets.

Hostility to technology has become such a familiar staple of our reading fare that rarely do we stop to consider how this new doctrine has so quickly and firmly gained its hold upon us. I believe that critical scrutiny of this strange and dangerous phenomenon is very much overdue. The founding father of the contemporary anti-technological movement is Jacques Ellul, whose book, *The Technological Society,* was published in France in 1954, and in the United States ten years later. When it appeared here, Thomas Merton, writing in *Commonweal,* called it "one of the most important books of this mid-century." In *Book Week* it was labeled "an essay that will likely rank among the most important, as well as tragic, of our time."

Ellul's thesis is that "technique" has become a Frankenstein monster that cannot be controlled. By technique he means not just the use of machines, but all deliberate and rational behavior, all efficiency and organization. Man created technique in prehistoric times out of sheer necessity, but then the *bourgeoisie* developed it in order to make money, and the masses were converted because of their interest in comfort. The search for efficiency has become an end in itself, dominating man and destroying the quality of his life.

The second prominent figure to unfurl the banner of anti-technology was Lewis Mumford. His conversion was particularly significant since for many years he had been known and respected as the leading historian of technology. His massive *Myth of the Machine* appeared in 1967 (Part I: *Technics and Human Development*) and in 1970 (Part II: *The Pentagon of Power*). Each volume in turn was given front-page coverage in *The New York Times Sunday Book Review*. On the first page of *Book World* a reviewer wrote, "Hereafter it will be difficult indeed to take seriously any discussion of our industrial ills which does not draw heavily upon this wise and mighty work." The reviewer was Theodore Roszak, who, as we shall see, was soon to take his place in the movement.

The next important convert was René Dubos, a respected research biologist and author. In *So Human an Animal,* published in 1968, Dubos started with the biologist's view that man is an animal whose basic nature was formed during the course of his evolution, both physical and social. This basic nature, molded in forests and fields, is not suited to life in a technological world. Man's ability to adapt to almost any environment has been his downfall, and little by little he has accommodated himself to the physical and psychic horrors of modern life. Man must choose a different path, said Dubos, or he is doomed. This concern for the individual, living human being was just what was needed to flesh out the abstract theories of Ellul and the historical analyses of Mumford. *So Human an Animal* was awarded the Pulitzer Prize, and quickly became an important article of faith in the anti-technology crusade.

In 1970 everybody was talking about Charles A. Reich's *Greening of America.* In paperback it sold more than a million copies within a year. Reich, a law professor at Yale, spoke out on behalf of the youthful counterculture and its dedication to a liberating consciousness-raising. Theodore Roszak's *Where The Wasteland Ends* appeared in 1972 and carried Reich's theme just a little further, into the realm of primitive spiritualism. Roszak, like Reich, is a college professor. Unlike *The Greening of America,* his work did not capture a mass audience. But it seemed to bring to a logical climax the anti-technological movement started by Ellul. As the reviewer in *Time* magazine said, "he has brilliantly summed up once and for all the New Arcadian criticism of what he calls 'postindustrial society.' "

There have been many other contributors to the anti-technological movement, but I think that these five—Ellul, Mumford, Dubos, Reich, and Roszak—have been pivotal.

They are united in their hatred and fear of technology, and surprisingly unanimous in their treatment of several key themes:

1. Technology is a "thing" or a force that has escaped from human control and is spoiling our lives.

2. Technology forces man to do work that is tedious and degrading.

3. Technology forces man to consume things that he does not really desire.

4. Technology creates an elite class of technocrats, and so disenfranchises the masses.

5. Technology cripples man by cutting him off from the natural world in which he evolved.

6. Technology provides man with technical diversions which destroy his existential sense of his own being.

The anti-technologists repeatedly contrast our abysmal technocracy with three cultures that they consider preferable: the primitive tribe, the peasant community, and medieval society.

Recognizing that we cannot return to earlier times, the anti-technologists nevertheless would have us attempt to recapture the satisfactions of these vanished cultures. In order to do this what is required is nothing less than *a change in the nature of man*. The anti-technologists would probably argue that the change they seek is really a return to man's *true* nature. But a change from man's present nature is clearly their fondest hope.

In the often-repeated story, Samuel Johnson and James Boswell stood talking about Berkeley's theory of the nonexistence of matter. Boswell observed that although he was satisfied that the theory was false, it was impossible to refute it. "I never shall forget," Boswell tells us, "the alacrity with which Johnson answered, striking his foot with mighty force against a large stone, till he rebounded from it—" 'I refute it *thus.*' "

The ideas of the anti-technologists arouse in me a mood of exasperation similar to Dr. Johnson's. Their ideas are so obviously false, and yet so persuasive and widely accepted, that I fear for the common sense of us all.

The impulse to refute this doctrine with a Johnsonian kick is diminished by the fear of appearing simplistic. So much has been written about technology by so many profound thinkers that the nonprofessional cannot help but be intimidated. Unfortunately for those who would dispute them, the anti-technologists are masters of prose and intellectual finesse. To make things worse, they display an aesthetic and moral concern that makes the defender of technology appear like something of a philistine. To make things worse yet, many defenders of technology are indeed philistines of the first order.

Yet the effort must be made. If the anti-technological argument is allowed to stand, the engineer is hard pressed to justify his existence. More important, the implications for society, should anti-technology prevail, are most disquieting. For, at the very core of anti-technology, hidden under a veneer of esthetic sensibility and ethical concern, lies a yearning for a totalitarian society.

The first anti-technological dogma to be confronted is the treatment of technology as something that has escaped from human control. It is understandable that sometimes anxiety and frustration can make us feel this way. But sober thought reveals that technology is not an independent force, much less a thing, but merely one of the types of activities in which people engage. Furthermore, it is an activity in which people engage because they choose to do so. The choice may sometimes be foolish or unconsidered. The choice may be forced upon some members of society by others. But this is very different from the concept of technology *itself* misleading or enslaving the populace.

Philosopher Daniel Callahan has stated the case with calm clarity:

> At the very outset we have to do away with a false and misleading dualism, one which abstracts man on the one hand and technology on the other, as if the two were quite separate kinds of realities. I believe that there is no dualism inherent here. Man is by nature a technological animal; to be human is to be technological. If I am correct in that judgment, then there is no room for a dualism at all. Instead, we should recognize that when we speak of technology, this is another way of speaking about man himself in one of his manifestations.

Although to me Callahan's statement makes irrefutable good sense, and Ellul's concept of technology as being a thing-in-itself makes absolutely no sense, I recognize that this does not put an end to the matter, any more than Samuel Johnson settled the question of the nature of reality by kicking a stone.

It cannot be denied that, in the face of the excruciatingly complex problems with which we live, it seems ingenuous to say that men invent and manufacture things because they want to, or because others want them to and reward them accordingly. When men have engaged in technological activities, these activities appear to have had *consequences,* not only physical but also intellectual, psychological, and cultural. Thus, it can be argued, technology is *deterministic.* It causes other things to happen. Someone invents the automobile, for example, and it changes the way people think as well as the way they act. It changes their living patterns, their values, and their expectations in ways that were not anticipated when the automobile was first introduced. Some of the changes appear to be not only unanticipated but undesired. Nobody wanted traffic jams, accidents, and pollution. Therefore, technological advance seems to be independent of human direction. Observers of the social scene become so chagrined and frustrated by this turn of events —and its thousand equivalents—that they turn away from the old commonsense explanations, and become entranced by the demonology of the anti-technologists.

In addition to confounding rational discourse, the demonology outlook of the anti-technologists discounts completely the integrity and intelligence of the ordinary person. Indeed, pity and disdain for the individual citizen is an essential aspect of anti-technology. It is central to the next two dogmas, which hold that technology forces man to do tedious and degrading work, and then forces him to consume things that he does not really desire.

Is it ingenuous, again, to say that people work, not to feed some monstrous technological machine, but, as since time immemorial, to feed themselves? We all have ambivalent feelings toward work, engineers as well as anti-technologists. We try to avoid it, and yet we seem to require it for our emotional well-being. This dichotomy is as old as civilization. A few wealthy people are bored because they are not required to work, and a lot of ordinary people grumble because they have to work hard.

The anti-technologists romanticize the work of earlier times in an attempt to make it seem more appealing than work in a technological age. But their idyllic descriptions of peasant life do not ring true. Agricultural work, for all its appeal to the intellectual in his armchair, is brutalizing in its demands. Factory and office work is not a bed of roses either. But given their choice, most people seem to prefer to escape from the drudgery of the farm. This fact fails to impress the anti-technologists, who prefer their sensibilities to the choices of real people.

As for the technological society forcing people to consume things that they do not want, how can we respond to this canard? Like the boy who said, "Look, the emperor has no clothes," one might observe that the consumers who buy cars and electric can openers could, if they chose, buy oboes and oil paints, sailboats and hiking boots, chess sets and Mozart records. Or, if they have no personal "increasing wants," in Mumford's phrase, could they not help purchase a kidney machine which would save their neighbor's life? If people are vulgar, foolish, and selfish in their choice of purchases, is it not the worst sort of cop-out to blame this on "the economy," "society," or "the suave technocracy"? Indeed, would not a man prefer being called vulgar to being told he has no will with which to make choices of his own?

Which brings us to the next tenet of anti-technology, the belief that a technocratic elite is taking over control of society. Such a view at least avoids the logical absurdity of a demon technology compelling people to act against their own interests. It does not violate our common sense to be told that certain people are taking advantage of other people. But is it logical to claim that exploitation increases as a result of the growth of technology?

Upon reflection, this claim appears to be absolutely without foundation. When camel caravans traveled across the deserts, there were a few merchant entrepreneurs and many disenfranchised camel drivers. From earliest historical times, peasants have been abused and exploited by the nobility. Bankers, merchants, landowners, kings, and assorted plunderers have had it good at the expense of the masses in practically every large social group that has ever been (not just in certain groups like pyramid-building Egypt, as Mumford contends). Perhaps in small tribes there was less exploitation than that which developed in large and complex cultures, and surely technology played a role in that transition. But since the dim, distant time of that initial transition, it simply is not true that advances in technology have been helpful to the Establishment in increasing its power over the masses.

In fact, the evidence is all the other way. In technologically advanced societies, there is more freedom for the average citizen than there was in earlier ages. There has been continuing apprehension that new technological achievements *might* make it possible for governments to tyrannize the citizenry with Big Brother techniques. But, in spite of all the newest electronic gadgetry, governments are scarcely able to prevent the antisocial actions of criminals, much less control every act of every citizen. Hijacking, technically ingenious robberies, computer-aided embezzlements, and the like, are evidence that the outlaw is able to turn technology to his own advantage, often more adroitly than the government. The FBI has admitted that young revolutionaries are almost impossible to find once they go "underground." The rebellious individual is more than holding his own.

Exploitation continues to exist. That is a fact of life. But the anti-technologists are in error when they say that it has increased in extent or intensity because of technology. In spite of their extravagant statements, they cannot help but recognize that they are mistaken, statistically, at least. Reich is wrong when he says that "decisions are made by experts, specialists, and professionals safely insulated from the feelings of the people." (Witness changes in opinion, and then in legislation, concerning abortion, divorce, and pornography.) Those who were slaves are now free. Those who were disenfranchised can now vote. Rigid class structures are giving way to frenetic mobility. The barons and abbots and merchant princes who treated their fellow humans like animals, and convinced them that they would get their reward in heaven, would be incredulous to hear the anti-technologists theorize about how technology has brought about an increase in exploitation. We need only look at the underdeveloped nations of our present era to see that exploitation is not proportionate to technological advance. If anything, the proportion is inverse.

Next we must confront the charge that technology is cutting man off from his natural habitat, with catastrophic consequences. It is important to point out that if we are less in touch with nature than we were—and this can hardly be disputed—then the reason does not lie exclusively with technology. Technology could be used to put people in very close touch with nature, if that is what they want. Wealthy people could have comfortable abodes in the wilderness, could live among birds in the highest jungle treetops, or even commune with fish in the ocean depths. But they seem to prefer penthouse apartments in New York and villas on the crowded hills above Cannes. Poorer people could stay on their farms on the plains of Iowa, or in their small towns in the hills of New Hampshire, if they were willing to live the spare and simple life. But many of them seem to tire of the loneliness and the hard physical labor that goes with rusticity, and succumb to the allure of the cities.

It is Roszak's lament that "the malaise of a Chekhov play" has settled upon daily life. He ignores the fact that the famous Chekhov malaise stems in no small measure from living in the country. "Yes, old man," shouts Dr. Astrov at Uncle Vanya, "in the whole district there were only two decent, well-educated men: you and I. And in some ten years the common round of the trivial life here has swamped us, and has poisoned our life with its putrid vapors, and made us just as despicable as all the rest." There is tedium in the countryside, and sometimes squalor.

Nevertheless, I personally enjoy being in the countryside or in the woods and so feel a certain sympathy for the anti-technologists' views on this subject. But I can see no evidence that frequent contact with nature is *essential* to human well-being, as the antitechnologists assert. Even if the human species owes much of its complexity to the diversity of the natural environment, why must man continue to commune with the landscapes in which he evolved? Millions of people, in ages past as well as present, have lived out their lives in city environs, with very little if any contact with "nature." Have they lived lives inherently inferior because of this? Who would be presumptuous enough to make such a statement?

The next target of the anti-technologists is Everyman at play. It is particularly important to anti-technology that popular hobbies and pastimes be discredited, for leisure is one of the benefits generally assumed to follow in the wake of technological advances. The theme of modern man at leisure spurs the anti-technologists to derision.

In their consideration of recreation activities, the anti-technologists disdain to take into account anything that an actual participant might feel. For even when the ordinary man considers himself happy—at a ball game or a vacation camp, watching television or listening to a jukebox, playing with a pinball machine or eating hot dogs—we are told that he is only being fooled into *thinking* that he is happy.

It is strategically convenient for the anti-technologists to discount the expressed feelings of the average citizen. It then follows that (1) those satisfactions which are attributed to technology are illusory, and (2) those dissatisfactions which are the fault of the individual can be blamed on technology, since the individual's choices are made under some form of hypnosis. It is a can't-lose proposition.

Under these ground rules, how can we argue the question of what constitutes the good life? The anti-technologists have every right to be gloomy, and have a bounden duty to express their doubts about the direction our lives are taking. But their persistent disregard of the average person's sentiments is a crucial weakness in their argument—particularly when they ask us to consider the "real" satisfactions that they claim ordinary people experienced in other cultures of other times.

It is difficult not to be seduced by the anti-technologists' idyllic elegies for past cultures. We all are moved to reverie by talk of an arcadian golden age. But when we awaken from this reverie, we realize that the anti-technologists have diverted us with half-truths and distortions. The harmony which the anti-technologists see in primitive life, anthropologists find in only certain tribes. Others display the very anxiety and hostility that anti-technologists blame on technology—as why should they not, being almost totally vulnerable to every passing hazard of nature, beast, disease, and human enemy? As for the peasant, was he "foot-free," "sustained by physical work," with a capacity for a "nonmaterial existence"? Did he crack jokes with every passerby? Or was he brutal and brutalized, materialistic and suspicious, stoning errant women and hiding gold in his mattress? And the Middle Ages, that dimly remembered time of "moral judgment," "equilibrium," and "common aspirations." Was it not also a time of pestilence, brigandage, and public tortures? "The chroniclers themselves," admits a noted admirer of the period (J. Huizinga), tell us "of covetousness, of cruelty, of cool calculation, of well-understood self-interest . . . . " The callous brutality, the unrelievable pain, the ever-present threat of untimely death for oneself (and worse, for one's children) are the realities with which our ancestors lived and of which the anti-technologists seem totally oblivious.

It is not my intention to assert that, because we live longer and in greater physical comfort than our forebears, life today is better than it ever was. It is this sort of chamber of commerce banality that has driven so many intellectuals into the arms of the anti-technological movement. Nobody is satisfied that we are living in the best of all possible worlds.

Part of the problem is the same as it has always been. Men are imperfect, and nature is often unkind, so that unhappiness, uncertainty, and pain are perpetually present. From the beginning of recorded time we find evidence of despair, melancholy, and ennui. We find also an abundance of greed, treachery, vulgarity, and stupidity. Absorbed as we are in our own problems, we tend to forget how replete history is with wars, feuds, plagues, fires, massacres, tortures, slavery, the wasting of cities, and the destruction of libraries. As for ecology, over huge portions of the earth men have made pastures out of forests, and then deserts out of pastures. In every generation prophets, poets, and politicians have considered their contemporary situation uniquely distressing, and have looked about for something—or someone—to blame. The anti-technologists follow in this tradition, and, in the light of history, their condemnation of technology can be seen to be just about as valid as the Counter-Reformation's condemnation of witchcraft.

But it will not do to say *plus ça change plus c'est la même chose,* * and let it go at that. We do have some problems that are unique in degree if not in kind, and in our society a vague, generalized discontent appears to

---

*Editors' note: "The more things change, the more they are the same."

be more widespread than it was just a generation ago. *Something* is wrong, but what?

Our contemporary problem is distressingly obvious. We have too many people wanting too many things. This is not caused by technology; it is a consequence of the type of creature that man is. There are a few people holding back, like those who are willing to do without disposable bottles, a few people turning back, like the young men and women moving to the counterculture communes, and many people who have not gotten started because of crushing poverty and ignorance. But the vast majority of people in the world want to move forward, whatever the consequences. Not that they are lemmings. They are wary of revolution and anarchy. They are increasingly disturbed by crowding and pollution. Many of them recognize that "progress" is not necessarily taking them from worse to better. But whatever their caution and misgivings, they are pressing on with a determination that is awesome to behold.

Our blundering, pragmatic democracy may be doomed to fail. The increasing demands of the masses may overwhelm us, despite all our resilience and ingenuity. In such an event we will have no choice but to change. The Chinese have shown us that a different way of life is possible. However, we must not deceive ourselves into thinking that we can undergo such a change, or maintain such a society, without the most bloody upheavals and repressions.

We are all frightened and unsure of ourselves, in need of good counsel. But where we require clear thinking and courage, the anti-technologists offer us fantasies and despair. Where we need an increase in mutual respect, they exhibit hatred for the powerful and contempt for the weak. The times demand more citizen activism, but they tend to recommend an aloof disengagement. We surely could use a sense of humor, but they are in the grip of an unrelenting dolefulness. Nevertheless, the anti-technologists have managed to gain a reputation for kindly wisdom.

This reputation is not entirely undeserved, since they do have many inspiring and interesting things to say. Their sentiments about nature, work, art, spirituality, and many of the good things in life, are generally splendid and difficult to quarrel with. Their ecological concerns are praiseworthy, and their cries of alarm have served some useful purpose. In sum, the anti-technologists are good men, and they mean well.

But, frightened and dismayed by the unfolding of the human drama in our time, yearning for simple solutions where there can be none, and refusing to acknowledge that the true source of our problems is nothing other than the irrepressible human will, they have deluded themselves with the doctrine of anti-technology. It is a hollow doctrine, the increasing popularity of which adds the dangers inherent in self-deception to all of the other dangers we already face.

# 12

# Technology and Human Values

## Melvin Kranzberg

Just when technology seems on the verge of banishing want and starvation, we find it called into question. The suspicion with which John Ruskin, William Morris, and Herman Melville regarded the machine in the nineteenth century has carried over into the twentieth. Counterbalancing H. G. Wells's belief in the beneficence of technology were the nightmare visions of the future contained in Çapek, Huxley, and Orwell. Most recently, such stalwart upholders of the humane tradition as Jacques Barzun, Lewis Mumford, and F. W. Leavis have exhibited the same ambivalence toward scientific and technological "progress."

Why is it that technology, which ministers to human needs and which has been regarded as a boon to mankind throughout most ages—and is still so regarded in the so-called underdeveloped areas—is viewed with such suspicion? Has technology changed? Has our value system changed?

Man himself is what he is as a result of technological change. Archeology, anthropology, biology, and psychology tell us that man could not have become *Homo sapiens* (man the thinker) had he not been at the same time *homo faber* (man the maker). Only by his possession and use of tools can we distinguish between man and "almost man." Man made tools, but tools also made man.

From the very beginning of our species, therefore, man has depended upon his technology. His attempt to master and control his physical environment is enshrined in the legend of Prometheus, who stole fire from the gods to bring it to mankind. Ever since then the march of civilization has been accom-

From *Virginia Quarterly Review* 40 (1964): 578–92. Reprinted by permission.

panied by technological advance—in terms of materials, from stone to bronze, from bronze to iron, from iron to steel; in terms of energy, from human muscle power to animals, to wind and water, to steam and oil, to rockets and nuclear power; in terms of machines, from hand tools to powered tools, to mass production lines, to computer-controlled factories.

For most of man's history, the term "humanistic" was used to distinguish what was human from what was brutal and coarse, or animal. But now we find that "humanist" is increasingly contrasted with "technology," and "humanistic" is used to distinguish everything else from science and technology. Indeed, the word "humanist" has almost become equated with ignorance of science and technology. The humanities have become the home of anti-rationalists who deny that rational attempts to deal with human material wants have any bearing upon man's pursuit of "the good life."

This change in the meaning of "humanistic," so that it is now equivalent to "spiritual" in contrast to "material," becomes even more confusing when we realize that some non-Western cultures, such as that of India, glorified because of their elevation of spiritual goals over materialistic ends, want to appropriate the technological paraphernalia of Western civilization while repudiating our so-called "humanistic" values. Yet the underdeveloped nations who attempt to borrow our technology are distressed to find that along with it come the humanistic values of our society. In other words, technology is part of the warp and woof of our civilization, and the humanistic cannot be separated from the technological.

The current questioning of the role and value of technology is nothing new in human affairs. Technological change has always created tensions within society. Today technological change is outpacing our capacity for social adjustment—a form of William Fielding Ogburn's "cultural lag"—and the pattern of change has become so complex that the "bleeding-heart humanists" find themselves incapable of understanding it.

A rough parallel can be found by studying the Industrial Revolution in England at the end of the eighteenth and beginning of the nineteenth centuries. Here the machine caused a rapid buildup of tension between owners and workers, a tension which reached its peak when the Luddites naïvely thought that they could combat change by destroying the new machines. Today we are faced with the "intellectual Luddites." They are not so naïve as to believe that social change can be prevented by destroying machines; instead, they attack the philosophical basis for technological change by calling into question its impact on human values.

In the nineteenth century William Morris proposed that Britain go back to cottage industry and an idyllic medieval pastoral life—that had never existed in actuality. John Ruskin also inveighed against the Industrial Revolution. Both believed that the material plenty contributed by machine production carried with it a cultural poverty. Today's "intellectual Luddites" are the spiritual descendants of Morris and Ruskin—concerned, articulate, but ineffectual.

It is not only the rate of change that worries critics, however. There is also the fear that contemporary technology represents something qualitatively new and dangerous to human values. Technology was welcomed when machines took the burden off men's backs and eased the strain on human muscles. Now that machines have proceeded to take some burdens off men's minds and to free men from dull and repetitive tasks, there is fear that the machine is making the human being obsolete.

In an ironic sense the machine is making possible the attacks upon it. In the past, technology has been primarily concerned with the human needs of food, clothing, and shelter. It still fulfills those needs, and so successfully that modern Western technology for the first time in history has produced a society which has not only a surplus of goods but a surplus of leisure as well. Living in an economy of abundance made possible by technology, we are now free to question technology in terms of its ability to meet those humanistic needs which go beyond our material desires.

What are these human values which the humanists believe are in such peril from the onslaught of technology? And what has been the actual impact of technology upon them?

Foremost among the humanistic values in Western civilization is our respect for the worth of the individual human being. Our religious concepts, our philosophies, our laws, our schools, and our economic system glorify the individual and are presumably aimed at making it possible for man to realize his full potential as a human being. Placing the individual as the basis of the value system is perhaps unique to Western culture. This elevation of the individual came relatively late—just two or three centuries ago—and even in very recent times, the individual has been subordinated to the social or economic rigidities of a particular nation or "race."

The level of technology in any period in history determines the way in which the majority of men earn their living, where they live, and how they spend the major portion of their time. Throughout antiquity—in Egypt, Mesopotamia, Greece, and Rome—manual labor was largely left to slaves, who were considered as property and had few rights as individuals. In the Middle Ages, windmills and waterwheels eased the human physical burden somewhat, but the serfs, who were numerically the largest group in the population, possessed few rights, and those only by virtue of the custom associated with their plot of land, not as individuals. Although the decline of feudalism loosened the bonds of serfdom, not until the political and social revolutions of the seventeenth and eighteenth centuries was the idea accepted that each individual possessed certain inalienable rights and that society would be directed toward the guarantee and maintenance of those rights.

At the same time that the state was being organized in behalf of the individual, great technological changes, lumped together under the term Industrial Revolution, were also taking place. Throughout history the home had been the production center. Farming, weaving, garment making—all were family endeavors centering around hearth and home. Industrialization uprooted this system, moved thousands of families into cities, and made factory labor the source of their livelihood. The Industrial Revolution not only changed the productive mechanisms of society but also transformed the individual's conditions of life.

What else did industrialization do to the individual? As a result of his urbanization, the working man, for the first time, was achieving a degree of political recognition, but the widespread feeling was that the price was the loss of his individuality on the production line. In the factory work was divided into separate units, and this "fracturing of work" took away from the work- man much of his pride in craftsmanship. The development of assembly-line techniques has exaggerated this trend, and now automation is separating the worker even further from the end product.

There is no question that this division of labor helped to make possible the enormous production of goods which raised the material conditions of living for the workers engaged in the manufacturing process. Thus the human imperative of satisfying material wants has been in part met by technological progress through the division of labor. But has the humanistic imperative of the dignity and worth of the individual personality in actuality been sacri- ficed thereby?

At times in the past, and in isolated instances today, the answer would have to be a limited "yes." But in the main, today and in the future the answer is an emphatic "no!" Instead of making man into a robot, as envisioned by Karel Çapek in "R.U.R.,"* automation is in the process of restoring human dignity by freeing man from the repetitious tasks which dull the human personality. One of the technological imperatives is efficiency: in pursuit of efficiency, industrial engineers and industrial management have been forced to focus upon the individual human being. Modern systems engineering must consider the human parameter in any engineering system. And, despite the dreadful connotation of the term, which makes one think that it is designed to "engineer" human beings, human engineering is actually concerned with the man-machine relationship. Its primary goal is to adapt the machine and the work process to the human mind and body. Thus any threat to the individ- ual arising from technology will tend to be counterbalanced by the technolog- ical demand for efficient production which depends upon the proper environ- ment for and the proper use of the individual human being.

Yet it must be recognized that some sacrifice of unbridled individualism is necessary if men are to work together. Technology makes compulsory some form of cooperation and understanding among human beings in order to carry on the productive process. If each worker were to follow his own bent, he might not awaken until noon or he might decide to go fishing instead of going to work; in either case, the production line would cease to function. Technology

*I.e., Rossum's Universal Robots (Ed.)

has therefore necessitated some kind of discipline in behalf of the performance of collective tasks.

However, the threat of technology to the individual lies not only in terms of the social discipline in the actual work process but also in the possible constraints upon human freedom. To some social thinkers, such as Lewis Mumford, certain trends in our contemporary technology point to the development of an "authoritarian technics." In the past this authoritarian technics "raised the ceiling of human achievement in both mass construction and mass destruction." Although marvelously dynamic and productive, authoritarian technics, with its command and utilization of science, is thought to be threatening to displace life, "transferring the attributes of life to the machine and the mechanical collective." In contrast to this is what Mumford calls "democratic technics," a small-scale method of production, "resting mainly on human skill and animal energy but always, even when employing machines, remaining under the active direction of the craftsman or the farmer."*

Mr. Mumford may be both right and wrong. There are many ways in which work processes may be organized, even at the most sophisticated levels of technology, and the choice is not necessarily between Mumford's antitheses. A strong case could be made to the effect that technology, while it may threaten to deprive man of one kind of freedom, actually enlarges human freedom in other dimensions. For millennia men lived under Mr. Mumford's "democratic technics" with its small-scale methods of production—and men were constantly in want. Only in our day with its highly organized, mass-production technology—Mumford's "authoritarian technics"—could men conceive of "freedom from want" as a rational goal and the keystone of international policy, as envisioned in the Atlantic Charter.

If we examine the development of democracy historically, we find that technology, far from destroying democracy, may have actually increased it. Iron has been hailed as the "democratic" metal by some writers, for the replacement of bronze by iron made possible the spread of improved technological devices and a better standard of living for the masses. At a later date we find that the great growth of democracy in the Western world was concomitant with the Industrial Revolution. And there are those Kremlinologists who tell us that an improved standard of living in the Soviet Union, made possible by the application of advanced technology, may help bring about a freer society there.†

Technological advance demands democracy in still another way. The institution of slavery, as anti-democratic an institution as one can possibly imagine, has been one of the victims of advancing technology. According to Gerard Piel, "Slavery became immoral when it became technologically obsolete."

---

*See Part 8, chapter 26 of this volume.

†A rather ironic statement when viewed against the light of actual events. It is only after the collapse of the Soviet economy and political system that there will be an earnest move to a free market system. (Ed.)

Despite this oversimplification—which overlooks the possibility of the exploitation of "wage slaves"—the historical fact is that technological developments made outright slavery unprofitable and thereby hastened its end.

Proof of the democratic tendencies of advancing technology is also to be seen in the progress toward integration in the southern United States. Here the development of a new industrial South is bringing an end to inequality. Lest we think that this situation is peculiar to our own country, may I also point out that the demands of a modern industrialized society in India have partly breached the caste system.

Besides its political and legal side, democracy has its social aspect. The advance of technology is closing the great gap between rich and poor. In our economy of abundance the poor can enjoy the same entertainment as the rich merely by flicking a switch, can also eat strawberries out of season simply by going to the nearest supermarket, can enjoy clothes which look and wear like those handtailored by a Paris couturier even though mass produced on New York's Seventh Avenue, can step into automobiles which take them to their destinations as quickly and surely as the Rolls-Royces of the wealthy. As David Potter has said, "When man gains a satisfactory income, acquires education, dresses himself and his wife in the standard clothes worn by all members of the community, sends his children to school . . . the system of classes itself, no longer natural, no longer inevitable, begins to seem unjust." Social democracy thus emerges from technological advance.

Another humanistic imperative is the creation and enjoyment of esthetic works—music, literature, art. Ever since the Industrial Revolution, artists, composers, and writers have attacked technology as creating ugliness and stifling artistic creativity. Yet the nineteenth century, when society was coming under the sway of industrial technology, produced a great new form of literary expression, the novel. It was also rich in poetry, in art, and in music. If industrialization is inimical to esthetic elements, how are we to account for the flourishing of the arts in the nineteenth century?

Once we realize that technology is not inherently harmful to the arts, we find two constructive ways in which technology has fulfilled the humanistic demand for cultivation of esthetic works. The first is that an advancing technology has made possible man's cultivation of the arts; the second is that there are esthetic elements within technology itself.

In a society where the subsistence level is marginal, cultivation of the arts is minimal. Only after elementary wants have been satisfied can men have the leisure to produce intellectual and artistic works of quality. In antiquity, the servile work of the masses produced a slight surplus which was appropriated by the ruling groups of society. They utilized this surplus to enjoy the "finer things" of life. Until the Industrial Revolution, literature and the arts were virtually an aristocratic monopoly.

The philosophers of antiquity recognized the need for leisure, made possible only by the surpluses produced by technology, in order to enable man to pursue intellectual and esthetic activity. In his *Politics,* Aristotle spoke of leisure as the highest condition of life: "[It] gives pleasure and happiness and enjoyment of life. These are experienced not by the busy man, but by those who have leisure. . . . There are branches of learning and education which we must study merely with the view to leisure spent in intellectual activity, and these are to be valued for their own sake. . . ." Because slaves had no leisure and because their entire time was spent in manual work, Aristotle denied them human status.

The importance of leisure as a basis for cultural activity is recognized today also. Arnold Wesker, the young British playwright, while deploring "this terrible cultural bankruptcy" of modern life, says, "Everything is marvelous about a welfare state, but the one thing that is wrong is that you have provided leisure for the community but nothing to fill it in. Today, people have more leisure, more money, and better houses. But this is where civilization begins." True, technology has now made it possible for everyone to have leisure for thought, but according to Sebastian de Grazia, our shrinking work week has left us with little net human gain. We have confused Aristotle's true leisure with free time and have filled our free hours with busy work. Instead of using our leisure to attain our highest mental development, as Aristotle would have us do, we spend most of our free time in pursuit of recreation—not to re-create ourselves, but to kill time.

Even though we must make allowances for human frailty, we still can see how the advance of technology has made it possible for more people to engage in esthetic and intellectual activities, transforming these from an aristocratic monopoly to mass participation in the "finer things" of life. Mass culture has been made possible not only by the free time granted by technology but by other technical advances—by long-playing records [and now compact discs], by art reproductions available, at low cost, by television and movies, the latter two representing new art forms developed through technology. Even in the United States, the attendance at concerts and at museums exceeds the attendance at organized baseball games; more books are being published every year; and the amount of money spent on the theater and the opera has almost doubled in a decade.

To the humanists, this argument is probably meaningless—largely because it is stated in numerical terms. Technology, they would say, provides only a quantitative rather than a qualitative advance in man's culture. They declaim against the debased esthetic tastes of the masses, and then they turn and attack the technological means by which that taste can be elevated.

My second point in regard to esthetics is the technological imperative which makes for the beauty of man's works in terms of functional design. In the nineteenth century, some poets and artists were much impressed by the scientific advances of the time; they tried to understand and utilize them in their descriptions of the world which they saw about them. Tennyson and Matthew Arnold employed scientific references and metaphors; science became a personal, metaphysical concern. Today we find new poets of the machine.

Our poets have let us down badly in interpreting our times to us. By refusing to consider the impact of science and technology, our men of letters are carrying on their intellectual life in a cultural vacuum. It is no wonder that they can communicate only with one another and complain that they feel alienated from a society whose culture they ignore.

It is shocking to realize that the poets regard the world of technology as a prosaic world. They do not recognize the beauty, the challenges, the human experience—the esthetics, if you will—of technology. Yet there they are, and in large measure. Architecture provides a good example, for men like Frank Lloyd Wright have developed technological means to produce new esthetic delights in the plastic arts. It is indeed ironical that the mathematical precision and symmetry of form which characterize our most advanced technological designs are based upon that mathematics which, along with music, Plato placed at the foundations of humanistic education. It is no wonder that Richard L. Meier claims, "The humanities seem to have cut themselves off from the modern lines of creativity in general cultural activity. Perhaps we are coming to a time when the humanities will be but a minor part of a human endeavor."

If the humanists no longer fulfill their role of interpreting nature and society to man, that task will be taken up by the social scientists and psychologists. Instead of reading poetry to acquaint ourselves with the wellsprings of human behavior and man's relations to nature, we will read pyschology. Instead of viewing drama and paintings which endeavor to interpret nature and man's relations to society, we will peruse sociological tracts and look at photographs. Indeed, we have already begun to do so, largely because the humanities have abandoned their traditional role and left a gap in the fulfillment of this humanistic imperative.

In ethics, too, technological advancement has made possible the fulfillment of some significant goals of society and at the same time has engendered new values.

It is the duty of everyone to aid his neighbor, we have long been told, and the relief of poverty and destitution has ever been a goal of the Christian social ethic. The productivity of today's technology now enables us to translate this into action domestically by social welfare measures and on an international scale through technical assistance programs.

Although technology provides us with the means to fulfill an injunction of Christian ethics, we find ourselves somewhat embarrassed by our abundance of material goods. Our theological preconceptions derived from the past leave us with feelings of guilt about our plenteous economy. The Biblical injunction, that man, through Adam, must earn his living by the sweat of his brow, seems to have been overimposed and incommunicable personal anguish and despair.

To make up for the failure of others to develop the human dimensions of technology, technologists must perforce educate themselves in what Simon Ramo calls "the greater engineeering." This involves a more responsive attitude to human and social demands in their ultimate implications, rather than the mere fulfillment of immediate demands. As Dr. Ramo says, "It is this bigger, overall, application of science to serve society that engineering now needs to be concerned with. . . . Now, more than ever, engineering efforts must be in proper match to social, industrial, economic, governmental, and psychological needs. So complex is the list of considerations that clearly we are not going to create the best engineers by teaching them the technical facts alone." In other words, some technologists are increasingly aware of the humanistic imperatives and are trying to do something about fulfilling them. Can the same be said of the humanists in understanding the demands of a technological society?

Let us recognize that the problems presented by technology are not simply technical in nature or solution but are the problems of all society and mankind. Technology does not exist in a vacuum; it develops in a social context, as do all other human activities. Let us realize also, that the problems presented by technology must be met by all men. Instead of being a mechanical master which determines man's destiny, or a Frankenstein's monster which threatens to destroy its creator, technology has always been, and still remains, an essential part of man. The question, therefore, is not whether man can master technology, the question is whether man—*Homo sapiens* and *homo faber*—can master himself. This is the technological imperative; this is the humanistic imperative.

## REFERENCES

De Grazia, Sebastian. *Of Time and Leisure*. New York: Twentieth Century Fund, 1962.

Meier, Richard L. *Science and Economic Development: New Patterns of Living*. 2d ed. Cambridge, Mass.: MIT Press, 1966.

Ogburn, William Fielding. *Social Change, with Respect to Culture and Original Nature*, 1922. Reprint New York: Dell Publishing Co., 1966.

Potter, David. *People of Plenty: Economic Abundance and the American Character*. Chicago: University of Chicago Press, 1954.

# 13

# The Role of Technology in Society

## Emmanuel G. Mesthene

SOCIAL CHANGE

### Three Unhelpful Views About Technology

While a good deal of research is aimed at discerning the particular effects
of technological change on industry, government, or education, systematic
inquiry devoted to seeing these effects together and to assessing their implications for contemporary society as a whole is relatively recent and does not
enjoy the strong methodology and richness of theory and data that mark more
established fields of scholarship. It therefore often has to contend with facile
or one-dimensional views about what technology means for society. Three such
views, which are prevalent at the present time, may be mildly caricatured
somewhat as follows.

The first holds that technology is an unalloyed blessing for man and society. Technology is seen as the motor of all progress, as holding the solution
to most of our social problems, as helping to liberate the individual from the
clutches of a complex and highly organized society, and as the source of
permanent prosperity; in short, as the premise of utopia in our time. This
view has its modern origins in the social philosophies of such nineteenth-century
thinkers as Saint-Simon, Karl Marx, and Auguste Comte. It tends to be held
by many scientists and engineers, by many military leaders and aerospace

From *Technology and Culture* 10, no. 4 (October 1969): 489–513. Copyright © 1969 by the Society
for the History of Technology. Reprinted by permission of the University of Chicago Press.

industrialists, by people who believe that man is fully in command of his tools and his destiny, and by many of the devotees of modern techniques of "scientific management."

A second view holds that technology is an unmitigated curse. Technology is said to rob people of their jobs, their privacy, their participation in democratic government, and even, in the end, their dignity as human beings. It is seen as autonomous and uncontrollable, as fostering materialistic values and as destructive of religion, as bringing about a technocratic society and bureaucratic state in which the individual is increasingly submerged, and as threatening, ultimately, to poison nature and blow up the world. This view is akin to historical "back-to-nature" attitudes toward the world and is propounded mainly by artists, literary commentators, popular social critics, and existentialist philosophers. It is becoming increasingly attractive to many of our youth, and it tends to be held, understandably enough, by segments of the population that have suffered dislocation as a result of technological change.

The third view is of a different sort. It argues that technology as such is not worthy of special notice, because it has been well recognized as a factor in social change at least since the Industrial Revolution, because it is unlikely that the social effects of computers will be nearly so traumatic as the introduction of the factory system in eighteenth-century England, because research has shown that technology has done little to accelerate the rate of economic productivity since the 1800s, because there has been no significant change in recent decades in the time period between invention and widespread adoption of new technology, and because improved communications and higher levels of education make people much more adaptable than heretofore to new ideas and to new social reforms required by technology.

While this view is supported by a good deal of empirical evidence, however, it tends to ignore a number of social, cultural, psychological, and political effects of technological change that are less easy to identify with precision. It thus reflects the difficulty of coming to grips with a new or broadened subject matter by means of concepts and intellectual categories designed to deal with older and different subject matters. This view tends to be held by historians, for whom continuity is an indispensable methodological assumption, and by many economists, who find that their instruments measure some things quite well while those of the other social sciences do not yet measure much of anything.

Stripped of caricature, each of these views contains a measure of truth and reflects a real aspect of the relationship of technology and society. Yet they are oversimplifications that do not contribute much to understanding. One can find empirical evidence to support each of them without gaining much knowledge about the actual mechanism by which technology leads to social change or significant insight into its implications for the future. All three remain too uncritical or too partial to guide inquiry. Research and analysis lead to more differentiated conclusions and reveal more subtle relationships.

## Some Countervailing Considerations

Two of the projects of the Harvard University Program on Technology and Society serve, respectively, to temper some exaggerated claims made for technology and to replace gloom with balanced judgment. Professor Anthony G. Oettinger's study of information technology in education* has shown that, in the schools at least, technology is not likely to bring salvation with it quite so soon as the U.S. Office of Education, leaders of the education industry, and enthusiastic computermen and systems analysts might wish. Neither educational technology nor the school establishment seems ready to consummate the revolution in learning that will bring individualized instruction to every child, systematic planning and uniform standards across 25,000 separate school districts, an answer to bad teachers and unmovable bureaucracies, and implementation of a national policy to educate every American to his full potential for a useful and satisfying life. Human fallibility and political reality are still here to keep utopia at bay, and neither promises soon to yield to a quick technological fix. Major institutional change that can encourage experimentation, flexibility, variety, and competition among educational institutions seems called for before the new technology can contribute significantly to education. Application of the technology itself, moreover, poses problems of scale-up, reliability, and economics that have scarcely been faced as yet.

By contrast, Professor Manfred Stanley's study of the value presuppositions that underlie the pessimistic arguments about technology suggests that predictions of inevitable doom are premature and that a number of different social outcomes are potential in the process of technological change. In other words, the range of possibility and of human choice implicit in technology is much greater than most critics assume. The problem—here, as well as in the application of educational technology—is how to organize society to free the possibility of choice.

Finally, whether modern technology and its effects constitute a subject matter deserving of special attention is largely a matter of how technology is defined. The research studies of the Harvard Program on Technology and Society reflect an operating assumption that the meaning of technology includes more than machines. As most serious investigators have found, understanding is not advanced by concentrating single-mindedly on such narrowly drawn yet imprecise questions as "What are the social implications of computers, or lasers, or space technology?" Society and the influences of technology upon it are much too complex for such artificially limited approaches to be meaningful. The opposite error, made by some, is to define technology too broadly by identifying it with rationality in the broadest sense. The term is then operationally meaningless and unable to support fruitful inquiry.

---

*Unless otherwise noted, studies such as Oettinger's, which are referred to in this [chapter], are described in the Fourth Annual Report (1967–68) of the Harvard University Program on Technology and Society.

We have found it more useful to define technology as tools in a general sense, including machines, but also including linguistic and intellectual tools and contemporary analytic and mathematical techniques. That is, we define technology as the organization of knowledge for practical purposes. It is in this broader meaning that we can best see the extent and variety of the effects of technology on our institutions and values. Its pervasive influence on our very culture would be unintelligible if technology were understood as no more than hardware.

It is in the pervasive influence of technology that our contemporary situation seems qualitatively different from that of past societies, for three reasons. (1) Our tools are more powerful than any before. The rifle wiped out the buffalo, but nuclear weapons can wipe out man. Dust storms lay whole regions waste, but too much radioactivity in the atmosphere could make the planet uninhabitable. The domestication of animals and the invention of the wheel literally lifted the burden from man's back, but computers could free him from all need to labor. (2) This quality of finality of modern technology has brought our society, more than any before, to explicit awareness of technology as an important determinant of our lives and institutions. (3) As a result, our society is coming to a deliberate decision to understand and control technology to good social purpose and is therefore devoting significant effort to the search for ways to measure the full range of its effects rather than only those bearing principally on the economy. It is this prominence of technology in many dimensions of modern life that seems novel in our time and deserving of explicit attention.

## How Technological Change Impinges on Society

It is clearly possible to sketch a more adequate hypothesis about the interaction of technology and society than the partial views outlined above. Technological change would appear to induce or "motor" social change in two principal ways. New technology creates new opportunities for men and societies, and it also generates new problems for them. It has both positive and negative effects, and it usually has the two *at the same time and in virtue of each other*. Thus, industrial technology strengthens the economy, as our measures of growth and productivity show. As Dr. Anne P. Carter's study on structural changes in the American economy has helped to demonstrate, however, it also induces changes in the relative importance of individual supplying sectors in the economy as new techniques of production alter the amounts and kinds of materials, parts and components, energy, and service inputs used by each industry to produce its output. It thus tends to bring about dislocations of businesses and people as a result of changes in industrial patterns and in the structure of occupations.

The close relationship between technological and social change itself helps to explain why any given technological development is likely to have both positive and negative effects. The usual sequence is that (1) technological advance creates a new opportunity to achieve some desired goal; (2) this requires (except in trivial cases) alterations in social organization if advantage is to be taken of the new opportunity, (3) which means that the functions of existing social structures will be interfered with, (4) with the result that other goals which were served by the older structures are now only inadequately achieved.

As the Meyer-Kain study has shown, for example, improved transportation technology and increased ownership of private automobiles have increased the mobility of businesses and individuals. This has led to altered patterns of industrial and residential location, so that older unified cities are being increasingly transformed into larger metropolitan complexes. The new opportunities for mobility are largely denied to the poor and black populations of the core cities, however, partly for economic reasons, and partly as a result of restrictions on choice of residence by blacks, thus leading to persistent black unemployment despite a generally high level of economic activity. Cities are thus increasingly unable to perform their traditional functions of providing employment opportunities for all segments of their populations and an integrated social environment that can temper ethnic and racial differences. The new urban complexes are neither fully viable economic units nor effective political organizations able to upgrade and integrate their core populations into new economic and social structures. The resulting instability is further aggravated by modern mass communications technology, which heightens the expectations of the poor and the fears of the well-to-do and adds frustration and bitterness to the urban crisis.

An almost classic example of the sequence in which technology impinges on society is provided by Professor Mark Field's study of changes in the system and practice of medical care. Recent advances in biomedical science and technology have created two new opportunities: (1) they have made possible treatment and cures that were never possible before, and (2) they provide a necessary condition for the delivery of adequate medical care to the population at large as a matter of right rather than privilege. In realization of the first possibility, the medical profession has become increasingly differentiated and specialized and is tending to concentrate its best efforts in a few major, urban centers of medical excellence. This alters the older social organization of medicine that was built around the general practitioner. The second possibility has led to big increases in demand for medical services, partly because a healthy population has important economic advantages in a highly industrialized society. This increased demand accelerates the process of differentiation and multiplies the levels of paramedical personnel between the physician at the top and the patient at the bottom of the hospital pyramid.

Both of these changes in the medical system are responsive to the new opportunities for technical excellence that have been created by biomedical technology. Both also involve a number of well-known costs in terms of some older desiderata of medical care. The increasing scarcity of the general prac-

‑titioner in many sections of the country means that people in need often have neither easy access to professional care nor the advantage of a "medical general manager" who can direct them to the right care at the right place at the right time, which can result both in poor treatment and a waste of medical resources. Also, too exclusive a concentration on technical excellence can lead to neglect of the patient's psychological well-being, and even the possibility of technical error increases as the "medical assembly line" gets longer.

The pattern illustrated by the preceding examples tends to be the general one. Our most spectacular technological successes in America in the last quarter of a century have been in national defense and in space exploration. They have brought with them, however, enthusiastic advocates and vested interests who claim that the development of sophisticated technology is an intrinsic good that should be pursued for its own sake. They thus contribute to the self-reinforcing quality of technological advance and raise fears of an autonomous technology uncontrollable by man. Mass communications technology has also made rapid strides since World War II, with great benefit to education, journalism, commerce, and sheer convenience. It has also been accompanied by an aggravation of social unrest, however, and may help to explain the singular rebelliousness of a youth that can find out what the world is like from television before home and school have had the time to instill some ethical sense of what it could or should be like.

In all such cases, technology creates a new opportunity and a new problem at the same time. That is why isolating the opportunity or the problem and construing it as the whole answer is ultimately obstructive of rather than helpful to understanding.

## How Society Reacts to Technological Change

The heightened prominence of technology in our society makes the interrelated tasks of profiting from its opportunities and containing its dangers a major intellectual and political challenge of our time.

Failure of society to respond to the opportunities created by new technology means that much actual or potential technology lies fallow, that is, is not used at all or is not used to its full capacity. This can mean that potentially solvable problems are left unsolved and potentially achievable goals unachieved, because we waste our technological reosurces or use them inefficiently. A society has at least as much stake in the efficient utilization of technology as in that of its natural or human resources.

There are often good reasons, of course, for not developing or utilizing a particular technology. The mere fact that it can be developed is not sufficient reason for doing so. The costs of development may be too high in the light of the expected benefits, as in the case of the project to develop a nuclear-powered aircraft. Or, a new technological device may be so dangerous in itself or so inimical to other purposes that it is never developed, as in the cases of

Herman Kahn's "Doomsday Machine" and the recent proposal to "nightlight" Vietnam by reflected sunlight.

But there are also cases where technology lies fallow because existing social structures are inadequate to exploit the opportunities it offers. This is revealed clearly in the examination of institutional failure in the ghetto by Professor Richard S. Rosenbloom and his colleagues. At point after point, their analyses confirm what has been long suspected, that is, that existing institutions and traditional approaches are by and large incapable of coming to grips with the new problems of our cities—many of them caused by technological change, as the Meyer-Kain study has reminded us—and unable to realize the possibilities for resolving them that are also inherent in technology. Vested economic and political interests serve to obstruct adequate provision of low-cost housing. Community institutions wither for want of interest and participation by residents. City agencies are unable to marshal the skills and take the systematic approach needed to deal with new and intensified problems of education, crime control, and public welfare. Business corporations, finally, which are organized around the expectation of private profit, are insufficiently motivated to bring new technology and management know-how to bear on urban projects where the benefits will be largely social. All these factors combine to dilute what may otherwise be a genuine desire to apply our best knowledge and adequate resources to the resolution of urban tensions and the eradication of poverty in the nation.

There is also institutional failure of another sort. Government in general and agencies of public information in particular are not yet equipped for the massive task of public education that is needed if our society is to make full use of its technological potential, although the federal government has been making significant strides in this direction in recent years. Thus, much potentially valuable technology goes unused because the public at large is insufficiently informed about the possibilities and their costs to provide support for appropriate political action. As noted, we have done very well with our technology in the face of what were or were believed to be crisis situations, as with our military technology in World War II and with our space efforts when beating the Russians to the moon was deemed a national goal of first priority. We have also done very well when the potential benefits of technology were close to home or easy to see, as in improved health care and better and more varied consumer goods and services. We have done much less well in developing and applying technology where the need or opportunity has seemed neither so clearly critical nor so clearly personal as to motivate political action, as in the instance of urban policy already cited. Technological possibility continues to lie fallow in those areas where institutional and political innovation is a precondition of realizing it.

## Containing the Negative Effects of Technology

The kinds and magnitude of the negative effects of technology are no more independent of the institutional structures and cultural attitudes of society than is realization of the new opportunities that technology offers. In our society, there are individuals or individual firms always on the lookout for new technological opportunities, and large corporations hire scientists and engineers to invent such opportunities. In deciding whether to develop a new technology, individual entrepreneurs engage in calculations of expected benefits and expected costs to themselves, and proceed if the former are likely to exceed the latter. Their calculations do not take adequate account of the probable benefits and costs of the new developments to others than themselves or to society generally. These latter are what economists call external benefits and costs.

The external benefits potential in new technology will thus not be realized by the individual developer and will rather accrue to society as a result of deliberate social action, as has been argued above. Similarly with the external costs. In minimizing only expected costs to himself, the individual decision maker helps to contain only some of the potentially negative effects of the new technology. The external costs and therefore the negative effects on society at large are not of principal concern to him and, in our society, are not expected to be.

Most of the consequences of technology that are causing concern at the present time—pollution of the environment, potential damage to the ecology of the planet, occupational and social dislocations, threats to the privacy and political significance of the individual, social and psychological malaise—are negative externalities of this kind. They are with us in large measure because it has not been anybody's explicit business to foresee and anticipate them. They have fallen between the stools of innumerable individual decisions to develop individual technologies for individual purposes without explicit attention to what all these decisions add up to for society as a whole and for people as human beings. This freedom of individual decision making is a value that we have cherished and that is built into the institutional fabric of our society. The negative effects of technology that we deplore are a measure of what this traditional freedom is beginning to cost us. They are traceable, less to some mystical autonomy presumed to lie in technology, and much more to the autonomy that our economic and political institutions grant to individual decision making.

When the social costs of individual decision making in the economic realm achieved crisis proportions in the great depression of the 1930s, the federal government introduced economic policies and measures many of which had the effect of abridging the freedom of individual decision. Now that some of the negative impacts of technology are threatening to become critical, the government is considering measures of control that will have the analogous effect of constraining the freedom of individual decision makers to develop and apply new technologies irrespective of social consequence. Congress is actively seeking to establish technology-assessment boards of one sort or another which it hopes may be able to foresee potentially damaging effects of technology on nature and man. In the executive branch, attention is being directed (1) to development of a system of social indicators to help gauge the social effects of technology, (2) to establishment of some body of social advisers to the president to help develop policies in anticipation of such effects, and generally (3) to strengthening the role of the social sciences in policy making.

Measures to control and mitigate the negative effects of technology, however, often appear to threaten freedoms that our traditions still take for granted as inalienable rights of men and good societies, however much they may have been tempered in practice by the social pressures of modern times: the freedom of the market, the freedom of private enterprise, the freedom of the scientist to follow truth wherever it may lead, and the freedom of the individual to pursue his fortune and decide his fate. There is thus set up a tension between the need to control technology and our wish to preserve our values, which leads some people to conclude that technology is inherently inimical to human values. The political effect of this tension takes the form of inability to adjust our decision-making structures to the realities of technology so as to take maximum advantage of the opportunities it offers and so that we can act to contain its potential ill effects before they become so pervasive and urgent as to seem uncontrollable.

To understand why such tensions are so prominent a social consequence of technological change, it becomes necessary to look explicitly at the effects of technology on social and individual values.

## VALUES

### Technology's Challenge to Values

Despite the practical importance of the techniques, institutions, and processes of knowledge in contemporary society, political decision making and the resolution of social problems are clearly not dependent on knowledge alone. Numerous commentators have noted that ours is a "knowledge" society, devoted to rational decision making and an "end of ideology," but none would deny the role that values play in shaping the course of society and the decisions of individuals. On the contrary, questions of values become more pointed and insistent in a society that organizes itself to control technology and that engages in deliberate social planning. Planning demands explicit recognition of value hierarchies and often brings into the open value conflicts which remain hidden in the more impersonal working of the market.

In economic planning, for example, we have to make choices between the values of leisure and increased productivity, without a common measure to help us choose. In planning education, we come face to face with the traditional American value dilemma of equality versus achievement: do we opt for equality and nondiscrimination and give all students the same basic education, or do we foster achievement by tailoring education to the capacity for learning, which is itself often conditioned by socioeconomic background?

The new science-based decision-making techniques also call for clarity: in the specification of goals, thus serving to make value preferences explicit. The effectiveness of systems analysis, for example, depends on having explicitly stated objectives and criteria of evaluation to begin with, and the criteria and objectives of specific actions invariably relate to the society's system of values. That, incidentally, is why the application of systems analysis meets with less relative success in educational or urban planning than in military planning: the value conflicts are fewer in the latter and the objectives and criteria easier to specify and agree on. This increased awareness of conflicts among our values contributes to a general questioning attitude toward traditional values that appears to be endemic to a high-technology, knowledge-based society: "A society in which the store of knowledge concerning the consequences of action is large and is rapidly increasing is a society in which received norms and their 'justifying' values will be increasingly subjected to questioning and reformulation."[1]

This is another way of pointing to the tension alluded to earlier, between the need for social action based on knowledge on the one hand, and the pull of our traditional values on the other. The increased questioning and reformulation of values that Williams speaks of, coupled with a growing awareness that our values are in fact changing under the impact of technological change, leads many people to believe that technology is by nature destructive of values. But this belief presupposes a conception of values as eternal and unchanging and therefore tends to confuse the valuable with the stable. The fact that values come into question as our knowledge increases and that some traditional values cease to function adequately when technology leads to changes in social conditions does not mean that values per se are being destroyed by knowledge and technology.

What does happen is that values change through a process of accommodation between the system of existing values and the technological and social changes that impinge on it. The projects of the Harvard Program in the area of technology and values are devoted to discovering the specific ways in which this process of accommodation occurs and to tracing its consequences for value changes in contemporary American society. The balance of this section is devoted to a more extended discussion of the first results of these projects.

### Technology as a Cause of Value Change

Technology has a direct impact on values by virtue of its capacity for creating new opportunities. By making possible what was not possible before, it offers individuals and society new options to choose from. For example, space technology makes it possible for the first time to go to the moon or to communicate by satellite and thereby adds those two new options to the spectrum of choices available to society. By adding new options in this way, technology can lead to changes in values in the same way that the appearance of new dishes on the heretofore standard menu of one's favorite restaurant can lead to changes in one's tastes and choices of food. Specifically, technology can lead to value change either (1) by bringing some previously unattainable goal within the realm of choice or (2) by making some values easier to implement than heretofore, that is, by changing the costs associated with realizing them.

Dr. Irene Taviss is exploring the ways in which technological change affects intrinsic sources of tension and potential change in value systems. When technology facilitates implementation of some social ideal and society fails to act upon this new possibility, the conflict between principle and practice is sharpened, thus leading to new tensions. For example, the economic affluence that technology has helped to bring to American society makes possible fuller implementation than heretofore of our traditional values of social and economic equality. Until it is acted upon, that possibility gives rise to the tensions we associate with the rising expectations of the underprivileged and provokes both the activist response of the radical left and the hippie's rejection of society as "hypocritical."

Another example related to the effect of technological change on values is implicit in our concept of democracy. The ideal we associate with the old New England town meeting is that each citizen should have a direct voice in political decisions. Since this has not been possible, we have elected representatives to serve our interests and vote our opinions. Sophisticated computer technology, however, now makes possible rapid and efficient collection and analysis of voter opinion and could eventually provide for "instant voting" by the whole electorate on any issue presented to it via television a few hours before. It thus raises the possibility of instituting a system of direct democracy and gives rise to tensions between those who would be violently opposed to such a prospect and those who are already advocating some system of participatory democracy.

This new technological possibility challenges us to clarify what we mean by democracy. Do we construe it as the will of an undifferentiated majority, as the resultant of transient coalitions of different interest groups representing different value commitments, as the considered judgment of the people's elected representatives, or as by and large the kind of government we actually have in the United States, minus the flaws in it that we would like to correct? By bringing us face to face with such questions, technology has the effect of calling society's bluff and thereby preparing the ground for changes in its values.

In the case where technological change alters the relative costs of implementing different values, it impinges on inherent contradictions in our value system. To pursue the same example, modern technology can enhance the values we associate with democracy. But it can also enhance another American value—that of "secular rationality," as sociologists call it—by facilitating the use of scientific and technical expertise in the process of political decision making. This can in turn further reduce citizen participation in the democratic process. Technology thus has the effect of facing us with contradictions in our own value system and of calling for deliberate attention to their resolution.

**The Value Implications of Economic Change**

In addition to the relatively direct effects of technology on values, as illustrated above, value change often comes about through the intermediation of some more general social change produced by technology, as in the tension imposed on our individualistic values by the external benefits and costs of technological development that was alluded to in the earlier discussion of the negative effects of technology. Professor Nathan Rosenberg is exploring the closely allied relationship between such values and the need for society to provide what economists call public goods and services.

As a number of economists have shown, such public goods differ from private consumer goods and services in that they are provided on an all-or-none basis and consumed in a joint way, so that more for one consumer does not mean less for another. The clearing of a swamp or a flood-control project, once completed, benefits everyone in the vicinity. A meteorological forecast, once made, can be transmitted by word of mouth to additional users at no additional cost. Knowledge itself may thus be thought of as the public good par excellence, since the research expenses needed to produce it are incurred only once, unlike consumer goods of which every additional unit adds to the cost of production.

As noted earlier, private profit expectation is an inadequate incentive for the production of such public goods, because their benefit is indiscriminate and not fully appropriate to the firm or individual that might incur the cost of producing them. Individuals are therefore motivated to dissimulate by understating their true preferences for such goods in the hope of shifting their cost to others. This creates a "free-loader" problem, which skews the mechanism of the market. The market therefore provides no effective indication of the optimal amount of such public commodities from the point of view of society as a whole. If society got only as much public health care, flood control, or knowledge as individual profit calculations would generate, it would no doubt get less of all of them than it does now or than it expresses a desire for by collective political action.

This gap between collective preference and individual motivation imposes strains on a value system, such as ours, which is primarily individualistic rather than collective or "societal" in its orientation. That system arose out of a simpler, more rustic, and less affluent time, when both benefits and costs were of a much more private sort than now. It is no longer fully adequate for our society, which industrial technology has made productive enough to allocate significant resources to the purchase of public goods and services, and in which modern transportation and communications as well as the absolute magnitude of technological effects lead to extensive ramifications of individual actions on other people and on the environment.

The response to this changed experience on the part of the public at large generally takes the form of increased government intervention in social and economic affairs to contain or guide these wider ramifications, as noted previously. The result is that the influence of values associated with the free reign of individual enterprise and action tends to be counteracted, thus facilitating a change in values. To be sure, the tradition that ties freedom and liberty to a laissez-faire system of decision making remains very strong, and the changes in social structures and cultural attitudes that can touch it at its foundations are still only on the horizon.

## Religion and Values

Much of the unease that our society's emphasis on technology seems to generate among various sectors of society can perhaps be explained in terms of the impact that technology has on religion. The formulations and institutions of religion are not immune to the influences to technological change, for they too tend toward an accommodation to changes in the social milieu in which they function. But one way in which religion functions is as an ultimate belief system that provides legitimation, that is, a "meaning" orientation, to moral and social values. This ultimate meaning orientation, according to Professor Harvey Cox, is even more basic to human existence than the value orientation. When the magnitude or rapidity of social change threatens the credibility of that belief system, therefore, and when the changes are moreover seen as largely the results of technological change, the meanings of human existence that we hold most sacred seem to totter and technology emerges as the villain.

Religious change thus provides another mediating mechanism through which technology affects our values. That conditions are ripe for religious change at the present time has been noted by many observers, who are increasingly questioning whether our established religious syntheses and symbol systems are adequate any longer to the religious needs of a scientific and secular society that is changing so fundamentally as to strain traditional notions of eternity. If they are not, how are they likely to change? Professor Cox is addressing himself to this problem with specific attention to the influence of technology in guiding the direction of change.

He notes that religion needs to come to terms with the pluralism of belief systems that is characteristic of the modern world. The generation of knowledge and the use of technology are so much a part of the style and self-image of our own society that men begin to experience themselves, their power, and their relationships to nature and history in terms of open possibility, hope, action, and self-confidence. The symbolism of such traditional religious postures as subservience, fatefulness, destiny, and suprarational faith begin then to seem irrelevant to our actual experience. They lose credibility, and their religious function is weakened. Secular belief systems arise to compete for the allegiance of men: political belief systems, such as communism; or scientific ones, such as modern-day humanism; or such inexplicit, noninstitutionalized belief complexes as are characteristic of agnosticism.

This pluralism poses serious problems for the ultimate legitimation or "meaning" orientation for moral and social values that religion seeks to provide, because it demands a religious synthesis that can integrate the fact of variant perspectives into its own symbol system. Western religions have been notoriously incapable of performing this integrating function and have rather gone the route of schism and condemnation of variance as heresy. The institutions and formulations of historical Christianity in particular, which once served as the foundations of Western society, carry the added burden of centuries of conflict with scientific world views as these have competed for ascendancy in the same society. This makes it especially difficult for traditional Christianity to accommodate to a living experience so infused by scientific knowledge and attitude as ours and helps explain why its adequacy is coming under serious question at the present time.

Cox notes three major traditions in the Judeo-Christian synthesis and finds them inconsistent in their perceptions of the future: an "apocalyptic" tradition foresees imminent catastrophe and induces a negative evaluation of this world; a "teleological" tradition sees the future as the certain unfolding of a fixed purpose inherent in the universe itself; a "prophetic" tradition, finally, sees the future as an open field of human hope and responsibility and as becoming what man will make of it.[2]

Technology, as noted, creates new possibilities for human choice and action but leaves their disposition uncertain. What its effects will be and what ends it will serve are not inherent in the technology, but depend on what man will do with technology. Technology thus makes possible a future of open-ended options that seems to accord well with the presuppositions of the prophetic tradition. It is in that tradition above others, then, that we may seek the beginnings of a religious synthesis that is both adequate to our time and continuous with what is most relevant in our religious history. But this requires an effort at deliberate religious innovation for which Cox finds insufficient theological ground at the present time. Although it is recognized that religions have changed and developed in the past, conscious innovation in religion has been condemned and is not provided for by the relevant theologies. The main task that technological change poses for theology in the next decades, therefore, is that of deliberate religious innovation and symbol reformulation to take specific account of religious needs in a technological age.

What consequences would such changes in religion have for values? Cox approaches this question in the context of the familiar complaint that, since technology is principally a means, it enhances merely instrumental values at the expense of expressive, consummatory, or somehow more "real" values. The appropriate distinction, however, is not between technological instrumental values and nontechnological expressive values, but among the expressive values that attach to different technologies. The horse-and-buggy was a technology too, after all, and it is not prima facie clear that its charms were different in kind or superior to the sense of power and adventure and the spectacular views that go with jet travel.

Further, technological advance in many instances is a condition for the emergence of new creative or consummatory values. Improved sound boxes in the past and structural steel and motion photography in the present have made possible the artistry of Jascha Heifetz, Frank Lloyd Wright, and Charles Chaplin, which have opened up wholly new ranges of expressive possibility without, moreover, in any way inhibiting a concurrent renewal of interest in medieval instruments and primitive art. If religious innovation can provide a meaning orientation broad enough to accommodate the idea that new technology can be creative of new values, a long step will have been taken toward providing a religious belief system adequate to the realities and needs of a technological age.

## Individual Man in a Technological Age

What do technological change and the social and value changes that it brings with it mean for the life of the individual today? It is not clear that their effects are all one-way. For example, we are often told that today's individual is alienated by the vast proliferation of technical expertise and complex bureaucracies, by a feeling of impotence in the face of "the machine," and by a decline in personal privacy. It is probably true that the social pressures placed on individuals today are more complicated and demanding than they were in earlier times. Increased geographical and occupational mobility and the need to function in large organizations place difficult demands on the individual to conform or "adjust." It is also evident that the privacy of many individuals tends to be encroached upon by sophisticated eavesdropping and surveillance devices, by the accumulation of more and more information about individuals by governmental and many private agencies, and by improvements in information-handling technologies such as the proposed institution of centralized statistical data banks. There is little doubt, finally, that the power, authority, influence, and scope of government are greater today than at any time in the history of the United States.

But, as Professor Edward Shils points out in his study on technology and the individual, there is another, equally compelling side of the coin. First, government seems to be more shy and more lacking in confidence today than ever before. Second, while privacy may be declining in the ways indicated above, it also tends to decline in a sense that most individuals are likely to approve. The average man in Victorian times, for example, probably "enjoyed" much more privacy than today. No one much cared what happened to him, and he was free to remain ignorant, starve, fall ill, and die in complete privacy; that was the "golden age of privacy," as Shils puts it. Compulsory universal education, social security legislation, and public health measures—indeed, the very idea of a welfare state—are all antithetical to privacy in this sense, and it is the rare individual today who is loath to see that kind of privacy go.

It is not clear, finally, that technological and social complexity must inevitably lead to reducing the individual to "mass" or "organization" man. Economic productivity and modern means of communication allow the individual to aspire to more than he ever could before. Better and more easily available education not only provides him with skills and with the means to develop his individual potentialities, but also improves his self-image and his sense of value as a human being. This is probably the first age in history in which such high proportions of people have *felt* like individuals; no eighteenth-century English factory worker, so far as we know, had the sense of individual worth that underlies the demands on society of the average resident of the black urban ghetto today. And, as Shils notes, the scope of individual choice and action today are greater than in previous times, all the way from consumer behavior to political or religious allegiance. Even the much-maligned modern organization may in fact "serve as a mediator or buffer between the individual and the full raw impact of technological change," as an earlier study supported by the Harvard Program has concluded.

Recognition that the impact of modern technology on the individual has two faces, both negative and positive, is consistent with the double effect of technological change that was discussed above. It also suggests that appreciation of that impact in detail may not be achieved in terms of old formulas, such as more or less privacy, more or less government, more or less individuality. Professor Shils is therefore attempting to couch his inquiry in terms of the implications of technological change for the balance that every individual must strike between his commitment to private goals and satisfactions and his desires and responsibilities as a public citizen. The citizens of ancient Athens seem to have been largely public beings in this sense, while certain segments of today's hippie population seem to pursue mainly private gratifications. The political requirements of our modern technological society would seem to call for a relatively greater public commitment on the part of individuals than has been the case in the past, and it is by exploring this hypothesis that we may enhance our understanding of what technology does to the individual in present-day society.

## ECONOMIC AND POLITICAL ORGANIZATION

### The Enlarged Scope of Public Decision Making

When technology brings about social changes which impinge on our existing system of values, it poses for society a number of problems that are ultimately political in nature. The term "political" is used here in the broadest sense: it encompasses all of the decision-making structures and procedures that have to do with the allocation and distribution of wealth and power in society. The political organization of society thus includes not only the formal apparatus of the state but also industrial organizations and other private institutions that play a role in the decision-making process. It is particularly important to attend to the organization of the entire body politic when technological change leads to a blurring of once clear distinctions between the public and private sectors of society and to changes in the roles of its principal institutions.

It was suggested above that the political requirements of our modern technological society call for a relatively greater public commitment on the part of individuals than in previous times. The reason for this, stated most generally, is that technological change has the effect of enhancing the importance of public decision making in society, because technology is continually creating new possibilities for social action as well as new problems that have to be dealt with.

A society that undertakes to foster technology on a large scale, in fact, commits itself to social complexity and to facing and dealing with new problems as a normal feature of political life. Not much is yet known with any precision about the political imperatives inherent in technological change, but one may nevertheless speculate about the reasons why an increasingly technological society seems to be characterized by enlargement of the scope of public decision making.

For one thing, the development and application of technology seems to require large-scale, and hence increasingly complex, social concentrations, whether these be large cities, large corporations, big universities, or big government. In instances where technological advance appears to facilitate reduction of such first-order concentrations, it tends instead to enlarge the relevant *system* of social organization, that is, to lead to increased centralization. Thus, the physical dispersion made possible by transportation and communications technologies, as Meyer and Kain have shown, enlarges the urban complex that must be governed as a unit.

A second characteristic of advanced technology is that its effects cover large distances, in both the geographical and social senses of the term. Both its positive and negative features are more extensive. Horsepowered transportation technology was limited in its speed and capacity, but its nuisance value was also limited, in most cases to the owner and to the occupant of the next farm. The supersonic transport can carry hundreds across long distances in minutes, but its noise and vibration damage must also be suffered willy-nilly by everyone within the limits of a swath 3,000 miles long and several miles wide.

The concatention of increased density (or enlarged system) and extended technological "distance" means that technological applications have increasingly wider ramifications and that increasingly large concentrations of people and organizations become dependent on technological systems. A striking illustration of this was provided by the widespread effects of the power blackout in the northeasten part of the United States. The result is not only that more and more decisions must be social decisions taken in public ways, as already noted, but that, once made, decisions are likely to have a shorter useful life than heretofore. That is partly because technology is continually altering the spectrum of choices and problems that society faces, and partly because any decision taken is likely to generate a need to take ten more.

These speculations about the effects of technology on public decision making raise the problem of restructuring our decision-making mechanisms—including the system of market incentives—so that the increasing number and importance of social issues that confront us can be resolved equitably and effectively.

## Private Firms and Public Goods

Among these issues, as noted earlier, is that created by the shift in the composition of demand in favor of public goods and services—such as education, health, transportation, slum clearance, and recreational facilities—which, it is generally agreed, the market has never provided effectively and in the provision of which government has usually played a role of some significance. This shift in demand raises serious questions about the relationship between technological change and existing decision-making structures in general and about the respective roles of government and business in particular. A project initiated under the direction of Dr. Robin Marris is designed to explore those questions in detail.

In Western industrialized countries, new technological developments generally originated in and are applied through joint stock companies whose shares are widely traded on organized capital markets. Corporations thus play a dominant role in the development of new methods of production, of new methods of satisfying consumer wants, and even of new wants. Most economists appear to accept the thesis originally proposed by Schumpeter that corporations play a key role in the actual process of technological innovation in the economy. Marris himself has recently characterized this role as a perceiving of latent consumer needs and of fostering and regulating the rate at which these are converted into felt wants.[3]

There is no similar agreement about the implications of all this for social policy. J. K. Galbraith, for example, argues that the corporation is motivated by the desire for growth subject to a minimum profit constraint and infers (1) a higher rate of new-want development than would be the case if corporations were motivated principally to maximize profit, (2) a bias in favor of economic activities heavy in "technological content" in contrast to activities requiring sophisticated social organization, and (3) a bias in the economy as a whole in favor of development and satisfaction of private needs to the neglect of public needs and at the cost of a relatively slow rate of innovation in the public sector.

But Galbraith's picture is not generally accepted by economists, and his model of the corporation is not regarded as established economic theory. There is, in fact, no generally accepted economic theory of corporate behavior, as Marris points out, so that discussions about the future of the system of corporate enterprise usually get bogged down in an exchange of unsubstantiated assertions about how the existing system actually operates. What seems needed at this time, then, is less a new program of empirical research than an attempt to synthesize what we know for the purpose of arriving at a more adequate theory of the firm. This is the objective of phase 1 of the Marris project.

On the basis of the resulting theoretical clarification, phase 2 will go on to address such questions as (1) the costs of a policy of economic growth, (2) the incommensurability of individual incentive and public will, (3) the desirable balance between individual and social welfare when the two are inconsistent with each other, (4) changes in the roles of government and industrial institutions in the political organization of American society, and (5) the consequences of those changes for the functions of advertising and competing forms of communication in the process of public education. In particular, attention will be directed to whether existing forms of company organization are adequate for marshaling technology to social purposes by responding to the demand for public goods and services, or whether new productive institutions will be required to serve that end.

We can hope to do no more than raise the level of discussion of such fundamental and difficult questions, of course, but even that could be a service.

## The Promise and Problems of Scientific Decision Making

There are two further consequences of the expanding role of public decision making. The first is that the latest information-handling of devices and techniques tend to be utilized in the decision-making process. This is so (1) because public policy can be effective only to the degree that it is based on reliable knowledge about the actual state of the society, and thus requires a strong capability to collect, aggregate, and analyze detailed data about economic activities, social patterns, popular attitudes, and political trends, and (2) because it is recognized increasingly that decisions taken in one area impinge on and have consequences for other policy areas often thought of as unrelated, so that it becomes necessary to base decisions on a model of society that sees it as a system and that is capable of signaling as many as possible of the probable consequences of a contemplated action.

As Professor Alan F. Westin points out, reactions to the prospect of more decision making based on computerized data banks and scientific management techniques run the gamut of optimism to pessimism mentioned in the opening of this [chapter]. Negative reactions take the form of rising political demands for greater popular participation in decision making, for more equality among different segments of the population, and for greater regard for the dignity of individuals. The increasing dependence of decison making on scientific and technological devices and techniques is seen as posing a threat to these goals, and pressures are generated in opposition to further "rationalization" of decision-making processes. These pressures have the paradoxical effect, however, not of deflecting the supporters of technological decision making from their course, but of spurring them on to renewed effort to save the society before it explodes under planlessness and inadequate administration.

The paradox goes further, and helps to explain much of the social discontent that we are witnessing at the present time. The greater complexity and the more extensive ramifications that technology brings about in society tend to make social processes increasingly circuitous and indirect. The effects of actions are widespread and difficult to keep track of, so that experts and sophisticated techniques are increasingly needed to detect and analyze social events and to formulate policies adequate to the complexity of social issues. The "logic" of modern decision making thus appears to require greater and greater dependence on the collection and analysis of data and on the use of technological devices and scientific techniques. Indeed, many observers would agree that there is an "increasiing relegation of questions which used to be matters of political debate to professional cadres of technicians and experts which function almost independently of the democratic political process."[4] In recent times, that process has been most noticeable, perhaps, in the areas of economic policy and national security affairs.

This "logic" of modern decision making, however, runs counter to that element of traditional democratic theory that places high value on direct participation in the political processes and generates the kind of discontent referred to above. If it turns out on more careful examination that direct participation is becoming less relevant to a society in which the connections between causes and effects are long and often hidden—which is an increasingly "indirect" society, in other words—elaboration of a new democratic ethos and of new democratic processes more adequate to the realities of modern society will emerge as perhaps the major intellectual and political challenge of our time.

**The Need for Institutional Innovation**

The challenge is, indeed, already upon us, for the second consequence of the enlarged scope of public decision making is the need to develop new institutional forms and new mechanisms to replace established ones that can no longer deal effectively with the new kinds of problems with which we are increasingly faced. Much of the political ferment of the present time—over the problems of technology assessment, the introduction of statistical data banks, the extension to domestic problems of techniques of analysis developed for the military services, and the modification of the institutions of local government—is evidence of the need for new institutions. It will be recalled that Professor Oettinger's study concludes that innovation is called for in the educational establishment before instructional technology can realize the promise that is potential in it. Our research in the biomedical area has repeatedly confirmed the need for institutional innovation in the medical system, and Marris has noted the evolution that seems called for in our industrial institutions. The Rosenbloom research group, finally, has documented the same need in the urban area and is exploring the form and course that the processes of innovation might take.

Direct intervention by business or government to improve ghetto conditions will tend to be ineffective until local organizations come ito existence which enable residents to participate in and control their own situation. Such organizations seem to be a necessary condition for any solution of the ghetto problem that is likely to prove acceptable to black communities. Professors Richard S. Rosenbloom, Paul R. Lawrence, and their associates are therefore engaged in the design of two types of organization suited to the peculiar problems of the modern ghetto. These are (1) a state- or area-wide urban development corporation in which business and government join to channel funds and provide technical assistance to (2) a number of local development corporations, under community control, which can combine social service with sound business management.

Various "ghetto enrichment" strategies are being proposed at the present time, all of which stress the need for institutional innovation of some kind and in many of which creation of one sort of another of community development corporation is a prominent feature. In none of these respects does our approach claim any particular originality. What does seem promising, however, is our effort to design a local development corporation that is at once devoted to social service and built on sound business principles.

These characteristics point to large and powerful organizations that can serve as engines of indigenous ghetto development. They would of course interact with "outside" institutions, not only those at various levels of government, but especially their counterpart state or area urban development corporations. They would not be dependent principally on such outside institutions, however, since they would be engines that, once started, could keep running largely on their own power. In economic terms, the local development corporations would become "customers" of business. In political terms, they would be partners of existing governmental structures. In broader social terms, they could become vehicles for integrating underprivileged urban communities into the mainstream of American society.

The design for the state or area urban development corporation, in Professor Rosenbloom's description, would be a new form of public-private partnership serving to pull together the resources and programs of the business sector, of universities and research institutions, of public agencies, and of community organizations. This corporation could act as a surrogate for the "invisible hand" of the market, able to reward the successes of the local development corporations through command of a pool of unrestricted funds. Since there is no necessary relationship between profitability and social benefit for economic venture in the ghetto, however, success would need to be measured, not in usual profit-and-loss terms, but in terms of such social indicators as employment levels, educational attainment, health statistics, and the like.

The collaborative arrangements we have entered into in New Jersey and in Boston offer us a welcome opportunity to test and develop some of our hypotheses and designs. In both of these programs, our research group is in a position to contribute know-how and advice, based on its understanding of organizational and corporate behavior, and to acquire insight and primary data for research that can prove useful in other contexts. As long ago as our first annual report, we announced the hope and expectation that the Harvard Program could supplement its scholarly production by adding a dimension of action research. New Jersey and Boston are providing us with our first opportunity to realize that objective.

## CONCLUSION

As we review what we are learning about the relationship of technological and social change, a number of conclusions begin to emerge. We find, on the one hand, that the creation of new physical possibilities and social options by technology tends toward and appears to require the emergence of new values, new forms of economic activity, and new political organizations. On the other hand, technological change also poses problems of social and psychological displacement.

The two phenomena are not unconnected, nor is the tension between them new; man's technical prowess always seems to run ahead of his ability to deal with and profit from it. In America, especially, we are becoming adept at extracting the new techniques, the physical power, and the economic productivity that are inherent in our knowledge and its associated technologies. Yet we have not fully accepted the fact that our progress in the technical realm does not leave our institutions, values, and political processes unaffected.

Individuals will be fully integrated into society only when we can extract from our knowledge not only its technological potential but also its implications for a system of values and a social, economic, and political organization appropriate to a society in which technology is so prevalent.

## NOTES

1. Robin Williams, "Individual and Group Values," *Annals of the American Academy of Political and Social Science* 37 (May 1967): 30.

2. See Harvey Cox, "Tradition and the Future," pts. 1 and 2, in *Christianity and Crisis* 27, nos. 16 and 17 (October 2 and 16, 1968): 218–20 and 227–31.

3. Robin Marris, *The Economic Theory of "Managerial" Capitalism* (Glencoe, Ill.: The Free Press, 1964).

4. Harvey Brooks, "Scientific Concepts and Cultural Change," in G. Holton, ed., *Science and Culture* (Boston: Houghton Mifflin, 1965), p. 71.

# Part Five

# Demystifying Autonomous Technology

# Introduction

Modern technology does appear to many to be a powerful, mysterious force radically and continuously transforming our world. The plausibility of this view, contrary to those expressed by the authors in the previous section, does not hinge on the reification of technology. The serious autonomous technology thesis does not attribute an evil intent to technology, but does claim that it develops in a mechanistic way free from any purpose. The next step in technological development is determined by the antecedent development, and this process in turn is *the* cause of all social change. As biological evolution seems random and purposeless, so does the evolution of technology.

The authors in this section, while not denying that the notion of autonomous technology illuminates an important factor in social change, argue that this is not the whole story. Technology is *a* cause, but not *the* cause. Clearly, some technological developments have escaped *humane* control, although this is not an inevitable consequence. In this sense, the defenders of modern technology are right; however, it is too facile to claim that the value of technology simply depends on how "we" choose to use it. Technologies are not ethically neutral; they are *designed* by human beings to serve other human beings' ends. The democratic control of technology demands an understanding of the multiple, interacting, dynamic causes and *reasons* behind the growth and deployment of technology. An adequate philosophy of technology thus requires the help of social scientists to uncover those points in the causal nexus where human values can, and do, exert themselves.

The danger in thinking of technology as autonomous is that it leads to a sense of hopelessness, or naïve optimism, in the face of modern developments. Although opponents of technology like Ellul employ this notion of autonomy in their criticism of modern development, it can be, and frequently is, used to silence all criticism. Such a mind-set obscures the fact that at bottom there is a man behind the machine; that an important factor underlying the design of machines consists of human, all too human, motives.

Michael Goldhaber summarizes in his criticisms of the autonomous technology thesis the kinds of argument offered by Ellul. A close examination of these arguments shows, however, that "technological progress is always guided by values and interests that come from outside technology." While technological inventions cannot be unmade—Schell is correct about the irreversibility of technology—this fact need not predetermine the future. The construction of nuclear arsenals was not the inevitable "next step" in technological development but a reflection of the fact that the destructive and deterrent power of nuclear energy has been more highly valued than its constructive, life-sustaining applications.

Technology is not value-free, nor, argues Goldhaber, is science. Even pure science is largely a social construction. While the scientist pursues knowledge, the ends being sought are dependent on his interests, and these in turn are affected by what research can get funded. Scientific theories are never "proved" by experiment, for this is always subject to interpretation. Referring to the philosopher of science Imre Lakatos, Goldhaber argues that rival explanatory systems operate much like the stock market. Choices are made on the basis of which system is likely to grow the fastest. This is not a mere metaphor, for the desire for profits fuels the direction of such scientific research. Science and technology are deeply interrelated in today's society, and to understand the direction both take, we must include the various ideological commitments that drive them.

Science and technology could be used to serve the interests of humanity as a whole. "Unfortunately," says Goldhaber, "the motives of profit, international competitiveness, national expansion, and perpetuating the power of the already powerful tend to prevail in the institutions that currently set the direction of innovation. Deep changes in these institutions are sorely needed."

Is "Star Wars," alias Ronald Reagan's Strategic Defense Initiative, the inevitable next step in scientific/technological development? William J. Broad gives us a case study of how, in Goldhaber's words, "technologists are complicit: many willingly help perpetuate the arms race because they benefit from it in terms of jobs and status."* In this context, "pure" science is "impure" at its very foundation.

The anti-hero of Broad's article, Peter Hagelstein, begins with the pure motive to understand, e.g., how lasers work, thinking that such research will have benevolent medical applications; but he ends up working on weapons systems which he initially thought to be evil. If one is a bright, ambitious young person who wants to be on the cutting edge of scientific research, one

---

*Such vested interests continue to exert pressure on Congress to fund high-tech weapons research despite the collapse of communism. Although the "Star Wars" budget has been reduced, the research aspect of the program continues.

must go where the enormously expensive and necessary technology is made available. Thus, the "system" co-opts individuals and manages to change their moral convictions. Hagelstein now comes to see weapons systems as "purely" interesting physics problems.

One might read this on the surface as an account of how technology has become autonomous. At a deeper level, however, it is clear that the money pouring into Livermore Labs was the result of a political decision on the part of President Reagan who, we need to add, found the arguments made by the "impure" scientist, Edward Teller, most persuasive. Further, while we can understand the causes for Hagelstein's changing his ethical views, these causes did not force or strictly determine such a change. Hagelstein could have refused, as many scientists have done, to do Star Wars research. The tragedy is that he seems to realize at the same time that little hope exists of an effective "technical fix" for offensive nuclear weapons.

Robert Heilbroner asks, "Do machines make history?" Was Karl Marx right when he said, "The hand mill gives you society with the feudal lord; the steam mill, society with the industrial capitalist"? The answer, Heilbroner believes, is yes in the sense that there is a necessary sequence in the development of technology, and clearly machines do affect in important ways the socioeconomic order. Although this cannot be proven beyond doubt, Heilbroner offers what he considers some convincing lines of argument.

Technology, however, is not a sufficient explanation of historical development. A variety of social factors are necessary to explain the explosive growth of technology, beginning with the Industrial Revolution. While the steam mill did not by itself give us industrial capitalism, it helped make this possible. However, Heilbroner does believe that technology has a distinct role to play in the composition and organization of the labor force. If Marx had "written that the steam mill gives you society with the industrial *manager*, he would have been closer to the truth."

Fundamentally, it is the laissez-faire ideology of capitalism and socialism committed to maximizing production that, according to Heilbroner, give the impression that technology is autonomous. Thus, so-called technological determinism is a problem unique to a certain historical period "in which the forces of technical change have been unleashed, but when the agencies for control or guidance of technology are still rudimentary."* It seems likely, he thinks, that in our own day the pace of technological change will accelerate in an uncontrolled fashion unless agencies of public control are greatly strengthened.

---

*Events occurring since Heilbroner's published warning (1967) have shown him to be prophetic. Only recently have we become aware of the incredibly reckless manner in which the government plants that are producing weapons-grade uranium have stored their radioactive wastes. In some cases they have simply vented their wastes into the atmosphere—this despite the fact that these facilities were "supervised" by the Atomic Energy Commission (AEC) and, since 1947, by the Department of Energy (DOE). Clearly, the health and safety of American citizens was a low priority in developing our nuclear arsenal.

David F. Noble argues that we cannot strengthen the public, democratic agencies to control technological development until we go beyond, i.e., see through, the prevailing myth of technological determinism. Combined with the myth of inevitable "progress," this doctrine blinds us to the fact that there are choices to be made in regard to technology. Technology does not "give us" capitalism, nor (against Heilbroner) a hierarchical bureaucratic structure of social relations. Technological development is neither uilinear nor autonomous, but (like Wartofsky's conception of science) a social process which reflects the dominant ideology of those who design technology.

This abstract notion of technological development as autonomous bespeaks a profound ignorance of the actual process that brings specific technologies into being. To refute the notion of technological determinism, Noble reconstructs the social history of a specific technology—the automation of machine tools, i.e, of the machines that are used to make machines. Although the push for automation may be explained by the desire for increased efficiency, the question is, why this specific technology, why numerically controlled machine tools rather than record-playback? There was a choice to be made here, and, on Noble's account, management opted for the development of NC (numerical control) tools, not in the interest of efficiency, but because such tools promised management increased control over the worker. Such "rationalization" of the modes of production is, of course, irrational from the workers' point of view, leading as it does to a tragic deskilling of the worker and a subsequent reduction in his autonomy. This was not an inevitable next step in some autonomous process, but a deliberate choice on the part of management.

The challenge for labor is to reject the claims made in the name of some autonomous, mystical technological "progress" and not merely to react to new developments, but to demand control of the design of new technologies. The larger end, for Noble, is "the eclipse of the capitalist system as a whole."

# 14

# Is Technology Autonomous?

## Michael Goldhaber

Technology is a human activity but it often seems to be a force of nature. There are a number of reasons for this.

1. Technology as a system always seems to improve on existing technology. Thus, if past technology has led to higher productivity, future technology, it is commonly assumed, will increase productivity still further.

2. Technological progress is based on competition among firms and nations. Thus, technology as a whole seems to work very much like the arms race: we fear the Japanese will beat us to the "Fifth Generation Computer," so we devote resources to the same end. Whatever advance we do make, whoever is behind will try to copy and build on to remain competitive. So we will have to forge ahead even faster.

3. Decisions about the future direction of technology seem to be made according to ideas in the air in the technological community, rather than by purely individual choices. Thus, for example, as it became possible to produce integrated circuits on a single silicon chip, seemingly obvious economic considerations led to producing a general purpose circuit, i.e., a digital computer processor, rather than specially designing a separate circuit for each different function. Likewise, the goal of higher speed, higher density circuits was also obvious to many in the field.

From *Reinventing Technology* by Michael Goldhaber. Reprinted by permission of the Institute for Policy Studies and Routledge and Kegan Paul.

4. On the other hand, inventions of great influence come from surprising sources, including individuals working on their own (e.g., Chester Carlson, inventor of what became the Xerox machine). Since these inventions obviously cannot be anticipated, there is apparently no way for the direction of technology to be controlled.

5. Technology builds on science, and scientists are supposedly led to their discoveries by nothing other than the nature of what they already know and their experimental and observational capabilities.

6. The results of prior technology are everywhere, often are incomprehensible to the lay person and act in unexpected ways, in this way resembling natural processes or living things. For example, without special instruments, it is as impossible to take apart a digital watch to see how it works as it would be to do the same with a housefly.

7. Finally, products of technology are now more feared than are natural forces. No one anticipates a natural disaster on the order of the "nuclear winter" that might result from nuclear war. (Indeed, theorized catastrophic collisions of the earth with asteroids, such as the one that is hypothesized to have caused the extinction of the dinosaurs, could now probably be prevented by utilizing existing space technology).

Do all these reasons hold? Is technology like a train leaving the station that we can hop onto or get left behind, but whose destination is beyond our control? If so, then it would be correct to speak of "sunrise" industries; it would be correct for politicians simply to urge improving the conditions for technology. At best, a more nuanced political approach to technology would only involve ameliorating its negative consequences.

The answer is that technology is not autonomous; the apparent relentless, natural forward motion of the field is in reality anything but that. Closer examination of the arguments advanced above (or of similar arguments elsewhere) will reveal a very different conclusion: technological progress is always guided by values and interests that come from outside technology. Let us proceed once more through the list above to see what has been left out of account.

1. The first five items concern technological innovation as a human process. Each of these points leaves unstated that there is a complex social—and therefore ultimately political—process by which technologists, scientists, industrialists, etc., decide on such questions as what constitutes an "improvement." A technological development is always planned for some social setting in which the improvements involved make sense. But what makes sense is always a matter of social consensus, in which a combination of cultural, economic, and ideological elements are socially evaluated to arrive at a set of priorities. For instance, in automobile design there are many possibilities of what might be considered improvements under different circumstances: cars could be faster, safer, use less gas per mile, be bigger

to hold more passengers in greater comfort, be smaller to be more easily parked, require less maintenance, or wear out faster (planned obsolescence).

Simply put, what constitutes an improvement is always a question of values and dominant interests, and it is never a purely technological issue. Even though technologists often seek numerical measures of performance by which to gauge improvements, what they choose to try to measure depends upon nontechnological factors. If pleasing working conditions were valued more highly than efficiency, for instance, it would be possible to arrive at a variety of numerically measurable quantities, which at least partially or indirectly would correlate with this concept. Technological progress could then be measured according to the new parameters.

If technologists were to operate without some guiding set of values, what would count as improvement would constantly change according to the particular measure that happened to catch their momentary attention. Even if they were to persist with some single measure, it would be more likely to be one of the huge number of socially meaningless possibilities than anything that could be called serious. For example, an auto designer might take as a criterion of perfection how close the weight of the brand new car was to exactly two tons; there would be no limit to improvement, for there would always be another decimal place of accuracy to consider. The effort might make for a real challenge to technical skills, but there would be no noticeable benefit to anyone else involved. Needless to say, no corporation or government agency would be likely to support the pursuit of such a goal—unless, mystified by technology, it thought it was doing something else. Technological frivility of this kind does take place, but only most rarely and accidentally could it have any important consequences. Technology is significant precisely when the goals it adopts are related to values and interests; then the question becomes what values and whose interests are being served.

The range of values that can motivate technological development is wide: from authoritarianism, racism, and destruction—witness Zyklon B poison gas in the Nazi concentration camps, machine guns, and the South African automated pass system; through corporate power, profitability and hierarchy—consider the assembly line, centralized data banks, large office buildings, and containerized shipping; to human equality (at least roughly)—as in mass transit or improvements in nutrition. Encouraging curiosity, extending life, facilitating playfulness, or enlarging democracy have all been goals as well. The values that matter most are those of the institutions and individuals with the greatest power to determine the direction of technology in our society. Overall, at present, these are the values of corporations and the goals of certain government agencies. But, as is especially evident in the latter case, these values and goals can be changed by different political choices.

2. Competition among nations or even between firms is not implicit in technology, and there is no reason technology has to be shaped accordingly. What is true is that technologists have commonly used the potential for competition, and the political weight commonly accorded it, as a basis for urging support for technological development. They have been fairly successful with this tactic, and, as a result, they have been expected to deliver in terms of advantages over the competition. But it does not therefore follow that such competition is either wise or unavoidable. In fact there are many instances of technological cooperation—for example, making air travel safe—that demonstrate it is possible for nations and corporations to break free of competitive patterns when it is widely acknowledged that they are harmful. The will to do so on a larger scale is a political question.

3. The foregoing should suggest that ideas "in the air" are there for more than purely technological reasons. A bread with triple the current calorie content may be technologically feasible; indeed, it is quite possible that a development in baking technology would point in that direction. But since our culture as a whole would accord little value to such an innovation, it would never be a serious focus for technologists. Clothing that would dissolve in the rain, a pill that would mimic the effects of hay fever, or assembly-line processes so designed that the sounds emanating from them provide renditions of all nine Beethoven symphonies may all be quite feasible, and might offer interesting challenges to technologists. None of them are "in the air," because the context of power and values in which technology is embedded makes these seem nonsensical at the same time as it finds sense in cruise missiles, space stations, and increasing productivity in an era of high unemployment.

4. Individual inventors, or even groups of inventors, can undoubtedly depart from dominant values. But for their inventions to have any significant impact they must be accepted by large corporations, venture capitalists, or government bureaucracies, then by some institution involved with distribution, and finally by some group of users or consumers. An inventor like Chester Carlson may have had difficulty finding a corporation willing to invest in developing his electrostatic photocopying (Xerox) process, but there was nothing remarkably eccentric in his awareness that others besides himself frequently could make use of copies of business letters and other documents. In the 1950s, few individual inventors would have worried about problems of energy conservation; likewise, an inventor of today would probably have little motivation to work on an idea of specific benefit to welfare mothers.

5. Since technical feasibility does not in itself determine the direction of technology, it is obvious that new scientific results do not either. The next section takes a closer look at science itself; though stemming from more complex motives than technology, science too turns out not to be autonomous.

6. This and the next point concern past technological developments already in place. Admittedly, the inventions cannot be unmade, but there is no reason they need determine the future. To a large extent, for example, the unintelligibility of present technology is a deliberate choice, for reasons ranging from laziness to the wish to extract high replacement and repair charges ("no user-serviceable parts inside"). It would be possible to put more effort into making each technological project comprehensible to its users; alternatively, new products could be designed with intelligibility as a goal. For— unlike nature—the design of modern products began with conscious understanding, and that can be made accessible.

7. As far as the dangers from nuclear war or other direct technological dangers are concerned, these demonstrate the power of technology but not its inevitability. The reason that weapons are so highly developed is a consequence of the fact that destructive power is both highly valued and easier to enunciate than the more complex set of values associated with sustaining and improving human life. Technologists are complicit: many willingly help perpetuate the arms race because they benefit from it in terms of jobs and status. But it is a national political choice that has made it easier to be assured recognition and employment in weapons development than in projects related to other values.

## THE PLACE OF SCIENCE

In policy as well as practice, science and technology are interlinked. A political approach to technology has to deal with science as well, in ways that take into account both the linkages and the important distinction\* between the two forms of activity.

Like technology, science is a characteristically modern kind of knowledge. Even more than technology, it is intrinsically open, in that for a scientific result

---

\*For readers approaching this subject for the first time, the following summary may be of help.

Very loosely, the distinction between science and technology is that if the immediate aim of technology is to achieve practical ends, then the immediate aim of science is increased understanding, or the accumulation of knowledge, especially the knowledge of nature. The term "research" may—again, loosely—be taken to describe science as an activity; "development" is the same for technology. Science or research are both often further subdivided into "basic" (or "pure") and "applied." This distinction has to do with the closeness with which the knowledge likely to be gained is consciously connected to specific possible technological applications. The discovery of nuclear fission involved basic research, but once the practical possibilities were recognized, subsequent experiments to aid in the construction of the atomic bomb were applied, even though an outside observer would have had difficulty seeing much difference in the laboratory procedures involved. Although for administrative purposes, the definitions may be made sharper, basic and applied efforts in fact shade into one another. Finally, it is, of course, unwise to read any moral connotation into the term "pure."

to be considered valid it must be reproducible. Reproducibility implies a set of published procedures that any other skilled scientist or group of scientists can use to duplicate the experiment or observation, regardless of any personal beliefs, virtues, conditions of birth, or particular location. All that is needed is some apparatus describable in numerical terms, often built with readily available parts, and itself understandable according to scientific explanation. Within a particular explanatory and conceptual framework, two very different-looking experimental setups may be said to lead to the same result.

What counts as a scientific explanation changes as theories change, but it characteristically involves natural objects and forces that lack intention, volition, or symbolic meaning—i.e., there are no gods, spirits, angels, demons, ghosts, portents, etc. Science assumes and reinforces a desacralized world view, one that is amenable to commercial development and bureaucratic management.

Technology is necessary for science—in effect, it is the source of scientific apparatus and at least some scientific procedures; and science is necessary for technology, in that it constantly offers new reproducible situations that can be converted into industrial scale forms, and in that through scientific explanation technologists are able to understand how to approach the goals that interest them. For example, the physics of Isaac Newton provides the basis for calculating the dynamics of the orbits of communications satellites, without which they could not be launched. The more "basic" or "pure" the science, the more its explanations are likely to tie together diverse phenomena, and the wider its potential use by technologists is likely to be.

Just as technologists are paid to innovate, scientists are paid to make new discoveries. (Again, scientists are not the only discoverers; poets, psychoanalysts, and investigative reporters all make discoveries different from science.) As a community, scientists can be said to be always seeking to discover the "natural laws" that lie behind appearances; since appearances include the currently accepted laws, in effect scientists, whether they recognize it or not, are always seeking to undermine the apparent limitations on actions those current laws suggest. In asking the question, "What is there?", scientists are really asking how does such and such work, with the implicit goal of understanding how it can be made to work differently. When Newton was trying to discover the physical laws underlying planetary motions, he was implicitly asking how to go about changing those orbits. Implicit in the study of hormones affecting human sexuality is the possibility of changing the nature of that sexuality (for instance, in sex-change operations). Thus, scientific exploration suggests and promotes new technologies (perhaps only for the far future); it may seem that this happens without any specific values or interests other than curiosity, but, again, closer examination suggests that is not so.

To indicate the deep way that values enter science, I shall adapt and summarize the most thoroughgoing account I know of—that of the late philosopher of science Imire Lakatos—on how scientists decide between rival theories. Scientific theories can never be proved or disproved by experiment,

since the connection between theory and experiment is always open to interpretation, and interpretations can always be modified or elaborated to account
for any disagreements or to explain away agreements. How then are better
theories selected?

Lakatos suggests that the scientific community functions like the stock
market, in that scientists choose between rival explanatory systems on the basis
of which ones are likely to undergo the fastest growth. That is, each explanatory system suggests some new concepts that relate to new kinds of experiments and observations; these in turn help suggest further elaborations and
modifications of the explanatory system and thus lead to still further experiments. The systems in which the payoff of interesting new concepts and interesting new experiments is likely to occur fastest have an obvious attraction for scientists since these will help not only in furthering their careers but
in placing them closer to heretofore undisclosed knowledge of nature and to
novel technological possibilities.

The catch in this explanation is the word "interesting." What is interesting remains a human question answerable differently by different people and
at different times. Since one very strong limitation of experimentation is what
experiments can be funded, and what social purposes are likely to command
the development of new technologies, what is scientifically interesting, and
therefore the character of the explanatory system that is likely to survive, will
be influenced by who has political or economic power and to what ends that
power is exercised.

The choice of explanatory system in which to pursue knowledge influences what experiments are done, and how they are to be interpreted. Thus,
the very nature of scientific knowledge and the set of known facts depends
in a very complex way on the power structure and values of the society that
is - in the final analysis - doing the asking. Since the choice among explanatory systems appears to be a decision about what is true and what is false,
truth turns out to be highly, if indirectly, dependent on the larger society of
the day.

Furthermore, it is of course not coincidental that the model of science
turns out to resemble the stock market. Ideologies of economic growth and
of the growth of scientific knowledge evolved at the same time and continually reinforced each other. Rather than splitting apart, these two systems are
actually tending towards each other, as exemplified in the recent introduction of genetic engineering stocks on the market. Profitability and scientific
truth easily become intertwined. Just as, at the leading edge of technology,
companies compete with one another to be the first to produce a new type
of commodity (e.g., the first "256,000 bit random access memory chip"—better known as the "256K RAM"—or the first human insulin genetically engineered into bacteria), so scientists compete with each other to be the first to
discover something anticipated by the current explanatory system (e.g., the
first hormones isolated in mammalian brains or the "top" quark). The sheer

joy of being first is common to both such enterprises; so is the increased like-lihood of obtaining not only recognition but funding as a result of demon-strating speed that can be related to fast growth—in the one case of profits, and in the other of the explanatory system itself.


## THE OVERALL DIRECTION OF SCIENCE AND TECHNOLOGY

So far in this chapter, technology and science might each appear to be a sin-gle seamless unit. The reality of course is far more complex. Some technolog-ical efforts focus on highly specific problems such as how to decontaminate the Three Mile Island reactor. The values and interests involved are usually easy to discern. But these specific projects normally make use of other tech-nologies that are less specific in scope. In the Three Mile Island case these would include technologies ranging from structural engineering to video trans-mission to chelate chemistry to radiation detection, among many others. Such technologies in turn involve others, such as the metallurgy of steel for the structure of a crane, semiconductor electronics for a video camera, and so on. These more general purpose technologies are in turn closely connected to applied science; at an even further remove, various basic sciences would be involved.

The further we go from specific applications, the more difficult it usu-ally is to ferret out the values and interests that underlie the activity. If we look at some particular laboratory, or at one person, or even one special field, the discernible motivations may be quite idiosyncratic. There may well be an engineer somewhere working on improving the color resolution of television screens because he or she would like to see the face of a certain performer better; there may be chemists who just love the smells associated with work-ing on certain compounds; there are computer scientists convinced that computers will help make all people equal. These individual motivations are not to be dismissed as necessarily irrelevant, but they also do not normally determine the overall direction of any particular field, much less the direction of science and technology as a whole.

Roughly speaking, each different subspeciality in science and technology may be viewed as a service to all the other subspecialities where it is applied. It takes on the sum total of the values and interests they serve, approximately in proportion to the degree of demand each application places on the particu-lar subspeciality in question. At each level in this process we must include the institutional interests of the members of the subspeciality and any related bureaucracy. Especially for the sciences, we must also include what might be termed ideological applications—thus the field of ecology may serve the val-ues of the environmental movement, and the field of sociobiology to some extent serves to support sexist ideas.

As each field then builds on past foundations, it continues in directions suggested by the values and interests it has been serving—that is, it expands more in directions helpful to those values than in other directions. In ways both subtle and direct, these values come to imbue the thinking of members of the subspeciality: thus, the value of increasing efficiency and raising productivity becomes central to the thinking of industrial engineers; computer scientists working with them will have these same values reinforced, and so on. The values and interests will also be embodied in the procedures, processes, and product designs emanating from each subspeciality.

When a technology or a science now is applied in a new way, the values and interests that have shaped it before will influence its suitability for the new application, and may even limit the ways the values and interests directly related to that application are served. For example, for most of their four-decade history, computer systems were developed to serve the needs of large, more or less bureaucratic organizations. Now the programs available for personal computers are being written as if the individual user will operate as a scaled-down version of a bureaucracy (with programs for "database management," "word processing," and balance sheets). This emphasis influences not only who can use such systems but how the users will come to view themselves.

Technology and science together both amplify and help perpetuate dominant values. To the extent that these values accord with the broad interests of humanity as a whole, with the needs of the downtrodden and ill-served, that is all to the good. Unfortunately, the motives of profit, international competitiveness, national expansion, and perpetuating the power of the already powerful tend to prevail in the institutions that currently set the direction of innovation. Deep changes in these institutions are sorely needed.

## REFERENCE

Lakatos, Imire. *The Methodology of Scientific Research Programs.* Cambridge University Press, 1978.

# 15

# The Secret Behind Star Wars

## William J. Broad

In the military, they are known as "skunk works"—an elite band of scientists and engineers laboring in secrecy on important projects. At the Lawrence Livermore National Laboratory, a federal site for the design of nuclear weapons and other advanced technologies, about 45 miles east of San Francisco, they are known variously as "O Group" or "Lowell's group" (after Lowell Wood, the founder). They are "eccentric and extraordinarily bright," says a high Livermore official. To a critic within Livermore who opposes the construction of new weapons, they are "bright young hotshots who are socially maladjusted. All their time and energy is spent on science."

I am at the Livermore laboratory to find out about O Group: young scientists, mostly in their 20s, at the forefront of the Pentagon's five-year, $26 billion search for an antimissile shield, known officially as the Strategic Defense Initiative and popularly as "Star Wars." The "Star Wars" venture is one of the biggest research programs in the history of Western civilization, an effort rivaling the Manhattan Project, which gave birth to the first nuclear weapon, and the Apollo moon program.

Unlike the Manhattan Project, which was shrouded in secrecy, the controversial "Star Wars" theory has been subjected to detailed public scrutiny. Yet, prior to May 1984, the time of my visit to Livermore, little was known about O Group, the creative heart of the weapons lab, or about its legendary Peter Hagelstein, who in 1979, when he was 24, came up with an

From *Star Warriors: The Secret Behind Star Wars* by William J. Broad. Copyright © 1985 by William J. Broad. Reprinted by permission of Simon and Schuster, Inc., and Sterling Lord Literistic, Inc.

inspired idea for a laser device which became a key component in the nation's "Star Wars" program and which has been heralded as the most innovative idea in nuclear weaponry since the hydrogen bomb.

Hagelstein's nuclear-pumped X-ray laser, the group's most dazzling success in the world of nuclear design, is meant to fire deadly beams across the heavens at the speed of light to destroy enemy missiles. First tested in a secret underground explosion in 1980, it helped inspire President Reagan's "Star Wars" speech of March 23, 1983, and has also helped to bring the Russians back to the negotiating table in Geneva.

As it turns out, Livermore's two dozen or so Star Warriors are anything but humorless scientists. They seem addicted to soft drinks and ice cream, and delight in black humor and pranks. Taking off on a greeting-card commercial, they like to say the bombs of Livermore are the way to "send the very best." They also like to tell the story of the time some of the lab's scientists slipped a 20-pound lead brick into Lowell Wood's briefcase. Wood unknowingly lugged it around the country for months until they let him in on the joke. A big, powerfully built man in his early 40s with a full beard and a crease in his nose, Wood is a protégé of Edward Teller, principal developer of the H-bomb. He founded O Group in the early 1970s.

Most of the members of "Lowell's group" are proud to lend their talents to the design of a new generation of nuclear arms. Their common goal is to use their technical skills to protect the nation from the horrors of nuclear war. They argue not only with critics who say that a switch to defense will touch off an expensive round of new offensive weaponry to penetrate the shields, but also with those who say that a nation with a good shield might be tempted to launch a first strike against an enemy's missiles. They do not see themselves as atomic scientists doomed to repeat the mistakes of the past. "We're working on weapons of life, ones that will save people from the weapons of death," says Larry West, who designs both supercomputers and nuclear weapons.

To West and his fellow researchers, Hagelstein's story is a saga of epic proportions. Hagelstein's name is often on the lips of O Group members. It is clear that unlike many of his peers, Hagelstein is a scientist for whom music and literature, as well as the ironies and ambiguities of life, are not mere distractions from the all-consuming goal of uncovering the powerful abstractions of science. He ran marathons in college and was on the swim team. He played the piano. He played violin in a string quartet during his freshman year at the Massachusetts Institute of Technology, joining its symphony orchestra. He loves French literature, not in translation but in the original French.

He appears to be the group's resident mystic and genius—elusive, brooding, like a character out of a Dostoyevsky novel. In fact, at his lowest moments after breaking up with his girlfriend, who was opposed to his working on nuclear weapons, his stereo played nothing but requiems by Brahms, Verdi, and Mozart. Lowell Wood remembers that Hagelstein's office sounded like a funeral parlor.

"He's an insomniac in general, but especially before important meetings," says Andy Weisberg, a close friend at the lab who designs nuclear war games to try to see if the Russians can outwit a defensive shield. "He works incredible hours the day before and then can't sleep, and shows up looking like a dead fish."

Larry West, a jovial extrovert, recalls with awe how Hagelstein in the 1970s had "millions of things . . . to do, all of which were very exotic and relied on the most advanced physical theory. He didn't even have a physics background. He learned the most advanced quantum physics by simply reading the technical literature, which was amazing. He worked that way for about seven or eight years."

Hagelstein, I am told, never wanted to work on weapons—not in the beginning at least. He wanted to win the Nobel Prize by creating the world's first laboratory X-ray laser, a device that would have no use in war but wide application in biology and medicine.

Regular light is made up of electromagnetic waves of many different frequencies and phases that often interfere with one another, just as waves on the ocean surface often cancel each other out. In contrast, waves of laser light have exactly the same frequency and direction and are perfectly in step with one another. They are a pounding rhythm of powerful light.

For decades the quest in laser making has been to construct devices of ever shorter wavelength. Whereas wavelengths of visible light range from about 7,000 to 4,000 angstroms (an angstrom is about 4 billionths of an inch), X-rays—which are not visible—are thought to measure less than 100 angstroms. A brilliant success in the X-ray region would be the achievement of a laser with a wavelength of 1 angstrom. Shorter wavelengths pack more punch. X-rays have 100 to 10,000 times more energy than visible light and react with matter in a different way. Light, for instance, does not penetrate human flesh while X-rays do.

Hagelstein's challenge was to use Livermore's powerful laboratory lasers, such as the Novette, to produce a laser in the neighborhood of 1 angstrom. His idea when he arrived at Livermore was that radiation of this extremely short wavelength would allow the holographic imaging of tiny molecules from the human body, providing clues to the riddle of cancer. Along the way, however, he got caught in a very different quest—and ended up inventing not a medical but a military laser.

For days, I tried to track down Hagelstein at his many haunts, but with no success. Instead, I talk to his peers and learn something of the weapons lab, an atomic metropolis of 8,000 people in a dry California valley of gentle hills and country roads. It was cofounded in the 1950s by Edward Teller and is today made up of hundreds of buildings and laboratories—a square mile of concrete, glass, and asphalt surrounded by barbed wire and armed guards.

On the fourth day of my visit, Hagelstein suddenly appears at the door of the small library in the Livermore complex that has become my "office."

He is taller than I expected (just over six feet), and not the painfully thin, ascetic man I imagined him to be. But his complexion is pale and his manner withdrawn. His shyness is unmistakable. He apologizes for not stopping by sooner.

Hesitantly at first, he tells his story. Peter Hagelstein grew up in Los Angeles and showed an early talent for mathematics, which his father, a mechanical engineer, encouraged. His parents broke up when he was about 10, and he eventually went to live with his mother.

At Canoga Park High School, he excelled in math, history, and the humanities, playing violin and viola and starting to write music. "I came to the conclusion that the interesting compositions were too hard to play and the ones I could play were too dull," Hagelstein recalls. "So I started writing my own. That started in 1971 and continues to this day."

Graduating in 1972 with a National Merit Scholarship, Hagelstein went to MIT to pursue an emerging interest in the physical sciences.

There he took a double load and, after two years, was ready to graduate from the department of electrical engineering and computer science. In the spring of 1974, he was admitted to MIT's graduate school. Rather belatedly, he began to look for a graduate fellowship. The one from the Fannie and John Hertz Foundation stood out as having one of the highest annual stipends of all: $5,000 plus full tuition. John D. Hertz—a poor immigrant's son made rich by his many business ventures, including Yellow Cab and Hertz rental cars—started the foundation in the 1940s as a way to challenge what he saw as threatening technical advances by the Soviet Union.

An interviewer for the foundation, Lowell Wood recommended Hagelstein not only for a Hertz fellowship but also for an internship at Livermore for the summer of 1975. Did Wood explain the nature of the laboratory? "He said that in some ways it was like anyplace else," Hagelstein replies. "He said they were working on lasers and laser fusion, which I had never heard of before, and he said there were computer codes out there that were like playing a Wurlitzer organ. It all sounded kind of dreamy."

At the age of 20, Hagelstein drove through the Livermore valley toward the lab. "The lab itself made quite an impression," he recalls, "especially the guards and barbed wire. When I got to the personnel department, it dawned on me that they worked on weapons here, and that's about the first I knew about it. I came pretty close to leaving. I didn't want to have anything to do with it. Anyway, I met nice people, so I stayed. The people were quite interesting."

In 1976, Hagelstein graduated from MIT with B.S. and M.S. degrees and proceeded to take up full-time work at Livermore. He also maintained his academic status, working toward a Ph.D. and receiving a yearly stipend from the Hertz Foundation.

In pursuing his goal at the lab to build the world's first laboratory X-ray laser for biomedical uses and thus win a Nobel Prize, Hagelstein hoped to have the use of Livermore's huge, multimillion-dollar lasers that generated powerful beams of visible light. But the laser group had no time for the shy graduate student, who was barred from using the lab's powerful machines.

So he pursued his X-ray project by learning physics, developing ideas, and writing computer codes late into the night. He mastered the intricacies of quantum mechanics, which, as an electrical engineer, he had passed over superficially at MIT. With the help of his trusty computer terminal, Hagelstein began to simulate the experiments he was denied in real life.

Hagelstein, however, was not the only person at Livermore to dream of X-ray lasers. For decades, the weapons enthusiasts at Livermore had envisioned using bombs to dig ditches, blast asteroids, create black holes, and "pump" all kinds of exotic beam weapons, including X-ray lasers.

Any electron (the negativly charged particles that form a part of all atoms), if properly jostled, will emit a particle of electromagnetic radiation, such as a photon of light or an X-ray. In a laser device, trillions of electrons are jostled all at once. The powerful Novette laser at Livermore jostles, or pumps, all its electrons with an intense burst of regular light.

In 1977, a senior Livermore physicist named George Chapline came up with a novel (and still highly classified) idea for building an X-ray laser pumped by a nuclear bomb. In one of those odd coincidences, that year also marked the release of the movie *Star Wars*.

The explosive test of Chapline's idea took place the next year at the Nevada Test Site, the government's tract for the underground detonation of nuclear weapons. Chapline's bomb went off, but the elaborate apparatus of detectors and sensors for measuring the output of the X-ray experiment broke down. No one knew whether Chaplines' innovative idea worked.

Months passed and plans were made for a second attempt, Chapline and the laboratory's senior bomb builders holding regular meetings throughout 1979 to discuss the impending test and to tie up any loose ends. Wood and Hagelstein were present at some of the discussions. Hagelstein's input was especially welcome, for he had worked for several years on laboratory X-ray lasers and knew the general theoretics of X-ray lasers better than anyone else. But Hagelstein's impulse was to resist. He hated bombs. He didn't want to be associated with anything nuclear. This feeling, moreover, was strongly reinforced by the woman he dated at the time, Josephine Stein.

They had met at MIT in the early 1970s while they were both in the symphony. She was a mechanical engineer who could talk about stress values or Schubert. He was a high achiever who excelled in sports, school, and music.

During the summer of 1978, Josie Stein moved from Cambridge to Berkeley to begin work on a master's degree at the University of California. She looked up Hagelstein in nearby Livermore and the two were soon seeing much of each other.

As Miss Stein learned about the lab and what it did, she became vocal in her opposition. She said bombs were bombs, and would always be agents of death and destruction. She encouraged Hagelstein to quit. She became militant, at one point marching with protestors outside Livermore's gates.

Hagelstein was sympathetic, but one day he accidentally started down a fateful path. It was during the summer of 1979 at one of Chapline's meetings. There Hagelstein let slip a suggestion (still highly classified) that changed forever the focus of the nation's nuclear X-ray laser program.

Typically, the day before the meeting Hagelstein had been on an around-the-clock work binge. Now, zonked from too much work and not enough sleep, his subconscious seemed to take over. He viewed himself from a distance, as if through the wrong end of a telescope. And there he was, saying something that had not been said before, something new in the arcane world of nuclear X-ray lasers.

"Then," Hagelstein continues, "I got my arm twisted to do a detailed calculation. I resisted doing it. There were political pressures like you wouldn't believe." He was asked to sit at his computer terminal day after day, pouring his special expertise into the calculation of what might happen when a certain set of hardware was pumped by a nuclear explosion. But he felt he had better things to do. His work on laboratory X-ray lasers was picking up speed. He was struggling to finish his Ph.D. Couldn't the mad bombers see he was busy?

Despite the protests of Josie Stein and his own apprehensions, Hagelstein went ahead and worked on the calculations for the nuclear-pumped X-ray laser. Why?

During this period, Hagelstein read *The Gulag Archipelago*, Aleksandr Solzhenitsyn's three-volume portrait of the nightmares of Soviet concentration camps. His peers have suggested to me that it turned him against the Russians and toward work on nuclear weaponry. But Hagelstein pooh-poohs this explanation, saying he was in no way naïve about the Russians, having read much Russian literature and history in high school and college. "I've got a fairly moody and depressive personality," he muses. "I read the *Gulag*. I'm afraid I like reading that kind of thing. I was depressed and it lifted my spirits."

As we talk, the factor Hagelstein emphasizes is his desire to build an X-ray laser, be it pumped by a laboratory laser or a nuclear bomb. And Chapline was threatening to become the first person in the world to create the innovative X-ray device. (For graduate students, says Wood, it's a "win-or-die" situation: ". . . There's no graceful second place. If somebody else publishes the definitive results in the area, they go back to zero and start over.")

Another factor was probably friendship. If he refused, his relationship with the Livermore lab might never be the same. Subtle changes might make him feel uncomfortable and compel him to leave. This would mean giving up his friends, his home, and one of the few places in the world where his special talents had been appreciated.

The young scientists of the group were close friends. They were smart and sassy. Being with them was fun. One day, they talked about buying Wood a costume of Darth Vader, the looming dark side of The Force in *Star Wars*. But they scrapped the idea, afraid Wood would actually wear it as he wandered the halls urging them to work harder.

The fabric of friendship extended even to the language they spoke. Classified projects led to classified jokes. After a while, the young scientists began to be cut off from the spontaneity of the outside world. A visitor could engage them in polite conversation, but so much of their world revolved around secret research that free-ranging discussions could take place only with those who had the proper security clearances. It was like the Gulag. Stalin's concentration camps were the only place in Russia where people could criticize the state. Freedom came only in captivity.

So Hagelstein sat at his terminal and worked on the calculations for the design of the bomb-pumped weapon. Lab officials quickly decided to include a test of Hagelstein's idea in the next underground experiment of Chapline's approach.

At this time, Hagelstein's relationship with Josie Stein started to fall apart. "At first I tended to agree with her," Hagelstein recalls, his voice edged with bitterness. "But she was terribly adamant." Although a parting of the ways was probably inevitable, he became very depressed.

The underground detonation itself occurred on November 14, 1980. Wood and Chapline were at the Nevada Test Site, worrying and fussing and sweating over the details. Hagelstein stayed behind in Livermore.

The test was a success for both Hagelstein and Chapline, but Hagelstein's results were vastly superior. To celebrate, Wood took Hagelstein and several other members of the group to the nearby town of Livermore and they all had ice cream at Baskin-Robbins.

For Hagelstein and the world, the successful X-ray test had huge implications. The name bestowed upon Hagelstein's creation was "Excalibur," referring to the Arthurian legend in which the young king-to-be pulls a magic sword from a stone.

Allusions to the nature of the top-secret device eventually appeared in the press. At its core is an H-bomb. A telescope tracks distant targets, feeding information to the device's computer which then aims the device at a target or targets. When detonated, the bomb emits radiation that speeds out spherically and strikes a series of long, thin metal rods—lasing wires. The radiation's impact causes these rods to emit powerful bursts of X-rays, capable of striking one or multiple targets—such as oncoming missiles—before the whole device is consumed in a nuclear fireball.

This device is a third-generation nuclear weapon, much more precise than the previous two generations, the atomic and hydrogen bombs. Powered by

A-bombs and H-bombs, third-generation weapons *channel* the explosive energy at their core toward targets rather than letting it escape in all directions.

After the successful underground test, many doors opened for Hagelstein. Most importantly, he gained access to the laboratory's big lasers. But, ironically, his original reason for pursuing research on X-ray lasers was vanishing. He felt that scientists working with electron microscopes and other devices had improved their techniques to the point where these tools were better suited to achieving the long-sought biomedical goals.

Hints of this turnaround were contained in Hagelstein's Ph.D. thesis, which he submitted to MIT in 1981 under the title "Physics of Short Wavelength Laser Design." Its 451 pages were thick with equations and scholarly references, but at one point the document broke from its esoteric pace to suggest "future applications" found in three works of science fiction.

In one of them, *Ringworld* by Larry Niven, a spaceship is hit by beam weapons as it approaches a foreign world.

"We have been fired upon," cries a crew member. "We are still being fired upon, probably by X-ray lasers. This ship is now in a state of war."

"An X-ray laser is invariably a weapon of war," says another crew member. "Were it not for our invulnerable hull, we would be dead."

For Hagelstein, the reference to death rays bespoke a deep change of attitude. "Writers of science fiction are supposed to look into the future," he says. "So I started looking to see what they had in mind for X-ray lasers. It turns out all the science-fiction references are to blowing things up. . . . It's fairly discouraging."

The science-fiction references are an ironic comment on the seeming futility of his loftier ambitions for the laboratory X-ray laser. His work is certainly the source of some pride, but Hagelstein appears to feel a deep ambivalence about his brainchild.

"My view of weapons has changed," he says with dry understatment. "Until 1980 or so, I didn't want to have anything to do with nuclear anything. Back in those days, I thought there was something fundamentally evil about weapons. Now I see it as an interesting physics problem." It is hardly the way a king-to-be should talk about his magic sword.

He shifts back and forth on the issue of whether a shield is feasible. His manner does not evoke visions of a high-tech warrior who believes that all problems can be solved with hardware. It suggests a troubled young man who prefers to ignore the military uses of his creation and, when he is asked to contemplate them, tends to see the limitations. As we talk, he stresses not technical solutions to the arms race but political ones, such as cultural exchanges between the superpowers.

"Defense is clearly interesting and feasible—I suppose if I say something like that they'll want to classify it," he says, with a trace of a smile. "With respect to whether it will make war less likely, I doubt that—I mean in terms of man's drives. You're not going to stop war. It would be very nice if we could develop a defense network that would blow away all Soviet ICBMs, but I don't think we can do that. We could take out some, but I don't think we could take out all of them. Even if we could, that would not stop war or get rid of the nuclear threat, people being what they are.

"I'm more or less convinced that one of these days we'll have World War III or whatever," he continues, looking grim. "It'll be pretty ugly. A lot of cities will get busted up. I don't really understand how in the world to defuse the situation or get rid of it. I tend to blame the Soviet government for a lot of it. But as these things go, our own government is sometimes more earthy than its voters realize or would like to know. When all is said and done, the Russians are not as flaky as we are in a lot of respects.

I bear no grudges, at least with respect to the Soviet people. In terms of making the situation better, I think something that would make a big difference is if there were large-scale cultural exchanges between the Soviets and us—so we could at least get to know one another. Maybe that would help. We're in a bad situation, though. And getting up a defensive system might help things somewhat. But it wouldn't keep cities from being obliterated."

# 16

# Do Machines Make History?

## Robert Heilbroner

The hand mill gives you society with the feudal lord; the steam mill, society with the industrial capitalist.

Karl Marx, *The Poverty of Philosophy*

That machines make history in some sense—that the level of technology has a direct bearing on the human drama—is of course obvious. That they do not make all of history, however that word is defined, is equally clear. The challenge, then, is to see if one can say something systematic about the matter, to see whether one can order the problem so that it becomes intellectually manageable.

To do so calls at the very beginning for a careful specification of our task. There are a number of important ways in which machines make history that will not concern us here. For example, one can study the impact of technology on the *political* course of history, evidenced most strikingly by the central role played by the technology of war. Or one can study the effect of machines on the *social* attitudes that underlie historical evolution: one thinks of the effect of radio or television on political behavior. Or one can study technology as one of the factors shaping the changeful content of life from one epoch to another: when we speak of "life" in the Middle Ages or today we define an existence much of whose texture and substance is intimately connected with the prevailing technological order.

From *Technology and Culture* 8 (1967): 335–45. Copyright © 1967 by the Society for the History of Technology. Reprinted by permission of The University of Chicago Press.

None of these problems will form the focus of this [chapter]. Instead, I propose to examine the impact of technology on history in another area—an area defined by the famous quotation from Marx that stands beneath our title. The question we are interested in, then, concerns the effect of technology in determining the nature of the *socioeconomic order*. In its simplest terms the question is: did medieval technology bring about feudalism? Is industrial technology the necessary and sufficient condition for capitalism? Or, by extension, will the technology of the computer and the atom constitute the ineluctable cause of a new social order?

Even in this restricted sense, our inquiry promises to be broad and sprawling. Hence, I shall not try to attack it head-on, but to examine it in two stages:

1. If we make the assumption that the hand mill does "give" us fedualism and the steam mill capitalism, this places technological change in the position of a prime mover of social history. Can we then explain the "laws of motion" of technology itself? Or to put the question less grandly, can we explain why technology evolves in the sequence it does?

2. Again, taking the Marxian paradigm at face value, exactly what do we mean when we assert that the hand mill "gives us" society with the feudal lord? Precisely how does the mode of production affect the superstructure of social relationships?

These questions will enable us to test the empirical content—or at least to see if there *is* an empirical content—in the idea of technological determinism. I do not think it will come as a surprise if I announce now that we will find *some* content, and a great deal of missing evidence, in our investigation. What will remain then will be to see if we can place the salvageable elements of the theory in historical perspective—to see, in a word, if we can explain technological determinism historically as well as explain history by technological determinism.

I

We begin with a very difficult question hardly rendered easier by the fact that there exist, to the best of my knowledge, no empirical studies on which to base our speculations. It is the question of whether there is a fixed sequence to technological development and therefore a necessitous path over which technologically developing societies must travel.

I believe there is such a sequence—that the steam mill follows the hand mill not by chance but because it is the next "stage" in a technical conquest of nature that follows one and only one grand avenue of advance. To put it differently, I believe that it is impossible to proceed to the age of the steam mill until one has passed through the age of the hand mill, and that in turn one cannot move to the age of the hydroelectric plant before one has mastered the steam mill, nor to the nuclear power age until one has lived through that of electricity.

Before I attempt to justify so sweeping an assertion, let me make a few reservations. To begin with, I am fully conscious that not all societies are interested in developing a technology of production or in channeling to it the same quota of social energy. I am very much aware of the different pressures that different societies exert on the direction in which technology unfolds. Lastly, I am not unmindful of the difference between the discovery of a given machine and its application as a technology—for example, the invention of a steam engine (the aeolipile) by Hero of Alexandria long before its incorporation into a steam mill. All these problems, to which we will return in our last section, refer however to the way in which technology makes its peace with the social, political, and economic institutions of the society in which it appears. They do not directly affect the contention that there exists a determinate sequence of productive technology for those societies that are interested in originating and applying such a technology.

What evidence do we have for such a view? I would put forward three suggestive pieces of evidence:

## 1. *The simultaneity of invention*

The phenomenon of simultaneous discovery is well known.[1] From our view, it argues that the process of discovery takes place along a well-defined frontier of knowledge, rather than in grab-bag fashion. Admittedly, the concept of "simultaneity" is impressionistic,[2] but the related phenomenon of technological "clustering" again suggests that technical evolution follows a sequential and determinate rather than random course.[3]

## 2. *The absence of technological leaps*

All inventions and innovations, by definition, represent an advance of the art beyond existing base lines. Yet, most advances, particularly in retrospect, appear essentially incremental, evolutionary. If nature makes no sudden leaps, neither, it would appear, does technology. To make my point by exaggeration, we do not find experiments in electricity in the year *1500*, or attempts to extract power from the atom in the year *1700*. On the whole, the development of the technology of production presents a fairly smooth and continuous profile rather than one of jagged peaks and discontinuities.

## 3. *The predictability of technology*

There is a long history of technological prediction, some of it ludicrous and some not.[4] What is interesting is that the development of technical progress has always seemed *intrinsically* predictable. This does not mean that we can lay down future timetables of technical discovery, nor does it rule out the possibility of surprises. Yet I venture to state that many scientists would be willing to make *general* predictions as to the nature of technological capability twenty-five or even fifty years ahead. This too suggests that technology follows a developmental sequence rather than arriving in a more chancy fashion.

I am aware, needless to say, that these bits of evidence do not constitute anything like a "proof" of my hypothesis. At best they establish the grounds on which a prima facie case of plausibility may be rested. But I should like now to strengthen these grounds by suggesting two deeper-seated reasons why technology *should* display a "structured" history.

The first of these is that a major constraint always operates on the technological capacity of an age, the constraint of its accumulated stock of available knowledge. The application of this knowledge may lag behind its reach; the technology of the hand mill, for example, was by no means at the frontier of medieval technical knowledge, but technical realization can hardly precede what men generally know (although experiment may incrementally advance both technology and knowledge concurrently). Particularly from the mid-nineteenth century to the present do we sense the loosening constraints on technology stemming from succesively yielding barriers of scientific knowledge —loosening constraints that result in the successive arrival of the electrical, chemical, aeronautical, electronic, nuclear, and space stages of technology.[5]

The gradual expansion of knowledge is not, however, the only order-bestowing constraint on the development of technology. A second controlling factor is the material competence of the age, its level of technical expertise. To make a steam engine, for example, requires not only some knowledge of the elastic properties of steam but the ability to cast iron cylinders of considerable dimensions with tolerable accuracy. It is one thing to produce a single steam machine as an expensive toy, such as the machine depicted by Hero, and another to produce a machine that will produce power economically and effectively. The difficulties experienced by Watt and Boulton in achieving a fit of piston to cylinder illustrate the problems of creating a technology, in contrast with a single machine.

Yet until a metal-working technology was established—indeed, until an embryonic machine-tool industry had taken root—an industrial technology was impossible to create. Furthermore, the competence required to create such a technology does not reside alone in the ability or inability to make a particular machine (one thinks of Babbage's ill-fated calculator as an example of a machine born too soon), but in the ability of many industries to change their products or processes to "fit" a change in one key product or process.

The necessary requirement of technological congruence[6] gives us an additional cause of sequencing. For the ability of many industries to co-operate in producing the equipment needed for a "higher" stage of technology depends not alone on knowledge or sheer skill but on the division of labor and the specialization of industry. And this in turn hinges to a considerable degree on the sheer size of the stock of capital itself. Thus the slow and painful accumulation of capital, from which springs the gradual diversification of industrial function, becomes an independent regulator of the reach of technical capability.

In making this general case for a determinate pattern of technological evolution—at least insofar as that technology is concerned with production—I do not want to claim too much. I am well aware that reasoning about technical sequences is easily faulted as *post hoc ergo propter hoc*. Hence, let me leave this phase of my inquiry by suggesting no more than that the idea of a roughly ordered progression of productive technology seems logical enough to warrant further empirical investigation. To put it as concretely as possible, I do not think it is just by happenstance that the steam mill follows, and does not precede, the hand mill, nor is it mere fantasy in our own day when we speak of the coming of the automatic factory. In the future as in the past, the development of the technology of production seems bounded by the constraints of knowledge and capabilty and thus, in principle at least, open to prediction as a determinable force of the historic process.

## II

The second proposition to be investigated is no less difficult than the first. It relates, we will recall, to the explicit statement that a given technology imposes certain social and political characteristics upon the society in which it is found. It is true that, as Marx wrote in *The German Ideology*, "A certain mode of production, or industrial stage, is always combined with a certain mode of cooperation, or social stage,"[7] or as he put it in the sentence immediately preceding our hand mill, steam mill paradigm, "In acquiring new productive forces men change their mode of production, and in changing their mode of production they change their way of living—they change all their social relations"?

As before, we must set aside for the moment certain "cultural" aspects of the question. But if we restrict ourselves to the functional relationships directly connected with the process of production itself, I think we can indeed state that the technology of a society imposes a determinate pattern of social relations on that society.

We can, as a matter of fact, distinguish at least two such modes of influence:

### 1. The composition of the labor force

In order to function, a given technology must be attended by a labor force of a particular kind. Thus, the hand mill (if we take this as referring to late medieval technology in general) required a work force composed of skilled or semiskilled craftsmen, who were free to practice their occupations at home or in a small atelier, at times and seasons that varied considerably. By way of contrast, the steam mill—that is, the technology of the nineteenth century—required a work force composed of semiskilled or unskilled operatives who could work only at the factory site and only at the strict time schedule enforced by turning the machinery on or off. Again, the technology of the electronic age has steadily required a higher proportion of skilled attendants; and the coming technology of automation will still further change the needed mix of skills and the locale of work, and may as well drastically lessen the requirements of labor time itself.

## 2.  The hierarchical organization of work

Different technological apparatuses not only require different labor forces but different orders of supervision and coordination. The internal organization of the eighteenth-century handicraft unit, with its typical man-master relationship, presents a social configuration of a wholly different kind from that of the nineteenth-century factory with its men-manager confrontation, and this in turn differs from the internal social structure of the continuous-flow, semi-automated plant of the present. As the intricacy of the production process increases, a much more complex system of internal controls is required to maintain the system in working order.

Does this add up to the proposition that the steam mill gives us society with the industrial capitalist? Certainly the class characteristics of a particular society are strongly implied in its functional organization. Yet it would seem wise to be very cautious before relating political effects exclusively to functional economic causes. The Soviet Union, for example, proclaims itself to be a socialist society although its technical base resembles that of old-fashioned capitalism. Had Marx written that the steam mill gives you society with the industrial *manager*, he would have been closer to the truth.

What is less easy to decide is the degree to which the technological infrastructure is responsible for some of the sociological features of society. Is anomie, for instance, a disease of capitalism or of all industrial societies? Is the organization man a creature of monopoly capital or of all bureaucratic industry wherever found. The questions tempt us to look into the problem of the impact of technology on the existential quality of life, an area we have ruled out of bounds for this paper. Suffice it to say that the similar technologies of Russia and America are indeed giving rise to similar social phenomena of this sort.

As with the first portion of our inquiry, it seems advisable to end this section on a note of caution. There is a danger, in discussing the structure of the labor force or the nature of intrafirm organization, of assigning the sole causal efficacy to the visible presence of machinery and of overlooking the invisible influence of other factors at work. Gilfillan, for instance, writes, "engineers have committed such blunders as saying the typewriter brought women to work in offices, and with the typesetting machine made possible the great modern newspapers, forgetting that in Japan there are women office workers and great modern newspapers getting practically no help from typewriters and typesetting machines."[8] In addition, even where technology seems unquestionably to play the critical role, an independent "social" element unavoidably enters the scene in the *design* of technology, which must take into account such facts as the level of education of the work force or its relative price. In this way the machine will reflect, as much as mold, the social relationship of work.

These caveats urge us to practice what William James called a "soft determinism" with regard to the influence of the machine on social relations. Nevertheless, I would say that our cautions qualify rather than invalidate the thesis that the prevailing level of technology imposes itself powerfully on the structural organization of the productive side of society. A foreknowledge of the shape of the technical core of society fifty years hence may not allow us to describe the political attributes of that society, and may perhaps only hint at its sociological character, but assuredly it presents us with a profile of requirements, both in labor skills and in supervisory needs, that differ considerably from those of today. We cannot say whether the society of the computer will give us the latter-day capitalist or the commissar, but it seems beyond question that it will give us the technician and the bureaucrat.

## III

Frequently, during our efforts thus far to demonstrate what is valid and useful in the concept of technological determinism, we have been forced to defer certain aspects of the problem until later. It is time now to turn up the rug and to examine what has been swept under it. Let us try to systematize our qualifications and objections to the basic Marxian paradigm:

### 1. *Technological progresss is itself a social activity*

A theory of technological determinism must contend with the fact that the very activity of invention and innovation is an attribute of some societies and not of others. The Kalahari bushmen or the tribesmen of New Guinea, for instance, have persisted in a neolithic technology to the present day; the Arabs reached a high degree of technical proficiency in the past and have since suffered a decline; the classical Chinese developed technical expertise in some fields while unaccountably neglecting it in the area of production. What factors serve to encourage or discourage this technical thrust is a problem about which we know extremely little at the present moment.[9]

### 2. *The course of technological advance is responsive to social reform*

Whether technology advances in the area of war, the arts, agriculture, or industry depends in part on the rewards, inducements, and incentives offered by society. In this way the direction of technological advance is partially the result of social policy. For example, the system of interchangeable parts, first introduced into France and then independently into England, failed to take root in either country for lack of government interest or market stimulus. Its success in America is attributable mainly to government support and to its appeal in a society without guild traditions and with high labor costs.[10] The general *level* of technology may follow an independently determined sequential path, but its areas of application certainly reflect social influences.

### 3. Technological change must be compatible with existing social conditions

An advance in technology not only must be congruent with the surrounding technology but must also be compatible with the existing economic and other institutions of society. For example, labor-saving machinery will not find ready acceptance in a society where labor is abundant and cheap as a factor of production. Nor would a mass production technique recommend itself to a society that did not have mass market. Indeed, the presence of slave labor seems generally to inhibit the use of machinery and the presence of expensive labor to accelerate it.[11]

These reflections on the social forces bearing on technical progress tempt us to throw aside the whole notion of technological determinism as false or misleading.[12] Yet, to relegate technology from an undeserved position of *primum mobile* in history to that of a mediating factor, both acted upon by and acting on the body of society, is not to write off its influence but only to specify its mode of operation with greater precision. Similarly, to admit we understand very little of the cultural factors that give rise to technology does not depreciate its role but focuses our attention on that period of history when technology is clearly a major historic force, namely Western society since 1700.

### IV

What is the mediating role played by technology within modern Western society? When we ask this much more modest question, the interaction of society and technology begins to clarify itself for us:

### 1. The rise of capitalism provided a major stimulus for the development of a technology of production

Not until the emergence of a market system organized around the principle of private property did there also emerge an institution capable of systematically guiding the inventive and innovative abilities of society to the problem of facilitating production. Hence the environment of the eighteenth and nineteenth centuries provided both a novel and an extremely effective encouragement for the development of an *industrial* technology. In addition, the slowly opening political and social framework of late mercantilist society gave rise to social aspirations for which the new technology offered the best chance of realization. It was not only the steam mill that gave us the industrial capitalist but the rising inventor-manufacturer who gave us the steam mill.

## 2. *The expansion of technology within the market system took on a new "automatic" aspect*

Under the burgeoning market system not alone the initiation of technical improvement but its subsequent adoption and repercussion through the economy was largely governed by market considerations. As a result, both the rise and the proliferation of technology assumed the attributes of an impersonal diffuse "force" bearing on social and economic life. This was all the more pronounced because the political control needed to buffer its disruptive consequences was seriously inhibited by the prevailing laissez-faire ideology.

## 3. *The rise of science gave a new impetus to technology*

The period of early capitalism roughly coincided with and provided a congenial setting for the development of an independent source of technological encouragement—the rise of the self-conscious activity of science. The steady expansion of scientific research, dedicated to the exploration of nature's secrets and to their harnessing for social use, provided an increasingly important stimulus for technological advance from the middle of the nineteenth century. Indeed, as the twentieth century has progressed, science has become a major historical force in its own right and is now the indispensable precondition for an effective technology.

It is for these reasons that technology takes on a special significance in the context of capitalism—or, for that matter, of a socialism based on maximizing production or minimizing costs. For in these societies, both the continuous appearance of technical advance and its diffusion throughout the society assume the attributes of autonomous process, "mysteriously" generated by society and thrust upon its members in a manner as indifferent as it is imperious. This is why, I think, the problem of technological determinism—of how machines make history—comes to us with such insistence despite the ease with which we can disprove its more extreme contentions.

*Technological determinism is thus peculiarly a problem of a certain historic epoch*—specifically that of high capitalism and low socialism—*in which the forces of technical change have been unleashed, but when the agencies for the control or guidance of technology are still rudimentary.*

The point has relevance for the future. The surrender of society to the free play of market forces is now on the wane, but its subservience to the impetus of the scientific ethos is on the rise. The prospect before us is assuredly that of an undiminished and very likely accelerated pace of technical change. From what we can foretell about the direction of this technological advance and the structural alterations it implies, the pressures in the future will be toward a society marked by a much greater degree of organization and deliberate control. What other political, social, and existential changes the age of the computer will also bring we do not know. What seems certain, however, is that the problem of technological determinism—that is, of the impact of machines on history—will remain germane until there is forged a degree of public control over technology far greater than anything that now exists.

## NOTES

1. See Robert K. Merton, "Singletons and Multiples in Scientific Discovery: A Chapter in the Sociology of Science," *Proceedings* of the American Philosophical Society 105 (October 1961): 470–86.

2. See John Jewkes, David Sawers, and Richard Stillerman, *The Sources of Invention* (New York: Norton, 1960 [paperback edition]), p. 227, for a skeptical view.

3. "One can count 21 basically different means of flying, at least eight basic methods of geophysical prospecting, four ways to make uranium explosive; . . . 20 or 30 ways to control birth. . . . If each of these separate inventions were autonomous, i.e., without cause, how could one account for their arriving in these functional groups?" S. C. Gilfallan, "Social Implications of Technological Advance," *Current Sociology* 1 (1952): 197. See also Jacob Schmookler, "Economic Sources of Inventive Activity," *Journal of Economic History* (March 1962): 1–20; and Richard Nelson, "The Economics of Invention: A Survey of the Literature," *Journal of Business* 32 (April 1959): 101–19.

4. Jewkes et al. (see note 2) present a catalogue of chastening mistakes (p. 230 f.). On the other hand, for a sober predictive effort, see Francis Bello, "The 1960s: A Forecast of Technology," *Fortune* 59 (January 1959): 74–78; and Daniel Bell, "The Study of the Future," *Public Interest* 1 (Fall 1965): 119–30. Modern attempts at prediction project likely avenues of scientific advance or technological function rather than the feasibility of specific machines.

5. To be sure, the inquiry now regresses one step and forces us to ask whether there are inherent stages for the expansion of knowledge, at least insofar as it applies to nature. This is a very uncertain question. But having already risked so much, I will hazard the suggestion that the roughly parallel sequential development of scientific understanding in those few cultures that have cultivated it (mainly, classical Greece, China, the high Arabian culture, and the West since the Renaissance) makes such a hypothesis impossible, provided that one looks to broad outlines and not to inner detail.

6. The phrase is Richard LaPiere's in *Social Change* (New York: McGraw-Hill, 1965), p. 263 f.

7. Karl Marx and Friedrich Engels, *The German Ideology* (London: Lawrence and Wisehart, 1942), p. 18.

8. Gilfillan (see note 3), p. 202.

9. An interesting attempt to find a line of social causation is found in E. Hagen, *The Theory of Social Change* (Homewood, Ill.: Dorsey Press, 1962).

10. See K. R. Gilbert, "Machine Tools," in Charles Singer, E. J. Holmwood, A. R. Hall, and Trevor I. Williams (eds.), *A History of Technology* (Oxford University Press, 1958), IV, chap. 14.

11. See LaPiere (note 6), p. 284; also H. J. Habbakuk, *British and American Technology in the 19th Century* (Cambridge University Press, 1962), *passim*.

12. As, for example, in A. Hansen, "The Technological Determination of History," *Quarterly Journal of Economics* (1921): 76–83.

# 17

# Social Choice in Machine Design:
# The Case of Automatically Controlled
# Machine Tools, and a Challenge for Labor

## David F. Noble

### BEYOND TECHNOLOGICAL DETERMINISM

The hard-sounding authority of the phrase *technological development* belies its ambiguity. However popular as an explanatory or justificatory device, the notion is but a convenient catch-all, signifying nothing and everything. With reference to human labor, our focus here, the term is commonly used, in a descriptive mode, to suggest the grand evolution of the material artifacts of "work" that set human beings off from the animal world. Alternatively, in a more modern setting, it is used to refer to an integral aspect of the capitalist process of accumulation, wherein costs are minimized and productivity is enhanced through the profitable substitution of machinery for labor. In a normative and teleological mode, the phrase is used to connote "progress," the steady upswing of human society characterized by freedom from want and toil and by greater human dignity, individual creativity, and autonomy. Or, in a less sanguine view, the same process is seen as the dehumanization of people through the progressive rationalization of labor, either as a routine aspect of capitalism (and thus the managerial quest for control, class hegemony, and intensified exploitation) or as an independent process in itself, called industrialization or modernization. The variations are endless.

From *Politics & Society* 8, nos. 3–4 (1978): 247–312. Reprinted by permission of the publisher.

As can readily be seen, each use of the term is pregnant with intent as well as content. More important for present purposes, all uses tend to have something in common: they reflect the habit of thought that will be referred to here as "technological determinism." However much technological development is understood to be mediated by (unwitting) human agency or tied, in its use, to an economic or social process like capital accumulation, it itself is nevertheless commonly comprehended as an essentially autonomous, unilinear, and causal process.

Technological determinism actually embraces two basic, interrelated notions: first, that technological development itself is a "given" that is self-generating and follows a single course; and second, that this process has effects "outside" it, usually referred to as "social impacts." In the first instance, technological development is seen to be essentially independent of social setting; however much it may be embedded in a particular time and place, its form reflects less these historical particulars than the extrapolation of its own immanent dynamic. In the second instance, technological cause is understood to be irreducible and to have singular effects and not others; moreover, the relation between cause and effect is seen to be automatic and inevitable (necessary)—and is more often assumed than demonstrated.[1] Of course, few would claim to be consistent technological determinists, in the precise philosophical meaning of the term; we are talking rather about a prevalent tendency, a subtle although commonplace habit of thought. Like all other determinisms, this habit denies a realm of human freedom; it views history not as a domain of possibilities but as a sequence of necessities.

Why such a tendency should exist is a subject for historical inquiry in itself. Perhaps foremost among the reasons is the common alienation from, and thus ignorance of, technology, on the part of those people who so often write about its supposed impacts. This is not anyone's fault, of course, but rather the result of the professional monopolization of technical knowledge, the industrial monopolization of professionals, and the general specialization and fragmentation of intellect. Thus, for many observers, technology remains mysterious, alien, and impenetrable, simply a given. And this appearance itself is reinforced by the market context in which technology often develops, where everything appears to happen by itself, automatically. But there are reasons why observers remain content with such a superficial view.

For apologists of the status quo, clearly, such a notion of automaticity absolves everyone of blame and responsibility and ratifies things as they are: they could not be any other way given the ineluctable march of technological progress. For lazy revolutionaries, who proclaim liberation through technology, and prophets of doom, who forecast ultimate disaster through the same medium, such notions offer justifications for inactivity. And, for the vast majority of us, numbed into a passive complicity in "progress" by the consumption of goods and by daily chants echoing the slogan of the 1933 World's fair—SCIENCE FINDS, INDUSTRY APPLIES, MAN CONFORMS—such conceptions provide a convenient, albeit often unhappy, excuse for resignation, for avoiding the always difficult task of critically evaluating our circumstances, of exercising our imagination and freedom. Finally, the habit of exaggerating the causal role of technology in history is readily, if subtly, adopted by historians for the simple reason that it makes their work, the writing of history, easier.

But technological determinism is not simply an intellectual shortcoming; it is politically dangerous. Depicting an inexorable, disembodied, and omnipotent historical force that rules out human action and choice, it fosters passivity, quiescence, and resignation, and their correlates, cynicism and despair. Moreover, as a confusion in thought, it generates artificial contradictions that confound effective action. For example, the labor movement's relation to technological development is an unnecessarily contradictory one. Union officials tend readily to welcome rationalization so long as such technological progress guarantees a bigger slice of the pie without jeopardizing jobs and membership. Workers on the shop floor, however—even those whose jobs have been "red circled" (guaranteed)—quite often see such rationalization less as a lightening of their load or as a bigger paycheck than as a loss of control and a tightening of managerial authority over them. Thus, a conflict arises: in general, union spokesmen tend to be "let it" while people on the shop floor tend to be "against it." The "it," however, is taken as a given, in the habit of technological determinism. Rarely, if ever, is the "it" viewed as a range of possibilities, a domain of human choices—at present the reserve of management—that might potentially provide for *both* increased productivity *and* greater shop floor worker control, depending upon the design. The contradictions arise, then, out of a false notion of a fixed technology, a notion symptomatic of technological determinism. (In this case, the notion is in part a reflection of the virtual exclusion of labor from the realm of technological decision-making, which thus leaves it in no position to recognize the extent to which technological development is the special product of managerial choices made to increase productivity through the enhancement of managerial, not worker, control.)

To the extent that social commentators and scholars simply accept this technology as inevitable and necessary, they ratify and legitimate the managerial choices that inform it. However unwitting they may be, their studies are thus partisan acts. The purpose of this [chapter] is to try to overcome the tendency of technological determinism, and the confusion and impotence it generates, by pointing up the possibilities inherent in technological development. It is a deliberately partisan effort, launched from the other side. Before we can ever hope confidently to strive to intervene in this important process, in order to reshape it according to different choices, we must convince ourselves that such choice is possible. And to do this, we must look at the choices that have already been made. Such an investigation, moreover, should make it quite apparent that, first, technological development itself is neither autonomous nor unilinear, and that, second, technological development as a "cause" is neither irreducible nor automatic.

To begin with, we must recognize that technological development is a social process in itself, that it is not only man-made but made of men (and, increasingly, of women, too). Elsewhere, in trying to understand the relationship between modern technology and capitalism, I have examined that social process in some detail, to identify the people who tend most often to give direction and shape to technological development (engineers), to explain how they obtained this important prerogative (professionalization), to describe the social context in which they learn to use it (technical education), to map out the institutional framework within which they exercise it (corporate research organizations, university laboratories, the patent system, a competitive market environment, etc.), and, finally, to articulate a dominant ideology of technical advance (an engineering ideology of profit-making and management).[2] In that study, it became clear that, as Seymour Melman observed, "if one wants to alter our technologies, the place to look is not to molecular structure but to social structure, not to the chemistry of materials but to the rules of man, especially the economic rules of who decides on technology."[3] Technological development, in short, is not an independent force impinging upon society from the outside, according to its own internal logic; rather, it is a social activity in itself, which cannot but reflect the particulars of its setting: the time, the place, the dream and purposes, the relations between people.[4]

But how does the technology reflect the social context, to what extent, and in what specific ways? Where is the imprint of the social activity that gave issue to it? Marx asserted that "instruments of labor not only supply a standard of the degree of development to which human labor has attained, but they are also indicators of the social conditions under which that labor is carried on."[5] How might we go about reading those indicators, and what do they indicate? One way, beyond merely examining the artifact and guessing at its intended use, is to try to recreate the social history of the technology, to reconstruct the choices that became frozen in the hardware. This would then make it possible to examine the ways in which these choice reflect the ideology and thus the soical position of the designers. But to look for choices, of course, requires that the assumption be made that technological development is not unilinear, that it could, potentially, follow any number of chosen courses. And the validity of this assumption rests upon the identification, and thus awareness, of possible alternatives.

If it is assumed that technological development is neither autonomous nor unilinear, what are the implications of these assumptions for the causal view of technological development? We discover now that the "impacts" of technology must follow not simply from the technology but from the design choices it embodies, choices that (fully intended or not) define or at least constrain subsequent choices in deployment. In short, technological development, however much it is a cause of social change, is never an irreducible, first cause.

It too has been caused, or, more correctly, chosen, as thus indirectly so have its "impacts."

However, and finally, to say that technologies embody human choices and that these choices reflect the intentions (desired impacts) of the designers—intentions that reflect the ideology (often inarticulate and prereflective) and thus social position of the designers—is not to say that these intentions (desired impacts) are automatically fully realized in the simple construction and use of the technology. Far from it. To end the investigation here, by simply extrapolating the impacts from the choices, would be to beg some of the most important questions and confuse mere intentions for the whole of reality (a common and convenient error). In actuality, the "impacts" are always determined subsequent to the introduction of the technology and in ways not altogether consistent with the intentions of designers. That is, if technology does not automatically "cause" a social effect, neither do the choices (intentions) that lie behind it.

The relation between cause and effect is always mediated by a complex and often conflictive social process, and it is this process, and not the technology or the choices that informed the technology, that determines the final outcome. This social process can be broken down into several aspects. Two of these have received considerable attention from industrial engineers and sociologists: the debugging (and possible minor redesign) of the physical technology following trial use, and the psychological, social, and organizational "adaptation" to the technology of those affected by it. A third aspect, often mistaken for (or dismissed as) "irrational fear of change" is the quite rational struggle on the part of those affected by the technology against the choices embodied in it and the impacts implied by them, a struggle that accurately reflects an objective conflict of interest between, say, machine operators and designers. It is here that we find the only point of entry for labor to register its choices in the process of technological development.

The following brief case history of the design, deployment, and subsequent use of a particular production technology—automatically controlled machine tools—is not meant to be a full account. Rather, it is presented in order to illustrate the points made above and, more importantly, to ground them in the historical and the concrete. Theorizing, however vital to our understanding, is never in itself sufficient to comprehend reality (much less to change it). In this social history, we will endeavor to: place the technology in its social setting, identify the designers, and indicate the loci of decision making wherein its shape was determined; identify the choices made in the *design* of the hardware and software systems, by examining selected and abandoned alternatives; explore how these choices reflected the social relations of production (the "horizontal" relations between large and small firms and between firms and the state, and the "vertical" relations between management and labor within the firm); examine the choices made in *deployment* subsequent to design (since in the case of a relatively portable technology like machine tools, deployment—

physical and institutional installations—is separable from design, and choices enter in at both stages of development to successively delimit possibilities and contribute to the final outcome); and examine closely the social process subsequent to installation in order to contrast the realities of that experience with the expectations implicit in the original design and deployment choices. Again, the whole purpose of this exercise is to move us beyond the facile and mystifying habit of technological determinism, and the sense of hopelessness that it mirrors and reinforces, by reawakening us to the possibilities.

## THE TECHNOLOGY: AUTOMATICALLY CONTROLLED MACHINE TOOLS

The focus here is a particular production technology, numerically controlled contouring machine tools.[6] It appears that the numerical control (NC) revolution in manufacturing, as it has been called, is leading, on one hand, to increased concentration in the metalworking industry and, on the other, to a reorganization of shop-floor activities within the larger firms in the direction of greater managerial control over production and, thus, over the work force. These changes are most often attributed to the advent of the new technology and are seen to follow logically, inevitably, as a consequence of it. At a Small Business Administration hearing on the impact of NC on small business in 1971, for example, one expert, the president of Data Systems Corporation, intimated that it was inevitable that "we will see some companies die, but I think we will see other companies grow very rapidly."[7] James Childs, president of the Numerical Control Society, was far less sanguine in his assessment of the situation, pointing out that "the technological gap is definitely growing and unless proper action is taken, will continue to grow until the small shop is extinct. Unless we are willing to allow a relatively few large shops to control the market . . . we must support the small shop."[8] Whatever the orientation, there was consensus among those in attendance that the metalworking industry was undergoing a change as a consequence of the new technology, a change that seemed to spell disaster for many of the smaller firms, which, in 1971, constituted 83 percent of the firms in the industry.[9] The most common reason cited for this trend was the inaccessibility of the new technology to the smaller shops, and this was explained in terms of the expense of NC machines (hardware) and the difficulties associated with programming them (software).

If the new technology was seen as having an important effect on the structure of a vital industry, that is, on the relations of production between firms, it was also seen as the cause of significant changes within shops. Indeed, it has been argued that smaller shops could not take advantage of NC because they were unwilling to undertake the social reorganization efforts that the new technology required.[10] Earl Lundgren, a sociologist who has studied the impact of NC on shop reorganization, insists, for example, that the successful employment of the new technology demands extensive training programs for parts programmers, the shift of shop-floor skills from the machinists to the parts programmers and methods personnel, the intensification of centralized control over all aspects of the production process, and a corollary, the detailed coordination of effort throughout the shop.[11] In the course of a site-visit survey of twenty-four NC using large- and medium-sized firms in 1978, I found much evidence that such a reorganization effort was underway, that in nearly every case management had attempted to transfer skill from the shop floor to the programming office, to tighten up lines of authority, and to extend control over all aspects of production, that is, to meet the social requirements of NC, requirements that signaled profound changes in the relations of production between management and labor.[12]

For the technological determinist, the story is pretty much told: NC leads to concentration in the metalworking industry and to a tightening of managerial control on the shop floor. All that remains to be done is to sit back and watch the inevitable process unfold. But for the critical historian of technology, the problem has merely been defined. The first question to be asked is, do these consequences really follow from this technological cause? Is the causal connection real? Do the cost and complexity of the new technology really have anything to do with the diffusion of it in the metalworking industry? Might a better explanation be that smaller firms have never even heard of NC because of their distance from the locus of technological change in the industry?[13] Along the same lines, is it really necessary to divide the programming and machine operating functions within the shop? Could programming, like other tooling, be done closer to the floor or by people on the floor? Does the new technology itself make such reorganization impossible?[14] For purposes of brevity, we will here assume that there *is* a sufficient degree of causal connection between the technology and its supposed effects to warrant further investigation.

This leads us to ask the next question: If *this* technology has these significant consequences, why *this* technology? Here I will limit myself to a single aspect of this problem. All would agree that technology affects the social relations of production; here I am turning that around to ask, how have the social relations of production defined the technology? Could it be the case that the new technology, which took shape within the context of these social relations, not only affects them but also reflects them? If the new technology was developed under the auspices of large firms within the metalworking industry, and under the auspices of management within these firms, is it just a coincidence that the technology serves to extend the market control of large firms within the metalworking industry and enhance managerial authority within the shop? Why did NC take the particular *form* that it did, a form that seems to have rendered it inaccessible to small firms, and *why only NC?* Are there other ways of automating machine tools?

Let us begin with the technology. A machine tool (say, a lathe or milling machine) is a machine used to cut away surplus material from a piece of metal to produce a part with the desired shape, size, and finish. Machine tools are really the guts of machine-based industry because they are the means whereby all machinery, including machine tools themselves, are made. Traditionally, the machine tool is operated by a machinist who transmits his skill and his purpose to the machine by means of cranks, levers, and handles. Feedback is achieved through hands, ears, and eyes. Throughout the nineteenth century, technical advances in machining developed by innovative machinists built some intelligence into the machine tools themselves, making them partially "self-acting": automatic feeds, stops, throw-out dogs, mechanical cams. These mechanical devices relieved the machinists of certain manual tasks; the machinist, however, retained control over the operation of the machine. Together with elaborate tooling—fixtures for holding the workpiece in the proper cutting position and jigs for guiding the path of the cutting tool—these design innovations made it possible for less skilled operators to use the machines to cut parts after they had been properly "set up" by more skilled men.[15] Still, the source of the intelligence was the skilled machinist on the floor. Another step in machine design was the advent of tracer technology, perfected during the 1930s and 40s, which involved the use of patterns, or templates; these were traced by an hydraulic or electronic sensing device, which in turn conveyed the information to a cutting tool, which reproduced the pattern in the workpiece. The template, then, was, in essence, the cam that contained the intelligence for the machine, intelligence that came from a patternmaker. Tracer technology made possible elaborate contour cutting, but it was still only a partial form of automation. You needed different templates for different surfaces on the same workpiece. During the 1940s, with the war-spurred development of a whole host of new sensing and measuring devices as well as precision servomotors, which made possible the accurate control of mechanical motion, people began to think about the complete automation of contour machining.

Automating a machine tool is different from automating, say, automotive manufacturing equipment, which is single-purpose, fixed automation, and cost effective only given a high volume of product and thus high demand. Machine tools are general purpose, versatile machines, used primarily for small-batch, low-volume production of parts. The challenge of automating machine tools, then, is to retain the versatility of the machine. The answer that evolved was the use of some medium—film, lines on paper, magnetic tape, punched cards of tape—that would store the intelligence and control the machine. To change the part produced, you had only to change the tape. The machine remained the same.

The automating of machine tools, then, involves two separate processes. You need machine controls, a means of transmitting information to the machine to make the tables and cutting tool move as desired. And you need a means of getting the information on the medium, the tape, in the first place. The real challenge was the latter. Machine controls were just another step in a known direction, an extension of gunfire control technology developed during the war. The tape preparation was something new. The first viable solution was record playback, a system developed in 1946–47 by General Electric and Gisholt and a few smaller firms.[16] It involved having a machinist make a part while the motions of the machine under his command were recorded on magnetic tape. After the first piece was made, subsequent identical parts could be made automatically by playing back the tape and reproducing the machine motions. John Diebold, the management consultant, among the first to write about such "flexible automation" in his book *Automation,* heralded record playback as "no small achievement . . . it means that automatic operation of machine tools is possible for the job shop—normally the last place in which anyone would expect even partial automation."[17] But record playback enjoyed only a brief existence, for reasons we shall explore. (It was nevertheless immortalized as the inspiration for Kurt Vonnegut's *Player Piano.*[18] Vonnegut was a publicist at G.E. at the time and saw the record-playback lathe he describes in the novel.)

The other solution to the medium-preparation problem was numerical control (NC). Although some trace its history back to the Jacquard loom of 1804, NC was actually of more recent vintage, the brainchild of a defense subcontractor for Bell Aircraft, John Parsons, and engineers at MIT subcontracted by Parsons.[19] Numerical control, first demonstrated in 1952, represented a dramatic departure in machine tool technology.[20] Record playback was, in reality, a multiplier of skill, a means of obtaining repeatability. The intelligence still came from the machinist who made the tape. Numerical control was based upon an entirely different philosophy of manufacturing. Here the specifications for a part, the information contained in the engineering blueprint, is broken down, first, into a mathematical representation of the part, then into a mathematical description of the desired path of the cutting tool, and ultimately, into hundreds or thousands of discrete instructions, translated for economy into a numerical code, which is read by the machine controls. The NC tape, in short, is a means of formally synthesizing the skill of a machinist, circumventing his role as the source of the intelligence of production (in theory). This new approach to machining was heralded by the National Commission on Technology, Automation and Economic Progress, as "probably the most significant development in manufacturing since the introduction of the moving assembly line."[21]

## CHOICE IN DESIGN: HORIZONTAL RELATIONS OF PRODUCTION

Numerical control appeared to potential users in the large aircraft contracting firms to be a valuable means of taking the intelligence of production, and thus control over production, off the shop floor. The new technology thus dovetailed nicely with their larger efforts to computerize company operations.[22] At the same time, in the intensely anti-Communist 1950s, NC looked like a solution to security problems, enabling management to remove the blueprints from the floor so that Communists could not get their hands on them. NC did appear to eliminate the need for costly jigs and fixtures and the templates required by tracer machining, and it did make possible the cutting of complex shapes that defied manual methods. But, additionally, and of equal importance, NC seemed to eliminate once and for all the problems of "pacing," to afford management greater control over production by replacing problematic time-study methods with "tape-time" (using the time it takes to run a part tape as the base for calculating rates) and replacing skilled machinists with more tractable "button-pushers," who would simply load and unload the automatic machinery. The intention is the important thing here. If, with hindsight, NC seems to have required organizational changes in the factory, changes that enhanced managerial control, it is because the technology was chosen, in part for just that purpose. This becomes even more clear when one looks at how the new technology was deployed.

## CHOICE IN DEPLOYMENT: MANAGERIAL INTENTIONS

There is no question but that management saw in NC the potential to enhance their authority over production and seized upon it, despite questionable cost effectiveness.[23] Machine tool builders and control manufacturers, of course, also promoted their wares along these lines; well attuned to the needs of their customers, they promised an end to traditional managerial problems. Thus the president of the Landis Machine Company, in a trade journal article entitled "How Can New Machines Cut Costs?" stressed that "with modern automatic controls, the production pace is set by the machine, not by the operator."[24] The advertising copy of the MOOG Machine Company of Buffalo, New York, similarly described how their new machining center "has allowed management to plan and schedule jobs more effectively," while pointing out, benevolently, that "operators are no longer faced with making critical production decisions."[25]

Machine tool manufacturers peddled their wares and the trade journals echoed their pitch.[26] Initially, potential customers believed the hype; they very much wanted to. Earl Lundgren, a sociologist, conducted surveys of user plants in the 1960s and concluded that "the prime interest in each subject company was the transfer of as much planning and control from the shop to the office as possible; . . . there was little doubt in all cases that management fully intended to transfer as much planning from the shop floor to the staff offices [methods enginners and programmers] as possible." Moreover, management believed that "under numerical control the operator is no longer required to take part in planning activities."[27]

In my own survey in 1978 of twenty-five plants in the Midwest and New England—including manufacturers of machine tools, farm implements, heavy construction equipment, jet engines and aircraft parts, and specialized industrial machinery—I observed the same phenomenon. Everywhere, management initially believed in the promises of NC promoters and attempted to remove all decision-making from the floor and assign unskilled people to NC machines, to substitute "tape-time" for problematic time studies to set base rates for piecework and measure output quotas, to tighten up authority by concentrating all mental activity in the office, and otherwise to extend detail control over all aspects of the production process.

This is not to say, however, that I drew the same conclusions that Lundgren did in his earlier survey. Characteristically for an industrial sociologist, he viewed such changes as *requirements* of the new technology whereas, in reality, they reflected simply the *possibilities* of the technology that were "seized upon," to use Harry Braverman's phrase, by management to realize particular objectives, social as well as technical. There is nothing inherent in NC technology, for example, that makes it *necessary* to assign programming and machine tending to different people (that is, to management and workers, respectively): the technology merely makes it *possible*. Management philosophy and motives alone make it necessary that the technology be deployed in this way, and this is another form of necessity entirely, namely, the (to their minds, forced) social choices of the powerful.

One illustration of managerial choice in machine deployment is provided by the experience of a large manufacturing firm near Boston. In 1968, owing to low worker morale, turnover, absenteeism, and the general unreliability of programming and machinery, the company faced what it termed a "bottleneck" in its NC lathe section. Plant managers were frantic to figure out a way to achieve the expected output from this expensive equipment. In that prosperous and reform-minded period they decided upon a job enlargement/enrichment experiment wherein machine operators would be organized into groups and their individual tasks would be extended. Although it was the hope of the company that such a reorganization would boost the morale of the men on the floor and motivate them to "optimize the utilization" of the machinery, the union was at first reluctant to cooperate, fearing a speed-up. The company was thus hard-pressed to secure union support for their program and instituted a bonus for all participants. At one of the earliest meetings between management and union representatives on the new program, the company spokesman for the plan began his discussion of the job-enlargement issue with the question (and thinly veiled threat), "Should we make the hourly people button-pushers or responsible people?" (Given the new technology, management believed it now had the choice.[28])

A second illustration of the managerial imperative behind technological determinism is provided in an interview I had with shop managers of a plant in Connecticut. Here, as elsewhere, much of the NC programming is relatively simple—the technology is used to machine simple parts formerly produced on conventional machinery (as opposed to complex three- to five-axis contour cutting such as of airfoils, etc.). Observing this, I asked the two men why the operators couldn't do their own programming. At first, they dismissed the suggestion as ridiculous, arguing that the operators would have to know how to set feeds and speeds, that is, be "industrial engineers." I countered this by pointing out that the same people probably set the feeds and speeds on conventional machinery, routinely making adjustments on the process sheet provided by the methods engineers in order to make out. They nodded. Then they said that the operators could not understand the programming language. This time I pointed out that the operators could often be seen reading the mylar tape—twice-removed information describing the machining being done —in order to know what was coming (especially to anticipate programming errors that could mess things up). Again, they nodded. Finally, they looked at each other and smiled, and one of them leaned over and confided, "we don't want them to." Here is the reality behind technological determinism.[29]

## REALITY ON THE SHOP FLOOR

In the discussions above on choice in design and deployment, we have endeavored to show why it is a mistake to view technological development as an autonomous or unilinear process. The evolution of any technology reflects the social relations that gave birth to it and follows from the human choices that inform it. But, as we argued at the outset, it would be an error to assume that we can now simply substitute one form of determinism for another, to suppose that, in having exposed the choices, we can now simply deduce the rest of reality (rather than just describe a part of it). For it would be as much a serious flaw in reasoning to extrapolate reality from the intentions that underlie the technology[30] as from the technology itself. Intentions are never so automatically realized, no more than desire is identical to satisfaction.

"In the conflict between employer and employed," John G. Brooks observed in 1903, "the 'storm center' is largely at this point where science and invention are applied to industry."[31] It is here, in the storm center, that the reality of NC is hammered out; it is here, in the storm center, where those who choose the technology finally come face to face with those who do not. It is their first confrontation with what philosophers call "other minds."

The introduction of NC control machinery has not been altogether uneventful, especially in plants where the machinists' union (such as the International Association of Machinists, the United Auto Workers, the United Electrical Workers, or the International Union of Electrical Workers) have had a long history. Work stoppages and strikes over rates for the new machinery were common in the 1960s. At General Electric, for example, there were strikes at several plants and one during the winter of 1965 shut down the entire Lynn, Massachusetts, plant for a month. Here we will focus less upon these overt expressions of conflict than upon more subtle indications that management dreams have tended to remain dreams: the use of "tape time" to replace time-studies; the deskilling of machine operators; and the question of control over production.

Early dreams of the use of tape time to set base rates and determine output proved fanciful. The machines could not produce parts to specifications without the repeated manual intervention of the operator, in the early machines to make tool offset adjustments and to correct for program errors and even now to insure a good finish to tolerance (especially with rough castings). At one large factory in New England, for example, where NC has been in use for nearly a quarter of a century, the machines are often used almost like manual machines. There is, in reality, a spectrum of manual intervention requirements depending upon the machine, the product, and the like, but the mythology that the tape ran the machine without the need for people was dispelled pretty early on—and along with it went the hope of using the tape to measure performance.

The deskilling of machine operators has, on the whole, not even taken place, for two reasons. First, as was mentioned, the assigning of labor grades and thus rates for the new machinery was, and is, a hotly contested issue, yet to be finally resolved one way or the other. Second (and the reason why skill levels on numerical control equipment are as high in nonunion shops as in union shops), any determination of skill requirements must take into account the actual degree of automaticity of the machinery and, as we have seen, this was not up to expectations. That is, management has had to have people on their machines who know what they are doing simply because the machines do *not* run by themselves, and they are very expensive. While it is true that many manufacturers initially tried to use unskilled people on the new equipment, they rather quickly saw their error and upgraded the classification (although in some places they merely gave the skilled operators a premium while retaining the lower formal classification, presumably in the hope that some day the skill requirements would actually drop to match the classification). It has been argued, moreover, that, in some ways, NC requires greater skill—as was suggested by the United Electical Workers in their UE *Guide to Automation* of 1960—because of the need to oversee the complex and rapid machining of parts, to constantly watch for "nonevents." Whether this is true or not is certainly debatable. One thing is not, though. The intelligence of production in machine shops has not yet been built into the machine or taken off the floor.

And this brings us, once again, to the question of control. In theory, the programmer prepares the tape (and thus sets feeds and speeds, thereby determining the rate of production), proofs it out on the machine, and then turns the show over to the operator who from then on simply presses start and stop buttons and loads and unloads the machine (using standard fixtures). This rarely happens in reality as was pointed out above. Machining to tolerances more often than not requires close attention to the details of the operation and frequent manual interventions through manual feed and speed overrides. This aspect of the technology, of course, reintroduces the control problem for management. Just as in the conventional shop, where operators are able to modify the settings specified on the work sheet (prepared by the methods engineer) in order to restrict output or otherwise "make out" (by running the machine harder), so in the NC shop, the operators are able to adjust feeds and speeds, for similar purposes.

Thus, if you walk into a shop you will often find feedrate override dials set uniformly at, say, 70 percent or 80 percent of tape-determined feedrate. In some places, this is called the "70 percent syndrome"; everywhere it is known as pacing, the collective restriction of output on the floor. To combat it, management sometimes programs the machines at 130 percent; sometimes they actually lock the overrides altogether to keep the operators out of the "planning process." But this, of course, gets management into serious trouble since interventions are required in many cases to get parts out the door.

To what extent the considerable amount of human intervention required for machining (and repairs) is attributable to the inherent unreliability of the technology itself is hard to assess. But it is certainly true that the technology develops shortcomings once it is placed on the shop floor, whether they were there in the original designs or not. Machines often do not do the job they are supposed to, and downtime is still excessive. Whether this is due to operator "adjustments" (or failures to adjust) or technical defects is hard to determine, but sabotage is an acknowledged problem. "I don't care how many computers you have they'll still have a thousand ways to beat you," lamented one manager in a Connecticut plant. "When you put a guy on an NC machine, he gets tempermental," another manager in Rhode Island complained. "And then, through a process of osmosis, the machine gets temperamental."

On the shop floor, it is not only the choices of management that have effects. The same antagonistic social relations that, in their reflection in the minds of designers, gave issue to the new technology, now subvert it in reality. This contradiction of capitalist production, of a Divided Humanity, presents itself most clearly to management as a problem of "worker motivation," and management's acceptance of this challenge is its own tacit acknowledgment that it does not have control over production, that it is still dependent upon the work force to turn a profit.

Thus, in evaluating the work of those whose intentions to wrest control over production from the work force informed the design and deployment of NC, we must take into account an article written by two industrial engineers in 1971. Appearing in *The Manufacturing, Engineering and Management Journal*, it was entitled "A Case for Wage Incentives in the NC Age." It makes it quite clear that the contradiction of capitalist production has not been eclipsed—computers or no computers.

Under automation, it is argued, the machine basically controls the manufacturing cycle, and therefore, the worker's role diminishes in importance. The fallacy in this reasoning is that if the operator malingers or fails to service the machine for a variety of reasons, both utilization and subsequent return on investment suffer drastically.

Basic premises underlying the design and development of NC machines aim at providing the capability of machining configurations beyond the scope of conventional machines. Additionally, they "deskill" the operator. Surprisingly, however, the human element continues to be a major factor in the realization of optimum utilization or yield of these machines. This poses a continuing problem for management, because a maximum level of utilization is necessary to assure a satisfactory return on investment.[32]

This same contradiction, faced by every capitalist since the emergence of the capitalist mode of production, was more succinctly, if inadvertently, expressed by another plant manager in Connecticut. With a colleague chiming in, he proudly described the elaborate procedure they had developed whereby every production change, even the most minor, had to be okayed by an industrial engineer. "We want absolutely no decisions made on the floor," he insisted; no operator was to make any change from the process sheets without the written authorization of a supervisor. A moment later, however, looking out onto the floor from his glass-enclosed office, he reflected upon the reliability of the machinery and the expense of parts and equipment and emphasized, with equal conviction, that "we need guys out there who can think."

## CONCLUSION: LABOR'S CHALLENGE REVISITED

We have here tried to get beyond the ideology of technological determinism by demystifying the development of a particular technology. The purpose of this exercise, as was indicated at the outset, was to regain confidence in the fact that technology consists of a range of possibilities; if certain human choices guided the course of its development in the past, other choices could steer it in the future. This done, we must turn again to the remaining two tasks: to study the possibilities and clarify new choices and to struggle to get in the position to make them.

It is time, it is imperative, that the labor movement as a whole begin to assume the responsibility for the design and deployment of technology—the organization of our shops, the structure of our jobs, the shape of our lives. For only by becoming self-reliant and assuming this responsibility can we regain the confidence to secure the power to exercise it. This challenge, now faced by all unions throughout industry (due, in part, to the homogenizing effect of management-designed automation, which diminishes the differences between industries and between shops and offices) was clearly, if rather modestly, summarized by an NC machine tool operator in a large shop in Massachusetts:

The introduction of automation means that our skills are being downgraded and instead of having the prospect of moving up to a more interesting job we now have the prospect of either unemployment or a dead-end job. [But] there are alternatives that unions can explore. We have to establish the position that the fruits of technological change can be divided up—some to the workers, not all to the management as is the case today. We must demand that the machinist rise with the complexity of the machine. Thus, rather than dividing his job up, the machinist should be trained to program and repair his new equipment—a task well within the grasp of most people in the industry.

Demands such as this strike at the heart of most management prerogative clauses which are in many collective bargaining contracts. Thus, to deal with automation effectively, one has to strike at another prime ingredient of business unionism: the idea of "let the management run the business." The introduction of NC equipment makes it imperative that we fight such ideas.[33]

This, in essence, is the challenge. Overt political and covert shop-floor resistance to the choices of management, which exploit the contradictions inherent in the capitalist mode of production, must be encouraged and enlarged; but these are not in themselves sufficient actions, given the current desperate corporate drive to rationalize industry and fight organized labor. It is no longer enough merely to respond to new methods nor even to anticipate the changes that are "coming down." The goal must be to gain control of, and thereafter redirect, the social process of technological development itself. And this end, of course, requires—as it contributes to—a larger transformation of the social relations of production and, thus, the eclipse of the capitalist system as a whole.

## NOTES

1. This assumption is not always correct. See, for example, Stephen Marglin, "What Do Bosses Do? The Origins and Functions of Hierarchy in Capitalist Production," and Katherine Stone, "The Origins of Job Structures in the Steel Industry," *The Review of Radical Political Economy* 6 (Summer 1974).

2. David F. Noble, *America by Design: Science, Technology and the Rise of Corporate Capitalism* (New York: Alfred A. Knopf, 1977).

3. Seymour Melman, "The Impact of Economics on Technology," *Journal of Economic Issues* 9, no. 1 (March 1975): 71.

4. It perhaps ought to be pointed out that it is a mistake to try to eclipse technological determinism by simply substituting for it another mechanical, say economic, determinism. Market factors are critical ingredients in the process of technological development, but they are not the only ones, nor, at times, even the most important ones. Sweeping economic explanations for technical advance, however logically consistent, provide only a framework for historical analysis, not a substitute for it. This history, like any other, is a complex of scientific, technical, sociological, economic, political, ideological, and cultural threads, all of which give direction to it. Thus we see the role of the government often rendering market considerations beside the point, fascination with remote control on the part of designers and their sponsors outweighing simple cost considerations, and a fetish for order, predictability, continuous-flow, power, or mathematical

elegance having more to do with the outcome than other, more practical economic concerns. In short, here the principle of parsimony can be too avidly applied.

5. Kark Marx, *Capital* (Moscow: Foreign Languages Press, 1959), 1:200.

6. The discussion here is restricted to the first few generations of NC (tape control); it does not include later developments such as Computer Numerical Control (CNC), Direct Numerical Control (DNC) or Flexible Manufacturing Systems (FMS), or any other aspects of computer Aided Design/Computer Aided Manufacture (CAD/CAM). These are subjects for another article.

7. U.S., Congress, Senate, Hearing before the Subcommittee on Science and Technology of the Select Committee on Small Business, *Introduction to Numerical Control and Its Impact on Small Business,* "Statement of Kenneth Stephanz," 92nd Cong., 1st sess., June 24, 1971, p. 76.

8. Ibid., letter from James Childs, p. 87.

9. Ibid. See statements of John C. Williams, Edward Miller, and Senator David Gambrell. For more information about the diffusion of NC tools, see Clifford Fawcett, "Factors and Issues in the Survival and Growth of the U.S. Machine Tool Industry" (Ph.D. diss., George Washington University, 1976); Jacob Sonny, "Technological Change in the U.S. Machine Tool Industry, 1947–1966" (Ph.D. diss., New School for Social Research, 1971); A. Romeo, "Interindustry Differences in the Diffusion of Innovations" (Ph.D. diss., University of Pennsylvania, 1973); "1976 American Machinist Inventory of Metalworking Equipment," *American Machinist,* December 1976; S. Kurlat, "The Diffusion of NC Machine Tools," Technical Memorandum, EIKONIX Corporation, April 1977; and Jack Rosenberg, "A History of Numerical Control, 1949–1973: The Technical Development, Transfer to Industry, and Assimilation," unpublished manuscript, October 1973.

10. Small Business Administration, "The Impact of NC on Small Business," (Washington, D.C.: Government Printing Office, 1971), p. 129. On organizational impacts of NC, see: Ervin M. Birt, "Organizational and Behavioral Aspects of NC Machine Tool Innovation" (M.S. thesis, Course XV, MIT, 1959); James J. Childs, "Organization of a Numerical Control Operation," *Mechanical Engineering* (May 1959): 61; and Earl F. Lundgren, "Effects of NC on Organizational Structure," *Automation* 76 (January 1969): 44–47.

11. Lundgren, "Effects of NC on Organizational Structure." In his study, Lundgren observed that, among other things, "there was little doubt in all cases that management fully intended to transfer as much planning from the shop floor to the staff offices as possible" and that "under NC the operator is no longer required to take part in planning activities." He concluded that therefore "a change in organization structure to define and formalize the relationships required by the NC technology is strongly indicated." See also L. K. Williams and C. B. Williams, "Impact of NC Equipment on Factory Organization," *California Management Review* 7 (Winter 1964): 25–34; R. C. Brewer, "Organizational and Economic Aspects of NC," *Engineer's Digest* 146 (August 1965): 103; William H. Bentley, "Management Aspects of NC," *Automation* 7 (October 1960): 64–70; Earl Lundgren and M. H. Sageger, "Impact of NC on First Line Supervision," *Personnel Journal* 46 (December 1967): 715.

12. This survey included primarily large- and medium-sized plants in the Midwest and New England of manufacturers of machine tools, farm implements, heavy construction equipment, jet engines, aircraft parts, and specialized industrial machinery.

13. On this point, see the letter from James Childs in *Introduction to Numerical Control and Its Impact on Small Business,* p. 87.

14. See, for example, Harry Braverman's discussion of the social possibilities of NC in his *Labor and Monopoly Capital* (New York: Monthly Review Press, 1974), p. 199.

15. The use of jigs and fixtures in metalworking date back to the early nineteenth century and were the heart of interchangeable parts manufacture, as Merritt Roe Smith has shown in *Harpers Ferry Armory and the New Technology* (Ithaca, N.Y.: Cornell University Press, 1976). But it was not until much later, around the turn of the century, that the "toolmaker" as such became a specialist, distinguished from machinists. The new function was a product of scientific management, which aimed to shift the locus of skill, and control, from the production floor,

and the operators, to the toolroom, as a matter of basic shop reorganization. But however much the new tools allowed management to employ less skilled, and thus cheaper, machine operators, they were nevertheless very expensive to manufacture and store, and they lent to manufacture a heavy burden of inflexibility—shortcomings that one Taylorite, Sterling Bunnell, warned about as early as 1914 (cited in David Montgomery, *Fall of the House of Labor: The Workplace, the State, and American Labor Activism* (Cambridge University Press, 1989). The cost savings that resulted from the use of cheaper labor were thus offset by the expense of tooling. Numerical control, as we will see, was developed, in part, to eliminate the costs and inflexibility of jigs and fixtures and, equally important, to take skill, and the control it implied, off the floor altogether. Here again, however, the expense of the solution was equal to or greater than the problem. It is interesting to note that in both cases, jigs and fixtures and numerical control, where very expensive new technologies were introduced to make it possible to hire cheaper labor, the tab for the conversion was picked up by the state, from the Ordnance Department in the early nineteenth century, to the Departments of the Army and Navy in World War I, to the Air Force in the second half of the twentieth century.

16. The discussion of the record-playback technology is based upon extensive interviews and correspondence with the engineers who participated in the projects at General Electric (Schenectady) and Gisholt (Madison, Wisconsin). For a brief description of the G.E. technology, see Lawrence R. Peaslee, "Tape-Controlled Machines," *Electrical Manufacturing Magazine*, November 1953, pp. 102–8. Key patents for the G.E. system include Orrin W. Livingston, "Record-Reproduce Programming Control System for Electric Motors," patent no. 2,755,422 (July 17, 1956); Lawrence R. Peaslee, "Programming Control System," patent no. 2,937,365 (May 17, 1960); and Lowell L. Holmes, "Magnetic Tape Recording Device," patent no. 2,755,160 (July 17, 1956). Key patents for the Gisholt system: Leif Eric de Neergaard, Frederic W. Olmstead, and Hans Trechsel, "Control System for Machine Tools Utilizing Magnetic Recording," patent no. 3,296,606 (January 3, 1967), and Leif Eric de Neegard, "Method and Means for Recording and Reproducing Displacements," patent no. 2,628,539 (February 17, 1953). For a post-NC view of the advantage of record-playback control, see Veljko Milenkovic, "Single-Channel Programmed Tape Motor Control for Machine Tools," patent no. 3,241,020 (March 15, 1966). Milenkovic's patent was used by the American Machine and Foundry Company (AMF) in the development of their "Versatran" robot. Industrial robots, like "unimates," are record-playback controlled.

17. John Diebold, *Automation* (New York: Van Nostrand, 1952), p. 88.

18. Kurt Vonnegut, *Player Piano* (New York: Delacorte Press), 1952. Kurt Vonnegut, letter to author, February 19, 1977.

19. This is why the Numerical Control Society's award given for significant advancements in the technology is called the Jacquard Award. In 1970, this award went to the developers of the first NC machine at MIT. See "How It All Began," *Metalworking Economics*, June 1970, p. 43. For general historical discussion of such automation, see Diebold, *Automation*; James R. Bright, "The Development of Automation," in *Technology in Western Civilization*, Kranzberg and Pursell (eds.), vol. 2, chap. 41; Braverman's chapter on "Machinery," in *Labor and Monopoly Capital*; and Ben Seligman, *Most Notorious Victory: Man in an Age of Automation* (Glencoe, Ill.: The Free Press, 1966), esp. pp. 122–27. For a more detailed history of NC, see Donald P. Hunt, "The Evolution of a Machine Tool Control System and Succeeding Developments" (M.S. thesis, course XV, MIT, 1959) and "A Numerically Controlled Milling Machine: Final Report to the U.S. Air Force in Construction and Initial Operation" (Servomechanisms Laboratory, MIT, July 30, 1952), pt. 1.

20. No effort will be made here to trace the early history of NC, which includes the work of Emanuel Scheyer, Max Schenker, Eric de Neegaard, and Fred Cunningham, among many others. Parsons is generally credited with having initiated the first successful hardware project, the one that, with the help of the Air Force, gave rise to the commerical development of NC.

21. Frank Lynn, Thomas Roseberry, and Victor Babich, "A History of Recent Technological Innovations," in *Technology and the American Economy*, ed. National Commission on Technology,

Automation, and Economic Progress (Washington, D.C.: Government Printing Office, 1966), vol. 2, *The Employment Impact of Technological Change*, app., p. 89.

22. Like most large companies that entered the computer age early, the aircraft firms were faced with a number of problems: first, how fully to utilize the computer (after payroll, then what?), and second, how to extract the information for data banks from the personnel who possessed it (whose jobs depended upon their access to or control over information). NC contributed to the solution of both problems: the use of APT absorbed about 50 percent of their computer capacity throughout the 1960s, and NC itself appeared to allow managers to circumvent shop floor personnel considerably.

23. The cost effectiveness of NC depends upon many factors, including training costs, programming costs, and computer costs, beyond mere time saved in actual chip-cutting or reduction in direct labor costs. The MIT staff who conducted the early studies on the economics of NC focused on the savings in cutting time and waxed eloquent about the new revolution. At the same time, however, they warned that the key to the economic viability of NC was a reduction in programming costs. Machine tool company salesmen were not disposed to emphasize these potential drawbacks, though, and numerous users went bankrupt because they believed what they were told. In the early days, however, most users were buffered against such tragedy by state subsidy. Today potential users are somewhat more cautious, and machine tool builders are more restrained in their advertising, tempering their promise of economic success with qualifiers about proper use, the right lot and batch size, sufficient training, and so on.

For the independent investigator, it is extremely difficult to assess the economic viability of such a technology. There are many reasons for this. First, the data are rarely available or accessible. Whatever the motivation—technical fascination, keeping up with competitors, and so on—the purchase of new capital equipment must be justified in economic terms. But justifications are not too difficult to come by if the item is desired enough by the right people. They are self-interested anticipations and thus usually optimistic ones. More importantly, firms rarely conduct postaudits on their purchases, to see if their justifications were warranted. Nobody wants to document his errors, and if the machinery is fixed in its foundation, that is where it will stay, whatever a postaudit reveals; you learn to live with it. The point here is that the economics of capital equipment is not nearly so tidy as economists would sometimes have us believe. The invisible hand has to do quite a bit of sweeping up after the fact.

If the data does exist, it is very difficult to get a hold of. Companies have a proprietary interest in the information and are wary about disclosing it for fear of revealing (and thus jeopardizing) their position vis-à-vis labor unions (wages), competitors (prices), and government (regulations and taxes). Moreover, the data, if it were accessible, is not all tabulated and in a drawer somewhere. It is distributed among departments, with separate budgets; and the costs of one are the hidden costs to the others. Also there is every reason to believe that the data that does exist is self-serving information provided by each operating unit to enhance its position in the firm. And, finally, there is the tricky question of how "viability" is defined in the first place. Sometimes, machines make money for a company whether they are used productively or not.

The purpose of this aside is to emphasize that "bottom line" explanations for complex historical developments, like the introduction of new capital equipment, are never in themselves sufficient, nor necessarily to be trusted. If a company wants to introduce something new, it must justify it in terms of making a profit. This is not to say, however, that profit making was its real motive or that a profit was ever made. In the case of automation, steps are taken less out of careful calculation than on the faith that it is always good to replace labor with capital, a faith kindled deep in the soul of manufacturing engineers and managers—as economist Michael Piore, for example, has shown. See his "The Impact of the Labor Market upon the Design and Selection of Productive Techniques within the Manufacturing Plant," *Quarterly Journal of Economics* 32 (1968). Thus, automation is driven forward, not simply by the profit motive, but by the ideology of automation itself, which reflects the social relations of production.

24. Grayson M. Stickell, "How Can New Machines Cut Costs?" *Tooling and Production*, August 1960, p. 61.

25. *MOOG Hydra-Point News*, Buffalo, New York, 1975.

26. Charles Weiner, former associate editor of *Tooling and Production Magazine* (one of the leading trade journals for the metalworking industry), authored several articles on numerical control in the early 1960s, one of which was based upon a "comprehensive survey of machine tool builders and control manufacturers." According to Weiner, all of his information for these articles came from the manufacturers themselves, and no effort was ever made to make an independent evaluation of NC for the readers of the magazine. Although the editors strove for credibility with production men in the metalworking industry, they were guided primarily, as are the editors of all controlled circulation magazines in the trade press, by the need to secure advertisements. Thus they tended to exaggerate the promise of a new technology, seconding the claims of advertisers, in order to appeal to a particular readership and, by so doing, to elicit further support from the advertisers of the new technology, the manufacturers themselves.

27. Lundgren, "Effects of NC on Organizational Structure."

28. This is not to say that the new technology actually enabled management to reduce people to button-pushers, a centuries-old dream of managers everywhere, and still get quality production out the door; it didn't. The point here is that, with the advent of NC, management began in earnest to think about (and make decisions about) redesigning jobs and reorganizing the production process on the assumption that the new technology gave them this capability.

29. This reality can be seen even more clearly in the case of the latest generation of NC machines, which come equipped with a small computer (hence the name: computer numerical control, CNC). With these machines, it has become possible to store programs right at the machine; more important, it is now possible to edit programs (or create them from scratch) on the shop floor by simply punching information into storage numerically (reminiscent of the old Gisholt Factrol system) or by moving the machine manually to the desired position and feeding the information into storage (a digitized version of record playback). In short, these new machines, created to overcome the programming problems of NC, are ideal for shop floor and operator control over the whole process. However, they are almost never used in this way. It is characteristic of the larger metalworking shops that operators are not permitted to edit the programs, much less to create new ones themselves. Management usually defends this policy by arguing that too many cooks spoil the stew.

30. This is an error that Harry Braverman tended to make in his path-breaking *Labor and Monopoly Capital*. As a result, the potential for class struggle was minimized. One is left merely with a juggernaut on the one side and impotence and despair on the other.

31. Brooks quoted by David Montgomery, *The Fall of the House of Labor* (see note 15), chap. 4, p. 1.

32. Martin R. Doring and Raymond C. Salling, "A Case for Wage Incentives in the NC Age," *Manufacturing Engineering and Management* 66, no. 6 (1971): 31.

33. Frank Emspak, "Crisis and Austerity in the Seventies," unpublished manuscript.

# Part Six
# Technology and Politics

# Introduction

If we are now convinced that technology is neither neutral nor ultimately autonomous, serious political, and moral, questions are posed for our consideration—not simply about the use of technology but about its design. Thus, the fundamental questions are not about technology per se, but about values. To cast the issue as an argument between those who are pro-technology and those who are anti-technology is to misdirect our attention from the basic dispute. Do you favor the existing sociopolitical constitution of society or do you think some fundamental changes ought to be made? As we shall see, our considered moral judgments about what constitutes a just society may be contradicted by the implicit political structure of modern technology, which hides under the cloak of inevitable "progress."

Norman Balabanian would agree with Noble that there is no technological determinism. What he calls for is a "paradigm shift" in the way we think about technology, that is, a radical change in our fundamental world view. It does not occur to us to question the motto of the 1933 World's Fair, "Science Finds—Industry Applies—Man Conforms." This traditional world view, according to Balabanian, accepts uncritically a whole cluster of assumptions about the nature of man in a capitalistic-technological society that simply will not fit the facts of experience. As we have seen, Ellul would think this motto correctly, and tragically, describes our situation. The "pro-technologists" we have read in Part 4 would also endorse this view, but be quite happy with this state of affairs. Both reactions are based upon a serious misunderstanding. There is no technological imperative that operates independently of human motives.

Balabanian hastens to add, however, that to think of "human" motives, to think of man in the abstract, papers over important moral distinctions, significant questions of distributive justice. Who wins and who loses from this technology? This new technology satisfies some persons, but possibly at the expense of others. The free choice of some may restrict others' choices. Contemporary technology "is intimately tied to matters of political power and social control . . . . "

We cannot cope with the serious crises we face by tinkering with technology. What is required is the democratization of the entire social order, a new paradigm. *Contra* Florman, Balabian argues this does not require a change in human nature, for Florman's view of man as a greedy, self-seeking egoist is merely a reflection of the capitalist ideology. We need to appeal to the best in persons, not the worst. The new paradigm calls for "a harmonious technology in a harmonious society . . . Science Discovers—Humanity Decides—Technology Conforms."

Jonathan Kwitny documents the case mentioned by Balabian to support his claim that new technologies are neither the inevitable next step in an autonomous process of technological development, nor simply the consequence of the free choice of consumers. Streetcars in many of our cities were not replaced by automobiles due not to a technological imperative but to a conspiracy on the part of large American corporations. What destroyed clean, efficient mass transit was good old-fashioned greed. This development was freely chosen by corporate managers and doubtless increased the freedom of large corporations, and their choice effectively eliminated significant choice for citizens. Consumers could choose what make of automobile to buy, but not whether to buy an automobile. Of course, consumers might have preferred private automobiles to mass transit in any case, but the point is that they were not given this choice.

Since the 1960s, people have increasingly demanded a voice in those decisions that affect their lives. However, the democratic control of modern, complex technology seems to require specialized scientific and technical knowledge that ordinary citizens simply do not have. So long as this esoteric knowledge was monopolized by vested interests, the people were essentially powerless. However, as scientists become involved in opposing specific developments, this monopoly of expertise is being broken.

What, as a matter of fact, is the political impact of expertise in current policy decisions? In addressing this question, Dorothy Nelkin follows the public controversy in two cases which she thinks are representative. Although there are differences in the details of these two cases, there are important similarities which can be generalized.

The authority of expert knowledge rests upon assumptions about scientific rationality. As we saw in Part 1, Schell claimed that pure science is guided by the structure of nature, not by any political motives on the part of the individual scientist. Thus, we believe that scientific knowledge is free from subjective value judgments, for it is publicly verified by a rigorous methodology. This seems to offer a way of depoliticizing public controversy; the "facts" speak for themselves. Rather than debate endlessly about what we ought to do, let's just look at the scientific "facts."

This model of scientific rationality is undermined, however, when the experts disagree. Nelkin is not claiming that there is no scientific knowledge, but in the cases she follows it is clear that there are a plethora of facts from which experts may select, as well as considerable uncertainty about what the facts themselves are. In addition, as Balabian has argued, the data always require interpretation. Opposing technical advice tends to cancel out the importance of such "knowledge," and reduces the authority of the experts.

Nelkin concludes that technical expertise is used by the partisan in a controversy to support what is at bottom a political position. Experts, once they become involved in a policy issue, are "just like everybody else"; they too have philosophical and ethical commitments. Although technical expertise can clarify, as well as confuse, the issues, policy decisions are essentially political.

Langdon Winner argues that although many political theorists in the history of Western thought have employed technological analogies, they thought the technological enterprise was completely separate from politics. If there was any relationship, it was from *technē* to *politeia*. That is, the construction of technology served as a model for the construction of political constitutions, for a "science" of politics. It did not occur to anyone until after the Industrial Revolution that *technē* might be *politeia*.

On Winner's view, modern technology has evolved without conscious political control. In this sense technology since the Industrial Revolution has tended to develop autonomously. However, we should note that Winner does not attribute a will to technology nor is he claiming that persons and their motives are not involved in this process. Further, while there are causes for this process, these are not to be understood deterministically. It could have been otherwise. What allows technology to develop without significant political control is what Winner has called elsewhere "somnabulism." We were unaware, due in part to traditional political thinking that separates technology and politics, that technology might incorporate a political structure. Although some of our founding fathers sounded the alarm, their warnings have been dismissed as mere romanticism.

Specific technologies have become interconnected to form in the modern world *"de facto* a constitution of a sociotechnological order." Winner thinks this state of affairs has come about not by design, but by the lack of conscious political awareness. The danger is that we now have an "authoritarian technics" that we would never knowingly vote into power. This "other constitution" may subvert our most cherished democratic values that are built into the political constitution. "Reverse adaptation" may give us *de facto* an inhumane, undemocratic society.

There is a growing awareness of the obvious hazards of some industrial technologies, but most attempts to control technology are superficial. If a technology is "efficient" and doesn't cause cancer, we give it the green light. What we refuse to recognize is that centralized systems of energy, for example, give us centralized systems of political power. Although efficiency and the price paid by the consumer is a factor, "perhaps we ought to ask whether or not that lowest cost design simply reproduces the large, centralized, uniform, automatic sociotechnical patterns that contribute to the ways people find themselves to be insignificant, not involved, powerless."

# 18

# Presumed Neutrality of Technology

## Norman Balabanian

Contemporary technological society is experiencing a profound multidimensional crisis. It was not always so. From at least the time of the Industrial Revolution in England, a general feeling of optimism pervaded Western society. It was commonly believed that the growth of scientific knowledge knew no limits, and that scientific knowledge could always be applied to the problems of society. Since science and technology were so successful in producing marvelous inventions, they could eventually solve any human problem.

This attitude was exemplified at the Chicago *Century of Progress* World's Fair in 1933. The motto of the Fair was: *Science Finds—Industry Applies— Man Conforms.* The guidebook to the Fair amplified further: "Science discovers, genius invents, industry applies, and man adapts himself, or is molded by, new things . . . . Individuals, groups, entire races of men fall into step with science and technology."

Such sentiments were not expressed in sorrow, but in obvious satisfaction. The irony that human beings should bend willingly to the dictates of a technological imperative, when for ages they have struggled to be free of human tyrants, seemed to escape the "happy technologists" of that day. A similar outlook survives among technological optimists of today, typified by Simon Ramo in *Century of Mismatch:*

From *Society* (March/April 1980). Copyright © 1980 by Transaction Periodicals Consortium, Rutgers University. Reprinted by permission.

> We must now plan on sharing the earth with machines . . . . But much more
> important is that we share a way of life with them . . . . We become partners.
> The machines require for their optimum performance, certain patterns of society.
> We too have preferred arrangements. But we want what the machines can furnish,
> and so we must compromise. We must alter the rules of society so that we and
> they can be compatible.[1]

There is no "compromise" here; it is not that the machine will be constructed
to be compatible with human processes, but that humanity must conform to
the machine and take on the machine's way of life.

For some time now, and at an increasingly rapid pace, many people have
begun to realize that the benefits flowing from science and technology to contemporary society have been purchased at a very high price. The social problems
associated with science and technology, which point up the nature of the crisis,
are well known. A brief, nonexhaustive taxonomy of crisis-level problems includes:

- *Environmental:* pollution, resource depletion, excess population;

- *Medical/Health:* dangers to health and safety from industrial production processes and from industrial products;

- *Psychological/Emotional:* substitution of machine values for human
  values; transformation of the nature of work from craftsmanship to
  meaninglessness, leading to worker alienation; a feeling of citizen powerlessness in the face of a complexity said to be understandable only
  by an expert elite, and thus, alienation from politics; social malaise exhibited in symptoms of increasing crime, senseless vandalism, anxiety,
  disharmony and tension, apathy and loss of a feeling of community;

- *Military:* potential nuclear annihilation through MAD (Mutual Assured
  Deterrence);

- *Social:* increasing centralization, bureaucratization, authoritarianism; diminishing real returns on immense capital requirements.

What do commentators mean when they use the term *technology?* The first
image conjured by the term is a machine, a physical object. This is an inadequate conception; like the term *society, technology* is an abstract concept. Society is not simply a collection of people but subsumes the interrelationships
among them. In the same way, technology is not simply a collection of machines but encompasses relationships among them and their uses. Tools, looms,
x-ray machines, nuclear reactors, refrigerators, and automobiles are all elements of technology. But if such objects are all that are comprehended by
the term *technology,* the imagination is impoverished indeed. Just as a single
word, or collection of words, cannot adequately represent the rich texture of
language, so also a single machine, or collection of machines, cannot adequately represent contemporary technology.

There are two serious omissions from the simple-minded notion of technology. One of these is the concept of *know-how*. Accumulated knowledge is as much a part of technology as a machine. In the view of Harvey Brooks, technology is nothing but certain kinds of know-how; technology "is not hardware but knowledge, including the knowledge not only of how to fabricate hardware to predetermined specifications and functions, but also of how to design administrative processes and organizations to carry out specified functions, and to influence human behavior toward specified ends."[2]

A more important omission is the concept of organization, of *system:* the organized structures; the mechanisms of management and control; the processes of production; the specific designs of the overall organizations and systems within which the machines are embedded; the linkages that tie together the physical objects—the "hardware"—with the social institutions—the software." Technology is not just the computer, for example, but large-scale computer networks linked through telecommunications systems; operating and managing sytems; data banks, the knowledge and programs to manipulate them, and the power implicit in their control. Any analysis of contemporary technological society which fails to understand this is deeply flawed.

## MODELS AND PREMISES

In going about their everyday lives, people carry in their heads models or paradigms of what the world is like, what society is like. Walter Lippmann noted that individuals create for themselves a *pseudoenvironment,* an internal representation of the world, built up over a lifetime. People's perceptions of events are determined by the images, the preconceptions, the premises that underlie this pseudoenvironment. Most people tend not to question these preconceptions, even when the consequences of acting in accordance with their images of reality lead to anomalies that the paradigm cannot reconcile.

In science, when such anomalies develop, creative thinkers question the old paradigm and its premises and develop a new image of the world based on a new way of looking at things. For example, Newtonian mechanics gave way to relativistic mechanics; the economic system of mercantilism of the fifteenth and sixteenth centuries gave way to the classical capitalist economic system of the eighteenth and nineteenth centuries, which in turn has given way to the neoclassical and Keynesian economic systems. The Keynesian analysis evolved because the world depression of the 1930s was a traumatic anomaly that the previous paradigm could not explain.

In everyday life, on another level, many people are aware of the anomalies between the rhetorically-cultivated presuppositions of the social system and the adverse effects of the realities they experience on the receiving end. Such people seriously question the premises on which the social system is founded; and sometimes this questioning leads to a violent "paradigm shift"—through revolution. But, more often than not, their questioning is "contained." Historically, whenever a paradigm shift has been necessary (in science or social structure) it has been resisted by those with an interest in the old paradigm (intellectual, emotional, or financial). It is difficult for people who have invested a lifetime in the service of a particular world view to switch to a different outlook. Even if they intellectually understand the need for it, their previous life leaves them unprepared to carry on comfortably in the new paradigm.

Contemporary technological society is now facing anomalies which the social and economic preconceptions cannot explain. These preconceptions are built into the social structure and culture. But reality cries out for a paradigm shift. It is essential to identify and critically examine the premises—sometimes explicit, but often hidden—that undergird the inadequate contemporary model. Some of the major premises are:

- *Self-Seeking Values:* The preferred behavior mode for human beings is pursuit of one's own self-interest. The foundation of the capitalist ethos is that such self-seeking behavior will lead to social good through the operation of an "invisible hand."

- *Elastic Wants:* Human wants are infinitely elastic; they expand without limit. It is necessary to have continual economic growth in order to satisfy them.

- *Man's Domination of Nature:* The physical world is there for man to subdue, conquer, dominate, subjugate, and exploit. By scientific knowledge, said Descartes, "We may be able to make ourselves masters and possessors of nature."

- *Neutrality of Technology:* Technology is morally and politically neutral; it is a mere tool which can be used for good or evil. If it is not used properly, man is to blame.

- *Freedom of Choice:* Individuals in our free market system have free choice. The root cause of such ills as wasteful consumption, urban congestion, pollution, and the design of inappropriate products lies in the free choice exercised by autonomous individuals.

Each of these undergirding pillars fails to withstand critical examination. They must all be rejected if transformation to a humane society is a goal. The first three refer to the presumed nature of human beings. Although I will devote some brief thoughts to them, the bulk of my analysis will be reserved for the last two.

The premise or assertion that self-seeking behavior is the preferred mode for humans tends to encourage an aggressive, contentious, noncooperative spirit; it cultivates self-aggrandizement, greed, and envy—looking out for Number One at the expense of the community. Its proponents say this is human nature and cannot be changed. The social structure fostered by this outlook is hierarchical, with individuals engaged in a scramble for status on the ladder of success, elbowing their lonely way to the top.

## HUMAN NATURE

The capitalist culture and social system require individuals to act in a self-centered, contentious manner. The proper operation of the system *demands* it. How convenient, then, to ascribe this attitude to basic human nature! Writing in 1930, John Maynard Keynes said: "For at least another hundred years we must pretend to ourselves and to everyone that fair is foul and foul is fair; for foul is useful and fair is not. Avarice and usury and precaution must be our gods."[3] Keynes thought that self-seeking should be encouraged because it was useful to the operation of the capitalist system. But he at least recognized that it was not laudable, and that you had to work at it to make avarice and greed appear as gods.

Is the greedy, status-seeking pursuit of self-interest a consequence of unalterable human nature? Demonstrating that it is not merely requires finding counterexamples. Have humans ever acted selflessly? If we could find any such cases (and we need only look to ordinary people in common situations to find many counterexamples) we would have to conclude that the proposition that self-seeking is unalterable human nature is, at the least, not proved. With a bit of further thought, we would have to say that some humans act selflessly, others selfishly; that any human sometimes acts one way, sometimes the other; that individuals often have conflicts within themselves as to whether they should respond to a given situation in a self-seeking manner or in a cooperative, communitarian manner. For each example of greedy, self-centered human behavior one can find an example of altruistic, other-directed, cooperative behavior. Without the cooperative and symbiotic working together of its millions of cells, the human body itself could not function. Far from being by nature selfish, humans can just as validly be assumed to be cooperative by nature. How they actually behave in given situations depends on their socialization, on the reinforcements they obtain for their behavior. If the culture, the social order, continually reinforces them for self-seeking behavior, for personal aggrandizement, the chances are they will act this way more often than not. An outside observer would then notice that most people, most of the time, behave in noncooperative, self-seeking, status-enhancing ways. The observer who concludes that such behavior is intrinsic human nature would be a naïve observer, indeed.

Sometimes the happy technologist will unknowingly concede this. Samuel Florman writes: "Man, for all his angelic qualities, is self-seeking and competitive."[4] There it is: a concession that humans have noble impulses as well as base ones. The real question becomes: which qualities should be cultivated and reinforced? It is not a question of changing human nature to something it is not, but arranging conditions so that people can more often exhibit, and behave in accordance with, their "angelic qualities" rather than their base ones.

Economists postulate that human wants are infinite and insatiable —no sooner has one want been served than another is stimulated; humans are not capable of saying "enough." Florman states that "contemporary man is not content because he *wants* more than he can ever have."[5] This being the case, goes the argument, it is essential to maintain economic growth and increasing levels of consumption. The serious flaw in these assertions is the failure to distinguish between those wants that are basic and absolute needs—such as food, clothing, shelter, sex—which humans will experience independent of the condition of other human beings around them, and those which are social and relative. It is clearly untrue that basic human needs cannot be satisfied. The sight of food is not tempting to a person who has just finished dinner. It is also clear that some basic human needs are not at present satisfied for a substantial fraction of the world's population. To this extent, growth is still needed; not generalized growth, but increase in those areas of production intended to satisfy basic needs of the poor.

The second category of wants may well be insatiable; but what is their nature? These wants are experienced only in a relative sense, only if a feeling of superiority to others is achieved, only if vanity and status are enhanced. These wants require continual comparison with others and feverish activity in pursuit of inequality. They are not ennobling but base. In a sane society, their pursuit would be discouraged. But in a society dominated by the capitalist ethos, they are encouraged and cultivated through high-powered promotion and persuasion. Herbert Marcuse refers to such wants as "false needs,"[6] not to deny that they exist but as a judgment of their worthiness. The flourishing of false needs is a reflection not on human nature but on the values consciously cultivated by the social system. It makes no sense actively to promote ego trips, feelings of vanity and prestige, desires for superiority and status, and then to demand economic growth in order to satisfy these desires—at the expense of the crises now being faced. Furthermore, the effort of satisfying these wants is doomed to failure. If people's satisfactions depend almost entirley on status, ego gratification, and feelings of superiority, then increasing levels of consumption cannot yield increasing satisfaction to society as a whole. The superiority and enhanced status of some implies the inferiority and reduced status of others.

The idea that human beings should have dominion over the earth and all that it contains (now extended to the entire universe) was an early tenet of Western civilization; it even carried Biblical sanction. And mankind has not been reticent in carrying out this injunction. But there are at least two fallacies in this outlook.

The first relates to depletion. Clearly, intrusive human activities carried out over a period of time can have, and have had, devastating effects on nature and on human society. In the past, the wholesale destruction of forests, improper cultivation leading to soil erosion, and other similar activities have had major effects on the present conditions of many parts of the earth. They have even partly caused flourishing civilizations to vanish. But the scale, intensity, and quality of current human interventions in nature dwarf those of the past. The disappearance of much of the earth's wealth seems to be imminent. Whatever utility the concept of domination, subjugation, conquest, exploitation, and control of nature by humans may have had in the past, it is now counterproductive. Rather than subjugating nature, human beings must learn to live in harmony with it, to cooperate with its processes. That does not mean that people must lie down supinely before nature, but that their activities should take nature's processes into account. Humans should avoid building their structures over faults in the earth's plate, for example. They should avoid building their towns in flood plains. Cooperating with nature also means understanding its limits and minimizing those activities that put pressure on them or use up its irreplaceable parts.

The second fallacy is the mistaken assumption that nature is one thing and human beings something else. That is false, of course; human beings are as much a part of nature as mountains and birds. If the earth were destroyed, human beings would cease to exist also. Human domination and exploitation of nature implies human domination and exploitation of other humans. Although this proposition was accepted in the past, slavery, imperialism, and other institutions of exploitation and domination should no longer be tolerated. Their rejection also implies the rejection of the parent concept: the subjugation of nature by humans.

Although champions of "advanced" technology—happy technologists— may approach their subjects from different perspectives, there is a common refrain to their individual verses that amounts to a litany of technology: technology is just a passive tool whose consequences depend on the use to which it is put; if technology is used harmfully, man is to blame; there are no values embodied in technology; technology plays an entirely passive role with respect to issues of power and control; the prime reasons for introducing innovations in production processes are increased efficiency and productivity; the prime reason for introducing innovations in products is to satisfy human needs. This litany of the happy technologist constitutes an ideology that is a collection of errors, illusions, and mystification presenting an inverted, truncated, distorted reflection of reality. It is also a set of values characteristic of a group; the integrated assertions, theories, and aims that constitute a sociopolitical program. The ideology of technology has purposes quite remote from explaining reality to members of society. It fails to take political power and economic interests into account and thus masks their predominant role. It promotes a model which ascribes to technology an objectivity, a value-neutrality, which technology does not in fact possess. A useful clue to the ideological nature of a statement purporting to be explanatory is the ascribing of action to vague collective nouns and pronouns, as in: *"Man"* is to blame;

"*Mind* determines the shape and direction of technology";[7] "If technology is sometimes used for bad ends, *all* bear responsibility . . . ";[8] ". . . make technology work as *our* servant";[9] "thus, *we* manufacture millions of products to enhance *our* physical comfort and convenience . . . . But in doing this, *we* overlook the need to plan ahead."[10]

Are we *all* equal in responsibility, or are some more equal than others? Who are the "we" who do the manufacturing? Is that the same "we" who forgot to plan? Doesn't somebody's profit enter the picture at all? Surely some specific minds shape technology, not an abstract "mind." The preceding manner of speaking conceals the existence of specific, powerful corporations whose activities in pursuit of their interests are major factors in the problems of our contemporary society.

## NEUTRALITY OF TECHNOLOGY

Some insight into the role played by technological ideology can be obtained by analogy, through an examination of the role of economics in our society. Like any other science, says John Kenneth Galbraith, the purpose of economics is understanding; in this case, understanding the economic system—how it works, the nature of money, etc. But economics also has an instrumental function—to serve the goals of those with power. It creates images in the minds of people—thus contributing to their model of society—which are not at all consonant with the reality of the economic system, at least with the more than fifty percent of the economy represented by what Galbraith calls the "planning system," the large corporations and their activities. The instrumental function is to induce people to behave as if the image were the reality. It is to conceal from people the true nature of most of the economy as a planned system (not free enterprise), with the planning done by a handful of large corporations in their own interest.[11] Like economics, technology also has two goals. Quite apart from their purpose "to enhance our physical comfort and convenience," technology and technical expertise serve an ideological, instrumental function. This function is, again, image-making and concealment, the covering of political and economic power in a cloak of technical objectivity. The image is created that decisions and actions serving the interests of those in power are simply the consequences of objective facts, carried out for such objective reasons as efficiency.

The ideological assertion is that technological innovations and their introduction serve the objective goals of efficiency, increase in productivity, and human needs satisfaction. To those holding the images of the dominant paradigm, this seems reasonable. But it does not stand up under close scrutiny. In his study of the development of the textile industry during the Industrial Revolution in Britain, David Dickson[12] shows that the rise of the factory system of production, the organization of work in factories, was largely a managerial necessity, rather than a technological one. It was done for the purpose of "curbing the insolence and dishonesty of men." The rising capitalist class made no bones about the introduction of specific machines having as its major purpose the subduing and disciplining of workers. Speaking of one invention in the textile industry, Andrew Ure, an early champion of the factory system, says, "This invention confirms the great doctrine already propounded, that when capital enlists science in her service, the refractory hand of labor will always be taught docility."[13] Technological innovation was not so much determined by concern for production efficiency as by management's desire to maintain fragmentation of workers, authoritarian forms of discipline, hierarchical structure, and regimentation. These same concerns are evident to the present day. After analyzing the demands that contemporary corporations impose on employees, Richard C. Edwards concludes that the complex hierarchy of the modern corporation grew not from the demands of technology but from the desire for greater control of workers.[14]

To a large extent, technological innovations in consumer products arise as a consequence of research and development (R&D) activities. Almost all R&D activities directed toward product development are carried out in the laboratories of large, technology-intensive corporations. The goals of these corporations, simply stated, are survival, growth in sales, and growth in profits.[15] All the activities of corporations—production, marketing, sales, *and* R&D —are carried out to reach these goals. Product innovation, no less than production or marketing, serves corporate purposes and would be carried out independent of social need.

Lack of need would not suffice to thwart the corporation's desire to increase sales and profit; if the market does not exist, it is developed—created, cultivated, and nourished.[16] Once the decision has been made to introduce an innovation in furtherance of corporate objectives, "developing the market" is thrown into high gear. The entire arsenal of persuasion is unleashed to convince potential consumers that the new innovation will not only perform the specific function for which the product is designed, but it will also enhance status, satisfy vanity, increase sexual appeal, etc. The result is to intensify these base impulses, and then to prey upon people's expectations that such impulses can be satisfied by the product. People are thus sold the idea that their self-worth is measured by the goods they possess, in general, and by this specific product, in particular.

Another dimension related to technological innovations appears when one seeks to determine the factors that guide the introduction of an innovation. The paramount consideration, of course, is profit; but why introduce one thing rather than another? On a superficial level, it seems that trial-and-error has something to do with it. In 1978, for example, the processed food industry introduced to the market some ten thousand new products. Of these, about eighty percent failed.[17] Was there a societal need for these products? Was "lower cost to the user" a criterion for developing, producing, and marketing them? In fact, pricing of all the corporation's products must reflect losses from those that failed. Hence, processed food prices generally must rise as a result of these innovations, quite contrary to the ideologically stated reason for product innovation.

The preceding analysis evaporates the claims of technological objectivity and value-neutrality. The nature of a society's technology is intimately related to issues of power and control, and reflects the dominant paradigm in terms of which reality is interpreted. A society in which economic growth is highly valued necessitates a particular kind of technology—one with a high level of innovation, quite independent of social need. Policies leading to economic expansion have to be reflected in the particular form of technology through which this expansion is achieved. Hierarchical forms of social control become reflected in the technology. The presumed neutrality of technology then lends legitimacy to social policies, however repressive.

Like other happy technologists, Ramo over and over again explicitly claims the value-neutrality of technology. But, without realizing it, he makes an amazing concession contradicting this position and acknowledging an instrumental function for technology. In reviewing the space program and justifying having spent large resources on this program, he concludes: "The pattern that we are developing—to be far-sighted, to be bold, to want to pioneer, to be willing to take some risks, to carry with us as a part of our way of life the exploration of the unknown—it is these habits that we cultivated when we carried out the space program."[18] This is a remarkable concession that a specific technological development had an agenda quite unrelated to the primary goal; that the program served the ideological purpose of cultivating certain habits. Can it be denied that less glorious-sounding attitudes than the ones admitted by Ramo—agreed, status-seeking, self-aggrandizement, contentiousness—are on the agenda? The general truth cannot be escaped: technology serves an instrumental function.

## INDIVIDUAL AUTONOMY

Not only is technology passive and neutral, according to the happy technologist, but whatever evil consequences are associated with the deployment of technology result from autonomous individuals exercising their free choice. Not only that, but people perversely go on using technology even though this fact lends to environmental degradation, depletion of resources, and other unpleasant things they themselves experience. A sampling of their assertions follows:

> *John Gardner:* Everyone lampoons modern technology but no one is prepared to give up his refrigerator.[19]

> *Samuel Florman:* However much we deplore our automobile culture, clearly it has been created by people making choices, not by a runaway technology.[20]

*Melvin Kranzberg:* That kind of spatial freedom (of the past in rural areas) vanished from the onrush of urbanism; but people apparently want to live together in large agglomerations.[21]

*Alvin Weinberg:* A social problem exists because many people behave, individually, in a socially unacceptable way . . . . Too many people drive cars in Los Angeles with its curious meteorology, and so Los Angeles suffocates from smog.[22]

*Emmanuel Mesthene:* The negative effects of technology . . . are traceable less to some mystical autonomy presumed to lie in technology and much more to the autonomy that our political and economic institutions grant to individual decision making.[23]

*Simon Ramo:* National control is really the only answer, and that can come only if a majority of Americans are willing to accept interference in their freedom to choose automobiles.[24]

These assertions constitute a second litany. To be generous, one would ascribe the origins of this assertion litany not to a deliberate agenda, ideologically promoted, but to a fundamental misunderstanding of the nature of technology. As noted earlier, the systems within which the separate components of technology (the machines) are incorporated are its essential features. Failure to understand that the term *technology* subsumes organized and integrated systems implies a profound misunderstanding of the nature of contemporary technology.

The term *lifestyle* designates the manner in which individuals go about their daily activities at home, at work, at play, etc. In American society there is a general perception that lifestyle is a matter of individual choice, at least for a vast majority. Disregarding economic means for a moment, people think that one can choose to lead a "bohemian" lifestyle or a "straight" one, to wear flashy clothes or sober ones, etc. But is one free to choose to have a refrigerator or not? Is it a simple matter of lifestyle choice or do other institutional arrangements of society impinge with demands of their own? Is it the kind of choice referred to by Justice Holmes when he said: "In its evenhanded majesty, the law forbids rich and poor alike to sleep under a bridge"?

A refrigerator (including freezer) performs several functions. It stores perishable food (a necessity) and cools beer or produces ice for cooling drinks (a comfort or luxury). The latter category is not an essential function. The desirability of cold beer, for example, is culturally or socially induced; other cultures (the British) find warm beer more desirable, so people in those societies do not need a refrigerator to perform this particular function. Consider another society—even a developed European society like France a decade or two ago—in which it is possible for people to purchase their perishable foods on a daily basis in markets or small shops, easily accessible and within walking distance of their homes, even in the largest cities. This option is not available to most contemporary Americans. The supermarket as a social institution, not within walking distance of most people, has its own imperatives. One buys for a week of eating, not for a day, so storage in a refrigerator becomes essential to living. It is a necessity induced by a lifestyle over which individuals have little control—an institutionalized lifestyle. To chide individuals for recalcitrance or perversity for their unwillingness to give up a refrigerator is to profoundly misjudge the nature of contemporary technology and its induced social change. No value judgment about the merits of different lifestyles is implied in this scenario. It is irrelevant to the argument whether or not a supermarket/refrigerator society has advantages over the other. The only question is: do individuals have autonomy to freely choose one or the other?

A similar and even stronger case can be made concerning the automobile. The question, again, is one of choice. Those who claim the existence of free choice gaze out at society as it exists at a given period of time, with the social structure and state of technology as they exist. Within this framework, they argue, individuals can choose. They can choose to buy this model car or that, this color or that, this upholstery material or that, this option or that. The one fact that belies all of this apparent freedom is that the majority of individuals cannot choose *not* to buy a car—if they also want to participate in the normal life of the society, such as going to work, buying food and clothing, etc.

Many communities in the U.S. had electric railway systems that served admirably in the first third of this century. It was not the autonomous choice of individuals that killed these existing urban and interurban mass public transportation systems and prevented their expansion and improvement. In more than one case they were purchased by automotive corporations (the major culprit being General Motors) and converted to motor buses, and then allowed to die in order to promote the use of the private automobile.[25] A case in point is Los Angeles. It had an extensive electric streetcar and interurban rail system in the early part of this century. During the 1920s the Pacific Electric Railway operated 1,200 miles of interurban rail service. When the population of the area was only one million in 1924, the system carried a volume of one hundred and nine million passengers. (By comparison, 45 years later when the population was eight to nine times greater, public transit buses carried only one hundred ninety million passengers annually.) The reason we have smog in Los Angeles, says Weinberg, is because too many people drive cars. A much more accurate reason is because General Motors bought the Pacific Electric Railway system and destroyed it. The single most important cause for not only the smog, but the fact that over half the land area of Los Angeles—including freeways, streets, driveways, parking lots, gas stations, sales rooms, etc.—is dedicated to the automobile, is the power of large corporations.

Simon Ramo decries federal "interference" in setting safety regulations, emission standards, etc., because it would control people's "freedom to choose automobiles." But many government laws and regulations have had, and continue to have, a major impact in instituting, cultivating, and maintaining the U.S. automobile culture. Among these are the investment tax credit that encouraged auto manufacturers to produce cars and the oil depletion allowance encouraged oil companies to produce fuel for the cars. But of far greater significance was the establishment and funding method of the federal interstate highway system in the late fifties. This was one of the most far-reaching acts of interference by government. Yet ideologically committed technologists like Ramo do not cry "control" when the actions of government favor the corporate interests.

People were not asked to debate the merits of different transportation systems and then choose what they favored. Specific corporate interests, in order to promote their own welfare, caused the current state of the U.S. transportation system. The design of the transportation system is not a consequence of two hundred million citizens exercising their free choice, but a handful of powerful groups pursuing their own interest. It is not descriptive of reality to say now that people have free choice of their mode of transportation. To set up the social system so that individuals are compelled to buy cars just in order to be active members of society, and then to sneer at them because they are unwilling to give up their cars, is to add insult to injury. It is like blaming the victim for the crime. For most people, most of the time, driving a car is not discretionary; it is mandatory.

Even within the context of a market and the regulation of technological developments by the market, is it possible accurately to describe the current status of specific technologies (e.g., the transportation system) as the consequence of untrammelled individual choice guiding the invisible hand? Market prices can be kept artificially low by transferring some of the costs associated with production or use from the manufacturer and/or user to third parties. This can be done in at least two ways—by subsidies from the government or by failure to account for "external costs" or negative "externalities." Both of these processes have operated extensively to distort price structures. Vast sums have been transferred to corporations in subsidies by the federal government, either directly (through grants and low-interest loans) or indirectly (through the taxing mechanism or having the government assume responsibility for certain components of technological systems, like highways and airports). For example, subsidies have been running at $10 billion annually just to the traditional energy industries; subsidies to the oil corporations alone have totalled more than $75 billion.

Economic activity involves producers and consumers, sellers and buyers. External costs are those undesirable effects upon other people resulting from these activities. Such costs can be tangible—such as cleaning bills and medical bills due to the effects of economic activity on the environment—or intangible, yet real. Inestimably huge external costs, both privately and socially borne, have been transferred to others. Purchasing decisions are influenced by prices that are artificially depressed in such ways. If this circumstance permits a large-scale technological development to take place, which then induces major changes in the way people live, would it be meaningful to assert that the detailed forms of the resulting society are consequences of individual free choice?

A cogent and compelling analysis of these issues is provided by James Carroll:

> [T]echnology often embodies and expresses political value choices that, in their operations and effects, are binding on individuals and groups, whether such choices have been made in political forums or elsewhere. . . . technological processes in contemporary society have become the equivalent of a form of law—that is, an authoritative or binding expression of social norms and values from which the individual or group may have no immediate recourse.[26]

Furthermore, says Carroll, there are often no appropriate political processes for "identifying and debating the value choices implicit in what appear to be technical alternatives." Technological processes are technically complex and occur in administrative organizations (either government agencies or corporations) to which citizens have no access. Ordinary people on the outside have neither the opportunity nor the means to identify the value questions, far less to resolve them in a public forum. *De facto*, the locus of the political value choices becomes the technological processes themselves; there is no public debate and issues are posed and resolved in technical terms. Individuals have no autonomous choice in the matter.

Is Kranzberg serious when he offers pure individual choice as the explanation for the specific way that Americans are distributed around the country? Did people leave the Dust Bowl in the thirties because of free choice? Were individuals consulted on the mechanization of the farms which drove farm workers away from the rural areas? The locations of industries will greatly influence where people live; were individuals consulted as to where specific industries should be located? Did the interests of huckstering land developers have nothing to do with luring people to southern California? Was it individual choice or the manipulation of specific corporate interests that caused the specific layout of Los Angeles where it is necessary to drive long distances just to carry on everyday activities?

The answers to all these questions are obvious. The design of cities, the locations of services, places of employment, shopping centers, etc., are all based on the private motor car as the dominant mode of transportation. Individuals in most places have little choice; they cannot decide to buy either at the supermarket or the corner grocery—they must buy at the supermarket because there are no longer many small stores. They cannot choose either to take mass transportation or drive a car—they are compelled to drive a car. They cannot choose to buy unpackaged, unwrapped, unboxed products because such products do not exist in most places. They cannot choose to recycle much of the waste materials (paper, glass, metal) they are compelled to bring into their homes because no recycling facilities are available in most places.

## NECESSARY HARMONY

Technology is not a neutral, passive tool devoid of values; it takes the shape of and, in turn, helps to shape, its embedding social system. The ideologically promoted neutral-tool/use-abuse model of technology conceals the issues of economic and political power relationships among different groups in society, and thus serves the instrumental function of legitimating the dominant ideology. In addition, contemporary technology, far from increasing freedom, limits individual autonomy and imposes a style of living about which individuals have little choice.

The needs to which technology is said to respond are induced by the social system. In a social order with different values and goals, the needs would be different and so the nature of technology would be correspondingly different. Thus, the crisis of contemporary society cannot be resolved if the contemporary form of technology remains dominant; it must be replaced by a technology of a different nature. Such technology is intimately tied to matters of political power and social control, changing the technology implies a profound change in the social order.

The crisis is not a crisis *within* technological society which can be overcome by patching up the system, but a crisis of the technological system *itself*. The major question is not *who* is to control the means of production, but *what* the means of production shall be; and *what* shall be produced. It is not *where* to locate the nuclear power plants, but *whether* to have nuclear power at all. It is not merely a question of possibly limiting growth but of radically altering the very nature of technology.[27] Contemporary technology is based on a narrowly conceived economic efficiency, on social control, and on profit. I would characterize the alternate technology needed as *harmonious* and based on different criteria. Harmonious technology would respect ecological values and be in symbiosis with nature. This does not mean that there would be no human intervention in nature, just that such interventions would not be destructive and exploitative, but in harmony with ecological values; consequently, harmonious technology would rely mainly on renewable energy and be minimally consumptive of nonrenewable resources. Harmonious technology would be responsive to direct social needs and would not require a hierarchical, exploitative, and alienating relationship among human beings. It would not oppress people nor treat them as appendages to machines, but would be satisfying to work with. Harmonious technolgoy would value durability and equality of products, decentralization of production, diversity—rather than monoculture—in agriculture, and pluralism in lifestyle and culture.

Accomplishing this transformation requires a new consciousness that sees the interrelations among the physical, biological, and social spheres; collectively they constitute a system of which humanity is a part. A new style of living which is in harmony with the natural world is also needed. A harmonious technology in a harmonious society is the goal. An appropriate motto might be: *Science Discovers—Humanity Decides—Technology Conforms.*

## NOTES

1. Simon Ramo, *Century of Mismatch* (New York: David McKay, 1970), p. 120.

2. Harvey Brooks, "The Technology of Zero Growth," *Daedalus* (Fall 1983): 139.

3. John Maynard Keynes, *Essays in Persuasion* (London), p. 372; reprint New York: Norton, 1953.

4. Samuel C. Florman, *The Existential Pleasures of Engineering* (New York: St. Martin's Press, 1976), p. 84.

5. Ibid., p. 75.

6. Herbert Marcuse, *One-Dimensional Man* (Boston: Beacon, 1964), p. 5.

7. Bruce O. Watkins and Roy Meador, *Technology and Human Values* (Ann Arbor Science, 1978), p. 55.

8. Ibid., p. 157.

9. Melvin Kranzberg and Carroll Pursell, *Technology in Western Civilization*, vol. 2 (Oxford University Press, 1967), p. 32.

10. Simon Ramo, *Cure for Chaos* (New York: David McKay, 1969), p. 1.

11. John Kenneth Galbraith, *Economics and the Public Purpose* (New York: Houghton Mifflin, 1973).

12. David Dickson, *The Politics of Alternative Technology* (Universe, 1974), pp. 71–83.

13. Andrew Ure, *The Philosophy of Manufacturers* (London, 1835); quoted in Dickson (see note 12), p. 80.

14. Richard C. Edwards, *Contested Terrain: The Transformation of the Workplace in the 20th Century* (New York: Basic Books, 1979).

15. J. K. Galbraith (see note 11).

16. R. M. Hall and F. S. Hill, Jr., *Introduction to Engineering* (New York: Prentice Hall, 1975), p. 24.

17. "The Great Consumer Rip-Off," Home Box Office television program, February 28, 1979.

18. *Century of Mismatch* (see note 1), p. 51.

19. John Gardner, Godkin Lecture at Harvard University, reported in the *New York Times*, March 30, 1969, section 4, p. 9E.

20. *The Existential Pleasures of Engineering* (see note 4), p. 60.

21. Kranzberg and Pursell (see note 9), p. 700.

22. Alvin Weinberg, "Can Technology Replace Social Engineering?" *University of Chicago Magazine* 59 (October 1966); reprinted in Albert H. Teich, *Technology and Man's Future* (New York: St. Martin's Press, 1977).

23. Emmanuel G. Mesthene, *Technological Change: Its Impact on Man and Society* (Harvard University Press, 1970), p. 40.

24. *Century of Mismatch* (see note 1), p. 117.

25. Bradford C. Snell, *American Ground Transport*, 1974. Prepared for the U.S. Senate Subcommittee.

26. James D. Carroll, "Participatory Technology," *Science* 171 (February 19, 1971): 647.

27. Ivan Illich, *Tools for Conviviality* (New York: Harper and Row, 1973).

# 19

# The Great Transportation Conspiracy

## Jonathan Kwitny

> What's good for General Motors is good for the country.
>
> Charles Wilson, 1953

When Charlie Wilson was toiling in the General Motors executive suite, earning his future Cabinet appointment as secretary of defense, GM, along with some of the oil companies, was steering the country toward its current energy predicament. Few remember it, but before the automobile companies became predominant, the country relied on centrally generated electricity for city transportation. It was relatively clean and energy-efficient. There were streetcars and off-street railways. There were also trackless trolleys—electric buses powered by overhead wires and able to maneuver through traffic.

Without realizing, much less debating the consequences, the country turned its transportation policy over to GM and its automotive allies. What followed was the destruction of mass transit: the country became almost totally reliant on the private automobile, with its necessary consumption of foreign oil. Of course, most people would consider it unfair to blame the demise of mass transit on several big corporations. They just manufactured the car and the bus—to the delight of millions.

But it wasn't that simple. When GM and a few other big companies created a transportation oligopoly for the internal-combustion engine—so convenient until the cheap gasoline ran out—they did not rely just on the obvious sales pitch. They conspired. They broke the law. This was all proved at a little-remembered trial in a federal court in Chicago, in 1949. After more than a month of sworn testimony, a jury convicted the corporations and several executives of criminal antitrust violations for their part in the demise of mass transit. The convictions were upheld on appeal.

In many places, mass transit didn't just die—it was murdered. No doubt the mass availability of the automobile inevitably would have changed travel habits to a great degree, but it will never be known to what extent electrified transport would have died on its own. The big conspirator companies were unwilling to entrust their fates to the market. Instead, they methodically removed the competition. In known violation of the Sherman Antitrust Act, they used their economic power to take over a small bus company and, through it, acquired and dismantled one electrified mass-transit system after another, replacing them with buses. The buses, besides being built and supplied by GM and the oil companies, never had the same appeal for riders that the electrified transit systems did, and merely added to the allure of the private car. Then the big companies that orchestrated the demise of the trolley tried to cover over their own tracks as surely as they covered over the tracks of many a rail line. The GM conspiracy case is a fine example of what can happen when important matters of public policy are abandoned by government to the self-interest of corporations—something that is occurring right now in the realm of energy.

References to the conspiracy over the years have been few and cursory. It was cited briefly in 1974 by Congressional-committee staff member Bradford Snell in "American Ground Transport," his report on monopolistic practices in the automobile industry. The committee published the report along with a reply by General Motors, which mostly repeated the defenses that the jury had chosen not to believe at the trial: that the dismantled electrified transit systems weren't profitable, and that the whole thing was an innocent effort to help a customer, the affiliated bus company.

There was no evidence in the committee report, or in an obscure book that mentioned the case last year, or in some occasional references Ralph Nader has made to the case, that the real transcript itself had been dug up and consulted. GM's reply said that because the indictment dealt with antitrust violations—"a close point of law," in GM's words—the case "lends no support" to the notion that GM induced the destruction of mass transit. The transcript of the trial, however, says otherwise.

The transcript and other evidence from the GM case are in two battered packing cartons in a federal warehouse near Chicago. That material makes this point beyond a reasonable doubt: There was for many years a criminal conspiracy behind our national transportation policy, and it was directed by some of the biggest corporations in the country. As spelled out in the court record, the conspirators did their work in many cities. They schemed from the mid-1930s through the 1940s. Electrified-rail mass-transit systems, which carried millions of riders, were bought and junked. Tracks literally were torn out of the ground, sometimes overnight. Overhead power lines were dismantled, and valuable off-street rights of way were sold.

After reading the testimony and court findings, I interviewed dozens of transit officials all over the country to find out if the old electrified system could have served us today with both convenience and savings in energy. No more than three of these officials were even aware of the GM conspiracy case, and none knew the details. They were, however, aware that a series of "mistakes" had been made in transportation planning back in the 1930s and 1940s.

What keeps millions of American city dwellers and suburbanites from greatly reducing their use of gasoline by riding transit lines today is the enormous cost of building new trolley systems. But evidence from the trial shows that this cost might have been, to a large degree, avoided. Transit officials who remember the rails, power lines, and generating stations that were once in place say these facilities, if left intact, could have formed the nucleus for a modern American transit system. Electrified trains and trackless trolleys are not only cheaper to run than automobiles, they are substantially cheaper to run than diesel buses. Riders tend to prefer them to buses. The differences in cost can be expected to widen with each oil-price increase and with the introduction of new power-conserving devices on railcars and trolleys. But in most American cities the rails and wires are gone.

Americans didn't need a lot of arm twisting to give up mass transit for the private car. Gasoline was twelve cents a gallon in the 1930s, and the air was clean. Although the internal-combustion engine was no doubt attractive, some big companies promoting the engine evidently considered the attraction insufficient for the product to succeed legitimately. The conspirators in this case included not only General Motors but also Standard Oil of California, Phillips Petroleum, Mack Manufacturing (the big truck maker), and Firestone Tire & Rubber, among others. Though all were convicted of antitrust violations for what they did, the token punishments they received scarcely marred the success of their venture.

Ironically, a Congressional antitrust action in 1935 was what made it possible for the conspiracy to succeed as easily as it did. The new law tried to break up electric-utility monopolies and required power companies to divest themselves of ancillary businesses. Most of the nation's transit systems had been started by electric-utility companies before the days of household power. By the 1930s, the retail sale of electricity had become the main business of these power companies, and transit was just a sideline. But the forced sell-off came just when the internal-combustion engine was ready to substitute for electrified transit.

It was at about this point that the GM conspirators got together with a tiny, family-owned bus service and tutored and bankrolled it as it gobbled up one trolley system after another. The front for GM was National City

Lines, Inc. After it had destroyed scores of rail and trolley systems on the pretext that buses would be more profitable, National City Lines showed its commitment by promptly getting out of the bus business and putting its assets into intercity trucking.

Perhaps the most striking example of what happened is in Los Angeles, which has become a frightening mutation of human life produced by the automotive gene. Though hard to believe now, Los Angeles once had a heavily used urban rail system extending from Newport Beach and Long Beach, through downtown, on to Pasadena, and into the San Fernando Valley—perhaps the best system in the country. The conspirators bought and dismantled it in stages during the 1940s. Taxpayers now are faced with building a similar system at a cost of billions. Year after year they have rejected the idea because of this cost.

Because the conspirators continued to deny the charges even after conviction, we are deprived of the kind of thorough narrative that might have been provided if even one guilty executive had crossed over and testified for the government. But the corporate letters and memoranda unearthed by federal prosecutors, and the explanations offered by the executives who tried to justify their actions in their own defense, tell a vivid enough story. It left the jury no reasonable doubt that the big motor, tire, and oil concerns knew they were breaking the law and acted deviously to cover up for it.

The story personalized itself in the unlikely career of E. Roy Fitzgerald, who quit school in the seventh grade to work, as irony would have it, in a railroad camp. In the 1920s he and two brothers saved up enough money to start a bus service over the two miles between Eveleth and Leonidas, Minnesota. By 1933 they had moved up to a somewhat longer intercity route, from Chicago to Paducah, Kentucky. That was when a GM salesman began talking to them about the virtues of local bus service, and persuaded them to buy the transit franchise in Galesburg, Illinois, which was for sale at the time. GM said it would be glad to help Fitzgerald and his brothers meet the purchase terms if they would agree to replace the existing streetcars with GM buses.

Fitzgerald apparently didn't know it, but GM had been trying to create a succcessful showcase for its buses for many years, according to the testimony of Irving Babcock, president of the GM truck and bus division. "We were having great difficulty in convincing the power companies to motorize and give up their streetcars," Babcock testified. So, he said, "I went to my executive committee and asked for an appropriation to invest $300,000 to help finance a few of these small cities." GM bought the transit systems in Kalamazoo and Saginaw, Michigan, and Springfield, Ohio, and proceeded to convert them from rail to bus.

But the transit industry missed the hint. Cities refused to give up their rail lines voluntarily, despite the presence of these showcases and the best efforts of GM salesmanship. So GM decided that more force-feeding was necessary, and to accomplish this in the best public-relations light, GM chose to stop buying transit systems directly and to act instead through an independent, or purportedly independent, bus operator. It was at this point that GM signed a deal with Roy Fitzgerald.

So Galesburg, too, lost its streetcars. Where there were rails one day, there was asphalt the next. The enthusiastic Fitzgerald caught wind of opportunities in a few more Illinois towns, and soon he was in Detroit, in the office of Babcock himself, to negotiate financing to take over the transit franchise in East St. Louis. Such direct dealing with the GM division president indicates that Fitzgerald was no ordinary customer. He had GM's money behind him, which made it easy to buy transit systems, particularly after Congress, in forcing utilities to divest, forced them onto the market. Undeniably, as GM's defense kept pointing out, urban railway companies suffered a profit drop-off in the 1930s, and some were losing money. But, as Herbert Listman, general sales manager of the bus division at GM, testified, the same was true of other businesseslduring the Depression—including bus lines.

On the strength of GM's checkbook, Fitzgerald moved from East St. Louis to Joliet, Illinois, where, he testified, "they discontinued operating streetcars in the city one night and we started operating modern buses . . . the next day." Quickly into the fold came Tulsa, Oklahoma; Jackson, Michigan; and Montgomery, Alabama. General Motors even provided engineering surveys showing Fitzgerald's operation just what to do. By 1936, Fitzgerald had moved into Beaumont and Port Arthur, Texas, and Cedar Rapids, Iowa. Again, rail lines were either torn up or paved over. Fitzgerald instructed the transit systems he was dealing with that he would buy in only "if a deal could be made with the city for complete bus operation—that we were not interested in operating streetcars."

The Fitzgerald bus systems were now big business, and clearly some kind of corporate structure was needed. Just as clearly, it was not really Fitzgerald's business, so he could not set up the corporate structure on his own. Early in 1936 he and his chief underling, Foster G. Beamsley, met in Detroit again with GM division president Babcock and sales manager Listman. They decided to form National City Lines, Inc., as a holding company for the various transit ventures. Obviously there would be further expansion—opportunities beckoned all over the map. Apparently hoping not to have to foot the bill for all this, the GM men suggested the National City Lines try to finance its expanison with bank loans and a public stock sale.

The result of these money-raising efforts over the next six months is significant because it contradicts the cover story that GM and the other conspirators later put forward. The companies argued in court that they had gone in with Fitzgerald to create modern, profitable bus lines out of broken-down rail systems. But the financial community disagreed at the time. The banks refused to lend any money. "They did not think it was the proper time," Fitzgerald explained on the witness stand. National City Lines did succeed in raising $1.9 million from a public stock sale, but only after agreeing to the most extreme terms—15 percent of the top as fees to the brokers, which was practically Mafia rates.

Moreover, $1.9 million wasn't nearly as much as was needed. So in October Fitzgerald and Beamsley were back in Babcock's office at GM for more capital. Also present was Glenn Traer, an executive from Greyhound, the bus company. Babcock later testified that GM had gone to Greyhound earlier to help pay for the takeover and destruction of some of the rail lines Fitzgerald had started with in Illinois. (Neither Greyhound nor any of its executives was charged in the conspiracy case.) Now Greyhound agreed to participate with GM in a much wider venture, but only if others were brought in to share the load. A lot of money would be needed. The B. F. Goodrich Company seemed a logical choice to approach because a tire concern would certainly benefit from transforming city railways into paved streets. But B. F. Goodrich declined to join the conspiracy. So Firestone was approached and agreed to come in. By their later actions, the conspirators appear to have been well aware that they were violating the Sherman Antitrust Act, which prohibits companies from joining together to restrain competition or to sabotage competitors.

But they were quite undeterred by the law, which may be a fair comment on its general effectiveness.

Eventually the conspirators invested about 10 million 1930s dollars in the plot. GM and Firestone stationed their own service personnel where Fitzgerald operated his buses. Stuart Moore, a Greyhound maintenance executive, was put on the National City Lines staff and board of directors to help supervise the conversion of the rail systems. At least one government regulator, who acknowledged at the trial that he had helped engineer official approval for what the GM conspirators did, was later made a paid consultant for the fraudulent holding company.

In midsummer of 1937, the conspirators resolved to expand the bus scheme to the Western states. But the financing problem remained, and Traer, the Greyhound executive, was sent out to raise cash. "Well," he reported back to Babcock, "I talked to investment houses, brokers, and private capital. . . . I couldn't get the money." If the city bus was indeed a brilliant new idea that was sweeping the country on its own merit, as the conspirators later contended, the country's capital markets were curiously slow to catch on. The only way the GM group could raise more money was to bring in more conspirators. An oil company seemed a logical bet, so Traer and Babcock went to Standard Oil of California.

"We could see . . . from our standpoint, it was going to create a market for our product—gasoline, lubricating oil, and greases," a Standard Oil executive recalled from the witness stand. "If the Fitzgeralds were able to accomplish anything along this line on the Pacific coast, then other people would do it, and that would open up even more markets for us," he said. So Standard Oil came in.

Then the conspirators went to Mack Trucks—GM's supposed direct competitor in the bus-making business. A Mack officer named Roy Hauer showed up on Roy Fitzgerald's farm in the winter of 1937–38 and agreed that the new law forcing electric companies to sell their transit businesses provided a rare opportunity. So officers from Mack Trucks, Standard Oil, and General Motors all met in the office of Greyhound Bus Lines in Chicago and decided who was going to pay Fitzgerald to dismantle the West Coast rail system.

Part of the deal was that Fitzgerald's operations would buy at least 42.5 percent of their buses from General Motors and 42.5 percent from Mack (an obvious Sherman violation), with the other 15 percent to be decided by need. At the trial, Fitzgerald said that the new bus lines promised to make big money for his investors; that was why they invested, he testified. But there were indications from the investing companies themselves that they expected their profits to come not from bus operations at all but from the sale of their products after electrified transit was destroyed. An internal memo at Mack, for example, spoke of a "probable loss" on the bus-line stock, but said it would be "more than justified" by "the business and gross profit flowing out of this move in years to come."

Nor does it appear that GM expected to make its principal profit from the sale of buses, the new form of mass transit. If it did, there is no satisfactory explanation in the trial record for why GM gave half the prospective bus business away to Mack, its supposed competitor. Another explanation, of course, is that the real profits were going to be made from the sale of cars (in Mack's case, trucks) after the destruction of mass transit opened the way for a huge public network of streets and highways. That this is what happened offers some justification for the explanation that it was intended.

The agreements under which the conspirators provided money did not require merely that all buses, tires, and petroleum products be purchased from the particular supplier who was putting up the cash. The contracts also specified that the transit systems could never buy another streetcar or any other piece of equipment that would "use any fuel or method of propulsion other than gasoline." (In the early 1940s, when the diesel bus came into vogue as a replacement for the older, gasoline-engine models, it was discovered that diesel equipment violated this restrictive clause. Accordingly, the clause was changed, specifically to permit the purchase of diesel fuel.)

As operations spread around the country, more capital was needed and the conspirators decided to bring in others who would benefit from what they were doing. A plan was devised to carve up the United States among various oil companies; each one was to be awarded a region in which it would supply the bus companies run by National City Lines. Texaco was approached to handle the Midwest and South; its sales department liked the idea, but the top executives turned it down, saying only, according to Fitzgerald's testimony, that they were "not interested."

Phillips 66 was offered the same deal and showed unrestrained enthusiasm. At the negotiations with Phillips, Fitzgerald was accompanied by R. S. Leonard, a finance officer of Firestone, and Victor Palmer, the treasurer of Standard Oil of California—a competitor of Phillips. The transaction was sealed personally by Frank Phillips, the petroleum company's founder and chairman, and Kenneth S. Adams, the president and heir to Phillip's position as head of the company. According to Fitzgerald, Phillips told him that "anywhere along the line that I might feel that his people were doing anything to us that might change this deal, he would be glad to have me come back and talk to him."

Meanwhile, the GM transit juggernaut rolled on. Butte, Montana; Fresno, Oakland, Stockton, and San Jose, California; Portsmouth and Canton, Ohio; Terre Haute, Indiana. In St. Louis, the whole electric utility had gone into bankruptcy receivership. Seven banks had taken over, and were glad to have an investor named Fitzgerald buy control of the streetcar system, which became a bus system.

Roy Fitzgerald was being made into the biggest transportation tycoon since Jay Gould. His capacity to manage it all was finally spread so thin that it was decided the West Coast portion should be split off and run separately. Victor Palmer left his job as treasurer of Standard Oil of California to take over the presidency of the West Coast bus systems, which were called Pacific City Lines. John L. Wilson, a Mack executive, was made president of the St. Louis system and was given seed money to buy and convert the Lincoln, Nebraska, transit system in his own name.

In general, the conspirators took great pains to disguise their involvement. They clearly didn't want the public to know who was really behind all the marvelous new transit systems that Roy Fitzgerald and General Motors were designing. Firestone executive Leonard wrote a chummy letter to Phillips stating that Firestone was keeping its transit investments secret by investing in the names of two employees acting as nominees, and hinting that Phillips might do the same thing (apparently Phillips didn't). At one point, even National City Lines, the front group, operated behind a front name of its own, the Andover Finance Company, in order "to make investments in situations beyond the legal limits," in the words of a Fitzgerald aide. Standard Oil of California made its investments in the name of two nominee companies, because, Standard's treasurer, Henry Judd, testified: "We didn't want to be criticized. . . . We didn't want to have the people in the community feel that if the service was not what they wanted . . . the complaints would rest with the Standard Oil Company of California." This seems strange behavior from companies that defended themselves on the grounds that they had performed noble public service by hastening the advent of the bus. At one point, B. F. Stradley, acting treasurer of Phillips, wrote to Harry L. Grossman, vice-president and secretary of GM's bus division:

> From our conversation, it appears there may be a difference of opinion between us in respect of the propriety and perhaps the legality of certain requirements which we have in mind in respect of the agreements covering the purchase of stock in American City Lines [a proposed National City Lines affiliate]. We shall be glad to present our views to you at any time . . . although it occurs to me that it might not be well to discuss the problem jointly with the American City Lines group since by so doing it would become obvious that our meeting was prearranged.

The same letter noted that the details of the transaction had already been discussed with Firestone.

Fitzgerald himself obviously knew that there was something wrong with talking to representatives of more than one supplier at a time, because from the witness stand he kept denying that he had ever done so. In the face of all the evidence, he insisted that he had merely gone around independently trying to raise money from the most logical investors he could think of, his suppliers. For example, there was a meeting in April 1939 to discuss the formation of an affiliate that later took over and wrecked the suburban Los Angeles rail transit system. Fitzgerald testified that the only people there were himself and Russell M. Riggins of Phillips. He specifically swore, on questioning, that R. S. Leonard of Firestone hadn't joined the discussions at all.

Yet the prosecution produced a letter from Riggins to Leonard saying, "It was a real pleasure to again have the opportunity to be with you" at what Riggins called "the big meeting last Monday," as a result of which "everything has been mutually agreed upon."

Sacramento, Salt Lake City, Portland, Tampa, Mobile, Baltimore, El Paso, and Spokane were taken over. The takeover of Los Angeles had been carefully plotted for a couple of years. In 1941, the Glendale and Pasadena railway systems were bought and transformed into all-bus operations according to an engineering plan drawn up by General Motors. The Long Beach system was bought and scrapped.

In its reply to the Congressional staff study's account of the Los Angeles takeover, GM argued that the bus-for-rail substitution there was accomplished gradually over four decades, starting before GM even got into the bus business. But the trial testimony of Henry C. Judd, treasurer of Standard Oil, was pretty blunt:

> Mr. Fitzgerald called me on the telephone [in December 1944]. He told me that they had made an offer for the purchase of the [downtown] Los Angeles railway, and that it had been accepted, and that he would like to have us put about $1 million into [the deal].

Besides its own contribution, Standard used its influence to pry loose another $5 million from Bank of America to finance the takeover.

Soon after the war, GM, Standard Oil, Firestone, and Phillips all got out of their stock ownership in the transit systems. Mack and Greyhound already were long gone. Victor Palmer, leaving the presidency of Pacific City Lines, was welcomed back to the executive payroll at Standard. Money had been made, all right, but not on transit company stock. As Herbert Listman, general sales manager for GM buses, testified, "It was the policy of General Motors to get out of all these investments. They were temporary finance plans. . . . They have served their purpose."

Soon, National City Lines was out of the bus business, too. What was left were cars.

Those indicted and convicted of violating the Sherman Antitrust Act were National City Lines, Pacific City Lines, Firestone Tire & Rubber, General Motors, Phillips Petroleum, Mack Manufacturing, Standard Oil of California, Federal Engineering (a Standard Oil subsidiary), E. Roy Fitzgerald, Foster G. Beamsley, H. C. Grossman (assistant secretary of GM), Henry C. Judd, L. R. Jackson (vice-president of Firestone), B. F. Stradley (secretary and treasurer of Phillips), and A. M. Hughes (vice-president and director of Phillips). These few took the rap for everyone involved.

Recalling the old rail network in Los Angeles, Gerald Haugh, currently general manager of the bus system in the city's Long Beach section, says, "It would be great if we had it all back again. It could have been modernized. You'd have tried to extend the rails out into those areas where people were buying. It would have been a hell of a lot cheaper than to do it today. It was a damn shame they took up the tracks."

As for the people who took up the tracks, they suffered little for it. U.S. District Judge William J. Campbell sentenced the guilty corporations to pay fines of $5,000 each (except for Federal Engineering, a Standard Oil subsidiary, which had to pay only $1,000). The guilty individuals paid fines of exactly $1 each. The defendants also had to pick up the court costs, which totaled a not too princely $4,220.78.

A few years after the trial, Julius and Ethel Rosenberg paid the death penalty for treason in a case that unfolded at about the same time as the GM conspiracy case. The Rosenbergs' crime, as it turned out, had no appreciable effect on the future of the country. On the other hand, what the transit conspirators did was destroy mass-transit systems that today could benefit millions of citizens and, ironically, make for improved national security by reducing reliance on foreign oil. And they did it for no greater cause than for their own profit.

# 20

# The Political Impact of Technical Expertise

## Dorothy Nelkin

Technologies of speed and power—airports, power generating facilities, high-ways, dams—are often a focus of bitter opposition. As these technologies become increasingly controversial, scientists, whose expertise forms the basis of technical decisions, find themselves involved in public disputes. This "public" role of science has generated concern both within the profession and beyond; for a scientist's involvement in controversial issues may violate the norms of scientific research, but have considerable impact on the political process. As scientists are called upon to address a wider range of controversial policy questions,[1] "problems of political choice [may] become buried in debate among experts over high technical alternatives."[2]

This [chapter] will discuss some of the implications of the increasing in-volvement of scientists in controversial areas. What is the role of experts in public disputes? How are they used by various parties to a controversy, and how do scientists behave once involved? Finally, what is their impact on the political dynamics of such disputes?

## THE ROLE OF EXPERTS

Scientists play an ambivalent role in controversial policy areas. They are both indispensible and suspect. Their technical knowledge is widely regarded as a

---

From *Social Studies of Science* 5 (1975): 189–205. Copyright © 1975 by Sage Publications. Reprinted by permission of the publisher.

source of power. "The capacity of science to authorize and certify facts and pictures of reality [is] a potent source of political influence."[3] Yet experts are resented and feared. While the reliance on experts is growing, we see a revival of Jacksonian hostility toward expertise, and of the belief that common sense is an adequate substitute for technical knowledge.[4]

The authority of expertise rests on assumptions about scientific rationality; interpretations and predictions made by scientists are judged to be rational because they are based on "objective" data gathered through rational procedures, and evaluated by the scientific community through a rigorous control process. Science, therefore, is widely regarded as a means by which to depoliticize public issues. The increasing use of expertise is often associated with the "end of ideology"; politics, it is claimed, will become less important as scientists are able to define constraints and provide rational policy choices.[5]

Policy makers find that it is efficient and comfortable to define decisions as technical rather than political. Technical decisions are made by defining objectives, considering available knowledge, and analyzing the most effective ways of reaching these objectives. Debate over technical alternatives need not weigh conflicting interests, but only the relative effectiveness of various approaches for resolving an immediate problem. Thus, scientific knowledge is used as a "rational" basis for substantive planning, and as a means of defending the legitimacy of specific decisions. Indeed, the viability of bureaucracies depends so much on the control and monopoly of knowledge in a specific area, that this may become a dominant objective.[6] Recent technological disputes, however, suggest that access to knowledge and expertise has itself become a source of conflict, as various groups realize its growing implications for political choice.

The past decade has been remarkable for the development of "advocacy politics";[7] consumer advocates, planning advocates, health care advocates, and environmental advocates have mobilized around diverse issues. Key slogans are "accountability," "participation," and "demystification." These groups share common concerns with the "misuse of expertise," the "political use" of scientists and professionals, and the implications of expert decision making for public action. Table 1 presents some statements of these concerns by various groups: radical scientists who have organized to develop "science for the people"; consumer advocates concerned with corporate accountability; advocacy planners who assist communities in expressing their local needs; and environmentalists and health professionals who demand "demystification of medicine."

Their criticism reflects a dilemma. The complexity of public decisions seems to require highly specialized and esoteric knowledge, and those who control this knowledge have considerable power. Yet democratic ideology suggests that people must be able to influence policy decisions that affect their lives. This dilemma has provoked a number of proposals for better distribution of technical information; expertise, it is argued, is a political resource and must be available to communities as well as to corporations, utilities, or developers.[8]

The increasing importance of technical information has also prompted analyses of the behavior of scientists as they are diverted to applied and controversial work.

For example, Allan Mazur suggests that the political (i.e., nonscientific) context of controversies crucially affects the activities of scientists, the way they present their findings, and thus their ultimate influence on decisions. Despite norms of political neutrality, claims Mazur, scientists behave just like anyone else when they engage in disputes; their views polarize and as a result the value of scientific advice becomes questionable. Thus, disputes among experts may become a major source of confusion for policy makers and for the public.[9] Guy Benveniste, focusing on the use of scientists by policy makers, suggests that "technical" decisions are basically made on political or economic grounds. Expertise is sought as a means of supporting particular policy programs; the selection of data and their interpretation are thus related to policy goals.[10] Similarly, King and Melanson argue that when knowledge is employed in the resolution of public problems, it is shaped, manipulated, and frequently distorted by the dynamics of the policy arena.[11]

These analyses emphasize the politicization of expertise. Details of two recent disputes in which "experts" were used by both project developers and critics provide an opportunity to develop these arguments, and then to explore the impact of experts on the political process. One of the disputes concerns the siting of an 830 megawatt nuclear power plant on Cayuga Lake in upstate New York; the other is the proposed construction of a new runway at Logan International Airport in East Boston, Massachusetts.

The power plant siting controversy began in June 1967, when the New York State Electric and Gas Company (NYSE&G) first announced its intention to build Bell Station.[12] Groups of scientists and citizens, concerned with the thermal pollution of Cayuga Lake, organized themselves to oppose the plant, and demanded that NYSE&G consider design alternatives that would minimize the damage to the lake caused by waste heat. They forced the utility to postpone its application for a construction permit, and to contract for additional research on the environmental impact of the plant. In March 1973, following consultants' recommendations, NYSE&G announced a power station plan that was essentially the same as its earlier controversial design. The company, however, was now armed with data from one and a half million dollars' worth of environmental research supporting its claim that the heat from Bell Station would not damage the lake. Yet once more there was concerted and well-informed public opposition, this time focused on radiation hazards. Four months later the company was forced to abandon its plan.

The proposed new 9,200-foot runway at Logan Airport was part of a major expansion plan that had been a source of bitter conflict in East Boston for many years.[13] Located only two miles from the center of downtown Boston in an Italian working-class community, this modern convenient airport is a source of extreme irritation, fear, and community disruption. The expansion policies of the Massachusetts Port Authority (Massport) have been opposed, not only by airport neighbors but also by Boston's city government and by state officials concerned with the development of a balanced transportation system. Here, as in the Cayuga Lake power plant siting debate, knowledge was used as a resource both by Massport, seeking justification for its expansion plans, and by those opposed to such plans. Massport's staff was backed by consultants who claimed that without expansion the airport would reach saturation by 1974, and that the new runway would cause no environmental damage. The opponents, primarily from the adjacent working-class neighborhood of East Boston, used technical advice provided by the city of Boston. Following pressure from the governor as well as from the mayor, Massport eventually deleted the proposed runway from the master plan for future airport development.

While this [chapter] will focus on similarities in the dynamics of these two disputes, it is necessary first to point out important differences. The community opposed to the power plant was a college town; the dispute was a middle-class environmental conflict, sustained by expertise from scientists in a nearby university who also lived in the area. In contrast, the opposition to the airport came primarily from a working-class neighborhood dependent on expertise provided by government officials who, for political and economic reasons, chose to oppose the airport development plans.

The technical aspects of the two disputes were also quite different. The power plant issue was embedded in a set of vague uncertainties and intangible fears about radiation; airpot expansion posed the concrete and direct threat of increased noise and land purchase. The main area of technical conflict in the former case was the potential environmental impact of the new power plant and the experts involved were mostly scientists and engineers. In the latter case the controversial issue was the validity of projections—whether the runway was really necessary at all—and the dispute involved economists and lawyers as well as engineers.

Despite such differences, the two cases have a great deal in common: the use of expertise, the style of technical debate, and the impact of experts on the political dynamics of the dispute are remarkably similar.

## THE USE OF EXPERTISE

Opposition to both the power plant and the airport developed in several stages. The developers (utility manager, airport manager) contracted for detailed plans on the construction of their proposed facility. As they applied for the necessary permits, affected groups tried to influence the decision. The developer in each case argued that plans, based on their consultants' predictions of future demands and technical imperatives concerning the location and design of the facility, were definitive, except perhaps for minor adjustments necessary to meet federal standards.

## Table 1.  Public concern with expertise

| Radical scientists | Consumer advocates | Environmentalists | Advocacy planners | Medical critics |
|---|---|---|---|---|
| **On the misuse of technology** | | | | |
| [We] feel a deep sense of frustration and exasperation about the use of [our] work. We teach, we do experiments, we design new things —and for what? To enable those who direct this society to better exploit and oppress the great majority of us? To place the technological reins of power in the hands of those who plunder. . . . | What is needed is a sustained public demand for a liberation of law and technology to cleanse the air by disarming the corporate power that turns nature against man. | Many believe that the advantages of our technology compensate for environmental degradation. . . . Some have faith that the laboratories that have delivered miracles can also provide the tools to remedy any problems man may face. But with technology's gifts to improve man's environment has come an awesome potential for destruction. | Advocacy planning may be one of the channels of action through which people may try to humanize their technical apparatus; to prevent the exercise of bureaucratic power from leading to a new diffuse despotism, in which power appears in the image of technical necessity. | Psychiatry and psychology are used as direct instruments of coercion against individuals. Under the guise of "medical methods," people are pacified, punished, or incarcerated. |
| **On the use of expertise** | | | | |
| Skills and talents of potentially enormous usefulness have been bent to destructive ends to guarantee expansion and protect imperialism. For the sake of the ruling class scientists and engineers have been turned into creators of destruction by the mechanisms of an economic and social system over which they can exert no control. | Too many of our citizens have little or no understanding of the relative ease with which industry has or can obtain the technical solutions . . . | It doesn't require special training to keep a broad perspective and to apply common sense. Thus, for every technically knowledgeable [person] there is a layman activist. . . . In fact, the technologist's training can stand in his way. There is a growing awareness that civilized man has blindly followed the technologists into a mess. | Even without administrative power, the advocate planner is a manipulator . . . . The planner may not be the first to identify "problems" of an urban area, but he puts them on the agenda and plays a large part in defining the terms in which the problem will be thought about— and those terms in effect play a large part in determining the solution. | Professionals often regard themselves as more capable of making decisions than other people even when their technical knowledge does not contribute to a particular decision. . . . Professionalism is not a guarantor of humane, quality services. Rather it is a code-word for a distinct political posture. |

**Table 1.** (contd.)

---

**On expertise and public action**

---

| | | | | |
|---|---|---|---|---|
| What we can hope is not that scientists can provide the people with an objective approach to build a better world, but that in the better world built by the people, scientists will be able to work in a more objective fashion, unfettered by elitism and the worst competitive aspects of present-day science. | An action strategy must embrace the most meticulous understanding of the corporate structure—its points of access, its points of maximum responsiveness, its specific motivational sources, and its constituencies. | The importance of the environmental movement's potential rests not only in what tangible results it can accomplish, but in its acting as a catalyst to start people working together. Alliances possible by organizing around environmental concerns stagger the mind of the seasoned community organizer. | Any plan is the embodiment of particular group interests . . . any group which has interests at stake in the planning process should have those interests articulated. . . . Planning in this view becomes pluralistic and partisan—in a word, overtly political. | Medicine should be demystified. . . . When possible, patients should be permitted to choose among alternative methods of treatment based upon their needs. Health care should be de-professionalized. Health care skills should be transferred to worker and patient alike. |

---

*Sources:* These statements are quotations from editorials and the popular literature circulated by such groups as SESPA, Nader's Raiders, Earth Day groups, and the Health Policy Advisory Center.

In the power plant controversy, scientists from Cornell University who lived in the community were the first to raise questions about the NYSE&G plan when it was announced in 1967. By mid-1968, their activity had built up sufficient political support to persuade NYSE&G to postpone its plans, and to undertake further environmental research.

A new sequence of events began in March 1973, when NYSE&G again announced its intention to build the plant and claimed that it was imperative to begin construction promptly. The company's consultants, Nuclear Utilities Services Corporation, had prepared a five-volume technical report. NYSE&G placed copies in local libraries, circulated a summary to its customers, and invited comments. The report supported NYSE&G's earlier plan for a plant involving a General Electric boiling water reactor with a once-through cooling system. The study concluded that cooling towers (which had been recommended by power plant critics in 1968) were economically unfeasible in the size range required for the plant, unsuited to the topography of the area, and would have a tendency to create fog. To develop an optimum design for a once-through cooling system, consultants designed a jet diffuser to provide rapid mixing of the heated discharge with the lake water. With this system, they argued that the plant would have an insignificant effect on the aquatic environment of Cayuga Lake. The consultants only briefly concerned themselves with the issue of radioactive wastes on the grounds that this was not a problem unique to Cayuga Lake; the report only stated that the effect would be substantially below current radiation protection standards.

NYSE&G organized an information meeting attended by 1,000 citizens, and for two hours summarized the highly technical material supporting its plans. This, however, was followed by two and one-half hours of angry discussion, and the utility's president announced that if public protest was likely to cause delay, they would build the plant at another site. He hoped, however, that the decision would be "based on fact and not on emotion."

The first organized response came from twenty-four scientists who volunteered to provide the public with a review and assessment of the utility's massive technical report.[14] Their review was highly critical and NYSE&Gs' consultants responded in kind (see below). Meanwhile, citizens' groups formed and the community polarized, as the company posed the issue in terms of "nuclear power *or* blackouts."

The airport case also involved experts on both sides of the controversy. Opposing forces mobilized in February 1971, at a public hearing required by the Corps of Engineers in order to approve Massport's request to fill in part of Boston Harbor. One thousand people attended and for ten hours scientists, politicians, priests, schoolteachers, and others debated the priorities which they felt should govern airport decisions. Massport's staff was backed by consultants, who claimed that without the runway the airport would reach saturation by 1974. Consultants provided a brief environmental statement arguing that the new runway would have no direct detrimental effects of ecological significance. The only environmental costs would be the elimination of ninety-three acres of polluted clam flats and two hundred and fifty acres of wildlife preserve—which constituted a hazard in any case because birds interfere with jets. Furthermore, because of the added flexibility, the runway would relieve noise and congestion caused by an expected increase in aircraft operations. Massport's claims were later buttressed by an environmental impact statement commissioned from Landrum and Brown, Airport Consultants, Inc. at a cost of $166,000. The study documented Massport's contention that the new runway was essential for safety and would be environmentally advantageous; it emphasized the positive contributions of Logan Airport—its economic importance to the City of Boston, and the reduction of noise that would result from increased runway flexibility.

The opposition was organized by a coalition of citizens' groups called the Massachusetts Air Pollution and Noise Abatement Committee. The issues raised were diverse. Neighborhood people spoke of the discomfort caused by aircraft operations, and of Massport's piecemeal and closed decision-making procedures. Environmentalists feared the destruction of Boston Harbor, and planners related airport decisions to general urban problems. Legal, economic, and technical experts became involved as the Mayor's office and the Governor evaluated Massport's claims. As in the power plant case, the conflict polarized as Massport posed the issue in terms of "airport expansion *or* economic disaster."

## THE STYLE OF TECHNICAL DEBATE[15]

In both cases the technical debate involved considerable rhetorical licence, with many insinuations concerning the competence and the biases of the involved scientists.[16] NYSE&G emphasized that the need for a nuclear power plant on Cayuga Lake was "imperative," that there would be a serious energy shortage if they did not proceed immediately with the plan, and that the impact of the plant on the local environment would be "insignificant." NYSE&G insisted on their unique technical competence to make this decision. "Our study is the most comprehensive study ever made on the lake. Opponents can create delays but are not required to assume responsibility. . . ."

However, the Cornell critics called NYSE&G's data "inadequate," "misleading," "non-comprehensive," and "limited in scope and inadequate in concept." Some of the critics provided data from other research that contradicted NYSE&G's findings. They emphasized that there was simply not enough known about deep-water lakes to assess the risks.

NYSE&G consultants countered by claiming that Cornell critics were unfamiliar with the scope and requirements of an environmental feasibility report; in particular, that the critics' review failed to distinguish between the goals of pure and applied research. "From an academic position a complete ecological model that predicted all possible relationships would be desirable, but this was neither feasible nor necessary for assessing the minor perturbations caused by one plant."

In fact, each group used different criteria to collect and interpret technical data. The two studies were based on diverse premises which required different sampling intervals and techniques. NYSE&G consultants, for instance, claimed that their water quality studies focused on establishing base-line conditions to predict the changes caused by the power plant; Cornell studies focused on limiting factors, such as the impact of nutrients on lake growth.

Scientists attacked each other with little constraint. Cornell reviewers accused NYSE&G consultants of value judgments that led to "glaring omissions," "gross inadequacies," and "misleading interpretations." Consultants referred to the Cornell report's "confusion resulting from reviewers reading only certain sections of the report," and "imaginative, but hardly practicable suggestions." The NYSE&G president accused the Cornell reviewers of bias: "It is of some interest that many of the individuals who participated in the Cornell review have taken a public position in opposition to nuclear plants. Philosophical commitment in opposition to nuclear generation may have made it difficult for these reviewers to keep their comments completely objective."[17]

A similar style of debate characterized the technical dispute over the airport runway. Expansion of Logan was recommended by consultants as "the best opportunity to realize a reduction of current social impact." Failure to expand the airport as proposed would cause delays, increase air pollution, reduce safety margins and have a "drastic" and "immeasurable" impact on the local economy—"an impact which the Boston area could not afford." Massport's environmental report described and rejected, one by one, alternatives proposed by airport opponents. Banning specific types of aircraft "interferes with interstate commerce." Limiting maximum permissible noise levels is "legally questionable," since the airport functions as part of a coordinated national system. A surcharge for noisy aircraft would be "useless" as economic leverage, since landings fees represent a negligible percentage of total airline expenses. Setting night curfews is "precluded" by the interdependence of flight schedules and aircraft utilization requirements: it would relegate Boston to a "second-class" airport and have "disastrous effects" on service to 65 per cent of the 267 cities served by Boston. Moreover, 70 per cent of the cargo business would be "negatively affected." Soundproofing neighboring houses and buildings would be "economically prohibitive" and have little effect. The *only* feasible solution to noise and environmental problems, according to the consultants' report, was an expanded runway system that would permit increased flexibility. Massport insisted on the validity of its expertise. "We are closer and more knowledgeable than any other group no matter what their intention may be, on what Logan Airport . . . what Metropolitan Boston, what the entire state of Massachusetts and New England needs."[18] And Massport consultants suggested their agreement with their client when, in a technical analysis of the airport's economic impact, they stated: "It is inconceivable that an enterprise of this magnitude can be treated other than with the most profound respect."[19]

Airport opponents called the Massport technical reports "the logical outcome of efforts directed toward narrow objectives." City consultants contended that authority to restrict aircraft noise was in fact limited neither by the FAA nor by the Massport enabling act, and that the FAA actually encouraged airport operators to restrict airport noise independently. They argued that Massport's assumptions concerning anticipated demand for increased airport capacity were questionable and in any case were subject to modification by consolidating schedules and dispersing general aviation flights. Massport's own raw data suggested that with a reasonable adjustment Logan Airport could accommodate a considerable increase in actual business, for aircraft were operating at an average of just under half capacity. Moreover, projections were based on the growth pattern of the 1960s. The decrease in air travel demand in 1970 could have been regarded either as a new data point or as an anomaly. Massport chose the latter interpretation, ignoring the 1970 slump. Their projections also ignored the possibility of competitive alternatives to air travel.[20]

Massport's figures concerning the economic impact of expansion and the consequences of a moratorium on expansion were debunked by critics as "blatant puffery." As for Massport's contention that the new runway would be environmentally advantageous, city representatives concluded that an expanded airfield would only expose new populations to intolerable noise. Instead, they recommended measures to increase capacity at Logan through scheduling adjustments and efforts to distribute the hours of peak demand by economic controls such as landing fees.

Differences were to be aired at a second round of public hearings scheduled for 10 July 1971. However, on 8 July, following a task-force study that recommended alternatives to expansion, Governor Sargent publicly opposed the construction of the new runway. Under these circumstances, the Corps of Engineers was unlikely to approve the project, so Massport withdrew its application for a permit and temporarily put aside its plans for the runway. A year and a half later, in February 1973, Massport deleted the proposed runway from the master plan for future airport development. Citing projections that were close to those used by airport opponents two years earlier, the Port Authority claimed that reevaluation of future needs indicated that the new runway was no longer necessary.

Both disputes necessarily dealt with a great number of genuine uncertainties that allowed divergent predictions from available data. The opposing experts emphasized these uncertainties; but in any case, the substance of the technical arguments had little to do with the subsequent political activity.

## THE IMPACT OF EXPERTISE ON POLITICAL ACTION

In both the airport and power plant controversy, it was the *existence* of technical debate more than its *substance* that stimulated political activity.[21] In each case the fact that there was disagreement among experts confirmed the fears of the community and directed attention to what they felt was an arbitrary decision-making procedure in which expertise was used to mask questions of political priorities.

The relationship between technical disputes and political conflict was most striking in the power plant case. Cornell scientists assessed the NYSE&G report with the intention of providing technical information to the public. They focused almost entirely on the issue of thermal pollution—the effect of the plant's heated effluent on Cayuga Lake. The citizens' groups, however, were most concerned with the issue of radiation. They had followed the considerable discussion in the press and in popular journals about the risks associated with the operation of nuclear reactors—risks that had not been as widely publicized at the time of the first controversy in 1968. Thus, the thermal pollution issue (which had dominated earlier controversy) became, in 1973, a relatively minor concern. Citizens, in contrast to the scientists who were advising them, focused on problems of transporting and disposing of nuclear wastes, on the reliability of reactor safety mechanisms, on reactor core defects that would allow the release of radioactive gases, and on the danger of human error or sabotage.

When the citizens' committee first met to establish a position on the issue, its newsletter concentrated entirely on the reactor safety issue.[22] This set the tone of subsequent discussion, in which three possible courses of action were considered: that the committee oppose construction of any nuclear plant on Cayuga Lake until problems of reactor safety and disposal of radioactive wastes were resolved; that it take up its 1968 position and oppose only the *current design* of Bell Station; or that it support NYSE&G plans. The first proposal, one of total opposition, won overwhelming support. The emphasis of citizens' groups thereafter was on the risks associated with nuclear power, despite the fact that the technical debate dealt mainly with the problem of thermal pollution.

The disputes between scientists, however, served as a stimulus to political activity. In the first place, the criticism by Cornell scientists neutralized the expertise of the power company. Simply suggesting that there were opposing points of view on one dimension of the technical problem increased public mistrust of the company's experts, and encouraged citizens to oppose the plant. Second, the involvement of scientists gave moral support to community activists, suggesting that their work would be effective. The citizens' groups called attention to NYSE&G's statement that if there were concerted opposition, the company would not go ahead with its plans. The ready support of local scientists led to substantial expectation in the community that the effort involved in writing letters and going to meetings would not be wasted.

As for the details of the technical dispute, they had little direct bearing on the dynamics of the case. Citizens trusted those experts who supported their position. People who supported NYSE&G voiced their trust in the consultants employed by the power company: "Let us allow the professionals to make the decisions that they get paid to make." And power plant critics used expertise only as a means to bring the issue back to its appropriate political context. The case was one of local priorities, they claimed; it was not a technical decision: "To say that our future is out of our hands and entrusted to scientists and technicians is an arrogant assumption. . . . We suggest that the opinions of area residents who care deeply about their environment and its future are of equal if not greater importance."[23]

In the airport case, the technical arguments served primarily to reinforce the existing mistrust of Massport among those opposed to airport expansion, and they were virtually ignored by those who supported Massport. Opinions about the necessity of the runway were well established prior to the actual dispute. In East Boston, Massport employees and local sports clubs which were supported by an airport community relations program defended the Port Authority's plans for a new runway and maintained their trust in Massport's competence. "In terms of efficient and competent operation, Massport is head and shoulders above other agencies."

Airport opponents, while benefiting from the advice provided by experts from the City of Boston, claimed the issue was a matter of common sense and justice. They defined the problem in terms of values (such as neighborhood solidarity) which are not amenable to expert analysis. "We need no experts. These people will verify themselves the effect of noise. . . . Massport is extremely arrogant. They do not have the slightest conception of the human suffering they cause and could not care less."[24]

Airport critics pointed out various technical errors and problems of interpretation in Massport's predictions and environmental impact statements; but this simply reconfirmed the community's suspicion of Massport, and further polarized the dispute. Later, these same experts who were sympathetic to East Boston's noise problem failed to convince the community to accept a Massport plan for a sound barrier. Despite advice that this would help to relieve their noise problem, the community chose to oppose construction of the barrier. Local activists feared that this was a diversion, and that if they accepted this project the community would somehow lose out in the long run. Thus, they disregarded expert opinion that this was a favorable decision, and the old mistrust prevailed.

## SUMMARY AND CONCLUSIONS

The two conflicts described above, over the siting of a power plant and the expansion of an airport, have several aspects in common. One can trace parallels, for instance, in the way the developers used expertise as a basis and justification of their planning decisions; how experts on both sides of the controversy entered the dispute and presented their technical arguments; and how citizens affected by the plan perceived the dispute. Similarities are evident in public statements, as developers, experts, and citizens expressed their concerns about various aspects of the decision-making process. These are compared in Table 2. These similarities, especially with respect to the use of scientific knowledge, suggest several related propositions which may be generalizable to other controversies involving conflicting technical expertise:

First, *developers seek expertise to legitimize their plans and they use their command of technical knowledge to justify their autonomy.* They assume that special technical competence is a reason to preclude outside public (or "democratic") control.

Second, *while expert advice can help to clarify technical constraints, it also is likely to increase conflict,* especially when expertise is available to those communities affected by a plan. Citizens' groups are increasingly seeking their own expertise to neutralize the impact of data provided by project developers.[25] Most issues that have become politically controversial (environmental problems, fluoridation, DDT) contain basic technical as well as political uncertainties, and evidence can easily be mustered to support or oppose a given proposal.

Third, *the extent to which technical advice is accepted depends less on its validity and the competence of the expert, than on the extent to which it reinforces existing positions.* Our two cases suggest that factors such as trust in authority, the economic or employment context in which a controversy takes place, and the intensity of local concern will matter more than the quality or character of technical advice.[26]

## Table 2.  Perspectives on decision making and expertise

|  | Power plant dispute | Runway dispute |
|---|---|---|
| **Developers** | | |
| On responsibility and competence for planning | Our study is the most comprehensive study ever made on the lake. Opponents can create delays but are not required to assume responsibility. | We are closer and more knowledgeable than any other group no matter what their intention may be, on what Logan Airport . . . what Metropolitan Boston . . . what New England needs. |
| On public debate | We have adopted a posture of no public debate. | We have competent staffs . . . I can't see any sense in having a public hearing . . . if it is to be by consensus that the authority operates. . . . |
| **Experts (consultants)** | | |
| On impact of project | Alternate approaches would have undesirable effects on the human environment . . . the proposed design should produce no significant impact. Actual individuals would be exposed to much lower doses than that due to normal habits. | Adverse environmental impact will result from failure to undertake this project as contrasted with the impact if the authority proceeds. Noise measurements of typical urban noise conditions . . . show that street level background noise overshadows taxiway noise. |
| On planning | Although an ecological model might be desirable from an academic viewpoint it is not felt to be necessary to provide an adequate assessment of the impact of the minor perturbation introduced by the proposed plant. | A master plan would be nothing more than an academic exercise . . . a study of this magnitude could never be justified for a small project of this nature. |
| **Experts (critics)** | | |
| On developers' data | Statements and conclusions were not justified and must therefore be regarded as nothing more than guesses. . . . The data base is not only inadequate, but misleading. | Analysis of the economic impact of Logan Airport shows demonstrated "blatant puffery" in the figures appearing in the report. |
| **Citizens (project supporters)** | | |
| On decision-making responsibility | Let us allow the professionals to make the decisions that they get paid to make. | In terms of efficient and competent operation, Massport is head and shoulders above other agencies. |
| **Citizens (project opponents)** | | |
| On decision-making responsibility | To say that our future is out of our hands and entrusted to scientists and technicians is an arrogant assumption. . . . We suggest that the opinions of area residents who care deeply about their environment and its future is of equal if not greater importance. | We need no experts. These people will verify themselves. . . . Massport is extremely arrogant. They do not have the slightest conception of the human suffering they cause and could not care less. |

**Table 2.** (contd.)

| On decision-making process | Were they using the power the people gave them to support their own feelings or those of private concerns? There is representative government in our country, but it sure isn't in our county. | What is really on trial here is not just the Port Authority, it is really the American system. Will it listen to spokesmen for the people and the people who speak for themselves? |
| --- | --- | --- |

Fourth, *those opposing a decision need not muster equal evidence.* It is sufficient to raise questions that will undermine the expertise of a developer whose power and legitimacy rests on his monopoly of knowledge or claims of special competence.

Fifth, *conflict among experts reduces their political impact.* The influence of experts is based on public trust in the infallibility of expertise. Ironically, the increasing participation of scientists in political life may reduce their effectiveness, for the conflict among scientists that invariably follows from their participation in controversial policies highlights their fallibility, demystifies their special expertise, and calls attention to nontechnical and political assumptions that influence technical advice.[27]

Finally, *the role of experts appears to be similar regardless of whether they are "hard" or "soft" scientists.* The two conflicts described here involved scientists, engineers, economists, and lawyers as experts. The similarities suggest that the technical complexity of the controversial issues does not greatly influence the political nature of a dispute.

In sum, the way in which clients (either developers or citizens' groups) direct and use the work of experts embodies their subjective construction of reality—their judgments, for example, about public priorities or about the level of acceptable risk or discomfort. When there is conflict in such judgments, it is bound to be reflected in a biased use of technical knowledge, in which the value of scientific work depends less on its merits than on its utility.

## NOTES

1. See discussion of the increased demands for expert decision-making in Garry Brewer, *Politicians, Bureaucrats and the Consultant* (New York: Basic Books, 1973). Also, Dean Schooler, Jr., in *Science, Scientists, and Public Policy* (Glencoe, Ill.: The Free Press, 1971), suggests that in the past, scientific influence has concentrated in government entrepreneurial areas such as space exploration, or in policy areas defined in terms of national security. The participation and influence of scientists has traditionally been rather minimal in policy areas with redistributive implications, e.g., social policy, transportation, and other issues subject to social conflict and competing political interests. As the public seeks technical solutions to social problems, and as scientists themselves become engaged in controversial public issues, this pattern is changing.

2. Harvey Brooks, "Scientific Concepts and Cultural Change," *Daedalus* 94 (Winter 1965):68.

3. Yaron Ezrahi, "The Political Resources of American Science," *Science Studies* 1(1971):121. See also Don K. Price, *Government and Science* (New York University Press, 1954).

4. For a discussion of the historical tradition of resentment of experts in the United States see Richard Hofstadter, *Anti-Intellectualism in American Life* (New York: Knopf, 1962).

5. See Robert Lane, "The Decline of Politics and Ideology in a Knowledgeable Society," *American Sociological Review* 31 (October 1966):649–62, and Daniel Bell, *The End of Ideology* (New York: The Free Press, 1960).

6. See discussion in Michel Crozier, *The Stalled Society* (New York: Viking Press, 1973), chapter 3. A vivid example of the importance of this tendency to monopolize knowledge occurred during the "energy crisis" with the realization that the large oil companies had nearly exclusive knowledge on the state of oil reserves.

7. I am using this term to describe a phenomenon that Orion White and Gideon Sioberg call "mobilization politics," in "The Emerging New Politics in America," in M.D. Hancock and Gideon Sjoberg (eds.), *Politics in the Post-Welfare State* (New York: Columbia University Press, 1972), p. 23.

8. Note for example the system of "scientific advocacy" proposed by John W. Gofman and Arthur R. Tamplin, *Poisoned Power* (Emmaus, Pa.: Rodale Press, 1971). A similar system is suggested by Donald Geesaman and Dean Abrahamson in "Forensic Science—A Proposal," *Science and Public Affairs (Bulletin of the Atomic Scientists)* 29 (March 1973):17. Thomas Reiner has proposed a system of community technical services in "The Planner as a Value Technician: Two Classes of Utopian Constructs and their Impact on Planning," in H. Wentworth Eldridge (ed.), *Taming Megalopolis,* vol. 1 (New York: Anchor Books, 1967). Based on systems similar to legal advocacy and expert witness in the courts, such proposals are intended to make technical advice more widely available to citizens' groups—usually through provision of public funds to underwrite the cost of expertise.

9. Allan Mazur, "Disputes between Experts," *Minerva* 11(April 1973):243–62.

10. Guy Benveniste, *The Politics of Expertise* (Boston, Mass.: Glendessary Press, 1972). See also Leonard Rubin, "Politics and information in the Anti-Poverty Programs," *Policy Studies Journal* 2 (Spring 1974):190–95.

11. Lauriston R. King and Philip Melanson, "Knowledge and Politics," *Public Policy* 20(Winter 1972):82–101.

12. For a history and analysis of this controversy see Dorothy Nelkin, *Nuclear Power and its Critics* (Ithaca, N.Y.: Cornell University Press, 1971); "Scientists in an Environmental Controversy," *Science Studies* 1(1971):245–61; and "The Role of Experts in a Nuclear Siting Controversy," *Science and Public Affairs* 30(November 1974):29–36.

13. Documentation of this conflict can be found in Dorothy Nelkin, *Jetport: The Boston Airport Controversy* (New Brunswick, N.J.: Transaction Books, 1974).

14. Two hundred copies of the critique were sent to libraries, citizens' groups, faculties at universities and colleges in the area, officials in state and federal agencies, political representatives in local, state and federal government, and newspapers.

15. Unless otherwise noted, the quotations that follow are from local environmental reports, memos, letters, and public hearings. They are statements by the opposing scientists involved in the controversy.

16. Mazur (see note 9) also documents the use of rhetoric in technical debates.

17. William A. Lyons, "Recommendations of the Executive Offices of New York State Electric and Gas Corporation to the Board of Directors" (July 13, 1973).

18. Edward King, Massport Executive Director, Testimony at US Corps of Engineers' "Hearings on the Application by the MPA for a Permit to Fill the Areas of Boston Harbor," February 26, 1971, mimeograph, p. 101.

19. Landrum and Brown, Inc., *Boston-Logan International Airport Environmental Impact Analysis,* February 11, 1972, section ix, 3.

20. A systematic critique of Massport's data was made by a commission chaired by Robert Behn (Chairman of Governor's Task Force on Inter-City Transportation), "Report to Governor Sargent," April 1971.

21. For further discussion of this point, see Nelkin, "The Role of Experts in a Nuclear Siting Controversy" (note 12).

22. CCSL (Citizens Committee to Save Cayuga Lake) *Newsletter* 6 (April 1973). This newsletter

reprinted in full a selection of well-informed articles—notably those by Robert Gillette in *Science* 176 (May 5, 1973); 177 (July 28, 1972, September 8, 1972, September 19, 1972, and September 22, 1972); and 179 (January 26, 1973).

23. Statement by Jane Rice cited in the *Ithaca Journal,* May 14, 1973, p. 1.

24. These statements are from testimony at US Corps of Engineers' Hearings (note 18). The ultimate expression of this kind of sentiment was, of course, the remark alleged to have been made by former Vice-President Spiro Agnew, responding to the report by the US Presidential Commission on Pornography and Obscenity: "I don't care what the experts say, I *know* pornography corrupts!"

25. For further discussion of the tactics of using expertise within the fluoridation controversy, for example, see Robert Crain et al., *The Politics of Community Conflict* (New York: Bobbs Merrill, 1969); and H. M. Sapolsky, "Science, Voters and the Fluoridation Controversy," *Science* 162 (October 25, 1968): 427–33.

26. The relation between beliefs and the interpretation of scientific information is analyzed in S. B. Barnes, "On the Reception of Scientific Beliefs," in Barry Barnes (ed.), *Sociology of Science* (Hammondsworth, Middlesex, England: Penguin Books, 1972), pp. 269–91.

27. See discussion of how controversy among scientists influences legislators in Barnes (note 26).

## 21

# Technē and Politeia:
# The Technical Constitution of Society

### Langdon Winner

At the beginning of Western political theory a powerful analogy links the practice of technology to that of politics. In his *Republic, Laws, Statesman*, and other discourses, Plato asserts that statecraft is a *technē*, one of the practical arts. Much like architecture, the building of ships, and other commonly recognized arts and crafts, politics is a field of practice that has its own distinctive knowledge, its own special skills. One purpose of Plato's argument was to discredit those who believed that the affairs of public life could be left to mere amateurs. But beyond that, it is clear that he thought the art of politics could be useful in the same way as any other *technē*, that is, it could produce finished works of lasting value. The works he had in mind were good constitutions, supremely well-crafted products of political architecture. *Politeia*, the title of the *Republic* in Greek, means the constitution of a polis, the proper order of human relationships within a city-state. The dialogue describes and justifies what Plato holds to be the institutional arrangements appropriate to the best *politeia*. He returns to this theme in the *Laws*, a discussion of the "second best" constitution, comparing his work to that of a well-established craft. "The shipwright, you know, begins his work by laying down the keel of the vessel and indicating her outlines, and I feel myself to be doing the same thing in my attempt to present you with outlines of human lives. . . . I

From *Philosophy and Technology*, Paul T. Durbin and Friedrich Rapp (eds.), pp. 97–111, D. Reidel. Copyright © 1983 by D. Reidel Publishing Company. Reproduced by permission of Kluwer Academic Publishers.

am really laying the keels of the vessels by due consideration of the question by what means or manner of life we shall make our voyage over the sea of time to the best purpose."[1]

In Plato's interpretation the analogy between technology and politics works in one direction only; *technē* serves as a model for politics, not the other way around. Having employed this notion for its own purposes, he took a further step, seeking to segregate the substance of politics from any other form of *technē* whatsoever. Thus, in the *Laws* he excludes craftsmen from positions of citizenship (because they already have an art that requires their full attention) and forbids citizens to enagage in any material craft (because citizenship makes its own full demands upon them—a judgment that reflects his supreme respect for the dedication *technē* involves and his suspicion of material pursuits in general. Evidently, it did not occur to Plato or to anyone else for a very long time that the analogy could at some point qualify in reverse, that *technē* itself might become a *politeia*, that technical forms of life might in themselves give powerful and authoritative shape to human affairs. If that ever did occur, what would the response of political theory be?

The one-sided comparison of technical and political creativity appears again in modern political thought. Writing in the *Social Contact*, Jean-Jacques Rousseau employs a mechanical metaphor to illuminate the art of constitution making. "A prince," he says, "has only to follow a model which the lawgiver provides. The lawgiver is the engineer who invents the machine; the prince is merely the mechanic who sets it up and operates it."[2] At another point in the book, Rousseau compares the work of the lawgiver to that of an architect. With a frustrated ambition reminiscent of Plato's, Rousseau offered himself as a political engineer or architect of exactly this kind, writing treatises on the constitutions of Corsica and Poland in the hope that his ideas might influence the founding of new states.

An opportunity of exactly that kind later became available to the founders of modern nation states, among them the leaders of the American Revolution. From the earliest rumblings of rebellion in the seventeenth century to the adoption of the Federal Constitution in 1787, the nation was alive with disputes about the application of political principles to the design of public institutions. Taking what they found useful from previous history and existing theories, thinkers like Madison, Hamilton, Adams, and Jefferson tried to devise a "science of politics," a science specifically aimed at providing knowledge for a collective set of architectonic skill. Thus, in *The Federalist Papers*, to take one example, we find a sustained discussion of how one moves from abstract political notions such as power, liberty, and public good to their tangible manifestations in the divisions, functions, powers, relationships, and limits of the Constitution. "The science of politics, . . ." Hamilton explains in *Federalist* No. 9, "like most other sciences, has received great improvement. The efficacy of various principles is now well understood, which were either not known at all, or imperfectly known to the ancients. The regular distribution of power into distinct departments; the introduction of legislative balances and checks; the institution of courts composed of judges holding their offices during good behavior; the representation of the people in the legislature by deputies of their own election: these are wholly new discoveries, or have made their principal progress towards perfection in modern times." Metaphors from eighteenth-century science and mechanical invention—e.g., "the ENLARGEMENT of the ORBIT within which such systems are to revolve"[3] and references to the idea of checks and balances—pervade *The Federalist Papers* and indicate the extent to which its writers saw the founding as the creation of an ingenious political mechanical device.

But even as the eighteenth century was reviewing the ancient analogy between technology and politics, even as philosopher statesmen were restoring the ancient art of constitution-making, another extremely powerful mode of institutionalization was taking shape in America and Europe. The Industrial Revolution with its distinctive ways of arranging people, machines, and materials for production very soon began to compete with strictly political institutions for power, authority, and the loyalties of men and women. *Technē* and *politeia*, long thought to be entirely separate phenomena within the category of human works, were drawing closer together.

Writing in 1781 in his *Notes on Virginia*, Thomas Jefferson noted the new force abroad in the world and commented upon its probable meaning for public life. The system of manufactures emerging at the time would, he argued, be incompatible with the life of a stable, virtuous republic. Manufacturing would create a thoroughly dependent rather than a self-sufficient populace. "Dependence," he warned, "begets subservience and venality, suffocates the germ of virtue, and prepares fit tools for the design of ambition." In his view the industrial mode of production threatened the "manners and spirit of a people which preserve a republic in vigor. A degeneracy in these is a canker which soon eats to the heart of its laws and constitution."[4] For that reason he advised, in this book at least, that Americans agree to leave the workshops in Europe.

There are signs that a desire to shape industrial development to accord with the principles of the republican political tradition continued to interest some Americans well into the 1830s. Attempts to include elements of republican community in the building of the factory town in Lowell, Massachusetts show this impulse at work.[5] But these efforts were neither prominent within economic patterns then taking shape nor successful in their own right. In the 1840s and decades since, the notion that industrial development might be shaped or limited by republican virtues—virtues of frugality, self-restraint, respect for the public good, and the like—dropped out of common discourse, echoed in the woeful lamentations of Henry David Thoreau, Henry Adams, Lewis Mumford, Paul Goodman, and a host of others now flippantly dismissed as "romantics" and "pastoralists."

In fact, the republican tradition of political thought had long since made its peace with the primary carrier of technical change, entrepreneurial capitalism. Moral and political thinkers from Machiavelli to Montesquieu and Adam Smith had argued that the pursuit of economic advantage is a civilizing, moderating influence in society, the very basis of stable government. Rather than engage the fierce passion for glory that often leads to conflict, it is better, so the argument goes, to convince people to pursue their self-interest, an interest that inclines them toward rational behavior.[6] The framers of the American constitution were, by and large, convinced of the wisdom of this formula. They expected that Americans would act in a self-interested manner, employing whatever instruments they needed to generate wealth. The competition of these interests in society would, they believed, provide a check upon the concentration of power in the hands of any one faction. Thus, in one important sense, republicanism and capitalism were fully reconciled at the time of the founding.

By the middle of the nineteenth century this point of view had been strongly augmented by another idea, one that to this day informs the self-image of Americans—a notion that equates abundance and freedom. The country was rich in land and resources; people liberated from the social hierarchies and status definitions of traditional societies were given the opportunity to exploit that material bounty in whatever ways they could muster. In this context, new technologies were seen as an undeniable blessing because they enabled the treasures to be extracted more quickly, because they vastly increased the product of labor. Factories, railroads, steamboats, telegraphs, and the like were greeted as the very essence of democratic freedom for the ways they rendered, as one mid-nineteenth century writer explained, "the conveniences and elegancies of life accessible to the many instead of the few."[7]

American society encouraged people to be self-determining, to pursue their own economic goals. That policy would work, it was commonly believed, only if there was a surplus that guaranteed enough to go around. Class conflict, the scourge of democracy in the ancient world, could be avoided in the United States because the inequalities present in society would not matter very much. Material abundance would make it possible for everybody to have enough to be perfectly happy. Eventually, Americans took this notion to be a generally applicable theory: economic enterprise driven by the engine of technical improvement was the very essence of human freedom. Franklin D. Roosevelt reportedly remarked that if he could put one American book in the hands of every Russian, it would be the Sears, Roebuck catalogue.

In this way of looking at things, the form of technology you adopt does not matter. If you have cornucopia in your grasp, you do not worry about its shape. Insofar as it is a powerful thing, more power to it. Anything that history, literature, philosophy, or long-standing traditions might have to suggest about the prudence one ought to employ in the shaping of new institutions can be thrown in the trash bin. Describing the Industrial Revolution in Britain, historian Karl Polanyi drew an accurate picture of this attitude.

"Fired by an emotional faith in spontaneity, the commonsense attitude toward change was discarded in favor of a mystical readiness to accept the social consequences of economic improvement, whatever they might be. The elementary truths of political science and statecraft were first discarded, then forgotten. It should need no elaboration that a process of undirected change, the pace of which is deemed too fast, should be slowed down, if possible, so as to safeguard the welfare of the community. Such household truths of traditional statesmanship, often merely reflecting the teachings of a social philosophy inherited from the ancients, were in the nineteenth century erased from the thoughts of the educated by the corrosive of a crude utilitarianism combined with an uncritical reliance on the alleged self-healing virtues of unconscious growth."[8] Indeed, by the late nineteenth century, an impressive array of scientific discoveries, technical inventions, and industrial motivations seemed to make the mastery of nature an accomplished fact rather than an idle dream. Many took this as a sign that all ancient wisdom had simply been rendered obsolete. As one chronicler of the new technology wrote in *Scientific American*: "The speculative philosophy of the past is but a too empty consolation for short-lived, busy man, and seeing with the eye of science the possibilities of matter, he has touched it with the divine breath of thought and made a new world."[9]

Today we can examine the world of interconnected systems in manufacturing, communications, transportation, and the like that have arisen over the past two centuries and appreciate how they form *de facto* a constitution of a sociotechnical order. This way of arranging people and things, of course, did not develop as the result of the application of any particular plan or political theory. It grew gradually and in separate increments, invention by invention, industry by industry, engineering project by engineering project, system by system. From a contemporary vantage point, nevertheless, one can notice some of its characteristics and begin to see how they embody answers to age-old political questions about membership, power, authority, order, freedom, justice, and the conditions of government. Several of the characteristics that matter in this way of seeing, characteristics that would have interested Plato or Rousseau or Madison, are, very briefly, the following.

First is the ability of technologies of transportation and communication to facilitate control over events from a single center or small number of centers. Largely unchecked by effective countervailing influence, there has been an extraordinary centralization of social control in large business corporations, bureaucracies and, lest we forget, the military.

Second is a tendency for new devices and techniques to increase the most efficient or effective size of organized human associations. Over the past century more and more people have found themselves living and working within technology-based institutions that previous generations would have called gigantic. Justified by impressive economics of scale and (economics or not) always an expression of the power that accrues to very large organizations, this gigantism has become an accustomed feature of the material and social settings of everyday life.

Third is the way in which the rational arrangement of sociotechnical systems has tended to produce its own distinctive forms of hierarchical authority. Legitimized by the felt need to do things in what seems to be the most efficient, productive way, human roles and relationships are structured in rule-guided patterns that involve taking orders and giving orders along an elaborate chain of command. Thus, far from being an expression of democratic freedom, the reality of the workplace tends to be undisguisedly authoritarian.

Fourth is the tendency of large, centralized, hierarchically arranged sociotechnical systems to crowd out and eliminate other varieties of social activity. Hence, industrial production placed craftwork in eclipse; technologies of modern agribusiness made small scale farming all but impossible; high speed transportation crowded out slower means of getting about. It is not merely that useful devices and techniques of earlier periods have been rendered extinct, but also that the patterns of social existence and individual experience based upon them have vanished as living realities.

Fifth are the various ways that large sociotechnical organizations exercise power to control the social and political influences that ostensibly control them. In a process that I have elsewhere described as "reverse adaptation," the human needs, markets, and political institutions that might regulate technology-based systems are often subject to manipulation by those very systems.[10] Thus, to take one example, psychologically sophisticated techniques of advertising have become an accustomed way of altering people's ends to suit the structure of available means, a practice that now affects political campaigns no less than campaigns to sell underarm deodorant (with similar results).

There are, of course, other characteristics of today's technological systems that can accurately be read as political phenomena; it is certainly true that there are factors other than technology which figure prominently in the developments I have mentioned. What I want to indicate is that as our society adopts one sociotechnical system after another, it answers *de facto* a number of the most important questions that political philosophers have asked about the proper order of human affairs. Should power be centralized or dispersed? What is the best size for units of organized social activity? What constitutes justifiable authority in human associations? Does a free society depend upon social uniformity or social diversity? What are appropriate structures and processes of public deliberation and decision making? For the past century or longer our answers to such questions have been primarily instrumental ones, expressed in an instrumental language of efficiency and productivity, physically embodied in instrumentalities that often seem to be nothing more than ways of providing goods and services.

For those who have adopted the formula of freedom through abundance, however, the traditional questions have ceased to matter. In fact, it has commonly been assumed that whatever happened to be created in the sphere of material/instrumental culture would certainly be compatible with freedom and democracy. This amounts to a conviction that all technology is inherently liberating, a very peculir belief indeed.

It is true that on occasion agencies of the modern state have attempted to "regulate" business enterprises and technological applications of various kinds.[11] On balance, however, the extent of that regulation has been modest at best. In the United States absolute monopolies are sometimes outlawed only to be replaced by enormous semi-monopolies no less powerful in their ability to influence the life of society. The history of regulation shows abundant instances in which the rules and procedures that govern production or trade were actually demanded by or later captured by the industries they supposedly regulate. In general, the rule of thumb has been: if a business makes goods and services widely available, at low cost with due regard for public health and safety and with a reasonable return on investment, all is well.

In recent times the question of recognizing possible limits upon the growth of technologies has had something of a revival. Many people are now prepared to entertain the notion that a given technology be limited: (1) if its application threatens public health or safety, (2) if its use threatens to exhaust some vital resource, (3) if it degrades the quality of the environment—air, land, and water, (4) if it threatens natural species and wilderness areas that ought to be preserved, and (5) if its application causes social stresses and strains. Along with the ongoing discussion about ways to sustain economic growth and prosperity, these are about the only matters of "technology assessment" that the general public, decision makers, and academics are prepared to take seriously at present.

While such concerns are valid ones, they do severely restrict the range of moral and political criteria that are permissible in public discussions of technological change. Several years ago I tried to register my discomfort on this score with some colleagues in computer science who were doing a study of the then novel electronic funds transfer systems. They had concluded that such systems contained the potential for redistributing financial power in the world of banking. Electronic money would make possible a shift of power from smaller local banks to large institutions of national and international finance. They asked me to suggest a way of arguing the possible dangers of this development to their audience of scholars and policy makers. In a letter to them I recommended that their research might try to show that under conditions of heavy, continued exposure, electronic funds transfer causes cancer in laboratory animals. Surely, that finding would be cause for concern. My ironic suggestion acknowledged what I take to be the central characteristic of socially acceptable criticism of science and technology in our time. Unless one can demonstrate conclusively that a particular technical practice will generate some physically evident catastrophe—cancer, destruction of the ozone layer, or some other—one might as well shut up.

Even criteria of that kind, however, may soon erode. In a style of analysis now being perfected in the United States and Europe, the outright banning of carcinogenic and mutagenic substances is now considered an overwrought policy. Rather than eliminate from human consumption any substance shown to cause cancer or birth defects in laboratory animals, we are asked to substitute "risk/benefit analysis." In that rapidly developing, highly qualified moral science, people are (in effect) asked to acknowledge cancer and birth defects as among the exhilarating risks—often compared to flying or mountain climbing!—we run in order to live in such a materially abundant society. Like our factories that need a dose of "reindustrialization" to bring them back to life, our nihilism is now being completely retooled, becoming at long last a truly rigorous discipline.

But even before risk/benefit analysis helps dissolve existing public norms of care and prudence—e.g., the Delaney clause of the Food and Drug Act—it is important to notice how very narrow attempts to guide or limit the direction of technological innovation have been up to this point. The development of techniques of technology assessment during the 1960s and 1970s did little to alter the widespread belief that ultimately what matters is economic growth and efficiency. As regards the substance of its many studies, the Office of Technology of Assessment established by the U.S. Congress could well change its name to the office of Economic Growth and Efficiency Research. Whatever hope there may have been for contemporary universities to produce critical reevaluations of science and technology have largely faded. Academic departments and programs in science, technology, and society have vastly improved our ability to generate intricate descriptions, explanations, and apologies for what scientific and technical institutions do. But such programs are, for the most part, completely sterile as regards any serious questioning of the central practices they study. Criticism of technology is taken to be a sign of bad taste, even bad collegiality, not to mention a threat to S.T.S. groups' sources of funding.

The renewed conversation about technology and society has continued to a point at which an obvious question needs to be asked: Are there no shared ends that matter greatly to us any longer than the desire to be affluent while avoiding the risk of cancer? It may be that the answer is "no." The prevailing social consensus seems to be that people love the life of high consumption, tremble at the thought that it might end, and are displeased about having to clean up the various messes that modern technology sometimes brings. To argue a moral position convincingly these days requires that one speak to (and not depart from) concerns of this kind. One must engage people's love of material well-being, their fascination with efficiency, or their fear of death. The moral sentiments that hold force, that can be played upon in attempts to change social behavior, are those described by Adam Smith and Thomas Hobbes. I do not wish to deny the validity of these sentiments, only to suggest that they comprise an extremely narrow set. We continue to disregard a problem that has been brewing since the earliest days of the Industrial Revolution—whether our society will find it possible to establish forms and limits for technological change, forms and limits that derive from a positively articulated idea of what society ought to be.

To aid our thinking about such matters, I would suggest we begin with a simple heuristic device. Let us suppose that every political philosophy in a given time implies a technology or set of technologies in a particular configuration for its realization. And let us recognize that every technology of significance to us implies a set of political commitments that one can identify if one looks carefully enough. To state it more directly, what appear to be merely instrumental choices are better seen as choices about the form of the society we continually build, choices about the kinds of people we want to be. Plato's metaphor, especially his reference to the shipwright, is one that a high technology age ought to take literally: we ought to lay out the keels of our vessels with due consideration to what means or manner of life we shall make our voyage over the sea of time to best purpose. The vessels that matter now are such things as communications systems, transit systems, energy supply and distribution systems, household instruments, biomedical technologies, and of course systems of industrial and agricultural production.

In one way or another, issues of this kind are addressed and settled in the course of technological change. Often they appear as subliminal or concealed agendas in discussions that seem to be about efficiency, productivity, abundance, profit, and market conditions. For instance, it is possible to read the dozens of sophisticated energy studies that have been done during the past ten years and interpret them for the social and political structures their analyses and recommendations imply. Will it be nuclear power administered by a benign priesthood of scientists? Will it be coal and oil brought to you by large multinational corporations? Will it be synthetic fuels, directly subsidized and administered by the state? Will it be the soft energy path brought to you by you and your neighbors?

Whatever one's position might be, the prevailing consensus requires that all parties argue their positions solely on grounds of efficiency. Regardless of how a particular energy solution will distribute social power, the case for or against it must be stated as a practical necessity that derives from demonstrable conditions of efficiency. Thus, even those who favor decentralist energy solutions feel compelled to rest their claims solely on the grounds: "This way is most efficient." Prominent among these now is Amory Lovins who writes, "While not under the illusion that facts are separable from values, I have tried to separate my personal preferences from my analytic assumptions and to rely not on modes of discourse that might be viewed as overtly ideological, but rather on classical arguments of economic and engineering efficiency (which are only tacitly ideological)."[12] In his book, *Soft Energy Paths*, Lovins notices "centrism, vulnerability, technocracy, repression, alienation," and other grave problems present in the existing energy sector. He sets out to compare "two energy paths that are distinguished by their antithetical social implications." Then he notes that basing energy decisions on social criteria may appear to involve a "heroic decision," that is "doing something the more expensive way because it is desirable on other more important grounds than internal cost."

But fear not. "Surprisingly," he writes, "a heroic decision does not seem to be necessary in this case, because the energy system that seems socially more attractive is also cheaper and easier."[13] But what if the analysis had shown the contrary? Would Lovins and others who play the energy policy game be prepared to give up the social advantages believed to exist along the soft energy path? Would they feel compelled by the logic of analytic, empirical demonstration to embrace "centrism, vulnerability, technocracy, repression, alienation," and the like? Here Lovins gives up ground that has in modern history again and again been abandoned as lost territory. It raises the question of whether even the best meaning among us are anything more than mere efficiency worshippers.

The same tendency stands out in the arguments of those who seek to defend democratic self-management and small scale technology. More often than not, they feel compelled to show their proposal is more efficient rather than endorse it on directly social or political grounds: that is, indeed, one way of catching people's attention; if you can get away with it, it is certainly the most convincing variety of argument. But victories won in this way are in other important respects great losses. For they affirm in our words, our very methodologies, that there are certain human ends that no longer dare speak their names in public. The silence grows deeper by the day.

As long as we respond reflexively to the latest "crisis," energy crisis or some other, as long as we persist in seeing the world as a set of discrete "problems" awaiting ingeniously concocted "solutions," the failure to consider the question of ends will continue. True, the idea that society might try to guide its own sociotechnical development according to preconceived articulations of form and limit has only a tiny constituency, no larger than that which existed among the utopians and social reformers of the early nineteenth century. It is, in fact, a matter of pride for many engaged in the scientific, technical, and financial aspects of innovation in material culture that we do not know where we are going until we get there. Nevertheless, it may still be possible to stand outside the stampede long enough to begin regaining our bearings.

My suggestion is that each significant area of technical/functional organization in modern society be seen as a kind of regime, *a regime of instrumentality*, under which we are obliged to live. Thus, there are a number of regimes of mass production, each with a structure that may be interpreted as a technopolitical phenomenon. There are a number of regimes in energy production and distribution, in petroleum, coal, hydroelectric, nuclear power, etc., each with a form that can be seen as a political phenomenon. There is, of course, the regime of network television and that of the automobile. If one were to identify and characterize all of the instrumental/functional sociotechnical systems of our society, all of our regimes of instrumentality and their complex interconnections, one would have a picture of a second constitution, one that stands parallel to and occasionally overlaps the constitution of political society as such. The important task becomes, therefore, not that of studying the "impacts" of technical change—a social scientific approach committed to a passive stance—but of evaluating the material and social infrastructures that specific technologies create for our life's activity.[14] We should try to imagine and seek to build technical infrastructures compatible with freedom, justice, and other crucial political ends.

One set of technical possibilities that I find interesting from this point of view are those involved in the development of photovoltaic systems. Here is a case in which the crucial choices have yet to be made. We can expect to see the events unfold in our lifetime with outcomes that could have many different dimensions. The short version of the story, as I would tell it, goes as follows. If solar cells become feasible to mass produce, if their price in installed systems comes down to a reasonable level (rather than being outrageously expensive when compared to other means of producing electricity), solar electricity can make a contribution to our energy needs. If it should occur that photovoltaic systems do become technically and economically feasible (and many working with such systems find the auspices good), then there will be—at least in principle—a choice about how to structure these systems.

One could, for example, build centralized photovoltaic farms that hook directly into the existing electrical grid like any other form of central power. One could produce fully stand-alone systems placed on the rooftops of homes, schools, factories, and the like. Or one could design and build intermediate sized ensembles, perhaps at a neighborhood level. In one way or another a number of questions will eventually be answered. Will society have photovoltaics in any substantial number at all? How large should such systems be? Who should own them? How should they be managed? Should they be "fully automatic"? Or should the producer/consumer of solar power be involved in activities of load management?

I believe that if one wants technical diversity as part of the infrastructure of freedom in the regime of renewable energy, then a disaggregated, decentralized design of photovoltaic power could be counted a positive good. In saying this, I would not ask anyone to make exorbitant economic sacrifices. But rather than pursue the lemming-like course of choosing only that system which gives the lowest cost kilowatt, perhaps we ought to ask whether or not that lowest cost design simply reproduces the large, centralized, uniform, automatic sociotechnical patterns that contribute to the ways people find themselves to be insignificant, not involved, powerless. To propose an innovation of this kind does not, by the way, presuppose that existing producers and suppliers of electricity are somehow evil. I am speaking of the kinds of patterns in material culture that eventually become forms of social life and individual experience, suggesting that we actively seek to create patterns that manifest (rather than mock) the idea of a good society.[15]

It goes without saying that the people now actively developing photovoltaics have no such questions in mind. Government subsidized research, development, and implementation processes in the United States now rest upon the explicit aim of finding that lowest cost kilowatt, and helping it be commercialized in the "private sector."[16] In the meantime, large multinational petroleum companies that have no particular interest in solar power have been buying up companies at work in this field; their motive seems to be a desire to control the configuration of whatever mix of energy sources this society eventually receives and to influence the rates of transition. Rather than simply echo what a growing number of journalists and scholars like to do when confronted with evidence of this kind, namely to look at a particular area of development and decry the role of capitalist corporations yet again, I believe it is important to reclaim the critical sense of possibilities. To keep alive our sense of which alternatives exist, why they matter and why they are not being chosen is the most important role that the study of technology and society can play right now. Otherwise, it seems to me, research and thinking of this kind can become little more than detached description or bitter lament.

In our time *techne* has at last become *politeia*. What appear to be merely useful artifacts are, from another point of view, underlying preconditions of social activity. Our instruments are institutions in the making. In a world already saturated by a myriad of devices and systems (with more and more on the horizon all the time), the modern idea that equates technology, material abundance, and freedom can only be a source of blindness. If our society is to recapture the power to determine consciously its own form (rather than flitter wildly about in pursuit of each new mechanical, electronic, or biotechnical novelty), each new technology of any significance must be examined with respect to the way it will become a durable infrastructure of human life. Insofar as the possibilities present in that technology allow it, the thing ought to be designed in both its hardware and social components to accord with a deliberately articulated, widely shared notion of a society worthy of our care and loyalty, a notion defined by an open, broadly based process of deliberation. If it is clear that the social contract implicitly created by implementing a particular generic variety of technology is incompatible with the kind of society we would deliberately choose, then that kind of device or system ought to be excluded from society altogether.

A crucial failure of modern political theory has been its inability or unwillingness even to begin this project: critical evaluation of society's technical constitution. The silence of modern liberalism on this issue is matched by an equally obvious neglect in Marxist theory. Both persuasions have enthusiastically sought freedom in sheer material plenitude, welcoming whatever technological means (or monstrosities) seemed to produce abundance fastest. It is, however, a serious mistake to construct one sociotechnical system after another in the blind faith that each will automatically be compatible with a free humanity. Many crucial choices about the form and limits of our regimes of instrumentality must be enforced at the time of the founding, at the genesis of new technology. It is here that our best purposes must be heard.

Through technological creation and in other ways, we make a world for each other to live in. Much more than we have acknowledged in the past, we must own our responsibility for what we are making.

## NOTES

1. Plato, *Laws* 7.803b, translated by A. E. Taylor, in *The Collected Dialogues of Plato*, Edith Hamilton and Huntington Cairns (eds.) (Princeton, N.J.: Princeton University Press, 1961), p. 1374.

2. Jean-Jacques Rousseau, *The Social Contract*, translated and introduced by Maurice Cranston (Harmondsworth, Middlesex, England: Penguin Books, 1968), p. 84.

3. Alexander Hamilton, Federalist No. 9, in *The Federalist Papers*, with an introduction by Clinton Rossiter (New York: Mentor Books, 1961), pp. 72–73.

4. Thomas Jefferson, *Notes on Virginia*, in *The Life and Selected Writings of Thomas Jefferson*, Adrienne Koch and William Peden (eds.) (New York: Modern Library, 1944), pp. 28–281.

5. See John Kasson, *Civilizing the Machine: Technology and Republican Values in America, 1776–1900* (New York: Grossman, 1976).

6. See Albert O. Hirschman, *The Passions and the Interests: Political Arguments for Capitalism before Its Triumph* (Princeton, N.J.: Princeton University Press, 1977).

7. Denison Olmsted, "On the Democratic Tendencies of Science, *Barnard's Journal of Education*, 1 (1855–1856), reprinted in *Changing Attitudes toward American Technology*, Thomas Parke Hughes (ed.) (New York: Harper & Row, 1975), p. 148.

8. Karl Polanyi, *The Great Transformation* (Boston: Beacon Press, 1957), p. 33.

9. "Beta" (Edward W. Byrn), "The Progress of Invention during the Past Fifty Years," *Scientific American* 75 (July 25, 1896), reprinted in Hughes (see note 7), pp. 158–59.

10. Langdon Winner, *Autonomous Technology: Technics-out-of-Control as a Theme in Political Thought* (Cambridge, Mass.: MIT Press, 1977).

11. A recent set of commentaries on the relative efficacy of regulation is contained in *The Politics of Regulation*, James Q. Wilson (ed.) (New York: Basic Books, 1980).

12. Amory B. Lovins, "Technology Is the Answer! (But What Was the Question?): Energy as a Case Study of Inappropriate Technology," discussion paper for the Symposium on Social Values and Technological Change in an International Context, Racine, Wis., June 1978, p. 1.

13. Amory B. Lovins, *Soft Energy Paths: Toward a Durable Peace* (Cambridge, Mass.: Ballinger, 1977), pp. 6–7.

14. See my argument in "Do Artifacts Have Politics?" *Daedalus* (Winter 1980): 121–36.

15. I suggest a way of addressing such issues in "Technologies as Forms of Life," in R. S. Cohen and M. W. Wartofsky (eds.), *Epistemology, Methodology, and the Social Sciences* (Norwell, Mass.: D. Reidel Publishing Company, 1983), pp. 249–63.

16. See for example, J. L. Smith, "Photovoltaics," *Science* 212, no. 4502 (June 26, 1981): 1472–78.

# Part Seven

# Alienated Labor

# Introduction

Working for most of us is a necessity, a means of earning our livelihood. But it is not merely a means, it is a way of life. To a considerable extent, we are what we do. Not only is our self-respect contingent upon the value we, and others, attribute to the work we do, but the nature and conditions of our employment are major determinants in our experience of the whole of life. If in our working life we find ourselves, to quote Winner, ". . . insignificant, not involved, powerless," this infects the very fabric of our existence.

Although the essays in this section focus on the nature of factory work, the analyses can be generalized and applied to a wide variety of occupations. Our society is rapidly shifting its economic base from manufacturing (the traditional smoke-stack industries) to hi-tech and service industries. However, work in all areas is increasingly organized on an industrial production model. There is even a push in higher education to increase efficiency. How many B.A.'s does this university crank out per faculty member? McDonald's is a highly integrated, efficient system of production and sales. Mass producing Big Macs is not essentially different from producing Mack trucks.

The concept of alienation has its roots in the philosophy of G. W. F. Hegel, but the most widely influential notion was that developed by the early Karl Marx in his discussion of alienated, or (in our translation) "estranged" labor. Since World War II "alienation" has been used by Marxists and non-Marxists alike in a variety of disciplines to describe a variety of phenomena. Unfortunately, it is difficult to discern any common meaning in all these uses. Some psychologists take "alienation" to signify a state characterized by feelings of powerlessness, loneliness, isolation, strangeness, and separation from one's society or self; a generalized feeling of meaninglessness and despair in the face of conditions over which one seems to have no control. On this account, it is a pathological condition that requires treatment.

Karl Marx, writing during the early stages of the Industrial Revolution, was deeply concerned about the dehumanizing conditions of work under the new system of industrial capitalism. Although it is labor that generates wealth, the laboring man does not receive this wealth, but only a minimal wage. The surplus goes toward capital accumulation. Thus, the rich get richer while the poor get poorer—economically *and* "spiritually."

Although scholars disagree about the precise meaning of "alienation" in the corpus of Marx's work, it is clear in our selection that alienation is not merely a subjective state of the worker. There are real, objective economic causes for "estranged" labor, and these lie in the property relations. Thus, it is capitalism that separates the laborer from (1) his product, (2) his "true" self, (3) his fellow workers, and (4) nature. The tragic consequence of this exploitation is that the worker ". . . does not affirm himself but denies himself, does not feel content but unhappy, does not develop freely his physical and mental energy but mortifies his body and ruins his mnd." Man becomes an animal, a commodity, merely another cost in the capitalists' ceaseless drive to increase profits.

Studs Terkel's *Working* consists of interviews with people from all walks of life. Although a few find their work to be a rich, creative, satisfying activity, the vast majority experience their jobs as a degrading and, if not back-breaking, a mind-numbing routine. Work for most is mere labor—a necessary means to a paycheck without any intrinsic satisfaction. In our selection, Mike Lefevre talks about his life as a steel worker, giving us a clear case of alienated labor—although it is clear that his job has not ruined his mind.

Mike is extraordinarily self-conscious and has thought seriously about those forces over which he has no control The problem as he sees it is not technology: "Machines can either liberate man or enslave 'im, because they're pretty neutral. It's man who has the bias to put the thing in one place or another." On the other hand he doesn't think communism is for the working man either: "That's where I couldn't buy communism. It's the intellectuals' utopia, not mine. I cannot picture myself singing to a tractor. . . ." The problem is not just the hard work, but the way work is organized and managed. But what can you do? "Who you gonna sock? You can't sock General Motors, you can't sock anybody in Washington, you can't sock a system."

Mr Lefevre feels trapped in a dehumanizing system and is tired, angry, and frustrated. Does he need psychological adjustment? Not on his view, for he says, "The day I get excited about my job is the day I go to a head shrinker." For him not to be alienated would be irrational.

How are we to understand "the system"? Is the alienation Marx describes the consequence of the means of production or property relations, of technology or capitalism? Marxists and non-Marxists alike have found the notion of alienated labor a most insightful perspective; however, they disagree about both the precise understanding of "alienation" and its causes.

According to Robert Blauner, a non-Marxist sociologist, the root causes of alienation derive from the nature of industrial society, from the requirements of an efficient technological system of production. Feelings of powerlessness, meaninglessness, social alienation, and self-estrangement vary considerably in various occupations and industrial settings. Blauner claims that workers do not want to own the means of production, for capitalist ownership is a constant in modern, Western industry and employees do not expect to have influence from this direction. Nor do most manual workers resent hierarchical lines of authority. This too is taken as a "given," and workers do not want responsibility for the overall operation. They are only concerned with those factors that impinge directly on the conditions of their own work, and these matters have been rather effectively handled by labor unions through collective bargaining—a development which Marx did not anticipate.

Of course, the extreme division of labor exemplified in assembly line production makes work boring, but for most the time passes quickly. The idea that work should be self-fulfilling is quite modern and is embraced primarily by those who are highly educated. Contrary to Terkel's *Working,* Blauner's study concludes that most workers are quite satisfied with their jobs even though they experience high levels of alienation. As production becomes increasingly automated, we can anticipate a reduction in alienated labor.

Harry Braverman argues that the degradation of work is not the result of technology but the direct and intended aim of the capitalist organization of labor. The extreme division of labor in modern industry does not on this account derive from a technological imperative but from the desire of management to "discipline" the work force. Although the division of labor is intended to increase production, and thus profit, more importantly it aims at controlling the worker.

In developing his argument, Braverman gives a rather detailed analysis of Frederick Winslow Taylor's principles of management. While these purport to be scientific, Braverman claims they reflect nothing more than the unfounded assumptions of capitalism. "It starts . . . not from the human point of view but from the capitalist point of view. . . ." It does not inquire as to the causes of a refractory work force, of "alienated" workers, but accepts this as a given, a "natural" condition. Although contemporary management techniques have modified some of Taylor's specific methods, it would be a serious mistake to think that the purposes have been altered.

Taylor was quite explicit as to the purposes of capitalist management: (1) to gain a monopoly of skill from the workers, (2) to use this knowledge to "cheapen the worker by decreasing his training and enlarging his output," and thus (3) "to control each step of the labor process and its mode of execution." These principles apply to the management of labor regardless of the level of technology, from the unskilled loading of pig iron to, as we saw Noble argue, the machine tool industry.

Is it, then, the property relations under capitalism that create alienated labor? It is clear that workers in the Soviet Union are at least as alienated as American workers. This state of affairs has been cited to support the thesis that it is the means of production, the technological system, that is the major determinant of alienated labor, not who owns the means of production. One need not accept the autonomous technology thesis to agree with Ellul that it is useless to rail against capitalism. Technology spells the end of such ideologies as capitalism—and socialism. The drive for efficiency demands a division of labor and thus assembly line production techniques, and this is a sufficient condition for alienated labor. Substituting the state for corporate ownership of the means of production changes nothing.

Blauner may be right that American workers do not want to own the industries which employ them or the responsibilities of management. However, this becomes most problematic, for Marx claimed that what we in fact want is largely a product of the economic system under which we live. The "true" interests of the workers have been subverted by propaganda and higher wages.

To cite the Soviet Union in support of Blauner's claim that technology is the basic cause of alienation won't do, for their industry has also been organized "scientifically." When Lenin invited Taylor to the Soviet Union to "rationalize" their industrial system, Braverman could argue that this insured alienated workers. Both capitalistic and communistic systems have managed labor in an authoritarian way. We must not confuse bureaucratic and totalitarian socialism with the ideal of genuine democratic socialism. Perhaps Mike Lefevre would feel less alienated if he and his fellow workers owned and controlled the steel mill, even if they decided that efficient production demanded a strict division of labor.

# √ 22

# Estranged Labor*

## Karl Marx

We have proceeded from the premises of political economy. We have accepted its language and its laws. We presupposed private property, the separation of labor, capital and land, and of wages, profit of capital and rent of land—likewise division of labor, competition, the concept of exchange-value, etc. On the basis of political economy itself, in its own words, we have shown that the worker sinks to the level of a commodity and becomes indeed the most wretched of commodities; that the wretchedness of the worker is in inverse proportion to the power and magnitude of his production; that the necessary result of competition is the accumulation of capital in a few hands, and thus the restoration of monopoly in a more terrible form; that finally the distinction between capitalist and land-rentier, like that between the tiller of the soil and the factory-worker, disappears and that the whole of society must fall apart into the two classes—the property *owners* and the propertyless *workers*.

Political economy proceeds from the fact of private property, but it does not explain it to us. It expresses in general, abstract formulae the *material* process through which private property actually passes, and these formulae it then takes for *laws*. It does not *comprehend* these laws—i.e., it does not demonstrate how they arise from the very nature of private property. Political economy does not disclose the source of the division between labor and capital, and between capital and land. When, for example, it defines the relationship of wages to profit, it takes the interest of the capitalists to be the ultimate

From *Economic and Philosophic Manuscripts of 1844 by Karl Marx, and the Communist Manifesto by Karl Marx and Frederick Engels,* translated by Martin Milligan. Prometheus Books, 1988.

*Estranged Labor—*Die entfremdete Arbeit.*

cause; i.e., it takes for granted what it is supposed to evolve. Similarly, competition comes in everywhere. It is explained from external circumstances. As to how far these external and apparently fortuitous circumstances are but the expression of a necessary course of development, political economy teaches us nothing. We have seen how, to it, exchange itself appears to be a fortuitous fact. The only wheels which political economy sets in motion are *avarice* and the *war among the avaricious—competition.*

Precisely because political economy does not grasp the connections within the movement, it was possible to counterpose, for instance, the doctrine of competition to the doctrine of monopoly, the doctrine of craft-liberty to the doctrine of the corporation, the doctrine of the division of landed property to the doctrine of the big estate—for competition, craft-liberty and the division of landed property were explained and comprehended only as fortuitous, pre-meditated, and violent consequences of monopoly, the corporation, and feudal property, not as their necessary, inevitable, and natural consequences.

Now, therefore, we have to grasp the essential connection between private property, avarice, and the separation of labor, capital, and landed property; between exchange and competition, value and the devaluation of men, monopoly and competition, etc.; the connection between this whole estrangement and the *money*-system.

Do not let us go back to a fictitious primordial condition as the political economist does, when he tries to explain. Such a primordial condition explains nothing. He merely pushes the question away into a gray nebulous distance. He assumes in the form of fact, of an event, what he is supposed to deduce—namely, the necessary relationship between two things—between, for example, division of labor and exchange. Theology in the same way explains the origin of evil by the fall of man; that is, it assumes as a fact, in historical form, what has to be explained.

We proceed from an *actual* economic fact.

The worker becomes all the poorer the more wealth he produces, the more his production increases in power and range. The worker becomes an ever cheaper commodity the more commodities he creates. With the *increasing value* of the world of things proceeds in direct proportion the *devaluation* of the world of men. Labor produces not only commodities: it produces itself and the worker as a *commodity*—and does so in the proportion in which it produces commodities generally.

This fact expresses merely the object which labor produces—labor's product—confronts it as *something alien,* as a *power independent* of the producer. The product of labor is labor which has been congealed in an object, which has become material: it is the *objectification* of labor. Labor's realization is its objectification. In the conditions dealt with by political economy this realization of labor appears as *loss of reality* for the workers; objectification as *loss of the object* and *object-bondage;* appropriation as *estrangement,* as *alienation.**

---

*Alienation—*Entäusserung.*

So much does labor's realization appear as loss of reality that the worker loses reality to the point of starving to death. So much does objectification appear as loss of the object that the worker is robbed of the objects most necessary not only for his life but for his work. Indeed, labor itself becomes an object which he can get hold of only with the greatest effort and with the most irregular interruptions. So much does the appropriation of the object appear as estrangement that the more objects the worker produces the fewer can he possess and the more he falls under the dominion of his product, capital.

All these consequences are contained in the definition that the worker is related to the *product of his labor* as to an *alien* object. For on this premise it is clear that the more the worker spends himself, the more powerful the alien objective world becomes which he creates over-against himself, the poorer he himself—his inner world—becomes, the less belongs to him as his own. It is the same in religion. The more man puts into God, the less he retains in himself. The worker puts his life into the object; but now his life no longer belongs to him but to the object. Hence, the greater this activity, the greater is the worker's lack of objects. Whatever the product of his labor is, he is not. Therefore the greater this product, the less is he himself. The *alienation* of the worker in his product means not only that his labor becomes an object, an *external* existence, but that it exists *outside him,* independently, as something alien to him, and that it becomes a power on its own confronting him; it means that the life which he has conferred on the object confronts him as something hostile and alien.

Let us now look more closely at the *objectification,* at the production of the worker; and therein at the *estrangement,* the *loss* of the object, his product.

The worker can create nothing without *nature,* without the *sensuous external world.* It is the material on which his labor is manifested, in which it is active, from which and by means of which it produces.

But just as nature provides labor with the *means of life* in the sense that labor cannot *live* without objects on which to operate, on the other hand, it also provides the *means of life* in the more restricted sense—i.e., the means for the physical subsistence of the *worker* himself.

Thus the more the worker by his labor *appropriates* the external world, sensuous nature, the more he deprives himself of *means of life* in the double respect: first, that the sensuous external world more and more ceases to be an object belonging to his labor—to be his labor's *means of life;* and secondly, that it more and more ceases to be *means of life* in the immediate sense, means for the physical subsistence of the worker.

Thus in this double respect the worker becomes a slave of his object, first, in that he receives an *object of labor,* i.e., in that he receives *work;* and secondly, in that he receives *means of subsistence.* Therefore, it enables him to exist, first, as a *worker;* and, second, as a *physical subject.* The extremity of this bondage is that it is only as a *worker* that he continues to maintain himself as a *physical subject,* and that it is only as a *physical subject* that he is a *worker.*

(The laws of political economy express the estrangement of the worker in his object thus: the more the worker produces, the less he has to consume; the more values he creates, the more valueless, the more unworthy he becomes; the better formed his product, the more deformed becomes the worker; the more civilized his object, the more barbarous becomes the worker; the mightier labor becomes, the more powerless becomes the worker; the more ingenious labor becomes, the duller becomes the worker and the more he becomes nature's bondsman.)

*Political economy conceals the estrangement inherent in the nature of labor by not considering the direct relationship between the worker* (labor) *and production.* It is true that labor produces for the rich wonderful things—but for the worker it produces privation. It produces palaces—but for the worker, hovels. It produces beauty—but for the worker, deformity. It replaces labor by machines—but some of the workers it throws back to a barbarous type of labor, and the other workers it turns into machines. It produces intelligence—but for the worker idiocy, cretinism.

*The direct relationship of labor to its products is the relationship of the worker to the objects of his production.* The relationship of the man of means to the objects of production and to production itself is only a *consequence* of the first relationship—and confirms it. We shall consider this other aspect later.

When we ask, then, what is the essential relationship of labor we are asking about the relationship of the *worker* to production.

Till now we have been considering the estrangement, the alienation of the worker only in one of its aspects, i.e., the worker's *relationship to the products of his labor.* But the estrangement is manifested not only in the result but in the *act of production*—within the *producing activity* itself. How would the worker come to face the product of his activity as a stranger, were it not that in the very act of production he was estranging himself from himself? The product is after all but the summary of the activity, of production. If then the product of labor is alienation, production itself must be active alienation, the alienation of activity, the activity of alienation. In the estrangement of the object of labor is merely summarized the estrangement, the alienation, in the activity of labor itself.

What, then, constitutes the alienation of labor?

First, the fact that labor is *external* to the worker, i.e., it does not belong to his essential being; that in his work, therefore, he does not affirm himself but denies himself, does not feel content but unhappy, does not develop freely his physical and mental energy but mortifies his body and ruins his mind. The worker therefore only feels himself outside his work, and in his work feels outside himself. He is at home when he is not working, and when he is working he is not at home. His labor is therefore not voluntary, but coerced;

it is *forced labor*. It is therefore not the satisfaction of a need; it is merely a *means* to satisfy needs external to it. Its alien character emerges clearly in the fact that as soon as no physical or other compulsion exists, labor is shunned like the plague. External labor, labor in which man alienates himself, is a labor of self-sacrifice, of mortification. Lastly, the external character of labor for the worker appears in the fact that it is not his own, but someone else's, that it does not belong to him, that in it he belongs, not to himself, but to another. Just as in religion the spontaneous activity of the human imagination, of the human brain and the human heart, operates independently of the individual—that is, operates on him as an alien, divine or diabolical activity—in the same way the worker's activity is not his spontaneous activity. It belongs to another; it is the loss of his self.

As a result, therefore, man (the worker) no longer feels himself to be freely active in any but his animal functions—eating, drinking, procreating, or at most in his dwelling and in dressing-up, etc.; and in his human functions he no longer feels himself to be anything but an animal. What is animal becomes human and what is human becomes animal.

Certainly drinking, eating, procreating, etc., are also genuinely human functions. But in the abstraction which separates them from the sphere of all other human activity and turns them into sole and ultimate ends, they are animal.

We have considered the act of estranging practical human activity, labor, in two of its aspects. (1) The relation of the worker to the *product of labor* as an alien object exercising power over him. This relation is at the same time the relation to the sensuous external world, to the objects of nature as an alien world antagonistically opposed to him. (2) The relation of labor to the *act of production* within the *labor* process. This relation is the relation of the worker to his own activity as an alien activity not belonging to him; it is activity as suffering, strength as weakness, begetting as emasculating, the worker's *own* physical and mental energy, his personal life or what is life other than activity—as an activity which is turned against him, neither depends on nor belongs to him. Here we have *self-estrangement,* as we had previously the estrangement of the *thing*.

We have yet a third aspect of *estranged labor* to deduce from the two already considered.

Man is a species being, not only because in practice and in theory he adopts the species as his object (his own as well as those of other things), but—and this is only another way of expressing it—but also because he treats himself as the actual, living species; because he treats himself as a *universal* and therefore a free being.

The life of the species, both in man and in animals, consists physically in the fact that man (like the animal) lives on inorganic nature; and the more universal man is compared with an animal, the more universal is the sphere of inorganic nature on which he lives. Just as plants, animals, stones, the air, light, etc., constitute a part of human consciousness in the realm of theory, partly as objects of natural science, partly as objects of art—his spiritual inorganic nature, spiritual nourishment which he must first prepare to make it palatable and digestable—so too in the realm of practice they constitute a part of human life and human activity. Physically man lives only on these products of nature, whether they appear in the form of food, heating, clothes, a dwelling, or whatever it may be. The universality of man is in practice manifested precisely in the universality which makes all nature his *inorganic* body —both inasmuch as nature is (1) his direct means of life, and (2) the material, the object, and the instrument of his life-activity. Nature is man's *inorganic body*—nature, that is, insofar as it is not itself the human body. Man *lives* on nature—means that nature is his *body,* with which he must remain in continuous intercourse if he is not to die. That man's physical and spiritual life is linked to nature means simply that nature is linked to itself, for man is a part of nature.

In estranging from man (1) nature, and (2) himself, his own active functions, his life-activity, estranged labor estranges the *species* from man. It turns for him the *life of the species* into a means of individual life. First it estranges the life of the species and individual life, and secondly it makes individual life in its abstract form the purpose of the life of the species, likewise in its abstract and estranged form.

For in the first place labor, *life-activity, productive life* itself, appears to man merely as a *means* of satisfying a need—the need to maintain the physical existence. Yet the productive life is the life of the species. It is life-engendering life. The whole character of a species—its species character—is contained in the character of its life-activity; and free, conscious activity is man's species character. Life itself appears only as a *means to life.*

The animal is immediately identical with its life-activity. It does not distinguish itself from it. It is *its life-activity.* Man makes his life-activity itself the object of his will and of his consciousness. He has conscious life-activity. It is not a determination with which he directly merges. Conscious life-activity directly distinguishes man from animal life-activity. It is just because of this that he is a species being. Or it is only because he is a species being that he is a Conscious Being, i.e., that his own life is an object for him. Only because of that is his activity free activity. Estranged labor reverses this relationship, so that it is just because man is a conscious being that he makes his life-activity, his *essential* being, a mere means to his *existence.*

In creating an *objective world* by his practical activity, in *working-up* inorganic nature, man proves himself a conscious species being, i.e., as a being that treats the species as its own essential being, or that treats itself as a species being. Admittedly animals also produce. They build themselves nests, dwellings, like the bees, beavers, ants, etc. But an animal only produces what it immediately needs for itself or its young. It produces one-sidedly, while man produces universally. It produces only under the dominion of immediate physical need, while man produces even when he is free from physical need and only truly produces in freedom therefrom. An animal produces only itself, while man reproduces the whole of nature. An animal's product belongs immediately to its physical body, while man freely confronts his product. An animal forms things in accordance with the standard and the need of the species to which it belongs, while man knows how to produce in accordance with the standard of every species, and knows how to apply everywhere the inherent standard to the object. Man therefore also forms things in accordance with the laws of beauty.

It is just in the working-up of the objective world, therefore, that man first really proves himself to be a *species being*. This production is his active species life. Through and because of this production, nature appears as *his* work and his reality. The object of labor is, therefore, the *objectification of man's species life:* for he duplicates himself not only, as in consciousness, intellectually, but also actively, in reality, and therefore he contemplates himself in a world that he has created. In tearing away from man the object of his production, therefore, estranged labor tears from him his *species life,* his real species objectivity, and transforms his advantage over animals into the disadvantage that his inorganic body, nature, is taken from him.

Similarly, in degrading spontaneous activity, free activity, to a means, estranged labor makes man's species life a means to his physical existence.

The consciousness which man has of his species is thus transformed by estrangement in such a way that the species life becomes for him a means.

Estranged labor turns thus:

(3) *Man's species being,* both nature and his spiritual species property, into a being *alien* to him, into a *means* to his *individual existence*. It estranges man's own body from him, as it does external nature and his spiritual essence, his *human* being.

(4) An immediate consequence of the fact that man is estranged from the product of his labor, from his life-activity, from his species being is the *estrangement of man* from *man*. If a man is confronted by himself, he is confronted by the *other* man. What applies to a man's relation to his work, to the product of his labor and to himself, also holds of a man's relation to the other man, and to the other man's labor and object of labor.

In fact, the proposition that man's species nature is estranged from him means that one man is estranged from the other, as each of them is from man's essential nature.*

---

*Species nature (and earlier species being)—*Gattungswesen:* man's essential nature—*menschlichen Wesen.*

The following short passages from Feuerbach's *Essence of Christianity* may help readers to understand the ideological background to this part of Marx's thought, and, incidentally, to see how Marx accepted but infused with new content concepts made current by Feuerbach as well as by Hegel and the political economists:

"What is this essential difference between man and the brute? . . . Consciousness—but consciousness in the strict sense; for the consciousness implied in the feeling of self as an individual, in discrimination by the senses, in the perception and even judgment of outward things according

The estrangement of man, and in fact every relationship in which man stands to himself, is first realized and expressed in the relationship in which a man stands to other men.

Hence within the relationship of estranged labor each man views the other in accordance with the standard and the position in which he finds himself as a worker.

We took our departure from a fact of political economy—the estrangement of the worker and his production. We have formulated the concept of this fact—*estranged, alienated* labor. We have analyzed this concept—hence analyzing merely a fact of political economy.

Let us now see, further, how in real life the concept of estranged, alienated labor must express and present itself.

If the product of labor is alien to me, if it confronts me as an alien power, to whom, then, does it belong?

To a being *other* than me.

Who is this being?

The *gods?* To be sure, in the earliest times the principal production (for example, the building of temples, etc., in Egypt, India and Mexico) appears to be in the service of the gods, and the product belongs to the gods. However, the gods on their own were never the lords of labor. No more was *nature.* And what a contradiction it would be if, the more man subjugated nature by his labor and the more the miracles of the gods were rendered superfluous by the miracles of industry, the more man were to renounce the joy of production and the enjoyment of the produce in favor of these powers.

---

to definite sensible signs, cannot be denied to the brutes. Consciousness in the strictest sense is present only in a being to whom his species, his essential nature, is an object of thought. The brute is indeed conscious of himself as an individual—and he has accordingly the feeling of self as the common center of successive sensations—but not as a species. . . . In practical life we have to do with individuals; in science, with species. . . . But only a being to whom his own species, his own nature, is an object of thought, can make the essential nature of other things or beings an object of thought. . . . The brute has only a simple, man a twofold life; in the brute, the inner life is one with the outer. Man has both an inner and an outer life. The inner life of man is the life which has relation to his species—to his general, as distinguished from his individual nature. . . . The brute can exercise no function which has relation to its species without another individual external to itself; but man can perform the functions of thought and speech, which strictly imply such a relation, apart from another individual. . . . Man is in fact at once I and Thou; he can put himself in the place of another, for this reason, that to him his species, his essential nature, and not merely his individuality, is an object of thought. . . . An object to which a subject essentially, necessarily relates, is nothing else than this subject's own, but objective nature. . . .

"The relation of the sun to the earth is, therefore, at the same time a relation of the earth to itself, or to its own nature, for the measure of the size and of the intensity of light which the sun possesses as the object of the earth, is the measure of the distance, which determines the peculiar nature of the earth. . . . In the object which he contemplates, therefore, man becomes acquainted with himself. . . . The power of the object over him is therefore the power of his own nature."

*(The Essence of Christianity,* by Ludwig Feuerbach, translated from the second German edition by Marian Evans, London, 1854, pp. 1-5.) (Ed.)

The *alien* being, to whom labor and the product of labor belongs, in whose service labor is done and for whose benefit the produce of labor is provided, can only be *man* himself.

If the product of labor does not belong to the worker, if it confronts him as an alien power, this can only be because it belongs to some *other man than the worker*. If the worker's activity is a torment to him, to another it must be *delight* and his life's joy. Not the gods, not nature, but only man himself can be this alien power over man.

We must bear in mind the above-stated proposition that man's relation to himself only becomes *objective* and *real* for him through his relation to the other man. Thus, if the product of his labor, his labor *objectified*, is for him an *alien*, hostile, powerful object independent of him, then his position towards it is such that someone else is master of this object, someone who is alien, hostile, powerful, and independent of him. If his own activity is to him an unfree activity, then he is treating it as activity performed in the service, under the dominion, the coercion and the yoke of another man.

Every self-estrangement of man from himself and from nature appears in the relation in which he places himself and nature to men other than and differentiated from himself. For this reason religious self-estrangement necessarily appears in the relationship of the layman to the priest, or again to a mediator, etc., since we are here dealing with the intellectual world. In the real practical world self-estrangement can only become manifest through the real practical relationship to other men. The medium through which estrangement takes place is itself *practical*. Thus through estranged labor man not only engenders his relationship to the object and to the act of production as to powers that are alien and hostile to him; he also engenders the relationship in which other men stand to his production and to his product, and the relationship in which he stands to these other men. Just as he begets his own production as the loss of his reality, as his punishment; just as he begets his own product as a loss, as a product not belonging to him; so he begets the dominion of the one who does not produce over production and over the product. Just as he estranges from himself his own activity, so he confers to the stranger activity which is not his own.

Till now we have only considered this relationship from the standpoint of the worker and later we shall be considering it also from the standpoint of the non-worker.

Through *estranged, alienated labor*, then, the worker produces the relationship to this labor of a man alien to labor and standing outside it. The relationship of the worker to labor engenders the relation to it of the capitalist, or whatever one chooses to call the master of labor. *Private property* is thus the product, the result, the necessary consequence, of *alienated labor*, of the external relation of the worker to nature and to himself.

*Private property* thus results by analysis from the concept of *alienated labor*— i.e., of *alienated man*, of estranged labor, of estranged life, of *estranged* man.

True, it is as a result of the *movement of private property* that we have obtained the concept of *alienated labor (of alienated life)* from political economy. But on analysis of this concept it becomes clear that though private property appears to be the source, the cause of alienated labor, it is really its consequence, just as the gods *in the beginning* are not the cause but the effect of man's intellectual confusion. Later this relationship becomes reciprocal.

Only at the very culmination of the development of private property does this, its secret, reemerge, namely, that on the one hand it is the *product* of alienated labor, and that secondly it is the *means* by which labor alienates itself, the *realization of this alienation.*

This exposition immediately sheds light on various hitherto unsolved conflicts.

(1) Political economy starts from labor as the real soul of production; yet to labor it gives nothing, and to private property everything. From this contradiction Proudhon* has concluded in favor of labor and against private property. We understand, however, that this apparent contradiction is the contradiction of *estranged labor* with itself, and that political economy has merely formulated the laws of estranged labor.

We also understand, therefore, that *wages* and *private property* are identical: where the product, the object of labor pays for labor itself, the wage is but a necessary consequence of labor's estrangement, for after all in the wage of labor, labor does not appear as an end in itself but as the servant of the wage. We shall develop this point later, and meanwhile will only deduce some conclusions.

A *forcing-up of wages* (disregarding all other difficulties, including the fact that it would only be by force, too, that the higher wages, being an anomaly, could be maintained) would therefore be nothing but *better payment for the slave,* and would not conquer either for the worker or for labor their human status and dignity.

Indeed, even the *equality of wages* demanded by Proudhon only transforms the relationship of the present-day worker to his labor into the relationship of all men to labor. Society is then conceived as an abstract capitalist.

Wages are a direct consequence of estranged labor, and estranged labor is the direct cause of private property. The downfall of the one aspect must therefore mean the downfall of the other.

(2) From the relationship of estranged labor to private property it further follows that the emancipation of society from private property, etc., from servitude, is expressed in the *political* form of the *emancipation of the workers;* not that *their* emancipation alone was at stake but because the emancipation of the workers contains universal human emancipation—and it contains this, because the whole of human servitude is involved in the relation of the worker

---

*Pierre-Joseph Proudhon (1809–1865). French journalist and socialist. (Ed.)

to production, and every relation of servitude is but a modification and consequence of this relation.

Just as we have found the concept of *private property* from the concept of *estranged, alienated labor* by analysis, in the same way every *category* of political economy can be evolved with the help of these two factors; and we shall find again in each category, e.g., trade, competition, capital, money, only a *definite* and *developed expression* of the first foundations.

Before considering this configuration, however, let us try to solve two problems.

(1) To define the general *nature of private property,* as it has arisen as a result of estranged labor, in its relation to *truly human, social property.*

(2) We have accepted the *estrangement of labor,* its *alienation,* as a fact, and we have analyzed this fact. How, we now ask, does *man* come to *alienate,* to estrange, *his labor?* How is this estrangement rooted in the nature of human development? We have already gone a long way to the solution of this problem by *transforming* the question as to the *origin of private property* into the question as to the relation of *alienated labor* to the course of humanity's development. For when one speaks of *private property,* one thinks of being concerned with something external to man. When one speaks of labor, one is directly concerned with man himself. This new formulation of the question already contains its solution.

*As to (1): The general nature of private property and its relation to truly human property.*

Alienated labor has resolved itself for us into two elements which mutually condition one another, or which are but different expressions of one and the same relationship. *Appropriation* appears as *estrangement,* as *alienation;* and *alienation* appears as *appropriation, estrangement* as true *enfranchisement.*

We have considered the one side—*alienated* labor in relation to the *worker* himself, i.e., the *relation of alienated labor to itself.* The *property-relation of the non-worker to the worker and to labor* we have found as the product, the necessary outcome of this relation of alienated labor. *Private property,* as the material, summary expression of alienated labor, embraces both relations—the *relation of the worker to work, to the product of his labor and to the non-worker,* and the relation of the *non-worker to the worker and to the product of his labor.*

Having seen that in relation to the worker who *appropriates* nature by means of his labor, this appropriation appears as estrangement, his own spontaneous activity as activity for another and as an activity of another, vitality as a sacrifice of life, production of the object as loss of the object to an alien power, to an *alien* person—we shall now consider the relation to the worker, to labor and its object of this person who is *alien* to labor and the worker.

First it has to be noted, that everything which appears in the worker as an *activity of alienation, of estrangement,* appears in the non-worker as a *state of alienation, of estrangement.*

Secondly, that the worker's *real, practical attitude* in production and to the product (as a state of mind) appears in the non-worker confronting him as a *theoretical* attitude.

*Thirdly,* the non-worker does everything against the worker which the worker does against himself; but he does not do against himself what he does against the worker.

Let us look more closely at these three relations.*

---

*At this point the first manuscript breaks off unfinished. (Ed.)

# 23

# Working

## Studs Terkel

Who built the seven towers of Thebes?
The books are filled with the names of kings.
Was it kings who hauled the craggy blocks of stone? . . .
In the evening when the Chinese wall was finished
Where did the masons go? . . .

Bertolt Brecht

It is a two-flat dwelling, somewhere in Cicero, on the outskirts of Chicago. He is thirty-seven. He works in a steel mill. On occasion, his wife Carol works as a waitress in a neighborhood restaurant; otherwise, she is at home, caring for their two small children, a girl and a boy.

At the time of my first visit, a sculpted statuette of Mother and Child was on the floor, head severed from body. He laughed softly as he indicated his three-year-old daughter: "She Doctor Spock'd it."

I'm a dying breed. A laborer. Strictly muscle work . . . pick it up, put it down, pick it up, put it down. We handle between forty and fifty thousand pounds of steel a day. (Laughs) I know this is hard to believe—from four hundred pounds to three- and four-pound pieces. It's dying.

You can't take pride any more. You remember when a guy could point to a house he built, how many logs he stacked. He built it and he was proud of it. I don't really think I could be proud if a contractor built a home for me. I would be tempted to get in there and kick the carpenter in the ass (laughs), and take the saw away from him. 'Cause I would have to be part of it, you know.

It's hard to take pride in a bridge you're never gonna cross, in a door you're never gonna open. You're mass-producing things and you never see the end result of it. (Muses) I worked for a trucker one time. And I got this tiny satisfaction when I loaded a truck. At least I could see the truck depart loaded. In a steel mill, forget it. You don't see where nothing goes.

I got chewed out by my foreman once. He said, "Mike, you're a good worker but you have a bad attitude." My attitude is that I don't get excited about my job. I do my work but I don't say whoopee-doo. The day I get excited about my job is the day I go to a head shrinker. How are you gonna get excited about pullin' steel? How are you gonna get excited when you're tired and want to sit down?

It's not just the work. Somebody built the pyramids. Somebody's going to build something. Pyramids, Empire State Building—these things just don't happen. There's hard work behind it. I would like to see a building, say, the Empire State, I would like to see on one side of it a foot-wide strip from top to bottom with the name of every bricklayer, the name of every electrician, with all the names. So, when a guy walked by, he could take his son and say, "See, that's me over there on the forty-fifth floor. I put the steel beam in." Picasso can point to a painting. What can I point to? A writer can point to a book. Everybody should have something to point to.

It's the not-recognition by other people. To say a woman is *just* a housewife is degrading, right? Okay. *Just* a housewife. It's also degrading to say *just* a laborer. The difference is that a man goes out and maybe gets smashed.

When I was single, I could quit, just split. I wandered all over the country,. You worked just enough to get a poke, money in your pocket. Now I'm married and I got two kids . . . (trails off). I worked on a truck dock one time and I was single. The foreman came over and he grabbed my shoulder, kind of gave me a shove. I punched him and knocked him off the dock. I said, "Leave me alone. I'm doing my work, just stay away from me, just don't give me the with-the-hands business."

Hell, if you whip a damn mule he might kick you. Stay out of my way, that's all. Working is bad enough, don't bug me. I would rather work my ass off for eight hours a day with nobody watching me than five minutes with a guy watching me. Who you gonna sock? You can't sock General Motors, you can't sock anybody in Washington, you can't sock a system.

A mule, an old mule, that's the way I feel. Oh yeah. See. (Shows black and blue marks on arms and legs, burns.) You know what I heard from more than one guy at work? "If my kid wants to work in a factory, I am going to kick the hell out of him." I want my kid to be an effete snob.

Yeah, mm-hmm. (Laughs). I want him to be able to quote Walt Whitman, to be proud of it.

If you can't improve yourself, you improve your posterity. Otherwise life isn't worth nothing. You might as well go back to the cave and stay there. I'm sure the first caveman who went over the hill to see what was on the other side—I don't think he went there wholly out of curiosity. He went there because he wanted to get his son out of the cave. Just the same way I want to send my kid to college.

I work so damn hard and want to come home and sit down and lay around. *But I gotta get it out.* I want to be able to turn around to somebody and say, "Hey, fuck you." You know? (Laughs.) The guy sitting next to me on the bus too. 'Cause all day I wanted to tell my foreman to go fuck himself, but I can't.

So I find a guy in a tavern. To tell him that. And he tells me too. I've been in brawls. He's punching me and I'm punching him, because we actually want to punch somebody else. The most that'll happen is the bartender will bar us from the tavern. But at work, you lose your job.

This one foreman I've got, he's a kid. He's a college graduate. He thinks he's better than everybody else. He was chewing me out and I was saying, "Yeah, yeah, yeah." He said, "What do you mean, yeah, yeah, yeah. Yes, *sir.*" I told him, "Who the hell are you, Hitler? What is this *"Yes, sir"* bullshit? I came here to work, I didn't come here to crawl. There's a fuckin' difference." One word led to another and I lost.

I got broke down to a lower grade and lost twenty-five cents an hour, which is a hell of a lot. It amounts to about ten dollars a week. He came over—after breaking me down. The guy comes over and smiles at me. I blew up. He didn't know it, but he was about two seconds and two feet away from a hospital. I said, "Stay the fuck away from me." He was just about to say something and was pointing his finger. I just reached my hand up and just grabbed his finger and I just put it back in his pocket. He walked away. I grabbed his finger because I'm married. If I'd a been single, I'd a grabbed his head. That's the difference.

You're doing this manual labor and you know that technology can do it. (Laughs.) Let's face it, a machine can do the work of a man; otherwise they wouldn't have space probes. Why can we send a rocket ship that's unmanned and yet send a man in a steel mill to do a mule's work?

Automation? Depends how it's applied. It frightens me if it puts me out on the street. It doesn't frighten me if it shortens my work week. You read that little thing: what are you going to do when this computer replaces you? Blow up computers. (Laughs.) Really. Blow up computers. I'll be goddamned if a computer is gonna eat before I do! I want milk for my kids and beer for me. Machines can either liberate man or enslave 'im, because they're pretty neutral. It's the man who has the bias to put the thing one place or another.

If I had a twenty-hour workweek, I'd get to know my kids better, my wife better. Some kid invited me to go on a college campus. On a Saturday. It was summertime. Hell, if I had a choice of taking my wife and kids to a picnic or going to a college campus, it's gonna be the picnic. But if I worked a twenty-hour week, I could go do both. Don't you think with that extra twenty hours people could really expand? Who's to say? There are some people in factories just by force of circumstance. I'm just like the colored people. Potential Einsteins don't have to be white. They could be in cotton fields, they could be in factories.

The twenty-hour week is a possibility today. The intellectuals, they always say there are potential Lord Byrons, Walt Whitmans, Roosevelts, Picassos working in construction or steel mills or factories. But I don't think they believe it. I think what they're afraid of is the potential Hitlers and Stalins that are there too. The people in power fear the leisure man. Not just the United States. Russia's the same way.

What do you think would happen in this country if, for one year, they experimented and gave everybody a twenty-hour week? How do they know that the guy who digs Wallace today doesn't try to resurrect Hitler tomorrow? Or the guy who is mildly disturbed at pollution doesn't decide to go to General Motors and shit on the guy's desk? You can become a fanatic if you had the time. The whole thing is time. That is, I think, one reason rich kids tend to be fanatic about politics: they have time. Time, that's the important thing.

It isn't that the average working guy is dumb. He's tired, that's all. I picked up a book on chess one time. That thing laid in the drawer for two or three weeks, you're too tired. During the weekends you want to take your kids out. You don't want to sit there and the kid comes up: "Daddy, can I go to the park?" You got your nose in a book? Forget it.

I know a guy fifty-seven years old. Know what he tells me? "Mike, I'm old and tired *all* the time." The first thing happens at work: When the arms start moving, the brain stops. I punch in about ten minutes to seven in the morning. I say hello to a couple of guys I like, I kid around with them. One guy says good morning to you and you say good morning. To another guy you say fuck you. The guy you say fuck you to is your friend.

I put on my hard hat, change into my safety shoes, put on my safety glasses, go to the bonderizer. It's the thing I work on. They rake the metal, they wash it, they dip it in a paint solution, and we take it off. Put it on, take it off, put it on, take it off, put it on, take it off. . . .

I say hello to everybody but my boss. At seven it starts. My arms get tired about the first half hour. After that, they don't get tired any more until maybe the last half-hour at the end of the day. I work from seven to three thirty. My arms are tired at seven thirty and they're tired at three o'clock. I hope to God I never get broke in, because I always want my arms to be tired at seven thirty and three o'clock. (Laughs.) 'Cause that's when I know that there's a beginning and there's an end. That I'm not brainwashed. In between, I don't even try to think.

If I were to put you in front of a dock and I pulled up a skid in front of you with fifty hundred-pound sacks of potatoes and there are fifty more skids just like it, and this is what you're gonna do all day, what would you think about—potatoes? Unless a guy's a nut, he never thinks about work or talks about it. Maybe about baseball or about getting drunk the other night or he got laid or he didn't get laid. I'd say one out of a hundred will actually get excited about work.

Why is it that the communists always say they're for the workingman, and as soon as they set up a country, you got guys singing to tractors? They're singing about how they love the factory. That's where I couldn't buy communism. It's the intellectuals' utopia, not mine. I cannot picture myself singing to a tractor, I just can't. (Laughs.) Or singing to steel. (Singsongs.) Oh whoop-dee-doo, I'm at the bonderizer, oh how I love this heavy steel. No thanks. Never hoppen.

Oh yeah, I daydream. I fantasize about a sexy blonde in Miami who's got my union dues. (Laughs.) I think of the head of the union the way I think of the head of my company. Living it up. I think of February in Miami. Warm weather, a place to lay in. When I hear a college kid say, "I'm oppressed," I don't believe him. You know what I'd like to do for one year? Live like a college kid. Just for one year. I'd love to. Wow! (Whispers) Wow! Sports car! Marijuana! (Laughs.) Wild, sexy broads. I'd love that, hell yes, I would.

Somebody has to do this work. If my kid ever goes to college, I just want him to have a little respect, to realize that his dad is one of those some-bodies. This is why even on—(muses) yeah, I guess, sure—on the black thing . . . (Sighs heavily.) I can't really hate the colored fella that's working with me all day. The black intellectual I got no respect for. The white in-tellectual I got no use for. I got no use for the black militant who's gonna scream three hundred years of slavery to me while I'm busting my ass. You know what I mean? (Laughs.) I have one answer for that guy: go see Rocke-feller. See Harriman. Don't bother me. We're in the same cotton field. So just don't bug me. (Laughs).

After work I usually stop off at a tavern. Cold beer. Cold beer right away. When I was single, I used to go into hillbilly bars, get in a lot of brawls. Just to explode. I got a thing on my arm here (indicates scar). I got slapped with a bicycle chain. Oh, wow! (Softly) Mmm. I'm getting older. (Laughs.) I don't explode as much. You might say I'm broken in. (Quickly) No, I'll never be broken in. (Sighs.) When you get a little older, you exchange the words. When you're younger, you exchange the blows.

When I get home, I argue with my wife a little bit. Turn on TV, get mad at the news. (Laughs.) I don't even watch the news that much. I watch Jackie Gleason. I look for any alternative to the ten o'clock news. I don't want to go to bed angry. Don't hit a man with anything heavy at five o'clock. He just can't be bothered. This is his time to relax. The heaviest thing he wants is what his wife has to tell him.

When I come home, know what I do for the first twenty minutes? Fake it. I put on a smile. I got a kid three years old. Sometimes she says, "Daddy, where've you been?" I say, "Work." I could have told her I'd been in Disneyland. What's work to a three-year-old kid? If I feel bad, I can't take it out on the kids. Kids are born innocent of everything but birth. You can't take it out on your wife either. This is why you go to a tavern. You want to release it there rather than do it at home. What does an actor do when he's got a bad movie? I got a bad movie every day.

I don't even need the alarm clock to get up in the morning. I can go out drinking all night, fall asleep at four, and bam! I'm up at six—no matter what I do. (Laughs.) It's a pseudo-death, more or less. Your whole system is paralyzed and you give all the appearance of death. It's an ingrown clock. It's a thing you get used to. The hours differ. It depends. Sometimes my wife wants to do something crazy like play five hundred rummy or put a puzzle together. It could be midnight, could be ten o'clock, could be nine thirty.

*What do you do weekends?*

Drink beer, read a book. See that one? *Violence in America.* It's one of them studies from Washington. One of them committees they're always appointing. A thing like that I read on a weekend. But during the weekdays, gee . . . I just thought about it. I don't do that much reading from Monday through Friday. Unless it's a horny book. I'll read it at work and go home and do my homework. (Laughs.) That's what the guys at the plant call it— homework. (Laughs.) Sometimes my wife works on Saturday and I drink beer at the tavern.

I went out drinking with one guy, oh, a long time ago. A college boy. He was working where I work now. Always preaching to me about how you need violence to change the system and all that garbage. We went into a hillbilly joint. Some guy there, I don't know him from Adam, he said, "You think you're smart." I said, "What's your pleasure?" (Laughs.) He said, "My pleasure's to kick your ass." I told him I really can't be bothered. He said, "What're you, chicken?" I said, "No, I just don't want to be bothered." He came over and said something to me again. I said, "I don't beat women, drunks, or fools. Now leave me alone."

The guy called his brother over. This college boy that was with me, he came, nudging my arm, "Mike, let's get out of here." I said, "What are you worried about?" (Laughs.) This isn't unusual. People will bug you. You fend it off as much as you can with your mouth and when you can't, you punch the guy out.

It was close to closing time and we stayed. We could have left but when you go into a place to have a beer and a guy challenges you—if you expect to go in that place again, you don't leave. If you have to fight the guy, you fight.

I just got outside the door and one of these guys jumped on me and grabbed me around the neck. I grabbed his arm and flung him against the wall. I grabbed him here (indicates throat), and jiggled his head against the wall quite a few times. He kind of slid down a little bit. This guy who said he was his brother took a swing at me with a garrison belt. He just missed and hit the wall. I'm looking around for my junior Stalin (laughs), who loves violence and everything. He's gone. Split. (Laughs.) Next day I see him at work. I couldn't get mad at him, he's a baby.

He saw a book in my back pocket one time and he was amazed. He walked up to me and he said, "You read?" I said, "What do you mean, I read?" "All these dummies read the sports pages around here. What are you doing with a book?" I got pissed off at the kid right away. I said, "What do you mean, all these dummies? Don't knock a man who's paying some-body else's way through college." He was a nineteen-year-old effete snob.

*Yet you want your kid to be an effete snob?*

Yes. I want my kid to look at me and say, "Dad, you're a nice guy, but you're a fuckin' dummy." Hell yes, I want my kid to tell me that he's not gonna be like me . . .

If I were hiring people to work, I'd try naturally to pay them a decent wage. I'd try to find out their first names, their last names, keep the company as small as possible, so I could personalize the whole thing. All I would ask a man is a handshake, see you in the morning. No applications, nothing. I wouldn't be interested in the guy's past. Nobody ever checks the pedigree on a mule, do they? But they do on a man. Can you imagine walking up to a mule and saying, "I'd like to know who his granddaddy was?"

I'd like to run a combination bookstore and tavern. (Laughs.) I would like to have a place where college kids came and a steelworker could sit down and talk. Where a workingman could not be ashamed of Walt Whitman and where a college professor could not be ashamed that he painted his house over the weekend.

If a carpenter built a cabin for poets, I think the least the poets owe the carpenter is just three or four one-liners on the wall. A little plaque: Though we labor with our minds, this place we can relax in was built by someone who can work with his hands. And his work is as noble as ours. I think the poet owes something to the guy who builds the cabin for him.

I don't think of Monday. You know what I'm thinking about on Sunday night? Next Sunday. If you work real hard, you think of a perpetual vaca-tion. Not perpetual sleep. . . . What do I think of on a Sunday night? Lord, I wish the fuck I could do something else for a living.

I don't know who the guy is who said there is nothing sweeter than an unfinished symphony. Like an unfinished painting and an unfinished poem. If he creates this thing one day—let's say, Michelangelo's Sistine Chapel. It took him a long time to do this, this beautiful work of art. But what if he had to create the Sistine Chapel a thousand times a year? Don't you think that would even dull Michelangelo's mind? Or if da Vinci had to draw his anatomical charts thirty, forty, fifty, sixty, eighty, ninety, a hundred times a day? Don't you think that would even bore da Vinci?

*Way back you spoke of the guys who built the pyramids, not the pharaohs, the unknowns. You put yourself in their category?*

Yes. I want my signature on 'em, too. Sometimes, out of pure meanness, when I make something, I put a little dent in it. I like to do something to make it really unique. Hit it with a hammer. I deliberately fuck it up to see if it'll get by, just so I can say I did it. It could be anything. Let me put it this way: I think God invented the dodo bird so when we get up there we could tell Him, "Don't you ever make mistakes?" and He'd say, "Sure, look." (Laughs.) I'd like to make my imprint. My dodo bird. A mistake, *mine*. Let's say the whole building is nothing but red bricks. I'd like to have just the black one or the white one or the purple one. Deliberately fuck up.

This is gonna sound square, but my kid is an imprint. He's my freedom. There's a line in one of Hemingway's books. I think it's from *For Whom the Bell Tolls*. They're behind the enemy lines, somewhere in Spain, and she's pregnant. She wants to stay with him. He tells her no. He says, "if you die, I die," knowing he's gonna die. But if you go, I go. Know what I mean? The mystics call it the brass bowl. Continuum. You know what I mean? This is why I work. Every time I see a young guy walk by with a shirt and tie and dressed up real sharp, I'm lookin' at my kid, you know? That's it.

# 24

# Alienation and Freedom

## Robert Blauner

No simple definition of alienation can do justice to the many intellectual traditions which have engaged this concept as a central explanatory idea. One basis of confusion is the fact that the idea of alienation has incorporated philosophical, psychological, sociological, and political orientations. In the literature on the theory of alienation, one finds statements of the desired state of human experience, assertions about the actual quality of personal experience, propositions which link attitudes and experience to social situations and social structures, and programs for the amelioration of the human condition. My own perspective in this investigation is chiefly sociological, or perhaps social-psychological, in that alienation is viewed as a quality of personal experience which results from specific kinds of social arrangements.[1]

This study also employs a multidimensional, rather than a unitary, conception of alienation. Alienation is a general syndrome made up of a number of different objective conditions and subjective feeling-states that emerge from certain relationships between workers and the sociotechnical settings of employment. Alienation exists when workers are unable to control their immediate work processes, to develop a sense of purpose and function which connects their jobs to the overall organization of production, to belong to integrated industrial communities, and when they fail to become involved in the activity of work as a mode of personal self-expression. In modern industrial employment, control, purpose, social integration, and self-involvement are all problematic. In this chapter we discuss how various aspects of the technology, work organization, and social structure of modern industry further the four types of alienation that correspond to these non-alienated states: powerlessness, meaninglessness, isolation, and self-estrangement.[2]

## POWERLESSNESS: MODES OF FREEDOM AND CONTROL IN INDUSTRY

A person is powerless when he is an object controlled and manipulated by other persons or by an impersonal system (such as technology), and when he cannot assert himself as a subject to change or modify this domination. Like an object, the powerless person reacts rather than acts. He is directed or dominated, rather than self-directing. The non-alienated pole of the powerlessness dimension is freedom and control. Freedom is the state which allows the person to remove himself from those dominating situations that make him simply a reacting object. Freedom may therefore involve the possibility of movement in a physical or social sense, the ability to walk away from a coercive machine process, or the opportunity of quitting a job because of the existence of alternative employment. Control is more positive than freedom, suggesting the assertion of the self-directing subject over such potentially dominating forces as employers or machine systems.

The degree of powerlessness a student imputes to manual workers in industry today depends not only on his sociological and political perspective but also on the aspects of freedom and control he selects as the most important. There are at least four modes of industrial powerlessness which have preoccupied writers on "the social question." These are (1) the separation from ownership of the means of production and the finished products, (2) the inability to influence general managerial policies, (3) the lack of control over the conditions of employment, and (4) the lack of control over the immediate work process. It is my contention that control over the conditions of employment and control over the immediate work process are most salient for manual workers, who are most likely to value control over those matters which affect their immediate jobs and work tasks and least likely to be concerned with the more general and abstract aspects of powerlessness.

The very nature of employment in a large-scale organization means that workers have forfeited their claims on the finished product and that they do not own the factory, machines, or often their own tools. Unlike the absence of control over the immediate work process, "ownership powerlessness" is a constant in modern industry, and employees, therefore, normally do not develop expectations for influence in this area. Today the average worker no more desires to own his machines than modern soldiers their howitzers or government clerks their file cabinets.[3] Automobile and chemical workers, by and large, do not feel deprived because they cannot take home the [Chevy Novas] or sulfuric acid they produce.

Orthodox Marxism saw the separation from the means of production as the central fact of capitalism, the inevitable consequence of which would be the worker's general alienation from society. This has not happened: manual workers have required only steady jobs, reasonable wages, and employee benefits to put down at least moderate stakes in society and industry. Yet, despite the lack of any conscious desire for control in this area, we cannot know for certain whether or not the worker's alienation from ownership unconsciously colors the whole quality of his experience in the factory, as Erich Fromm, for one, argues.[4] The appeal of small-business ownership, stronger among manual than white-collar employees, suggests that there may be many workers like the automobile worker Ely Chinoy quotes, for whom employment itself is inherently alienating:

> The main thing is to be independent and give your own orders and not have to take them from anybody else. That's the reason the fellows in the shop all want to start their own business. Then the profits are all for yourself. When you're in the shop, there's nothing for yourself in it. So you just do what you have to do in order to get along. A fellow would rather do it for himself. If you expend the energy, it's for your benefit then.[5]

Like the separation from ownership, another facet of industrial powerlessness, the lack of control over decision-making, is also common to the modern employment relationship. Large-scale organizations are hierarchical authority structures with power concentrated at the top, and manual workers have little opportunity to control the major decisions of the enterprise. And unlike the worker quoted above, most employees do not seem to resent this aspect of powerlessness, which they also tend to accept as a "given" of industry. The average worker does not want the responsibility for such decisions as what, for whom, and how much to produce; how to design the product; what machinery to buy; how to distribute jobs; or how to organize the flow of work. It is only when these decisions directly affect his immediate job and work load that he expects his labor organization to influence policy in his behalf—as the recent labor-management conflicts over work rules indicate.

A number of industrial reform movements have attempted to counteract this aspect of powerlessness. Early in the twentieth century, the classical advocates of workers' control—the socialist followers of Rosa Luxembourg in Germany, the American IWW, the French syndicalists, and the British shop-stewards' movements—raised the slogan of industrial democracy. But as labor reform movements became more sophisticated, they realized that large-scale production organizations cannot be governed directly and en masse. The sponsors of direct democracy gave way to the advocates of representative democracy and participation in management. The most important recent examples of this trend are "joint consultation" in England, codetermination in Germany, and the workers' councils of eastern Europe.[6] Yet the experience of these representative systems suggests that it is only the delegate or the participator, not the average worker, who actually feels he is influencing major decisions. Even those progresssive firms which have encouraged mass participation in shop councils find that the average employee confines his interest to his own job and work group and leaves participation in the overall plant to a select few.[7]

A third aspect of industrial powerlessness, the lack of control over conditions of employment, is considerably more meaningful to American workers. Selig Perlman's characterization of the American working class as more "job conscious" than "class conscious" suggests that control of the opportunity for work itself within the oligarchic industrial system has been historically more relevant than the two more "revolutionary" aspects of control discussed above.[8]

Under early capitalism, the worker could be hired and fired at will by impersonal forces of the market and personal whims of the employer. As a commodity subject to supply and demand factors, his employment depended on the extent of his skills and the phase of the business cycle. This is no longer the case. The most important innovations sponsored by American labor unions have been aimed at reducing the historic inequality of power in the contractual situation of employment. Collective bargaining, the contract, grievance procedures, arbitration, seniority provisions, hiring halls, and now "guaranteed annual wages" have all been partially successful attempts to increase the control of employees over their conditions of employment.

In addition, a number of economic changes have greatly reduced the worker's powerlessness in this area. The severity of periodic economic crises has diminished as industry and government have imposed major checks on the anarchy of a free competitive system. Technological requirements have increased the need for more skilled and responsible workers. Thus, the large corporation has recognized the advantage of a more permanent work force to its pursuit of economic stability and higher productivity.

As a result of these changes in economic life, technology, corporation policy, and union power, the worker's control over his employment is increasing in what Ralf Dahrendorf calls "post-capitalist society." The *worker*, who in classical capitalism was considered virtually a commodity or a cost of production and treated as a *thing*, is giving way to the *employee*, a permanent worker who is viewed much more as a *human being*. Many employees have job security based on seniority provisions or a *de facto* "common law" right to their jobs. The employment relationship no longer reflects merely the balance of power; it is more and more determined by a system of institutional justice.[9]

Economic security is not distributed equally in the industrial structure, for the trends outlined above have not developed evenly. Some firms, industries, and specific occupations are extremely unstable in employment, whereas others provide virtual tenure in jobs. Empirical studies constantly emphasize the important part which regularity of employment plays in workers' evaluations of particular jobs and companies.[10] As an area of significant concern for manual workers, control over employment conditions will be analyzed in the four industrial comparisons, with the major emphasis on variations in control over the immediate work process.

Both sociologists and socialists, in their emphasis on the assembly-line work situation, have provided much data on the powerlessness of the worker in the face of a dominating technological system. Despite the fact that the assembly line is not the representative work milieu, these scholars have rightly emphasized the central importance of the worker's relation to technology as a major condition of alienation. For when a worker is dominated and controlled by the machine system in the very process of his work, he, in effect, becomes reduced to a mechanical device. Reacting to the rhythms of technology rather than acting in some independent or autonomous manner, he approaches most completely the condition of *thingness*, the essence of alienation.

Studies of the assembly line show that workers greatly resent the dominance of technology and constantly try to devise ways to gain some measure of control over the machine system. The resentment against this kind of powerlessness may reflect an awareness of its special degrading and humiliating features, as well as the knowledge that there are many alternative kinds of work situations in factory employment.[11]

The variations in control over the immediate activity of work are a principal focus of the present study. We shall analyze each of the four factory work settings in terms of its characteristic tendency to impose restrictions and to permit freedom of action in a number of specific areas directly related to the job. Whether a worker controls his sociotechnical environment depends on his freedom of movement, freedom to make choices, and freedom from oppressive constraints. It is necessary to specify this final aspect of industrial powerlessness more precisely by distinguishing those individual freedoms which are the components or elements of control over the immediate activity of work. Of these, the most important is control over the *pace* of work.

A basic distinction can be made between those jobs which are machine-paced, with the rhythms of work and the timing of the operator's action depending on the speed of the machine or machine process, and those which are man-paced, in which the worker himself can vary the rhythms of his actions.[12] This distinction can be seen in two occupations outside the factory. The man who takes money or issues tickets at the toll plaza of a bridge or highway has virtually no control over the pace of his work, since it is determined by the flow of traffic. He can only respond. An unskilled clerk in an office who adds columns of figures all day on an adding machine, however, has considerable control over his work pace. Often he can slow down, speed up, or take a break at his own discretion, although supervisors and other clerks might have some influence over his work pace.

Control over the pace of work is critical because it sets a man apart from the machine system of modern technology. The pace of work is probably the most insistent, the most basic, aspect of a job and retaining control in this area is a kind of affirmation of human dignity. This freedom is also crucial because it influences other work freedoms.

For example, when a man can control his work rhythm, he can usually regulate the degree of *pressure* exerted on him. Some work environments, like automobile and textile factories, are characterized by considerable pressure, while others, like print shops and chemical plants, have a relaxed atmosphere. In addition, *freedom of physical movement* is much more likely when a worker controls his own work rhythm and also when he is relatively free from pressure. In American industry today many jobs require the worker to stay close to his station for eight hours a day, while others permit a great deal of moving around the plant. The automobile assembly line is again an extreme example of restricted physical movement, whereas the work milieu of the print shop permits a high degree of this freedom. Many manual workers consider free movement quite important; the rather common preference of manual workers for truck-driving, railroad, and construction work rather than factory jobs often represents an aversion to physically confining "inside" work.

Control over work pace generally brings some *freedom to control the quantity of production.* Of course, workers cannot keep their jobs without a minimum production. But many are able to vary the hourly and daily output greatly,[13] while others have no power at all to control this. Similar to this is the freedom to control the *quality* of one's work. When a man sets his own pace and is free from pressure, as are craft printers, he can take the pains to do a job up to his standards of workmanship; in machine-paced systems with high-speed production, a worker's desire to put out quality work is often frustrated, as is the case with many automobile assemblers.

A final component of control over the immediate work process refers to *techniques.* In mass production there is generally little opportunity to make choices as to how to do one's job, since these decisions have been already made by engineers, time-study men, and supervisors. In other industrial settings, however, jobs permit some selection of work methods. There, workers can solve problems and use their own ideas.

These individual task-related freedoms—control over pace, freedom from pressure, freedom of physical movement, and the ability to control the quantity and quality of production and to choose the techniques of work—together make up control over the immediate work process. When rationalized technology and work organization do not permit the active intervention of the worker at any of these points, the alienating tendencies of modern industry, which make the worker simply a responding object, an instrument of the productive process, are carried to their furthest extremes.

## MEANINGLESSNESS: PURPOSE AND
## FUNCTION IN MANUAL LABOR

A second dimension of alienation in industrial employment is meaninglessness. Bureaucratic structures seem to encourage feelings of meaninglessness.
As division of labor increases in complexity in large-scale organization, individual roles may seem to lack organic connection with the whole structure
of roles, and the result is that the employee may lack understanding of the
coordinated activity and a sense of purpose in his work.

Karl Mannheim saw meaninglessness emerging in bureaucracies as a result of the tension between "functional rationalization" and "substantial rationality." Functional rationalization refers to the idea that in a modern organization everything is geared to the highest efficiency. The number of tasks and
procedures required for a product or a service are analyzed, and the work
is organized so that there is a smooth flow and a minimum of costs. The
rationale of the technical and social organization is comprehended fully only
by a few top managers (and engineers in the case of a factory), if indeed by
anyone at all. But along with the greater efficiency and rationality of the whole,
the substantial rationality of the individuals who make up the system declines.
The man who has a highly subdivided job in a complex factory and the clerk
working in a huge government bureau need only know very limited tasks.
They need not know anyone else's job and may not even know what happens
in the departments of the organization next to them. They need not know
how their own small task fits into the entire operation. What results is a decline in the "capacity to act intelligently in a given situation on the basis of
one's own insight into the interrelations of events."[14]

Meaning in work depends largely on three aspects of the worker's relationship to the product, process, and organization of work. The first factor
is the character of the product itself. Working on a unique and individuated
product is almost inherently meaningful. It is more difficult to develop and
maintain a sense of purpose in contributing toward a standardized product,
since this inevitably involves repetitive work cycles. The second point is the
scope of the product worked on. It is more meaningful to work on the whole,
or a large part, of even a standardized product than to perform one's tasks
on only a small part of the final product. Third, purpose and function increase when the employee's job makes him responsible for a large span of
the production process, rather than a small restricted sphere.

Tendencies toward meaninglessness therefore stem from the nature of
modern manufacturing, which is based on standardized production and a division of labor that reduces the size of the worker's contribution to the final
product. Whereas many independent craftsmen of the preindustrial era made
the entire product themselves, from the first step in the operations to the last,
an automobile assembler may spend all his time putting on headlights and
never have anything to do with any other operation. These alienating tenden-

cies may be overcome when job design or technological developments result in a wide rather than a narrow scope of operations for the employee. Purpose may also be injected into relatively fractionalized jobs when the worker develops an understanding of the organization's total function and of the relation of his own contribution to that larger whole. However, such understanding is less likely to lead toward a sense of purpose and function if the worker's responsibilities and scope of operations remain narrow.

Like powerlessness, meaninglessness is unequally distributed among manual workers in modern industry. The nature of an industry's technology and work organization affects the worker's ability to wrest a sense of purpose from his work task—substantial irrationality is not the fate of all modern factory employees. This mode of alienation is most intensified when production is carried out in large plants. In the small factory it is easier for the worker to see the relationship of his contribution to the enterprise as a whole. Team production also reduces meaninglessness. It is easier for factory workers to develop a sense of purpose when they are members of work crews which carry out the job jointly than for employees who do their work individually. Finally there is less alienation in process technology than in batch or assembly methods of production. In the former system, work is organized in terms of an integrated process rather than in terms of subdivided tasks, and the worker's span of responsibility and job assignment is enlarged. An increased sense of purpose and function in work for the blue-collar employee may be one of the most important by-products of automation, since this technical system brings about smaller factories, production by teams rather than individuals, and integrated process operations.

## SOCIAL ALIENATION: INTEGRATION AND MEMBERSHIP IN INDUSTRIAL COMMUNITIES

In contrast to Marx, who emphasized the powerlessness of workers in modern industry and saw the solution to the modern social problem in "restoring" control to the workers over their conditions of work, the French sociologist Emile Durkheim saw *anomie* (normlessness) and the breakup of integrated communities as the distinguishing feature of modern society. The massive social processes of industrialization and urbanization had destroyed the normative structure of a more traditional society and uprooted people from the local groups and institutions which had provided stability and security.

The transition to industrialism brought about tendencies toward social alienation, not only in the larger society but also in factories and mills. Although the use of physical force and the threat of starvation as "incentives" expressed the callousess of many industrialists, it also reflected the fact that there was as yet no basis for an industrial community. With normative integration absent, machine-breaking, sabotage, strikes, and revolutionary activity not only represented protest against unbearable conditions but expressed the fact that workers had not yet developed a sense of loyalty to industrial enterprise or commitment to the new social role of factory employee.

In advanced industrial societies like the United States, the social alienation in factory employment characteristic of the early period has been greatly reduced. Even workers who lack control over their immediate work task and experience difficulty in achieving meaning and self-expression in the job may be spared the alienation of isolation, which implies the absence of a sense of membership in an industrial community. Membership in an industrial community involves commitment to the work role and loyalty to one or more centers of the work community. Isolation, on the other hand, means that the worker feels no sense of belonging in the work situation and is unable to identify or uninterested in identifying with the organization and its goals.

An industrial community is made up of a network of social relationships which are derived from a work organization and which are valued by the members of the community. For many factory workers the plant as a whole is a community, a center of belongingness and identification, which mitigates feelings of isolation. It is quite common for workers to come to a factory thirty minutes early every day to relax in the company of their friends. It has been argued that the human contacts of the plant community are critical in making work which is in other ways alienating bearable for mass production workers.[15] Beginning with the work of Elton Mayo and his associates, much research in industrial sociology has documented the role of informal work groups in providing a sense of belonging within the impersonal atmosphere of modern industry.

An industrial community also has a structure of norms, informal and formal rules, which guide the behavior of its members. Industrial organizations differ in the extent of normative integration, and this is important in determining the employee's sense of belonging to a cohesive work community. Industrial organizations are normatively integrated when there is consensus between the work force and management on standards of behavior, expectations of rewards, and definitions of fair play and justice, and when there are agreed-upon "rules of the game" which govern the relations between employees and employers. The norms and practices through which workers are disciplined and laid off, assigned wage rates relative to the earnings of others, and awarded promotions, are especially critical. These matters affect the worker's sense of equity with respect to the allocation of rewards and the standards of distributive justice and therefore often determine his sense of alienation from, or integration in, the industrial enterprise.

Although the maturation of industrial society has generally reduced the worker's isolation, the implications of bureaucratic organization for social alienation are somewhat mixed. Bureaucracy's norm of impersonal administration emphasizes formal procedures, and in many cases this creates a feeling of distance between workers and management. And the bureaucratic principle of the rational utilization of all resources to maximize organizational goals furthers the tendency to view employees as *labor*, as means to the ends of profit and company growth. But bureaucratic administration also enhances normative consensus through its emphasis on universalistic standards of justice and "fair treatment" and thus makes it possible for employees to acquire the status of industrial citizenship. It is probably the policy and practices of individual firms, unique historical and economic conditions, and particularly the technological setting,[16] that determines whether bureaucratization increases or decreases social integration in a specific situation.

Industries vary not only in the extent but also in the basis of normative integration and in the key institutions which are the center of the work community and the focus of worker loyalties. It is important to stress that the company need not be the major focus of the industrial community, as the advocates of what has been called "managerial sociology" tend to assume. In some cases, occupational groups and unions, in other situations, the local community as a whole, are more important presently and potentially. [An] analysis of [various] industries [would suggest that they] devise their own specific solutions to the problem of social alienation.

## SELF-ESTRANGEMENT

Self-estrangement refers to the fact that the worker may become alienated from his inner self in the activity of work. Particularly when an individual lacks control over the work process and a sense of purposeful connection to the work enterprise, he may experience a kind of depersonalized detachment rather than an immediate involvement or engrossment in the job tasks. This lack of present-time involvement means that the work becomes primarily instrumental, a means toward future considerations rather than an end in itself. When work encourages self-estrangement, it does not express the unique abilities, potentialities, or personality of the worker. Further consequences of self-estranged work may be boredom and monotony, the absence of personal growth, and a threat to a self-approved occupational identity.

Self-estrangement is absent in two main situations: when the work activity, satisfying such felt needs as those for control, meaning, and social connection, is inherently fulfilling in itself; or when the work activity is highly integrated into the totality of an individual's social commitments. Throughout most of history, the problem of work has been dealt with in the latter manner. Adriano Tilgher, a historian of work ideologies, finds that the idea that work should be a creative fulfilment is peculiarly modern, with origins in the Renaissance. In many previous civilizations work was viewed as some kind of unpleasant burden or punishment.[17] Our modern feeling that work should be a source of direct, immediate satisfaction and express the unique potential of the individual is probably a result of its compartmentalization in industrial society.

In preindustrial societies "uninteresting" work was highly integrated with other aspects of the society—with ritual, religion, family, and community or tribal relationships, for example. Therefore it could not become simply a means to life, because it was an immediate part of life's main concerns.

A number of fateful social changes have contributed to the compartmentalization of work. Most basic was the market economy which, in severing the organic connection between production and consumption, between effort and gratification, set the stage for the instrumental attitude toward work.[18] Second, the physical separation of household and workplace—an essential condition for the development of capitalism and bureaucratic organization, as Weber stressed—produced a hiatus between work life and family life. Third, with the secularization of modern society, the importance of the religious sanction in work motivation has declined; work and religion are now separated. Fourth, with the specialization brought about by industrial organization and the anonymity which urbanization has furthered, the average man's occupational role is not well known or understood: work is now separated from the community, as well as from the family and religion. Finally, the decline of the hours of work and the increase in living standards mean that less of life is devoted simply to problems of material existence. Time, energy, and resources are now available for other aspects of life,[19] which compete with work for emotional loyalties and commitments.

Self-estrangement is experienced as a heightened awareness of time, as a split between present activity and future considerations. Non-alienated activity consists of immersion in the present; it is involvement. Alienated activity is not free, spontaneous activity but is compulsive and driven by necessity. In non-alienated activity the rewards are in the activity itself; in alienated states they are largely extrinsic to the activity, which has become primarily a means to an end. Marx expressed these notions in his early work on alienation, the *Economic and Philosophical Manuscripts*:

> In his work, therefore, [the worker] does not affirm himself but denies himself, does not feel content but unhappy, does not develop freely his physical and mental energy but mortifies his body and ruins his mind. The worker therefore only feels himself outside his work, and in his work feels outside himself. He is at home when he is not working, and when he is working he is not at home. His labor is therefore not voluntary, but coerced; it is *forced labor*. It is therefore not the satisfaction of a need; it is merely a *means* to satisfy needs external to it. Its alien character emerges clearly in the fact that as soon as no physical or other compulsion exists, labor is shunned like the plague. External labor, labor in which man alienates himself, is a labor of self-sacrifice, of mortification.[20]

Since self-estranged activity is a means to an end rather than an end in itself, the satisfaction is in the future rather than the present, and the tone of feeling approaches *detachment* rather than involvement. The man on the assembly line is thinking about that beer he will have when the whistle blows;

the packing-house worker at Hormel goes home from work "so he can accomplish something for that day."[21] The meaning of the job for the automobile worker is not the intrinsic activity itself but that "new car" or "little modern house," which the paycheck, itself a future reward, brings closer.[22]

Lack of involvement results in a heightened time-consciousness. If it were possible to measure "clock-watching," this would be one of the best objective indicators of this mode of alienation. The "over-concern" with time is central to Fred Blum's perceptive discussion of alienation in a meat-packing plant and suggests that self-alienation is widespread in this kind of work. When Blum asked these workers whether they get bored on the job, a common response was that boredom was not a serious problem because "the time passes."

> How could the passage of time possibly neutralize the monotony of the job? Whatever the answer may be, there is no doubt that the time does, as a rule, pass fast. A large majority of workers, when asked: "When you are at work does the time generally pass slow or fast?" indicated that it usually passes quickly. Only a small minority feels that the time goes slowly. Many workers, however, intimated that sometimes the passage of time is slow and sometimes fast.[23]

On the other hand, involvement in work may come from control, for association with others, and from a sense of its purpose. A man who is controlling his immediate work process—regulating the pace, the quantity of output, the quality of the product, choosing tools or work techniques—must be relatively immersed in the work activity. For most employees, when work is carried out by close-knit work groups, especially work teams, it will be more intrinsically involving and rewarding. And involvement and self-fulfilment is heightened when the purpose of the job can be clearly connected with the final end product or the overall goals and organization of the enterprise. On the other hand, there is no necessary causal relation between social alienation and self-alienation. A worker may be integrated in the plant community and loyal to the company and still fail to achieve a sense of involvement and self-expression in his work activity itself.

When work is not inherently involving it will be felt as monotonous.[24] The extensive industrial research on monotony[25] suggests the high degree of self-estrangement in factory employment. Unfortunately, the studies are so scattered that they do not permit an overall assessment of the amount of felt monotony in the labor force. But the concern of industrial psychologists in England, France, Germany, and America with this topic, stimulated by management anxieties over dips in output, indicates that present-time involvement is a precarious thing, especially in repetitive jobs.[26]

Many industrial commentators feel that most modern jobs cannot be intrinsically involving and the best solution would be to make them so completely automatic that a worker would be free to daydream and talk to his workmates. Evidently, we are still far from this outcome, since the Roper survey, based on a representative sample of 3,000 factory workers, found that only 43 percent could do their work and keep their minds on other things most of the time. The most unsatisfactory situation seems to be the job which is not intrinsically interesting and yet requires rather constant attention.

Still, such work does not necessarily result in intense or even mild dissatisfaction. The capacity of people to adapt to routine repetitive work is remarkable. It is quite likely that the majority of industrial workers are self-estranged in the sense that their work is not particularly involving and is seen chiefly as a means to livelihood. Yet research in job satisfaction suggests that the majority of workers, possibly from 75 to 90 percent, are reasonably satisfied with such jobs.[27] Thus, the typical worker in modern industrial society is probably satisfied *and* self-estranged.

Self-estranged workers are dissatisfied only when they have developed *needs* for control, initiative, and meaning in work. The average manual worker and many white-collar employees may be satisfied with fairly steady jobs which are largely instrumental and non-involving, because they have not the need for responsibility and self-expression in work. They are therefore relatively content with work which is simply a means to the larger end of providing the paychecks for lives organized around leisure, family, and consumption.

One factor which is most important in influencing a man's aspirations in the work process is education. The more education a person has received, the greater the need for control and creativity. For those with little education, the need for sheer activity (working to "keep occupied") and for association are more important than control, challenge, and creativity.[28]

Finally, self-estranging work threatens a positive sense of selfhood because it fosters a damaging rather than an affirmative occupational identity. In a traditional society with little individuation, identity, the answer to the question "Who am I?" was not a problem for the masses of people. Identity, to the extent that this concept[29] was meaningful in such a society, was largely provided through the kinship system, which means that it was not a matter of choice. In a modern industrial society in which there is marked occupational, social, and geographical mobility and in which considerable freedom of choice exists among various conflicting value systems, the development of personal identity is an ongoing creative process.

An industrial society tends to break down many important past sources of loyalty, such as extended kinship, local, regional, and even ethnic attachments. In their place, occupation becomes a more important element of general social standing, since more than any other attribute it influences the income and style of life a person leads. While people construct a sense of identity by a synthesis of early childhood identifications with a large number of later commitments and loyalties,[30] occupational identity has probably become a much more significant component of total identity in modern society than in the past. In an industrial society, it is primarily occupational status which is ranked superior and inferior grades by the spontaneous processes of stratification. The estimates of the community and other men about the jobs we hold therefore greatly affect our own estimates of self-worth.

In general, working-class jobs in the United States have lower status than white-collar and professional ones. For this reason many factory workers are ambivalent about their work and do not find that occupational identity contributes to feelings of self-esteem and self-approval. In such a situation, there is probably a tendency to de-emphasize occupation and work as important components of selfhood and to stress in their place other loyalties and statuses, such as ethnic identifications and family relations.[31] Perhaps an indication of this dissatisfaction with working-class status is the fact that 59 percent of the factory workers in the Roper study said that they would choose *different* occupations if they were able to "start all over again at the age of 15." In contrast, 80 or 90 percent of those in various professional occupations would reenter the *same* line of work if given a free choice.[32]

Self-estranging work compounds and intensifies this problem of a negative occupational identity. When work provides opportunities for control, creativity, and challenge—when, in a word, it is self-expressive and enhances an individual's unique potentialities—then it contributes to the worker's sense of self-respect and dignity and at least partially overcomes the stigma of low status. Alienated work—without control, freedom, or responsibility—on the other hand simply confirms and deepens the feeling that societal estimates of low status and little worth are valid.

The theory of alienation has been and continues to be a fruitful perspective on the world of work, but it must be pointed out that it is a limited perspective. With all its social-psychological subtleties, it does not fully comprehend the complexities and ambiguities of the inner meaning of work to the individual. As a polemic, it therefore condemns too much, and as a vision, promises too much.

Because it ignores what might be called the bipolar or two-sided ambivalence of work, alienation theory cannot totally explain the relationship between work and human happiness. For even the most alienated work is never totally unpleasant, never completely rejected by the worker. Necessity and force is never the whole story. The very worst jobs are rarely only means to exist but often become ends in themselves in some regard. Marx's conception of the function of work for man was too narrow, or perhaps too philosophical: he did not accept as essential the myriad of functions that even alienated work plays in the life-organization of human beings. Observation and research have disproved his statement that "as soon as no physical or other compulsion exist, labor is shunned like the plague." The need for sheer activity, for social intercourse, and for some status and identity in the large society keeps even unskilled workers on the job after they are economically free to retire.[33]

Work is inherently ambivalent also at the opposite pole of freedom and non-alienation. Even in the most unalienated conditions, work is never totally pleasurable; in fact, the freest work, that of the writer or artist, usually involves long periods of virtual self-torture. Such non-alienated work is never completely an end in itself; it is never totally without the element of necessity. As Henri DeMan wrote in a profound study of the meaning of work:

> Even the worker who is free in the social sense, the peasant or the handicrafts-man, feels this compulsion, were it only because while he is at work, his activities are dominated and determined by the aim of his work, by the idea of a willed or necessary creation. Work inevitably signifies subordination of the worker to remoter aims, felt to be necessary, and therefore involving a renunciation of the freedoms and enjoyments of the present for the sake of a future advantage.[34]

## SUMMARY AND CONCLUSION

We have discussed four types of alienation often experienced by manual workers in industry. What do these dimensions have in common on a more general level? Basic to each one is the notion of fragmentation in man's existence and consciousness which impedes the wholeness of experience and activity. What distinguishes the separate dimensions is that they are based on different principles of division or fragmentation. Each dimension has its unique opposite, or non-alienated state, which implies a kind of organic wholeness in the quality of experience. Finally, each alienated state makes it more probable that the person (or worker) can be "used as a thing."

The split in man's existence and consciousness into subject and object underlies the idea of *powerlessness*. A person is powerless when he is an object controlled and manipulated by other persons or by an impersonal system (such as technology) and when he cannot assert himself as a subject to change or modify this domination. The non-alienated pole of the powerlessness dimension is the state of freedom and control.

*Meaninglessness* alienation reflects a split between the part and the whole. A person experiences alienation of this type when his individual acts seem to have no relation to a broader life-program. Meaninglessness also occurs when individual roles are not seen as fitting into the total system of goals of the organization but have become severed from any organic connection with the whole. The non-alienated state is understanding of a life-plan or of an organization's total functioning and activity which is purposeful rather than meaningless.

*Isolation* results from a fragmentation of the individual and social components of human behavior and motivation. Isolation suggests the idea of general societal alienation, the feeling of being in, but not of, society, a sense of remoteness from the larger social order, an absence of loyalties to intermediate collectivities. The non-alienated opposite of isolation is a sense of belonging and membership in society or in specific communities which are integrated through the sharing of a normative system.

*Self-estrangement* is based on a rupture in the temporal continuity of experience. When activity becomes a means to an end, rather than an end in itself, a heightened awareness of time results from a split between present engagements and future considerations. Activity that is not self-estranged, but self-expressive or self-actualizing, is characterized by involvement in the present-time context. Self-estrangement also entails a separation between work life and other concerns. When work is self-estranging, occupation does not contribute in an affirmative manner to personal identity and selfhood, but instead is damaging to self-esteem.

Thus the four modes of alienation reflect different "splits" in the organic relationship between man and his existential experience: the subject-object, the part-whole, the individual-social, and the present-future dichotomies. Each makes it more possible to use people as means rather than as ends. Since "things" rather than human beings are normally used as means, alienation tends to turn people into things: thus thingness, in addition to fragmentation, is another common denominator of the various meanings of alienation.

In sum, a person is more likely to be used as an object under these conditions: (1) when he is powerless and lacks control; (2) when his role is so specialized that he becomes a "cog" in an organization; and (3) when he is isolated from a community or network of personal relations which would inhibit impersonal treatment. The result of being a means for the ends of others is that for himself, his (own) activity becomes only a means rather than a fulfilling end.

These *fragmentations* in man's experience all seem to have resulted from basic changes in social organization brought about by the Industrial Revolution. That is why the alienation concept has a peculiarily modern ring. Few people in preindustrial societies seem to be alienated (the powerlessness of the masses might be the exception); in a bureaucratic mass society we are likely to regard huge numbers of people as alienated. Thus, the breadth of the alienation concept is due to the fact that it reflects the social conditions and consequences of the transition to an industrial society.[35] And conversely, when one studies the stabilization and reintegration of industrial societies in their more mature, advanced phases (a common perspective today of students of social organization), one is studying the conditions through which alienation is either overcome or rendered bearable for individuals and relatively harmless for society.

Within the world of work, the relative stabilization of an advanced industrial society has diminished some of the more glaring instances of alienation characteristic of the period of early industrialization in which Marx wrote. Yet the tendency to use people as things still persists in modern industry. And perhaps this is inevitable, since the nature of industrial organization is such that workers are productive resources and, therefore, to some degree, means to organizational goals.

But despite the common features of modern employment relations, industrial environments vary markedly in their alienating tendencies. Whether a worker approaches the state of being merely a commodity, a resource, or an element of cost in the productive process depends on his concrete relation to technology, the social structure of his industry, and its economic fortunes. The industry a man works in is fateful because the conditions of work and existence in various industrial environments are quite different.

## NOTES

1. Although my main approach is not philosophical, it will become clear that the problems which I analyze attain their relevancy from a personal value system. Along with Marx, Erich Fromm (*The Sane Society* [New York: Rinehart & Co., 1955]), and Chris Argyris (*Personality and Organization* [New York: Harper & Bros., 1957]), I assume that work which permits autonomy, responsibility, social connection, and self-actualization furthers the dignity of the human individual, whereas work without these characteristics limits the development of personal potential and is therefore to be negatively valued.

2. For identifying the dimensions of alienation I am indebted to an article by Melvin Seeman, "On the Meaning of Alienation," *American Sociological Review* 24 (1959): 783–91. The author helps clarify this confused area by distinguishing five different ways in which the alienation concept has been utilized in sociological theory and social thought. He attempts to restate the concepts of powerlessness, meaninglessness, normlessness, isolation, and self-estrangement in terms of a modern vocabulary of expectations and rewards. I have made a rather free adaptation of his discussion, redefining a number of his categories so that they better fit the industrial situation, an application Seeman does not himself make. I have not treated normlessness as a separate dimension but consider some of its implications in my discussion of isolation.

In the earliest discussion of alienated labor, Karl Marx also took a multidimensional approach and distinguished economic, psychological, sociological, and philosophical aspects of alienation. In the *Economic and Philosophical Manuscripts of 1844* (Moscow: Foreign Languages Publishing House, n.d., [and Buffalo, N.Y.: Prometheus Books, 1988]), the youthful Marx analyzed how the intitutions of capitalism, private property, market economy, and money alienated the worker from the product of his work, in the process or activity of work, from other human beings and from his own human nature.

Again, the connection between some of Marx's dimensions and those employed in the present chapter is clear.

3. It was Max Weber in his classic analysis of bureaucracy who expanded Marx's concept of the industrial worker's separation from the means of production to all modern large-scale organizations. Civil servants are separated from the means of administration; soldiers from the means of violence; and scientists from the means of inquiry. Hans Gerth and C. W. Mills, *From Max Weber: Essays in Sociology* (New York: Oxford University Press, 1946), p. 50.

4. Fromm (see note 1).

5. Ely Chinoy, *Automobile Workers and the American Dream* (New York: Doubleday & Co., 1955), pp. xvi–xvii.

6. Hugh Clegg, *A New Approach to Industrial Democracy* (Oxford: Basil Blackwell, 1960), p. 5.

7. E. Jaques, *The Changing Culture of the Factory* (London: Tavistock Publications, 1951), and F. Blum, *Toward a Democratic Work Process* (New York: Harper & Bros., 1953). A most notable exception to this generalization seems to be the Scanlon plan which encourages workers to make suggestions for increasing efficiency, cutting costs, and raising profits through a system of company-wide meetings and a group bonus plan. Probably best suited for small companies,

it has been remarkably successful in a number of cases. See, for example, Frederick Lesieur (ed.), *The Scanlon Plan* (New York: John Wiley & Sons, 1958).

8. S. Perlman, *A Theory of the Labor Movement* (New York: August M. Kelley, 1949).

9. This guiding idea informs the work of Philip Selznick, *Law, Society, and Industrial Justice* (New York: Russell Sage Foundation, 1969). See also Howard Vollmer, *Employee Rights and the Employment Relationship* (Berkeley: University of California Press, 1960).

10. Combining data from sixteen studies of employee attitudes, Herzberg and his collaborators found that security was the most important factor of ten job factors. See F. Herzberg et al., *Job Attitudes: Review of Research and Opinion* (Pittsburgh, Pa.: Psychological Service of Pittsburgh, 1957), p. 44.

11. The high degree of importance which workers place on control of their immediate job conditions is attested to by numerous investigations. The economists Joseph Shister and Lloyd Reynolds found that among two large samples of workers, "independence and control" were the most important elements among eleven job characteristics accounting for both satisfaction and dissatisfaction with their present jobs. *Job Horizons* (New York: Harper & Bros., 1949), p. 7. In his study of a gypsum plant Alvin Gouldner attributed the outbreak of a wildcat strike to the company's abrogation of an "indulgency pattern," an informal situation in which the workers had maintained a great deal of freedom and control in their immediate job realm. *Wildcat Strike* (Yellow Springs, Oh.: Antioch Press, 1954). In a survey of the literature on occupational differences in job satisfaction, the present writer found that variations in the degree of control over the conditions of work was the most important single factor accounting for these differences. "Work Satisfaction and Industrial Trends in Modern Society," in Walter Galenson and Seymour Martin Lipset (eds.), *Labor and Trade Unionism* (New York: John Wiley & Sons, 1960), pp. 345–49.

Among other studies of workers' attitudes which confirm the importance of control are Theodore Purcell, *The Worker Speaks His Mind on Company and Union* (Cambridge, Mass: Harvard University Press, 1954), p. 103; Gladys Palmer, "Attitudes toward Work in an Industrial Community," *American Journal of Sociology* 63 (1957): 24; and Nancy C. Morse and Robert S. Weiss, "The Function and Meaning of Work and the Job," *American Sociological Review* 20 (1955): 191–98.

12. John Dunlop, *Industrial Relations Systems* (New York: Henry Holt & Co., 1958), pp. 152–53.

13. This has been a common research finding in industrial sociology since the Western Electric study dramatized the fact. See especially the studies of Donald Roy—for example, "Quota Restriction and Goldbricking in a Machine Shop," *American Journal of Sociology* 57 (1952): 427–42.

14. K. Mannheim, *Man and Society in an Age of Reconstruction* (New York: Harcourt, Brace & Co., 1940), p. 59, cited in Seeman (see note 2), p. 786.

15. "Only the human contacts bring a touch of variety into the monotony of the daily work. . . . If you speak to a worker who has been sick for some time, and could not go to work, and he asks about the 'fellows' in the gang—then you realize the secret attraction which the plant has for many workers . . . . The shop community is a major factor making the experience of work more positive." Blum (see note 7), p. 77.

16. Technology has an important impact on social alienation because it determines a number of aspects of industrial structure that affect cohesion and integration: the occupational distribution of the blue-collar labor force, the economic cost structure of the enterprise, the typical size of plant, and the existence and structure of work groups.

17. Adriano Tilgher, *Work: What It Has Meant to Men through the Ages* (New York: Harcourt, Brace & Co., 1930).

18. Hannah Arendt emphasizes this factor as the basic precondition of alienation. See *The Human Condition* (Chicago: University of Chicago Press, 1958), especially pp. 79–174.

19. It has been often pointed out that the reduction of hours of work is only relevant to the past century or two. In the Middle Ages as much or more leisure time existed as at the

present. See Harold Wilensky, "The Uneven Distribution of Leisure: The Impact of Economic Growth on 'Free Time,' " *Social Problems* 9 (1961): 33–34.

20. K. Marx (see note 2), pp. 72–73.

21. Blum (note 7).

22. Chinoy (note 5).

23. Blum (note 7), p. 82.

24. Of course, many people do not find monotonous work objectionable.

25. A brilliant discussion is found in Georges Freidmann, *Industrial Society* (Glencoe, Ill.: Free Press, 1955), pp. 120–55.

26. Monotony, of course, is quite relative in the sense that minor alterations in the work routine or general situation (a new tool or a superintendent passing by) may give interest to a workday which, from an intellectual's vantage point, would appear the height of tedium.

27. Blauner, in Glaneson and Lipset (see note 11).

28. Morse and Weiss (see note 11); Eugene Friedmann and Robert Havighurst, *The Meaning of Work and Retirement* (Chicago: University of Chicago Press, 1954). Herzberg and his collaborators also report that those in non-manual occupations and the more educated are more concerned with intrinsic job features (Herzberg et al. [see note 10], p. 54.)

Besides education, other important factors are intelligence, personality, and occupation itself. For the most part, white-collar and professional work involves more variety, control, purpose, and responsibility than blue-collar work. It is to some degree the work itself which a person secures that instills him with specific kinds of needs to be satisfied or frustrated in the work situation. A manual worker whose work does not involve such qualities, whose education has not awakened such aspirations, and whose opportunities do not include realistic alternatives, will not develop the need for intrinsically fulfilling work.

29. Erik Erikson, "The Problem of Ego Identity," *Journal of the American Psychoanalytic Association* 4 (1956).

30. Ibid.

31. In her study of unskilled workers in a shipyard, Katherine Archibald has vividly documented their obsession with ethnic categorization, *Wartime Shipyard* (Berkeley: University of California Press, 1947), pp. 40–127. The importance of kinship relations to manual workers has been noted by many researchers.

32. Blauner, in Galenson and Lipset (see note 11), p. 343.

33. E. Friedmann and R. Havighurst (see note 28). Morse and Weiss found that 80 percent of a national sample said they would keep working if they inherited enough money to live comfortably (see note 11).

34. H. DeMan, *Joy in Work* (London: George Allen & Unwin, 1929), p. 67.

35. Note the similarity between this statement of alienation theory and the standard sociological analyses of modern industrial society (from Toennies to Parsons) which stress the predominance of instrumental over expressive orientations, of means over ends, of technology and organization over family and community.

# 25

# Scientific Management

## Harry Braverman

The classical economists were the first to approach the problems of the organization of labor within capitalist relations of production from a theoretical point of view. They may thus be called the first management experts, and their work was continued in the latter part of the Industrial Revolution by such men as Andrew Ure and Charles Babbage. Between these men and the next step, the comprehensive formulation of management theory in the late nineteenth and early twentieth centuries, there lies a gap of more than half a century during which there was an enormous growth in the size of enterprises, the beginnings of the monopolistic organization of industry, and the purposive and systematic application of science to production. The scientific management movement initiated by Frederick Winslow Taylor in the last decades of the nineteenth century was brought into being by these forces. Logically, Taylorism belongs to the chain of development of management methods and the organization of labor, and not to the development of technology, in which its role was minor.*

Scientific management, so-called, is an attempt to apply the methods of science to the increasingly complex problems of the control of labor in rapidly growing capitalist enterprises. It lacks the characteristics of a true science because its assumptions reflect nothing more than the outlook of the capitalist with

    *It is important to grasp this point, because from it flows the universal application of Taylorism to work in its various forms and stages of development, regardless of the nature of the technology employed. Scientific management, says Peter F. Drucker, "was not concerned with technology. Indeed, it took tools and techniques largely as given."[1]

regard to the conditions of production. It starts, despite occasional protestations to the contrary, not from the human point of view but from the capitalist point of view, from the point of view of the management of a refractory work force in a setting of antagonistic social relations. It does not attempt to discover and confront the cause of this condition, but accepts it as an inexorable given, a "natural" condition. It investigates not labor in general, but the adaptation of labor to the needs of capital. It enters the workplace not as the representative of science, but as the representative of management masquerading in the trappings of science.

A comprehensive and detailed outline of the principles of Taylorism is essential to our narrative, not because of the things for which it is popularly known—stopwatch, speed-up, etc.—but because behind these commonplaces there lies a theory which is nothing less than the explicit verbalization of the capitalist mode of production. But before I begin this presentation, a number of introductory remarks are required to clarify the role of the Taylor school in the development of management theory.

It is impossible to overestimate the importance of the scientific management movement in the shaping of the modern corporation and indeed all institutions of capitalist society which carry on labor processes. The popular notion that Taylorism has been "superseded" by later schools of industrial psychology or "human relations," that it "failed"—because of Taylor's amateurish and naïve views of human motivation or because it brought about a storm of labor opposition or because Taylor and various successors antagonized workers and sometimes management as well—or that it is "outmoded" because certain Taylorian specifics like functional foremanship or his incentive-pay schemes have been discarded for more sophisticated methods: all these represent a woeful misreading of the actual dynamics of the development of management.

The forms of management that existed prior to Taylorism, which Taylor called "ordinary management," he deemed altogether inadequate. His descriptions of ordinary management bear the marks of the propagandist and proselytizer: exaggeration, simplification, and schematization. But his point is clear:

> Now, in the best of the ordinary types of management, the managers recognize frankly that the . . . workmen, included in the twenty or thirty trades, who are under them, possess this mass of traditional knowledge, a large part of which is not in the possession of management. The management, of course, includes foremen and superintendents, who themselves have been first-class workers at their trades. And yet these foremen and superintendents know, better than any one else, that their own knowledge and personal skill falls far short of the combined knowledge and dexterity of all the workmen under them. The most experienced managers frankly place before their workmen the problem of doing the work in the best and most economical way. They recognize the task before them as that of inducing each workman to use his best endeavors, his hardest work, all his traditonal knowledge, his skill, his ingenuity, and his good will—in a word, his "initiative," so as to yield the largest possible return to his employer.[2]

As we have already seen from Taylor's belief in the universal prevalence and in fact inevitability of "soldiering," he did not recommend reliance upon the "initiative" of workers. Such a course, he felt, leads to the surrender of control: "As was usual then, and in fact as is still usual in most of the shops in this country, the shop was really run by the workmen and not by the bosses. The workmen together had carefully planned just how fast each job should be done." In his Midvale battle, Taylor pointed out, he had located the source of the trouble in the "ignorance of the management as to what really constitutes a proper day's work for a workman." He had "fully realized that, although he was foreman of the shop, the combined knowledge and skill of the workmen who were under him was certainly ten times as great as his own."[3] This, then, was the source of the trouble and the starting point of scientific management.

We may illustrate the Taylorian solution to this dilemma in the same manner that Taylor often did: by using his story of his work for the Bethlehem Steel Company in supervising the moving of pig iron by hand. This story has the advantage of being the most detailed and circumstantial he set down, and also of dealing with a type of work so simple that anyone can visualize it without special technical preparation. We extract it here from Taylor's *The Principles of Scientific Management*:

One of the first pieces of work undertaken by us, when the writer started to introduce scientific management into the Bethlehem Steel Company, was to handle pig iron on task work. The opening of the Spanish War found some 80,000 tons of pig iron placed in small piles in an open field adjoining the works. Prices for pig iron had been so low that it could not be sold at a profit, and therefore had been stored. With the opening of the Spanish War the price of pig iron rose, and this large accumulation of iron was sold. This gave us a good opportunity to show the workmen, as well as the owners and managers of the works, on a fairly large scale the advantages of task work over the old-fashioned day work and piece work, in doing a very elementary class of work.

The Bethlehem Steel Company had five blast furnaces, the product of which had been handled by a pig-iron gang for many years. This gang, at this time, consisted of about 75 men. They were good, average pig-iron handlers, were under an excellent foreman who himself had been a pig-iron handler, and the work was done, on the whole, about as fast and cheaply as it was anywhere else at that time.

A railroad switch was run out into the field, right along the edge of the piles of pig iron. An inclined plank was placed against the side of a car, and each man picked up from his pile a pig iron weighing about 92 pounds, walked up the inclined plank and dropped it on the end of the car.

We found that this gang were loading on the average about 12½ long tons per man per day. We were surprised to find, after studying the matter, that a first-class pig-iron handler ought to handle between 47 and 48 long tons per day, instead of 12½ tons. This task seemed to us so very large that we were obliged to go over our work several times before we were absolutely sure that we were right. Once we were sure, however, that 47 tons was a proper day's work for a first-class pig-iron handler, the task which faced us as managers under the modern scientific plan was clearly before us. It was our duty to see that the 80,000 tons of pig iron was loaded on to the cars at the rate of 47 tons per man per day, in place of 12½ tons, at which rate the work was then being done. And it was further our duty to see that this work was done without bringing on a strike among the men, without any quarrel with the men, and to see that the men were happier and better contented when loading at the new rate of 47 tons than they were when loading at the old rate of 12½ tons.

Our first step was the scientific selection of the workman. In dealing with workmen under this type of management, it is an inflexible rule to talk to and deal with only one man at a time, since each workman has his own special abilities and limitations, and since we are not dealing with men in masses, but are trying to develop each individual man to his highest state of efficieny and prosperity. Our first step was to find the proper workman to begin with. We therefore carefully watched and studied these 75 men for three or four days, at the end of which time we had picked out four men who appeared to be physically able to handle pig iron at the rate of 47 tons per day. A careful study was then made of each of these men. We looked up their history as far back as practicable and thorough inquiries were made as to the character, habits, and the ambition of each of them. Finally we selected one from among the four as the most likely man to start with. He was a little Pennsylvania Dutchman who had been observed to trot back home for a mile or so after his work in the evening, about as fresh as when he came trotting down to work in the morning. We found that upon wages of $1.15 a day he had succeeded in buying a small plot of ground, and that he was engaged in putting up the walls of a little house for himself in the morning before starting to work and at night after leaving. He also had the reputation of being exceedingly "close," that is, of placing a very high value on a dollar. As one man whom we talked to about him said, " A penny looks about the size of a cart-wheel to him." This man we will call Schmidt.

The task before us, then, narrowed itself down to getting Schmidt to handle 47 tons of pig iron per day and making him glad to do it. This was done as follows. Schmidt was called out from among the gang of pig-iron handlers and talked to somewhat in this way:

"Schmidt, are you a high-priced man?"

"Vell, I don't know vat you mean."

"Oh yes, you do. What I want to know is whether you are a high-priced man or not."

"Vell, I don't know vat you mean."

"Oh, come now, you answer my questions. What I want to find out is whether you are a high-priced man or one of these cheap fellows here. What I want to find out is whether you want to earn $1.85 a day or whether you are satisfied with $1.15, just the same as all those cheap fellows are getting."

"Did I vant $1.85 a day? Vas dot a high-priced man? Vell, yes, I vas a high-priced man."

"Oh, you're aggravating me. Of course you want $1.85 a day—everyone wants it! You know perfectly well that that has very little to do with your being a high-priced man. For goodness' sake answer my questions, and don't waste any more of my time. Now come over here. You see that pile of pig iron?"

"Yes."

"You see that car?"

"Yes."

"Well, if you are a high-priced man, you will load that pig iron on that car tomorrow for $1.85. Now do wake up and answer my question. Tell me whether you are a high-priced man or not."

"Vell—did I got $1.85 for loading dot pig iron on dot car tomorrow?"

"Yes, of course you do, and you get $1.85 for loading a pile like that every day right through the year. That is what a high-priced man does, and you know it just as well as I do."

" Vell, dot's all right. I could load pig iron on the car tomorrow for $1.85, and I get it every day, don't I?"

"Certainly you do—certainly you do."

"Vell, den, I vas a high-priced man."

"Now, hold on, hold on. You know just as well as I do that a high-priced man has to do exactly as he's told from morning till night. You have seen this man here before, haven't you?"

"No, I never saw him."

"Well, if you are a high-priced man, you will do exactly as this man tells you tomorrow, from morning till night. When he tells you to pick up a pig and walk, you pick it up and you walk, and when he tells you to sit down and rest, you sit down. You do that right straight through the day. And what's more, no back talk. Now a high-priced man does just what he's told to do, and no back talk. Do you understand that? When this man tells you to walk, you walk; when he tells you to sit down, you sit down, and you don't talk back to him. Now you come on to work here tomorrow morning and I'll know before night whether you are really a high-priced man or not."

This seems to be rather rough talk. And indeed it would be if applied to an educated mechanic, or even an intelligent laborer. With a man of the mentally sluggish type of Schmidt it is appropriate and not unkind, since it is effective in fixing his attention on the high wages which he wants and away from what, if it were called to his attention, he probably would consider impossibly hard work. . . .

Schmidt started to work, and all day long, and at regular intervals, was told by the man who stood over him with a watch, "Now pick up a pig and walk. Now sit down and rest. Now walk—now rest," etc. He worked when he was told to work, and rested when he was told to rest, and at half-past five in the afternoon had his 47½ tons loaded on the car. And he practically never failed to work at this pace and do the task that was set him during the three years that the writer was at Bethlehem. And throughout this time he averaged a little more than $1.85 per day, whereas before he had never received over $1.15 per day, which was the ruling rate of wages at that time in Bethlehem. That is, he received 60 percent higher wages than were paid to other men who were not working on task work. One man after another was picked out and trained to handle pig iron at the rate of 47½ tons per day until all of the pig iron was handled at this rate, and the men were receiving 60 percent more wages than other workmen around them.[4]*

---

*Daniel Bell has recorded this event as follows: "But it was in 1899 that Taylor achieved fame when he taught a Dutchman named Schmidt to shovel forty-seven tons instead of twelve and a half tons of pig iron a day. Every detail of the man's job was specified: the size of the

The merit of this tale is its clarity in illustrating the pivot upon which all modern management turns: the control over work through the control over the *decisions that are made in the course of work*. Since, in the case of pig-iron handling, the only decisions to be made were those having to do with time sequence, Taylor simply dictated that timing and the results at the end of the day added up to his planned day-task. As to the use of money as motivation, while this element has a usefulness in the first stages of a new mode or work, employers do not, when they have once found a way to compel a more rapid pace of work, continue to pay a 60 percent differential for common labor, or for any other job. Taylor was to discover (and to complain) that management treated his "scientific incentives" like any other piece rate, cutting them mercilessly so long as the labor market permitted, so that workers pushed to the Taylorian intensity found themselves getting little, or nothing, more than the going rate for the area, while other employers—under pressure of this competitive threat—forced their own workers to the higher intensities of labor.*

Taylor liked to pretend that his work standards were not beyond human capabilities exercised without undue strain, but as he himself made clear, this pretense could be maintained only on the understanding that unusual physical specimens were selected for each of his jobs:

> As to the scientific selection of the men, it is a fact that in this gang of 75 pig-iron handlers only about one man in eight was physically capable of handling 47½ tons per day. With the very best of intentions, the other seven out of eight men were physically unable to work at this pace. Now the one man in eight who was able to do this work was in no sense superior to the other men who were working on the gang. He merely happened to be a man of the type of the ox—no rare specimen of humanity, difficult to find and therefore very highly prized.

---

shovel, the bite into the pile, the weight of the scoop, the distance to walk, the arc of the swing, and the rest periods that Schmidt should take. By systematically varying each factor, Taylor got the optimum amount of barrow load."[5] In the face of so much circumstantial detail, one hesitates to inquire whether Professor Bell can imagine handling a 92-pound pig iron on a shovel, let alone what sort of an "arc of the swing" one could manage, or how a "barrow" would handle a whole "scoop" of them. The point here is not that anyone may be tripped up by the use of secondary sources, or get his stories mixed, or have never seen a pig of iron; the point is that sociologists, with few exceptions, deem it proper to write about occupations, work, skills, etc., without even bare familiarity. The result is what one would get from a school of literary critics who never read the novels, plays, poems they write about, but construct their theories entirely on the basis of responses to questionnaires put to "scientifically selected samples" of readers. Bell's error is only the grandfather of a long line of such misapprehensions, which become truly extraordinary as more complex forms of work are dealt with. In this situation, management can—and gleefully does—tell academics anything it pleases about the evolution of work, skills, etc.

*In his classic study of scientific management undertaken in 1915 for the United States Commission on Industrial Relations, Robert F. Hoxie pointed out that most rate cutting in shops which had installed a formal system of scientific management took place indirectly, by creating new job classifications at lower rates, etc. He concludes that under scientific management "what amounts to rate cutting seems to be almost of necessity an essential part of its very nature."[6]

On the contrary, he was a man so stupid that he was unfitted to do most kinds of laboring work, even. The selection of the man, then, does not involve finding some extraordinary individual, but merely picking out from among very ordinary men the few who are especially suited to this type of work. Although in this particular gang only one man in eight was suited to doing the work, we had not the slightest difficulty in getting all the men who were needed—some of them from inside the works and others from the neighboring country—who were exactly suited to the job.[7]*

Taylor spent his lifetime in expounding the principles of control enunciated here, and in applying them directly to many other tasks: shoveling loose materials, lumbering, inspecting ball bearings, etc., but particularly to the machinist's trade. He believed that the forms of control he advocated could be applied not only to simple labor, but to labor in its most complex forms, without exception, and in fact it was in machine shops, bricklaying, and other such sites for the practice of well-developed crafts that he and his immediate successors achieved their most striking results.

From earliest times to the Industrial Revolution the craft or skilled trade was the basic unit, the elementary cell of the labor process. In each craft, the worker was presumed to be the master of a body of traditional knowledge, and methods and procedures were left to his or her discretion. In each such worker reposed the accumulated knowledge of materials and processes by which production was accomplished in the craft. The potter, tanner, smith, weaver, carpenter, baker, miller, glassmaker, cobbler, etc., each representing a branch of the social division of labor, was a repository of human technique for the labor processes of that branch. The worker combined, in mind and body, the concepts and physical dexterities of the speciality: technique, understood in this way, is, as has often been observed, the predecessor and progenitor of science. The most important and widespread of all crafts was, and throughout the world remains to this day, that of farmer. The farming family combines its craft with the rude practice of a number of others, including those of the smith, mason, carpenter, butcher, miller, and baker, etc. The apprenticeships required in traditional crafts ranged from three to seven years, and for the farmer of course extends beyond this to include most of childhood, adolescence, and young adulthood. In view of the knowledge to be assimilated, the dexterities to be gained, and the fact that the craftsman, like the professional, was required

---

*Georges Friedmann reports that in 1927 a German physiologist, reviewing the Schmidt experience, calculated that the level of output set by Taylor could not be accepted as a standard because "most workers will succumb under the pressure of these labors."[8] Yet Taylor persisted in calling it "a pace under which men become happier and thrive."[9] We should also note that although Taylor called Schmidt "a man of the type of the ox," and Schmidt's stupidity has become part of the folklore of industrial sociology, Taylor himself reported that Schmidt was building his own house, presumably without anyone to tell him when to stand and when to squat. But a belief in the original stupidity of the worker is a necessity for management; otherwise it would have to admit that it is engaged in a wholesale enterprise of prizing and fostering stupidity.

to master a specialty and become the best judge of the manner of its application to specific production problems, the years of apprenticeship were generally needed and were employed in a learning process that extended well into the journeyman decades. Of these trades, that of the machinist was in Taylor's day among the most recent, and certainly the most important to modern industry.

As I have already pointed out, Taylor was not primarily concerned with the advance of technology (which, as we shall see, offers other means for direct control over the labor process). He did make significant contributions to the technical knowledge of machine-shop practice (high-speed tool steel, in particular), but these were chiefly by-products of his effort to study this practice with an eye to systematizing and classifying it. His concern was with the control of labor at any given level of technology, and he tackled his own trade with a boldness and energy which astonished his contemporaries and set the pattern for industrial engineers, work designers, and office managers from that day on. And in tackling machine-shop work, he had set himself a prodigious task.

The machinist of Taylor's day started with the shop drawing, and turned, milled, bored, drilled, planed, shaped, ground, filed, and otherwise machine- and hand-processed the proper stock to the desired shape as specified in the drawing. The range of decisions to be made in the course of the process is— unlike the case of a simple job, such as handling of pig iron—by its very nature enormous. Even for the lathe alone, disregarding all collateral tasks such as the choice of stock, handling, centering and chucking the work, layout and measuring, order of cuts, and considering only the operation of turning itself, the range of possibilities is huge. Taylor himself worked with twelve variables, including the hardness of the metal, the material of the cutting tool, the thickness of the shaving, the shape of the cutting tool, the use of a coolant during cutting, the depth of the cut, the frequency of regrinding cutting tools as they became dulled, the lip and clearance angles of the tool, the smoothness of cutting or absence of chatter, the diameter of the stock being turned, the pressure of the chip or shaving on the cutting surface of the tool, and the speeds, feeds, and pulling power of the machine.[10] Each of these variables is subject to broad choice, ranging from a few possibilities in the selection and use of a coolant, to a very great number of effective choices in all matters having to do with thickness, shape, depth, duration, speed, etc. Twelve variables, each subject to a large number of choices, will yield in their possible combinations and permutations astronomical figures, as Taylor soon realized. But upon these decisions of the machinist depended not just the accuracy and finish of the product, but also the pace of production. Nothing daunted, Taylor set out to gather into management's hands all the basic information bearing on these processes. He began a series of experiments at the Midvale Steel Company, in the fall of 1880, which lasted twenty-six years, recording the results of between 30,000 and 50,000 tests, and cutting up more than 800,000 pounds of iron and steel on ten different machine tools reserved for his experimental use.* His greatest difficulty, he reported, was not testing the many variations, but holding eleven variables constant while altering the conditions of the twelfth. The data were systematized, correlated, and reduced to practical form in the shape of what he called a "slide rule" which would determine the optimum combination of choices for each step in the machining process.[12] His machinists thenceforth were required to work in accordance with instructions derived from these experimental data, rather than from their own knowledge, experience, or tradition. This was the Taylor approach in its first systematic application to a complex labor process. Since the principles upon which it is based are fundamental to all advanced work design or industrial engineering today, it is important to examine them in detail. And since Taylor has been virtually alone in giving clear expression to principles which are seldom now publicly acknowledged, it is best to examine them with the aid of Taylor's own forthright formulations.

## FIRST PRINCIPLE

"The managers assume . . . the burden of gathering together all of the traditional knowledge which in the past has been possessed by the workmen and then of classifying, tabulating, and reducing this knowledge to rules, laws, and formulae. . . ."[13] We have seen the illustrations of this in the cases of the lathe machinist and the pig-iron handler. The great disparity between these activities, and the different orders of knowledge that may be collected about them, illustrate that for Taylor—as for managers today—no task is either so simple or so complex that it may not be studied with the object of collecting in the hands of management at least as much information as is known by the worker who performs it regularly, and very likely more. This brings to an end the situation in which "Employers derive their knowledge of how much of a given class of work can be done in a day from either their own experience, which has frequently grown hazy with age, from casual and unsystematic observation of their men, or at best from records which are kept, showing the quickest time in which each job has been done."[14] It enables management to discover and enforce those speedier

---

*Friedmann so far forgets this enormous machine-shop project at one point that he says: "This failure to appreciate the psychological factors in work is at least partially explained by the nature of the jobs to which Taylor exclusively confined his observations: handlers of pig iron, shovel-laborers, and navvies."[11] He was led to this error by his marked tendency to side with the psychological and sociological schools of "human relations" and work adjustment which came after Taylor, and which he always attempts to counterpose to Taylorism, although, as we have pointed out, they operate on different levels. In general, Friedmann, with all his knowledge of work processes, suffers from a confusion of viewpoints, writing sometimes as a socialist concerned about the trends in capitalist work organization, but more often as though the various forms of capitalist management and personnel administration represent scrupulous efforts to find a universal answer to problems of work.

methods and shortcuts which workers themselves, in the practice of their trades or tasks, learn or improvise, and use at their own discretion only. Such an experimental approach also brings into being new methods such as can be devised only through the means of systematic study.

This first principle we may call the *dissociation of the labor process from the skills of the workers*. The labor process is to be rendered independent of craft, tradition, and the workers' knowledge. Henceforth it is to depend not at all upon the abilities of workers, but entirely upon the practices of management.

## SECOND PRINCIPLE

"All possible brain work should be removed from the shop and centered in the planning or laying-out department. . . ."[15] Since this is the key to scientific management, as Taylor well understood, he was especially emphatic on this point and it is important to examine the principle thoroughly.

In the human, as we have seen, the essential feature that makes for a labor capacity superior to that of the animal is the combination of execution with a conception of the thing to be done. But as human labor becomes a social rather than an individual phenomenon, it is possible—unlike in the instance of animals where the motive force, instinct, is inseparable from action—to divorce conception from execution. This dehumanization of the labor process, in which workers are reduced almost to the level of labor in its animal form, while purposeless and unthinkable in the case of the self-organized and self-motivated social labor of a community of producers, becomes crucial for the management of purchased labor. For if the workers' execution is guided by their own conception, it is not possible, as we have seen, to enforce upon them either the methodological efficiency or the working pace desired by capital. The capitalist therefore learns from the start to take advantage of this aspect of human labor power, and to break the unity of the labor process.

This should be called the principle of the *separation of conception from execution,* rather than by its more common name of the separation of mental and manual labor (even though it is similar to the latter, and in practice often identical). This is because mental labor, labor done primarily in the brain, is also subjected to the same principle of separation of conception from execution: mental labor is first separated from manual labor and, as we shall see, is then itself subdivided rigorously according to the same rule.

The first implication of this principle is that Taylor's "science of work" is never to be developed by the worker, always by management. This notion, apparently so "natural" and undebatable today, was in fact vigorously discussed in Taylor's day, a fact that shows how far we have traveled along the road of transforming all ideas about the labor process in less than a century, and how completely Taylor's hotly contested assumptions have entered into the conventional outlook within a short space of time. Taylor confronted this question—why must work be studied by the management and not by the worker himself; why not *scientific workmanship* rather than *scientific management*?—repeatedly, and employed all his ingenuity in devising answers to it, though not always with his customary frankness. In *The Principles of Scientific Management,* he pointed out that the "older system" of management

> makes it necessary for each workman to bear almost the entire responsibility for the general plan as well as for each detail of his work, and in many cases for his implements as well. In addition to this he must do all of the actual physical labor. The development of a science, on the other hand, involves the establishment of many rules, laws, and formulae which replace the judgment of the individual workman and which can be effectively used only after having been systematically recorded, indexed, etc. The practical use of scientific data also calls for a room in which to keep the books, records, etc., and a desk for the planner to work at. Thus all of the planning which under the old system was done by the workman, as a result of his personal experience, must of necessity under the new system be done by the management in accordance with the laws of the science; because even if the workman was well suited to the development and use of scientific data, it would be physically impossible for him to work at his machine and at a desk at the same time. It is also clear that in most cases one type of man is needed to plan ahead and an entirely different type to execute the work.[16]

The objections having to do with physical arrangements in the workplace are clearly of little importance, and represent the deliberate exaggeration of obstacles which, while they may exist as inconveniences, are hardly insuperable. To refer to the "different type" of worker needed for each job is worse than disingenuous, since these "different types" hardly existed until the division of labor created them. As Taylor well understood, the possession of craft knowledge made the worker the best starting point for the development of the science of work; systematization often means, at least at the outset, the gathering of knowledge which *workers already possess*. But Taylor, secure in his obsession with the immense reasonableness of his proposed arrangement, did not stop at this point. In his testimony before the Special Committee of the House of Representatives, pressed and on the defensive, he brought forth still other arguments:

> I want to make it clear, Mr. Chairman, that work of this kind undertaken by the management leads to the development of a science, while it is next to impossible for the workman to develop a science. There are many workmen who are intellectually just as capable of developing a science, who have plenty of brains, and are just as capable of developing a science as those on the managing side. But the science of doing work of any kind cannot be developed by the workman. Why? Because he has neither the time nor the money to do it. The development of the science of doing any kind of work always required the work of two men, one man who actually does the work which is to be studied and another man

who observes closely the first man while he works and studies the time problems and the motion problems connected with this work. No workman has either the time or the money to burn in making experiments of this sort. If he is working for himself no one will pay him while he studies the motions of someone else. The management must and ought to pay for all such work. So that for the workman, the development of a science becomes impossible, not because the workman is not intellectually capable of developing it, but he has neither the time nor the money to do it and he realizes that this is a question for the management to handle.[17]

Taylor here argues that the systematic study of work and the fruits of this study belong to management for the very same reason that machines, factory buildings, etc., belong to them; that is, because it costs labor time to conduct such a study, and only the possessors of capital can afford labor time. The possessors of labor time cannot themselves afford to do anything with it but sell it for their means of subsistence. It is true that this is the rule in capitalist relations of production, and Taylor's use of the argument in this case shows with great clarity where the sway of capital leads: Not only is capital the property of the capitalist, but *labor itself has become part of capital.* Not only do the workers lose control over their instruments of production, but they must now lose control over their own labor and the manner of its performance. This control now falls to those who can "afford" to study it in order to know it better than the workers themselves know their own life activity.

But Taylor has not yet completed his argument: "Furthermore," he told the Committee, "if any workman were to find a new and quicker way of doing work, or if he were to develop a new method, you can see at once it becomes to his interest to keep that development to himself, not to teach the other workmen the quicker method. It is to his interest to do what workmen have done in all times, to keep their trade secrets for themselves and their friends. That is the old idea of trade secrets. The workman kept his knowledge to himself instead of developing a science and teaching it to others and making it public property."[18] Behind this hearkening back to old ideas of "guild secrets" is Taylor's persistent and fundamental notion that the improvement of work methods by workers brings few benefits to management. Elsewhere in his testimony, in discussing the work of his associate, Frank Gilbreth, who spent many years studying bricklaying methods, he candidly admits that not only *could* the "science of bricklaying" be developed by workers, but that it undoubtedly *had been:* "Now, I have not the slightest doubt that during the last 4,000 years all the methods that Mr. Gilbreth developed have many, many times suggested themselves to the minds of bricklayers." But because knowledge possessed by workers is not useful to capital, Taylor begins his list of the desiderata of scientific management: "First. The development—by the management, not the workmen—of the science of bricklaying."[19] Workers, he explains, are not going to put into execution any system or any method which harms them and their workmates: "Would they be likely," he says, referring to the pig-iron job, "to get rid of seven men out of eight from their own gang and retain only the eighth man? No!"[20]

Finally, Taylor understood the Babbage principle better than anyone of his time, and it was always uppermost in his calculations. The purpose of work study was never, in his mind, to enhance the ability of the worker, to concentrate in the worker a greater share of scientific knowledge, to ensure that as technique rose, the worker would rise with it. Rather, the purpose was to cheapen the worker by decreasing his training and enlarging his output. In his early book, *Shop Management,* he said frankly that the "full possibilities" of his system "will not have been realized until almost all of the machines in the shop are run by men who are of smaller caliber and attainments, and who are therefore cheaper than those required under the old system."[21]

Therefore, both in order to ensure management control and to cheapen the worker, conception and execution must be rendered separate spheres of work, and for this purpose the study of work processess must be reserved to management and kept from the workers, to whom its results are communicated only in the form of simplified job tasks governed by simplified instructions which it is thenceforth their duty to follow unthinkingly and without comprehension of the underlying technical reasoning or data.

## THIRD PRINCIPLE

The essential idea of "the ordinary types of management," Taylor said, "is that each workman has become more skilled in his own trade than it is possible for any one in the management to be, and that, therefore, the details of how the work shall best be done must be left to him." But, by contrast: "Perhaps the most prominent single element in modern scientific management is the task idea. The work of every workman is fully planned out by the management at least one day in advance, and each man receives in most cases complete written instructions, describing in detail the task which he is to accomplish, as well as the means to be used in doing the work. . . . This task specifies not only what is to be done, but how it is to be done and the exact time allowed for doing it. . . . Scientific management consists very largely in preparing for and carrying out these tasks."[22]

In this principle it is not the written instruction card that is important.*

---

*This despite the fact that for a time written instruction cards were a fetish among managers. The vogue for such cards passed as work tasks became so simplified and repetitious as to render the cards in most cases unnecessary. But the concept behind them remains: it is the concept of the direct action of management to determine the process, with the worker functioning as the mediating and closely governed instrument. This is the significance of Lillian Gilbreth's definition of the instruction card as "a self-producer of a predetermined product."[23] The worker as producer is ignored; management becomes the producer, and its plans and instructions bring the product into existence. This same instruction card inspired in Alfred Marshall, however, the curious opinion

Taylor had no need for such a card with Schmidt, nor did he use one in many other instances. Rather, the essential element is the systematic preplanning and precalculation of all elements of the labor process, which now no longer exists as a process in the imagination of the worker but only as a process in the imagination of a special management staff. Thus, if the first principle is the gathering and development of knowledge of labor processes, and the second is the concentration of this knowledge as the exclusive province of management—together with its essential converse, the absence of such knowledge among the workers—then the third is the *use of this monopoly over knowledge to control each step of the labor process and its mode of execution.*

As capitalist industrial, office, and market practices developed in accordance with this principle, it eventually became part of accepted routine and custom, all the more so as the increasingly scientific character of most processes, which grew in complexity while the worker was not allowed to partake of this growth, made it ever more difficult for the workers to understand the processes in which they functioned. But in the beginning, as Taylor well understood, an abrupt psychological wrench was required.* We have seen in the simple Schmidt case the means employed, both in the selection of a single worker as a starting point and in the way in which he was reoriented to the new conditions of work. In the more complex conditions of the machine shop, Taylor gave this part of the responsibility to the foremen. It is essential, he said of the gang bosses, to "nerve and brace them up to the point of insisting that the workmen shall carry out the orders exactly as specified on the instruction cards. This is a difficult task at first, as the workmen have been accustomed for years to do the details of the work to suit themselves, and many of them are intimate friends of the bosses and believe they know quite as much about their business as the latter."[25]

Modern management came into being on the basis of these principles. It arose as theoretical construct and as systematic practice, moreover, in the very period during which the transformation of labor from processes based on skill to processes based upon science was attaining its most rapid tempo.

---

that from it, workers could learn how production is carried on: such a card, "whenever it comes into the hands of a thoughtful man, may suggest to him something of the purposes and methods of those who have constructed it."[24] The worker, in Marshall's notion, having given up technical knowledge of the craft, is now to pick up the far more complex technical knowledge of modern industry from his task card, as a paleontologist reconstructs the entire animal from a fragment of a bone!

*One must not suppose from this that such a psychological shift in relations between worker and manager is entirely a thing of the past. On the contrary, it is constantly being recapitulated in the evolution of new occupations as they are brought into being by the development of industry and trade, and are then routinized and subjugated to management control. As this tendency has attacked office, technical, and "educated" occupations, sociologists have spoken of it as "bureaucratization," an evasive and unfortunate use of Weberian terminology, a terminology which often reflects its users' view that this form of government over work is endemic to "large-scale" or "complex" enterprises, whereas it is better understood as the specific product of the capitalist organization of work, and reflects not primarily scale but social antagonisms.

Its role was to render conscious and systematic, the formerly unconscious tendency of capitalist production. It was to ensure that as craft declined, the worker would sink to the level of general and undifferentiated labor power, adaptable to a large range of simple tasks, while as science grew, it would be concentrated in the hands of management.

## NOTES

1. Peter F. Drucker, "Work and Tools," in Melvin Kranzberg and William H. Davenport (eds.), *Technology and Culture* (New York: New American Library, 1972), pp. 192–93.

2. Frederick Winslow Taylor, *The Principles of Scientific Management* (New York and London: Greenwood, 1947; reprint 1972), p. 32.

3. Ibid., pp. 48–49, 53.

4. Ibid., pp. 41–47.

5. Daniel Bell, *Work and Its Discontents,* in *The End of Ideology* (Glencoe, Ill.: Free Press, 1960), p. 227.

6. Robert F. Hoxie, *Scientific Management and Labor* (New York and London, 1918; reprint New York: Kelley, 1966), pp. 85–87.

7. *The Principles of Scientific Management,* pp. 61–62.

8. Georges Friedmann, *Industrial Society: Emergence of the Human Problems of Automation* (1955; reprint New York: Arno Press, 1977), p. 55.

9. Taylor, *Shop Management* (1911), p. 25; reprint Darby, Pa.: Arden, 1980.

10. *The Principles of Scientific Management,* pp. 107–109.

11. Friedmann, *Industrial Society,* p. 63.

12. *The Principles of Scientific Management,* p. 111.

13. Ibid., p. 36.

14. Ibid., p. 22.

15. *Shop Management,* pp. 98–99.

16. *The Principles of Scientific Management,* pp. 37–38.

17. *Taylor's Testimony before the Special House Committee,* in *The Principles of Scientific Management,* pp. 235–36.

18. Ibid.

19. Ibid., pp. 75, 77.

20. *The Principles of Scientific Management,* p. 62.

21. *Shop Management,* p. 105.

22. *The Principles of Scientific Management,* pp. 63, 39.

23. Lillian Gilbreth, *The Psychology of Management* (1914), in *The Writings of the Gilbreths,* William R. Spriegel and Clark E. Myers (eds.) (Homewood, Ill.: R. D. Irwin, 1953), p. 404.

24. Alfred Marshall, *Industry and Trade* (London: Macmillan, 1919, 1932), pp. 391–93.

25. *Shop Management,* p. 108.

# Part Eight

# Appropriate Technology

# Introduction

The concept of appropriate technology integrates many of the strands of thought we have been considering. Contrary to some critics, advocates of appropriate technology are not anti-technology but opposed to those forms of technology that they consider in some sense to be inappropriate in the modern world. Thus, in contrast to large-scale, complex, centralized systems of technology they propose an alternative.

Although there is considerable controversy among the proponents of appropriate technology (AT), implicit in some of these perspectives is a vision of the good life, the good society, and the good earth; a vision strikingly different from the traditional values of industrial capitalism. While not denigrating technology as a means of satisfying our basic needs, it rejects the view that the meaning of life is to be found in the consumption of ever increasing "goods" pouring forth in mindless profusion from modern industry. The good life is characterized instead by meaningful work, harmony with one's fellowman, and a non-exploitative attitude toward nature; a life in which we are actively engaged in shaping our own life and justly concerned with the welfare of distant peoples and future generations. Human fulfillment requires a renewed sense of community.

The orthodox faith that technological growth would continue to satisfy increasing consumer demands in an endless cycle received a serious blow in the early seventies. Using state-of-the-art computer technology, a study called *Limits to Growth* predicted catastrophic disaster if present trends continued. Given the exponential growth in population, there was no way future demands on resources could be met, even assuming the development of new technologies to provide, for example, unlimited sources of energy. There are finite, and not too distant, limits to growth. Technological fixes merely postpone, and ultimately exacerbate, the coming ecological crisis. While the methodology behind this study was severely criticized, it accomplished its major purpose, which was to stimulate public discussion.

The energy crisis (actual or contrived) during this period gave real bite to the idea that there might be limits to "progress." The *Global 2000 Report*, completed at the behest of President Jimmy Carter, reaffirmed the central conclusions of *Limits to Growth*, moving Carter to urge Americans to conserve energy by setting back their thermostats. Urging such belt-tightening measures was a major contributory factor in Carter's unpopularity. Did he not believe in the American dream of unlimited growth, of continuously increasing prosperity?

Apparent shortages of natural resources, growing awareness of the ecological consequences of industrial production, the failure of advanced military technology to win the "war" in Vietnam—all combined to transform the idea of appropriate technology into a grass-roots movement. Organizations devoted to developing and using small-scale, decentralized technology sprang up in many sections of the country. Although public concern about finite resources fluctuates wildly in response to events in the Persian Gulf and the apparent supply of oil, increasing awareness about environmental problems has kept the appropriate technology movement alive.

The idea that there is an authoritarian aspect to technology can be traced to Lewis Mumford and the publication in 1934 of his *Technics and Civilization*. According to Mumford, the roots of modern technology are to be found prior to the Industrial Revolution in the harnessing of human power. The model for large-scale technological systems can be seen in the system of monarchy and in the efficient organization of manpower in military armies with their division of labor and hierarchical chains of command. Employed in "civil engineering," it was this hierarchically organized "megamachine" that built the pyramids. The "secret" to its efficient running were whips and chains, not new mechanical inventions.

Visible whips and chains have disappeared in modern technology, only to be replaced by the system itself. Having rejected the divine right of kings, we now come to worship at the shrine of technological progress. Even the high priests of science, the technological élite, and the captains of industry are trapped in their own system. When Mumford says, "The center of authority . . . now lies in the system itself," he is subscribing to a version of the autonomous technology thesis.

According to Mumford, authoritarian technics represent a clear and present danger to our democratic institutions, but the future is not determined. What may give the appearance of determinism is that we have bought into the system, the consumer society, sacrificing our democratic ideals for material prosperity. But we could choose otherwise. Alternatives exist.

Democratic technics existed prior to authoritarian technics and continue to this day. These man-centered technologies are relatively weak, but are most resourceful and durable. They offer viable alternatives to the large-scale systems that threaten them. While not wanting to deny the material benefits of large-scale systems, Mumford thinks it is time to put people at the center of our concerns. "There are large areas of technology that can be redeemed by the democratic process, once we have overcome the infantile compulsions and automations that now threaten to cancel our our real gains."

Carrol Pursell applies Mumford's distinction to the American experience. In his brief history of technology's application to early America, Pursell argues that the ideals of the American political revolution initially held hope for a democratic industrial revolution, but have been progressively subverted by the development of technology along authoritarian lines. This history shows that technology does not simply affect social institutions, but *is* a social institution. Pursell agrees with Mumford that there is no inevitability in the course of technological development and cites various points where key players chose the authoritarian path. Pursell emphatically rejects the version of the autonomy thesis that claims technology evolves according to its internal logic independent of human choices. We could have developed a democratic technics, and it is indeed still possible to do so. Reiterating Mumford, he claims the very survival of democratic society is at stake.

E. F. Schumacher's *Small is Beautiful* appeared at a most propitious time —1973—and gave a powerful impetus to the appropriate technology movement. In our selection he argues that modern economics (a crucial factor in the perpetuation of large-scale authoritarian technology) reverses means and ends, regarding labor as a mere item of cost to be reduced to a bare minimum, if not eliminated entirely through automation. Even if we provide adequate welfare, Schumacher argues, unemployment is inhumane, for meaningful work is fundamental to a meaningful existence. To regard work as a mere means in the blind imperative to increase production has disastrous consequences for people, for peace, and for the planet. The aim of production should not be the maximization of consumption, but the production of goods and services necessary for a *becoming* existence.

The central concern is for a democratic, person-centered control of technology. Although Schumacher emphasizes that "small is beautiful," he acknowledges that "big" may also be appropriate if it is adapted to satisfy genuine human needs and remains firmly under democratic control.

Samuel C. Florman thinks small is ridiculous. As he sees it, people like Schumacher and the British energy expert Amory B. Lovins are hopelessly confused. Smallness has no intrinsic value. Technological development is driven by human needs and choices in a free-market economy. Big technology survives because it is the most efficient. If people didn't want it, we wouldn't have it. The only rational standard for evaluating technologies is efficiency, a factor rejected by the small-is-beautiful advocates.

Although Florman recognizes serious problems with the uses of technology, the answers are not to be found in smallness. Perhaps Florman is right when he claims that,". . . diversity and freedom, at least in the United States, are protected and encouraged by strong institutions." Was not President Reagan's promise to reduce the size of the federal government, to get the government off "our" backs, code for giving free reign to big business?

Perhaps Schumacher has an overly romantic view of Buddhism, given the poverty of people in some Eastern societies. Is there not a role for technology to free persons from back-breaking labor and poverty? He is certainly reactionary when he claims a woman's place is in the home. But, is Florman correct when he says, ". . . the thrift being preached lends itself to a smallness of spirit?"

While small may be beautiful, this seems a vague and insufficient criterion of appropriate technology. Many critics have argued that there is no coherent notion of what constitutes an "appropriate" technology. Many critics have argued that there is no coherent notion of what constitutes an "appropriate" technoloy. Reviewing the literature, they simply find various authors pushing various technological fixes for various reasons. The movement seems to have degenerated into a fixation with do-it-yourself hardware and a romantic back-to-the-earth idealism.

Contrary to these critics, Thomas Simon thinks that an adequate definition can be constructed for "appropriate" technology and lists what he takes to be the four fundamental conditions: (1) environmental soundness, (2) labor intensity, (3) small scale, and (4) decentralization. Each condition, he claims, is necessary, and together they are sufficient for a technology to be deemed appropriate. These are relatively clear criteria, but they are ". . . interdependent conditions that must be explained together when evaluating a particular technique."

The crucial problem with AT is not a matter of specifying the criteria for what "appropriate" means, says Simon, but political. He agrees with Winner (and many of the people whose work we have examined) that "technical choices are, in fact, political." Simon thinks Winner is wrong, however, in thinking that AT offers an alternative political philosophy. If AT's defenders discuss politics at all, Simon thinks they embrace the status quo, and thus are not much different from the advocates of high technology (such as Florman).

In defending his position Simon analyzes the conditions he has stated for AT in order to show that the debate is not about the nature of various technologies, but about values—about what political philosophy we ought to adopt. All too often proponents of AT assume a kind of technological determinism, as though technology were an alternative to politics. From Simon's political perspective, conditions for appropriate technology *ought* to be: (1) ecological, (2) liberatory, (3) indigenous, and (4) medical.

The importance of Simon's discussion, I think, lies not in the value of his claim that AT does not give us an alternative political philosophy—for a wide diversity of views are found in this movement—but in his emphasis on the fact that our choices are fundamentally normative. "Philosophically, the first and most most important goal is an adequate politics of technological choice."

# 26

# Authoritarian and Democratic Technics
## Lewis Mumford

"Democracy" is a term now confused and sophisticated by indiscriminate use, and often treated with patronizing contempt. Can we agree, no matter how far we might diverge at a later point, that the spinal principle of democracy is to place what is common to all men above that which any organization, institution, or group may claim for itself? This is not to deny the claims of superior natural endowment, specialized knowledge, technical skill, or institutional organization: all these may, by democratic permission, play a useful role in the human economy. But democracy consists in giving final authority to the whole, rather than the part; and only living human beings, as such, are an authentic expression of the whole, whether acting alone or with the help of others.

Around this central principle clusters a group of related ideas and practices with a long foreground in history, though they are not always present, or present in equal amounts, in all societies. Among these items are communal self-government, free communication as between equals, unimpeded access to the common store of knowledge, protection against arbitrary external controls, and a sense of individual moral responsibility for behavior that affects the whole community. All living organisms are in some degree autonomous, in that they follow a life-pattern of their own; but in man this autonomy is an essential condition for his further development. We surrender some of our autonomy when ill or crippled: but to surrender it every day on every occasion would be to turn life itself into a chronic illness. The best life possible—and

From *Technology and Culture* 5, no. 1 (1964): 1–8. Copyright © 1964 by the Society for the History of Technology. Reprinted by permission of the University of Chicago Press.

here I am consciously treading on contested ground—is one that calls for an ever greater degree of self-direction, self-expression, and self-realization. In this sense, personality, once the exclusive attribute of kings, belongs on democratic theory of every man. Life itself in its fullness and wholeness cannot be delegated.

In framing this provisional definition I trust that I have not, for the sake of agreement, left out anything important. Democracy, in the primal sense I shall use the term, is necessarily most visible in relatively small communities and groups, whose members meet frequently face to face, interact freely, and are known to each other as persons. As soon as large numbers are involved, democratic association must be supplemented by a more abstract, depersonalized form. Historical experience shows that it is much easier to wipe out democracy by an institutional arrangement that gives authority only to those at the apex of the social hierarchy than it is to incorporate democratic practices into a well-organized system under centralized direction, which achieves the highest degree of mechanical efficiency when those who work it have no mind or purpose of their own.

The tension between small-scale association and large-scale organization, between personal autonomy and institional regulation, between remote control and diffused local intervention, has now created a critical situation. If our eyes had been open, we might long ago have discovered this conflict deeply embedded in technology itself.

I wish it were possible to characterize technics with as much hope of getting assent, with whatever quizzical reserves you may still have, as in this description of democracy. But the very title of this [chapter] is, I confess, a controversial one; and I cannot go far in my analysis without drawing on interpretations that have not yet been adequately published, still less widely discussed or rigorously ciriticized and evaluated. My thesis, to put it bluntly, is that from late neolithic times in the Near East, right down to our own day, two technologies have recurrently existed side by side: one authoritarian, the other democratic, the first system-centered, immensely powerful, but inherently unstable, the other man-centered, relatively weak, but resourceful and durable. If I am right, we are now rapidly approaching a point at which, unless we radically alter our present course, our surviving democratic technics will be completely suppressed or supplanted, so that every residual autonomy will be wiped out, or will be permitted only as a playful device of government, like national balloting for already chosen leaders in totalitarian countries.

The data on which this thesis is based are familiar; but their significance has, I believe, been overlooked. What I would call democratic technics is the small-scale method of production, resting mainly on human skill and animal energy but always, even when employing machines, remaining under the active direction of the craftsman or the farmer, each group developing its own gifts, through appropriate arts and social ceremonies, as well as making discreet use of the gifts of nature. This technology had limited horizons of achievement, but, just because of its wide. diffusion and its modest demands, it had great powers of adaptation and recuperation. This democratic technics has under-pinned and firmly supported every historical culture until our own day, and redeemed the constant tendency of authoritarian technics to misapply its powers. Even when paying tribute to the most oppressive authoritarian regimes, there yet remained within the workshop or the farmyard some degree of autonomy, selectivity, creativity. No royal mace, no slave-driver's whip, no bureaucratic directive left its imprint on the textiles of Damascus or the pottery of fifth-century Athens.

If this democratic technics goes back to the earliest use of tools, authoritarian technics is a much more recent achievement: it begins around the fourth millennium B.C. in a new configuration of technical invention, scientific ob-servation, and centralized political control that gave rise to the peculiar mode of life we may now identify, without eulogy, as civilization. Under the new institution of kingship, activities that had been scattered, diversified, cut to the human measure, were united on a monumental scale into an entirely new kind of theological-technological mass organization. In the person of an absolute ruler, whose word was law, cosmic powers came down to earth, mobilizing and unifying the efforts of thousands of men, hitherto all-too-autonomous and too decentralized to act voluntarily in unison for purposes that lay beyond the village horizon.

The new authoritarian technology was not limited by village custom or human sentiment: its herculean feats of mechanical organization rested on ruthless physical coercion, forced labor, and slavery, which brought into exis-tence machines that were capable of exerting thousands of horsepower centuries before horses were harnessed or wheels invented. This centralized technics drew on inventions and scientific discoveries of a high order: the written record, mathematics and astronomy, irrigation and canalization: above all, it created complex human machines composed of specialized, standardized, replaceable, interdependent parts—the work army, the military army, the bureaucracy. These work armies and military armies raised the ceiling of human achievement: the first in mass construction, the second in mass destruction, both on a scale hitherto inconceivable. Despite its constant drive to destruction, this totalitarian technics was tolerated, perhaps even welcomed, in home territory, for it created the first economy of controlled abundance: notably, immense food crops that not merely supported a big urban population but released a large trained mi-nority for purely religious, scientific, bureaucratic, or military activity. But the efficiency of the system was impaired by weaknesses that were never overcome until our own day.

To begin with, the democratic economy of the agricultural village resisted incorporation into the new authoritarian system. So even the Roman Empire found it expedient, once resistance was broken and taxes were collected, to consent to a large degree of local autonomy in religion and government. Moreover, as long as agriculture absorbed the labor of some 90 percent of the population, mass technics were confined largely to the populous urban centers. Since authoritarian technics first took form in an age when metals were scarce and human raw material, captured in war, was easily convertible into machines, its directors never bothered to invent inorganic mechanical substitutes. But there were even greater weaknesses: the system had no inner coherence: a break in communication, a missing link in the chain of command, and the great human machines fell apart. Finally, the myths upon which the whole system was based—particularly the essential myth of kingship—were irrational, with their paranoid suspicions and animosities and their paranoid claims to unconditional obedience and absolute power. For all its redoubtable constructive achievements, authoritarian technics expressed a deep hostility to life.

By now you doubtless see the point of this brief historical excursus. That authoritarian technics has come back today in an immensely magnified and adroitly perfected form. Up to now, following the optimistic premises of nineteenth-century thinkers like Auguste Comte and Herbert Spencer, we have regarded the spread of experimental science and mechanical invention as the soundest guarantee of a peaceful, productive, above all democratic, industrial society. Many have even comfortably supposed that the revolt against arbitrary political power in the seventeenth century was causally connected with the industrial revolution that accompanied it. But what we have interpreted as the new freedom now turns out to be a much more sophisticated version of the old slavery: for the rise of political democracy during the last few centuries has been increasingly nullified by the successful resurrection of a centralized authoritarian technics—a technics that had in fact for long lapsed in many parts of the world.

Let us fool ourselves no longer. At the very moment Western nations threw off the ancient regime of absolute government, operating under a once-divine king, they were restoring this same system in a far more effective form in their technology, reintroducing coercions of a military character no less strict in the organization of a factory than in that of the new drilled, uniformed, and regimented army. During the transitional stages of the last two centuries, the ultimate tendency of this system might be in doubt, for in many areas there were strong democratic reactions; but with the knitting together of a scientific ideology, itself liberated from theological restrictions or humanistic purposes, authoritarian technics found an instrument at hand that has now given it absolute command of physical energies of cosmic dimensions. The inventors of nuclear bombs, space rockets, and computers are the pyramid builders of our own age: psychologically inflated by a similar myth of unqualified power, boasting through their science of their increasing omnipotence, if not omniscience, moved by obsessions and compulsions no less irrational than those of earlier absolute systems: particularly the notion that the system itself must be expanded, at whatever eventual cost to life.

Through mechanization, automation, cybernetic direction, this authoritarian technics has at last successfully overcome its most serious weakness: its original dependence upon resistant, sometimes actively disobedient servomechanisms, still human enough to harbor purposes that do not always coincide with those of the system.

Like the earliest form of authoritarian technics, this new technology is marvelously dynamic and productive: its power in every form tends to increase without limits, in quantities that defy assimilation and defeat control, whether we are thinking of the output of scientific knowledge or of industrial assembly lines. To maximize energy, speed, or automation, without reference to the complex conditions that sustain organic life, have become ends in themselves. As with the earliest forms of authoritarian technics, the weight of effort, if one is to judge by national budgets, is toward absolute instruments of destruction, designed for absolutely irrational purposes whose chief by-product would be the mutilation or extermination of the human race. Even Ashurbanipal and Genghis Khan performed their gory operations under normal human limits.

The center of authority in this new system is no longer a visible personality, an all-powerful king: even in totalitarian dictatorships the center now lies in the system itself, invisible but omnipresent: all its human components, even the technical and managerial elite, even the sacred priesthood of science, who alone have access to the secret knowledge by means of which total control is now swiftly being effected, are themselves trapped by the very perfection of the organization they have invented. Like the pharaohs of the Pyramid Age, these servants of the system identify its good with their own kind of well-being: as with the divine kind, their praise of the system is an act of self-worship; and again like the king, they are in the grip of an irrational compulsion to extend their means of control and expand the scope of their authority. In this new systems-centered collective, this Pentagon of power, there is no visible presence who issues commands: unlike Job's God, the new deities cannot be confronted, still less defied. Under the pretext of saving labor, the ultimate end of this technics is to displace life, or rather, to transfer the attributes of life to the machine and the mechanical collective, allowing only so much of the organism to remain as may be controlled and manipulated.

Do not misunderstand this analysis. The danger to democracy does not spring from any specific scientific discoveries or electronic inventions. The human compulsions that dominate the authoritarian technics of our own day date back to a period before even the wheel had been invented. The danger springs from the fact that, since Francis Bacon and Galileo defined the new methods and objectives of technics, our great physical transformations have been effected by a system that deliberately eliminates the whole human personality, ignores the historical process, overplays the role of the abstract intelligence, and makes control over physical nature, ultimately control over man himself, the chief purpose of existence. This system has made its way so insidiously into Western society that my analysis of its derivation and its intentions may well seem more questionable—indeed more shocking—than the facts themselves.

Why has our age surrendered so easily to the controllers, the manipulators, the conditioners of an authoritarian technics? The answer to this question is both paradoxical and ironic. Present-day technics differs from that of the overtly brutal, half-baked authoritarian systems of the past in one highly favorable particular: it has accepted the basic principle of democracy, that every member of society should have a share in its goods. By progressively fulfilling this part of the democratic promise, our system has achieved a hold over the whole community that threatens to wipe out every other vestige of democracy.

The bargain we are being asked to ratify takes the form of a magnificent bribe. Under the democratic-authoritarian social contract, each member of the community may claim every material advantage, every intellectual and emotional stimulus he may desire, in quantities hardly available hitherto even for a restricted minority: food, housing, swift transportation, instantaneous communication, medical care, entertainment, education. But on one condition: that one must not merely ask for nothing that the system does not provide, but likewise agree to take everything offered, duly processed and fabricated, homogenized and equalized, in the precise quantities that the system, rather than the person, requires. Once one opts for the system no further choice remains. In a word, if one surrenders one's life at source, authoritarian technics will give back as much of it as can be mechanically graded, quantitatively multiplied, collectively manipulated and magnified.

"Is this not a fair bargain?" those who speak for the system will ask. "Are not the goods authoritarian technics promises real goods? Is this not the horn of plenty that mankind has long dreamed of, and that every ruling class has tried to secure, at whatever cost of brutality and injustice, for itself?" I would not belittle, still less deny, the many admirable products this technology has brought forth, products that a self-regulating economy would make good use of. I would only suggest that it is time to reckon up the human disadvantages and costs, to say nothing of the dangers, of our unqualified acceptance of the system itself. Even the immediate price is heavy; for the system is so far from being under effective human direction that it may poison us wholesale to provide us with food or exterminate us to provide national security, before we can enjoy its promised goods. Is it really humanly profitable to give up the possibility of living a few years at Walden Pond, so to say, for the privilege of spending a lifetime in *Walden Two?* Once our authoritarian technics consolidates its powers, with the aid of its new forms of mass control, its panoply of tranquilizers and sedatives and aphrodisiacs, could democracy in any form survive? That question is absurd: life itself will not survive, except what is funneled through the mechanical collective. The spread of a sterilized scientific intelligence over the planet would not, as Teilhard de Chardin so innocently imagined, be the happy consummation of divine purpose: it would rather ensure the final arrest of any further human development.

Again: do not mistake my meaning. This is not a prediction of what *will* happen, but a warning against what *may* happen.

What means must be taken to escape this fate? In characterizing the authoritarian technics that has begun to dominate us, I have not forgotten the great lesson of history: prepare for the unexpected! Nor do I overlook the immense reserves of vitality and creativity that a more humane democratic tradition still offers us. What I wish to do is to persuade those who are concerned with maintaining democratic institutions to see that their constructive efforts must include technology itself. There, too, we must return to the human center. We must challenge this authoritarian system that has given to an under-dimensioned ideology and technology the authority that belongs to the human personality. I repeat: life cannot be delegated.

Curiously, the first words in support of this thesis came forth, with exquisite symbolic aptness, from a willing agent—but very nearly a classic victim!—of the new authoritarian technics. They came from the astronaut, John Glenn, whose life was endangered by the malfunctioning of his automatic controls, operated from a remote center. After he barely saved his life by personal intervention, he emerged from his space capsule with these ringing words: "Now let man take over!"

That command is easier to utter than obey. But if we are not to be driven to even more drastic measures than Samuel Butler suggested in *Erewhon,* we had better map out a more positive course: namely, the reconstitution of both our science and our technics in such a fashion as to insert the rejected parts of the human personality at every stage in the process. This means gladly sacrificing mere quantity in order to restore qualitative choice; shifting the seat of authority from the mechanical collective to the human personality and the autonomous group; favoring variety and ecological complexity, instead of stressing undue uniformity and standarization; above all, reducing the insensate drive to extend the system itself, instead of containing it within definite human limits and thus releasing man himself for other purposes. We must ask, not what is good for science or technology, still less what is good for General Motors or Union Carbide or IBM or the Pentagon, but what is good for man: not machine-conditioned, system-regulated, mass-man, but man in person, moving freely over every area of life.

There are large areas of technology that can be redeemed by the democratic process, once we have overcome the infantile compulsions and automatisms that now threaten to cancel out our real gains. The very leisure that the machine now gives in advanced countries can be profitably used, not for further commitment to still other kinds of machine, furnishing automatic recreation, but by doing significant forms of work, unprofitable or technically impossible under mass production: work dependent upon special skill, knowledge, aesthetic sense. The do-it-yourself movement prematurely got bogged down in an attempt to sell still more machines; but its slogan pointed in the right direction, provided we still have a self to do it with. The glut of motor cars that is now destroying our cities can be coped with only if we redesign our cities to make fuller use of a more efficient human agent: the walker. Even in childbirth, the emphasis is already happily shifting from an officious, often lethal, authoritarian procedure, centered in hospital routine, to a more humane mode, which restores initiative to the mother and to the body's natural rhythms.

The replenishment of democratic technics is plainly too big a subject to be handled in a final sentence or two: but I trust I have made it clear that the genuine advantage our scientifically based technics has brought can be preserved only if we cut the whole system back to a point at which it will permit human alternatives, human interventions, and human destinations for entirely different purposes from those of the system itself. At the present juncture, if democracy did not exist, we would have to invent it, in order to save and recultivate the spirit of man.

# 27

# The American Ideal of a Democratic Technology

## Carroll Pursell

In 1815 Thomas Jefferson, asked to comment on a steam engine developed by a fellow American, compared it to those he had seen in Europe, and articulated the American ideal of a democratic technology scaled to human needs:

> I see, indeed, in yours, the valuable properties of simplicity, cheapness, and accomodation to the small and numerous calls of life, and the calculations of its power appear sound and correct. . . . The importance of your construction will be enhanced by the consideration that a smaller engine, applicable to our daily concerns, is infinitely more valuable than the greatest which can be used only for great objects. For these interest the few alone, the former the many. I once had an idea that it might perhaps be possible to economize the steam of a common pot, kept boiling on the kitchen fire until its accumulation should be sufficient to give a stroke, and although the strokes might not be rapid, there would be enough of them in the day to raise from an adjacent well the water necessary for daily use; to wash the linen, knead the bread, beat the hominy, churn the butter, turn the spit, and do all other household offices which require only a regular mechanical motion. The unproductive hands now necessarily employed in these, might then increase the produce of our fields. . . . Of how much more value would this be to ordinary life than Watts and Bolton's thirty pair of millstones to be turned by one engine. . . .[1]

From *The Technological Imagination: Theories and Fictions,* ed. Teresa de Laurentis, Andreas Huyssen, and Kathleen Woodward (Madison, Wis.: Coda Press, Inc., 1980).

Jefferson's remarks serve to remind us that throughout American history there has been a continuing (though never dominant) realization that, as Lewis Mumford phrased it, "those who are concerned with maintaining democratic institutions" must see to it that their "constructive efforts. . . include technology itself."[2] Never triumphant, but never completely disappearing, this same desire for a technology scaled to human needs and aptitudes has reappeared in recent times in the movement for what is called Appropriate Technology. Both the dream and its antithetical nightmare have best been described, I think, by Mumford—in the whole body of his work, but most succinctly in his 1964 essay titled "Authoritarian and Democratic Technics." "My thesis," he wrote, "is that from late neolithic times in the Near East, right down to our own day, two technologies have recurrently existed side by side: one authoritarian, the other democratic, the first system-centered, immensely powerful, but inherently unstable; the other man-centered, relatively weak, but resourceful and durable."[3]

Authoritarian technics, wrote Mumford, was centralized and "drew on inventions and scientific discoveries of a high order: the written record, mathematics and astronomy, irrigation and canalization; above all, it created complex human machines composed of specialized, standardized, replaceable, interdependent parts—the work army, the military army, the bureaucracy." From the beginning these "work armies and military armies raised the ceiling of human achievement" in both construction and destruction. In our time these technics have provided the masses with an astonishing array and abundance of material goods, but, as Mumford warns, "by progressively fulfilling this part of the democratic promise, our system has achieved a hold over the whole community that threatens to wipe out every other vestige of democracy."[4]

Opposed to this is a democratic technics, which, in Mumford's words, is characterized by "the small scale method of production, resting mainly on human skill and animal energy but always, even when employing machines, remaining under the active direction of the craftsman or the farmer, each group developing its own gifts, through appropriate arts and social ceremonies, as well as making discrete use of the gifts of nature."[5]

The conflict between these two technics has waxed and waned throughout recorded history, but its modern intensification began at the same time as our United States. Brooke Hindle has called the simultaneity of the American and Industrial Revolutions "one of the staggering coincidences of American history."[6] Mumford is more apprehensive than excited by the juxtaposition: "At the very moment Western nations threw off the ancient regime of absolute government, operating under a once-divine king," he wrote, "they were restoring this same system in a far more effective form in their technology, reintroducing coercions of a military character no less strict in the organization of a factory. . . ."[7] The resulting conflict had two facets, both of which have drawn attention throughout our history. In order to insure the survival of democracy one must preserve a democratic technics, but to do this, first, one must keep authoritarian technics from concentrating in the hands of the few, and second, one must at the same time provide easy access to a democratic technology for the many.

The prospect was hopeful during the years of the Early Republic and, as Hugo Meier and others have pointed out, it soon became a major canon of our American faith that democracy and technology were symbiotic, that political, social, and economic liberty would cause technology to flourish, and that technology in turn would help defend and extend such liberty.[8] Asserting in 1792 that *"free* governments are the only *asylum* and nursery for *science* and the *arts,"* Joseph Barnes explained that:

> Free governments have always been found most disposed to encourage the rise and progress of science, and the arts; for this obvious reason, that in republican governments *merit* alone is, or *ought* to be the *standard* for character; which necessarily *excites* that *laudable* spirit of emulation, so essential to society; and which never fails to produce celebrated philosophers, statesmen, husbandmen, and artists; the necessary effect of which, is, not only, the promotion of science and useful arts, but, the *happiness* of men,—the primary, the grand *object* of their existence.

Summarizing his argument, he maintained that *"Philosophy* being the *source* of liberty—*liberty,* of all the *improvements* in science and the arts; the improvements in science and the arts, of all the *real accomplishments* of the human species; consequently, *philosophy* is *essentially* the source of all virtue. . . ."[9] Benjamin Franklin's gesture with regard to his Pennsylvania Fire-Place exemplifies this faith in the interdependence between philosophy, or democracy, and technology. Instead of accepting a patent proffered by the governor of his colony, he advertised it in a pamphlet complete with drawings, description, and instructions to masons for setting it up. He declined the patent, he said, "from a Principle which has ever weigh'd with me on such Occasions, viz. That as we enjoy great Advantages from the Invention of others, we should be glad of an Opportunity to serve others by any Invention of ours, and this we should do freely and generously."[10]

Other factors fostered a democratic technics during this period. The nation had recently been set up as a republic, not a monarchy, and a standing army had been rejected. Moreover, so long as technology relied upon the energy of sun and water, the triumph of authoritarian technics appeared unlikely, or at least avoidable. The potential energy of woods and farm land, falling water and blowing wind was widely and all but freely available, the technology to harness these sources of energy was cheap and widely known, and the sources themselves of such energy could not be monopolized. Even the coming of the American system of manufactures seemed to strengthen the democratic nature of American technology. In 1849 the touring Scottish chemist James F. W. Johnston visited an agricultural fair in Syracuse, New York, and noted that "the general character of the implements was economy in construction and in price, and the exhibition was large and interesting." Ploughs, hayrakes, forks, scythes, and cooking-stoves," he said, "were very abundant, and many of them well and beautifully made." The "potato grips and forks, of various kinds, cut from sheet-steel, were very elastic, light, strong, and cheap."[11] Only a few years later Joseph Whitworth and George Wallis wrote that "labor-saving machines are most successfully employed in the manufacture of agricultural implements. In a plough manufactory at Baltimore, eight machines are employed on the various parts of the woodwork. With these machines seven men are able to make the wooden parts of thirty ploughs per day." One result of the extension of the American system from small arms to the manufacture of plows was that the implements made at his factory sold for from $2.50 to $7.[12] Surely the democratic nature of agriculture technology during the nineteenth century, and therefore its relatively low price, was as important as free land in extending a nation of yeoman farmers across a continent.

The American system, of course, with its machine designers and tenders, did not encompass the entirety of American technology. Many areas (farming and the building trades spring to mind) long resisted the intrusion of machine logic. This is one reason why many Americans were able (even when they were not forced) to move from job to job with easy proficiency. Whitworth and Wallis noted that "the citizen of the United States knows that matters are different with him [than with workers in Britain], and seems really to pride himself in not remaining over long at any particular occupation, and being able to turn his hand to some dozen different pursuits in the course of his life."[13] Karl Marx at one point quoted a Frenchman who had moved to San Francisco: "I was firmly convinced that I was fit for nothing but letterpress printing. . . . Once in the midst of this world of adventurers who change their occupation as often as they do their shirt, egad, I did as the others. As mining did not turn out remunerative enough, I left for the town where in succession I became a typographer, slater, plumber, etc. In consequence of thus finding out that I am fit for any sort of work I felt less of a mollusk and more of a man."[14]

Not content to leave well enough alone, however, Americans wanted to progress, and progress was away from this democratic technic. Early in the century Oliver Evans had confidently asserted that "we see by daily experience, that every art may be improved."[15] Late in the century, when Mark Twain's Hank Morgan gained power in King Arthur's Court he recorded that "the very first official thing I did, in my administration—and it was on the very first day of it, too—was to start a patent office; for I knew that a country without a patent office and good patent laws was just a crab, and couldn't travel any way but sideways and backwards." "The first thing you want in a new country," he concluded, "is a patent office; then work up your school system; and after that, out with your newspaper."[16] Little wonder that an anonymous scribbler was inspired by an industrial exhibition in 1828 to write these lines:[17]

Genius of Art! What achievements are thine—
   To delight and astonish the mind
The efforts of knowledge and fancy combine;
   But triumph to thee is assigned.
How high swell the bosoms of patriots with pride,
To behold the rich treasures which here are supplied;
   While Invention's bright wand
   In the artisan's hand,
Points to glory the freemen of Freedom's own land.

But authoritarian technics were not so easily ignored. The power fantasies of such inventors and social engineers as J. A. Etzler had a democratic appeal but an authoritarian promise. In 1841 Etzler published a sequel to his book *Paradise* in which he attempted to prove, "from experience:—How to cultivate 20,000 acres by one machine and three or four men, with a capital of less than one dollar per acre, in the most superior mode—how to clear land from trees, stumps, roots and stones; fill and drain swamps, make dams, canals, ditches, roads, and perform any kind of work in the ground; build houses, and furnish as much inanimate power as desired, for ever, for any place and any station-ary machine—all by the same system." In an appeal that was to be echoed many times over the next century in America, Etzler besought: "Ye, who are poor and of the laboring class, do not be alarmed at this invention. It will not deprive you of your poor pittance for sustaining life, obtainable now by your petty drudg-ery. When 20,000 acres of garden can be cultivated by three or four men, with but one dollar capital (once every year) per acre, you may easily become share-holders of joint stock companies, by paying from twenty to thirty dollars, and even this small sum, partly or entirely, in work of from one to three months, once for ever, and then enjoy the produce of from ten to twenty acres for each share, without further trouble or expense—and then live like gentlemen and la-dies, to much better purposes than those of a dull animal in a tread mill."[18] It is surely significant that talk to mechanical slaves increased precisely at the time human slavery was increasingly condemned. The extension of modern technology to agriculture came not only through the introduction of labor-sav-ing machines, but also through the rebirth of the work armies of the ancient Near East. In their recent book on slavery, *Time on the Cross,* Robert Fogel and Stanley Engerman point out that the regimen of the large southern planta-tion was "more like a modern assembly line than . . . the routine in many fac-tories in the antebellum era." Indeed they go so far as to assert that "the great plantations were the first large, scientifically managed business enterprises," and that black slaves were "the first group of workers to be trained in the work rhythms which later became characteristic of industrial society."[19]

The giant railroad companies of the period were also sources of the grow-ing authoritarian technics, rationalizing for their own needs and convenience everything from business forms to political corruption and the establishment of local time. Significantly, railroads were among the earliest corporations to make systematic use of industrial scientists. Just as significant, for many Americans, was the fact that such technics were welcomed despite their anti-democratic tendencies. Speaking in the aggregates necessary to authoritarian technics, the astronomer and political economist Simon Newcomb insisted first that "the question whether the effect of any policy is good or bad depends very largely upon whether it increases or dimishes the sum total of the products necessary for human welfare," and then that "carrying passengers forty miles an hour for two or three cents a mile is a fact which outweighs all we can say about watered stocks."[20]

Thus, in one field of American endeavor after another, what Mumford called "the machine and the mechanical collective" triumphed over democratic technics.[21] The arts of war and self-government were revolutionized. Agriculture, the backbone of democratic technics, was industrialized, mechanized, made energy-intensive and ever-more efficient. Farmers who could not compete with the new technological system of machines, irrigation, and fertilizers fled to the cities and became dependent upon those who remained behind. These, in their turn, however prosperous, were locked into a tightening circle of technological restraints.[22] But nowhere was the process more obvious and dramatic than in the area of transportation. The balanced systems of a previous era were replaced by a primary reliance on one machine, the automobile. In its production first man-the-maker was rationalized through the technics of Fordism, then man-the-consumer was rationalized through the technics of Sloanism.[23] With transportation, as with food and most other of life's needs, Americans were asked—or forced—to accept efficient, increased production with its machine logic and rhythms. For economic growth had always been seen in America as a substitute for social justice. As Frederick Winslow Taylor told a congressional committee in 1912, under the benign rule of his new scientific management "both sides take their eyes off the division of the surplus as the all-important matter, and together turn their attention toward increasing the size of the surplus until this surplus becomes so large that it is unnecessary to quarrel over how it shall be divided."[24] It was, in short, what Mumford has called the "magnificent bribe." By accepting the new technics, and by living "under the democratic-authoritarian social compact, each member of the community may claim every material advantage. . . . But on one condition: that he must not merely ask for nothing that the system does not provide, but likewise agree to take everything offered, duly processed and fabricated, homogenized and equalized, in the precise quantities that the system, rather than the person, requires."[25]

Not everyone, of course, acquiesced willingly in this compact. In 1896 a Minnesota state senator wrote disgustedly to Ignatius Donnelly:

> While we think, brag of it, how far we are ahead of any former civilization, I for one am disgusted of the bragging and the boasting and simply believe it is not true. . . .

> I have heard it asserted that the printing Press, telegraph etc. have educated the masses, that the direful relapse will not come again as in the past. . . .
>
> Bosh! Our would be masters have a corner on the whole outfit of the inventions, and they are now just as much employed to the destruction of human rights as formerly, in the absence of those inventions, the people's ignorance was used as a means.[26]

But this corporate and political monopolization of the very technology which was supposed to preserve the people's liberty, as recently described by David Noble in his book *America by Design,*[27] was one of the problems which motivated those who had some vision of a democratic technics. One promising area of reform was thought to be in electricity. By 1915 engineers were confident they could transmit economical amounts of electricity up to one hundred miles from central stations—far enough to provide nearly all Americans with adequate, flexible, cheap, clean energy. The fact that as late as 1935 less than ten percent of farms were so served, and the fact that rates in the United States were substantially higher than, for example, in Canada, led some critics to see in a reform of the electrical utility industry a new opportunity to fulfill the dream of a democratic technics. In the 1920s Morris L. Cooke, the Progressive engineer, produced for Governor Pinchot of Pennsylvania a comprehensive Giant Power plan which, without making power generation public, would have accomplished the twin goals of cheap and abundant available energy.[28] After a limited start in the Tennessee Valley Authority (1933), the Rural Electrification Administration, set up in 1935 with Cooke as its first director, finally succeeded in pushing rural lines to nearly all American farms.[29] Paradoxically, the coming of electricity tended as often as not merely to tie the individual farmer more closely into spreading national networks of communication and the agribusiness industry. As James Carey and John Quirk have pointed out in their article "The Mythos of the Electronic Revolution," the progressive "faith that electricity will exorcise social disorder and environmental disruption, eliminate political conflict and personal alienation, and restore ecological balance and a communion of man with nature," has unfortunately proved as baseless as the nineteenth-century hope that iron and steam would, as Timothy Walker put it in 1831, "perform all the drudgery of man, while he is to look on in self-complacent ease."[30] One fault was that while electricity might supply the clean, abundant, cheap, and divisible power needed for a democratic technology, it was provided by an increasingly authoritarian technics, the private power utilities. And although during the Great Depression many democratizing measures were introduced into the Congress, which sought to break the monopoly that big business (including private power utilities) had on research talent and technical expertise of the nation, none of them were adopted.[31] When the nation began its defense mobilization in 1940, that effort followed the lines of the status quo rather than the possibilities inherent in a world war for democracy.

Led by Vannevar Bush, the nation's spokesmen for science and technology deliberately chose to follow two cardinal principles in gearing up for war: first, the Axis was to be defeated as soon as possible; and second, insofar as possible, the mobilization was to be carried on with no disruption of the domestic status quo. What this last commitment meant was that since most research and development were concentrated, during the prewar period, in private industry—and within private industry within a very few large firms—the war effort was to be carried out largely in terms advantageous to the most powerful institutions in America. Thus, wartime spending for new science and technology was channeled largely through such corporations as General Motors, AT&T, and General Electric, and through such educational institutions as Harvard, MIT, and the University of California.[32]

Such an elitist mobilization was not inevitable. Indeed, hearings before the Kilgore committee during the war witnessed a steady stream of protestors who charged that American technology was being underutilized, and that research and development funds were being unnecessarily concentrated to make the nation's rich even richer.[33] Critics such as I. F. Stone and Bruce Catton pointed out that a democratic war effort was the best quarantee of a democratic postwar society.[34] The resulting legislation suggested by the Kilgore committee would have drafted patents, laboratories, and research brains, but, as in the previous decade, those who stood to benefit from the growing centralized technics were strong enough to bury such reformist proposals. On the eve of the war Waldemar Kaempffert, science editor of *The New York Times,* worried that "mass consumption, mass recreation, mass distribution of energy, and the collectivist utilization of identical things are impossible without control of mass production, without organization. The inventors have standarized behavior, pleasures, tastes. There is less freedom than there was a century ago because of invention; there will be still less tomorrow."[35] When the war was over, the stage was set for a corporate intensification of these trends.

At the same time, the decade of the late fifties and early sixties saw the rediscovery of a host of problems which Americans had thought long since solved. Betty Friedan's book *The Feminine Mystique* (1963) demonstrated that women's rights had not been secured totally by the right to vote. Ralph Nader's *Unsafe at Any Speed* (1965) attacked the most American of machines and recalled the continuing abuses of corporate responsibility. Michael Harrington reminded the nation of the existence of *The Other America* (1962), that third of the nation which still lived in poverty. And Rachel Carson, in her book *Silent Spring* (1962), proved that the Progressive conservation crusade had not solved all of the nation's environmental problems. This rediscovery and revitalization of the idea of a democratic technics rested on no one book (though several struck the same theme), but rather grew with the resurgence of environmental concern, the development of the so-called counterculture, and with the successive revelations of technological arrogance in such diverse but critical places as Detroit, Vietnam, and the board rooms of the petroleum industry. In 1967 the late Paul Goodman mourned the "betrayal of the promise of independent scientific technology" envisioned by the idealists of the nineteenth century. "They thought," he wrote, "of science as humble, brave, and austere, and of technology as circumspect, neat, and serviceable. Working by its own morale, scientific technology should by now have simplified life rather than complicated it, emptied the environment rather than cluttered it, and educated an inventive and skillful generation rather than a conformist and inept one."[36] In a later essay Goodman called upon technicians to fulfill their proper roles as moral philosophers, acting with foresight, caution, and prudence.[37]

Many of those who today advocate a technology characterized by foresight, caution, and prudence, are to be found working under the banner of Appropriate (or Alternative or Intermediate) Technology. Popularly identified with the late British economist E. F. Schumacher and his slogan, "Small is Beautiful," the movement is often focused on Third World nations. VITA, for example, the Volunteers in Technical Assistance, founded in 1959, advises developing countries on the "use of skill and materials that are locally available, or if equipment has to be imported, on designs that can be repaired by the village craftsman."[38] Better known groups have concentrated on our own problems of *over-development*. Private efforts such as the New Alchemy Institute on Cape Cod and the Farallon Institute in California have gained some notoriety for their work. The founder of the latter group, Sim Van der Ryn [was] appointed State Architect of California by Governor Jerry Brown, himself an avowed disciple of Schumacher. Van der Ryn has established within his agency a new Office of Appropriate Technology which is attempting to influence other state agencies to adopt such technologies as solar power.[39] At the federal level, a newly funded National Center for Appropriate Technology is being established in Butte, Montana. In describing its effort, *Science* magazine gave as good a definition of the subject as we are likely to find: "Appropriate technology generally means technology that is small, easy to understand and maintain, cheap, dependent on local resources, and fitted to local needs. It makes heavy use of renewable resources . . . and makes minimal demands on capital and on nonrenewable environmental and energy resources."[40] Thomas Jefferson could hardly put it better. Today the poet Gary Snyder echoes his concerns.

But this redefinition for our own time of the traditional ideal of a democratic technology answers only half the problem. There is a real danger that, as in the past, the technology that begins as democratic will be quickly absorbed into a larger authoritarian context. The history of energy use in America provides a case in point.

As mentioned above, during most of its first century, the United States depended upon widely available, easily harnessed energy sources: wind, water, wood (now called more gloriously "biomass"), and animal. They were, in terms of our definition, "small, easy to understand and maintain, cheap, dependent on local resources, and fitted to local needs." Since 1850, however, our consumption of energy has multiplied more than thirty times, and whereas wood sup-

plied ninety percent of our needs in 1850, by 1900 coal had become the dominant fuel (providing seventy percent) and by 1950 oil and natural gas were
the leading contributors (with 55.5 percent).[41] Not only had we become an energy-intensive society, but the source of that energy was increasingly nonrenewable and, as importantly, was increasingly vulnerable to monopolization.

Potentially, the emphasis of Appropriate Technology on solar and wind
power to provide for our energy needs is a progressive step toward reestablish-
ing the democratic nature of our energy mix. The potential, however, remains
only that, and there is increasing evidence that it too might well become
authoritarian. Ralph Nader has quipped that "if twenty years ago title to the
sun had been given to Exxon, with a depletion allowance, we'd have solar
energy today."[42] In effect, the government is today doing something much
like that. As *Science* magazine has reported, "government planners seem to
have trouble grasping" the point that solar power is "fundamentally different
from other [dominant energy] sources. Solar energy is democratic. It falls on
everyone and can be put to use by individuals and small groups of people."
Instead, the government's "research program has emphasized large central
stations to produce solar electricity in some distant future and has largely ignored small solar devices for producing on-site power."[43] It is obvious that
on-site solar power would provide a democratic alternative to the energy monopolies, while plans for orbiting reflectors and "power towers" would enhance
their position. As *Science* comments, "the centerpiece of the government's solar
energy program is proceeding from small to large tests in a fashion that is
remarkably parallel to the well-established pattern of nuclear reactor development. Big facilities, big expenditures, and a multidecade development program all characterize the program of centralized solar thermal generating
stations."[44] Much the same story appears in the government's miniscule wind
energy program.[45] Thus the fact is that this authoritarian pattern grows not
out of the nature of the technology itself (solar and wind resources are by
their very nature democratic) but rather from the larger social technics which
prevail in this country.

Looking back over the course of American history, the role played by technology in bringing us to our present state is both obvious and too little studied.
Scholars such as Hugo Meier have illuminated the predominant belief that
American technology and democracy were not only compatible but mutually
dependent.[46] John Kouwenhoven has maintained that this democratic technology in fact defines the unique nature of American culture.[47] Leo Marx
has brilliantly described and analyzed those voices of dissent which attempted
to come to grips with both the pastoral and the industrial.[48] John Higham
has suggested that by the mid-nineteenth century the United States had moved
from a primordial, through an ideological, to a technological context for its
national identity.[49] As we build upon these studies, however, it is important
to keep several major points in mind. First, to an important degree, the Ameri-

can experience in this regard has been "advanced," but not entirely unique. Lewis Mumford has found the roots of authoritarian technics in the ancient Middle East and, in his monumental study of the *Myth of the Machine,* has traced the evolution of what he calls the pentagon of power.[50] Similarly, Lynn White has insisted, persuasively I think, that the roots of ecological crisis are not uniquely American, but extend back to fantasies of power originating in the medieval period.[51] Second, it is important to remember that the voices of Jefferson and Thoreau, Mumford and Goodman, do not belong simply to an archaic and inert past, but are part of a *continuing tradition* of perception that technology does not simply affect social institutions, it *is* a social institution and, as such, is of proper concern to those who would preserve our democratic liberties. Third, it should also be obvious that technology is not indivisible, is not autonomous, and does not contain some inner logic which makes inevitable the kind of world in which we find ourselves. Indeed, the traditions of technology—simplicity, cheapness, and accommodation—are *those very virtues which Jefferson saw as characterizing a democratic technics.* That we have today a megamachine displaying exactly the opposite characteristics is not due to the logic of technology, but to some other force at work in American society. Finally, it is important to remember that this whole question is one of more than simple academic interest: the very survival of our democratic society is dependent upon an understanding of those forces working to destroy it. Authoritarian technics tend to an integration and uniformity which inevitably create a social and natural environment which is not only unpalatable but unstable as well. Openness and diversity, characteristics of a democratic technics, are essential for the kind of successful adaptations which our society must make to survive.

## NOTES

1. Thomas Jefferson, Letter to George Fleming, December 29, 1815, *The Writings of Thomas Jefferson,* H. A. Washington (ed.) (Washington: Taylor and Maury, 1854), II: 1–15, 504–5, 507.

2. Lewis Mumford, "Authoritarian and Democratic Technics," *Technology and Culture,* 5 (Winter 1964): 7. [Part 8, chapter 26 in this volume.]

3. Ibid, p. 2.

4. Ibid, pp. 3, 6.

5. Ibid, pp. 2–3.

6. Brooke Hindle, *Technology in Early America* (Chapel Hill: University of North Carolina Press, 1966), pp. 17–18.

7. Mumford, p. 4.

8. Hugo Meier, "Technology and Democracy, 1800–1860," *Mississippi Valley Historical Review* 43 (March 1957): 618–40. For other efforts to tie technology to American thought and character see Hugo A. Meier, "American Technology and the Nineteenth-Century World," *American Quarterly* 10 (Summer 1958): 116–30; John E. Sawyer, "The Social Basis of the American System of Manufacturing," *Journal of Economic History* 14 (Fall 1954): 361–79; Morrell Heald, "Technology in American Culture," *Stetson University Bulletin* 62, no. 3 (October 1962): 1–18; and Marvin

Fisher, "The Iconology of Industrialism, 1830–60," *American Quarterly* 13 (Fall 1961): 347–64.

9. Joseph Barnes, *Treatise on the Justice, Policy, and Utility of Establishing an Effectual System for Promoting the Progress of Useful Arts by Assuring Property in the Products of Genius*. . . (Philadelphia: Francis Bailey, 1792), pp. 9–10.

10 Benjamin Franklin, *An Account of the Newly Invented Pennsylvanian Fire-Place* (Philadelphia: 1744), p.v. Quoted in Thomas R. Adams's introduction to the 1973 reprint (Boston: G. K. Hall and Co.).

11. James F. W. Johnston, *Notes on North America: Agricultural, Economical, and Social* (Edinburgh: W. Blackwood & Sons, 1851), I: 160–61.

12. Joseph Whitworth and George Wallis, *The Industry of the United States in Machinery, Manufactures, and Useful and Ornamental Arts* (London: n.p., 1854), pp. 19–20.

13. Ibid, p. vi.

14. Quoted in Daniel Bell, *Work and Its Discontents* (New York: League for Industrial Democracy, 1970), p. 43.

15. Oliver Evans, *The Young Mill-Wright and Miller's Guide* (Octoraro, Pa.: Francis Bailey, 1807), p. 355.

16. Mark Twain, *A Connecticut Yankee in King Arthur's Court* (New York: Signet, 1963), pp. 58–59.

17. "An Ode," 1828, published at an industrial exhibition. copy kindly provided by Bruce Binclair, University of Toronto.

18. John Adolphus Etzler, *The New World: or, Mechanical System to Perform the Labors of Man and Beast by Inanimate Powers, That Cost Nothing for Producing and Preparing the Substances of Life*. . . (Philadelphia: C. F. Stollmeyer, 1841), p. 4.

19. Quoted in C. Vann Woodward, rev. of *Time on the Cross: The Economics of American Negro Slavery*, by Robert Fogel and Stanley Engerman, *New York Review of Books*, May 2, 1974, pp. 5–6.

20. Simon Newcomb, *A Plain Man's Talk on the Labor Question* (New York: Harper and Bros. 1886), pp. 28, 61.

21. Mumford, p.6.

22. For two excellent short articles on the recent history of American agribusiness, and the food it produces, see Jim Hightower, "Hard Tomatoes, Hard Times: Failure of the Land Grant College Complex," *Society* 10 (November–December 1972): 10–11, 14, and 16–22; and Daniel Zwerdling, "Death for Dinner," *New York Review of Books*, February 21, 1974, pp. 22–24.

23. I take the terms Fordism and Sloanism from the excellent book by Emma Rothschild, *Paradise Lost: The Decline of the Auto-Industrial Age* (New York: Random House, 1973). See also James J. Flink, "Three Stages of American Automobile Consciousness," *American Quarterly* 24 (October 1972): 451–73.

24. "Taylor's Testimony Before the Special House Committee" (1912), in Frederick Winslow Taylor, *Scientific Management* (New York: Harper & Bros., 1947), pp. 29–30.

25. Mumford, p.6.

26. Quoted in Norman Pollack, *The Populist Response to Industrial America* (New York: Norton, 1966), p.22.

27. David F. Noble, *America by Design: Science, Technology, and the Rise of Corporate Capitalism* (New York: Alfred A. Knopf, 1977).

28. See Jean Christie, "Giant Power: A Progressive Proposal of the Nineteen-Twenties, *Pennsylvania Magazine of History and Biography* 96 (October 1972): 480–507. For a later episode in Cooke's career, see Jean Christie, "The Mississippi Valley Committee: Conservation and Planning in the Early New Deal," *The Historian* 32 (May 1970): 449–69.

29. See the official history of the REA, *Rural Lines—USA: The Story of the Rural Electrification Administration's First Twenty-Five Years, 1935–1960*, USDA Misc. Pub. No. 811 (Washington D.C.: GPO, 1960), p. 36.

30. James W. Carey and John J. Quirk, "The Mythos of the Electronic Revolution," *The American Scholar* 39 (Spring 1970): 219–41 and (Summer 1970): 395–424; Timothy Walker "De-

fense of Mechanical Philosophy," *North American Review* 23 (July 1832): 122–36.

31. See for example H. R. 1536, 75th Cong., I sess., introduced by Jennings Randolph: "A Bill to aid and promote scientific research of a basic character upon which the inception and development of new industries or the expansion of established industries may be dependent, to encourage increased effort on the part of individuals toward the further advancement of scientific knowledge and discovery and for other purposes."

32. See Carroll Pursell, "Alternative American Science Policies during World War II," in *World War II: An Account of its Documents,* James E. O'Neill and Robert W. Krauskopf (eds.) (Washington, D.C.: Howard University Press, 1976), pp. 151–62.

33. One of Kilgore's pieces of legislation was S. 2721, 77th Cong. 2 sess. For the text, and some of the hearings, see James L. Penick, Jr., et al., *The Politics of American Science: 1939 to The Present,* 2d ed. (Cambridge, Mass.: MIT Press, 1972), pp. 82–95.

34. I. F. Stone, *Business as Usual: The First Year of Defense* (New York: Modern Age Books, 1941); Bruce Catton, *War Lords of Washington* (New York: Harcourt, Brace & Co., 1948).

35. Waldemar Kaempffert, *Science Today and Tomorrow* (New York: Viking, 1939), pp. 261–62.

36. Paul Goodman, "The Morality of Scientific Technology," *Dissent* 14 (January–February 1967).

37. Paul Goodman, "Can Technology Be Humane?" *New York Review of Books,* November 20, 1969, pp. 27–34. For some examples and problems, see Ralph Nader et al. (eds.), *Whistle Blowing: The Report of the Conference on Professional Responsibility* (New York: Grossman Publishers, 1972).

38. *Science* 188 (6 June 1975): 1000.

39. For an interview with Van der Ryn see "What is Appropriate Technology?" *Cry California* 12 (Summer 1977): 30–32.

40. "NCAT: Appropriate Technology with a Mission," *Science* 195 (March 4, 1977): 857.

41. Earl Cook, "The Flow of Energy in an Industrial Society," in *Energy and Power* (San Francisco: W. H. Freeman & Co., 1971), p. 85.

42. Quoted in *Santa Barbara News-Press,* April 21, 1974, p. B1, cols. 1 & 2.

43. "Solar Energy Research: Making Solar After the Nuclear Model?" *Science* 197 (July 15, 1977): 241.

44. Ibid.

45. "Wind Energy: Large and Small Systems Competing," *Science* 197 (September 2, 1977): 971–73; and "Windmills: The Resurrection of an Ancient Energy Technology," *Science* 184 (June 7, 1974): 1055–58.

46. Meier, "Technology and Democracy, 1800–1860" and "American Technology and the Nineteenth-Century World" (see note 8).

47. John A. Kouwenhoven, *The Arts in Modern American Civilization* (New York: Norton Library, 1967).

48. Leo Marx, *The Machine in the Garden: Technology and the Pastoral Ideal in America* (New York: Oxford University Press, 1964). See also his "American Institutions and Ecological Ideals," *Science* 170 (November 27, 1970): 945–52. For British writers, see Herbert L. Sussman, *Victorians and the Machine: The Literary Response to Technology* (Cambridge, Mass.: Harvard University Press, 1968).

49. John Higham, "Hanging Together: Divergent Unities in American History," *Journal of American History* 61 (June 1974): 5–28.

50. Lewis Mumford, *The Myth of the Machine: Technics and Human Development* (New York: Harcourt, Brace & World, 1967) and *The Myth of the Machine: The Pentagon of Power* (New York: Harcourt, Brace, Jovanovich, 1970). Also see his "Apology to Henry Adams," *Virginia Quarterly Review* 38 (Spring 1962): 196–217.

51. Lynn White, Jr., "The Historical Roots of our Ecologic Crisis," *Science* 155 (March 10, 1967): 1203–7.

# 28

# Buddhist Economics

## E. F. Schumacher

"Right Livelihood" is one of the requirements of the Buddha's Noble Eight-fold Path. It is clear, therefore, that there must be such a thing as Buddhist economics.

Buddhist countries have often stated that they wish to remain faithful to their heritage. So Burma: "The New Burma sees no conflict between religious values and economic progress. Spiritual health and material wellbeing are not enemies: they are natural allies."[1] Or: "We can blend successfully the religious and spiritual values of our heritage with the benefits of modern technology."[2] Or: "We Burmans have a sacred duty to conform both our dreams and our acts of our faith. This we shall ever do."[3]

All the same, such countries invariably assume that they can model their economic development plans in accordance with modern economics, and they call upon modern economists from so-called advanced countries to advise them, to formulate the policies to be pursued, and to construct the grand design for development, the Five-Year Plan or whatever it may be called. No one seems to think that a Buddhist way of life would call for Buddhist economics, just as the modern materialist way of life has brought forth modern economics.

Economists themselves, like most specialists, normally suffer from a kind of metaphysical blindness, assuming that theirs is a science of absolute and invariable truths, without any presuppositions. Some go as far as to claim that economic laws are as free from "metaphysics" or "values" as the law of gravitation. We need not, however, get involved in arguments of methodology.

Instead, let us take some fundamentals and see what they look like when viewed by a modern economist and a Buddhist economist.

There is universal agreement that a fundamental source of wealth is human labor. Now, the modern economist has been brought up to consider "labor" or work as little more than a necessary evil. From the point of view of the employer, it is in any case simply an item of cost, to be reduced to a minimum if it cannot be eliminated altogether, say, by automation. From the point of view of the workman, it is a "disutility"; to work is to make a sacrifice of one's leisure and comfort, and wages are a kind of compensation for the sacrifice. Hence the ideal from the point of view of the employer is to have output without employees, and the ideal from the point of view of the employee is to have income without employment.

The consequences of these attitudes both in theory and in practice are, of course, extremely far-reaching. If the ideal with regard to work is to get rid of it, every method that "reduces the work load" is a good thing. The most potent method, short of automation, is so-called "division of labor" and the classical example is the pin factory eulogized in Adam Smith's *Wealth of Nations*.[4] Here it is not a matter of ordinary specialization, which mankind has practised from time immemorial, but of dividing up every complete process of production into minute parts, so that the final product can be produced at great speed without anyone having had to contribute more than a totally insignificant and, in most cases, unskilled movement of his limbs.

The Buddhist point of view takes the function of work to be at least threefold: to give a man a chance to utilize and develop his faculties; to enable him to overcome his egocenteredness by joining with other people in a common task; and to bring forth the goods and services needed for a becoming existence. Again, the consequences that flow from this view are endless. To organize work in such a manner that it becomes meaningless, boring, stultifying, or nerve-racking for the worker would be little short of criminal; it would indicate a greater concern with goods than with people, an evil lack of compassion and a soul-destroying degree of attachment to the most primitive side of this worldly existence. Equally, to strive for leisure as an alternative to work would be considered a complete misunderstanding of one of the basic truths of human existence, namely that work and leisure are complementary parts of the same living process and cannot be separated without destroying the joy of work and the bliss of leisure.

From the Buddhist point of view, there are therefore two types of mechanization which must be clearly distinguished: one that enhances a man's skill and power and one that turns the work of man over to a mechanical slave, leaving man in a position of having to serve the slave. How to tell the one from the other? "The craftsman himself," says Ananda Coomaraswamy, a man equally competent to talk about the modern West as the ancient East, "can always, if allowed to, draw the delicate distinction between the machine and the tool. The carpet loom is a tool, a contrivance for holding warp threads at a stretch for the pile to be woven round them by the craftsmen's fingers; but the power loom is a machine, and its significance as a destroyer of culture lies in the fact that it does the essentially human part of the work."[5] It is clear, therefore, that Buddhist economics must be very different from the economics of modern materialism, since the Buddhist sees the essence of civilization not in a multiplication of wants but in the purification of human character. Character, at the same time, is formed primarily by a man's work. And work, properly conducted in conditions of human dignity and freedom, blesses those who do it and equally their products. The Indian philosopher and economist J. C. Kumarappa sums the matter up as follows:

> If the nature of the work is properly appreciated and applied, it will stand in the same relation to the higher faculties as food is to the physical body. It nourishes and enlivens the higher man and urges him to produce the best he is capable of. It directs his free will along the proper course and disciplines the animal in him into progressive channels. It furnishes an excellent background for man to display his scale of values and develop his personality.[6]

If a man has no chance of obtaining work he is in a desperate position, not simply because he lacks an income but because he lacks this nourishing and enlivening factor of disciplined work which nothing can replace. A modern economist may engage in highly sophisticated calculations on whether full employment "pays" or whether it might be more "economic" to run an economy at less than full employment so as to ensure mobility of labor, a better stability of wages, and so forth. His fundamental criterion of success is simply the total quantity of goods produced during a given period of time. "If the marginal urgency of goods is low," says Professor [John Kenneth] Galbraith in *The Affluent Society,* "then so is the urgency of employing the last man or the last million men in the labor force."[7] And again: "If . . . we can afford some unemployment in the interest of stability—a proposition, incidentally, of impeccably conservative antecedents—then we can afford to give those who are unemployed the goods that enable them to sustain their accustomed standard of living."

From a Buddhist point of view, this is standing the truth on its head by considering goods as more important than people and consumption as more important than creative activity. It means shifting the emphasis from the worker to the product of work, that is, from the human to the subhuman, a surrender to the forces of evil. The very start of Buddhist economic planning would be a planning for full employment, and the primary purpose of this would in fact be employment for everyone who needs an "outside" job: it would not be the maximization of employment nor the maximization of production. Women, on the whole, do not need an "outside" job, and the large-scale employment of women in offices or factories would be considered a sign of serious economic failure. In particular, to let mothers of young children work in factories while the children run wild would be as uneconomic in the eyes of a Buddhist economist as the employment of a skilled worker as a soldier in the eyes of a modern economist.

While the materialist is mainly interested in goods, the Buddhist is mainly interested in liberation. But Buddhism is "The Middle Way" and therefore in no way antagonistic to physical well-being. It is not wealth that stands in the way of liberation but the attachment to wealth; not the enjoyment of pleasurable things but the craving for them. The keynote of Buddhist economics, therefore, is simplicity and nonviolence. From an economist's point of view, the marvel of the Buddhist way of life is the utter rationality of its pattern— amazingly small means leading to extraordinarily satisfactory results.

For the modern economist this is very difficult to understand. He is used to measuring the "standard of living" by the amount of annual consumption, assuming all the time that a man who consumes more is "better off" than a man who consumes less. A Buddhist economist would consider this approach excessively irrational: since consumption is merely a means to human well-being, the aim should be to obtain the maximum of well-being with the minimum of consumption. Thus, if the purpose of clothing is a certain amount of temperature comfort and an attractive appearance, the task is to attain this purpose with the smallest possible effort, that is, with the smallest annual destruction of cloth and with the help of designs that involve the smallest possible input of toil. The less toil there is, the more time and strength is left for artistic creativity. It would be highly uneconomic, for instance, to go in for complicated tailoring, like the modern West, when a much more beautiful effect can be achieved by the skillful draping of uncut material. It would be the height of folly to make material so that it should wear out quickly and the height of barbarity to make anything ugly, shabby, or mean. What has just been said about clothing applies equally to all other human requirements. The ownership and the consumption of goods is a means to an end, and Buddhist economics is the systematic study of how to attain given ends with the minimum means.

Modern economics, on the other hand, considers consumption to be the sole end and purpose of all economic activity, taking the factors of production— land, labor, and capital—as the means. The former, in short, tries to maximize human satisfactions by the optimal pattern of consumption, while the latter tries to maximize consumption by the optimal pattern of productive effort. It is easy to see that the effort needed to sustain a way of life which seeks to attain the optimal pattern of consumption is likely to be much smaller than the effort needed to sustain a drive for maximum consumption. We need not be surprised, therefore, that the pressure and strain of living is very much less in, say, Burma than it is in the United States, in spite of the fact that the amount of labor-saving machinery used in the former country is only a minute fraction of the amount used in the latter.

Simplicity and nonviolence are obviously closely related. The optimal pattern of consumption, producing a high degree of human satisfaction by means of a relatively low rate of consumption, allows people to live without great pressure and strain and to fulfil the primary injunction of Buddhist teaching: "Cease to do evil; try to do good." As physical resources are everywhere limited, people satisfying their needs by means of a modest use of resources are obviously less likely to be at each other's throats than people depending upon a high rate of use. Equally, people who live in highly self-sufficient local communities are less likely to get involved in large-scale violence than people whose existence depends on world-wide systems of trade.

From the point of view of Buddhist economics, therefore, production from local resources for local needs is the most rational way of economic life, while dependence on imports from afar and the consequent need to produce for export to unknown and distant peoples is highly uneconomic and justifiable only in exceptional cases and on a small scale. Just as the modern economist would admit that a high rate of consumption of transport services between a man's home and his place of work signifies a misfortune and not a high standard of life, so the Buddhist economist would hold that to satisfy human wants from faraway sources rather than from sources nearby signifies failure rather than success. The former tends to take statistics showing an increase in the number of ton/miles per head of the population carried by a country's transport system as proof of economic process, while to the latter—the Buddhist economist—the same statistics would indicate a highly undesirable deterioration in the *pattern* of consumption.

Another striking difference between modern economics and Buddhist economics arises over the use of natural resources. Bertrand de Jouvenel, the eminent French political philosopher, has characterized "Western man" in words which may be taken as a fair description of the modern economist:

> He tends to count nothing as an expenditure, other than human effort; he does not seem to mind how much mineral matter he wastes and, far worse, how much living matter he destroys. He does not seem to realize at all that human life is a dependent part of an ecosystem of many different forms of life. As the world is ruled from towns where men are cut off from any form of life other than human, the feeling of belonging to an ecosystem is not revived. This results in a harsh and improvident treatment of things upon which we ultimately depend, such as water and trees.[8]

The teaching of the Buddha, on the other hand, enjoins a reverent and nonviolent attitude not only to all sentient beings but also, with great emphasis, to trees. Every follower of the Buddha ought to plant a tree every few years and look after it until it is safely established, and the Buddhist economist can demonstrate without difficulty that the universal observation of this rule would result in a high rate of genuine economic development independent of any foreign aid. Much of the economic decay of southeast Asia (as of many other parts of the world) is undoubtedly due to a heedless and shameful neglect of trees.

Modern economics does not distinguish between renewable and non-renewable materials, as its very method is to equalize and quantify everything by means of a money price. Thus, taking various alternative fuels, like coal, oil, wood, or water power: the only difference between them recognized by modern economics is relative cost per equivalent unit. The cheapest is automatically the one to be preferred, as to do otherwise would be irrational and "uneconomic." From a Buddhist point of view, of course, this will not do; the essential difference between nonrenewable fuels like coal and oil on the one hand and renewable fuels like wood and water power on the other cannot be simply overlooked. Nonrenewable goods must be used only if they are indispensable, and then only with the greatest care and the most meticulous concern for conservation. To use them heedlessly or extravagantly is an act of violence, and while complete nonviolence may not be attainable on this earth, there is nonetheless an ineluctable duty on man to aim at the ideal of nonviolence in all he does.

Just as a modern European economist would not consider it a great economic achievement if all European art treasures were sold to America at attractive prices, so the Buddhist economist would insist that a population basing its economic life on nonrenewable fuels is living parasitically, on capital instead of income. Such a way of life could have no permanence and could therefore be justified only as a purely temporary expedient. As the world's resources of nonrenewable fuels—coal, oil, and natural gas—are exceedingly unevenly distributed over the globe and undoubtedly limited in quantity, it is clear that their exploitation at an ever-increasing rate is an act of violence against nature which must almost inevitably lead to violence between men.

This fact alone might give food for thought even to those people in Buddhist countries who care nothing for the religious and spiritual values of their heritage and ardently desire to embrace the materialism of modern economics at the fastest possible speed. Before they dismiss Buddhist economics as nothing better than a nostalgic dream, they might consider whether the path of economic development outlined by modern economics is likely to lead them to places where they really want to be. Towards the end of his courageous book *The Challenge of Man's Future,* Professor Harrison Brown of the California Institute of Technology gives the following appraisal:

> Thus we see that, just as industrial society is fundamentally unstable and subject to reversion to agrarian existence, so within it the conditions which offer individual freedom are unstable in their ability to avoid the conditions which impose rigid organization and totalitarian control. Indeed, when we examine all of the foreseeable difficulties which threaten the survival of industrial civilization, it is difficult to see how the achievement of stability and the maintenance of individual liberty can be made compatible.[9]

Even if this were dismissed as a long-term view there is the immediate question of whether "modernization," as currently practiced without regard to religious and spiritual values, is actually producing agreeable results. As far as the masses are concerned, the results appear to be disastrous—a collapse of the rural economy, a rising tide of unemployment in town and country, and the growth of a city proletariat without nourishment for either body or soul.

It is the light of both immediate experience and long-term prospects that the study of Buddhist economics could be recommended even to those who believe that economic growth is more important than any spiritual or religious values. For it is not a question of choosing between "modern growth" and "traditional stagnation." It is a question of finding the right path of development, the Middle Way between materialist heedlessness and traditionalist immobility, in short, of finding "Right Livelihood."

## NOTES

1. *The New Burma* (Economic and Social Board, Government of the Union of Burma, 1954).
2. Ibid.
3. Ibid.
4. Adam Smith, *Wealth of Nations*.
5. Ananda K. Coomaraswamy, *Art and Swadeshi* (Madras: Ganesh & Co.).
6. J. C. Kumarappa, *Economy of Permanence*, 4th ed. (Rajghat, Kashi: Sarva-Seva Sangh Publication, 1958).
7. John Kenneth Galbraith, *The Affluent Society* (Hammondsworth, Middlesex, England: Penguin Books Ltd., 1962).
8. Richard B. Gregg, *A Philosophy of Indian Economic Development* (Ahmedabad: Navajivan Publishing House, 1958).
9. Harrison Brown, *The Challenge of Man's Future* (New York: Viking Press, 1954).

# 29

# Small Is Dubious

## Samuel C. Florman

Last April, while reading the papers the morning after the President's energy address to the nation, I was struck by a statement attributed to Mr. Carter's pollster and adviser, Patrick Caddell: "The idea that big is bad and that there is something good to smallness is something that the country has come to accept much more today than it did 10 years ago. This has been one of the biggest changes in America over the past decade."

Since the nation had just been exhorted to embark on the most herculean technological, economic, and political enterprises, this reference to smallness seemed to me to be singularly inapt. Waste is to be deplored, of course, and inefficiency. But bigness? I had not realized that the small-is-beautiful philosophy had reached the White House.

A few days after the Carter speech, I had an opportunity to attend a lecture by E. F. Schumacher, the author of *Small Is Beautiful,* the book that, since its publication in 1973, has become the Koran of the antitechnology movement. I listened, bemused, as Dr. Schumacher depicted a United States in which each community would bake its own bread and develop its own resources, a nation of self-reliant craftsmen where interstate transport would practically disappear. The energy crisis could be solved, Schumacher maintained, only be replacing our sprawling network of industrial metropolises with numerous small-scale production centers. Schumacher's audience listened, entranced.

It was clear that the energy crisis was giving new life to an idea which otherwise might have died a natural death.

On my way home, I found myself thinking about a telephone call I had received a few weeks earlier from a consultant to the power industry. He was concerned about an article entitled "Energy Strategy: The Road Not Taken?" by Amory B. Lovins, a British physicist, which had appeared in the October 1976 issue of *Foreign Affairs*. The article, which argued the small-is-beautiful position forcefully, had been extensively quoted in the international press, entered into the Congressional Record, discussed in *Business Week,* and been the subject of the most reprint requests ever received by *Foreign Affairs,* surpassing even the famous George Kennan "Mr. X" piece.

Opposition has not been slow to rally. The man who called me put together a collection of rebuttal essays prepared by people prominent in the fields of energy, academe, industry, and labor. This imposing pamphlet has been circulated in large quantities wherever its sponsor fears the Lovins article might have made an impression. It appears that the metaphysical struggle between small and big—reminiscent of the argument over the number of angels that can dance on the head of a pin—has become a real issue.

The small-is-beautiful believers, as exemplified by the Lovins article, commence their campaign with a critique of our existing energy technology, especially our nationwide grid of electrical power. The deficiencies of this system are obvious enough. Electricity is created in huge central plants by boiling water to run generators. Whether the heat that boils the water is furnished by oil, coal, gas, nuclear energy, or even by solar energy, a great deal of energy is wasted in the process, and even more is lost in transmission over long lines. By the time the electricity arrives in our home or factory and is put to use, about two-thirds of the original energy has been dissipated. In addition, the existence of what Lovins calls "the infrastructure" of the power industry itself —tens of thousands of workers occupying enormous office complexes—costs the system more energy, and costs the consumer more money.

The proposed solution, which on first hearing sounds fairly sensible, is the creation of small, efficient energy-creating installations in the buildings where the energy is used, or at most at the medium scale of urban neighborhoods and rural villages. Direct solar plants are the preferred system, although Lovins also mentions small mass-produced diesel generators, wind-driven generators, and several other technologies still in the developmental stage.

Yet, despite the advantages of this sytem, the new "soft" technologies, to use Lovins's term, would entail the manufacture, transport, and installation of millions of new mechanisms. This cannot but be a monumental undertaking requiring enormous outlays of capital and energy. Then these mechanisms will have to be maintained. We all resent the electric and phone companies, but, when service is interrupted, a crew of competent men arrives on the scene to set things right. Lovins assures us that the solar collectors or windmills in our homes will be serviced by our friendly, independent neighborhood mechanic, a prospect which must chill the blood of anyone who has ever had to have a car repaired or tried to get a plumber in an emergency. As for Americans becoming self-reliant craftsmen, as Schumacher assures us we can, this idea sounds fine in a symposium on the human condition, but it overlooks the enormous practical and psychological difficulties that stand in its way. The recently attempted urban homesteading program, for example, was based on this very appealing concept. Abandoned houses were to be turned over to deserving families at no cost, just as land was made available to homesteaders in the last century. The program failed because most poor families simply were not capable of fixing up the houses.

Another hope of the small-is-beautiful advocates is that great savings can be realized by eliminating the administrations, or "middlemen" of the utility companies. But in the real world it appears that the middleman does perform a useful function. How else can we explain the failure of the cooperative buying movement, which is based on the idea that people can band together to eliminate distribution costs? The shortcomings of large organizations are universally recognized, and "bureaucratic" has long been a synonym for "inefficient." But, like it or not, large organizations with apparently superfluous administrative layers seem to work better than small ones. Chain stores are still in business, while mom-and-pop stores continue to fail. Local power companies, especially, are a vanishing breed. Decisions made in the marketplace do not tell us everything, but they do tell us a lot more than the fantasies of futurist economists.

This is not to say that the situation cannot change. If a handy gadget becomes available that will heat my house economically using wind, water, sunlight, or moonlight, I will rush out to buy it. On the other hand, if the technological breakthroughs come in the power-plant field—perhaps nuclear fusion or direct conversion of sunlight to electricity—then I will be pleased to continue my contractual arrangements with the electric company.

Such an open-minded approach has no appeal to Lovins. Quoting Robert Frost on two roads diverging in a wood, he asserts that we must select one way or the other, since we cannot travel both. The analogy is absurd, since we are a pluralistic society of more than 200 million people, not a solitary poet, and it has been our habit to take every road in sight. Will it be wasteful to build power plants that may soon be obsolete? I think not. If a plant is used for an interim period while other technologies are developed, it will have served its purpose. If it is never used at all, it will still have been a useful component of a contingency plan. When billions of dollars are spent each year on constantly obsolescing weapons which we hope we will never have to use, it does not seem extravagant to ask for some contingency planning for our life-support systems.

Our resources are limited, or course, and we want to allocate them sensibly. At this time it is not clear whether the most promising technologies are "hard" or "soft" or, as is most likely, some combination of both. The "soft" technologies are not being ignored. The Administration's energy program contains incentives for solar heat installations by individual homeowners. Research and development funds are being granted to a multitude of experimental projects. At the same time, we are working on improvements to our conventional systems. What else could a responsible society do? We must assume that the technologies which prevail will be those which prove to be most cost-effective and least hazardous. Improper political pressures may be a factor, but these have a way of cancelling each other out. A new product attracts sophisticated investors, and before long there is a new lobbyist's office in Washington. The struggle for markets and profits creates a jungle in which the fittest technologies are likely to survive.

Technological efficiency, however, is not a standard by which the small-is-beautiful advocates are willing to abide. Lovins makes this clear when he states that even if nuclear power were clean, safe, and economic, "it would still be unattractive because of the political implications of the kind of energy economy it would lock us into." As for making electricity from huge solar collectors in the desert, or from solar energy collected by satellites in outer space—these also will not do, "for they are ingenious high-technology ways to supply energy in a form and at a scale inappropriate to most end-use needs." Finally, he admits straight out that the most important questions of energy strategy "are not mainly technical or economic but rather social and ethical."

So the technological issue is found to be a diversion, not at all the heart of the matter. The *political* consequences of bigness, it would appear, are what we have to fear. A centralized energy system, Lovins tell us, is "less compatible with social diversity and personal freedom of choice" than the small, more pluralistic, approach he favors.

But diversity and freedom, at least in the United States, are protected and encouraged by strong institutions. Exploitation thrives in small towns and in small businesses. Big government and big labor unions, for all their faults, are the means by which we achieve the freedoms we hold so dear.

When big organizations challenge our well-being, as indeed they do—monopolistic corporations, corrupt labor unions, et al.—our protection comes, not from petty insurrections, but from that biggest of all organizations, the federal government. And when big government itself is at fault, the remedy can only be shakeups and more sensible procedures, not elimination of that bureaucracy which is a crucial element of our democracy. Does it not seem absurd, and quite late in the day, to speak of losing our political freedom through the growth of federally supervised utility companies, when we long ago agreed to give up our individual militias, and entrust the national defense to a national army? The small-is-beautiful philosophy makes just as little sense politically as it does technologically.

The next argument that Schumacher and Lovins present is the social one. Even if large organizations "work" technically and politically, it is claimed, they do not work socially. The subtitle to *Small Is Beautiful* is "Economics As If People Mattered." Only in small social groups, apparently, is it possible for people to "matter." Schumacher and Lovins would not appear to have read such books as *Winesburg, Ohio; Spoon River Anthology;* and *Main Street,* with their picture of the American small town as a petty, cramped, and spiteful community. Cities and small towns will always have their defenders, but the constantly discussed question about whether it is "better" to live in the city, the country, or the suburbs is a matter of taste which cannot be settled by self-appointed intellectual mandarins.

Perhaps what lies at the heart of the new worship of smallness is an increasing revulsion against the ugliness of much of industrial America. Dams, highways, and electric transmission lines, once the symbol of a somewhat naïve commercial boosterism, are now depicted as vulgar. But this association of bigness with lack of taste is not warranted. The colossal works of man are no more inherently vulgar than the small works are inherently petty. We prize robustness in life as well as delicacy. Rousseau, coming upon a Roman aqueduct, had this to say:

> The echo of my footsteps under the immense arches made me think I could hear the strong voices of the men who had built it. I felt lost like an insect in the immensity of the work. I felt, along with the sense of my own littleness, something nevertheless which seemed to elevate my soul; I said to myself with a sigh: "Oh! that I had been born a Roman!"

Economic and social arguments aside, Schumacher and Lovins maintain that their philosophy is founded on a base of moral conviction, of thrift, simplicity, and humility. We have sinned by being wasteful, ostentatious, and arrogant. Thus smallness becomes a symbol of virtue.

For a moment, as at every step along the way, we are inclined to agree. The message has an appeal. The problems of our age—the environmental crisis, the energy crisis, the depletion of our natural resources—are, we suspect, caused by our profligacy. Improvidence, it would appear, has become the cardinal sin.

But even the most useful moral precepts—such as patriotism—often have a dark underside. In the present instance, the thrift being preached lends itself to a smallness of spirit. (The day after President Carter's first energy message I heard the radio commentator Paul Harvey question the "waste" of gasoline for busing school children.) The humility propoed evokes those Oriental attitudes which counsel the masses to accept their wretched lot. Such fatalistic beliefs may be useful in adding a measure of serenity to our private lives, but they are insidious elements to inject into debates on public policy.

Much of the debate over big versus small recalls the Lilliputians going to war over the question of whether eggs should be opened at the big or little end. *Smallness,* after all, is a word that is neutral—technologically, politically, socially, aesthetically, and, of course, morally. Its use as a symbol of goodness would be one more entertaining example of human folly were it not for the disturbing consequences of the arguments advanced in its cause.

# 30

# Appropriate Technology
# and Inappropriate Politics

## Thomas Simon

## INTRODUCTION

Over the past two decades "appropriate technology" has been used as code for new ways of thinking about the social implications of technological choice. Appropriate technology is seen variously: as a means of ushering in a New Age, as an alternative to high technology, as a social movement, and, by some, as utopian delusion. The debate over appropriate technology is raising some of the most difficult questions facing a philosophy of technology, including: "the relationship between technology and development, between ideology and industrialization, and more fundamentally, between man and machine."[1] Yet, the most critical question is seldom explicitly addressed in this debate: what is and what should be the political philosophy underlying the appropriate technology movement?

Before providing my own answer to that question we need to get clear about just what appropriate technology is. Some critics charge that appropriate technology is a grab bag of vague ideas, which resist any attempts to provide definitional coherence. According to this view,

> [Appropriate] technology is not a coherent philosophy. It is a collection of a large
> number of ideas and concepts, many of them quite incoherent, almost as diverse

From *Technology and Contemporary Life,* ed. Paul T. Durbin, pp. 107–28. Copyright ©1988 Kluwer Academic Publishers, Dordrecht, Holland. Reprinted by permission.

as the name of the outlook: intermediate technology, humane technology, a new alchemy, peoples' technology, radical hardware, biotechnics, etc. Each of these names emphasize a different aspect of the new technology: workers' control, demystification of expertise, reform of work rules, low specialization, development under the condition of low capital, local or regional self-sufficiency, balanced economic development, resource conservation, low energy use, reduced technological risks, and so on.[2]

Contrary to this assessment, I will argue that methodological coherence can be given to the appropriate technology (AT) proposals. To do this, I will first look at what proponents of AT indicate as their agenda, and then I will undertake a rational reconstruction of the aims and assumptions of this agenda. In other words, prevailing AT ideas and practices can be used to define a methodologically adequate concept of AT.

Armed with a clear definition of AT we should be in a position to differentiate appropriate technology from its close kin—ecotechnology, liberatory, indigenous, intermediate, and radical technologies. Each of these might be seen to emphasize a different definitional feature than AT emphasizes. This approach, however, will be shown to be misleading.

In the final section of the [chapter] I will demonstrate that the problem with AT (and its kindred conceptions) is not methodological adequacy but rather the problem is the political foundation of the particular philosophy of technology. Appropriate technologists debate high technologists in terms of the features of their differing technologies. Likewise some ecotechnologists, liberatory technologists, etc., debate appropriate technologists in terms of the features of their differing technologies. This, however, is the wrong debate. The debate should not be over the features of the technologies. The debate is covertly and should be overtly a political debate. Failure to recognize the political nature of the debate leads critics to see a hodgepodge among these differing conceptions of technology. Recognizing the political nature of these different conceptions results in AT being judged politically inadequate. Before making the case for its political inadequacy let us first demonstrate the methodological adequacy of AT.

## DEFINING APPROPRIATE TECHNOLOGY

When you read the AT literature and come across definitions of appropriate technology such as "technology with a human face"[3] and "whatever is appropriate,"[4], you can immediately see the need for some definitional clarity. Those AT proponents with some methodological sophistication use three definitional tactics: providing ostensive definitions, listing evidentiary features, and specifying necessary and sufficient conditions. While I will argue that the last tactic is the most convincing, the others are worth describing since the discussion sheds further light on the AT movement.

## A. Ostensive Definitions

Some appropriate technologies readily concede the difficulties in providing a clear definition of AT: "Although we do not know how to define it, we do know an appropriate technology when we see one."[5] There is something to this attitude. After all, whatever the definitional complexities, the differences between a bulldozer and an oxplough or between a nuclear power plant and kerosene lanterns are readily apparent.

Nevertheless, there are cases where we cannot simply see the difference between an appropriate technology and other forms of technology. What, for example, is the most appropriate technology for maize-grinding in Kenya— mortar and pestle, hand operated mill, hammer mills, or roller mills?[6] Making this determination by simply looking at the candidate technologies is doomed from the outset.

The ostensive-definitional strategy reflects an attitudinal bias which needs to be borne in mind when assessing AT. The attitude manifests itself in the impatient "Let's get on with it" directive typically issued by technologists of all varieties. Generally, the technologist wants to give priority to doing over knowing. Problems cannot await the plodding intellectualization of philosophers and theoreticians. It is important to note that there are many proponents of appropriate technologies who subscribe to this attitude. This should underscore the point that appropriate technologists are first and foremost technologists, a point which is developed further in this [chapter].

While I have some sympathy with the technologists' attitude, this attitude rules out a certain fundamental line of inquiry. If I say "Let's get on with it" to practically any kind of project, I am thereby cutting off the questioning of the project itself, its underlying assumptions and implications. For appropriate technologists this can involve a refusal to examine the broader social/political context of technology introduction.

The tactic of providing ostensive definitions avoids the task of developing a political philosophy of technology, implying that techniques, at least "appropriate" ones, are politically benign and, perhaps, inherently good. This political avoidance behavior is also evident, although less blatantly so, in the other definitional approaches. Before showing that, I want briefly to describe a "Let's get on with it" attitude among philosophers, comparable to the one found among technologists. Philosophers have little patience with extended treatments of ostensive definitions since they are so quickly dismissed in the philosophical literature. However, what is obvious in one discipline is not so obvious in another. Many practically oriented technologists take ostensive definitions seriously, and philosophers should at least be willing to give the technologists the benefit of the doubt.

## B. Evidentiary Features

Other commentators offer as a definitional strategy a shopping list of features which, supposedly, can be expected to be found in the appropriate technology store. No one feature or set of features is regarded as necessary or sufficient for appropriate technology, but the addition of each feature is argued to increase our inductive confidence that a candidate technology is appropriate. A solar satellite would presumably have relatively few of these features, while active solar heating and, certainly, passive solar design can be comfortably situated in the AT camp. What are these discriminating features?

No single list is found in the AT literature. Huelphinil proposes fifteen features;[7] Robin Clark proposes thirty-five, the longest list. Both lists seek to distinguish an appropriate technology society from a hard technology one. An AT-organized society emphasizes: functionality for all time, communal units, local bartering, and integration of young and old. In contrast, hard technology breeds: functionality for a limited time only, nuclear families, worldwide trade, and alienation of young from old. [Romesh K.] Diwan and [Dennis] Livingston, trying to order the chaos, group the features from various lists in the following way:

> In terms of material aspects of AT production, "Appropriateness" connotes the use of renewable sources of energy and recyclable materials, minimum destructive impact on the environment, and maximum utilization of local resources. In terms of the modes of production, AT fabrication should take place close to the resource base, using processes which are labor intensive (capital saving), small scale, amenable to user participation and/or worker management, and located close to points of consumption. In terms of application, AT connotes assimilation with local environmental and cultural conditions. It does not overwhelm the community, but is comprehensible, accessible, and easy to maintain.[8]

Despite some progress achieved by this grouping, the list approach in general confronts a number of methodological problems. One is "how incompatible [features] are to be combined."[9] Let us take two features from Diwan and Livingston's list, viz., minimum destructive impact on the environment, and small scale. Rybczynski[10] proposes "the flush toilet, the throwaway container, the aerosol can, . . . and deforestation" as counterexamples to the claim made by AT proponents, like Schumacher, that small-scale devices are environmentally benign compared to large-scale ones. Small-scale devices can have a considerable negative environmental impact. (Later we will see how a better definitional strategy can meet this objection.)

Moreover, some items that we might find intuitively unacceptable as appropriate technologies qualify under the list approach. For example, do we find a description of an appropriate technology in the following?

It will be large enough for the family but small enough for the individual to run and care for. It will be constructed of the best materials, by the best men to be hired, after the simplest designs that engineering can devise. But it will be so low in price that no man will be unable to own one—and enjoy with his family the blessing of hours of pleasure in God's great open spaces.[11]

Appropriate technology features abound in this description: small scale, simplicity, economical, amenable to mastery and maintenance by local people, etc. Yet, this was Henry Ford's description of the universal car, the Model T, hardly a fitting exemplar for AT enthusiasts. Similar descriptions can be found among nuclear power proponents, who are typically archenemies of AT advocates. As an example take the 1946 claim of Weinberg, Wigner, and Young, that "nuclear power plants [would] make feasible a greater decentralization of industry."[12]

Again, as in the case of ostensive-definitional tactics, something more than methodology is amiss here. [Langdon] Winner[13] correctly derides the paradise-for-Christmas versus the sordid-perils-of-modernity lists as shallow social criticism. Oddly enough, all the good things in life are found under the appropriate technology tree while all the evils group themselves under the "high technology" label. Just as we found beneath the "Let's get on with it" technologist's impatience with theory a refusal to deal with social and political issues, so we find here a social-political criticism disguised as a debate over types of technologies. When proponents of appropriate technology present these lists, they presuppose both a particular critique of current society and a proposal for a better society. Yet, the critique and proposal are never made explicit. Instead, we are to accept or reject them in terms of technological choices.

One final methodological problem besetting the evidentiary feature strategy is the inability to determine which features are central. For example, is using local resources, which results in destroying a rain forest, more important than environmental preservation? In the next section we will examine a strategy that helps overcome some of the methodological problems apparent in the other two strategies. Yet, this third strategy, while making some progress, also fails to confront the problem of providing a political foundation.

## C. Conditions

The following is a sample of typical definitions of appropriate technology in the literature:

—Technology which is decentralized, small in scale, labor intensive, amenable to mastery and maintenance by local people, and harmonious with local cultural and environmental conditions.[14]

—We emphasize four criteria: smallness; simplicity; capital cheapness; and nonviolence.[15]

—Besides its [AT's] ability to offer to every member of society the fullness of the *summum bonum,* it offers to everyone also the dignity of work needed to attain it.[16]

—It is conducive to decentralization, compatible with the laws of ecology, gentle in its use of scarce resouces, and designed to serve the human person instead of making him the servant of machines.[17]

—AT as content has come to be applied to a special class of technology as systems: those incorporating energy-eficiency, labor-intensive, small-scale, decentralized technologies.[18]

From this widely variegated list, it is easy to sympathize with the charge that AT is an incoherent hodgepodge. Nevertheless, an adequate definition, accept-able to most AT proponents, can be salvaged from these proposals. If the above proposals are examined not as an unmanageable list of features but as alternative sets of conditions, it is possible, through selecting the best set of conditions, to devise an adequate definition of AT. However, as I will try to show, this definition, despite its methodological adequacy, falls far short of providing a much-needed political critique. Moveover, when the political foundations are fleshed out, they are found wanting.

My strategy in this section is to focus on DeForest's proposed set of conditions. Why I have chosen DeForest's set will become more evident when a final assessment of the definition is given in the next section. At this stage, suffice it to say that DeForest provides a manageable list of conditions, which overlap to some extent or another with almost every other definitional proposal of AT that I have seen. Nevertheless, DeForest's list needs fine-tuning. Each condition is therefore examined to determine how the set might contribute to a manageable and defensible framework for AT. The final step is to develop my critique of AT in terms of its being either politically impotent or politically inadequate.

1. *Energy Efficiency:* This condition is central to two of AT's kindred spirits, soft technologies and biotechnics. The key feature of these technologies is (un-like their counterparts, hard technologies) that "they are matched in *energy quality* to end-use needs."[19] In accord with this analysis, nuclear power is a highly inefficient means of heating homes since the end-use does not require such a high-grade form of energy. Similarly, home water heating is better done with natural gas than electricity since natural gas heats the water directly where-as a conversion process is required to produce electricity. Mismatching end-use typifies hard energy technologies.

2. *Environmental Soundness:* However valuable an analysis in terms of energy efficiency might be, it is not broad enough to capture the concerns of many AT proponents. Energy efficiency is important to appropriate technologists but not as important as environmental soundness. For example, the insulat-ing and ventilating properties of Third World homes is not an issue for AT

proponents. In contrast, there is a great deal of discussion within the AT literature about the conceivable environmental impact of introducing tractors into a region.[20] Accordingly, a technology is evaluated in terms of its impact on the immediate environment. Therefore, there are good grounds for rejecting energy efficiency as too narrow a condition for defining AT. Furthermore, where energy efficiency is a consideration, it can be subsumed under environmental soundness.

3. *Labor Intensity:* Almost every proponent of AT includes some form of labor—as opposed to capital—intensity as a minimum requirement (i.e., as a necessary condition) for AT. For example:

> Instead of concentrating on labor-saving devices, which has been the whole trend of modern technology, can you turn your attention to capital-saving devices, because it is capital that is lacking in developing countries, not labor.[21]

Nuclear power and large farm tractors are capital intensive technologies, resulting in few workers employed. AT proponents oppose these options when other technologies can be deployed to carry out work which expands employment.

> Because more people are employed, the benefits of growth will be spread more widely, and this wider distribution of income will contribute greatly to sparking demand for marketable goods in other industries.[22]

(The founder of the AT movement, E. F. Schumacher,[23] makes the case for a Buddhist economics which is not preoccupied with marketable production. A thorough reading of the AT literature, however, reveals that Schumacher is an exception on this point.)

4. *Small Scale:* Schumacher outlined, in *Small Is Beautiful,* the parameters of the AT movement, which McRobie sought to implement in *Small Is Possible.*[24] Since the publication of Schumacher's book, homage is repeatedly paid to the virtues of smallness; bigness takes on an almost immoral character. But recognizing the importance of smallness for AT is one thing; getting a clear sense of what smallness means is quite another. Schumacher regards smallness as a relative concept, necessary to offset the currently reigning "idolatry of giantism." Beyond that consensus smallness is used ambiguously throughout the AT literature to apply to production,[25] equipment,[26] or markets.[27] AT proponents see these three senses of smallness in terms of factors enabling people to attain control and as meeting the demands of the market.

5. *Decentralization:* Again, it is difficult to find a clearcut meaning of this term. Does decentralization mean that production units are widely dispersed spatially rather than concentrated in special regions? Does it mean putting factories in the rice paddies?[28] Or does it mean that decisions about work and production are to be made at the lowest levels of production? AT propo-

nents use "decentralization" in two senses, viz., as a decision about where the technology should be placed, and as decision about worker control.

6. *My Definition:* Summarizing the analysis so far, a modified version of DeForest's definition can be proposed. Appropriate technology will be taken to incorporate the following characteristics:

   (1) environmental soundness;

   (2) labor intensity;

   (3) small scale; and

   (4) decentralization.

These are conjunctively sufficient conditions for defining AT with no one condition sufficient in itself. Also, these conditions are disjunctively necessary for AT. Thus, this is a coherent set of conditions which capture (for the most part) what AT proponents mean when they talk about AT.

## D. Adequacy of the Definition

The proposed definition more or less captures what most proponents are trying to express about the features and qualities of AT. As a further defense of the modified DeForest proposal, I would argue that any proposed alternative condition would be either vaguer than any of the accepted conditions, subsumable under one of those conditions, or objectionable in its own right. For example, McRobie's claim that AT should be nonviolent is vague. Labor-intensive technologies are easy to recognize: nonviolent ones are difficult to discern.

Many other proposed conditions can be subsumed under one or more of the accepted ones. For example, operating according to the accepted conditions will involve the use of renewable sources of energy and maximum use of local resources. Furthermore, adhering to these conditions generally yields a flexible, low-cost technology with a rural emphasis. In fact, many AT advocates use small scale as a condition because it is thought to result in a rural emphasis.

Finally, other candidate conditions can be readily dismissed. "Simplicity of operation" is just too problematic. The division of labor certainly simplifies operations. Are assembly lines, then, models of appropriate technology? I hardly think so. In summary, the accepted conditions include most of the features AT proponents want and exclude the undesirables.

More importantly, these conditions enable AT theorists to rebut previously telling charges. A number of critics argue against AT by taking each condition in isolation and then showing how that condition is not acceptable. This tactic has been used, for example, against the small-is-beautiful thesis. The smallness of a production process does not prevent environmental and human destruction on a massive scale. However, this violates the environmental soundness condition. Similarly, the criticism that a small slave system is more environmentally sound than a large factory farm is refuted by noting that a slave system violates the decentralization condition, giving workers some control over the process.

Also, some critics have sought to pit the conditions against one another, showing their mutual inconsistency.[29] As noted above, Rybczynski[30] proposes the aerosol can and deforestation as counterexamples to Schumacher's claim that small-scale devices are always more enviornmentally sound than large-scale ones. [Harvey] Brooks[31] follows a similar line, arguing the incompatibility of environmental soundness and decentralization. Response to these criticisms is straightforward. While the conditions are related (small-scale is generally, but not always, more environmentally sound than large-scale production), they are interdependent conditions that must be explained together when evaluating a particular technique. To take one of the alleged counterexamples, the aerosol can does not qualify as AT because it violates the condition of environmental soundness, since it is partially responsible for ozone depletion.

Thus far, I have demonstrated that prevailing AT ideas and practices can be used to define a methodologically adequate concept of AT. At this stage, it should be at least clear what people are talking about when they use the term "appropriate technology." From a definitional vantage point, AT can avoid the charge of representing an incoherent hodgepodge by appeal to a relatively clear set of conditions. Accepting that a defensible definition of AT can be rendered, we are now in a position to examine more fundamental criticisms of AT. Difficulties with AT are found, not in specifying what types of technology qualify as AT, but in constructing adequate philosophical, particularly political, foundations of AT.

## THE POLITICAL FOUNDATIONS OF
## AT AND RELATED TECHNOLOGIES

The real problem with AT is not methodological. The problem is political. On the one hand, Winner is correct in claiming that technological choices are, in fact, political.

> Choices about supposedly neutral technologies—if "choices" they ever merit being called—are actually choices about the kind of society in which we shall live.[32]

On the other hand, Winner is incorrect in thinking that AT offers an alternative political philosophy. AT proponents generally explicitly refuse to address political questions. To the extent that they do, AT political philosophy is not altogether that different from the political philosophy espoused by high technology advocates.

There are exceptions to this political failure within the AT movement. However, within AT that debate often takes on the character of a technological, not a political, debate. Ecotechnology, liberatory, indigenous, and intermediary technologies are thought to emphasize different features of the technologies. So, Sardar and Rosser-Owen,[33] quoted at the outset of this [chapter], are partially on target in criticizing these formulations for simply emphasizing different aspects of the new technology. Some of the proponents of these alternative formulations are guilty of that. But what they are really trying to do (some self-consciously) is construct an alternative philosophy of technology, emphasizing particularly the political aspects.

In what follows, I will try to articulate that philosophy in the course of showing that the debate between AT and these related technologies has been miscast as a debate over features of technology. Although I will examine each condition separately, my purpose is not to isolate them unwittingly but rather to reveal the political complex underlying each. I will be contrasting aspects of political philosophies, not features of technologies.

## A. Environmental Soundness vs. Ecotechnology

It is not simply a quirk in linguistic habits when AT proponents speak of environmental rather than ecological impact. The choice in phrasing reflects a specific political philosophy. Yet, even AT's commitment to environmental concerns is questionable. Environmental concerns are given lip service, but seldom is there an extended description of actual environmental impact in AT case studies. But let us assume environmental awareness in AT practices.

In coining the term "ecotechnology," [Murray] Bookchin[34] makes an important distinction between the environmental and the ecological, not as features of the technology but rather as philosophies. Environmentally, a technology is regarded as a relatively isolated device whose impact on the environment can be more or less precisely calculated. Ecologically, a technology is regarded as "functionally integrated with human communities as part of a shared biosphere of people and nonhuman life forms."[35] Bookchin reveals the important philosophical difference between these when he characterizes the concern of AT proponents over the impact of technology as

> . . . within the context of environmentalism which tends to reflect instrumentalist sensibility in which nature is viewed merely as a passive habitat, an agglomeration of external objects and forces, that must be made more serviceable for human use irrspective of what these uses may be.[36]

When environmental issues are discussed in the AT literature, they are couched in this instrumental framework and not in a broader ecological context, whose conscious goal is promoting the integrity of the biosphere.

Environmental soundness and ecological integrity are not two comparable features of technologies. Underlying each are different political philosophies. AT proponents, for the most part, do not challenge the existing political power structure except for advocating some degree of popular control over the technology. According to Bookchin:

> To speak of "Appropriate Technology". . . without *radically* challenging the political "technologies," the media "tools," and the bureaucratic "complexities" that have turned these concepts into elitist "art forms" is to completely betray their revolutionary promise as a challenge to the existing social structure.[37]

In other words, without an explicit alternative political philosophy AT offers little alternative beyond accommodation.

## B.  Labor Intensiveness vs. Liberatory Technology

While putting people to work is a noble undertaking, the labor intensity condition becomes problematic when AT is compared to liberatory technology, also developed by Bookchin.[38] A primary liberating function of technology is that it can free people from toil and drudgery. Bookchin bemoans the ineffectiveness of earlier revolutionary movements in their inability to alter conditions and structures of scarcity. Failures of the past might be avoided, he argues, as we enter a post-scarcity phase of history where technology is available to relieve people of having to slave for subsistence.

Some of Bookchin's liberatory technology examples are highly debatable; for example, controlled thermonuclear reactions for mining, and genetic improvements of food plants. It is unclear how truly liberatory these are, and I have other reservations about this analysis. Notwithstanding challenges that can be made to his liberatory technology philosophy, it seems clear that AT is not predicated on the same labor-technology relation.

For example, AT exhibits a myopic emphasis on manual labor rather than on the liberation potential of technology. Work is glorified as evidenced by this description of ten beggars employed through the use of AT:

> They are completely rehabilitated now. They are well-dressed; they are happy; and are now completely different people. . . . It just shows that if one has the imagination, almost anything can be done.[39]

Technology is cast in the role of rehabilitation, which translates as "put people to work." Unemployment, from this perspective, is taken as a consistently overriding factor in technological choice. But a technology freeing people of arduous tasks can be just as important as one creating jobs. After reading AT literature it is difficult to avoid the feeling that major labor-saving technologies are reserved for the First and not the Third World.

Further problems arise with the AT view of manual labor. For not only is there an emphasis on production, but even more narrowly there is a focus on the male productive functions of technology. Only the male aspects of technological development—innovation, design, construction, supply—are given attention. The other side of technology—daily operation, maintenance, use, care, responsibility—are ignored. An heroic image is fostered which finds little if any serious value in the nurturing functions. There is clearly a sexual division of labor between those features of technologies most commonly associated with males and those associated with females.

Devastating consequences, including the failure of many AT projects, result from the sexual division of technology in the AT movement. In the 1970s, windmills were sprouting up all over the northeastern part of the United States, including one atop a rehabilitated building in the New York City Loisada project. That was the exciting phase. Now few of these windmills are turning because, among other things, no one thought to maintain them. The dull, nurturing phase was bypassed. Likewise those technologies impacting primarily on women, such as reproduction, cooking, sanitation, and education, take a back seat to the gadgetry and engineering feats needed to build appropriate technologies.

Much of the critique just presented comes from [Arnold] Pacey's *The Culture of Technology*.[40] Yet, Pacey refuses to apply this critique to AT. I find nothing in AT practices to exonerate it from his charges.

It would appear that AT is not liberatory by design. Freeing people from work and addressing nurturing activities are not a central concern in the AT framework. So, labor intensity betrays something deeper about the AT movement than its concern to employ people. The AT movement has certainly been influenced by the environmental movement. Comparable influences, however, from the libertarian and feminist movements are not as evident or prominent.

## C. Small Scale vs. Indigenous Technologies

A convenient way to highlight the political bias underlying the small-scale condition is to introduce another variant of AT, intermediate technology. Although there are differences between appropriate and intermediate technologies, these do not need to concern us here. The important thing is that intermediate technology stands politically in marked contrast to indigenous technology.

Commonsensically, intermediate means between low and high. The lower rung of the ladder—cheap, primitive, indigenous technology—is contrasted with the higher rung—expensive, mass-produced, foreign-based technology. Intermediate technology, recognizing "the economic boundaries and limitations of poverty,"[41] presumably lies somewhere between these two extremes. It is allegedly a progressive step above traditional technologies, and a step below high technology in that it is "production by the masses," not mass production.

So, when AT advocates proclaim that small is beautiful, the smallness condition is generally thought not applicable to indigenous technologies, despite the fact that these indigenous technologies generally satisfy all of the conditions. The reason for this is that despite Schumacher and despite some direct AT disclaimers to the contrary, the AT movement, in the final analysis, is capitalist. Generally, appropriate technologists focus on questions of productivity and expanding market structures. Production of useful commodities for the market is positively valued. Accordingly, crafting religious artifacts, which might encourage community cohesion and discourage marketable production, does not constitute an AT activity.

The AT bias against indigenous technologies is nicely illustrated by the following example of grain storage silos in Africa:

> Many different types of traditional granary or silo exist, most of them built with mud walling. However, in some places there has been heavy loss of grain through the depradations of rats, insects, dampness, and mold, and this has contributed to food shortages and malnutrition. Initially, it was assumed that such inefficiency was an inevitable part of the traditional technology, which was dismissed as almost worthless.[42]

Because of the bias against traditional technologies the immediate action taken was to design concrete and metal alternatives to the indigenous ones. However, in this particular case AT innovations proved a failure, and attention was turned to the more nurturing task of suggesting "detailed improvements that would make maintenance easier"[43] on the traditional silos. Among AT practitioners this was a rare return to indigenous techniques.

Again, what is at stake here is not a choice between two kinds of technology, small-scale appropriate or indigenous technologies. Rather constrasting philosophies about indigenous people are at stake. Paternalism in the form of "knowing what is best for the natives" is readily apparent among AT practitioners. AT proponents emphasize learning and adopting techniques which replace or notably upgrade a community's technical capacity. But the reverse is hardly ever the case: learning from and adopting indigenous technologies. This is most evident in the area of medicine. Western medicine does not hold a monopoly over healing. We could learn a great deal from indigenous medical theories and practices. Yet, as with almost all appropriate technologies, the important thing is not what we can learn from the indigenous people but what we can teach them.

Small scale is not an innocent condition of AT. Small scale, when conceived principally in terms of the production of marketable goods, not only yields a bias against indigenous technologies; it also hides an antipathy toward the powers and abilities of the very people it claims to help.

## D.  Decentralization vs. Radical Technology

Of the related versions—ecotechnology, liberatory, and indigenous technology —radical technology is preferable. This is not because it emphasizes a superior feature of technologies. In fact, it is just the opposite. Radical technology is least likely to be construed as only a philosophy about technology. On the surface, it makes little sense to search for the radical features of technological things. Radical technology is preferable because it is first and foremost a political philosophy which encompasses the political aspects of ecotechnology, liberatory, and indigenous technology.

At this stage I need to counter a possible objection. By isolating the AT conditions I seem guilty of the very charge I lodged against the critics of AT. This claim is easily met by noting that, unlike the case with replies to other critics, AT proponents in this case do not have the option of appealing to the virtues of one condition in order to offset the criticized vices of another. For example, the ecotechnologist's criticism of AT, that it only considers environmental problems in isolation, is not countered by appeal to labor intensity or any of the other conditions. Moreover, radical technologists try to overcome the problem of pitting one form of domination against another by searching for the common roots of domination.

Although some attention is paid to the importance of political considerations in making technological choices, politics is regarded by AT proponents as secondary to the technology itself. Indeed, technology seems to be conceived as a substitute for politics.

> The choice of technology is the most important collective decision confronting any country. *It* is a choice that determines who works and who does not; that is, who gets income, new skills, self-reliance. *It* determines where work is done, whether concentrated in cities or more decentralized in smaller units; that is, *it* determines the kind of infrastructure required, and the whole quality of people's lives. *It* determines the ownership of industry; huge technologies are available only to the rich and powerful, whereas small technologies are tools in the hands of the poor.[44]

In ascribing these awesome powers to "it," McRobie's characterization of technological choice certainly has undertones of technological determinism: supply the Third World with the right kind of technology, and their lot will be improved. Form (engineering, technology) can be substituted for content (values, politics). Instead of the murky waters of values and politics people can turn to the relatively clear waters of engineering and technology. Seen in this light, it is not at all clear whether AT is an alternative to the technocracy esteemed within high technology circles; both appropriate technology and high technology advocates seem to be cut from the cloth of "technology pushers."

Radical technologies reject the technocratic approach, proposing that political choices of what type of society to live in, not the choice of a technology, is "the most important collective decision confronting any country."[45] Technological choice is seen as first and foremost a political choice. Technology does not simply appear on the scene as an exogenous circumstance necessitating a particular social choice.

> For the process of technological development is essentially social, and thus there is always a large measure of indeterminacy, of freedom, within it. Beyond the very real constraints of energy and matter exists a realm in which human thoughts and actions remain decisive. Therefore, technology does not necessitate. It merely consists of an evolving range of possibilities from which people choose.[46]

The preoccupation of AT proponents with the qualities of technique ignores the existence of political power, of who decides and for whose benefit.

While AT philosophy seeks to avoid direct engagement of the problem of political power, this does not mean that it is without a specific political stance. AT proponents may shun political debates and feign political neutrality, but as I have tried to show there is a political philosophy and agenda underlying the AT movement. In general, by refusing to challenge and confront the political *status quo,* the politics of AT is largely one of accommodation and reform.

Some AT advocates interpret the decentralization condition in the explicitly political sense of "amenable to mastery and maintenance by local people."[47] Nevertheless, closer examination of this interpreation shows that the idea of *control* by local people is entirely absent, and in AT practice local people seldom, if ever, take control of technological development. Decentralization in AT projects seems to be largely managerial and presupposes a technical hierarchy of AT innovators forming one class and AT implementers another. So, even where the political philosophy of AT is made relatively explicit, it no more actually challenges the political power structure than does high technology.

The aim of AT is to increase the number of technological choices, not necessarily to challenge any existing political structures.

> What the [AT] proponents are trying to do is to open up the spectrum and find solutions which are better suited to local conditions. The aim is generally not to replace the existing industrial system—but to promote technological innovation in the areas where it has been, until now, either weak or ineffective.[48]

AT differs from high technology more in terms of the range of technological choices presented than in the array of political options debated.

Reformist politics coupled with the failure to take into account or challenge the political/social context of technical application has resulted in some AT projects becoming instruments of class domination. For example, in India only wealthy farmers in one region are able to make use of a methane gas plant.[49] The two people able to afford a solar pump now monopolize the sale of previously free water in a Mauritanian village.[50] Small irrigation machines in Gao, Mali, enable farmers to sell enormous quantities of melons to Parisian tables, while food crops for local people are in short supply. (For further examples, see Lappé and Collins.[51])

An example of the failure to account for political context but with a different result is provided by [David] Elliott.[52] While working for an environmental group, he invented a hand-held radiation backscatter device which would measure the water content of a coal pile, resulting in more efficient utilization of coal. The device, however, proved highly unpopular among plant managers since their promotions depended on their coal-burning efficiency rating. They could easily improve this rating on their own by reducing the water level in the coal. An "objective" measuring device would spoil this political maneuvering. In this case, an AT device's introduction was resisted because it would diminish the political power of management.

Without explicit nonreformist politics, the AT movement will always remain indifferent to political outcomes, and this exacerbates the problem of technological hierarchy and dominance. As a condition of AT, "decentralization is reduced to a mere technical stratagem for concealing hierarchy and domination."[53]

## E. Advantages of Radical Technology

I do not want to leave the impression that the radical technology proposal only gets its strength from its critique of AT. Radical technology is a rich and powerful political philosophy in its own right. Although obviously I do not have the space to provide a full rendering of its theory and practices, an outline of its basic tenets can be given.

How does radical technology combine ecotechnology, liberatory, and indigenous technologies as political philosophies? There are two main foundation stones supporting the radical technology framework. The first consists of a theoretical critique of and concerted opposition to domination. Domination comes in many different forms. Economic, political, gender, and race forms are a few of the more commonly recognized varieties of domination. Radical technology develops an analysis of each of these and their interrelationships. Moreover, radical technologists seek to reveal the connection between these forms of human domination and domination of nature: "The attempt to dominate nature stems from the domination of human by human."[54] Any political philosophy choosing to ignore the domination of nature is doomed to foster the growth of domination structures rather than combatting them. So, radical technology combines ecotechnology and liberatory technology by providing a general critique of domination.

Empowerment, the second foundation stone of radical technology, means providing people with control over their institutions and practices. As we have seen AT practices can result in wresting technological control from people. The AT movement's major concession to popular control is a very weak interpretation of decentralization. In contrast empowerment is central to radical technology.

However, by promoting empowerment radical technologists do not thereby romanticize indigenous technologies and their accompanying political/social structures. Traditional practices can not only engender the domination of nature, they can also be forms of domination in themselves. Yet, my own hypothesis is that the traditional examples of domination count for little in the overall structure of domination. Nevertheless, the radical technologists should be aware of all forms of domination.

Radical technology (RT) is superior to appropriate technology because unlike the AT program the RT agenda is first and foremost an explicit political philosophy. Anything else evades the basic issues confronting any philosophy of technology. The issues are political and not technological in nature, where politics is defined as "any persistent pattern of human relationships that involve to a significant extent power, rule, or authority."[55] To see the issue of technological choice as not involving these relationships is to avoid seeing reality.

Moreover, RT is superior to AT in its political stance. Although AT proponents do make a habit of making their political beliefs explicit, they do have them. Overall the AT political philosophy is to advocate very moderate piecemeal reform of the existing power structures. Yet, it is just these power structures which are impediments to a just, egalitarian, and democratic development of technology.

## CONCLUSION

Contrary to Sardar and Rosser-Owen, AT is a coherent philosophy. It is not "a collection of a large number of ideas and concepts, many of them quite incoherent."[56] A coherent program can be found in the prevailing ideas and practices of the AT movement.

Yet, the problem, by this analysis, is not the development of a coherent AT program. Attention to each definitional strategy showed that the AT movement has failed to develop its political side. Under the guise of insisting on ostensive definitions, a technocratic impatience with political questions was uncovered. Listing evidentiary features turned out to be an inappropriate way of giving political criticism, and qualities of techniques were elevated as political ends in themselves.

Finally, political problems were found even with the methodologically adequate set of conditions of AT that I proposed. With its environmental soundness condition AT, unlike ecotechnology, treats environmental problems as subsidiary, as isolated ones for which technical fixes can be found. AT proposals refuse to confront the broader, political problem of dominating nature. By emphasizing the labor-intensive quality of technology, AT is not liberatory in the sense of freeing people from arduous tasks nor in the sense of developing nurturing aspects of technology. The small-scale condition is prone to an emphasis on marketable production and consequently devalues indigenous technologies and alternative economic forms and goals. The AT program as a whole exhibits a very muted and reformist sense of politics which neglects the political/social implications of its use.

Appropriate technology is often called alternative technology. To an extent, that claim is valid. High technologists and appropriate technologists deal with different technologies. However, it is delusional to think that AT offers very much of an alternative philosophy of technology—particularly when one factors in the political components of that philosophy. A truly alternative philosophy of technology requires the development of an ecological, liberatory, and thereby radical political foundation for technological choice. Philosophically, the first and most important goal is an adequate politics of technological choice.

## NOTES

1. Witold Rybczynski, *Paper Heroes* (Garden City, N.Y.: Doubleday, 1980), p. v.

2. Ziauddin Sardar and Dawud G. Rosser-Owen, "Science Policy and Developing Countries," in I. Spiegel-Rösing and D. Prive (eds.), *Science, Technology, and Society* (Beverly Hills, Calif.: Sage, 1977), p. 564.

3. E. F. Schumacher, *Small Is Beautiful* (New York: Harper & Row, 1973).

4. W. W. Ndongho and S. O. Anyang, "The Concept of 'Appropriate Technology'," *Monthly Review* 37, no. 9 (1981).

5. Nicholas Jequier, *Appropriate Technology: Problems and Promises* (Paris: Organization for Economic Cooperation and Development, 1976).

6. Frances Stewart, *Technology and Underdevelopment* (Boulder, Colo.: Westview Press, 1977), chapter 9.

7. In Tom De Wilde, "Some Social Criteria for Appropriate Technology," in R. Congdon (ed.), *Introduction to Appropriate Technology* (Emmaus, Pa.: Rodale Press, 1977), pp. 161–63.

8. Romesh K. Diwan and Dennis Livingston, *Alternative Development Strategies and Appropriate Technology* (New York: Pergamon Press, 1979).

9. J. van Brakel, "Appropriate Technology: Facts and Values," in P. Durbin (ed.), *Research in Philosophy & Technology* (Cambridge, Mass.: MIT Press, 1977), p. 392.

10. Rybczynski, *Paper Heroes* (see note 1), p. 20.

11. Quoted in Rybczynski, p. 19.

12. As quoted in Zolmay Khalilzad and Cheryl Bernard, "Energy: No Quick Fix for a Permanent Crisis," *The Bulletin of the Atomic Scientists* 36, no. 10 (1980): 15–20.

13. Langdon Winner, "Building a Better Mousetrap: Appropriate Technology as a Social Movement," in F. Long and A. Oleson (eds.), *Appropriate Technology and Social Values* (Cambridge, Mass.: Bollinger, 1980), p. 40.

14. Rashid Shaikh, "Commentary: Reflections of AT in India," *Science for the People* 13, no. 2 (1981): 26.

15. George McRobie, *Small Is Possible* (New York: Harper & Row, 1981), p. 36.

16. Leopold Kohn, "Appropriate Technology," in S. Kumar (ed.), *The Schumacher Lectures* (New York: Harper & Row, 1980), p. 190.

17. Schumacher, *Small Is Beautiful* (see note 3), p. 145.

18. Paul H. DeForest, "Technology Choice in the Context of Social Values—A Problem of Definition," in Long and Oleson, *Appropriate Technology and Social Values* (see note 13), p. 13.

19. Amory B. Lovins, *Soft Energy Paths* (New York: Harper & Row, 1977), p. 39.

20. Anil Date, "Understanding Appropriate Technology," in P. Ghosh (ed.), *Appropriate Technology in Third World Development* (Westport, Conn.: Greenwood Press, 1984).

21. McRobie, *Small Is Possible* (see note 15), p. 4.

22. Sarah Jackson, "Economically Appropriate Technologies for Developing Countries: A Survey," in P. Ghosh, *Appropriate Technology in Third World Development* (see note 20), p. 80.

23. Schumacher, *Small Is Beautiful* (see note 3).

24. See note 15.

25. David Dickson, *The Politics of Alternative Technology* (New York: Universe Books, 1974), p. 106.

26. McRobie, *Small Is Possible* (see note 15), p. 36.

27. Steward, *Technology and Underdevelopment* (see note 6), pp. 102–103.

28. Frances Moore Lappé and Joseph Collins, *Food First* (New York: Ballantine, 1978), p. 170.

29. Langdon Winner, "Building a Better Mousetrap: Appropriate Technology as a Social Movement," in Long and Oleson, *Appropriate Technology and Social Values* (see note 13).

30. Rybczynski, *Paper Heroes* (see note 1), p. 21.

31. Harvey Brooks, "A Critique of the Concept of Appropriate Technology," in Long and Oleson, *Appropriate Technology and Social Values* (see note 13).

32. Langdon Winner, "The Political Philosophy of Alternative Technology," in A. Teich, ed., *Technology and the Future* (New York: St. Martin's Press, 1986), p. 315.

33. Sardar and Rosser-Owen, "Science Policy and Developing Countries," in Spiegel-Rössing and Price, *Science, Technology, and Society* (see note 2).

34. Murray Bookchin, *Toward an Ecological Society* (Montreal: Black Rose Books, 1980).

35. Ibid., p. 109.

36. Ibid., p. 58.

37. Murray Bookchin, *The Ecology of Freedom* (Palo Alto, Calif.: Cheshire Books, 1982), p. 243.

38. Murray Bookchin, *Post-Scarcity Anarchism* (Palo Alto, Calif.: Ramparts Press, 1971).

39. Paul R. Lofthouse, "Industrial Liaison," in Congdon, *Introduction to Appropriate Technology* (see note 7), p. 156.

40. Arnold Pacey, *The Culture of Technology* (Oxford: Basil Blackwell, 1983).

41. Schumacher, *Small Is Beautiful* (see note 3), p. 179.

42. Pacey, *The Culture of Technology* (see note 40), p. 151.

43. Ibid.

44. McRobie, *Small Is Possible* (see note 15; emphasis mine—Ed.).

45. Peter Harper and Godfrey Boyle (eds.), *Radical Technology* (New York: Pantheon, 1976), p. 8.

46. Dabid Noble, *Forces of Production: A Social History of Industrial Automation* (New York: Knopf, 1984), p. xiii.

47. Shaikh, "Commentary: Reflections on AT in India" (see note 14).

48. Jequier, *Appropriate Technology: Problems and Promises* (see note 5).

49. Shaikh, "Commentary: Reflections on AT in India" (see note 14).

50. Jequier, *Appropriate Technology: Problems and Promises* (see note 5).

51. Lappé and Collins, *Food First* (see note 28).

52. David Elliott, "Energy Policy: Gut Reactions and Rationalists," unpublished manuscript, 1985.

53. Bookchin, *Toward an Ecological Society* (see note 34).

54. Ibid., pp. 66–67; William Leiss, *Domination of Nature* (Boston: Beacon, 1977).

55. Robert Dahl, *After the Revolution* (New Haven, Conn.: Yale University Press, 1970), p. 16.

56. Sardar and Rosser-Owen, "Science Policy and Developing Countries," in Spiegel-Rösing and Price, *Science, Technology, and Society* (see note 2), p. 564.

# Part Nine

# The Human Prospect

# Introduction

Many of the essays in this volume have focused on the enormous problems we face and may, collectively, present a rather depressing picture of the human prospect; but there remain grounds for optimism. None of the authors whom we have included predict an inevitably tragic outcome. Even Jacques Ellul's work is to be read as a cautionary tale about what may happen only *if* we do not change our ways of thinking. Perhaps the most telling criticism of studies such as *Limits to Growth* is that they do not make adequate provision in their models for political change. The future cannot be understood as a simple extrapolation of current trends. This is not to deny that events have causes, but to make the point that choices are causes. Choices matter.

Science, technology, politics, and human values are intimately related in the modern world. Neither science nor technology is autonomous in any strict sense. Both are in important respects social constructs, reflecting choices both in terms of what research gets funded and in the design and use of specific technologies. However, the structure of nature does impose limits. Political will cannot put a space shuttle into orbit against physical laws. And while we cannot fool nature, nature herself, as revealed through further discoveries, may surprise and frustrate traditional modes of thinking. As we have seen argued, scientific revolutions involve paradigm shifts in total world views. Facts and values, physics and metaphysics, are inextricably linked.

Although the distinction Jonathan Schell made in Part 1 between scientific and social revolutions is a generally useful one, we need to realize that scientific revolutions are not the only sources of surprise. Not even the most astute students of Soviet affairs could have foreseen the events of the last few years in Central and Eastern Europe. After forty-five years of military confrontation between the United States and the Soviet Union, the Cold War is over. In an astonishingly short period of time, the geopolitical structure of our world has been radically transformed. If we can now worry less about the thermonuclear destruction, perhaps we can begin to do more about saving the planet from the any other causes of environmental contamination.

Schell rightly observes that the uniquely modern predicament has its origins in scientific knowledge; however, as Barbara Ward argues in "The Final Constraints," it is our increasing scientific understanding of the fragility of the life-sustaining ecosystem that is causing us to rethink our technologically exploitative attitude toward nature. It is scientists who are blowing the whistle and warning us of the final constraints upon our military and industrial uses of technology. Although technology has been used to plunder the planet, it can also play an important role in monitoring the health of the biosphere, in disseminating scientific information, and in verifying international agreements.

Global problems require global solutions. Therefore, the biggest obstacle to "progress for a small planet" remains the increasingly outmoded concept of national sovereignty. Can we generate the political will to engage in international cooperation even when this requires the sharing of sovereignty? Ward does not underestimate the magnitude of the world's problems, but argues that "we have the duty to hope." Fear may initiate action, but only hope can sustain us in working for a harmonious world in which the world's goods are equitably distributed among all people.

Is this an overly romantic vision? Soviet President Mikhail Gorbachev thinks not. In his absolutely unprecedented speech before the General Assembly (excerpted here), he voices support for virtually all the central points that Ward has made. The new realities demand that we radically revise our traditional mode of thinking, and acting. Nuclear weapons reveal the absolute limits of military power. Force can no longer be an instrument of national policy. Only through international cooperation can we eliminate nuclear and chemical weapons, reduce conventional forces, protect the environment, reduce conflicts in the Third World, and move to eliminate global poverty. The survival of our planet requires both the de-ideologizing of international relations and a strengthened role for The United Nations.

Gorbachev affirms the Universal Declaration of Human Rights and claims that the Soviet Union is moving rapidly to restructure its laws to assure compliance with these principles. Glasnost (openness, democracy) and perestroika (restructuring) are linked in Gorbachev's thinking as he attempts to lead a cultural revolution. It is indicative of the rapidity of change that in 1988 Gorbachev was talking like a socialist and invoking the authority of Lenin. Today Gorbachev's prime concern is the speed with which the Soviets can shift to a free-market economy.

Arnold Pacey would find much to admire in Gorbachev's speech. Although Pacey's call for a cultural revolution is made from a Western perspective, it applies to us all in many respects: bureaucratic inertia and vested interests in perpetuating the status quo are the same whether the system be corporate capitalism or state socialism. In both kinds of society there is widespread alienation from the "system." But also in both there are "new realities" which demand fundamental change. We are, perhaps, in the midst of a cultural revolution.

In the Soviet Union the idea of openness is a new one. Pacey remains solidly within the Western liberal democratic tradition when he urges an extension of our democratic ideals to the economic and technological order. More genuine participatory democracy is necessary to restructure those authoritarian systems that control technology. But this alone is not sufficient. To develop and use technology in the interests of people requires a revolutionary consciousness; one that integrates our vision of technology, that recognizes that there is not value-free inquiry, and that sees beneath technical issues to the underlying normative questions.

Although Pacey uses the language of revolution, it is important to emphasize that it is a *cultural* revolution he advocates, in which education is to play a major role in reforming our institutions and the *practice* of technology. Rejecting any linear view that claims there is a single determinant of social change, Pacey likewise rejects the idea that there is any single solution to the world's problems. There is no one best way, small or big, low-tech, or high, Buddhist or materialist; no environmentalist blueprint or technocratic plan, whether capitalist or socialist. All these perspectives contribute to expanding our awareness, but we need to think about them, as Pacey says, "dialectically." Democracy, as he sees it, is opposed to any dogmatic ideology: it demands a respect for a plurality of ideas—but with a "stress on need-oriented values."

The prospects for a humane cultural revolution seem good, Pacey thinks. We should not underestimate the power of people at the grass-roots level to organize the effect changes in governmental policies. Nor, I think, should we disallow the power of imaginative leaders to effect significant change in direction. "We have the duty to hope." However, there is work to be done and informed choices to be made.

What will save us is not some one best way, but "openness, democracy, and diversity." Referring to the Elizabethan essayist Francis Bacon, Pacey concludes ". . . that knowledge and technique should be perfected and governed in love; and that the fruits of knowledge should be used, not for 'profit, or fame or power. . . but for the benefit and use of life.' "

## 31

# The Final Constraints

## Barbara Ward

If we were to depend solely upon the record of our political history, we could well doubt whether any widening of understanding and solidarity to a planetary level was even conceivable. Wars and rumors of wars, fierce tribal, communal, and national loyalties, fear and hatred of the stranger, pillage and destruction—are these not to an overwhelming extent the tragic determinants of human destiny? Why should we hope for anything different today? Surely we should need some quite new concept of reality, some revolutionary upheaval in past habits of thought, even to suppose that we could escape from the old "melancholy wheel" of ever repeated conquest, decline, defeat, and conquest again.

But it is at least just possible that such a concept is beginning to gather strength in our imagination. Still perhaps no more self-evident than human rights at the time of Magna Carta, or anticolonialism in 1775, yet it has begun to make its first impact on human thinking, with results which may over time prove to be as unpredictably radical and hopeful. This is the concept, made increasingly explicit by new methods and tools of scientific research, of the entirely inescapable physical interconnectedness of the planet which the human race must share if it is to survive.

Precisely those areas where immensity and distance have seemed to reign—climates, oceans, atmosphere—are beginning to be seen as profoundly interdependent systems in which the cumulative behavior of the inhabitants of the planet, the various activities of each seemingly separate community, can become

From *Progress for a Small Planet* by Barbara Ward, by permission of W. W. Norton & Company, Inc. Copyright © 1979 by the International Institute for Environment and Development.

the common destiny of all. This is not to say that earlier philosophers and sages have not sensed this underlying unity and spoken, with virtual unanimity, of a universal moral order—of human respect, of modesty and restraint, of Lao-tzu's "frugality" and "compassion." But these were dreams and visions. The radical change of the last century is the discovery that in literal, unchangeable scientific fact, interdependence is a reality and—what is an even more vital insight—that the connections which underlie it do not depend upon vast forces and changes alone. Rather, so delicate is much of the environment, so precarious are its balances, that human actions and interactions (especially now that they are armed with the forces of modern science) can have vast, potentially catastrophic and even irreversible effects. The whole picture is not clear. Systematic monitoring is only just beginning. Moreover, only a third of humanity has so far plunged into the full-scale technological organization of society which, in its first century or so, has been based upon a totally blind and exploitative reaction to the planet's own life-support systems. We are thus, in the most fundamental sense, at a hinge of history. If we can learn from the growing evidence of destructive risk in our present practices to determine that the next phase of development shall respect and sustain and even enhance the environment, we can look to a human future. If on the contrary we have learned so little that every present trend toward pollution, disruption, decay, and collapse is merely to be enhanced by its spread all round the planet, then the planet's own capacity to sustain such insults will be ineluctably exceeded. This fact cannot be too sharply underlined. All of the policies, all of the strategies outlined in [recent years], have been designed to lessen environmental strain, to increase reliance on safe and renewable sources of energy, to maintain a planet that is in balance between its needs, its demands, and its numbers. Taken separately, they may not appear to strike at the central issue of human survival. Cumulatively they do.

Our global atmosphere and regional climates are maintained by forces which would seem to be on a scale virtually to exclude human influence or intervention. The planet's mean temperature is maintained by the balance between incoming solar radiation that is absorbed and eventually reradiated back into space and that which is reflected. Within the general balance, the poles absorb less solar radiation than the tropics. The uneven absorption of solar radiation by the earth's surface causes the winds to develop, and this vast continuous interchange, complicated by the effects of the earth's spinning on its axis, gives us the specific climates of particular regions, all entirely integrated into the total system and thus, one might guess, on too vast a scale to be affected save very locally by the pygmy acts of man.

But the balance is not, over geological time, at all stable. Evolution went forward together with a changing atmosphere and changing temperatures. For much of its existence, the planet had no ice caps at all and an atmosphere lacking free oxygen. For the last two million years, there has been a succession of prolonged glacial epochs, or ice ages. We are recovering from the last ice age, eight to ten thousand years ago, which at its peak brought glaciers to Missouri. The whole climatic system may be vast, but it is influenced by many physical factors—among them, the carbon dioxide and dust concentration in the atmosphere, the cloud cover, and the earth's reflectivity, or "albedo." The largest, stablest seesaw in the world can be budged by shifting weight a few inches at one of its edges. Similarly, human intervention within a complex climatic system, if it takes place, as it were, at the edge of the planetary balance, might have catastrophic effects—a cooling down to another ice age, a heating up which could partially melt the ice caps and swamp lower-lying lands as the sea level rises. Some meteorologists put the potentially catastrophic average annual temperature change at no more than 3 degrees centigrade either way.

The difficulty at present is that although we know that changes *are* being brought about by human activities—for instance, the explosive growth in our use of energy in the last two centuries—it is much more difficult to be certain of the effects. Burning fossil fuels and cutting down forests for firewood has the effect of putting more carbon dioxide into the atmosphere, since these processes release the carbon locked up within the fossil fuel and within the wood. The concentration of carbon dioxide in the atmosphere has gone up by 12 percent since 1860, and of that, 5 percent was added in the last two decades. This trend will continue as more forests are cleared and fossil-fuel consumption goes on growing. And what is the effect? Here the debate begins. The increased carbon dioxide concentration helps a general warming-up process, since it absorbs some of the heat given off by sun-warmed lands and oceans which would otherwise be lost into space. To this indirect warming effect should be added thermal pollution, the heat produced by burning fossil fuels and uranium, since all the fuels we consume end up as waste heat in the atmosphere.

But this warming up is partially offset by the effect of other human activities—for instance, particle pollution by such substances as the sulphates massively released in the burning of fossil fuels. However, since these substances are linked to cancer and respiratory disease, most efforts at conservation are now designed to prevent them from escaping from their source—the power plant, factory, or automobile engine—and no one is likely to advocate their release in order to offset possible warming up of the planet, especially when one remembers that some particle pollution can itself contribute to the warming-up process instead of compensating for it. In short, the effect of particulate matter on the temperature of the atmosphere is variable and unpredictable, and it must be offset by placement of the maximum emphasis on conservation and on a steady shift to the renewable energy resources—sun, wind, falling water—which involve no thermal, carbon dioxide, or particulate pollution. Massive reafforestation to provide fuel for the poor and to protect fragile soils will also help to reabsorb some of the carbon lost through deforestation. Fuel conservation reduces both carbon dioxide and thermal pollution in that less fuel is used to do the same task. And tapping renewable energy sources leaves nature's own climatic system to operate without destabilizing human encroachment.

The argument is only reinforced by the degree to which, in spite of our massive increases in scientific understanding of atmospheric phenomena, we still do not understand fully the incredible complexities and interactions within all the biosphere's natural systems. Only recently have we learned of the role of the ocean's phytoplankton and the plant's processes of photosynthesis in building up the atmospheric concentration of oxygen. The release of oxygen allowed the build-up of the ozone layer (ozone being a form of oxygen), which alone protects organic life from the sun's potentially lethal ultraviolet radiation. Recently, two classes of man-made pollutants have been found to react with the ozone layer, decreasing its protective effect—nitrogen oxides, coming mainly from fleets of supersonic aircraft, massive increases in the use of nitrogen fertilizer, and the combustion of fossil fuels; and chlorofluorocarbons, used as refrigerants and as propellants for aerosol sprays. Both have the capacity to float up through the various layers of the atmosphere and attack the ozone. Yet even a 10 percent reduction of ozone content could increase the incidence of skin cancer by anything from 7 to 50 percent. Thus at the global level we rediscover the effects of ignorance, the chemical risks, which we have already seen at work within domestic societies.

Action at the national level has begun. The Swedish government has banned the manufacture and import of virtually all aerosols containing chlorofluorocarbons. The United States federal government has severely restricted their use. Several major manufactures of aerosol sprays have voluntarily switched to alternative propellants. But the daunting question is whether anything like a global agreement on nonuse can be achieved before dangerous ozone reduction has occurred.

As with the atmosphere, so with the oceans—on the face of it, they are so vast, so all-embracing, so seemingly independent of minute human interventions, that it is difficult for the imagination to see them as a single, interconnected natural system, vulnerable enough in its essential function of supporting life to be tampered with and even put at risk. Organic life evolved under the protection of the oceans; plants and animals moved from sea to rock to carry the evolution of organic life to the whole globe. The 70 percent of the earth's surface that remains the water's share, receives all the earth's detritus, breaks it down so its components are recycled, operates with the sun the giant purifying cycle of water desalination which returns the runoff of springs, lakes, and rivers in the form of rain for the whole world's harvests. And all the while it is moderating extreme temperatures—cooling the tropics, bringing warmer currents to chilly regions, and thus ensuring the habitability of a large part of the earth's surface. How could any system on such a scale be influenced by what must surely seem to be, in comparison, the all but marginal activities of human beings?

But once again, the growing insights of scientific research give us far more than visions of majesty and power. Vast the oceans may be, but like the atmosphere and climates, they contain critical points of vulnerability and fragility.

The areas under greatest pressure from our activities are precisely those where such pressure can do most damage. Traditional fishing grounds no longer provide fish for all who want it. The world's fish catch tripled between 1950 and 1970, reaching an annual total of seventy million tons. It then fell sharply in the early seventies, and in 1974 and 1975 could not exceed the 1970 figure despite expanded fleets and greatly intensified efforts to catch the fish. Depleted fish stocks have led to international conflicts such as the British-Icelandic "cod wars" and to governmental restrictions on both domestic and foreign fishing fleets in newly defined teritorial waters. This does not mean that the oceans' full capacity to produce food has been reached or even approached. Indeed, we fish only for certain choice species, with very considerable wastage in getting even these from the boat to the customer. But it does mean that traditional attitudes toward unrestricted fishing are having to be completely rethought. Take another example. At the beginning of the 1970s, less than 20 percent of the world's oil drilling was done out at sea. By the 1980s, the figure may have increased to over 50 percent, with some of the drilling in polar regions, where oil spills could have lasting, unpredictable, and almost certainly risky consequences. And while oil drilling increases, the scale of carriers used round the world to transport the oil goes up comparably. As late as 1948, no oil tanker was larger than 29,000 tons. Now we find monsters of over half a million tons, and even, on some demented drawing board, an 800,000-ton dinosaur. Yet by all but universal agreement, the training of crews and the handling of equipment are inadequate. The arrangements for insurance and salvage are on a ludicrously meager scale. A single disaster like that of the *Amoco Cadiz*—due, it seems, to poor navigation, inadequate countermeasures, and even mid-disaster squabbling over salvage—can let loose 200,000 tons of oil on an unoffending coast. Yet on some of the busiest tanker lanes in the world the vessels' masters ignore lane regulations and sail perilously close to rocky shores—as with the *Amoco Cadiz*. Even the regulations that have been adopted by the relevant world body—the Intergovernmental Maritime Consultative Organization—are usually evaded by delays in signing conventions. In addition, ship operators can register their vessels under "flags of convenience," such as those of Panama and Liberia, and thus gain from cheaper labor rates, lower construction and repair standards, and a far slacker imposition of fines and penalties for noncompliance with regulations.

And oil tankers present only one of the major risks in sea-borne trade. Add ships with nuclear wastes, add the new effluents of a planet industrialized not by a third of its people but by all of them, add the new prospects of deep-sea mining with (a dream still no doubt, but creeping into the blueprints) nuclear power stations *in situ,* processing minerals in mid-ocean, add in short the incorporation of the ocean systems into full technological activity of every kind, and is it really irrational to fear that even the oceans' productivity might suffer? The most productive ocean areas are the continental shelves adjoining the land masses. Most of the marine catch comes from these. And because of their shallowness and their proximity to land they receive the worst of technological society's water-borne wastes. Nor can any state, with Canute-like pretensions of sovereignty, bid other people's pollutions keep away. As the "moving waters" go to their work around the planet, here at least unity is incontestable. We have no choice but to share.

But how can we do so? Do not the sheer scale and immensity of atmosphere and ocean make it all but inconceivable that human beings should keep any sort of check upon the consequences of their own innumerable activities? It is one thing to give voice to the rhetoric of interdependence. But what hope is there of providing the concept with force and content sufficient for it to begin its fundamental task—that of changing the climate of our imagination, of clarifying our perception of the interconnections and interactions in our single planetary home?

But here all need not be darkness and discouragement. In the last two decades, the conquest of space and the infinite elaboration of instruments for tracing terrestrial and extraterrestrial movements—of air, of water, of heat, of changing tree cover, of areas of increasing desiccation (not to speak of the precise location of possible oil-bearing strata deep in the oceans or of surreptitious tankers emptying their bilges in contravention of agreed conventions)—all these new satellites and monitors have come just in time to give mankind a new and accurate picture of planetary events and changes which even thirty years ago were wholly beyond human assessment and comprehension. Whatever the would-be secrecy of certain societies and systems, the physical behavior of human beings is becoming increasingly open to view. So are the physical underpinnings of all their activities. People are now less likely to create, say, irreversible pollutions or desiccations or erosions by pure inadvertence. They have a clearer picture of how human activity affects the biosphere, even if there remain particular uncertainties, as with, for instance, the effect of inadequately tested chemicals still brought onto the market every year.

And however slowly and unwillingly, people do seem to be leaning away from some of the old arrogant sovereign habits of the past and realizing, marginally and cautiously, that the old ways no longer work. In all this effort to create what one can perhaps call a planetary awareness, the United Nations Environment Program (UNEP), working closely with other organizations of the United Nations—the World Meteorological Office (WMO), the Food and Agriculture Organization, the World Health Organization, the regional commissions—is taking the lead in what must be, of very necessity, the first stage in some sort of world control of conservation, antipollution activities, and sane resource management. Its Global Environmental Monitoring System (GEMS) covers many of the relevant fields. On land, it coordinates and links research and monitoring, usually in collaboration with local research stations, on such critical matters as soil cover, inroads on tropical forests, the spread of deserts. In the oceans, it coordinates the monitoring of the entry of effluents and poisons into the marine environment, with special emphasis on the steadily growing emissions of petroleum hydrocarbons from ships, from land-based installations, from the exhausts of the world's rising fleet of motor vehicles. In the air, data on chemical content, turbidity, and the amount of carbon dioxide are being collected, in collaboration with WMO, and regularly published. In addition, the movements of pollution in the air—including such rising dangers as acid rain—are being studied in GEMS on a regional basis (where the gravest impacts are most likely to occur). The Economic Commission for Europe has become an early partner in this extension of UNEP's work with WMO, and research centers in Norway and the Soviet Union are also partners in the venture.

Acquiring the information is the first step. The next is to ensure that governments and other organizations are fully informed. An International Referral System for sources of environmental information has been set up by UNEP, and with it works an International Registry of Potentially Toxic Chemicals. Since a great majority of the developing countries still lack their own monitoring and information services, these UNEP systems have special significance for the Third World, and their establishment is perhaps one more hopeful signal that not all the errors of the early industrializing powers need be repeated by those who are coming after them.

Accurate information, widespread dissemination—neither would have been conceivable even two decades ago. But the biggest hurdle remains—the problem of obtaining action, a readiness by means of internationally shared sovereignty, expressed in formal conventions, to eliminate the dangers and undertake the positive activity, the "spring cleaning" of so much that is damaged and toxic in our small and vulnerable world. One should not for a moment underestimate the importance of monitoring and knowledge. They are essential for the formulation of effective policies. Equally important are the mechanisms for ensuring that the policies are followed. It is simply because satellites and other surveillance systems can be developed to trace delinquent tankers that controls over illegal oil spills can now be envisaged. It is because aerial reconnaissance and the various forms of radar already exist that it can make sense to suggest that in narrow waters, ships, like aircraft approaching airports, should be strictly kept to lanes established for them by a local authority. Yet although the new scientific instruments make effective cooperation possible, they do not ensure it. For that, there must be a new commitment to the whole concept of joint constructive work at the planetary level.

And here just possibly we may find that we have reached the last and most fateful of all barriers to survival. We know—although we cannot imaginatively grasp the fact—that each year we spend $400 billion on the means of destroying one another. Our planet—and we ourselves—can be blasted back to little more than the bare and crumbling rock from which, over evolutionary aeons, we emerged. Indeed, so ludicrous is the scale of our "overkill" that we have at our disposal the equivalent of several tons of TNT for every person on the planet. But we have hardly the barest counterimage of working together to build up our capacities for coexistence, to create that community of feeling which can spring from common goals and common efforts, that dedication that can grow from working together with care and patience, that experience at every level of shared effort—building the village, the town, the shrine, the temple, the city, creating the common symbols and places and vistas of order and dignity—in which all can take pride and all can love.

If one looks about, almost with depair, at the poised missiles and bomber fleets, one wonders where in all the ludicrous apparatus of fear and hatred one unifying counteraim of wisdom and loyalty can be found. Yet perhaps that wisdom, beginning in fear, can precisely be the realization that in a shared biosphere, no one will escape nuclear destruction, and that loyalty can be built, from however small a beginning, from a shared effort to keep that biosphere in a life-creating, life-enhancing, and life-preserving state. A fragile hope? The first microorganism must have seemed minute enough in the vast wash of the primitive oceans. Yet it had within it the seed of life. Let us at least be bold enough to hope and, where we can, begin to act.

And there is one further reason for moving our angle of vision from the sheer immensity of our environmental interdependence on to specific instances of particular acts and functions in particular places. Again and again in human history, it is the concrete example, the flash of individual insight, the last stroke of the brush on the masterpiece, that has brought life, new light, and new understanding into existence. Are there anywhere in our present experience of our geophysical interdependence those single instances of risk and opportunity which may suddenly have the power to precipitate human imagination into a new level of awareness, bringing with it entirely new reserves of courage and readiness to act? The oceans are, we know, all finally enclosed seas, all without exits for man's wastes and pollutions. They are therefore a complete paradigm of an interdependence we cannot evade or deny. But the whole system is on too large a scale for the flash of vision and insight we need to experience. Can we work to a smaller but still relevant scale? Are there more exact, more comprehensive parables among our actions waiting to be interpreted? Have we anywhere a picture vivid and compelling enough to make us, not in cliché but in reality, see with new eyes?

Once again it is perhaps in one part of the work of UNEP that such an instance can be found. From its earliest days of preparation, its directors have been aware that some of the world's most abused natural systems are to be found among the regional seas and enclosed waters of the planet. The Mediterranean, the Caribbean, the Gulf of Guinea, the Caspian, Lake Baikal, the Great Lakes—all are under pressure, and the kinds of pressure are once again just the sort of encroachments which world-wide industrialization for all the planet's peoples might inflict on the ultimate enclosed water—the whole oceanic system. We are, as it were, seeing through the wrong end of the telescope the vision of disorder and breakdown that might become global in scale if technological society at the same time tripled its numbers, its industrialization, its chemical and power installations, and multiplied by as much again the effluents discarded into rivers, lakes, and oceans—and left everything else unchanged. Of the various seas for which UNEP is now preparing action plans for monitoring and control, we can take the Mediterranean, because the processes of degeneration have gone far, because it in almost perfect geographical fashion illustrates the planet's North/South split, and because—in March 1978—a setback occurred to these plans of absolutely critical importance to our whole understanding of the world's dilemmas in conservation and development.

First, then, the degree of actual and potential pressure—population on the coast, already at 100 million, is likely to double in the next twenty years. But in addition, 100 million tourists crowd in every year, and their number will rise, bringing with it, on present showing, even more wall-to-wall hotels rounding every bay, with totally inadequate sanitary arrangements. And 120 coastal cities already empty their sewage into the sea, virtually without treatment. On the Northern side, industrialization has come like an inundation in the last two decades, with thousands of factories drawn to the shores to take advantage of no-cost dumping of waste products. Oil pollution as the tankers ply their way from Suez is reckoned to be about 300,000 tons a year, and land-based installations are adding at least 130,000 tons of hydrocarbon wastes annually. Add all this together—municipal sewage, industrial effluents, oil pollution—and it is not surprising to learn that the small bacteria whose task it is to decompose all the filth and put it harmlessly back into the food chains are already being threatened in some areas by lack of enough oxygen for the tasks of decomposition (i.e., enough oxygen to satisfy the so-called biochemical oxygen demand, or BOD). This danger signal is already flashing at a time when the Southern states have comparatively few settlements and industries on their shores. Without radical redirection of policy, the Mediterranean could be no more than a few years away from being a place from which a fishing industry worth $700 million per year will have vanished, as well as tourists who will no longer tolerate oily beaches and the risks of hepatitis or even cholera along with their Greek temples and bathing resorts.

The response of UNEP has been rapid. By 1975, it had persuaded most of the coastal nations (even those in a state of some degree of hostility toward one another) to come together and to agree that their common problems required common action—systematic monitoring (to take place in what soon grew to be eighty research centers in fifteen different countries) and plans to share information about development and environmental policies at the national level. At a conference the following year, two protocols were agreed upon—one to restrict dumping of toxic pollutants from ships, the other to make joint action possible in emergencies. The essential preliminaries—accurate knowledge, its dissemination—were under way.

But in 1978 came the highly significant setback, when the coastal nations failed to agree on limiting land-based pollution. Three-quarters of the pollution in the Mediterranean is land-based, and the bulk of it comes from Italy, France, and Spain. The Southern states found themselves being asked to accept stringent and expensive pollution controls when they were not responsible for most of the existing pollution and their part of the Mediterranean was relatively clean. The attempt to secure agreed-upon uniform standards broke down. Monitoring would continue. The states would meet in eighteen months. But the most important part of the action plan had proved unacceptable.

And here surely in straightforward down-to-earth reality we have the basic dilemma of any joint effort to see in the threatened world environment a cause of shared concern and a reason for acting together in time to enjoy now and to leave to future generations a beautiful and inhabitable planet. The dilemma is that three-quarters of mankind, having had little or nothing to do with the various threats and degradations, can now see no reason for helping to pay to clean up a natural environment they did not themselves do much to pollute. Yet the rich on the whole have as little sense that the bill is really theirs. But let us suppose that at the Mediterranean consultations, the funds for development had been easily and obviously available for installing treatment plants and effluent controls. Would there have been much deadlock about safe treatment and common standards? It is surely significant that in the more cooperative atmosphere of the Persian-Arabian Gulf, a six million dollar fund has already been set up not only for joint monitoring of the effects of coastal installations but for more rational management of development, with, for example, the optimum siting of settlements and industry and the introduction of modern sewage and effluent-treatment systems. The very nations for whom the expenditure of $400 billion a year on arms is a matter of course apparently cannot agree to a joint Mediterranean fund financed mainly by the developed nations. We can apparently envisage subsidized weapons systems for the poorer nations—indeed, we compete to supply them. But sewage-treatment plants, effluent-control technology, ensuring marine integrity—these apparently lie beyond our mental grasp. The contrast is all the more devastating in that UNEP's estimate for the total cost of controlling land-based pollution—the major expense in cleaning up the Mediterranean—is $10 billion, little more than a week's expenditure on world armaments.

But the final irony is that accepted responsibility, common consultation, and joint work are the only sure routes away from ultimate conflict. Each constructive joint scheme that is made to function is a step away from catastrophe. Cleaning the Mediterranean and the other regional seas, accepting a regime for the oceans with common environmental laws in the new exclusive economic zones and a joint authority for the remaining seabed, a worldwatch for the forests and a reversal of the world's trend to deforestation, UNEP's already articulated plan to hold back the encroachment of the deserts, the development of Asia's vast water resources, a world tax system for providing capital for investment in basic human needs, the siting and building of communities on a human scale—how vast the prospects of peaceful construction could become, from farm to federation, from village to metropolis, if human faith and loyalty could grow to match the irreversible geophysical unity of our shared and single planet. We cannot change its nature. It envelops us, provides for us, sustains us. Our only choice is to preserve it in cooperative ventures or to end it and ourselves in a common ruin.

These are not clichés of any kind of political rhetoric. We can surely see that there is really only one central factor of doubt in our present debates. We are not irretrievably threatened by what are usually thought of as the most implacable constraints. Any lack of resources can be countered by conservation and care, while a sane use of science's immeasurable virtuosity can vastly increase useful materials and maintain the renewable resources that already exist. Energy is not a problem, given the breathing space for invention provided by the careful use of the still remaining reserves of fossil fuels and the promise of steady availability of energy derived directly or indirectly from the sun. Even the most widely canvassed risk—excessive population—has already been shown to be manageable, provided health, literacy, jobs, and hope are open to all the world's peoples.

No, the only fundamentally unsolved problem in this unsteady interregnum between imperial ages which may be dying and a planetary society which struggles to be born is whether the rich and fortunate are imaginative enough and the resentful and underpriviledged poor patient enough to begin to establish a true foundation of better sharing, fuller cooperation, and joint planetary work. The significance of the Mediterranean setback is quite simply that it underlines how little those nations with the genuine power to act—for conservation, against pollution, for the shared commons—are yet ready to confront the cost, minimal though it is compared with the gargantuan wastes of war. In short, no problem is insoluble in the creating of a balanced and conserving planet save humanity itself. Can it reach in time the vision of joint survival? Can its inescapable physical interpendence—the chief new insight of our century—induce that vision? We do not know. We have the duty to hope.

# 32

# The Problem of Mankind's Survival

## Mikhail S. Gorbachev

### THE LIMITS OF POWER

The world in which we live today is radically different from what it was at the beginning or even in the middle of this century. And it continues to change as do all its components.

The advent of nuclear weapons was just another tragic reminder of the fundamental nature of that change. A material symbol and expression of absolute military power, nuclear weapons at the same time revealed the absolute limits of that power.

The problem of mankind's survival and self-preservation came to the fore . . . .

It is obvious, for instance, that the use or threat of force no longer can or must be an instrument of foreign policy. This applies above all to nuclear arms, but that is not the only thing that matters. All of us, and primarily the stronger of us, must exercise self-restraint and totally rule out any outward-oriented use of force.

That is the first and the most important component of a nonviolent world as an ideal which we proclaimed together with India in the Delhi Declaration and which we invite [everyone] to follow . . . .

The new phase also requires de-ideologizing relations among states. We are not abandoning our convictions, our philosophy or traditions, nor do we urge anyone to abandon theirs.

But neither do we have any intention to be hemmed in by our values.

That would result in intellectual impoverishment, for it would mean rejecting a powerful source of development—the exchange of everything original that each nation has independently created.

In the course of such exchange, let everyone show the advantages of their social system, way of life, or values—and not just by words or propaganda, but by real deeds.

That would be a fair rivalry of ideologies. But it should not be extended to relations among states.

## ROMANTIC? NO, REALISTIC

We are, of course, far from claiming to be in possession of the ultimate truth. But, on the basis of a thorough analysis of the past and newly emerging realities, we have concluded that it is on those lines that we should jointly seek the way leading to the supremacy of the universal human idea over the endless multitude of centrifugal forces, the way to preserve the vitality of this civilization, possibly the only one in the entire universe.

Could this view be a little too romantic? Are we not overestimating the potential and the maturity of the world's social consciousness? We have heard such doubts and such questions both in our country and from some of our Western partners.

I am convinced that we are not floating above reality.

We regard prospects for the near and more distant future quite optimistically.

Just look at the changes in the [Soviet Union's] relations with the United States. Little by little, mutual understanding has started to develop and elements of trust have emerged, without which it is very hard to make headway in politics.

In Europe, these elements are even more numerous. The Helsinki process is a great process.

## NEW VIGOR AT THE U.N.

I am convinced that our time and the realities of today's world call for internationalizing dialogue and the negotiating process.

This is the main, the most general conclusion that we have come to in studying global trends that have been gaining momentum in recent years, and in participating in world politics.

In this specific historical situation we face the question of a new role for the United Nations.

We feel that states must to some extent review their attitude to the United Nations, this unique instrument without which world politics would be inconceivable today.

The recent reinvigoration of its peacemaking role has again demonstrated the United Nations' ability to assist its members in coping with the daunting challenges of our time and working to humanize their relations . . . .

External debt is one of the gravest problems. Let us not forget that in the age of colonialism the developing world, at the cost of countless losses and sacrifices, financed the prosperity of a large portion of the world community. The time has come to make up for the losses that accompanied its historic and tragic contribution to global material progress.

We are convinced that here, too, internationalizing our approach shows a way out.

Looking at things realistically, one has to admit that the accumulated debt cannot be repaid or recovered on the original terms.

## THE BURDEN OF WORLD DEBT

The Soviet Union is prepared to institute a lengthy moratorium of up to 100 years on debt servicing by the least developed countries, and in quite a few cases to write off the debt altogether.

As regards other developing countries, we invite all to consider the following:

- Limiting their official debt servicing payments depending on the economic performance of each of them or granting them a long period of deferral in the repayment of a major portion of their debt.

- Supporting the appeal of the United Nations Conference on Trade and Development for reducing debts owed to commercial banks.

- Guaranteeing government support for market arrangements to assist in Third World debt settlement, including the formation of a specialized international agency that would repurchase debts at a discount.

The Soviet Union favors a substantive discussion of ways to settle the debt crisis at multilateral forums, including consultations under the auspices of the United Nations among heads of government of debtor and creditor countries.

International economic security is inconceivable unless related not only to disarmament but also to the elimination of the threat to the world's environment. In a number of regions, the state of the environment is simply frightening . . . .

Let us also think about setting up within the framework of the United Nations a center for emergency environmental assistance. Its function would be promptly to send international groups of experts to areas with badly deteriorating environment.

The Soviet Union is also ready to cooperate in establishing an international space laboratory or manned orbital station designed exclusively for monitoring the state of the environment.

In the general area of space exploration, the outlines of a future space industry are becoming increasingly clear.

The position of the Soviet Union is well known: activities in outer space must rule out the appearance of weapons there. Here again, there has to be a legal base. The groundwork for it—the provisions of the 1967 treaty and other agreements—is already in place . . . .

We have put forward our proposal to establish it on more than one occasion. We are prepared to incorporate within its system our Krasnoyarsk radar station. A decision has already been taken to place that radar under the authority of the U.S.S.R. Academy of Sciences.

Soviet scientists are prepared to receive their foreign colleagues and discuss with them ways of converting it into an international center for peaceful cooperation by dismantling and refitting certain units and structures, and to provide additional equipment.

The entire system could function under the auspices of the United Nations.

The whole world welcomes the efforts of this organization, its Secretary General, and his representatives in untying knots of regional problems.

Allow me to elaborate on this.

Paraphrasing the words of the English poet [John Donne whom] Hemingway took as an epigraph to his famous novel, I will say this: The bell of every regional conflict tolls for all of us.

This is particularly true, since those conflicts are taking place in the Third World, which already faces many ills and problems of such magnitude that is has to be a matter of concern to us all.

The year 1988 has brought a glimmer of hope in this area of our common concerns as well. This has been felt in almost all regional crises. On some of them, there has been movement. We welcome it and we did what we could to contribute to it . . . .

I would like to join the voice of my country in the expressions of high appreciation of the significance of the Universal Declaration of Human Rights adopted on December 10, 1948.

Today, this document retains its significance. It, too, reflects the universal nature of the goals and objectives of the United Nations.

The most fitting way for a state to observe this anniversary of the declaration is to improve its domestic conditions for respecting and protecting the rights of its own citizens.

Before I inform you on what specifically we have undertaken recently in this respect I would like to say the following.

Our country is going through a period of truly revolutionary uplifting.

The process of perestroika is gaining momentum. We began with the formulation of the theoretical concept of perestroika. We had to evaluate the nature and the magnitude of problems, to understand the lessons of the past and express that in the form of political conclusions and programs. This was done.

Theoretical work, a reassessment of what is happening, the finalization, enrichment, and readjustment of political positions have not been completed. They are continuing.

But it was essential to begin with an overall concept, which, as now confirmed by the experience of these past years, has generally proved to be correct and which has no alternative.

For our society to participate in efforts to implement the plans of perestroika, it had to be democratized in practice. Under the sign of democratization, perestoika has now spread to politics, the economy, intellectual life, and ideology.

## ECONOMIC CHANGES AT HOME

We have initiated a radical economic reform. We have gained experience. At the start of next year the entire national economy will be redirected to new forms and methods of operation. This also means profoundly reorganizing relations of production and releasing the tremendous potential inherent in socialist property.

Undertaking such bold revolutionary transformations, we realized that there would be mistakes, and also opposition, that new approaches would generate new problems. We also foresaw the possibility of slowdowns in some areas.

But the guarantee that the overall process of perestroika will steadily move forward and gain strength lies in a profound democratic reform of the entire system of power and administration.

With the recent decisions by the Supreme Soviet on amendments to the Constitution and the adoption of the Law on Elections, we have completed the first stage of the process of political reform.

Without pausing, we have begun the second stage of this process with the main task of improving the relationship between the center and the republics, harmonizing interethnic relations on the principles of Leninist internationalism that we inherited from the Great Revolution, and at the same time reorganizing the local system of Soviet power.

A great deal of work lies ahead. Major tasks will have to be dealt with concurrently.

We are full of confidence. We have a theory and a policy, and also the vanguard force of perestoika—the party, which also is restructuring itself in accordance with new tasks and fundamental changes in society as a whole.

What is most important is that all our peoples and all generations of citizens of our great country support perestroika.

## BUILDING BY REBUILDING

We have become deeply involved in building a socialist state based on the rule of law.

Work on a series of new laws has been completed or is nearing completion.

Many of them will enter into force as early as in 1989, and we expect them to meet the highest standards from the standpoint of ensuring the rights of the individual.

Soviet democracy will be placed on a solid normative base. I am referring, in particular to laws on the freedom of conscience, glasnost, public associations and organizations, and many others.

In places of confinement there are no persons convicted for their political or religious beliefs.

Additional guarantees are to be included in the new draft laws that rule out any form of persecution on those grounds.

Naturally this does not apply to those who committed actual criminal offenses or state crimes such as espionage, sabotage, terrorism, etc., whatever their political or ideological beliefs.

Draft amendments to the penal code have been prepared and are awaiting their turn. Among the articles being revised are those related to capital punishment.

The problem of exit from and entry to our country, including the question of leaving it for family reunification, is being dealt with in a humane spirit.

## HELSINKI AND THE HAGUE

As you know, one of the reasons for refusal to leave is a person's knowledge of secrets. Strictly warranted time limitations on the secrecy rule will now be applied. Every person seeking employment at certain agencies or enterprises will be informed of this rule. In case of disputes, there is a right of appeal under the law.

This removes from the agenda the problem of the so-called "refuseniks."

We intend to expand the Soviet Union's participation in the United Nations and Conference of Security and Cooperation in Europe human rights monitoring arrangements. We believe that the jurisdiction of the International Court of Justice at the Hague as regards the interpretation and implementation of agreements on human rights should be binding on all states.

We regard as part of the Helsinki process the cessation of jamming of all foreign radio broadcasts beamed at the Soviet Union.

Overall, this is our credo. Political problems must be solved only by political means; human problems, only in a humane way.

## REDUCTIONS IN ARMED FORCES

Now let me turn to the main issue—disarmament, without which none of the problems of the coming century can be solved . . . .

Today, I can report to you that the Soviet Union has taken a decision to reduce its armed forces.

Within the next two years their numerical strength will be reduced by 500,000 men. The numbers of conventional armaments will also be substantially reduced. This will be done unilaterally, without relation to the talks on the mandate of the Vienna meeting.

By agreement with our Warsaw Treaty allies, we have decided to withdraw by 1991 six tank divisions from East Germany, Czechoslovakia, and Hungary, and to disband them.

Assault landing troops and several other formations and units, including assault crossing units with their weapons and combat equipment, will also be withdrawn from the groups of Soviet forces stationed in those countries.

Soviet forces stationed in those countries will be reduced by 50,000 men and their armaments, by 5,000 tanks.

All Soviet divisions remaining, for the time being, in the territory of our allies are being reorganized. Their structure will be different from what it is now; after a major cutback of their tanks it will become clearly defensive.

At the same time, we shall reduce the numerical strength of the armed forces and the numbers of armaments stationed in the European part of the Soviet Union.

In total, Soviet armed forces in this part of our country and in the territories of our European allies will be reduced by 10,000 tanks, 8,500 artillery systems, and 800 combat aircraft.

Over these two years we intend to reduce significantly our armed forces in the Asian part of our country, too. By agreement with the government of the Mongolian People's Republic a major portion of Soviet troops temporarily stationed there will return home.

In taking this fundamental decision the Soviet leadership expresses the will of the people, who have undertaken a profound renewal of their entire socialist society.

## THE ECONOMY OF DISARMAMENT

We shall maintain our country's defense capability at a level of reasonable and reliable sufficiency so that no one might be tempted to encroach on the security of the Soviet Union and our allies.

By this action, and by all our activities in favor of demilitarizing international relations, we wish to draw the attention of the international community to yet another pressing problem—the problem of transition from the economy of armaments to an economy of disarmament.

Is conversion of military production a realistic idea? I have already had occasion to speak about this. We think that, indeed, it is realistic.

For its part, the Soviet Union is prepared to do these things:

- In the framework of our economic reform we are ready to draw up and make public our internal plan of conversion;

- In the course of 1989 to draw up, as an experiment, conversion plans for two or three defense plants;

- To make public our experience in providing employment for specialists from military industry and in using its equipment, buildings, and structures in civilian production.

It is desirable that all states, in the first place major military powers, should submit to the United Nations their national conversion plans.

It would also be useful to set up a group of scientists to undertake a thorough analysis of the problem of conversion as a whole and as applied to individual countries and regions and report to the secretary-general of the United Nations, and subsequently, to have this matter considered at a session of the General Assembly.


## FUTURE RELATIONS WITH U.S.

And finally, since I am here on American soil, and also for other obvious reasons, I have to turn to the subject of our relations with this great country. I had a chance to appreciate the full measure of its hospitality during my memorable visit to Washington exactly a year ago.

The relations between the Soviet Union and the United States of America have a history of five and a half decades. As the world changed, so did the nature, role, and place of those relations in world politics.

For too long a time they developed along the lines of confrontation and sometimes animosity—either overt or covert.

But in the last few years the entire world could breath a sigh of relief thanks to the changes for the better in the substance and the atmosphere of the relationship between Moscow and Washington.

No one intends to underestimate the seriousness of our differences and the toughness of outstanding problems. We have, however, already graduated from the primary school of learning to understand each other and seek solutions in both our own and common interests.

## ELIMINATING NUCLEAR ARMS

The Soviet Union and the United States have built the largest nuclear and missile arsenals. But it is those two countries that, having become specifically aware of their responsibility, were the first to conclude a treaty on the reduction and physical elimination of a portion of their armaments which posed a threat to both of them and to all others.

Both countries possess the greatest and the most sophisticated military secrets. But it is those two countries that have laid a basis for and are further developing a system of mutual verification both of the elimination of armaments and of the reduction and prohibition of their production.

It is those two countries that are accumulating the experience for future bilateral and multilateral agreements.

We value this. We acknowledge and appreciate the contribution made by President Ronald Reagan and by the members of his administration, particularly Mr. George Shultz.

All this is our joint investment in a venture of historic importance. We must not lose this investment, or leave it idle.

## LOOKING TO THE BUSH YEARS

The next U.S. administration, headed by President-elect George Bush, will find in us a partner who is ready—without long pauses or backtracking—to continue the dialogue in a spirit of realism, openness, and good will, with a willingness to achieve concrete results working on the agenda which covers the main issues of Soviet-U.S. relations and world politics.

I have in mind, above all, these things:

- Consistent movement toward a treaty on 50 percent reductions in strategic offensive arms while preserving the ABM treaty;

- Working out a convention on the elimination of chemical weapons—here, as we see it, prerequisites exist to make 1989 a decisive year;

- And negotiations on the reduction of conventional arms and armed forces in Europe.

I also have in mind economic, environmental and humanistic problems in their broadest sense . . . .

I would like to believe that our hopes will be matched by our joint effort to put an end to an era of wars, confrontation and regional conflicts, to aggressions against nature, to the terror of hunger and poverty as well as to political terrorism.

This is our common goal and we can only reach it together.

# 33

# Cultural Revolution

## Arnold Pacey

### DEMOCRACY AND INFORMATION

Two principal issues have emerged from previous chapters,* one intellectual and the other political. The intellectual issue concerns the way value systems inform world views, and how they support beliefs about resources, the arms race, the Third World, and technology itself. The political issue concerns the totalitarian nature of many of the institutions which control technology; it is associated with the difficulty encountered at almost every level, of opening any real dialogue between experts and users, technocrats and parliamentarians, planners and people. On the government level, the growth of bureaucracy "has tended to shunt parliament away from the center of political life. The executive apparatus functions increasingly without adequate political control."[1] That has led to a widespread sense of political impotence, and some loss of faith in elected government, and so to the growth of protest movements concerned with the environment, the arms race, and nuclear energy.

In both Europe and America, the feeling that totalitarian institutions were taking over was forcibly expressed in the unrest of the late 1960s (especially 1968) and the early 1970s, and in response to this there have been modest reforms. In several countries, legislators have improved their ability to scrutinize bureaucratic action and technology policy (in Britain, since 1979, through strengthened Parliamentary select committees). There have also been moves

---

*See Part 2, chapter 5.

to reduce the secrecy that surrounds many decisions; citizens' rights of access to some categories of official information have been recognized in law, first in the Scandinavian countries, then by the American Freedom of Information Act (1967), and later in West Germany (1973) and France (1978). In addition, there have been deliberate efforts to open up public debate on nuclear energy. In Sweden, from 1973, the government encouraged the formation of study circles to examine the nuclear issue, and some eight thousand of these local citizens' groups became active. In Britain, a National Energy Conference was held in 1976 as part of an effort by the minister responsible, Tony Benn, to widen the scope of public discussion. In Austria, there was an extended campaign to inform the public on the nuclear energy issue which ended in 1978 with a referendum that halted the nation's nuclear program.

A study of these developments, commissioned by the European Economic Community, has led Jean-Jacques Salomon to put forward an optimistic vision of technology as a European enterprise, carried forward in an increasingly cooperative spirit by an informed, participating public.[2] This is a liberal vision firmly rejecting all determinist concepts and emphasizing technology as a social process, just as open to democratic control as any other social process—if people will appreciate it this way. To secure that appreciation, Salomon advocates more education in science for everybody, and better training for the professionals with regard to the social and economic aspects of technology. His hope is for a healing of the divide between the two cultures based on science and the humanities.

This is a progressive vision, but too much is claimed for the more open decision-making procedures as they so far exist, and the intellectual issues concerning differing world views and values remain largely untouched. Salomon recognizes that there are important value-conflicts that cannot be resolved simply by making more information available, but argues that when vigorous debate takes place and there is open participation, perceptions are broadened; expert opinions then no longer appear exclusively technical, but are seen to involve subjective judgments and political preferences as well as technical fact. Dorothy Nelkin has described controversies concerning an airport extension and a nuclear energy plant in the United States, where open debate in itself exposed the values built into the experts' technical assessments.[3] There is thus a case for saying that the development of procedures for participation is by itself forcing a change in intellectual perspectives; professionals are forced to abandon the esoteric and sacred land of scientific facts for the real world, where facts and values are mixed.

This may be partly right, but may also lead to a complacent view of what participation can achieve. Despite the recognition that facts are always entwined with value judgments, there is still an assumption that only one kind of technical information is at issue, and that the way to promote public participation in technology policy is to ensure the information is widely shared and debated. But any knowledge at all presupposes a world view, and the problem about sharing information is that where world views are in conflict, there will be little agreement about what kinds of knowledge are relevant and valid. Thus one problem at present is that although the framework for debate has opened a little, not much real dialogue takes place—because the different viewpoints that need to interact are not recognized. For example, when technologists submit information to parliamentary committees or public inquiries, they have been known to suggest that their particular proposals are the only rational answer to the problem in hand, and that any other would be "irrational" or even "illegitimate." At the same time, a public inquiry may be conducted on the assumption that the very diverse evidence heard can all be related to a single frame of reference. Often this is done by imposing economic reference points on everything, perhaps by assigning a money value to a botanically unique habitat[4] or an ancient church.

At other inquiries, one may observe a public demonstration of the intellectual habit where available information is simply not perceived and is effectively destroyed in order to achieve a coherent view. This seems to have happened at the inquiry into Britain's Windscale nuclear reprocessing project in 1977 where evidence that did not fit a particular concept of "technical fact"[5] was given little weight. As in Dorothy Nelkin's case-studies, the inquiry evidence certainly exposed the values built into technical arguments. But in the absence of any concept of how to accommodate dissident values, the debate was rather like a discussion between the blind and the deaf—people who perceive different kinds of reality and have no way of discovering how they interconnect.

In this respect, commentators[6] have noticed a sharp contrast in concept between the Windscale inquiry and the roughly simultaneous Canadian inquiry into the proposed Mackenzie Valley pipeline. Here, Judge Berger's report pointed out that at least three different sets of values had a bearing on the question— values concerned firstly with the northern frontier, secondly with lifestyle and land, and thirdly with wilderness and environment. Having recognized these values, Berger was then able to suggest an agenda for decision making, indicating that value-conflicts and claims about land should be resolved before a decision about the pipeline could be taken.

Among the European experiments with widened forms of participation, those which seem to have come nearest to making allowance in their procedures for fundamentally different scales of value may perhaps be found in The Netherlands. Six universities there have opened science shops to provide expert advice—and counterexpert advice—to citizens and community groups worried about environmental issues. At government level, proposals for major physical development projects are discussed by advisory groups representing several mutually opposed points of view, and government ministers must reply to their comments before a parliamentary decision is taken.[7] The concept of counterinformation implied by this is perhaps the idea we most badly need, to make clear the point that there is no uniquely correct information. Basic observations and measurements can be factual and neutral, but interpretations, future projections, plans and designs never are—neither is the decision about what to observe and measure. All these are rooted in world views and values, and where the latter differ, the same facts will have different meanings. Agreed facts about rising carbon dioxide levels in the atmosphere have different meanings for different specialists and there is no agreement about whether there is a major problem here. Agreed facts about pollution or nuclear accidents are reassuring to some people, alarming to others. Counterinformation relates partly to different interpretations of the same data; partly, though, it can compensate for the way experts are trained not to perceive, or to ignore some categories of readily available information.

Even taking a limited view based on economic efficiency, governments, in their own interest, need to listen to "multiple voices" and take account of "multiple public views."[8] The public interest is only rarely unitary; so the exercise of rationality is "a more complex and variable process than any conceivable amalgam of 'expert' inquiries."[9]

All this is illustrated in a more restricted but equally clear way by the evaluations of household appliances carried out by some consumer organizations. Such research is based on values and assumptions different from those motivating the manufacturers of the equipment, and sometimes generates information that is new to them.[10] Yet quite a number of people feel that the values of the consumer groups are themselves too narrowly related to efficiency, safety, and price, and that not enough consideration is given to the relevance of products for low-income groups, or to their environmental impact. Thus it has been said of the British Consumers' Association, publishers of *Which?* magazine, that they are sometimes just as dogmatic and inflexible as any bureaucracy, "representing only a narrow range of middle class consumer society." Among other comments is the suggestion that there could be a *Counter-Which?* magazine to assess products less on the basis of technical efficiency than with regard to the environment, social welfare, the Third World, and so on.[11]

## INSTITUTIONS AND EDUCATION

The task of creating more open and democratic forms of technology-practice cannot be limited to establishing procedures through which public opinion may influence policy and planning. There are issues on which people do not want to participate actively but where it is still very desirable for decisions to accommodate widely different points of view arising from different values and frames of reference.

One subsidiary controversy at the Mackenzie Valley inquiry was connected with the engineering design of pipelines laid in arctic soils, and arose from a phenomenon known as frost heave. Calculations and experiments had been done to check the magnitude of the forces this generated, but the results were in dispute. Even on this specialist problem, then, there were conflicts of information and counterinformation. Judge Berger noted that: "Much of the specialist knowledge and expertise that is relevant to these matters is tied up with the industry and its consultants. This situation is untenable. . . . Government cannot rely solely on industry's ability to judge its own case."[12] On a matter such as this, public participation is barely relevant, but decisions still need to be based on diverse and independent research activity.

Berger thus strongly urged the Canadian government "to make itself more knowledgeable in matters involving major innovative technology." Much the same advice could be given to the British government in relation to its nationalized industries. On energy matters, for example, the Atomic Energy Authority has for long been in a privileged position in advising the Department of Energy. There is an especial need for its influence to be countered by a strong, independent energy agency concerned with energy use, consumer interests, and conservation. There is also a case for devolving much more responsibility to the regional electricity boards in order to diversify innovation, and to encourage initiatives like those of Midlands Electricity.

More important, though, is the need for more public interest research by independent bodies, especially bodies representative of minority and environmental interests, and of low-income groups. As we have seen, such research is already done in science shops and by some consumer groups. In addition, very valuable studies have been made by Greenpeace on chemical waste dumping in the North Sea, by Friends of the Earth on nuclear power, and by World-Watch on deforestation. But beyond the campaigning style of these latter, often aimed mainly at producing short, polemical publications, there is need for public interest studies with a long-term commitment. The Stockholm International Peace Research Institute (SIPRI) is a good example, and public interest research on arms control is perhaps a more urgent need than anything else. We have already seen how the arms race is sustained by phoney intelligence, and counterinformation is needed to offset this. Another example is the Political Ecology Research Group, which since 1976 has specialized on nuclear energy questions, providing an independent consultancy service which is used by a wide variety of people—local community groups, broadcasting media, the Union of Concerned Scientists (of the United States), and the Lower Saxony State Government (in Germany).[13]

One topic on which public interest research can be particularly important is food, drugs, and chemicals. Government regulation of the relevant industries is often fairly tight, but is limited by national boundaries, and is evaded when corporations transfer their activities from one country to another. Thus as tobacco advertising is increasingly restricted within the industrialized countries, sales campaigns in the Third World intensify. Agricultural chemicals which are restricted, "on safety grounds in the rich countries are freely available in the poor, where the risks are greatest."[14] A drug which is sold in Africa and Asia as a medicine for children, and vigorously promoted there by an American corporation is known to be "of no value to children—may actually harm them—

and the marketing procedures would be forbidden by law in the U.S."[15] The public interest group exposing this scandal—Social Audit—also points to abuses in British sales of milk powder, vitamin pills, and hair-care products. The size of the problem is illustrated by one country's attempt to control it. In 1982, Bangladesh announced a ban on 1,500 different drugs, of which 237 were described as harmful and the rest as unnecessary.

One query that has been raised is, how far can one go in encouraging research oriented to many different viewpoints before the result is confusion? Raymond Williams, for example, suggests that in a socialist country committed to central planning, it might be reasonable to suggest that "there should never be less than two independently prepared plans."[16] For people used to linear modes of thought, this sounds like a recipe either for disaster or complete paralysis. But if there is to be any democracy in decision making, alternatives have to be explicit and fully researched. This is a prerequisite for choice. And it need not lead to confusion if alternative views interact in a dialectic of mutual adjustment. If this were recognized, in nations of whatever political complexion, public interest research and critical science would be seen to have a validity and importance in their own right, and would attract support from research councils and foundations. As it is, such work is mainly perceived as a form of opposition to private corporations and government, and thus gains little support from official quarters.

In his vision of a cooperative European commitment to technology based on public participation and a free flow of information, Jean-Jacques Salomon does not fully confront this issue. But he does comment usefully on the importance of better education in science and technology, not only for the citizen but also for the professional. In particular, he makes the point that unless professional technologists are more aware of the socioeconomic implications of their work, they will remain locked in illusions of value-free technical rationality, believing that there is only one right answer to every problem. And holding those views, they will not understand how public choice and participation in decision making can ever make sense.

One may see in detail how the idea of value-free rationality has been perpetuated simply by looking at the textbooks from which many among the present generation of engineers were taught. Most are strongly directed towards the concept of technology as problem-solving discipline capable of finding "optimum solutions" and "right answers" to strictly technical problems. For example, the textbooks from which I was supposed to learn soil mechanics[17] discussed the design of embankments, dams, foundations, and highways almost entirely without giving examples of real dams or highways, so questions of context and socioeconomic background could never arise. Textbook writers also favored a very formal style which emphasized the internal logic of the subject. Their model seemed to be Euclid's geometry, with its definitions and axioms, and its logical build-up of theorem upon theorem. An example which follows this pattern very closely, taking Newton's laws of motion as its axioms, is a text on "mechanical technology" used in teaching technicians for the Ordinary National Certificate.[18] In this work, the abstraction employed in the effort to seem totally rational and value-free is taken to such extremes that no real machine is mentioned, and engine components such as flywheels are referred to only as "rigid bodies."

Thought about in this way, technology is quite literally neutral—one might even say sterile. Not surprisingly then, some engineers speak of their formative years as a mind-dulling, disabling experience; it is they who have used the term tunnel vision[19] and in one extreme case, have talked about the need for an engineers liberation' movement.[20] Samuel Florman refers to the stultifying influence of engineering schools in America, where "the least bit of imagination, social concern, or cultural interest is snuffed out under a crushing load of purely technical subjects."[21]

In many respects, these problems are now better handled. Better textbooks are available. New professional journals discuss technology-practice and its social context, and in Britain, enhanced or enriched engineering degree courses include an extra year of study with emphasis on management and business studies, longer periods of industrial experience, and in some universities, much more design and project work. Elsewhere, there are new courses on science, technology, and society (STS).

But this is only a beginning. The additional training in management studies does not automatically mean that engineers have a more rounded, interdisciplinary approach. It may mean that they simply learn fragments of two disciplines without adequately making connections between them. In fact, a central difficulty for the teacher or textbook writer is that if he discusses social context and organization as a sociologist would, he loses touch with real nuts and bolts and practical technology. But if he presents the technical content of a problem in a conventional manner, there is no satisfactory way of bringing in the organizational aspect at all. In other words, bridges are not built between the two cultures simply by tacking extra subjects onto a conventional technical education. The whole philosophy of such training has to be rethought, textbooks and all, in order to present an integrated vision of technology-practice rather than a tunnel vision focused only on its technical aspects.

One way of overcoming these problems may be found through the new design disciplines which have developed within technology itself. They have led to renewed emphasis on design as part of the training of engineers, and several authors make the point that this helps to tie course content to a social background.[22] Apart from that, however, the design disciplines and the soft system approach which goes with them can have an influence on the overall structure of teaching. An example is the Open University's very wide-ranging foundation course in technology, which has a mainstream component dealing with issues in technology, and tributary components providing basic teaching in mathematics, materials, chemistry, electricity, and so on.

The aim of presenting an integrated vision of technology which some of these approaches illustrate has been at the center of my own work for the last dozen years. That needs to be mentioned, because it is this work which has led to the somewhat personal view of technology put forward [here]. Apart from some teaching on the course just mentioned, formative experience has included project work with engineering students; exposure to courses on design technology and agricultural engineering; and multidisciplinary editorial work on subjects ranging from public standpost water supplies[23] to human ecology.[24] In all of this, it has seemed particularly important to find ways of breaking through professional boundaries, to develop broader insights in collectively written texts,[25] and to think about extending the same multidisciplinary approach to field surveys and planning.[26]

Three short practical manuals can also be mentioned as tributaries which have fed the mainstream of [our research].[27] Taken together, they could almost form a companion volume, illustrating what the concept of technology-practice may mean in specific applications, and applying the notion of technology as the management of process to specific problems of husbandry and maintenance. The manuals were also written with the defects of conventional textbooks in mind; where the latter are narrowly technical, the manuals attempt a unified view of how the technical and organizational aspects of water supply or nutrition projects are related; and where textbooks are deliberately abstract, the manuals quote identifiable case-studies from Brazil and Botswana, India and Zaire. Through the case-studies rather than by analysis, the user's viewpoint is brought in, forcing one to notice how technology-practice depends on ordinary people, not just experts, and how experts from different disciplines need to collaborate: engineers with social workers, doctors with horticulturists. The contribution of these small booklets is modest indeed, but I do claim one thing for them: that they show how the philosophy of technology may have practical application; it is not just a literary formulation.

## FRAMES OF REFERENCE

Previous paragraphs suggest a random list of recommendations for minor reforms in technology-practice based on a strengthening of public interest research and improvements in technical education. But these suggestions have implications that run counter to the conventional wisdom. They indicate a plurality of approaches rather than one right answer. They present technical fact and engineering design as expressions of world views and values, not of neutral rationality. Thus for any of these reforms to be carried through with conviction, and for it to have the desired effect, there must be a fairly fundamental shift in the frame of reference we use when thinking about technology and the world in which it is applied. This might entail a fairly small adjustment. But it may prove to be a sufficiently radical change to merit description as a change in levels of awareness, an awakening to new insights, or even a cultural revolution. In the philosophers' jargon, it might be seen as the adoption of a new paradigm—a new pattern for organizing ideas.

Such terms are relevant because the most fundamental choices in technology are not those between solar and nuclear energy, appropriate and high technique. They are choices between attitudes in mind. We may cultivate an exploratory, open view of the world, or we may maintain a fixed, inflexible outlook, tied to the conventional wisdom, in which new options are not recognized.

This need to pose choices about attitudes, including world views and the concept of technology itself, makes it particularly appropriate to talk about cultural revolution. And although I do not employ this term in quite the same sense as socialists do, there is still much to be learned from that direction. Socialists talk about revolutionary awareness. We require this especially with respect to awareness of the possibilities for future progress and choice in technology. Moreover, we require it to be an awareness that is shared by everybody because, as Aldo Leopold says, "all men, by what they think about and wish for, in effect wield all tools."[28] Or as the socialist writer Raymond Williams[29] has put it, the "cultural revolution insists . . . that what a society needs, before all . . . is as many as possible conscious individuals." This, he makes clear, is a first requirement for countering the trend towards technocratic decision making.

Williams defines the central task of a socialist cultural revolution as, "the general appropriation of . . . the intellectual forces of knowledge and conscious decision," for the service of the community; he sees it also as a more "effective response to . . . general human needs, in care and relationships, and in knowledge and development." One thinks of the improvements in health achieved in [the Indian state] Kerala partly through the openness of local democracy, and partly through a widening of literacy, and a growing awareness among women especially of what they can do to help themselves. In both respects, this is "the general appropriation of knowledge." And as Williams says, the "cultural revolution . . . will be deeply sited among women or it will not, in practice, occur at all." Many professionals in technology, I have argued, have tended to be diverted away from the service of basic needs and good husbandry through their greater interest in technological virtuosity. The potential contribution of women—and of insights from some non-Western communities —lies in the fact that they represent areas of life where technological virtuosity has not yet become dominant.

To speak about cultural revolution is inevitably to recall the China of Mao Zedong during the late 1960s. It is now usual to decry the events of this cultural revolution, but they are still a relevant example. Mao was disturbed by three widening divisions in Chinese society—between town and country, between worker and peasant, and between mental and manual labor. He hoped to bridge these gaps by making education more practical, by sending students and professional people to work in agriculture, by training peasants as barefoot doctors, and by encouraging dialogue between workers and management in factories. My concern is with some very similar divisions in Western technological society, and especially the division between the expert sphere and the user sphere. Many aspects of the Chinese approach are pertinent to this, but whereas Mao sought to bridge the gap by rapid change involving brutal compulsion, I share Williams's view that what we are concerned with is a long revolution based on educational development as well as ideological campaigning.

In this context, it is worth remembering that other crucial phases in the development of Western technology arose out of experiences of awakening to new possibilities, some of which may justly be called cultural revolutions, [e.g.,] the voyages of Columbus and his contemporaries, and the scientific revolution of the seventeenth century. Among more directly relevant examples are the new ideas about economics and production that developed in the eighteenth century and contributed to the organizational innovations of the first industrial revolution. Mary Douglas describes this phase as a "realization which transfixed thoughtful minds in the eighteenth century and onwards . . . that the market is a system with its own immutable laws."[30] There was a boldness of illumination about the way this idea was grasped and analyzed, and for people engaged in trade and industry, a sense of revelation about the new potential open to them. Reading the correspondence of James Watt's associates and other early industrialists,[31] one may still feel their sense of discovery and see how a shift in awareness concerning socioeconomic organization fed ideas into factory development and engineering innovation.

The cultural revolution that we may find occurring today will also involve the exhilaration of discovering new insights. In the 1970s, one could sense this among advocates of the use of solar energy and renewable resources. Today there are other new enthusiasms, such as that which, in 1982, gave Britain more microcomputers in schools and homes, and more teletext users per head of population than any other nation. Such things are bound to change perceptions of technology, and to awaken new awareness of the possibilities open to us, but perhaps only in trivial ways.

A more fundamental aspect of current industrial change is the impact on employment. Between 1971 and 1981, Britain lost 1.3 million jobs in ten major industries ranging from automobiles and chemicals to mining and textiles. By 1990, these same industries could lose another 0.5 million workplaces. But new microelectronics industries seem likely to create less than 0.1 million new jobs by 1990,[32] and the only other major prospects for expanded employment are in the arms industries and construction. Whether the consequence of reduced employment is social unrest, or whether instead there is an erosion of the work ethic and a growing feeling that it no longer matters if one has a job, then either way, the change in perceptions of industry and technology must be vast.

But the central preoccupation of any modern cultural revolution must surely be centered on what one university engineer has described as "the mainspring of technological misdirection."[33] This is the impulse to go on inventing, developing, and producing regardless of society's needs. The result is that we create systems of organized waste in electricity supply, consumer goods, and food production, and above all, in the arms race.

But conventional world views disguise much of this and make it seem logical and necessary; they hide the real nature of the technological imperative. Thus the most important part of any cultural revolution—the biggest shift in perceptions and paradigms—could be a reconstruction of world views so that the irrationality of our present pattern of technological progress is no longer hidden. Before pursuing this point, though, we ought first to ask whether a fundamental change in the technological imperative is possible, even if we were more aware of how that imperative is conventionally disguised?

Some authors advocate change that seems too radical to be credible. They portray Western man as an "unbound Prometheus,"[34] crazy about science and machines, and pursuing his white whales of technological achievement wildly and obsessively. They see the historical roots of this attitude in the Judaeo-Christian tradition, with its work ethic and its teachings about man's dominion over nature. And they conceive cultural revolution as a turning away from this outlook to something more contemplative and gentle, drawing on Eastern types of wisdom, and on Buddhist insights.

One does not have to be a slavish adherent of the conventional wisdom to take alarm at any such suggestion of a wholesale rejection of Western thought. It might involve the rejection of liberal values also, and of enlightenment and reason, and even of the basis of modern advances in health and welfare. To advocate anything that could involve this seems as absurd as the more extreme aspects of the nineteenth century's romantic reaction against industry.

The point is taken, but yet there remains the problem of unrelenting drives in technology that make many of us secretly want an arms race, that make us thrill to the risks of advanced nuclear technology, or which draw us into adventure on the frontiers of environmental conquest. Some Eastern cultures demonstrate an avoidance of these particular obsessions, and might help us find a new balance in Western thought without necessarily abandoning any part of it. The point here is that there is a doubleness in Western attitudes and a dialectic between opposed points of view. Beside the half of us that is fascinated by high technology, there is another half already partially in tune with Buddhism. Beside Western man, with his virtuosity drives, there is also Western woman, seemingly less enthralled by such impulses. Beside [Francis] Bacon's comments on science as dominion over natures, there is also Bacon's more insistent view that knowledge should be applied in works of compassion, and "for the benefit and use of life." Beside the heroic engineers who have built "cathedrals, railroads, and space vehicles to demonstrate the adventuring spirit of man," there have also been engineers who saw their vocation as a social and humanitarian one, like "John Smeaton, who stressed 'civil' engineering as opposed to the military branch (and) William Strutt, who attempted to create a technology of social welfare applicable in hospitals and homes."[35]

For those inclined to find all the faults of Western civilization in its religious tradition, we may note that the same doubleness of vision is to be found there as well. Beside Christ the King, celebrated by daringly engineered cathedrals, motivating crusades, and colonial conquests, there is also Jesus the carpenter, healing the sick, concerned for the hungry, and washing his followers' feet. The challenge we ought to recognize in Eastern religions, or in the basic-needs economies of Kerala and Sri Lanka, is a challenge to tip the balance in the West's traditional dialectic from conquest and virtuosity towards a point where we can perhaps feel our kinship with Buddhism, and where the work of women and craftsmen, of meeting needs and caring, becomes much more important.

It is worth making these points in terms that refer to religion and may seem rather literary, because our vision and values, even in this calculating, atheistic age, find their power to move us partly through rhetoric and symbolism. It sometimes seems that it is the most hardheaded engineers who talk most freely about their work as cathedral-building. And in the most urgent of our technological dilemmas, the nuclear arms race, women have altered the whole atmosphere of debate by actions that are both heroic and symbolic. A small party of women camped at the gates of a U.S. Air Force base in Britain throughout one of the coldest winters on record to protest against cruise missiles, and sustaining their protest into a second winter, make clear that it is not sufficient just to look at the issue simply in terms of power politics and technology. A similar awareness was generated on a more restricted scale by the Scandinavian women who carried their protest across Russia in the summer of 1982. Identical protests by men would have commanded much less respect in Britain, and would probably not have gained entry to Russia. When women take the lead, it is widely if intuitively recognized that their action represents a distinctive set of values, and not just the immaturity of some overgrown student cause.

## WORLD VIEWS AND WAVES OF PROGRESS

The question of nuclear weapons illustrates nearly all the key issues I have tried to tackle. Not only is this a field where technological imperatives and virtuosity drives have an ample scope, but there are also many questions to be asked about the roles played by professional technologists and by totalitarian organizations. Scientists' pressure groups, defense bureaucracies, and large-scale industry wield power almost beyond political control. President Eisenhower warned against it; retired defense experts such as Herbert York and Solly

Zuckerman have repeatedly raised the alarm; but the only thing that seems ever to move it is sustained, persistent, continuous, vociferous, peacefully disruptive public campaigning. One may regret the use of extra-parliamentary tactics, but faced with a totalitarian military-industrial system that makes its decisions in an extra-parliamentary way, the people have only this resort if they are to exercise their proper sovereignty.

It has been said that during the last decade, most really big initiatives have come from the people: governments have followed where people have led. With regard to environmental concerns, or ending the Vietnam war, or progress in women's rights, "what was politically opposed or neglected became so strongly supported by ordinary people that governments were led to treat it as good politics."[36] Similarly, nuclear energy in the United States has been made uneconomic by . . . public protest."[37] Some such claims can even be made with regard to the limited Test Ban Treaty of 1963. George Kistiakowsky records Britain's early resistance to any such agreement.[38] But Britain had a strong Campaign for Nuclear Disarmament which publicized the dangers of fallout from nuclear tests; not least because of this pressure, the British government eventually played a constructive part in the negotiations.

But to say all this is not to advocate unilateral disarmament nor even a nuclear freeze. It is merely to point out what difficulties face the public in getting its voice heard; and I mention it as a particular instance where the questions raised earlier about the role of dialogue in technological issues ought to be applied. In order to go beyond this and form an opinion about what level of defense is required, we have to consider another point that applies generally to most technology. This is that the world view we use in deciding what kinds of technique to use is a view which must include perspectives on human organization and their international context as well as specific concepts of technology.

In the age of Columbus, a shift in awareness came to many Europeans as a result of the discovery of a new continent, and due to the circumnavigation of Africa and the expansion of trade with Asia. In today's world, we perhaps need the altered frames of reference that could come through rediscovering these same continents. That would mean ceasing to lump them together in the ugly portmanteau concept of the Third World. Then instead of seeing these countries as full of backward people living a "soup kitchen" existence, we might find that much may be learned from them, especially from the non-industrialized but culturally rich countries.

If such voyages of rediscovery were ever to reach the Soviet Union, they would certainly confirm that this nation presents a special and serious danger, and that it cannot make sense for the West to carry out any sort of extensive, one-sided disarmament.* But we may also discover that the Soviet threat has

---

*We should note that it is now the Soviet Union that has initiated such voyages of rediscovery. (Ed.)

been partly induced by the West's own policies, and that Russia has been encouraged to behave dangerously by being perpetually distrusted, vilified, and spoken of openly as the enemy even in the absence of war.

The West has strong vested interests whose prosperity depends on preparation for war, and the problem we may need to recognize is that in some respects, the United States and Russia need each other, and manipulate each other's hostility in order to justify their commitments to virtuosity-oriented technology. Field Marshal Michael Carver points to the type of reconstruction of ideas required if we are to move away from this situation by quoting the former U.S. ambassador in Moscow, George F. Kennan.[39] The behavior of the Russian leadership, he says, is partly "a reflection of our own treatment" of them. If we continue to view the Russians as implacable enemies, dedicated to "nothing other than our destruction—that, in the end, is how we shall assuredly have them." To view Soviet Russia as eaten up with an absolute malevolence is to allow "intellectual primitivism and naïveté" to distort our own frame of reference. A first step in revising our views would be to seek a better understanding of Russian civilization, not just in terms of ideology, but by considering its history, traditions, and national experience, noting, perhaps, the marked continuity between Tsarist and Soviet ways . . . .

Along with the responsibility to understand Russian civilization, there is also a responsibility to better understand our own. In part, that means removing the disguises we use to hide the real reasons for much of our technology. We are told, for example, that some of the earliest nuclear weapons were made because "it would have been contrary to the spirit of modern science and technology to refrain voluntarily from the further development of a new field of research, however dangerous." So when the utilitarian or military purpose of the work was overtaken by events, that did not mean the project's cancellation. Instead, new grounds were found "for the political and moral justification of its continuance."[40] It is this business of inventing reasons to justify research and invention that has created many aspects of the world view we now take for granted . . . .

But in a short, exploratory [study], many parts of the argument are inevitably left incomplete. This is particularly regrettable where the more positive, constructive themes are concerned. One of these is the possibility of articulating the values of end use and basic human need more fully, so that they have greater influence in shaping future technology. Here, the most important point stressed is the role played by women, but a point left unexamined is the connection that ought to exist between need-oriented values and environmental concerns.

More fundamental, however, is the suggestion that the very concept of technology itself is open to revision. Technologists have made the world more dangerous simply by doing what they conceive to be their job—especially regarding the development of weapons. If this is so, cultural revolution needs to be carried to the point where these experts conceive their jobs differently, and understand technology differently also. Many people have recognized the problem, and some relevant ideas are in circulation, often under the banner of appropriate technology. But much of the discussion has been incoherent, even rhetorical, and to get beyond this stage and begin to explore new styles for Western technology, we need to go further in questioning ideas of what technology is about. Is it mainly about making things? Or is it about managing the natural processes of growth and decay in which we are involved? Given that a balance is needed in engineering between construction and maintenance, and in medicine between cure and prevention, where should that balance be struck? How should we use the concept of technology-practice, with its ideas about the interaction of technical and organizational innovations?

It would be wrong to claim that questions of this sort can lead to a concept so comprehensive as to displace entirely the more conventional view of technology as a quest to innovate and venture, to construct and develop. Again we need to think dialectically: this is not a matter of defeating one concept by another, but of tipping the balance away from the virtuosity concept towards the process view.

Freeman Dyson[41] sees the options in technology as "a choice of two styles, which I call the grey and the green." If the grey style is typified by physics, plutonium, and bureaucracy, the green is represented by biology, horse manure, and community. But he adds that we cannot simply replace all the grey high technology by a green approach and more appropriate technology. We cannot suppose that the ideology of "Green is beautiful" will save us "from the necessity of making difficult choices." If human needs are to be met, we require both grey and green; if they are to be met in a civilized, humane way, we require a continuous, active dialogue, not the one right answer offered by either of the opposite points of view. Nuclear energy is not the one right answer required if all human needs are to be supplied, but neither is its total abandonment.

If this sounds like fence-sitting, let it be said that I personally not only lean toward environmental causes, but have a low-energy, near-vegetarian lifestyle which scarcely requires nuclear energy for its support. But those are my own preferences, and it would be wrong to insist that this kind of lifestyle is the only satisfactory outcome of a decision-making process in which a great diversity of people and organizations must participate. One of the best of many reports on the energy question insists that the first priority in this sphere is open, pluralistic debate—otherwise "projects may come to be decided either by financial overlords on what are believed to be purely economic grounds, or by scientists and engineers on grounds of 'technical sweetness'."[42] The one right answer and the simple formula are always suspect, whether economically motivated or technically sweet, whether monetarist, socialist, or antinuclear. Individually, we must live by the light of our own awareness, while valuing a plurality of view in the community. Openness, democracy, and diversity are what will save us, not some environmentalist blueprint, nor any technocratic plan. Again Mao Zedong was right in theory if clumsy in practice, for he spoke about walking on two legs, that is, combining different approaches, including both complex techniques and community enterprises.

One possible interpretation of the context of these debates is that we have experienced four waves of industrial revolution during the last two centuries, and that the recession of the early 1980s is the pause which heralds a fifth. During the recession, technical innovation is proceeding apace, and there seems a good chance that ultimately some cluster of institutional and technical developments will fall into place to provide a new pattern for growth. One may even see, again with Freeman Dyson, what techniques could be involved: "We shall find the distinction between electronic and biological technology becoming increasingly blurred." Both deal with the fundamentals of information. In both, solar energy can he harnessed particularly effectively. Both allow us to fulfill many of the needs of industrial society using much less energy and other resources than we do now.

The prospects seem good, but a fifth wave of industrial change is not to be beneficiently achieved simply by letting innovation in microelectronics and biology run its course. There are choices to be made about the social and cultural aspects of new and evolving forms of technology-practice, about the institutions which manage technology, and about how the new techniques are applied in the user sphere. In looking at the possible options, attention may turn to the nations of the Pacific rim, where some of the new technology is currently being developed, and where much of its hardware is manufactured. These nations seem to have had remarkable success, but one may feel that theirs has become an excessively materialist culture, overemphasizing economic values. Confronted with this criticism from a Westerner, one Japanese retorted: "better a materialist culture than a weapons culture."[43]

Perhaps, though, we can do better than both through a humanitarian stress on need-oriented values, not just as a cozy idealism, nor as a search for "one right answer," but as a strengthening contribution to a continuing dialectic. For three centuries, people have been turning to Francis Bacon for ideas about the goals and methods of science and technology; and Bacon was motivated by a "love of God's creation . . . pity for the suffering of man, and striving for innocence, humility and charity."[44] He felt that knowledge and technique should be perfected and governed in love; and that the fruits of knowledge should be used, not for "profit, or fame or power . . . but for the benefit and use of life."

## NOTES

1. Stephen Cotgrove, *Catastrophe or Cornucopia: the Environment, Politics, and the Future* (Chichester and New York: John Wiley, 1982), pp. 71, 74.

2. Jean-Jacques Salomon, *Promethée empêtré [Prometheus Bound]* (Paris: Seuil, 1982).

3. Dorothy Nelkin, "The Political Impact of Technical Expertise," *Social Studies of Science* 5 (1975): 35–54. [And see Part 6, chapter 20 of this volume.]

4. An instance of this at the Cow Green reservoir in northern England; it seemed that rare flowers and industrial production were being measured on a single scale of values. See Cotgrove, *Catastrophe,* pp. 86–87.

5. Robert Walgate, "Mr. Justice Parker and Technical Fact," *Nature* (London) 272 (March 23, 1978):300–301; Martin Stott and Peter Taylor, *The Nuclear Controversy: a Guide to the Issues of the Windscale Inquiry* (London: Town and Country Planning Association with the Political Ecology Research Group, 1980).

6. Guild Nichols, *La technologie contestée* (Paris: OECD, 1979), pp. 73–82, compares the Windscale and Mackenzie Valley inquiries.

7. Salomon, *Promethée,* chapter 4.

8. P. D. Henderson, "Two British Errors . . . Some Possible Lessons," *Oxford Economic Papers* 29 (1977): 159–205.

9. Raymond Williams, *Problems in Materialism and Culture* (London: Verso Editions and New Left Books, 1980), pp. 264–65.

10. Jeremy Mitchell, "The Consumer Movement and Technological Change," in *The Politics of Technology,* Godfrey Boyle, David Elliott, and Robin Roy (eds.) (London: Longman, 1977), p. 210.

11. Ibid., p. 212; also David Farrar and Alice Crampin, private communications, 1982.

12. Thomas R. Berger, *Northern Frontier, Northern Homeland: The Report of the Mackenzie Valley Pipeline Inquiry* (Ottawa: Ministry of Supply and Services, 1977), I: 21.

13. *PERG, 1977–79: A Report on the Activities of the Political Ecology Research Group* (Oxford: PERG, 1979).

14. David Bull, *A Growing Problem: Pesticides and the Third World Poor* (Oxford: Oxfam, 1982), pp. 38, 93.

15. Charles Medawar and Barbara Freese, *Drug Diplomacy* (London: Social Audit, 1982); also Charles Medawar, *Insult or Inquiry?* (London: Social Audit, 1979).

16. Williams, *Problems* (note 9), pp. 264–65.

17. G. N. Smith, *Elements of Soil Mechanics,* 3rd ed. (London: Crosby Lockwood Staples, 1974); P. L. Capper and W. F. Cassie, *The Mechanics of Engineering Soils,* 5th ed. (London: Spon, 1969); T. W. Lambe and R. V. Whitman, *Soil Mechanics* (New York: John Wiley, 1969).

18. G. D. Redford, J. G. Rimmer, and D. Titherington, *Mechanical Technology: A Two-Year Course* (London: Macmillan, 1969).

19. Duncan Mara, "The Influence of Conventional Practice on Design Capabilities," in *Sanitation in Developing Countries,* Arnold Pacey (ed.) (Chichester and New York: John Wiley, 1978), p. 75.

20. S. B. Watt, "Letters," *New Civil Engineer* 15 (June 1978):53.

21. Samuel C. Florman, *The Existential Pleasures of Engineering* (New York: St. Martin's Press, 1976), p. 92.

22. Gordon L. Glegg, *The Design of Design* (Cambridge: Cambridge University Press, 1969); Victor Papanek, *Design for the Real World* (London: Thames and Hudson, 1972; Paladin, 1974), p. 39; Bruce O. Watkins and Roy Meador, *Technology and Human Values* (Ann Arbor, Mich.: Ann Arbor Science, 1977), p. 161.

23. *Public Standpost Water Supplies,* The Hague, International Reference Center for Community Water Supply, Technical Paper 13, 1979.

24. Robert Chambers, Richard Longhurst, and Arnold Pacey, *Seasonal Dimension to Rural Poverty* (London: Frances Pinter, 1981).

25. *Water for the Thousand Millions,* written by the Water Panel of the Intermediate Technology Development Group . . . compiled and edited by Arnold Pacey (Oxford: Pergamon Press, 1977).

26. Arnold Pacey, "Taking Soundings for Development and Health," *World Health Forum* 3 (1982): 38–47.

27. Arnold Pacey, *Hand-Pump Maintenance,* 1977, rev. ed., 1980; *Gardening for Better Nutrition,* 1978; *Rural Sanitation: Planning and Appraisal,* 1980, all from Intermediate Technology Publications, London.

28. Aldo Leopold, *A Sand County Almanac* (New York: Oxford University Press, 1949; reprint 1979), pp. 67–68.

29. Williams, *Problems* (note 9), pp. 255–72.

30. Mary Douglas, *Implicit Meanings: Essays in Anthropology* (London: Routledge & Kegan Paul, 1975), pp. 232–33.

31. See, for example, R. S. Fitton and A. P. Wadworth, *The Strutts and the Arkwrights* (Manchester: Manchester University Press, 1958).

32. Philip Beresford, "The High Tech Jobs Harvest," *Sunday Telegraph,* December 12, 1982, reporting data from Warwick University Institute for Employment Research.

33. M. J. L. Hussey, "Has the 20th Century the Technology It Deserves" *Journal of the Royal Society of Arts* 120 (December 1971): 4.

34. One of the best available histories of industrialization in Europe is *The Unbound Prometheus: Technological Change and Industrial Development in Western Europe from 1750,* by D. S. Landes (Cambridge: Cambridge University Press, 1969).

35. Arnold Pacey, "Engineering the Heroic Art," in *Great Engineers and Pioneers in Technology,* vol. 1, Roland Turner and Steven L. Goulden (eds.) (New York: St. Martin's Press, 1981), p. xxi.

36. Richard Jolly, "The Brandt Report," *Journal of the Royal Society of Arts* 130 (December 1981):45, 55.

37. Editorial, "Nothing Is Even More Expensive," *Nature* (London) 299 (September 23, 1982):287.

38. See George B. Kistiakowsky, *A Scientist at the White House* (Cambridge, Mass: Harvard University Press, 1976), p. xxvi.

39. Michael Carver, *A Policy for Peace* (London: Faber & Faber, 1982), pp. 97–98, quoting articles by Kennan in the *New York Review of Books* (January 21, 1982) and in *Foreign Affairs* (Spring 1982).

40. Robert Jungk, *Brighter than a Thousand Suns,* trans. James Cleugh (London: Gollancz and Hart Davies, 1958; Harmondsworth: Penguin Books, 1960), p. 159.

41. Freeman J. Dyson, *Disturbing the Universe* (New York: Harper & Row, 1979), pp. 196, 227.

42. Council for Science and Society, *Deciding about Energy Policy* (London: CSS [3/4 St Andrews Hill], 1979), pp. 4–5.

43. Making the same comparison in more measured tones, other authors have said that whereas Japan has integrated its technology policy with its economic planning, the U.S. and UK governments have tended to treat technology policy as "a special aspect of defense, with heavy prestige overtones"; see Christopher Freeman, John Clarke and Luc Soete, *Unemployment and Technical Innovation* (London: Frances Pinter, 1982), p. 199.

44. J.R. Ravetz, *Scientific Knowledge and its Social Problems* (London: Oxford University Press, 1971), pp. 434–36.

# NOTES

NOTES

# NOTES

# NOTES

# NOTES

# NOTES

# NOTES

# NOTES

# NOTES

# NOTES

# NOTES

# NOTES

# NOTES